UNDERSTANDING
AND TROUBLESHOOTING
THE MICROPROCESSOR

James W. Coffron

PRENTICE-HALL, INC., Englewood Cliffs, New Jersey 07632

Library of Congress Cataloging in Publication Data

COFFRON, JAMES.
  Understanding and troubleshooting the microprocessor.

  (His Prentice-Hall series in microprocessor technology)
  Includes index.
  1. Microprocessors. I. Title. II. Series.
  TK7895.M5C63   621.3819'58'3   79-20950
  ISBN 0-13-936625-3

Dedication

To all of my family, my heartfelt gratitude, affection and appreciation:

  Lillian Coffron, Julia and Albert Ashby—Grandparents
  Julie and Al Coffron—Parents
  John, Mike and Wayne—Brothers
  And to Carol, Jeff and Kelley—my wife, son, and daughter
  who help me live each day with joy

Prentice-Hall Series in Microprocessor Technology by James W. Coffron

© 1980 by Prentice-Hall, Inc., Englewood Cliffs, N.J. 07632

All rights reserved. No part of this book may be reproduced in any form or by any means without permission in writing from the publisher.

Printed in the United States of America
10 9 8 7 6 5 4 3 2 1

Editorial production by M.L. McAbee
Interior design by Judith Winthrop
Cover design by Zeppi Long
Manufacturing Buyer: Gordon Osbourne

Prentice-Hall International, Inc., *London*
Prentice-Hall of Australia Pty. Limited, *Sydney*
Prentice-Hall of Canada, Ltd., *Toronto*
Prentice-Hall of India Private Limited, *New Delhi*
Prentice-Hall of Japan, Inc., *Tokyo*
Prentice-Hall of Southeast Asia Pte. Ltd., *Singapore*
Whitehall Books Limited, *Wellington, New Zealand*

CONTENTS

FOREWORD vii

PREFACE ix

OVERVIEW OF THE WORLD OF MICROPROCESSORS 1

1 Introduction: What Is a Microprocessor? 6

    1-1 The General Nature of a Microprocessor System 7
    1-2 General Organization of Electronics Systems 10
    1-3 Some Basic Vocabulary Essential to Microprocessor Systems 12
    1-4 How to Convert Octal and Hexadecimal Codes in Binary Communication 30
    1-5 How to Read Data Sheets and Static Electrical Parameters of Digital Devices 21
    1-6 The Role of Symbolism in Understanding Computers 30

2 Semiconductor Memories for the Microprocessor 35

2-1 Static Memory Devices: Organization and Characteristics 35
2-2 Troubleshooting Memory Systems 53
2-3 Dynamic Memory Systems 59
2-4 Use of Memory Devices in Microprocessor Systems 65
2-5 Read Only Memory 72
2-6 Programmable Read Only Memories 72
2-7 Erasable Programmable Read Only Memory 74

3 Construction of a Keyboard and Introduction of Timed Data Input to the Microprocessor 77

3-1 The Keyboard and Data Transfer Functions 77
3-2 Troubleshooting the Keyboard Circuit 99
3-3 Interfacing the Keyboard Circuit to the Memory 104
3-4 Display Section 108
3-5 Checking the Memory System 110

4 The 8080 Microprocessor as a CPU 129

4-1 Reading Data from Memory 129
4-2 Writing Data to Memory 135
4-3 Writing Data to an External Circuit 138
4-4 Reading Data from an External Circuit 139
4-5 Performing an Internal Register Manipulation 140

5 Microprocessor Input and Output (I/O) 142

5-1 Addressed Port I/O 144
5-2 Device/Port I/O Architecture 149
5-3 Linear Select I/O Architecture 152
5-4 Memory Mapped I/O Architecture 153
5-5 Communication Between the 8080 and the Various I/O Architectures 154

Contents v

6 Programming the 8080 166

6–1 Definitions 168
6–2 8080 Instructions 170
6–3 Logic Instructions 173
6–4 MemoryStack 175
6–5 I/O Instructions 179
6–6 Branching Instructions 181

7 Microprocessor Circuit Application: Problem Definition, Relationship of Software Instructions to Hardware Operation 190

7–1 Statement and Elements of the Problem 190
7–2 Reading Data Bytes 192
7–3 Modifying Data Bytes for Display 193
7–4 Writing Data in the General Output Display 202

8 Static Stimulus Testing and Other Troubleshooting Techniques 212

8–1 Troubleshooting Digital Equipment Compared with Troubleshooting Analog Equipment 213
8–2 Static Stimulus Testing 214
8–3 Construction and Use of a Mobile I/O Port 222
8–4 Troubleshooting Systems with Read Only Memory 226
8–5 Localizing Trouble in a Microprocessor System 227

9 Taking Advantage of LSI: Advanced Features of an 8080 System 234

9–1 8224 Clock Generator and Drive 234
9–2 The 8228 System Controller and Bus Driver 239
9–3 The 8212 8-Bit Input/Output Port 241
9–4 4-Bit Parallel Bidirectional Bus Driver 243
9–5 Advanced Microprocessor Concepts 244
9–6 Extending Read and Write Access Time 248
9–7 Interrupting the 8080 253
9–8 Priority Interrupt 259

10   An Advanced Microprocessor Application   261

    10–1   Statement of the Problem   *261*
    10–2   The MM5314 Digital Clock Chip   *262*
    10–3   I/O Interface to the 5314 Clock Chip   *266*
    10–4   Software to Control the System   *270*
    10–5   Troubleshooting the System   *286*

Appendix A   289
Appendix B   319

FOREWORD

The day of the microprocessor is here. According to many sources, the development of the microprocessor and the microcomputer systems it makes possible will constitute a second computer revolution, larger and more extensive in numbers, applications, and dollar volume than what we have seen to date. Such claims raise impressive vistas indeed, grand in scale and far-reaching in effect. As it looks now, these predictions will almost certainly prove to be true, and most probably conservative. We are currently seeing the leading edge of the microprocessor and microcomputer revolution, and major changes appear to confirm those early predictions.

Almost any well-informed person is aware of the existence of the microcomputer and has heard some of the claims made for its possibilities. But there are few experts in the field, and not many people have had an opportunity to work closely with microprocessor systems. This is certain to change. The truth is that the microprocessor has intimidated most of us somewhat, largely because of our ignorance concerning it. Interest is high and constantly growing, however, and there is much curiosity surrounding all aspects of microprocessor system organization and applications.

James Coffron is a young engineer who is an expert in the use of microprocessors and the design of systems in which microprocessors play a central role. He understands such systems on both the engineer's and the technician's level because he has worked as both a Senior Applications Engineer and, enroute to his engineering degree, as a Senior Electronics Technician. Mr. Coffron holds an AS Degree in Electronics from Foothill College, and BSEECS and

MSEE degrees from the University of Santa Clara. He is a member of Eta Kappa Nu, Engineering Honorary Fraternity, and is the author of *Getting Started in Digital Troubleshooting*, 1979, Reston Publishing Co., Inc.

In the ten years that I have known James Coffron I have watched his career develop with great interest. He possesses a unique ability to grasp the essence of complex and highly sophisticated systems and translate theoretical concepts into practical hardware and applications. Mr. Coffron is well qualified to write on the subject of troubleshooting by virtue of his training, experience, and personal interests. His abilities and analytical skills have grown steadily since his days as an Electronics Technician, and he has not lost sight of the problems technicians face, nor of the kind of help needed to maintain and improve their effectiveness. He is keenly interested in education and has taught classes in digital theory, mathematics, and other phases of electronics at Foothill College and in industry.

One of the things I admire most about James Coffron is his ability to describe complex circuits and systems in a way that makes them seem simple. In Chapter 8 of this book, for example, he adds notably to the literature of digital troubleshooting by showing how Static Stimulus Testing, as he terms it, can bring the power and simplicity of static testing to logic circuits, with great potential for saving troubleshooting time. He uses language that is readable to anyone with a modest understanding of electronics and digital theory.

I believe you will find this book to be the clearest explanation yet available of all of the elements that make up a microprocessor system, how they work, and how they relate to each other to form a practical working system whose potential uses are enormous.

WILLIAM E. LONG
Foothill College
Los Altos Hills, California

PREFACE

The purpose of this book is to dispel the mystery that surrounds microprocessors and microprocessor systems. It shows how each element of the microprocessor system relates to the microprocessor chip, beginning with the DC power supply and continuing through each peripheral function. As each element is discussed, it is carefully analyzed to show what it must do, how it is organized to accomplish it's function, and how to check it when trouble develops.

As the use of microprocessors has grown, the need to improve the literature has grown with it. Manufacturers' data sheets provide necessary information, yes, but they are not intended to convey understanding of the total system or how various elements relate to each other. The person seeking an understanding of microprocessors and peripheral elements needs a source of information that brings all this information together in one place, written in understandable language.

This book is written for anyone who is curious, who desires to know about microprocessors solely for personal satisfaction, or whose job may entail knowing and understanding microprocessor systems. No prior knowledge of microprocessor circuits is required. A background understanding of digital electronics is necessary, and at the technician level or better is ideal, and should be attained prior to undertaking a study of microprocessor systems. Given this background, an individual should be able to develop a working knowledge and good understanding of the principles and elements of a microprocessor system. For anyone who may feel hesitant, a review of timing circuits such as flip flops and counters will be helpful.

For easier analysis and understanding, this book divides the microprocessor chip into subcircuits. Each subcircuit is then introduced for discussion at the appropriate point. This is a different approach from that of the literature on the market today, which discusses the entire processor at once, which constitutes a major difficulty. The number of subcircuits and the complexity of the microprocessor chip tend to intimidate the reader. By breaking the microprocessor into subcircuits, much of the mystery and complexity is dispelled, and a major part of the difficulty that goes with studying large systems as a unit is avoided. A hardware trainer that parallels the text and utilizes this approach has been developed and is available from Creative Microprocessor Systems, Inc.* Also in preparation is a Laboratory Manual for this textbook.** The Laboratory Manual is designed to be used with any general microprocessor trainer, although it uses the CMS hardware trainer as an example.

Since debugging is closely allied with troubleshooting, any comprehensive discussion of debugging inevitably leads into a discussion of troubleshooting. How to troubleshoot an entire system is shown through discussion of selected topics specifically chosen to illustrate the troubleshooting process. Here readers learn what to expect to find when faced with a new microprocessor system for the first time. With a little practice in applying the techniques and information presented in the book, readers should be able to troubleshoot microprocessor systems successfully.

Throughout, this book stresses a practical approach to using the microprocessor. For example, it explains how to connect the microprocessor to perform some useful function (i.e., to design simple microprocessor circuits). The 8080 is used as the basis for microprocessor discussions because it is the microprocessor in widest general use today. All circuits described in this book are constructed using standard digital devices that are commonly available. This approach was adopted so that everyone can have an opportunity to build the system discussed and understand fully what is involved in making a microprocessor work. Beginners in microprocessors will probably want to experiment by building some circuits so they can see for themselves. In industry, fewer parts would be used to produce the same system. In fact, Chapter 9 discusses special digital devices that can be used to reduce the number of separate devices, or "can count," in a system. This is standard practice in industry.

There can be no doubt that the potential of microprocessor systems is only beginning to unfold. If the predictors are right, the second computer revolution is now under way.

In past years, people beyond count have helped to prepare me to write this book. To all of you I say thanks; I have not forgotten how much you helped.

I also wish to make special mention of some of the people who contributed greatly to the realization of the manuscript and the book: To Barbara

---

*Creative Microprocessor Systems, Inc. P. O. Box 1538 Los Gatos, CA 95030
**Laboratory Experiments for Microprocessor Systems (Crane and Long) © 1980 by Prentice-Hall, Inc. College Division, Englewood Cliffs, NJ 07632.

Godwin and Laura Livingston, who typed it; to Dave Dowding and Al French, who helped with the hardware; to F. Richard Vasquez for his photography; to Margaret McAbee, whose help and guidance was invaluable as Production Editor; and to Zeppi Long, for her creative art work in conceiving and producing the cover design.

Finally, I want to thank Bill Long for his enormous efforts and contributions to the finished product. One may safely say that without Bill's help and encouragement I would still be working on the manuscript.

JAMES W. COFFRON

OVERVIEW OF THE WORLD OF MICROPROCESSORS

To put microprocessors in perspective, let us begin with a few quotes: "Now under way is a new expansion of electronics into our lives, a second computer revolution that will transform ordinary products and create many new ones . . . its applications are just beginning to explode, setting off reverberations that will affect work and play, the profitability and productivity of corporations, and the nature of the computer industry itself."[1] "The microprocessor represents truly low-cost computing. Its economics are so compelling that microcomputers are serving not only in many applications where computing power was previously too costly but also in applications where . . . computer control was formerly unthinkable."[2] "By 1986 the number of electronic functions incorporated into a wide range of products each year can be expected to be 100 times greater than it is today."[3]

When these claims for microprocessors were made, they sounded extravagant; and to some, they still do. But anyone who is in a position to know what is happening in microprocessor technology today will tell you that we are entering another rapid growth era in electronics whose ultimate limits can only be guessed. What is quite clear, is that those early predictions are proving to be remarkably sound and on target.

[1]Gene Bylinsky, "Here Comes The Second Computer Revolution," *Fortune*, Vol. XCII, No. 5 Nov., 1975).
[2]Hoo-Min D. Toong, "Microprocessors," *Scientific American*, Vol. 237, No. 3 (Sept., 1977).
[3]Robert N. Noyce, "Microelectronics," *Scientific American*, Vol. 237, No. 3 (Sept., 1977).

Dr. James Arnold is a research scientist with Varian Associates in Palo Alto, California, and also teaches an introductory class in *Microprocessor Systems* at Foothill College. Dr. Arnold has this to say: "Any technological company that doesn't use microprocessors in their engineering design is going to fall out of the business, because most major instrument companies have substantial efforts going on in microprocessors".[4]

When Dr. M. E. Hoff, Jr., of Intel Corporation in Santa Clara, California, came up with an innovative solution to a problem that confronted him in 1969 he could scarcely have envisioned the impact that his ideas would have on the information processing field ten years later. For the first year or two that Intel produced the 4004, the first microprocessor that grew out of Hoff's work, it was largely ignored in the marketplace. Some people regarded it as just another new integrated circuit, some thought it too exotic to be practical, while others began to experiment with it, think about it, and use it in a few applications.

To awaken designers to the potential of their new product, Intel decided to offer seminars to teach interested engineers. It is reported that several thousand engineer-designers availed themselves of this training, with the result that the second computer revolution was assured. Today the 8080 is the microprocessor that is in widest general use. It is considered a second generation microprocessor and was introduced by Intel in 1973. There are many companies now in the microprocessor field, and we may expect to see greater capabilities emerge as refinements and advances in the state of the art are incorporated in future generations of the microprocessor.

It's an eye-opener to consider the growth of the digital market with the introduction of each significant new technological advance. In the vacuum tube era, it has been estimated that the annual growth rate of the digital market approximated 10 percent. With the introduction of the transistor the growth rate accelerated to around 18 percent, which more than doubled to about 38 percent with the introduction of the integrated circuit. Now, with the introduction of the microprocessor we may look forward to yearly gains of 50 percent or more if the geometric rise in annual growth rate proceeds as projected.

The growth in importance of microprocessor-based systems is shown in the theme of the 1978 WESCON (Western Electronics Show and Convention) held in Los Angeles in September, 1978. Titled *Micro Encounter*, the convention featured a special exhibit displaying the winners of the new Microprocessor Applications Center and Awards Program. This program encompasses eight categories of microprocessor use: office equipment and devices, home appliances, automobile controls, production controls, process and quality controls, energy conserving devices, home computer systems, and games and toys. All of this

---

[4] Dr. Arnold is quoted in the Foothill College Schedule of Classes, Fall Quarter, 1978.

constitutes mounting evidence that the microprocessor-inspired second computer revolution is solidly established now and leading another dazzling display of growth in the electronics field.

We are not well prepared to deal with such growth rates, especially on the hardware technician level. Massachusetts Institute of Technology's Professor Hoo-Min D. Toong, in his *Scientific American* article,[5] comments about this: "Literally millions of maintenance workers who at this moment may never have heard of microprocessors, much less seen one, must quickly become acquainted with them and become reasonably expert in their testing and replacement." Professor Toong, it should be noted, made this remark in describing the anticipated need for qualified technicians *in automobile repair shops alone*.

In the rapid growth phase of any new enterprise the front does not always advance evenly. Some areas must expand before others for practical reasons. We have seen this repeatedly in electronics with the transistor, the integrated circuit, the digital computer, and the hand-held calculator, to mention just a few. So it is with the microprocessor. In this case the area of software advanced first.

In order for any of us to use the microprocessor we must first know how to make it work. That is, we must know how to instruct it, how to get information into and out of the circuits, and how to communicate with the system in language that the machine understands. This means software and programming. Thus a typical user has a primary need to master any required software ahead of the hardware if, indeed, he ever needs to learn the details of hardware at all.

Educators who deal with microprocessor systems turned their attention early to the development of suitable software. Manufacturers also contribute heavily to software programming in promoting their products. The result is that a choice of good software learning material is now available. Most schools that have responded to the growing need for microprocessor skills have established courses with a predominantly software orientation.

Because the full volume of the microprocessor flood has yet to crest, the need for technicians to maintain microprocessor systems has not yet reached maximum urgency. No one doubts that these systems will occasionally malfunction, or that analysis and repair will some day be required. But exactly how the need should (or can) be met is not so widely agreed upon. One solution calls for training personnel to the skill level necessary as they are needed. This is the traditional approach. But this has the drawback that it takes considerable time and tends to follow the need, sometimes lagging so far behind that it limits growth. To counteract this situation, or in the event the shortage of skilled people persists or becomes chronic, another solution is appearing. This trend calls for the design and use of sophisticated testing machines and techniques that avoid the need for

---

[5] Hoo-Min D. Toong, "Microprocessors."

large numbers of highly skilled operators because of the volume one machine and one operator can handle. Or, alternately, the testing machine is designed so that it can be operated satisfactorily by a low-skilled person. The drawback of this approach is that the machines tend to be quite costly and hence not available to any but a few carefully selected individuals. What is needed is low cost, effective, practical troubleshooting techniques and tools that can be employed by an average skill level technician at the point of need and in the small shop.

Various troubleshooting techniques and equipment are often mentioned in connection with microprocessors and other digital systems. Among them we find signature analysis, the logic analyzer, and microprocessor development system, to name just three. Each of these aims at the same goals—fault analysis, isolation of the trouble site, and repair—via different approaches. Consequently, each system has its own particular advantages and disadvantages. In skilled hands, any one approach will be more effective than any other technique of troubleshooting in *unskilled* hands.

Signature analysis is a powerful and effective troubleshooting technique, but plans to utilize it must be taken into account and incorporated in the original design of the equipment with which it is to be used. Equipment designed without specific provision for signature analysis cannot easily be retrofitted to use it afterwards. Signature analysis has the additional drawback that the core of the system under test must be operable in order to use it.

The logic analyzer concept requires the diagnosis of hardware faults through analysis of software performance (i.e., by analyzing a failure of the system to execute software instructions properly). The equipment for logic analysis has many leads and is cumbersome to work with. As with signature analysis, the logic analyzer requires that the core of the system under test be operable in order to use it.

The troubleshooting system chosen for detailed description in this book (Chapter 8) is straightforward in concept, does not require exotic or cumbersome equipment, does not require that the core of the system under test be working, does not require as strong a mastery of software as do other systems, is not limited to systems specifically designed for it, and does not depend on the interpretation of fleeting and elusive pulses seen on an oscilloscope screen. It does require, as do all systems, a firm knowledge of what should be there at strategic points in the hardware of the system under test.

Every troubleshooting system has its place, its unique combination of strengths and weaknesses. Static stimulus testing was selected for detailed presentation not because it was the only troubleshooting system, nor even the most powerful, but because in the author's opinion it was the simplest, most practical, most generally applicable, and most easily interpreted troubleshooting technique appropriate to an introductory text. This observation comes from experience.

The power, time, and cost-saving potentials of static stimulus testing when properly applied are significant and have been demonstrated repeatedly in practical hardware debugging and fault-finding.

1

INTRODUCTION: WHAT IS A MICROPROCESSOR?

In this chapter we will discuss the concept of a microprocessor without going into great technical detail about any single one on the market today. Instead we will present a view of microprocessors that will allow one to understand how they fit into circuits designed to use them. Our discussion is calculated to provide beginning technicians with basic guidelines that may be followed in understanding microprocessor systems regardless of the type of microprocessor used.

Many microprocessor systems used in industry today have a number of points in common. This book will provide the background necessary to recognize common circuit blocks that one may expect to find in each new microprocessor encountered in practice. This chapter is the entry point to reach this goal. It will allow the reader to relate the microprocessor to already familiar topics and thus eliminate the "fear of the unknown" one usually has when venturing into new territory. After familiar ground has been established, we provide all of the technical details one needs in order to understand, analyze, and troubleshoot circuits that use a microprocessor.

The term microprocessor refers to a VLSI (Very Large Scale Integrated) circuit. Most microprocessors today are fabricated using MOS (Metal Oxide Semiconductor) technology. The microprocessor is a single "chip" contained in a package. The number of leads on the package, and the package style, will vary from manufacturer to manufacturer. Although it consists of many circuits, the device is very small physically. It may be used to process information, or it may be the central processor unit in a system. Hence the name microprocessor.

1-1 The General Nature of a Microprocessor System

Each microprocessor on the market today is constructed to contain a number of different digital functional blocks. We are not going to discuss these logic blocks at this time. Instead, we will show how a microprocessor's function in a circuit is analogous to another function with which we are all familiar, that of the troubleshooter. To present this, let's look at and examine what happens when a technician follows a checkout procedure, or set of instructions.

The essential parts of this "human" system are:

1. The checkout procedure (Data input to be interpreted)
2. The technician (Interpretation section, or CPU)
3. The function the technician performs (Data output as signals from the CPU after interpretation)

This system is shown in Figure 1-1.

Let's discuss each of the three parts of the system and show how they relate to one another. First the checkout procedure. Anyone who has had to write or follow a checkout procedure knows that it is a sequence of instructions which, when followed, will produce a meaningful result. If these instructions are to be of value, they must be interpreted in one, and only one, way. If these instructions are not *exact*, then we have no way of determining what the final result will be. Each instruction is dependent on the instruction preceding it being followed in the same precise manner the author intended. Let us call this checkout procedure the input to the system shown in Figure 1-1.

Next is the technician's role in the system shown in Figure 1-1. This part of the system is very important. The technician must read the written instructions carefully. The procedure instructions must be written in a language that the technician can interpret and understand so that, based on that interpretation, the technician can perform some action. Hence the need for the instructions to be VERY EXACT. But the technician is the key. He or she reads the instructions and by a very complicated mental process interprets them and performs an action.

The third part of the system shown in Figure 1-1 is the output. This output is the final action based on the instruction read by the technician and the interpretation of the instruction. The action taken by the technician must be predictable at all times.

One may not have thought of a technician who is following a checkout procedure in quite this way, or in this much detail before, but this accurately describes what happens in troubleshooting.

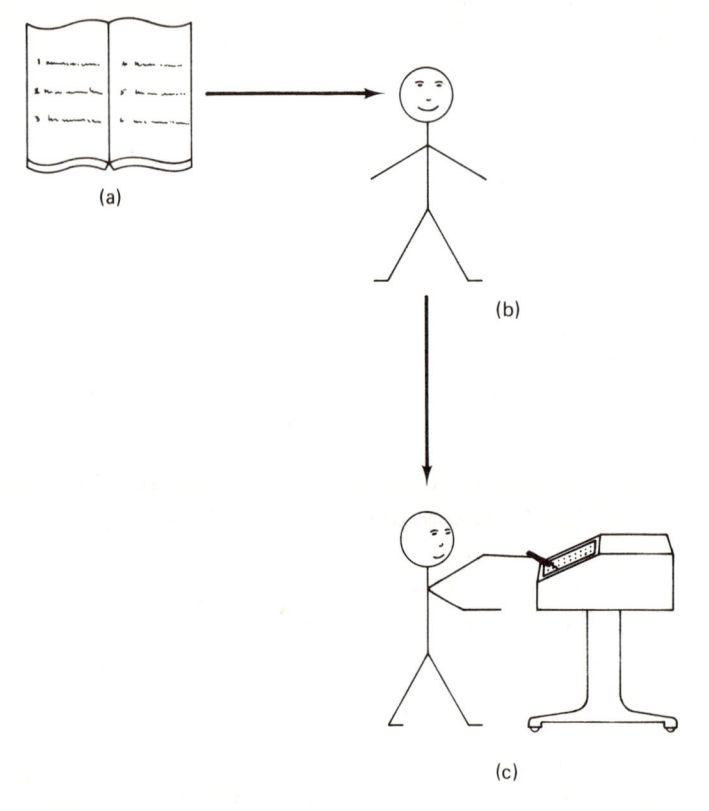

Figure 1-1 (a) Written checkout procedure (input data to be interpreted) (b) The technician (data interpretation section, or CPU) (c) Action of technician after interpretation of data input (output)

Let's turn now to a general microprocessor system. (The word *system* as used here means any circuit or combination of circuits that uses a microprocessor device, not necessarily a large computer system.) The general microprocessor system may also be described as having three basic parts. This system is shown in Figure 1-2.

The three parts of the microprocessor system shown in Figure 1-2 correspond exactly in function to the "human" system shown in Figure 1-1. The physical makeup of each part of the microprocessor system is different from the system of Figure 1-1, of course. We will now discuss each part of the system shown in Figure 1-2 and show how it relates in function to the system just discussed.

First, the input part of the microprocessor system is constructed of some type of semiconductor memory (Fig 1-2a). The memory may or may not be inside the microprocessor chip. This may be Random Access Memory (RAM), Read Only Memory (ROM), Programmable Read Only Memory (PROM), or Erasable Pro-

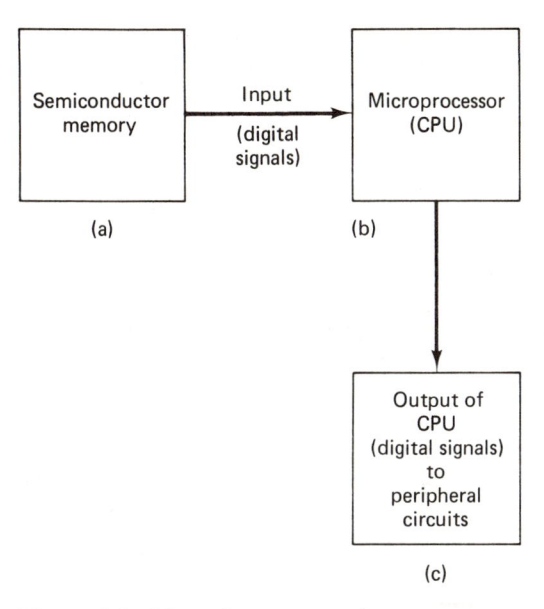

```
┌─────────────┐    Input      ┌─────────────┐
│Semiconductor│──(digital────▶│Microprocessor│
│   memory    │   signals)    │   (CPU)     │
└─────────────┘               └──────┬──────┘
      (a)                      (b)   │
                                     │
                                     ▼
                              ┌─────────────┐
                              │  Output of  │
                              │     CPU     │
                              │(digital signals)│
                              │     to      │
                              │ peripheral  │
                              │  circuits   │
                              └─────────────┘
                                    (c)
```

Figure 1-2 Three basic parts of a microprocessor system: (a) Semiconductor memory (data input to be interpreted) (b) Microprocessor (data interpretation section, or CPU) (c) Output signals from the CPU after interpretation of data input

grammable Read Only Memory (EPROM). (A detailed discussion of semiconductor memory is given in Chapter 2 of this book, so it is not necessary at this point for the reader to understand the types of memories we have just mentioned and how they are used.

The semiconductor memory contains the set of instructions that are used to instruct the interpreting section of the system. These instructions are written in a language that the interpreting section can understand and, in effect, they direct the system. The system will always do (if possible) what the instructions call for. If an instruction is out of sequence, the system has no way of knowing it is not right, and its response will be out of sequence.

The second part of the system is the interpreting section (Fig 1-2b). This is the microprocessor, or central processing unit (CPU). The microprocessor interprets the instruction input and performs some action based on the instruction.

The third part of the system is the output section (Fig 1-2c). The microprocessor interprets the input instruction and then performs some action. The action is in the form of digital outputs. The digital outputs of the microprocessor will change according to the input instructions.

One may see from this analogy between a microprocessor and a technician following a checkout procedure that the microprocessor's job is in all cases to interpret the input instructions and perform some action based on these instructions. *No matter what system the microprocessor is designed into, its main function does not change.* The part of a "microprocessor-based" system that makes the system itself unique consists of the external circuits that the microprocessor controls as it does its job of interpreting instructions and changing its output.

It may further be seen from Figure 1-2 that the microprocessor *is* the central processor of digital information. That is, the input instructions seldom go directly to the output section of Figure 1-2. The output section seldom "talks" directly to the instruction section. Most information exchanges between input and output in a microprocessor-based system are executed via the microprocessor. It is because of this central location for processing of information that the microprocessor is referred to as the Central Processor Unit, or simply CPU. Large computer systems have a CPU, but it may not be a microprocessor. The term CPU refers to the digital function of a section of hardware in a system. If the microprocessor performs that function, then it may be called a CPU. But remember, not all CPUs are microprocessors.

1-2 General Organization of Electronics Systems

We should recall that microprocessor systems are electronics systems, and as such, they conform to the organizational plan of virtually all electronics systems. That is, electronics systems are electrical systems: they have an input *transducer* to transform signal energy from its original form into an electrical signal, they have a means of amplifying or processing the electrical signal in some desired way, and they have an output transducer to transform the processed electrical signal energy into a form that is meaningful and useful to us. This is shown graphically in Figure 1-3.

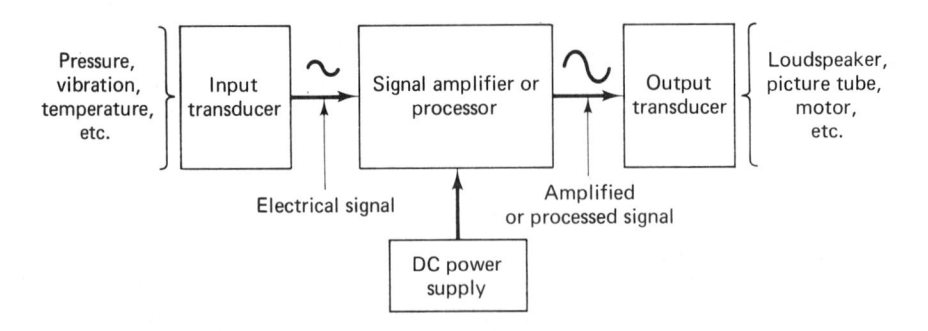

Figure 1-3 Functional organization typical of all electronics systems

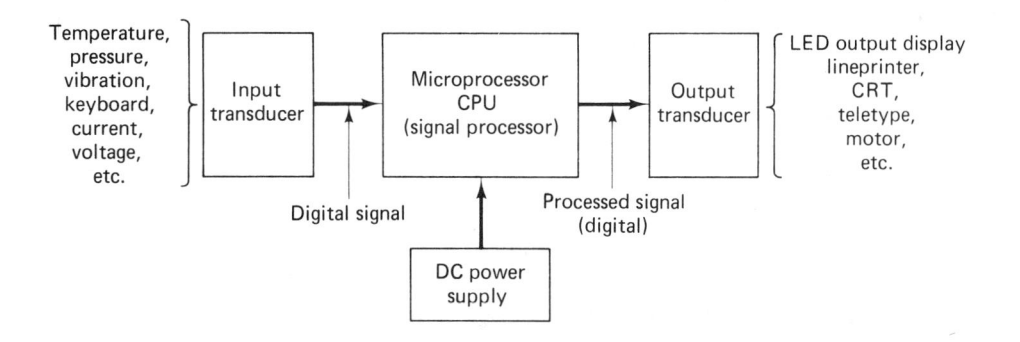

Figure 1-4 Functional organization typical of most microprocessor systems

There is one more essential part of all electronics systems, a power supply. In almost every electronics system, operating power is provided by a DC voltage source of proper voltage level, current capacity, regulation, and impedance to meet the requirements of the equipment it serves.

The organization of a microprocessor system is shown in Figure 1-4. Note that it conforms generally to the organizational plan of electronics systems shown in the preceding figure. For closer comparison, we have indicated some specifics typical of a microprocessor system, such as the keyboard and other functional blocks. Each of these parts—keyboard, signal processor, output display unit—will be carefully explored and discussed in the chapters ahead.

The only part of the microprocessor system that we will not examine closely is the power supply. For our purposes it is enough to know that a power supply must be there and functioning properly in order for the rest of the system to operate satisfactorily. Four observations about the power supply are worth remembering, however:

1. Output voltage of the power supply is DC voltage. (Look at schematics and manufacturer's specifications to find the specified voltage value.)
2. The amount of ripple is very small. (Specifications will tell the maximum permissible amount, usually in peak-to-peak values of voltage.)
3. DC voltage variation should not exceed specified limits as the system is operated. (Look to specifications to find out what these limits are. Most power supplies include voltage regulation circuits to hold output voltage values steady.)
4. When a power supply fails to meet its specifications, the trouble may be in either the power supply or the load.*

*See Chap. 1, *Getting Started in Electronic Troubleshooting*, Reston Publishing Co., 1979.

11

We mention these things about the DC power supply at this time because the schematics of digital systems usually take the power supply for granted. They assume that whoever looks at a schematic will know that a power supply is there, even though it may not be shown or mentioned. It is one of those items that is simply "understood" by experienced workers in the field, who sometimes forget that a person new to digital electronics does not understand this. Therefore, when checking out a malfunctioning microprocessor system, one should make measurements early to determine that the power supply is operating and that its voltage level is indeed what should be there. Trying to find trouble in the rest of the system is a waste of time if the power supply output is improper, because the system *cannot* operate as designed if this voltage is not correct. Check for satisfactory power supply output voltage first! Many digital systems have more than one power supply, which provide different levels of DC output voltage, provide different polarites of voltage with respect to ground, meet different requirements of different loads, and provide isolation between loads that might interfere with each other if connected to a common power supply. *Be sure to check all power supplies.*

1-3 Some Basic Vocabulary Essential to Microprocessor Systems

In working with microprocessors we encounter new terms that are associated with these devices. Some of these new terms that will be of value for the beginner are introduced in this section. Other terms will be introduced in later chapters of this book as they are needed. The terms introduced here are selected because of their value to the inexperienced microprocessor technician.

Bit: A bit is a single digital signal or "line" that usually performs some special function in a digital circuit. Examples of the use of the word bit are:

- "The least significant bit." (LSB) This is the single digital line that has the smallest value of $2^0 = 1$ in a binary sequence.
- "The most significant bit." (MSB) This is the digital line that has the largest value of 2^{n-1} where n is the maximum number of digital lines under discussion. For instance, if we were talking about four digital lines, then the "most significant bit" is the fourth line in the sequence. The least significant bit is the first line in the sequence.

Another example of the use of the word "bit" is in a phrase like, "the carry bit." This describes a particular digital line that has the function of carry. Do not be concerned at this point about the meaning of the word carry. We have introduced it here solely for demonstration purposes. The term bit still refers to a single digital line in a system.

Nibble: The term *nibble* refers to a group of 4 bits. The 4 bits of the group usually have some function in common. Groups of 4 bits are used often in microprocessor circuits. An example of a nibble would be 4 address lines input to a memory. The address lines A_0, A_1, A_2, A_3, as a group would be considered to be a nibble. There are also references to the least significant nibble and the most significant nibble. This is a shorthand way of describing the lower 4 bits of a group of more than 4 bits. It is also used for describing the 4 highest numbered bits in a group of more than 4 bits.

Byte: The term *byte* refers to a group of 8 bits that usually have some function in common. Many microprocessors process one byte of digital information at a time. This means the microprocessor is performing its function based on 8 bits of input information and 8 bits of output information. All processing performed on the 8 bits is done in parallel.

I/O: This abbreviation stands for the words Input/Output. It is used extensively in microprocessor systems to describe certain logic blocks related to input and output functions.

Common I/O: This term usually refers to a single set of digital lines that can be used for both inputting and outputting digital information. The technique of sharing digital lines for this purpose is common in microprocessors and semiconductor memories. It reduces the number of physical connections that have to be made to a device package. It is a useful technique because the information on a digital signal line is usually needed for only a brief period of time; the rest of the time the system "does not care" what information is on the signal line. A detailed discussion of common I/O lines relating to semiconductor memories is given in Chapter 2 of this book. Discussion of common I/O lines relating to microprocessors is presented in Chapter 3.

Active Pull-up Device: This refers to a digital device that has an active component pulling the output to a logical 1 voltage level. See Figure 1-5 for a diagram of an active pull-up output structure.**

**See Chap. 1, *Getting Started in Digital Troubleshooting*, Reston Publishing Co., 1979.

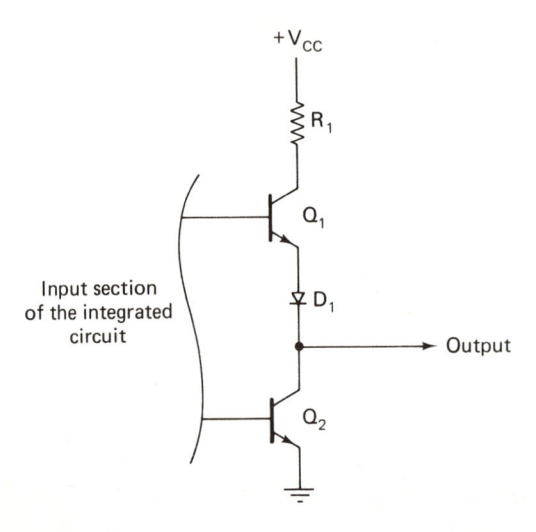

Figure 1-5 Active pull-up output structure of a TTL IC

Passive Pull-up Device: This refers to a digital device that has a passive component pulling up the output to a logical 1 voltage level. The passive device is usually a resistor. See Figure 1-6 for a diagram of a passive pull-up output structure.

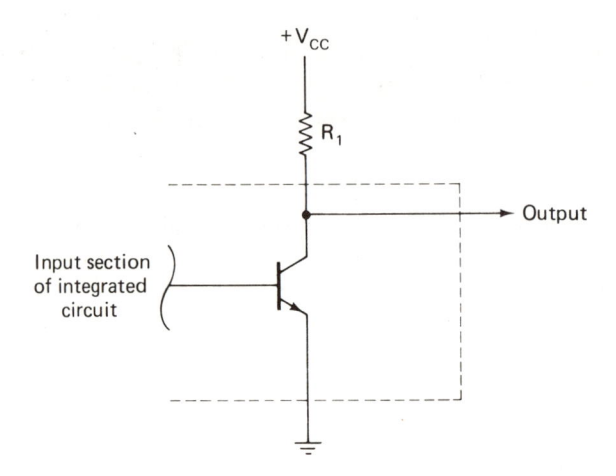

Figure 1-6 Passive pull-up output structure of a TTL IC. Resistor R1 is external to the device package (open collector device).

Tri-state Device: This refers to a digital device that has a third (tri) state on the output. The first two states are logical 1 and logical 0. The third state is "off," or the high impedance state. One reason for the use of a tri-state device is that it permits a digital line to be used as a common I/O line. The line might look as shown in Figure 1-7.

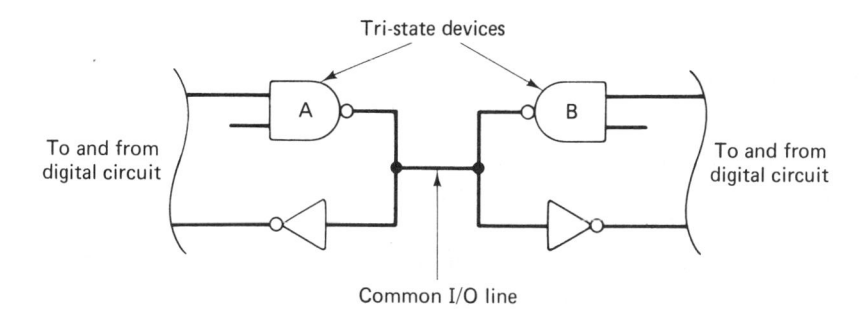

Figure 1-7 A typical example of how device outputs of tri-state devices can be connected on an I/O line

Notice that when we are inputting information into a common I/O line from device B we do not want the output of A to interfere. When we wish to use the common line as an input line, we must disable the output of A by putting device A in the tri-state mode. Device A is now in a high impedance state, and the common line can be driven safely by output B which is connected in parallel with it.

By using tri-state techniques the electronics industry has been able to take advantage of the speed and drive capability associated with active pull-up devices. At the same time, the use of a common I/O line reduces the number of pins needed on a device and hence the number of signal lines needed to perform the same function.

Buffer: The term *buffer* refers to a digital device that increases the output drive capability of one digital signal line. In effect, both the Iout (0) and Iout (1) are increased. The technique of buffering a digital signal is used when a single output line must drive many input lines. Common applications are on memory address input lines. Buffering is also used when interfacing most MOS devices to T^{2}L devices because of the difference in input and output currents for each family of logic. See Figure 1-8 for a diagram of a buffer in use.

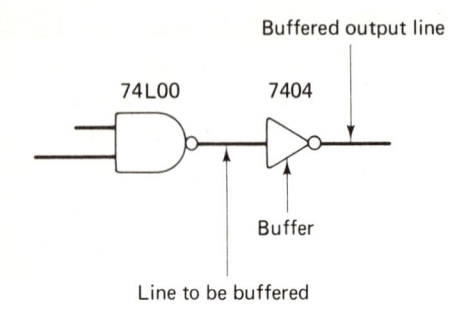

Figure 1-8 The 74L00 device can sink only 2 milliamperes. If this output is to drive several TTL standard inputs, we must increase the output drive capability of this line. The 7404 can be driven by 2 milliamperes and it can sink 16 milliamperes. There are special devices on the market that can sink more than 16 milliamperes (7437, 7438, 7406, for examples).

1-4 How to Convert Octal and Hexadecimal Codes in Binary Communication

The octal and hexadecimal codes are those most commonly used to communicate binary information from humans to computers. These codes are easy to translate into pure binary. For our purposes we will not need to perform arithmetic in the octal or hexadecimal number system. The only use we make of these codes is for ease of communication. We do need to know how to translate from octal to binary and from binary to octal. We also need to know how to translate from hexadecimal to binary and back to hexadecimal again. The hexadecimal, decimal, and binary codes are given in Table 1-1. The conversion techniques follow.

TABLE 1-1
HEXADECIMAL AND BINARY EQUIVALENTS
OF COMMON DECIMAL NUMBERS

Decimal	Hexadecimal	Binary
0	0	0000
1	1	0001
2	2	0010
3	3	0011
4	4	0100
5	5	0101
6	6	0110
7	7	0111
8	8	1000
9	9	1001
10	A	1010
11	B	1011
12	C	1100
13	D	1101
14	E	1110
15	F	1111

Sec. 1-4 *How to Convert Octal and Hexadecimal Codes in Binary Communication* **17**

Octal Code: Let us use an example and Figure 1-9 to show how to translate from binary to octal. Suppose we need to translate a 16-bit number from binary to octal. Such a number is shown in Figure 1–9(a). The sequence of events for the translation follows:

1. Starting from the LSB (least significant bit) count 3 bits in to the left and draw a vertical line (Figure 1-9(b).)
2. We then convert this 3-bit binary number to its decimal equivalent. (The only possible choices are digits 0–7.)
3. We then repeat the process of dividing the 16-bit number into groups of three bits each, as shown in Figure 1-9(c), proceeding from LSB to MSB.
4. If less than 3 bits are in the last group, simply insert zeros at left as place holders. Figure 1-9(d) shows the complete translation of the 16-bit binary number into octal.

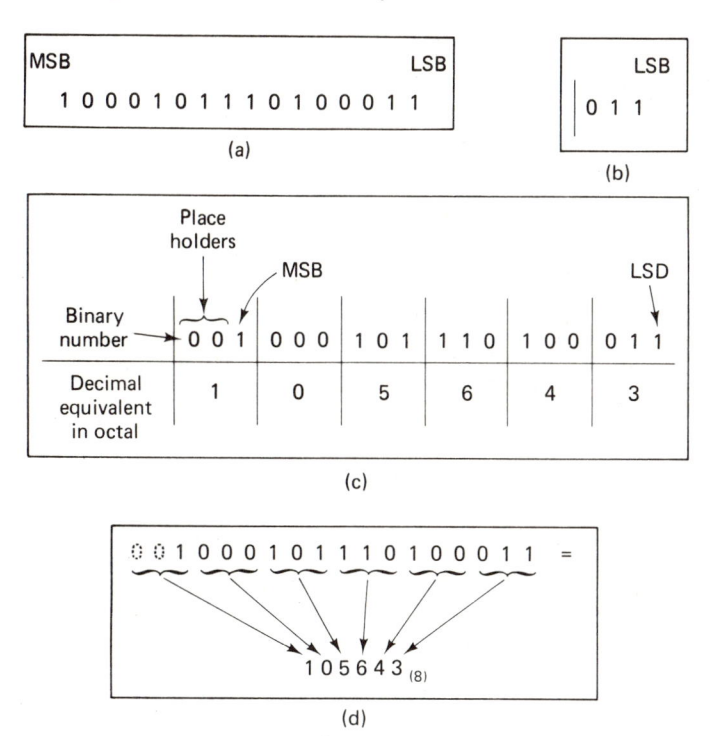

Figure 1-9 Conversion of a binary number into octal: (a) Write the binary number to be converted into octal. (b) Convert least significant 3 bits first (c) Divide the binary word into groups of 3 bits and translate each group of 3 bits into its decimal equivalent, proceeding from right to left. (d) Binary number translated into its octal equivalent

Here is another example. In Figure 1-10 the binary number is shown with the octal equivalent beneath in (b). Notice that the number of bits in the binary number does not matter. Just add zeroes at left as place-holders. If these steps are followed, the technique works every time. With a little practice such conversions can be made mentally in moments.

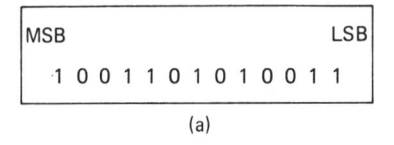

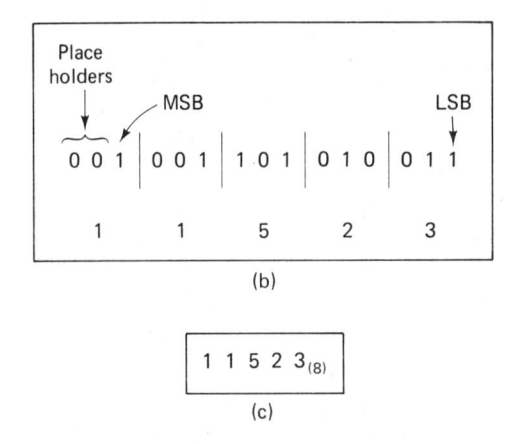

```
MSB                      LSB
 1 0 0 1 1 0 1 0 1 0 0 1 1
```
(a)

```
Place
holders
   |     MSB              LSB
   ↓    ↙                  ↓
 0 0 1 | 0 0 1 | 1 0 1 | 0 1 0 | 0 1 1
   1       1       5       2       3
```
(b)

$1\ 1\ 5\ 2\ 3_{(8)}$

(c)

Figure 1-10 (a) Binary number to be converted into octal (b) Divide number into groups of 3 bits, starting with the LSB (c) Final octal equivalent of binary number in (a)

Let us now reverse this process to translate from the octal to binary. Again we will demonstrate with an example and an illustration. Let's convert the octal number shown in Figure 1-11(a). The steps for conversion are:

1. Write the octal number (a) and then draw lines between each individual digit as shown.
2. Under each digit write the 3-bit binary equivalent. This is easy to do since the digits only go from 0–7.
3. When this is complete, read the binary number from left to right. The MSB is on the left.

```
          ┌─────────────────┐
          │ MSD       LSD   │
          │  3 4 6 2₍₈₎     │
          └─────────────────┘
                 (a)
```

Octal number	3	4	6	2
Binary equivalent	0 1 1	1 0 0	1 1 0	0 1 0

(b)

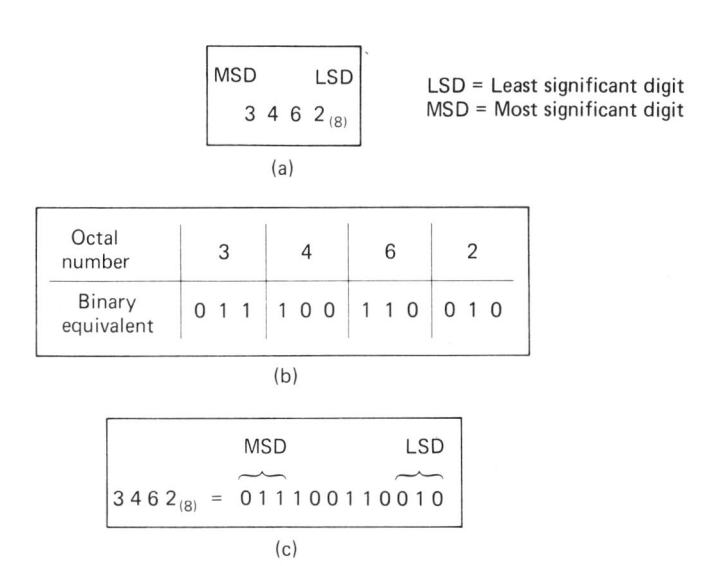

```
              MSD           LSD
      3 4 6 2₍₈₎ = 0 1 1 1 0 0 1 1 0 0 1 0
```
(c)

Figure 1-11 (a) Octal number to be converted (b) Conversion from octal to binary (c) Statement of equivalency, showing MSD and LSD

Another example of octal to binary conversion is shown in Figure 1-12.

One can see from these examples how quickly a large binary number can be rewritten as an octal number. With a little practice the conversions between these two number systems can be done in your head.

```
           ┌──────────┐
           │ 7 3 6 5₍₈₎│
           └──────────┘
               (a)
```

7	3	6	5
1 1 1	0 1 1	1 1 0	1 0 1

(b)

```
   7 3 6 5₍₈₎ = 1 1 1 0 1 1 1 1 0 1 0 1
```
(c)

Figure 1-12 (a) Octal number to be converted to binary (b) Binary equivalent of each octal digit (c) Binary equivalent of the octal number

Hexadecimal Code: The conversion between hexadecimal and binary codes is performed in similar fashion to the octal conversions we have just discussed. The major difference is that four bits are used in hexadecimal code while only three are used in octal code. The hexadecimal code is given in Table 1-1. The hexadecimal code is usually chosen only where the number of bits in the binary number is an exact multiple of four. This is common in microprocessor systems where the number of bits is either four, eight or sixteen. An example of converting from binary to hexadecimal is given in Figure 1-13. The steps for the conversion are similar to the binary to octal conversion except that four bits are used instead of three. This makes the conversion a little harder than octal because now there is a possibility of digits from 0–F.

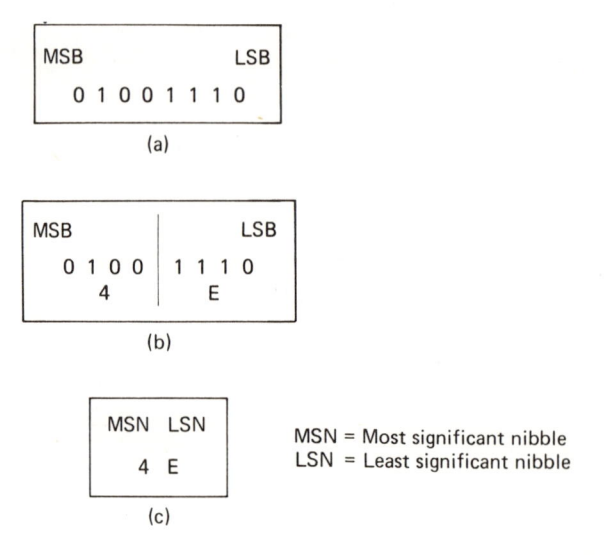

```
MSB              LSB
0 1 0 0 1 1 1 0
```
(a)

```
MSB        |     LSB
0 1 0 0    | 1 1 1 0
   4       |    E
```
(b)

```
MSN  LSN
 4    E
```
(c)

MSN = Most significant nibble
LSN = Least significant nibble

Figure 1-13 (a) **Binary number to translate into hexadecimal code** (b) **The binary number divided into groups of 4 bits with the hexadecimal equivalent of each 4 bits** (c) **The hexadecimal equivalent of the binary number in (a).**

To reverse the conversion, from hexadecimal to binary, the following procedure is used:

1. Write the digits of the hexadecimal number, and then draw a line separating each individual digit (Figure 1-14).
2. Write the binary equivalent of the hexadecimal number below each digit.
3. After all digits have been translated into binary, write the entire binary number, starting with the MSB as the leftmost digit.

$$\boxed{D\ 0\ 5_{(16)}}$$

(a)

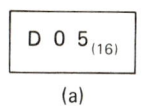

MSN		LSN
D	0	5
1101	0000	0101

MSB .... LSB

(b)

$$D\ 0\ 5_{(16)} = 1\ 1\ 0\ 1\ 0\ 0\ 0\ 0\ 0\ 1\ 0\ 1$$

(c)

Figure 1-14 (a) Hexadecimal number to be converted into binary (b) Each "hex" digit is translated into its binary equivalent (4 bits) (c) binary equivalent of the hexadecimal number in (a)

One should practice these conversions and become familiar with the octal number system and the hexadecimal number system. Most of the literature and data sheets for microprocessors and related devices assumes that readers know these number systems.

1-5 How to Read Data Sheets and Static Electrical Parameters of Digital Devices

Manufacturers' data sheets are vital to the design function and the repair and maintenance function. For the design engineers these data sheets provide device specifications that set forth the recommended operating conditions and safety limits, electrical parameters or characteristics, and the physical characteristics. The engineers cannot function effectively without the information they provide; if there were no data sheets the required information would have to be developed or another source found in order for the work to be done. Data sheets and specifications are equally valuable to troubleshooters who are responsible for system checkout and maintenance. Without specifications, a troubleshooter has no way to tell if a device or system is, or is not, performing as it is supposed to perform, because there are no "standards" at hand with which to compare measurements and data acquired. To work effectively in the electronics field, one needs to read and understand data sheets to learn the capabilities, characteristics, needs, and limitations of a particular device. Often, trouble in a system is due to a device that fails to meet its specifications in one or more ways.

We have chosen the data sheet for the SN 7400 series of T²L devices for detailed examination. This is shown in Figure 1-15. Each parameter will be discussed in the order in which it appears on this data sheet.

Parameter	Conditions	Min	Typ	Max	Units
Input diode clamp voltage	V_{CC} = 5.0 V, T_A = 25°C, I_{IN} = −12 mA			−1.5	V
Logical "1" Input voltage	V_{CC} = Min	2.0			V
Logical "0" Input voltage	V_{CC} = Min			0.8	V
Logical "1" Output voltage	V_{CC} = Min V_{IN} = 0.8 V, I_{OUT} = −400 μA	2.4			V
Logical "0" Output voltage	V_{CC} = Min V_{IN} = 2.0 V, I_{OUT} = 16 mA			0.4	V
Logical "1" Input current	V_{CC} = Max V_{IN} = 2.4 V			40	μA
Logical "1" Input current	V_{CC} = Max V_{IN} = 5.5 V			1	mA
Logical "0" Input current	V_{CC} = Max V_{IN} = 0.4 V			−1.6	mA
Output short circuit current	V_{CC} = Max V_{IN} = 0, V_0 = 0 V DM74XX / DM54XX	−20 / −18		−55	mA
Supply current— Logical "0"	V_{CC} = Max V_{IN} = 5.0 V		3	5.1	mA
Supply current— Logical "1"	V_{CC} = Max V_{IN} = 0 V		1	1.8	mA
Propagation delay time to logical "0", t_{pd0}	V_{CC} = 5.0 V, T_A = 25°C, C = 50 pF		8	15	ns
Propagation delay time to logical "1", t_{pd1}	V_{CC} = 5.0 V, T_A = 25°C, C = 50 pF		13	25	ns

Figure 1-15 Data sheet for 7400 TTL NAND gate

Sec. 1-5   *How to Read Data Sheets and Static Electrical Parameters of Digital Devices*   23

Input Diode Clamp Voltage: This should never exceed -1.5 volts. The input diodes are built-in protective diodes that are connected to the input lines of a device to keep or "clamp" input voltage from exceeding -1.5 volts with respect to ground. These diodes are incorporated in the IC as a part of the device chip. See Figure 1-16 for details.

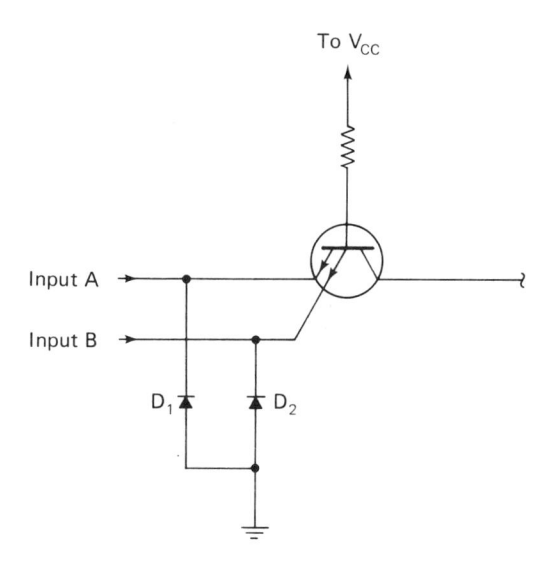

Figure 1-16   Location of input clamp diodes D1,D2 on a typical TTL input structure

Logical 1 Input Voltage: This is the minimum input voltage level (2.0 V) that will be recognized by the device as a valid logical 1 input voltage. This is illustrated in Figure 1-17.

Logical 0 Imput Voltage: This is the maximum input voltage level that will be recognized by the device as a valid logical 0 input voltage (Figure 1-17). Note carefully that the minimum logical 1 input voltage and the maximum logical 0 input voltage are NOT the same value. When the measured input voltage in a circuit falls outside the valid voltage boundaries for logical 1 or logical 0, the device itself is suspect, and more checks need to be made to pinpoint the trouble.

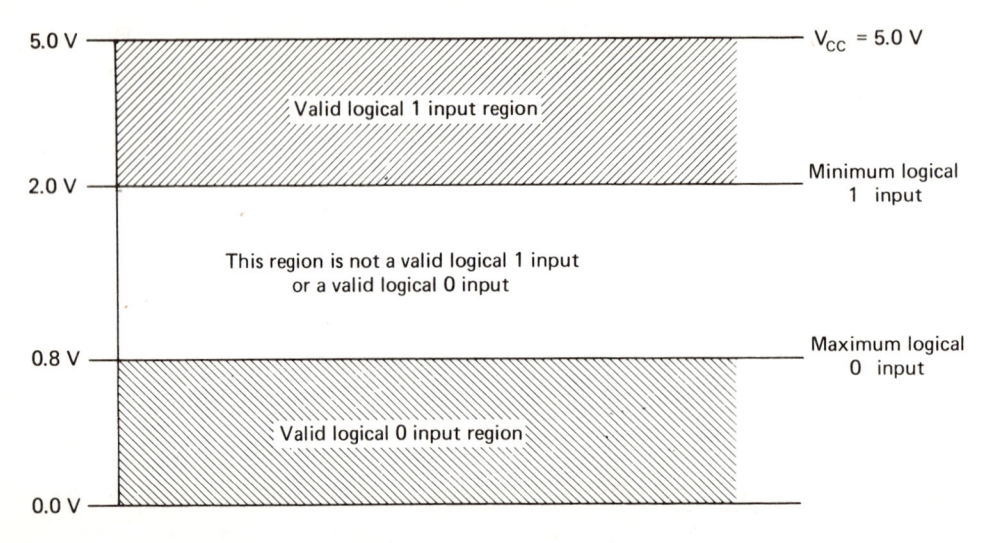

Figure 1-17 Boundaries of valid input voltages equal to logical 1 and logical 0

Logical 1 Output Voltage: To be valid logical 1, output voltage should not be less than 2.4 volts. This specification is given for active pull-up devices only. See Figure 1-18.

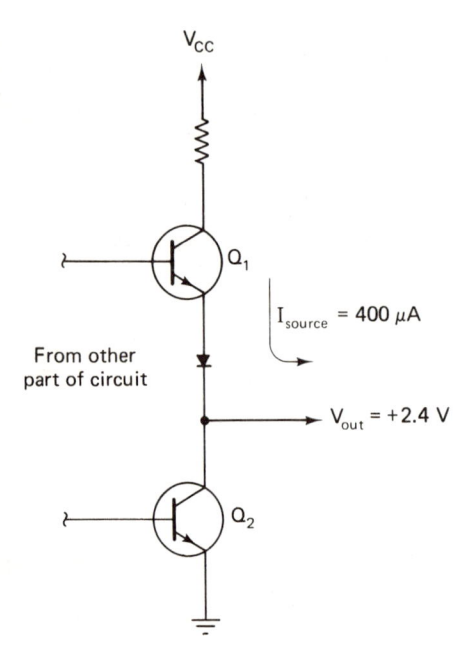

Figure 1-18 Active pull-up output structure in which transistor Q1 turns on and pulls the output line toward V_{CC}

24

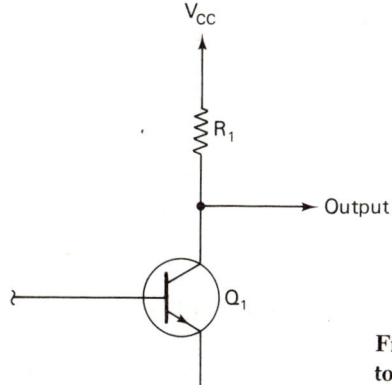

Figure 1-19 Passive pull-up output structure in which transistor Q1 turns off and resistor R1 pulls the output toward V_{CC}. In TTL devices, resistor R1 is *not* inside the device package.

Logical 0 Output Voltage: This is the maximum logical 0 output voltage of the device (0.4 volt) when 16 mA of output current is flowing. In other words, we can say that the output voltage should not exceed 0.4 volt when the output current is 16 mA; if it does, the device is not operating within its specifications. See Figures 1-19, and 20 to illustrate the definition in terms of hardware.

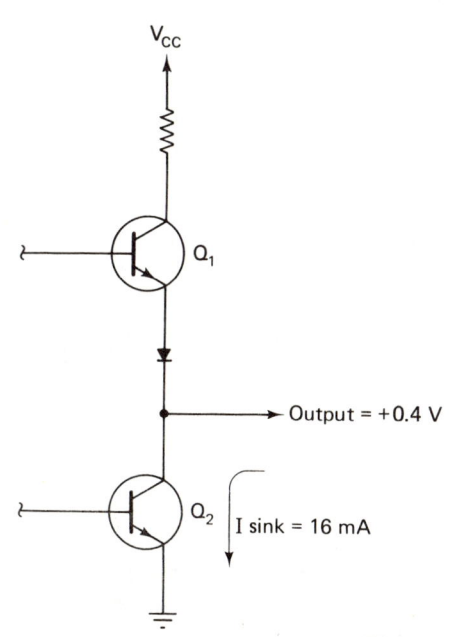

Figure 1-20 With transistor Q2 on and Q1 off, the output can sink 16 mA and not rise above +0.4 V

Logical 1 Input Current: This is the maximum input current to the device (40 µa) when the input voltage level equals 2.4 volts. This current is carried by the input line and comes from an external source. Note on Figure 1-15 that a specification of input current is also given for a different input voltage (1 mA @ 5.5 volts). See Figures 1-20, 21.

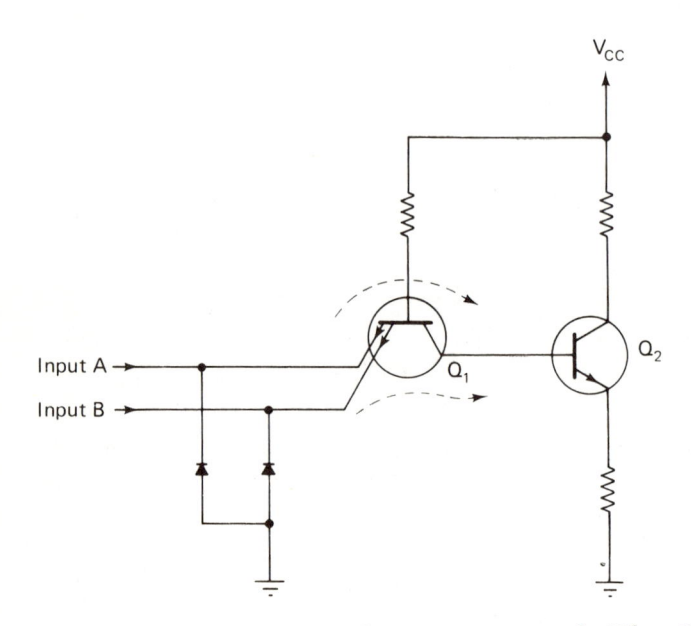

Figure 1-21 Logical 1 input current path. When Q1 goes into the inverted active mode, the input lines must supply the inverted collector current **Iin A** and **Iin B**

Logical 0 Input Current: This is the input current (−1.6 mA) when the input voltage level equals 0.4 volt. These last four specifications are used to determine the "fan out"—a term used to describe how many devices of the same type can be driven by the output from one. Fan out is illustrated in Figure 1-22 and is calculated as follows:

For logical 0, output voltage = 0.4 V @ 16 − mA
For logical 0, input current = −1.6 mA @ 0.4 V

Thus, fan out for logical 0 = 16 mA/−1.6 mA = 10. This means that the output of a single device is sufficient to drive the inputs of 10 similar devices.

For logical 1, output voltage = 2.4 V @ −400 µA
For logical 1, input current = 40 µA @ 2.4 V

Sec. 1-5 *How to Read Data Sheets and Static Electrical Parameters of Digital Devices* 27

Thus, fan out for logical 1 = −400 μA/40 μA = 10. This number of devices of fan out for logical 1 agrees with the calculation of fan out for logical 0. Notice in both calculations that the (−) sign denotes current direction only.

If one device supplies or "sources" a certain amount of current, another device (or devices) must accept or "sink" that current. The output current rating of the SN7400 is 10 times the input current rating, i.e., the fan out = 10. Figure 1-22 illustrates this.

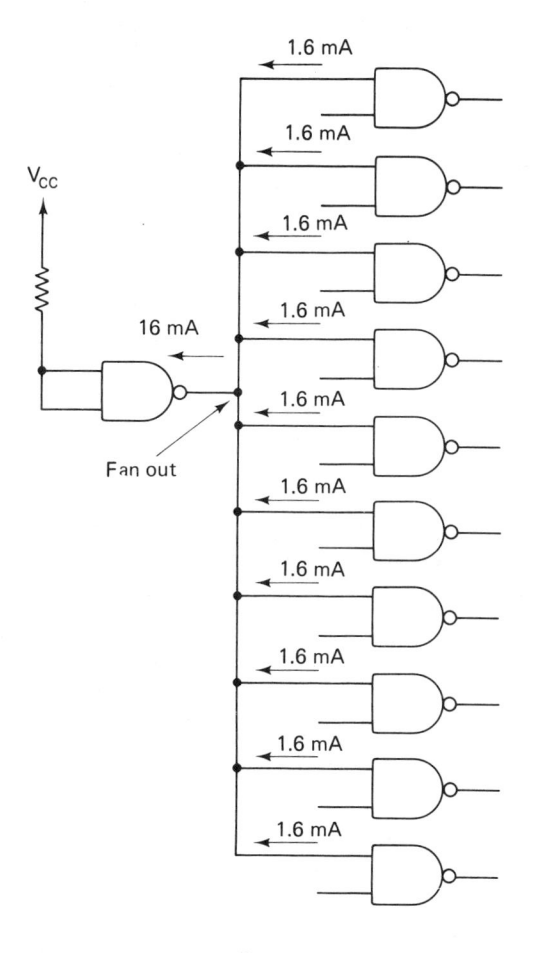

Figure 1-22 Fan out of 10, showing origins of all currents. Fan out = 16 mA/−1.6 mA = 10 devices

Output Short-circuit Current: With the output shorted to ground while the device is in the logical 1 state, the output current is specified to be between 20 and 55 mA (Figure 1-23). When the data sheet (Figure 1-15) specifies output short-circuit current, it implies that the device incorporates *short-circuit protection*. It also means that the device is an active pull-up type.

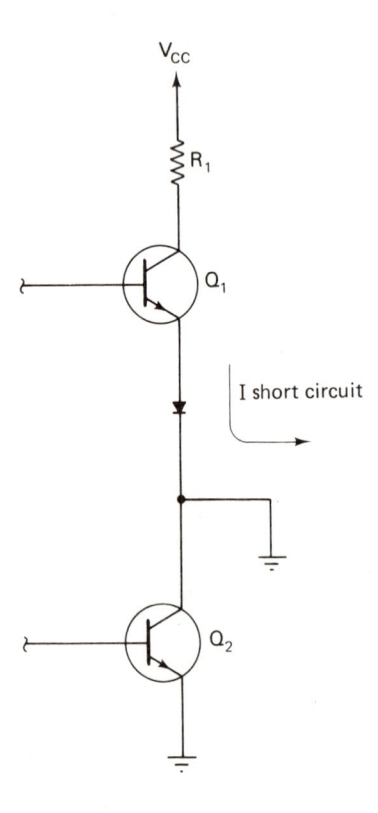

Figure 1-23 Q1 on and Q2 off with the output connected (shorted) to ground. Resistor R1 will limit the current to a value between 20–55 mA, providing short-circuit protection.

Supply Current Logical 0: This is the amount of current the DC power supply (V_{cc}) must furnish when only one output is at the logical 0 level (Figure 1-24). If two outputs are at logical 0 level, the power supply must provide twice as much current as the data sheet specifies.

Supply Current Logical 1: This is the amount of current the DC power supply (V_{cc}) must furnish when only one output is at the logical 1 level (Figure 1-25). Figure 1-26 illustrates "worst case" supply current when all gates are in the logical 0 state.

Anyone who works with digital integrated circuits needs to know and understand their specified parameters in order to work effectively; engineers use this information in designing circuits, and technicians depend on them to indicate "what should be there."

$I_{V_{CC}} = I_{G1} + I_{G2} + I_{G3} + I_{G4}$

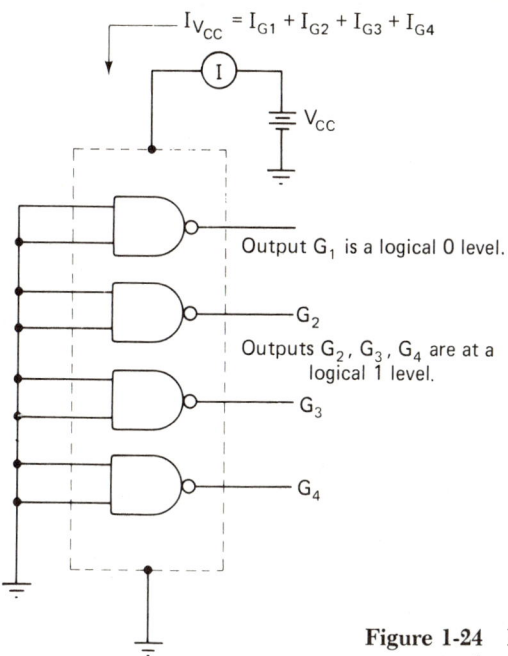

Output G_1 is a logical 0 level.

G_2

Outputs G_2, G_3, G_4 are at a logical 1 level.

G_3

G_4

Figure 1-24 Measurement of supply current logical 0, with G1 output in the logical 0 state

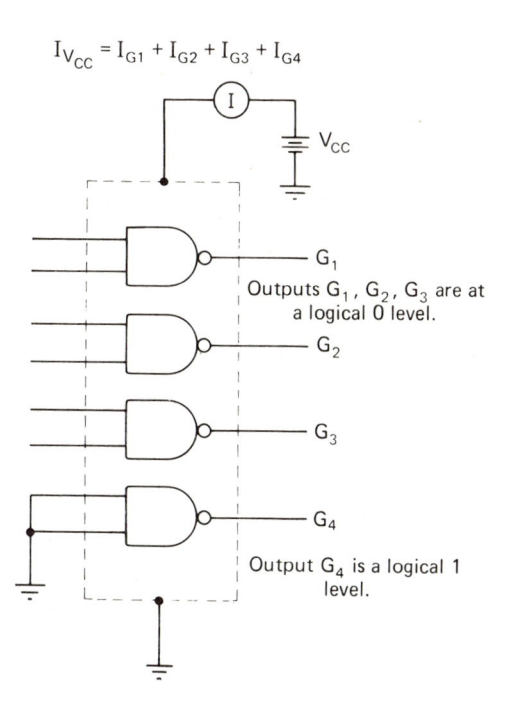

$I_{V_{CC}} = I_{G1} + I_{G2} + I_{G3} + I_{G4}$

G_1

Outputs G_1, G_2, G_3 are at a logical 0 level.

G_2

G_3

G_4

Output G_4 is a logical 1 level.

Figure 1-25 Measurement of supply current logical 1, with G4 output in the logical 1 state

29

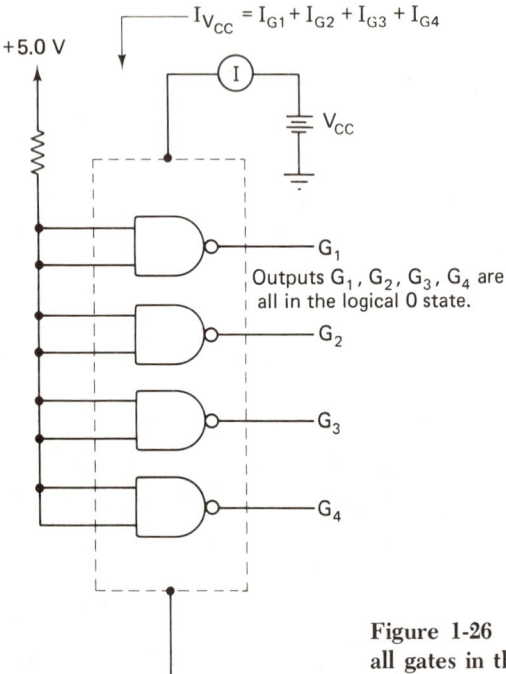

Figure 1-26 Measurement of worst case supply current with all gates in the logical 0 output state

1-6 The Role of Symbolism in Understanding Computers

The extent to which we use symbols in our daily lives is not appreciated until we consciously direct our attention to it. Symbols serve us so widely and so well that we take them for granted and seldom give them a passing thought. We use symbols every day, and we dream in symbols at night. Our memory and thought processes would be impossible without using symbols. Every experience, everything we understand about our past, present, and future environment is held in our minds in symbol form. All of our aspirations and plans for the future are directly dependent on the manipulation of information that is stored in our memory as symbols. Take the word "tree," for example. "Tree" evokes individual images for each of us. But the word "tree" is not the tree itself, nor is the image that it brings to mind. Even if we are born blind we have images in our minds of what a tree is, derived from remembered images produced by our senses of touch, smell, and hearing. Just to think about a tree involves the manipulation of information in different forms:

- the word "tree" is composed of individual letters, each one a symbol and an abstraction;

Sec. 1-6   *The Role of Symbolism in Understanding Computers*   31

- a picture of a tree involves shape, color, size, and relation to the earth. Yet none of these symbols *are* the tree, nor are the carbon of the letters, nor the pigment of the picture nor the symbols that are stored inside our heads. These stored symbols in memory have a different form, and still they represent the same actual tree.

What we are faced with here is the realization that we deal with "hard" information in many different symbolic ways. Language is an example. When we speak we use sounds to represent the actual tree, and we use different sounds to represent the same tree in different languages. Going further, a man's voice and a woman's voice employ different frequencies when they say the word "tree." Any thoughtful examination of the extent and manner in which all of us use symbols will almost certainly bring some surprises in this very basic, taken-for-granted area.

To comprehend and understand digital equipment and computers it is very important to realize that they simply handle information in the form of digital (or binary) symbols. Once this is understood, it is apparent that computers are just another information-handling type of machine in which information or data is represented in the form of digital symbols, which may be stored as an electrical charge on (or not on) a capacitor, as a transistor that is turned on or off, or as a spot that is magnetized or not magnetized, to mention just a few possibilities.

Whatever we want the computer to "remember" must be accurately described first and then translated into digital symbols before it can be "stored" in the computer memory. When we wish to "recall" the stored information, we go to the memory location where it is stored to retrieve it (access the memory). Stored information is recovered in digital symbol form, of course, and we must change it to whatever other symbolic form we desire for use.

We can, if we wish, represent the alphabet in digital or binary form. We might number the letters in digital sequence from 1 to 26 as follows:

A	00001		N	01110
B	00010		O	01111
C	00011		P	10000
D	00100		Q	10001
E	00101		R	10010
F	00110		S	10011
G	00111		T	10100
H	01000		U	10101
I	01001		V	10110
J	01010		W	10111
K	01011		X	11000
L	01100		Y	11001
M	01101		Z	11010

Now we can spell tree in binary/digital symbols: 10100 10010 00101 00101. It can be stored, retrieved, processed, moved, and re-translated into LED (light emitting diode) read-out, CRT (cathode ray tube) display, or printed page as we wish. We can even instruct the computer to give us a graphic picture of a tree on the CRT display or printed page if we prefer.

A point to remember is that whatever we want the computer to do or remember must be translated into binary form. Not only that, but the information to be handled must be precise and *exact*, and our instructions to the computer must be stated in exactly the right *form* and exactly the right *sequence*. Digital equipment does exactly what it is told to do in exactly the same sequence; any error in "programming" shows up as an error in output.

By storing information in memory, selectively moving and/or retrieving and processing it, our microprocessor can act upon instructions to make decisions.

If we are to take advantage of the capabilities the computer offers, we need to learn "computer language" in order to program the machine and instruct it about what we wish it to do. It is well worth the time and effort it takes to do this for those interested in enlarging their own capabilities.

The three major areas we must face when we ask ourselves what we need to master to become skilled in computers are:

1. *The hardware*: that is, the circuits, power supply, digital logic elements, keyboard and other information-handling input mechanisms, plus a variety of output devices such as the line printer, CRT display; LED indicators, and so on.
2. *The software*: that is, the language and instructions that get information into and out of the computer and enable the computer to process information in a way that will fulfill the user's objectives—in short, how to "talk" to the computer in the (digital/binary) language the computer understands.
3. *The applications*: that is, the nature and elements of problems for which the computer, when thoughtfully applied, offers a better way of solution than available alternative methods. It also involves understanding the capabilities (and limitations) of computers well enough to use one's imagination to generate new ideas and ways of using hardware for applications that may not have been thought of before.

The discussion of hardware runs throughout this book. If the workings of hardware are thoroughly understood, troubleshooting effectiveness is dramatically increased, software instructions and programming are easier because the steps make more sense, and application potentials are far more clear, because applications depend on hardware and software as the enabling factors.

The software aspect is also discussed at various points in the book, with Chapter 6 providing the heaviest emphasis on program instructions.

The applications aspect is a bit more elusive because it depends on some command of both hardware and software. It is, however, vital to anyone with curiosity of imagination who would like to help turn the pages of history to get a glimpse of what the future holds. We shall attempt to suggest the nature of some applications possibilities by presenting, at selected places in the book where they are most appropriate, illustrative examples of ways to use microprocessor systems.

In this chapter we have introduced the concept of a microprocessor, some of the specific vocabulary, an overview of the electronics system, and a review of the codes that are used in the "microprocessor" world. This introduction is meant to put the reader at ease and to offer reassurance that microprocessors are not a subject for intellectual fear. They are powerful devices and have many applications, yet the ability to use and work with these devices is within the abilities of a digital technician or hobbyist. Once the basics of using and understanding these very large scale integrated circuit devices are understood, the fun begins. Microprocessors will open new territories for fertile imaginations, of that we may all be sure!

Review Questions

1. What are the three major parts of a general microprocessor system? Discuss the relationships between these parts.

2. Which part of a general microprocessor system makes the system unique? Why?

3. What is the function of a Central Processing Unit?

4. Write a sentence in which the term "bit" is used as it relates to a piece of digital hardware.

5. Define the following terms:
   a. byte
   b. nibble
   c. I/O
   d. common I/O

6. Why would one use tri-state devices?

7. Convert the following octal numbers to a 10-bit binary number.
   a. 703
   b. 1362
   c. 51

8. Convert the following binary numbers to octal numbers:
    a. 110010001
    b. 001010
    c. 11101101111100

9. Convert the following hexadecimal numbers to binary numbers:
    a. F3
    b. 15CD
    c. 21A9

10. Convert the following binary numbers to hexadecimal numbers:
    a. 10011111
    b. 0011011
    c. 011100001100

11. What four IC electrical parameters are used in the calculation of fan out?

12. Using the alphabet given in Section 1-6, write the word *digital* in binary.

2

SEMICONDUCTOR MEMORIES FOR THE MICROPROCESSOR

Semiconductor memories are an integral part of any microprocessor circuit or system. As shown in Chapter 1, a simple microprocessor system may be divided into three major sections:

1. The input instruction,
2. The Central Processor Unit (CPU), and
3. Input-output (I/O) and peripheral equipment.

The semiconductor memory is most often seen in the input instruction section.

In this chapter we will discuss the concept of a memory and a memory system in detail. We will also show techniques for troubleshooting these special digital devices. Finally, the structure of a small memory system will be examined and its operation explained in detail.

One should understand how a semiconductor memory works and why special timing considerations must be observed to use these devices effectively. If this is thoroughly understood, integrating these devices into a microprocessor system will be a much easier task for anyone; for the serious beginner especially, such an understanding is a requirement.

2-1 Static Memory Devices: Organization and Characteristics

We begin our discussion by dividing memories into two major types, *static memories* and *dynamic memories*. We will first discuss static memories in detail, then proceed to dynamic memories. *Static memories* are those that retain the information, without the need to refresh that information at frequent time intervals. Static memories are simpler than dynamic memories in their operating characteristics. As long as DC power is applied to the device, a static memory will retain all of the information stored in it. No other input signals are required. However, when the power is turned off, this information is lost. These memories are called *volatile memories*. Often memories that retain their information after the power is turned off are called *non-volatile*. The first type of memory that we will discuss will be a static, volatile, semiconductor memory.

The term *memory* comes from the fact that these electronic devices can "remember" information that was electrically stored in the unit. This means that not only can information be electrically stored in a memory, but it can also be electrically retrieved. (A memory device is hardly useful if it can store information but never use that stored information.) Our discussion here will center on the type of memory that permits both storage and retrieval of information, because if one can understand these types of memories, understanding other types is much easier.

When information is stored in a semiconductor memory we say it is "written" into the memory. When information is retrieved from a semiconductor memory we say it is "read" from the memory. These two functions are the only two things that are done to static memories. The device can be written into, or it can be read from.

The writing of information into a memory is done in a "WRITE CYCLE." Reading information from a memory is done in a "READ CYCLE." The term *cycle* is defined as a fixed period of time required to perform the functions of *writing into* or *reading from* a memory. By the phrase, writing into a memory, we imply that electrical data is being stored in the memory. This electrical data or information is stored as a level of DC voltage. One DC voltage level corresponds to a "1" being stored in the memory. A different DC voltage level corresponds to a "0" being stored in the memory.

If data is to be stored in a memory, there must be some physical connection to the memory to allow this function to take place. In semiconductor memories data is entered on a "DATA IN" input pin on the physical device. Further, when data is read from a memory, there must be some physical means to bring out the data. Data being read from a memory is read from a "DATA OUT" output pin.

There must be four major physical connections on a semiconductor memory if it is to be of use. These connections provide for POWER input (VCC), DATA INPUT (DI), DATA OUTPUT (DO), and READ or WRITE cycle (R/W). These connections are shown in block diagram form in Figure 2-1. The single READ/WRITE (R/W) input pin defines a memory cycle as being a memory read or a

```
                    Power (V_CC)
                         ↑
                    ┌─────────┐
Data in    ───────▶│         │──────▶ Data out
  (DI)             │         │         (DO)
                   └─────────┘
                         ↑
                   Read/Write (R/W)
```

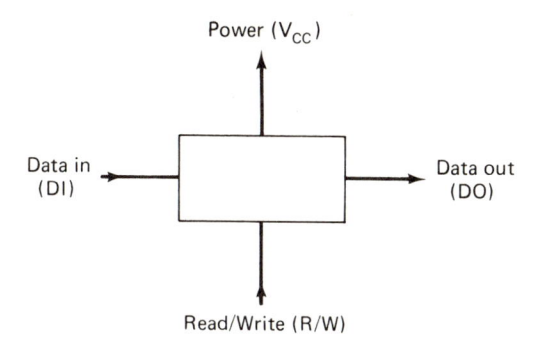

Figure 2-1 Block diagram of a 1-bit memory

memory write cycle. The 1-bit memory shown in Figure 2-1 is capable of storing and reading out only one bit of information at any time. The term *bit* is used to mean how many different items of information, or bits, can be stored in a single memory.

Now, let's consider a memory that is larger than one bit. Our new memory will be made to store 16 bits of information; however, it will store *only one of the 16 bits per write cycle*. Moreover, no particular sequence will be required. This memory will be capable of storing any one of the 16 bits at random, and reading any one of them at random. This means that it need not write the information in a certain order, nor must it read information from the memory in a certain order.

To accomplish this larger task, the physical connections to the memory still include power, data in, data out, and read/write, and another set of connections must be added. These extra connections or pins allow us to select a particular physical location for each bit of data to be stored in the memory chip.

This means that within this memory chip there are different physical locations where each bit of information can be stored. The added connections provide access to the location or "address" for any bit of information in the memory. The extra pins that allow us to do this are called "ADDRESS PINS." Each physical location in the memory has a unique address. Since there are 16 bits of information, 16 unique addresses are needed. This requires that four address pins be added to the model of Figure 2-1. The number of physical locations a memory has for storing information can be calculated by knowing the number of address pins. Here's how to do it.

$$\text{Number of storage locations} = 2^{(\text{number of address pins})}$$
$$= 2^{(4)}$$
$$= 16$$

This formula will be adjusted slightly later in the chapter.

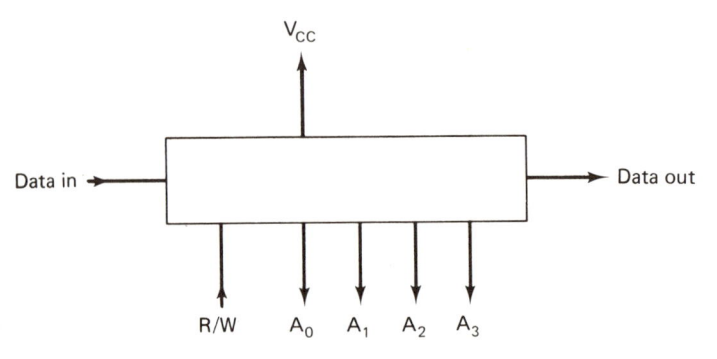

Figure 2-2 Block diagram of a 16-bit memory

The new diagram or model of the memory is shown in Figure 2-2. By applying one of 16 unique address codes (0–15) to these 4 address pins, data can be written into or read out of that physical location. All other pins on our model still perform the same functions as in the earlier model.

Now that we have a block form model of a memory chip it would be helpful if we mentally constructed, or "realized," with hardware a memory that will behave electrically as our model.

This memory will be constructed with standard logic devices. With this realized model we can show how each physical location in the memory could be made accessible, or "accessed," in order to write information into, or read information from it. We will also show some important timing relationships that exist in memory devices. By showing the timing that applies to this memory, the reason for these relationships will become very clear.

The first piece of the memory we will construct will be the physical locations for the information to be stored. D (or delay) flip flops will be used for this function. Since there are 16 bits of information to be stored, 16 D flip flops will be required. The 16 D flip flops will be arranged in a "4 × 4" array. This refers to the physical arrangement of storage locations internal to the memory chip. Figure 2-3 shows the 16 D flip flops in a 4 × 4 array. Notice that each of these flip flops has a *clock line* labeled "C," and a D input and Q output, labeled "D" and "Q" respectively. The D input of each device will be the path for data to be entered into the storage location. The Q output will be the path for data to be read from that storage location. There must also be a means provided for writing data into or reading data out of a single location, or D flip flop.

To accomplish this we must assign a unique address code or location code to every storage element in the memory. The assignment of these unique codes will be derived from giving each location a position in the 4 × 4 array. The position of each D flip flop can be located in a unique row and a unique column of the 4 × 4 array. This is shown in Figure 2-4.

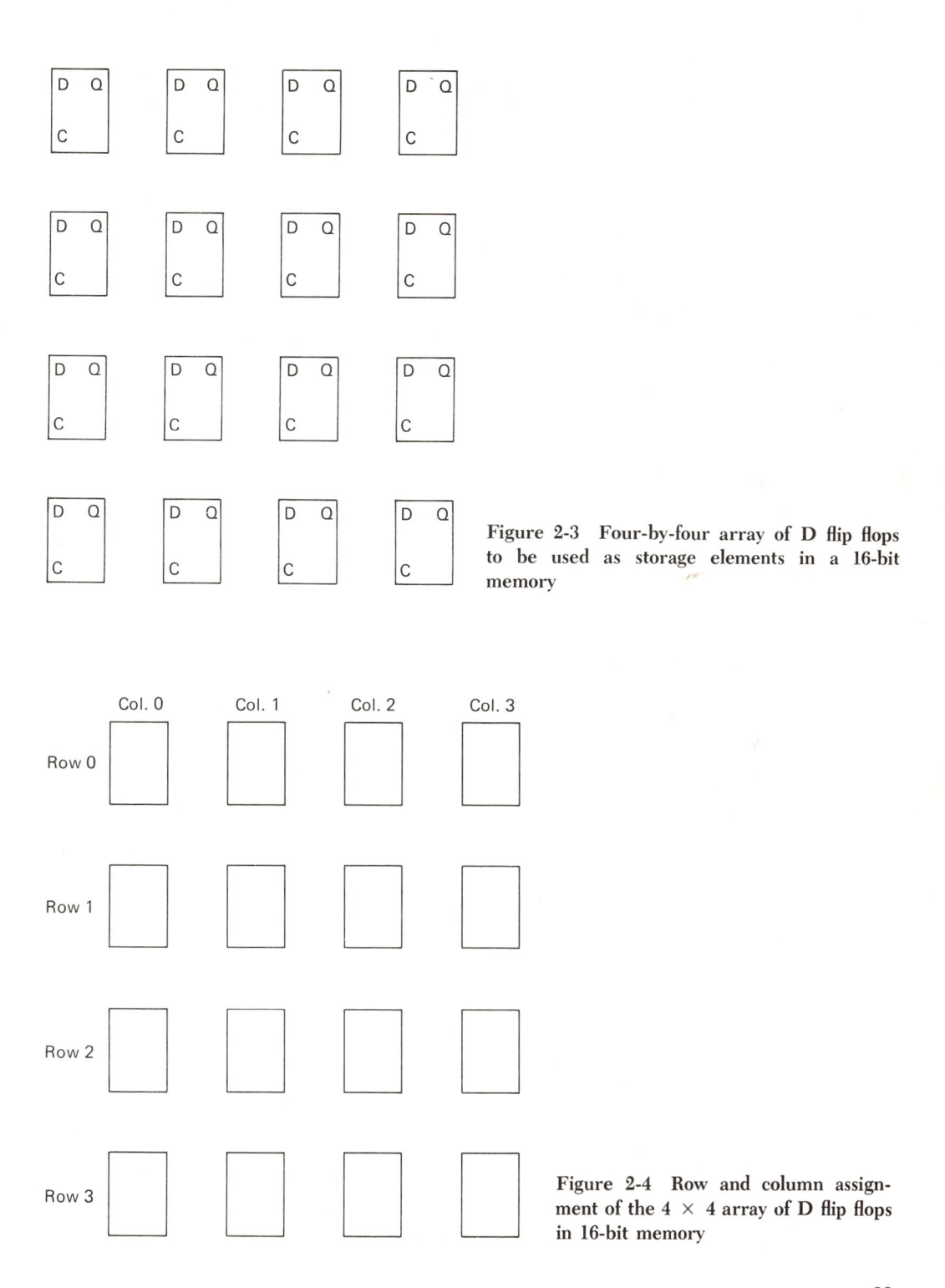

Figure 2-3 Four-by-four array of D flip flops to be used as storage elements in a 16-bit memory

Figure 2-4 Row and column assignment of the 4 × 4 array of D flip flops in 16-bit memory

The rows are numbered, starting with row zero. The columns are numbered, starting with column zero. Figure 2-4 shows the customary row and column numbering of a 4 × 4 array.

With this numbering procedure, or "convention," it is possible to assign a 2-bit binary code to each row from 0–3, and to each column from 0–3. If we then use a 4-bit address code to define the exact location, the first two bits will identify a unique row and the second two bits will identify a unique column. The total 4-bit address code will correspond to a unique storage location (D flip flop) in the memory. This location is at the intersection of the row and column defined by the address code. An example of an address code could be 1001. The location circle in Figure 2-5 is the location in the array that was defined by the address code 1001.

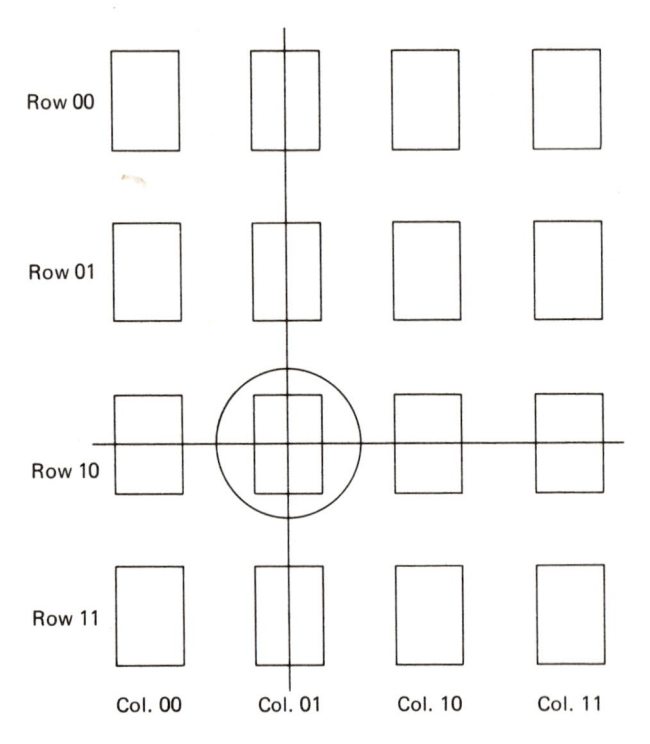

Figure 2-5 Location circled is the location requested by memory address code 1001.

The part of the address code that selects a unique column is called a column address. The part of the address code that selects a unique row is called the row address. The column and row addresses are subsets of the memory address.

Sec. 2-1   *Static Memory Devices: Organization and Characteristics*   **41**

As mentioned earlier, any element may be selected in any sequence. This means that any location may be selected at random, and we can gain access for reading or writing into that location at random. Memories with this type of storage location selection are called "RANDOM ACCESS MEMORIES," or "RAMs."

We can select any location in RAMs simply by applying or inputting the correct address code. We have yet to show how this selection is physically accomplished. To start with, let's "construct" the ability to write data into a 16-bit RAM. *To write data into a RAM we apply data to the D input of the flip flop, and then a pulse to the clock input of the particular flip flop where we want the information to be stored.* The reason is that data can be applied to the D input of the D flip flop, but none will be written or stored in the D flip flop until a clock pulse is applied. This lets us apply data to all 16 D flip flops at the same time, but we are required to clock only the D flip flop where we want the data to be stored. We will assume that the clock pulse needed to clock data into the D flip flop will resemble Figure 2-6.

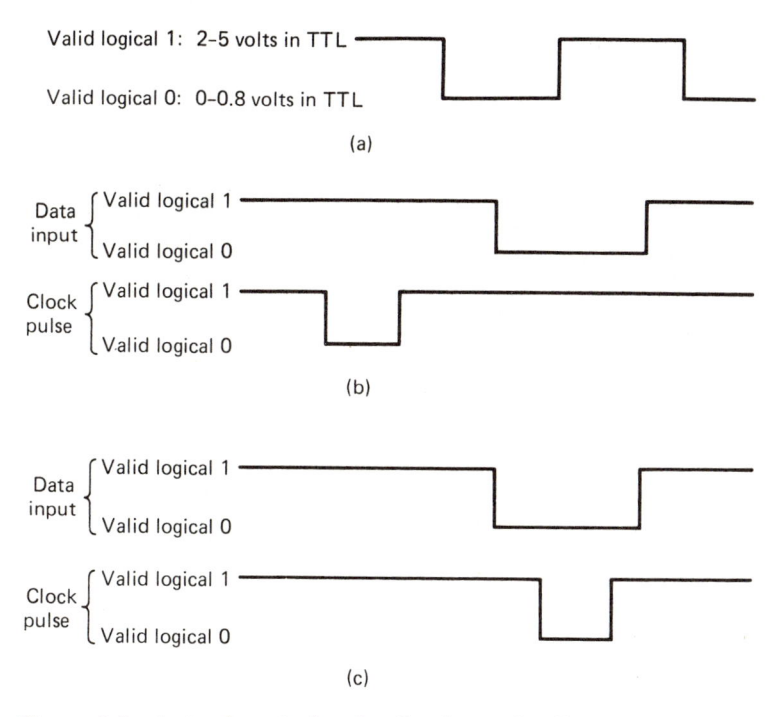

Figure 2-6   Active low clock pulse for the D flip flops in the 4 × 4 array

Remember that in the D flip flop data will stay at the Q output until another clock pulse is applied at the clock input. When data is written into a single D flip flop in the 4 × 4 array, the data stays there until a new bit of data is written into that same location.

We require some decoding circuits for the clock inputs to select a single D flip flop. These circuits will enable us to store data in a single flip flop. A design for decoding is shown in Figure 2-7. This may or may not be the technique used in building RAMs in industry. It is shown only to illustrate how decoding on a RAM could take place. At left, the clock "in" signal pulse is directed to the correct row by the row address demultiplexer. This pulse then enters another set

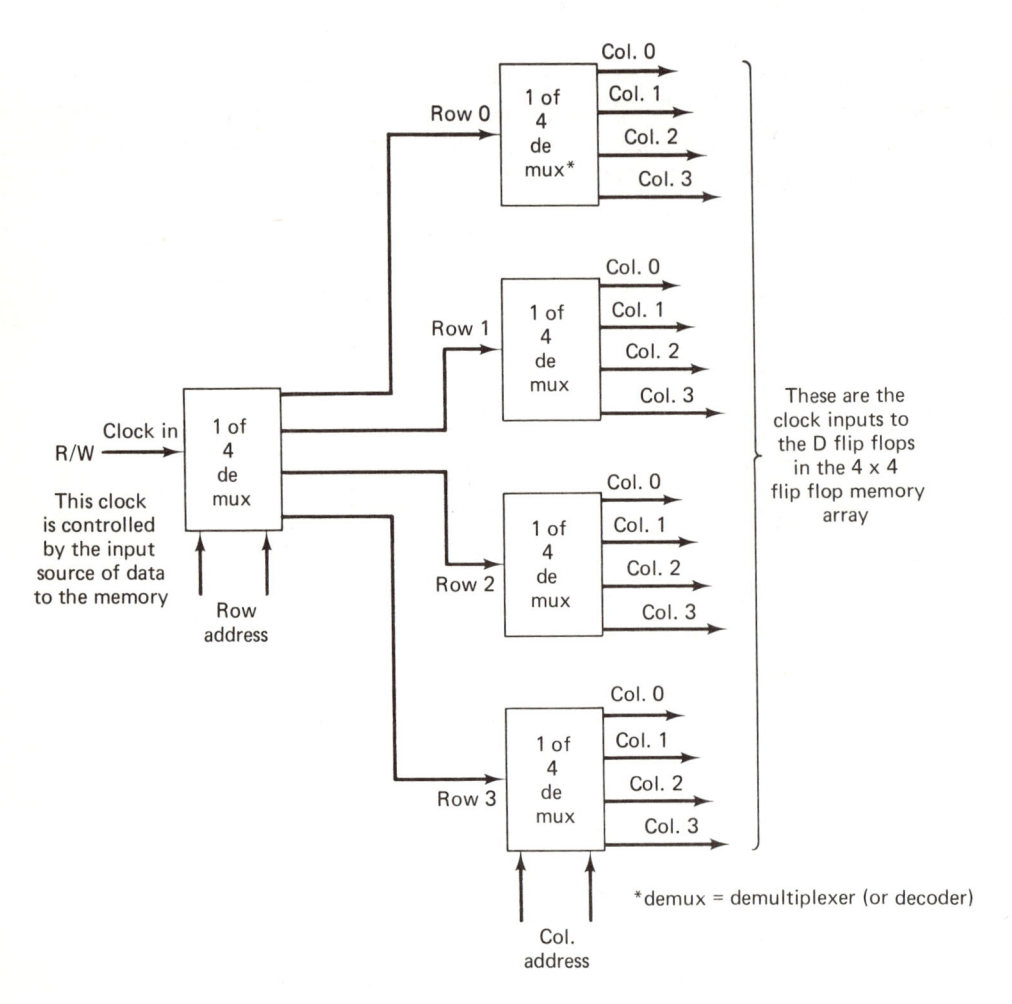

Figure 2-7 Write pulse clock decode for the 4 x 4 array. Note that only one path will be activated at any given address 0-15.

Sec. 2-1   *Static Memory Devices: Organization and Characteristics*   43

of decoders that uses the column address to select the correct column. In this way the single clock input can be directed to any of the 16 D flip flops. This is how data can be written into any of the sixteen storage elements in the array, simply by the application of the correct memory address code.

Now we shall examine how data can be read from any location in the memory. To accomplish this, the reverse procedure of the clock input decoder architecture is used. The block diagram for this is shown in Figure 2-8. Notice that the column address is used to select which column 0–3 is to be output of the first 1-of-4 multiplexer. Then the row address is used to determine which row of the selected column will send output to the data output pin of the entire memory.

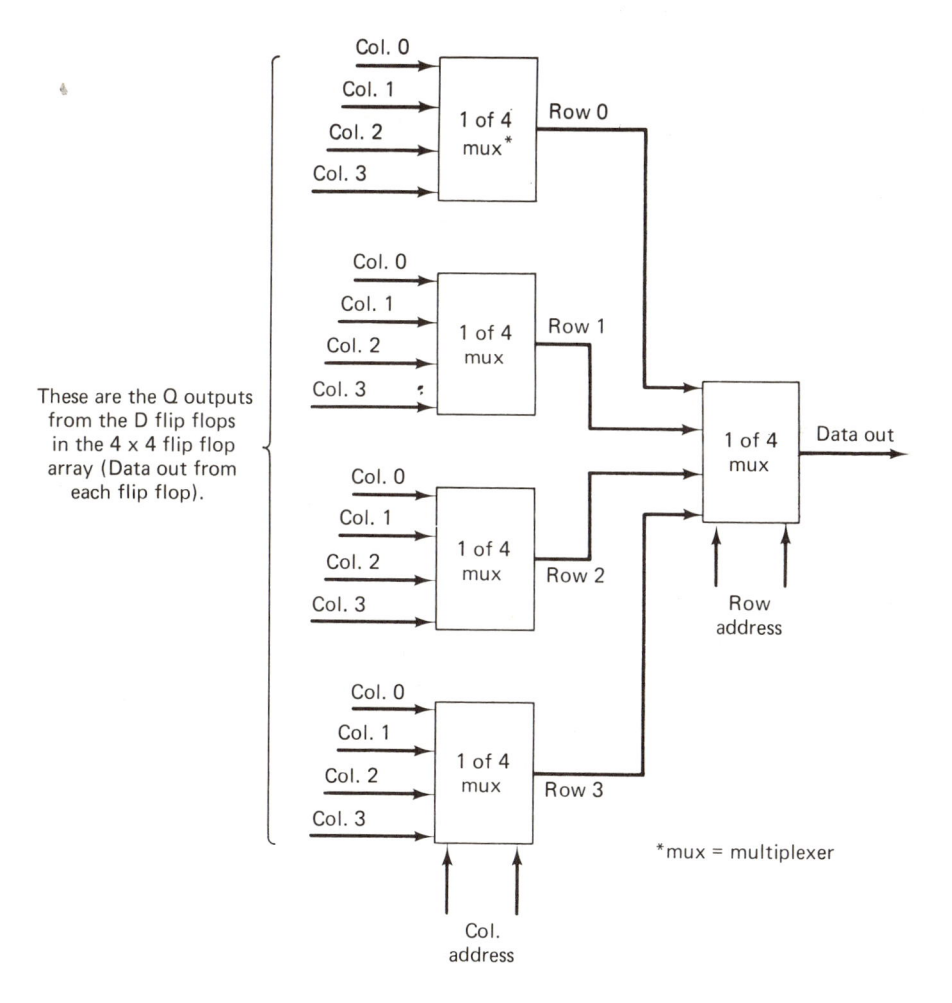

Figure 2-8 DATA OUT decode circuit for the 4 × 4 memory array

Further, it should be understood that the clock decoders and the data out select circuits are just combinational logic blocks. By connecting the individual pieces of this memory together as in Figure 2-9 we can see the complete 16-bit RAM. The portion of the circuit inside the dotted lines is the part to which a user of memory chips has no access. Access can only be gained through the R/W, Data In, Data Out, and Address lines shown earlier in Figure 2-2.

Referring to this circuit diagram, let's examine the timing relationships of different electrical signals and show why they exist as they do. The first term we will discuss is the general term *read access time*. In words, read access time is the time it takes for the data to be present or "valid" at the output pin of the memory after the request for the data has been electrically given to the memory.

In the circuit of Figure 2-9, the request for data out is complete after all address lines are at the proper logic level. The proper logic level is a logical 1 or

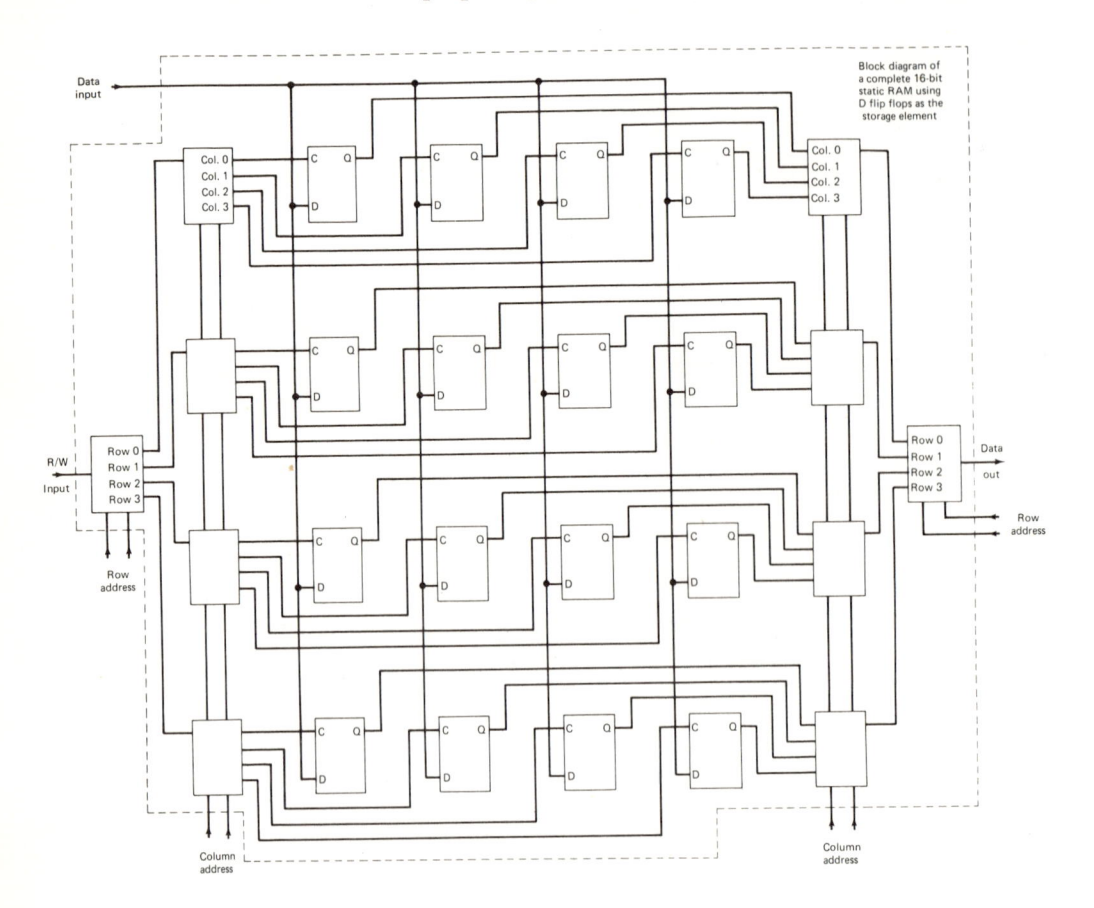

Figure 2-9 Block diagram of a complete 16-bit static RAM, using D flip flops as the storage element

Sec. 2-1   Static Memory Devices: Organization and Characteristics   45

a logical 0 level, depending on the desired address code. The time for data out to be present at the data output pin is when data out is at the proper logic level. This means if data out should be a logical 0, then access time is measured from the stable address input to the valid logical output of the memory. Figure 2-10 shows a timing diagram representation of read access time.

The cross part of the signal shown in Figure 2-10 represents the time where the address code is stable. The reason for the cross is to show that the address pin can be stable in the logical 1 or the logical 0 level. The cross at data out represents the point in time where data out becomes valid. The cross also means that data out can be valid in the logical 1 or the logical 0 level. Read access time is measured from the cross of the address input to the cross at the data output as shown in Figure 2-10.

*These axes are not normally shown on memory data sheets. It is "understood" that they are there.

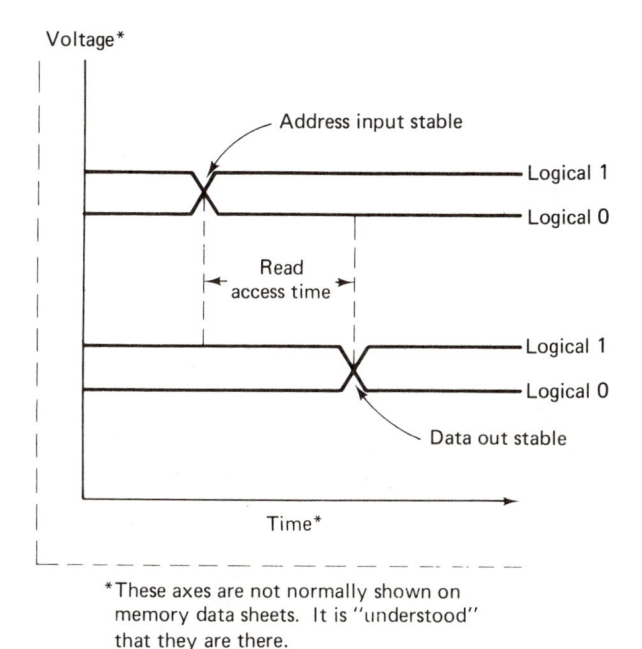

Figure 2-10 Timing diagram of read access time for a static semiconductor memory (These axes are not shown on memory data sheets normally. It is understood that they are there.)

Data sheets on memories will refer to read access time by different names, but its meaning is constant. A question that naturally arises is "why is there a read access time?" For an answer to this question let's examine the data output circuit of Figure 2-9.

Notice that when an address code is input to the memory the combinational logic circuit must stabilize. There are gate delays that must propagate through the entire output logic. Remember that it takes some time, however small, for a voltage to change from one value to another. This is the origin and reason for read access time in static semiconductor memories.

Another important timing relationship that exists in memories is the relationship between applying an address code and the write clock for writing into a single location in the memory. After an address is applied to the memory we must wait a fixed length of time for the system to stabilize before we can apply a write clock pulse. This timing relationship is shown by the timing diagram of Figure 2-11.

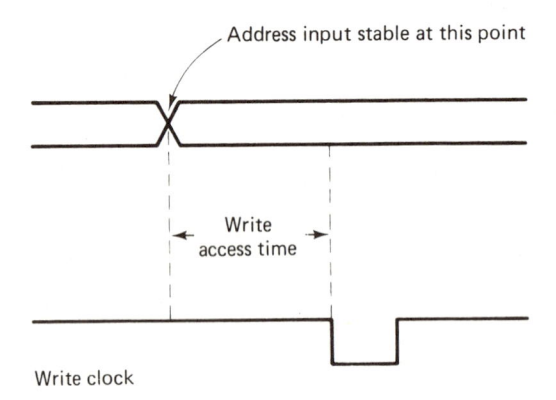

Figure 2-11 Timing diagram showing write access time for a static semiconductor memory

This waiting time exists to give the clock decoders enough time to respond correctly to the requested address code. If we do not wait for the clock decoders to settle, then data may transfer into a storage element that was not requested. This time is called *write access time*. Again, many data sheets will refer to this time by a different name such as T_{wac} but its meaning and origin are constant.

Since we are applying a clock pulse to a D flip flop or some type of flip flop storage element, there is a time specification on the minimum pulse width of the active portion of the clock. In the circuit presented in this discussion, the active portion of the write clock is the logical 0 level. The specification of write pulse clock width is meant for the logical low portion of the write clock. The specification of a minimum pulse width is called T_{wp}. In words, T_{wp} is the *write enable pulse width*. The symbol T_{wp} is used commonly on most memory data sheets to represent the write pulse width. See Figure 2-12 for a timing diagram representation of T_{wp}.

Another timing relationship that is important in memories is the time relationship between signals on the data input pin and the write pulse clock pin. In any storage element such as a flip flop, there is a data-in setup time and data-in hold time. *Data-in setup time* refers to the length of time data in must be present

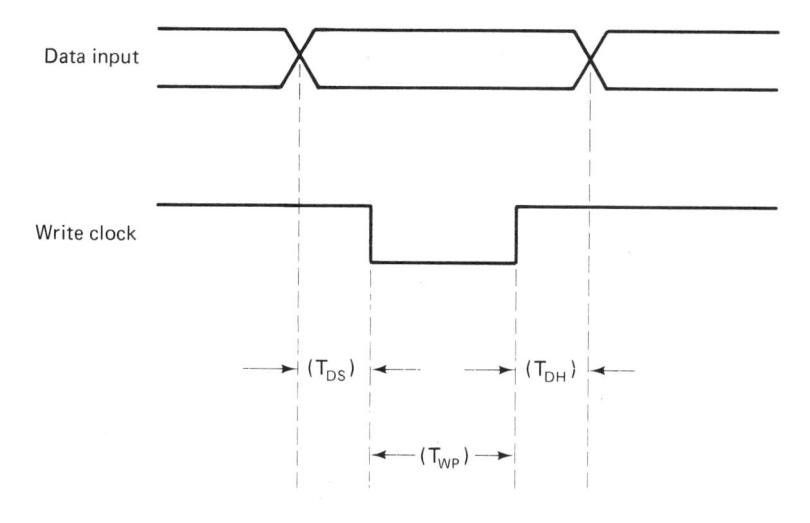

Figure 2-12 T_{DH} = Data hold time
T_{DS} = Data setup time
T_{wp} = Write enable pulse width

(valid) before a write pulse clock can be applied. *Data-in hold time* refers to the length of time data-in must stay present (valid) after the write pulse goes away. These timing relationships are shown in the timing diagram of Figure 2-12.

Data-in setup time is called T_{ds}. *Data-in hold time* is called T_{dh}. These times represent the same physical characteristics in a memory chip as they do in the individual flip flops.

We have presented a memory that can store sixteen unique bits of data, one bit at a time. The memory can also read sixteen unique bits of data, one bit at a time. Furthermore, any of the sixteen bits can be accessed at random. A complete word description of this type of memory is a "16 × 1 STATIC RAM." The "16" in the description refers to the number of unique address codes that can be applied to the memory. The "1" in the description refers to the number of data input and output lines the memory has. When we were discussing the storage capacity of the memory earlier, it was said that the number of storage locations was equal to:

$$2^{\text{(number of address pins)}}$$

This equation now must be modified to the following:

Number of storage locations =
$2^{\text{(number of address pins)}} \times$ (number of data input pins)

For example, many memories are organized differently than 16 × 1. Some typical memories are organized as 16 × 4, 256 × 4, 1024 × 1,

47

1024 × 4, 4096 × 1, 16384 × 1. In each case the first number refers to the number of unique address codes. The second number refers to how many data input pins are on the memory. The total storage capacity of the memory may be computed by simply multiplying the (number of unique address locations) × (the number of data input pins). Thus, the total storage capacity of a 256 × 4 RAM is equal to 1024 bits.

There are larger memory systems that are organized as 16384 × 32 or 1024 × 16, to name just two. These larger memory systems are made up of smaller memory chips. To show how this can be accomplished, let's take an example. Suppose we want to construct a 4096 × 4 memory system. The chips we will use to build this system will be organized as 1024 × 1. To reach the storage capacity of a 4096 × 4 memory system, we will need to use sixteen of the 1024 × 1 RAMs. Physically these sixteen RAMs will be organized as shown in Figure 2-13.

The question now arises as to how to interconnect these memories to make the larger memory. The larger memory is 4096 × 4. This means we have 4096 unique address codes. We need to determine how many address lines are required to obtain the 4096 address codes. It was given earlier that the number of address codes = 2^x, where x = the number of address pins. We want to solve the above equation for the number of address pins, when we are given the number of address codes. To solve this equation the following procedure is used:

$$4096 = 2^x$$

Take the log (4096) = x (log (2)) common logarithm to the base 10 of both sides of the equation,

$$x = \log(4096)/\log(2)$$
$$x = 3.6123/.30103$$
$$x = 12$$

Now that we know the number of address pins, a block diagram of the large memory can be drawn. This block diagram is shown in Figure 2-14.

The smaller RAMs 1024 × 1 have only 10 address pins. Our system needs 12 address pins. Two address pins must be added to the system. The question is: How do we get two more address pins? We will connect all address pins of the 1024 × 1 RAMs in a "daisy chain" fashion. That is, by *daisy chain* we mean that A_0 of all RAMs will be connected together, all A_1 of all RAMs will be connected together, etc. Doing this will leave us with 10 address lines for the memory. Since there are four rows of 1024 × 1 RAMs, the additional two address pins our system requires will select which row of the four is wanted. The solution we

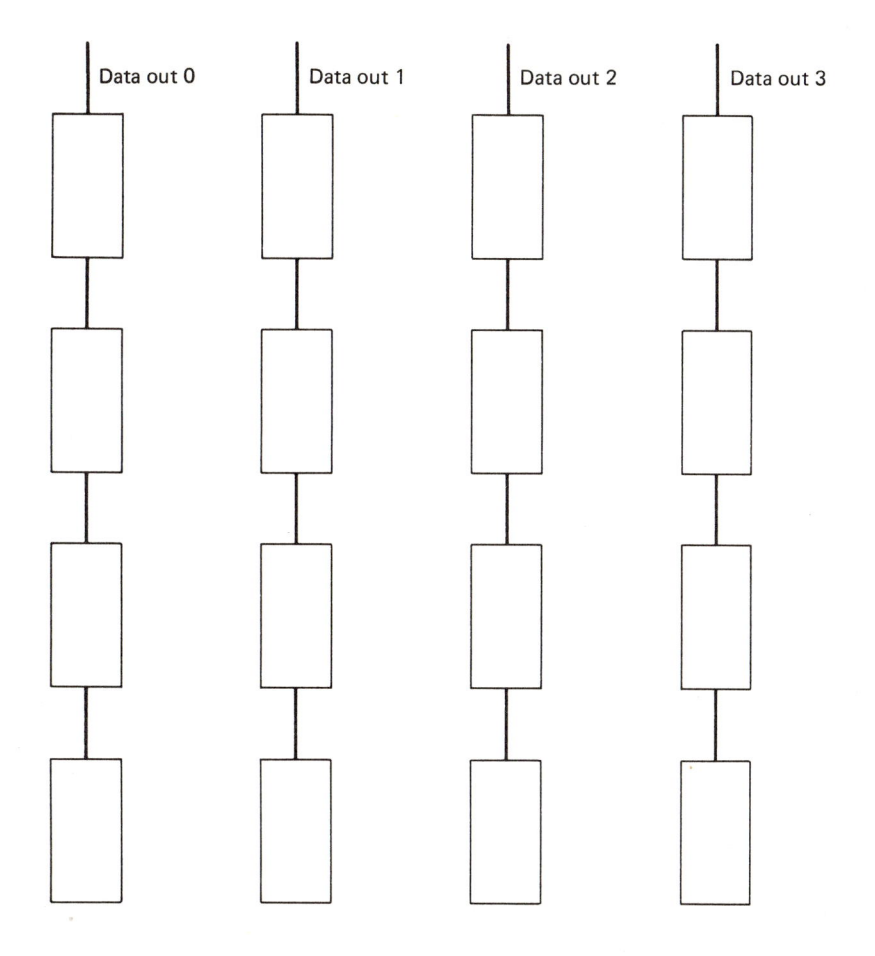

Figure 2-13 Sixteen 1024 × 1 bit memories arranged in à 4 × 4 array

are about to describe is a method commonly used to select only a few memory devices out of a large array.

To allow the selection of a particular device an additional input pin is constructed on most memory chips. This pin is called "chip select." When the chip select pin is active, the memory of that chip can be read from and written into. When the chip select pin is non-active, the memory will not accept data, nor can data be retrieved from the device. Also, when the select pin is non-active the data output pin(s) go into a high impedance state. This means that output pins on different memories can be physically connected together without disturbing each other. The controlling output will be the output of that chip which has its chip select pin in the active mode.

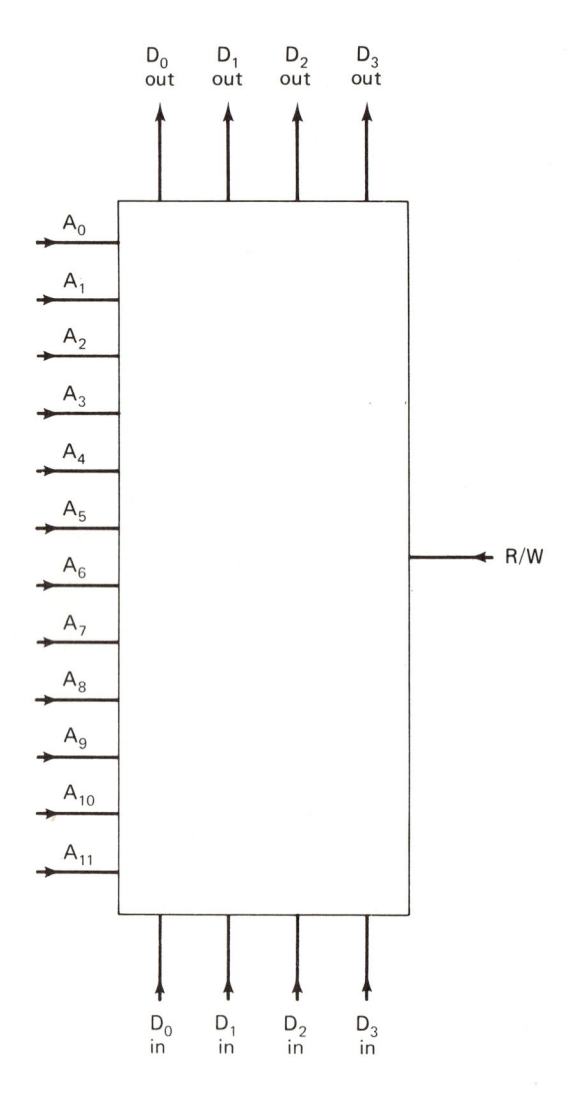

Figure 2-14 Block diagram of the 4096 × 4 bit memory

Referring to Figure 2-15, when point A = logical 0, chip 1 is selected. Because of the inverter in the input line, at this same time chip 2 is deselected (non-active). The output of chip 2 will go into a high impedance state. This high impedance state is sometimes referred to as "TRI-STATE." "Tri" because this is not a logical 1 state or a logical 0 state, but a *third* state of an output. When chip 2 goes into a high impedance state the output of chip 1 will control the output of

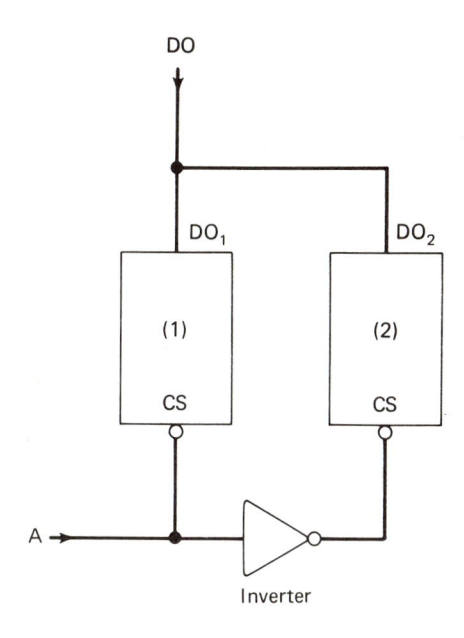

Figure 2-15 Two memories that have their data out connected together. Notice that the CHIP SELECT (CS) input pins of memory 1 and memory 2 will never be enabled at the same instant because of the inverter inserted in the circuit.

the circuit. This means that whatever the output of chip 1 may be, the circuit output will be the same. When point A goes to a logical 1 the output of chip 1 will go to a high impedance state, and chip 2 will be the controlling output.

It is by the use of the chip select pin that memory systems are able to use more address pins than the number of address pins on any given RAM. Using this information about the chip select pin, we will now show how the 1024 × 1 RAMs will be connected to realize the 4096 × 4 memory system that is wanted.

Referring to Figure 2-16, notice that the uppermost address bits A_{10}, A_{11} control the chip selects of all the memories. Only one row of devices is selected at any time. This allows the data-out pins to be connected together in parallel as shown. In this memory, address locations 0-1023 will be directed to the first row of 1024 × 1 RAMs. Address locations 1024-2047 will be directed to the second row of 1024 × 1 RAMs. Address locations 2048-3071 will be directed to the third row of 1024 × 1 RAMs. Finally, address locations 3072-4095 will be directed to the fourth row of 1024 × 1 RAMs. The upper two address bits, A_{10} and A_{11}, control which row the data in will be directed to. The lower ten address

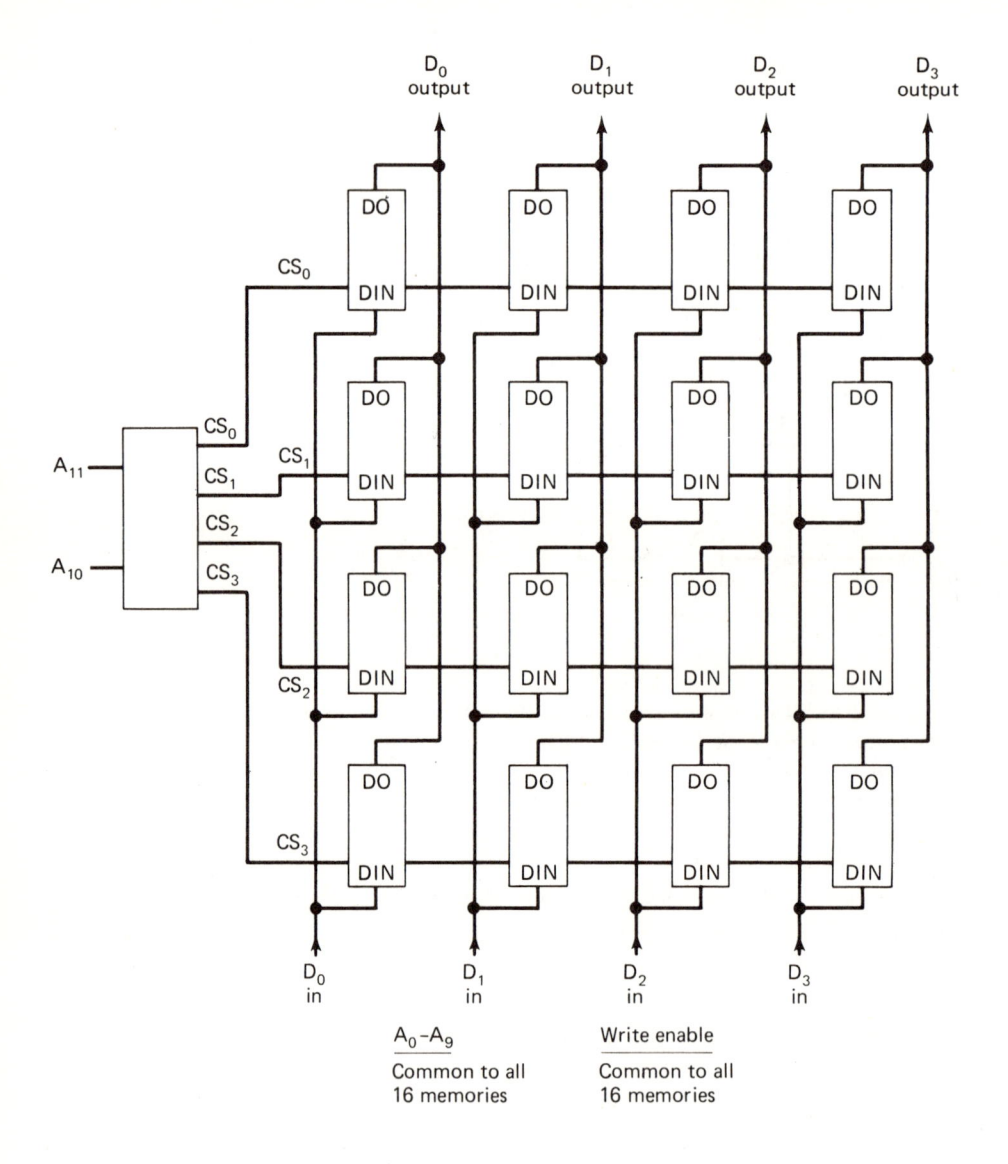

Figure 2-16 Complete 4096 × 4 static RAM array constructed, using sixteen 1024 × 1 static RAMs

bits, A_0 through A_9, direct the data to a specific address within the 1024 legal address locations of the selected row. This is a single example of an expanded memory system, but many memory systems use this structure as the basic architecture of the system.

52

2-2 Troubleshooting Memory Systems

After this introduction to the organization of static RAMs, let's discuss some methods for troubleshooting memory chips and memory systems. First, it is safe to say that memories are very difficult devices to troubleshoot. They have many storage locations and any of these locations can be defective. In troubleshooting memories the first step is to check general performance. If the system of memory chips has the basic elements of power and properly timed address inputs, data inputs, and read and write inputs present, then we can proceed to a more detailed troubleshooting process. If these basic inputs are missing from the memory or memory system, it is a waste of time and effort to try to troubleshoot further until the problem with the basic inputs has been cleared up. The first basic input characteristic to check for is proper timing. By timing we mean the time relationships between data inputs and clock inputs discussed earlier in this chapter. With an oscilloscope, check to insure that all of the input signals are present, and that they have the correct time relationships to one another. Figure 2-17 shows a flow diagram of what signals to check, and in what order they should be checked.

To make this check, it is necessary to make the system in which the memory is contained provide the input signals. The reason for this is simply that this is how the system would be functioning if it were working properly. The problem may not be in the memory system at all, but rather in the part of the system that provides the stimulus to the memory. To differentiate whether the fault is in memory, or external to the memory in the input signal circuits, the overall system must be put in a timing loop. The timing loop in any system should do the following:

1. apply a write pulse at every memory cycle
2. increment (change) the address location at every memory cycle
3. apply alternating 1s and 0s to the data input terminals.

By placing the overall system in a timing loop it will allow repeated applications of the input signals. This will make the observations of these signals with an oscilloscope much easier. It is impossible when discussing general troubleshooting to give a definite procedure for placing a system in a timing loop that will satisfy every system. The fact is, there are many different systems, every one requiring a different set of instructions for the generation of this timing loop. The best this book can do is to give guidelines for what signals the timing loop must provide. It will then be left to the troubleshooter to learn the particular system and what procedures it requires to set up an appropriate timing loop.

By applying a write pulse at every memory cycle the troubleshooter can determine if the write pulse width is correct and within the specification of the

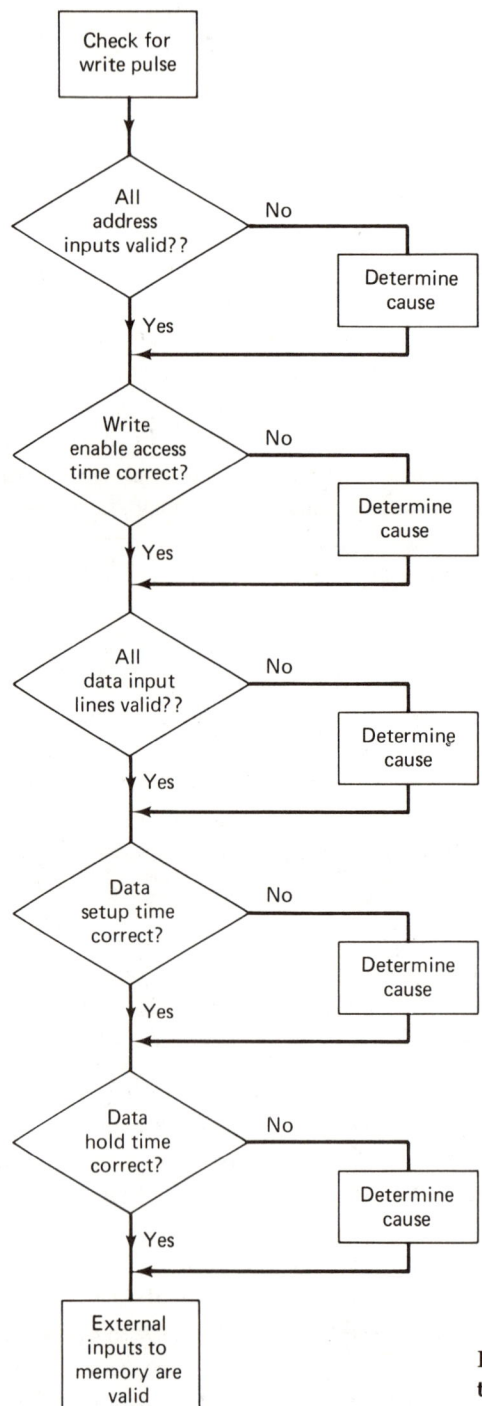

Figure 2-17 Flowchart showing signals to check on a memory to insure external inputs to memory are valid.

system. The troubleshooter can also determine if the voltage levels for the write pulse are correct. Lastly, the troubleshooter can check to determine whether the write pulse is happening at the correct time in the memory cycle. That is, is the write enable access time correct for this particular system or device?

By incrementing the address each cycle, the troubleshooter can determine if each address input is capable of switching from a logical low to a logical high level. If the address pins *all* switch, a check can be made to determine if they switch at the correct time in the memory cycle. Address inputs will often be loaded excessively and will not switch, remaining always at a logical 1 or a logical 0 level.

It is wise to check *all address pins* on each device of a large memory system. An address may be connected to a circuit, but a trace on the PC board may be broken, or the pin of the device may not be in a socket correctly and the address signal that is on the PC board may not be reaching a pin. So, whenever possible, check the address inputs at each address pin of each memory chip. This may take extra time, but it will pay off by making certain that all address inputs are present at the device terminals.

In troubleshooting never assume that any input is present! Always check to make certain—then you will not have to backtrack in the troubleshooting process.

With data input directed to switch from a logical 1 to a logical 0 level at each memory cycle, the troubleshooter can determine if data in actually does switch from a valid logical 1 to a valid logical 0. At the same time, the pulse width of the data in can be checked, as well as the time of T_{ds} and T_{dh} with respect to the write enable pulse. *All timing parameters should be checked against the system specifications.*

It is possible to check the timing at all pins of all devices simply by putting the memory system into a timing loop. Suppose we find an address input line that is always low, and this address input line never switches. The address input line will probably be connected to many memory devices in the same circuit. The simple 4096 × 4 memory that we constructed has each of the lower order ten address lines connected to sixteen memory devices. Any one of these sixteen devices could be defective and holding down the address input as a result. If this is ever the case, then you as a troubleshooter must know how to approach this type of problem. Here are some guidelines for doing just that.

1. The address input pulse is always the output of some other part of the system. This other part could be defective. Or there could be a fault in the interconnections, or in other inputs or elements connected in parallel. Do not assume that the input itself is bad without first making sure that other possible causes are not at fault. Isolate the address signal, and check to see if this output

switches as it should. If, after isolation, the signal does switch, then you must start isolating the inputs of the memory devices that are connected to this signal.

2. Since there are many address pins connected together, the troubleshooter does not want to cut or unsolder every input pin until he finds the defective memory if this can be avoided. Remember that one shorted device in a parallel arrangement shorts the whole line and can keep many devices from working properly. When a short is indicated the first step is to localize where the problem is physically located on the board. This can be done by a technique that might be called "isolating by halves." An example of this technique follows.

Suppose that 10 memories were daisy chained together. By daisy chain it is meant that one device is connected to the next, that all 10 devices are connected in parallel. You as a troubleshooter must determine which of the parallel branches is defective. If the devices are daisy chained, first cut the input trace so that half the devices are connected to the address stimulus and half the devices are not. Now look at the address input again. If the address input switches as it should, then you know that one of the five devices that are isolated from the address input is defective, and that the five devices that were not isolated do not have shorted inputs. If, after isolation, the address input fails to switch, then you know that the problem is in one of the five devices that were not isolated. Either way, you are troubleshooting half as many devices as you were before. Figure 2-18 shows the technique of "halving."

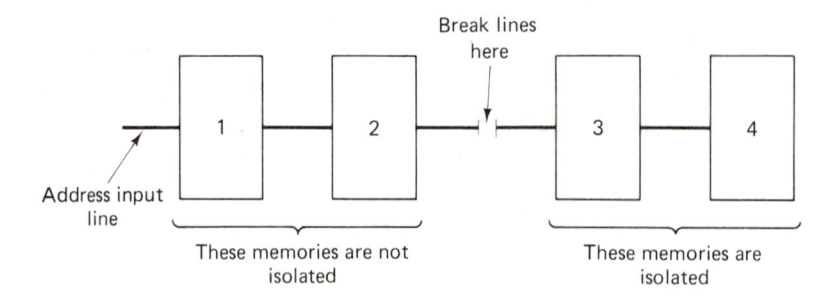

Figure 2-18 Fault discovered by breaking an address that is "daisy chained" to many memories in a memory system. If memory 1 or 2 is shorted, the input line will still show the fault; if memory 3 or 4 is shorted, the input line will now respond correctly.

Sec. 2-2 Troubleshooting Memory Systems

Now that you know which five of the ten devices includes the defective device you can make another cut in the section containing the fault to isolate part of it. After isolation, reconnect the signal to one part and make the same address check as you did before. Using this technique it is quite easy to isolate the bad device in a short time.

Checking for signal at the memory device inputs and outputs with the system in a timing loop is the quickest way to find some of the major problems that occur in a memory system. But what if the problem is not as obvious as a stuck input to the memory? Suppose that just a single storage location in the memory is defective. This type of problem can be difficult to find. There is an addressing sequence that can be followed, however, that will find a defective storage location quite easily.

This finding of faulty storage locations, or "cells," is accomplished by a test that will insure that all cells can be written into and read from without changing the information stored in any other cells. This addressing sequence is called a *march addressing pattern*. The reason for this designation is that we will be "marching" a logical 1 or a logical 0 sequentially through the memory under test. Described in words, the march pattern will:

1. Write a 0 into *every* location in the memory
2. Read location 0 *only* and test for data output equal to 0 from location 0
3. Write a 1 into location 0 *only*
4. Increment the address input by one to the next sequential location
5. Read the next location and check for data output equal to 0
6. Write a 1 into that location just checked for 0 in Step 5
7. Repeat Steps 4–6 until all address codes have been checked for a 0 and have had a 1 written into them.

After completion of Step 7 we have insured that all storage locations can store a 0, and have that 0 read from that location. However, to insure that no information was disturbed in any storage location when we wrote a 1 into each location after checking it for 0, the memory must be read again. This time we will be testing for a 1 to be read from the memory. These steps are described in Steps 8–13.

8. Read location 0 only and test for data output equal to 1 from location 0
9. Write a 0 into location 0 only
10. Increment the address input by one to the next location in the sequence

11. Read the next location and check for data output equal to 1. (We had written 1 into the location in Steps 3–6; this 1 should still be there unless it was disturbed when we wrote 0 into the previous location in Step 9.)
12. Write a 0 into the location just checked in Step 11
13. Repeat Steps 10–12 until all address codes have been checked for a 1 and have had a 0 written in them.

After concluding Step 13 with no errors found, we will have insured that the memory can read and write a 1 into each location without disturbing the information in any other storage location. *Notice that we had to make two complete passes of all storage locations in the memory to be certain that the memory could store and retrieve both logical 0 and logical 1 in each location successfully.* We must do this because of the way the march pattern checks the data output. When checking a storage location for data output, we never check storage locations with an address code lower than the code presently being tested. When reading or writing from a particular location information may be changed in storage locations that were previously checked and thought good. The second pass at the memory will allow us to check all of the storage locations that were not checked again on the first pass.

A good point of this march pattern addressing sequence is that the system will find the problem for us. In order to implement this addressing sequence, the memory system must be capable of changing the addresses under program control. If we can program the address sequence and the R/W input on a cycle-by-cycle basis, this technique will greatly aid in troubleshooting memories. Many memory systems allow us to do this. If the system we are using has the capabilities of this type of testing, it will be worth the effort to learn how to implement this march pattern.

If at any time when we are testing we find a storage location that has the wrong information in it, the test should stop. The address that failed to test correctly is defective, and an error will be displayed.

An example of how this addressing sequence works follows: Suppose that a particular address is defective, and that the address line A_3 inside the memory chip is always at logical 1 level. The address input to the chip has been checked and found to be working correctly, indicating the problem is inside the chip where the user has no control or access. The visible result is that when the march addressing pattern just described is run, the machine stops with address 15 displayed. This indicates a failure at this address in the memory. The machine will have stopped on this defective location for any one of several possible reasons that are internal to the memory chip. The only way to correct the problem is to replace the defective integrated circuit (IC).

2-3 Dynamic Memory Systems

So far we have talked about static memories and static memory systems. We now direct our attention to the other class of memories, dynamic memories. The major difference between a static memory and a dynamic memory is the "refresh" needed for dynamic memories. Dynamic memories retain information stored in them for only a limited period of time. This is approximately two milliseconds, depending on the ambient temperature of the device. After that time the information will be lost. This means that the information must be refreshed at regular time intervals just to keep the information in the memory correct.

Let's take a closer look at the structure of dynamic semiconductor memories. What we will see is an overall view of a dynamic memory device. There are many different dynamic memories on the market today, and probably none of them has the exact architecture that will be described here. The intent in this discussion is to give the reader a good intuitive feel for the major characteristics of dynamic memories. The first part we will examine is the storage element.

You will recall that the static memory storage cell is the flip flop. A typical dynamic memory storage element is a metal oxide semiconductor (MOS) capacitor. This capacitor is either charged to a given voltage, or the charge is removed. When the capacitor is charged, this corresponds to a logical 1 being stored in the cell. If the charge is intentionally removed from the capacitor, this corresponds to storing a logical 0 into the cell. If the storage element were an ideal capacitor, the charge would remain on the capacitor indefinitely; but the storage element is not ideal, so a certain amount of charge leakage is associated with it. The actual storage element may be thought of as a capacitor in parallel with a resistor. This is shown in Figure 2-19.

If an initial charge is put on the capacitor, the charge will have a leakage

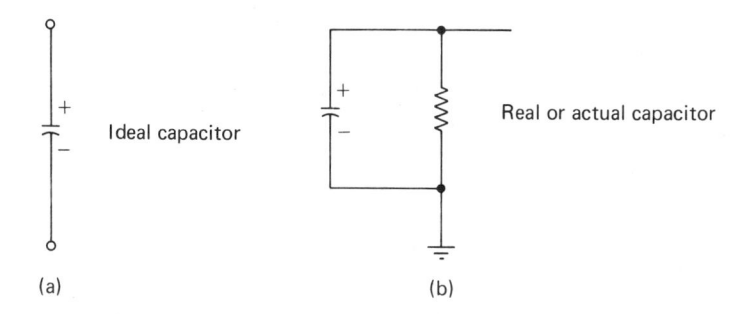

Figure 2-19 Simple model of a storage cell for a dynamic semiconductor memory (a) Ideal capacitor has a perfect dielectric and hence no leakage. (b) Actual capacitor has leakage, since the dielectric is never a perfect insulator.

path, and the voltage across the capacitor will start to decay as a function of the capacitor value and the resistor value. A true dynamic memory storage element is much more sophisticated than this simple model, but this is a good first approximation. More importantly, this model will help in the understanding of dynamic memory operation.

Now that a model of the storage cell has been introduced, let us see how these elements are arranged to form the memory array. The dynamic storage array is shown in Figure 2-20. While the array shown is for a 4 × 4 dynamic

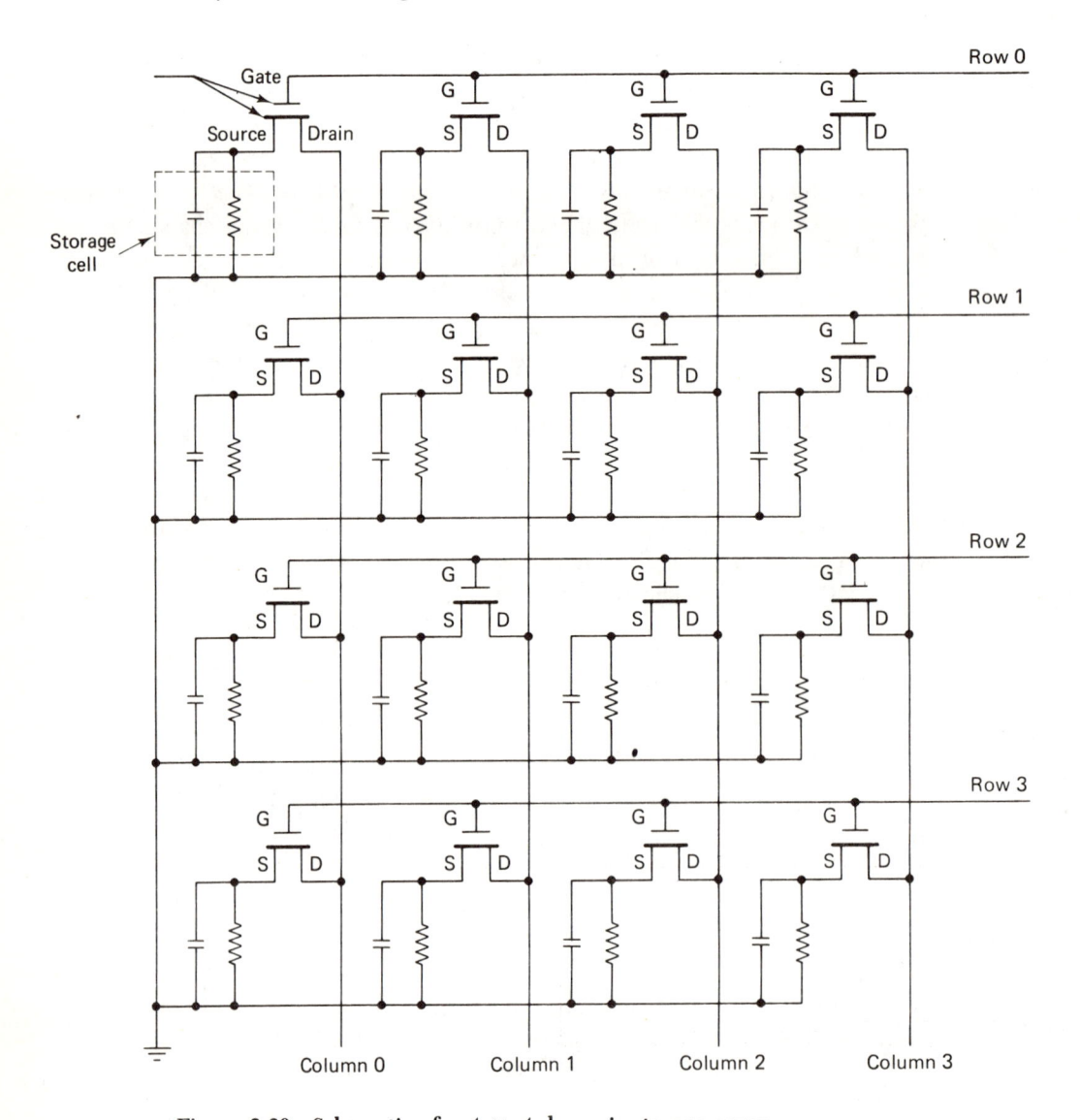

Figure 2-20 Schematic of a 4 × 4 dynamic storage array

Sec. 2-3   *Dynamic Memory Systems*   61

memory array, this array can be expanded to form any size necessary. The 4 × 4 array is shown only to make the concept clear. Notice that the MOS transistor gates are all tied to a common row line, and the drains are all tied to a common column line.

The row decoding is similar to the row decoding that was shown for the static memory. The row address is usually the lower order address bits of the entire address word. This means that for a 4 × 4 dynamic memory there would be four address inputs. The two LSB (least significant bits) of the address input, (A_0, A_1) would be the two bits of the row address. The reason for this will be shown as our discussion proceeds. See Figure 2-21 for the row address inputs.

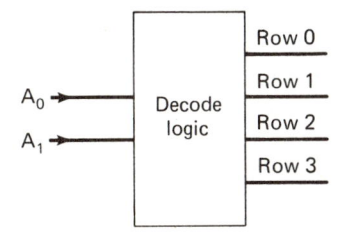

Figure 2-21 Block diagram of the row decode logic used in a dynamic RAM

Assume that a row address has been applied to the memory. This means that each column line is connected to a storage element. Look again at Figure 2-19. Remember that the information is stored as a charge on a capacitor. Every time a load is connected to the storage capacitor, some of the charge leaks off the capacitor. To read the information some type of device is needed that has a high input impedance so it will not excessively affect the charge stored on the capacitor. To accomplish this a device known as a *sense amplifier* is connected to each column line in the dynamic memory. See Figure 2-22 for a diagram of the sense amplifier connection.

These sense amplifiers read the information on the column lines. Their output is a logical 1 or logical 0 voltage, depending on the amount of charge on the storage element. There are various methods that the sense amplifiers use to interrogate the columns. One is for the sense amplifiers to connect a discharge path to the column lines and detect any charge changes in that path. See Figure 2-23.

By this method the sense amplifier connects a resistor (R_L) and measures the voltage that occurs across R_L. If there is a certain level of voltage across R_L the sense amplifier detects a logical 1 stored in the memory. If there is little voltage across R_L the sense amplifier interprets this as a logical 0 stored in the memory. See Figure 2-24.

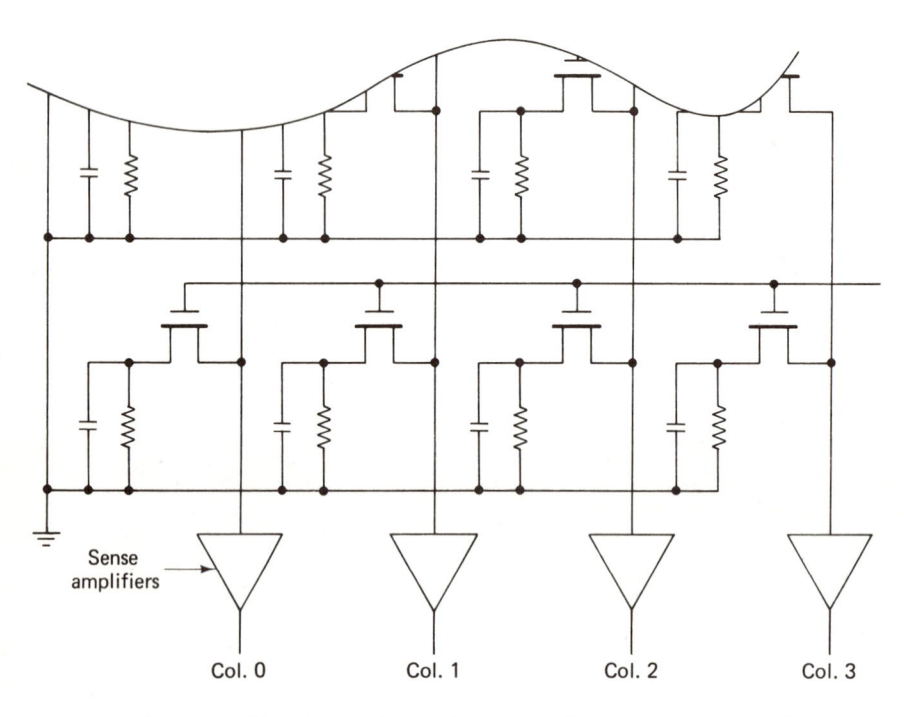

Figure 2-22 Column lines of a dynamic storage array with sense amplifiers connected to the column lines

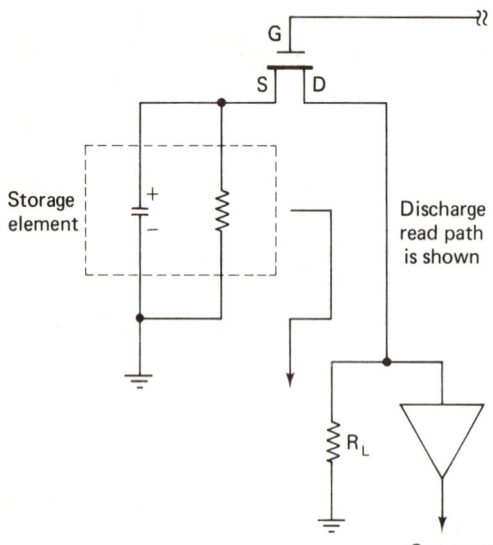

Figure 2-23 Schematic of the discharge path for reading the information in a single storage cell in a dynamic RAM

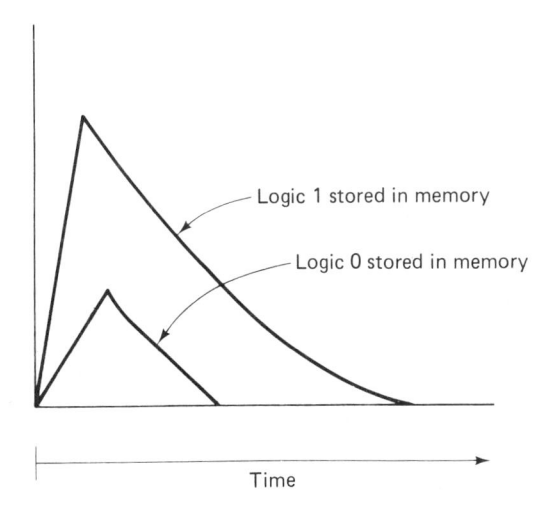

Figure 2-24 Voltage waveforms produced by the discharging of a storage cell. No voltage levels are shown, because they vary with the different manufacturers of the same device.

Note that this is a *destructive read* operation. By reading the information in the memory, the information is lost. The information must be restored to the value it was, if it is not to be lost completely. (Remember that we read an entire row of the memory at one time.) The column address selects which of the sense amplifiers will deliver the final data to the data output pin.

The output of the sense amplifiers is connected back to the column lines of the memory to restore the information from the row that was read. This puts a charge back on the storage cell if there was a charge on it before the read cycle took place. It does not put any charge on the cell if none was on it before the read cycle.

Note that if the memory was in a write cycle, the information that would go back to the column line would not be the sense amplifier output, but rather the information on the data input pin. The column address, along with the write enable pin, determines the path for the data in. See Figure 2-25 for the selection of data in and information restore in a dynamic memory.

Notice that the only way to refresh the information in memory is to read or write from the memory. If information is put into the dynamic memory and not accessed for a few milliseconds, all of that information will disappear as the storage capacitors lose all of the charge on them. To refresh the entire memory all that is needed is to access only the row address of all rows in the memory. Recall that an entire row is read and refreshed every memory read or write cycle. This is why the row addresses are usually the LSB's of the memory address.

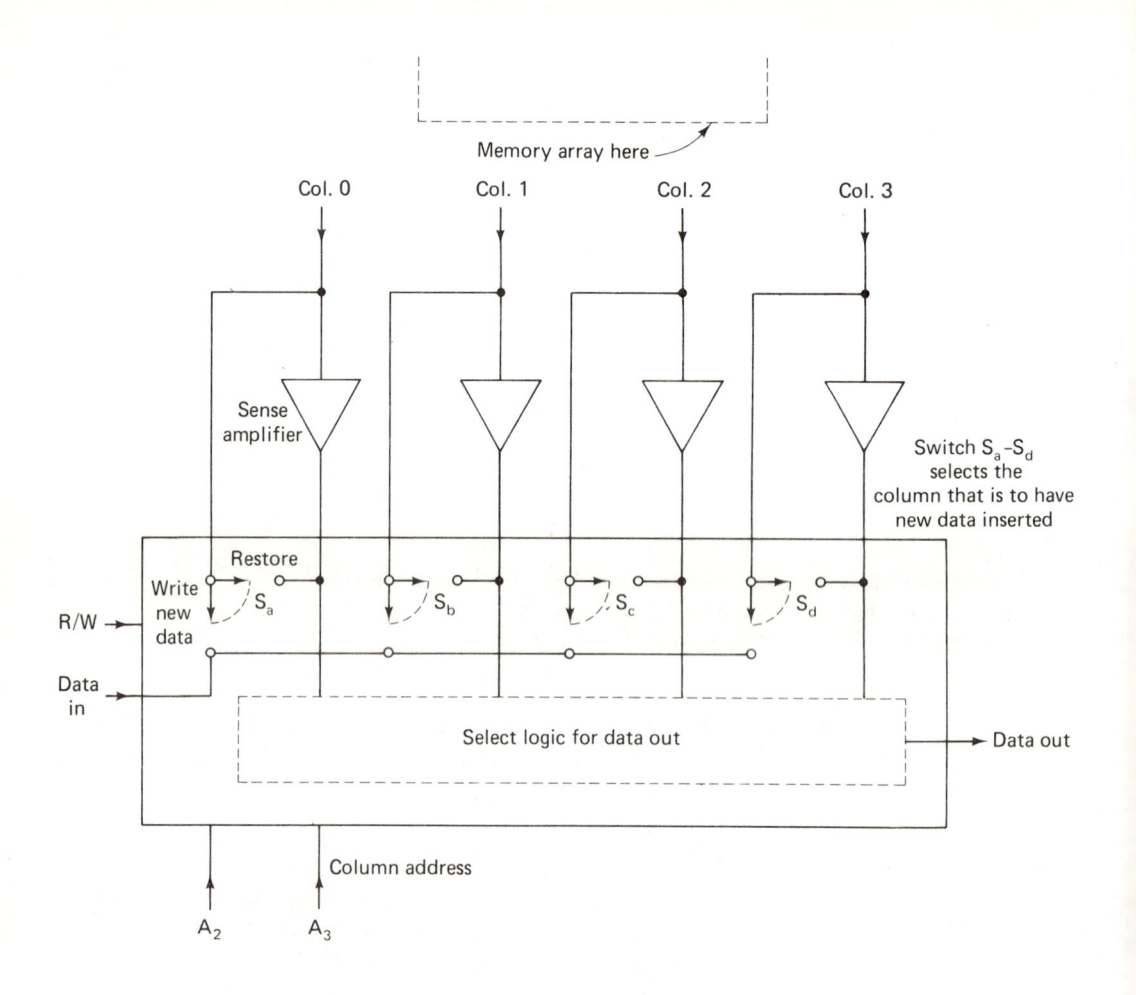

Figure 2-25 Block diagram of the column decode circuitry. The column decoder circuit selects which column will be directed to data out during a read cycle. The column decoder also directs data into the correct column during a write cycle. During a read cycle, Sa-Sd are in the refresh mode. During a write cycle, one switch is connected to the data-in line.

In dynamic memory systems external hardware is built in to keep track of when the memories need to be refreshed. When that time comes, the refresh hardware should automatically interrupt the system operation and cycle through the LSB or lower order address pins of the dynamic memory.

The question may arise: Why use dynamic memories since they are so difficult? The answer is quite clear. The storage element may be as simple as a single MOS transistor—compare this to a static memory that may use up to eight bipolar transistors per storage cell. As a result the power dissipation is greatly reduced for dynamic RAMs. Also the density is increased, which provides more information storage per unit of area on a dynamic RAM. There are available on the market MOS dynamic RAMs organized as 65536 × 1. This large a RAM would be difficult if not impossible without the use of dynamic memory technology.

Refreshing data in storage is just another potential trouble spot for dynamic memories. Not only does a troubleshooter have to insure that all timing signals are present, but also that the dynamic memory is being refreshed at the correct time. *Dynamic memories must be refreshed.* It is up to a troubleshooter to find out how this is accomplished on the particular piece of equipment that is to be repaired.

Dynamic memory systems can also be put into a timing loop described earlier for the static memory. The same signal checks apply. An additional signal to check for on dynamic memories is the *refresh circuitry*. The timing loop should allow the troubleshooting of this circuit also. The loop will cycle continually, showing that the memory board needs to be refreshed.

The march addressing pattern discussed earlier for the static memory also works equally well for dynamic memory systems.

2-4 Use of Memory Devices in Microprocessor Systems

Now that static and dynamic semiconductor memories have been discussed, we will introduce some key points in their use with microprocessors. The main focus will now concern entering data into memory (write operation) and retrieving data from memory (read operation). For this discussion we will assume that the address lines are stable and that we need not concern ourselves with either read or write access times.

We make these assumptions so as to focus on a single concept at a time (namely, reading and writing data in a semiconductor memory). Later we will discuss in detail how memory address inputs are generated, and what considerations must be given to read and write access times.

To begin, we must visualize how the semiconductor memory is physically connected to the entire system. For now, we will show the address inputs to memory but not where they come from. Look at Figure 2-26, where we recognize all the necessary digital inputs and outputs of a memory. These are:

1. Data-input lines
2. Data-output lines
3. Address-input lines
4. W/R line

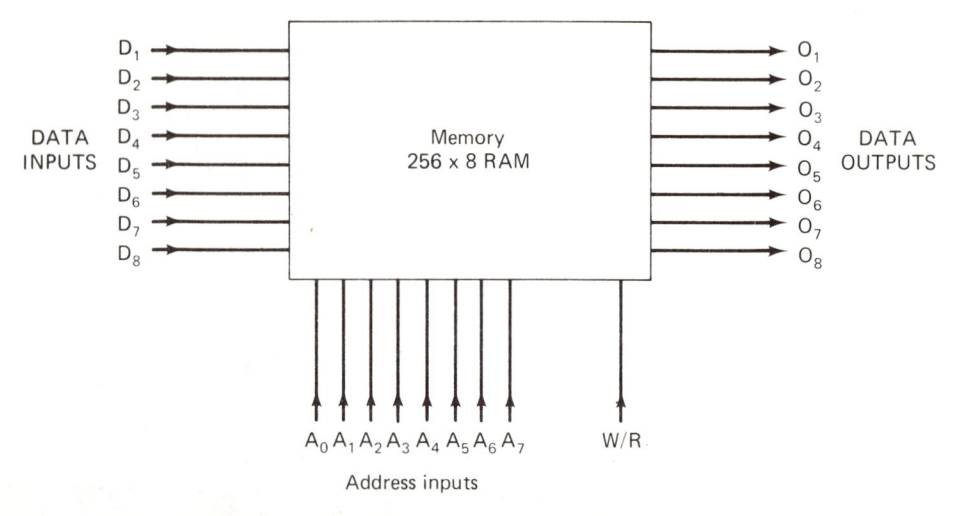

Figure 2-26 Block diagram of a memory, showing all important input and output lines

The power supply pins of a memory are not shown on the schematic usually. However, there will be a note somewhere on the schematic that indicates what pins of the memory device are designated for power input. We will now turn our attention to the signals Data In, Data Out and W/R.

When the memory is connected to a microprocessor CPU, the main path for data out from memory leads into the microprocessor. The main path for data into the memory comes from the microprocessor. This is shown in Figure 2-27.

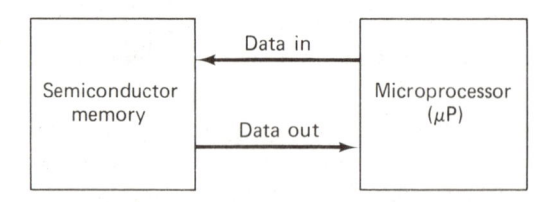

Figure 2-27 Main path for data in and data out for the memory is via the microprocessor

Let us suppose that our memory has 8 "Data In" lines and 8 "Data Out" lines. This is a typical number of lines in a microprocessor system. The 8080 microprocessor device, which we will concentrate on in this book, uses this number of input and output lines. If the data coming into the memory from the

Sec. 2-4 Use of Memory Devices in Microprocessor Systems

microprocessor and the data going out from the memory to the microprocessor were to have separate digital lines, 16 pins would be required on the microprocessor. See Figure 2-28 for details.

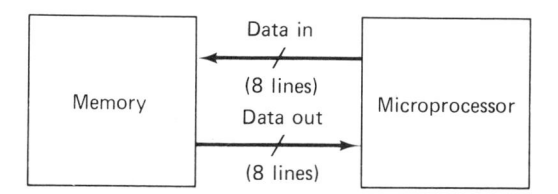

Figure 2-28 Sixteen physical digital lines could be used for a memory that has 8 data-in and 8 data-out lines.

This is not the case in the 8080 microprocessor; this device has only 8 pins, which are used for both Data In and Data Out. If one thinks about this, it makes sense because we do not enter data at the same time that we read data, and vice versa. Therefore, the 8 signal lines are named I/O (Input/Output) lines, and are further described as Data I/O lines. They are grouped together because of their similar function and are given the collective name of Data I/O Bus, or simply *Data Bus*.

All data flows on this bus. Sometimes the data flows into the microprocessor *from* the memory and sometimes the data flows out of the microprocessor *into* the memory. *These two directions of data flow never occur at the same instant in time.*

This system structure looks as shown in Figure 2-29. What does this type of structure require of the memory? We see that there are only 8 physical lines to the memory block for data in and data out. This means that the number of physical connections at the memory have been reduced from 16 to 8.

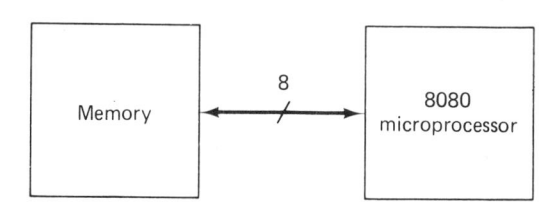

Figure 2-29 Only eight physical signal lines are needed if each line performs both the data-in and data-out function (I/O) for the memory.

How is this accomplished? We will show how it is accomplished for a single input and output line of the memory, then expand this concept to 8 lines that are identical. To make understanding easier we are using static RAMs for this discussion. Figure 2-30(a) shows one data input line and one data output line. We wish to make the circuit look as shown in Figure 2-30(b).

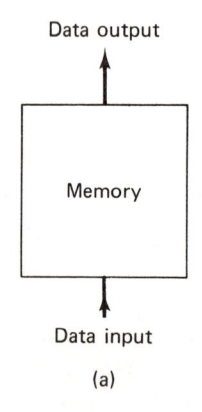

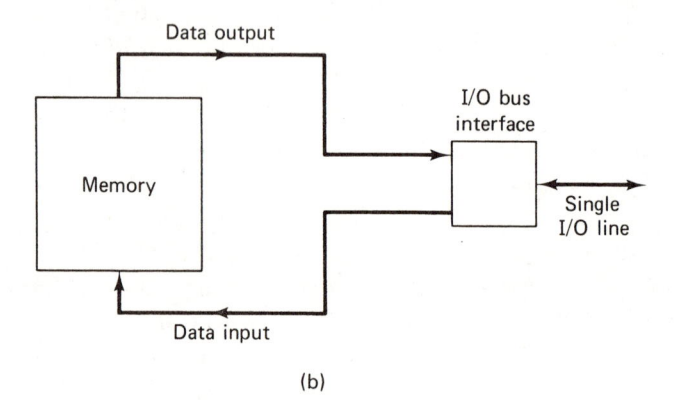

Figure 2-30 (a) Typical memory with separate data-in and data-out lines (b) I/O structure for one data-in and data-out line.

We need to know what type of data flow will be on the I/O line. There are two types:

1. Data into memory (from the processor)
2. Data from memory (to the processor)

To know which type is on line we need another line that indicates either type 1 or type 2 data flow. This is shown in Figure 2-31, as the "control" line.

```
                  Data out
    ┌─────────┐─────────────→┌──────────┐
    │         │              │ I/O interface
    │ Memory  │              │   μP?    │ ←→
    │         │              │          │
    └─────────┘←─────────────└──────────┘
                  Data in          ↑
                                Control
                                  line
```

Logical 1 = Data on I/O line
             from memory

Logical 0 = Data on I/O line
             to memory

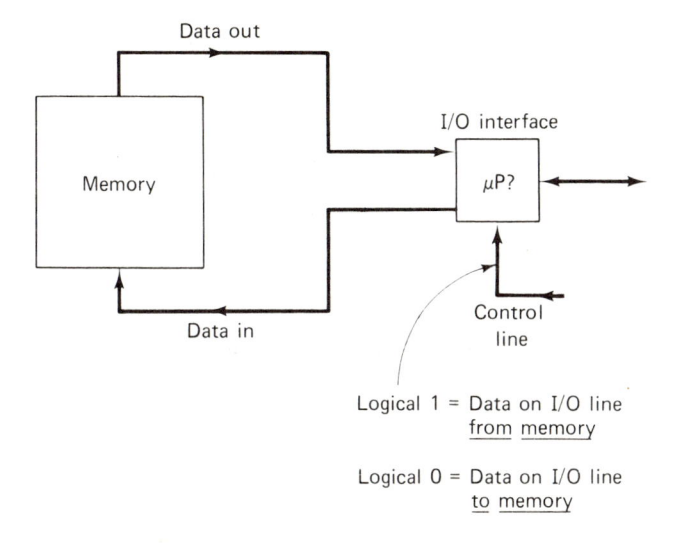

Figure 2-31 The control line is added to control what data on the I/O line is to be used for at any given instant in time.

The control line originates from the microprocessor, which governs the activities on the data I/O bus. When the microprocessor is receiving data from memory the control line is a logical 1. When the microprocessor is generating input data to memory the control line is a logical 0.

Now we will construct the hardware necessary to accomplish the data I/O bus *interface* for one data input and output line. A diagram of the single data I/O interface is shown in Figure 2-32(a). If we use standard T²L devices for this interface, the circuit will look as shown in Figure 2-32(b).

The following discussion describes in detail how the circuit of Figure 2-32(b) works. If the control line carries a logical 1, then input pin 2 shows a logical 1. This enables gate A and allows data from memory to be the controlling factor on the data I/O line. The dotted line in Figure 2-32(b) represents the data flow direction under these conditions.

The inverter B is in series with gate A which produces non-inverted data from the memory at the output of the data I/O line. Two inversions must occur: one at the inverter and one at the gate. Notice further that the data going to the memory will logically track the 1 or 0 data on the I/O line. This is of no concern because the data internally stored in the memory will not change until a write enable signal is issued to the memory. We are reading data from the memory under these conditions so a write enable signal will never occur. If we could observe the data input pin on the memory with an oscilloscope, we would see it switching from logical 1 to logical 0. At the same time the write enable pin on

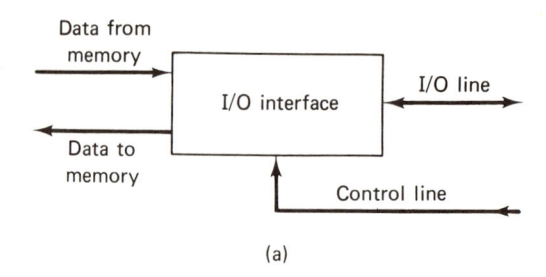

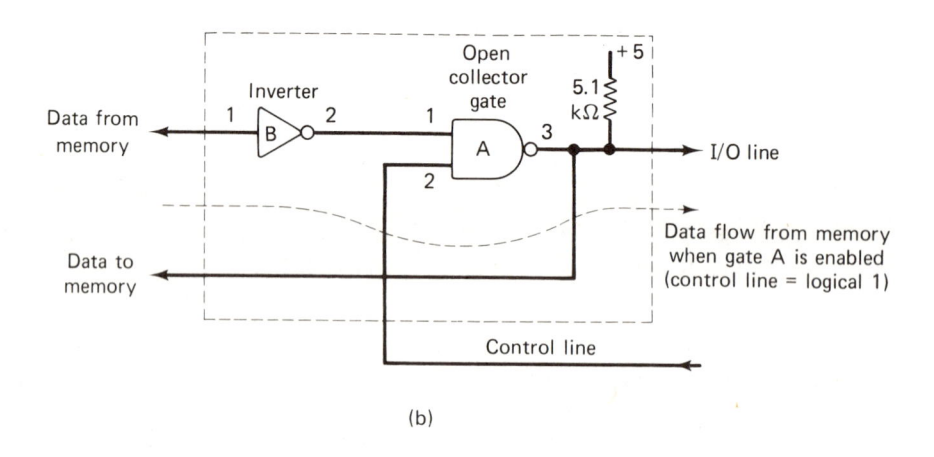

Figure 2-32 (a) Block diagram of an I/O interface for a single data-in and data-out line. (b) Hardware realization of the block diagram in (a)

the memory would be a steady logical 1 or logical 0, whichever the condition for a read data on the memory.

Now let us examine what happens when we enter data into the memory. First, the control line goes to a logical 0, "disabling" gate A and changing its output to a logical 1. More important than the output going to a logical 1, is the fact that the output of gate A is effectively "turned off." (Remember that an open collector device has a single npn transistor as its output structure. When this transistor is turned off, the data I/O line can be driven from some other source without creating a problem.) See Figure 2-33. Keeping this in mind, when gate A of Figure 2-33 is disabled, we see that some other device, which is connected in parallel with the output of gate A, now determines the output. This alternate output usually originates from the microprocessor. Now the data-in line to memory may be driven to a logical 1 or a logical 0, and the data out of the memory will not affect it because the data-out path to the I/O line is disabled.

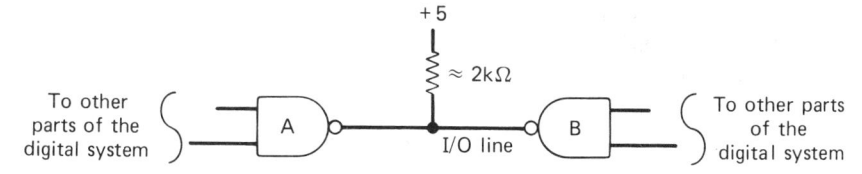

Figure 2-33 Either device output A or device output B can control the I/O line at different instants in time. In this figure, gate A is disabled and gate B is enabled.

The problem of interfacing memory devices to an I/O bus is a common one in microprocessor systems, so common, in fact, that special integrated circuits have been designed and built to solve this problem. We will discuss these special digital circuits in Chapter 9 titled "Taking Advantage of LSI." For now it is only necessary to understand and define the problem and the solution given. Once we know what the problem is, we find that its solution can take many forms. The solution presented here shows how this problem could be solved, using standard logic devices with which the reader should be familiar. By approaching the problem in this way we do not enter too many new variables into a new concept. The main focus is to get a good, intuitive feel for "what should be there." Our concern is, when a semiconductor memory is interfaced to a microprocessor, what should one look for in the hardware of that interface?

We find that some memories are designed with the interface circuits built into the integrated circuit. These memories have a characteristic called *common I/O*. This term differentiates them from memories that have *separate I/O*. So far we have discussed only memories with separate I/O. Figure 2-34(a) shows a block diagram of a memory with separate I/O; Figure 2-34(b) shows a memory with common I/O.

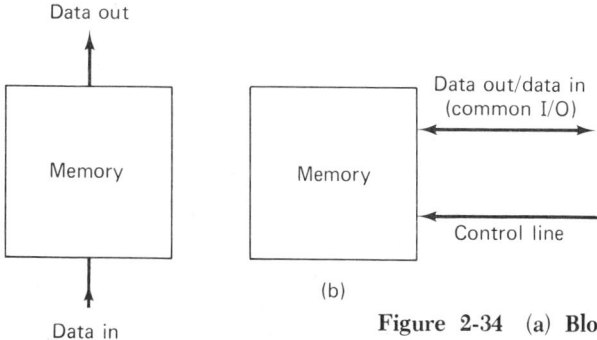

Figure 2-34 (a) Block diagram of a memory with separate data-in, data-out lines (b) Block diagram of a memory with common data-in and data-out lines.

2-5 Read Only Memory

After one has become familiar with a random access memory, understanding the operation of other types of semiconductor memory is a much easier task. The Read Only Memory (ROM) can be thought of as a subset of the RAM. In the RAM one can both enter and retrieve data. In a ROM one can only retrieve data. The data is stored in the memory when the device is built. ROMs are used often in microprocessor systems when one has a static, unchanging set of instructions. They are very useful in applications such as "look up tables" and character generators. When a set of input instructions or data is no longer in the process of being changed, the data is said to be *"static."* It is this kind of data that is built into the ROM. The advantage of a ROM over a RAM is that when power is turned off to the memory, the information in a ROM is not lost.

A familiar ROM is a T^2L device like a 7442 BCD to 7-segment decoder driver. (See Appendix A for the data sheet on this digital device.) The BCD inputs are the address inputs to this ROM, and the 7-segment outputs are the outputs of this ROM.

ROMs have only a *read access* time. This time is defined exactly the same as for a RAM. They do not have a write access time because one cannot write data into a ROM. Since ROMs can only be read, the construction of the internal memory cell is much less complex than that of a RAM. This allows information storage in a ROM to be denser than that for a RAM; that is, there is more data storage per unit of chip area. (Some typical ROMs are organized as 512×8, 1024×8, 2048×8, 4096×8.) From these numbers one can see that up to 16 bits of data storage is typical for a ROM.

2-6 Programmable Read Only Memories

Another type of ROM is the Programmable Read Only Memory (PROM). This type of semiconductor device does not have information in it when it is constructed. Each location is initially set to logical 1 or logical 0. Information can be programmed into these devices by applying special voltages to certain pins of the device. To show what happens when a PROM is programmed take a simple example. The concept discussed is accurate, but since manufacturers each have their own type of physical construction, the details of programming a PROM may vary from device to device.

Sec. 2-6 Programmable Read Only Memories

Each cell of a PROM has what is called a "fuse" in it. The one shown in Figure 2-35(a) is shaped like a common fuse and is, in reality, a conducting strip. To program the PROM, an amount of current is applied to the fuse sufficient to blow it if desired. When the fuse is blown, the strip of metal actually melts and separates (Figure 2-35(b)). Sometimes in PROMs the fuse does not blow well enough, and the metal only separates for a brief period of time. After this time the metal again makes contact, and the programmed information is lost. This process of the metal remaking contact once the fuse is blown is sometimes referred to as "grow back."

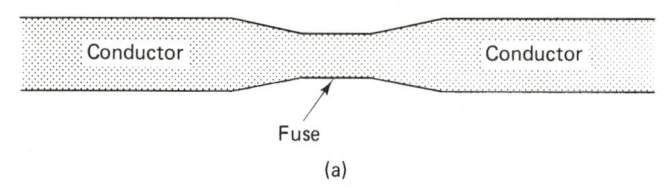

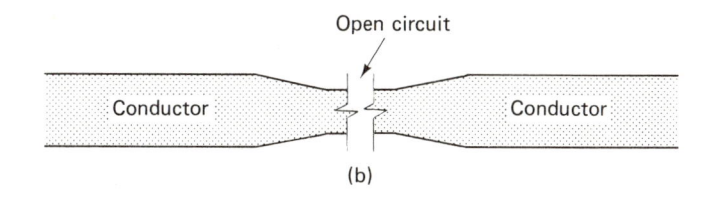

Figure 2-35 A "fuse" in a PROM as it is initially constructed by the manufacturer (b) The fuse after it has been blown

In Figure 2-36, if the fuse were blown the data in the cell would change from logical 1 to logical 0. (Note that only those cells are programmed in which the information differs from the initial information.) The drawback of a PROM is

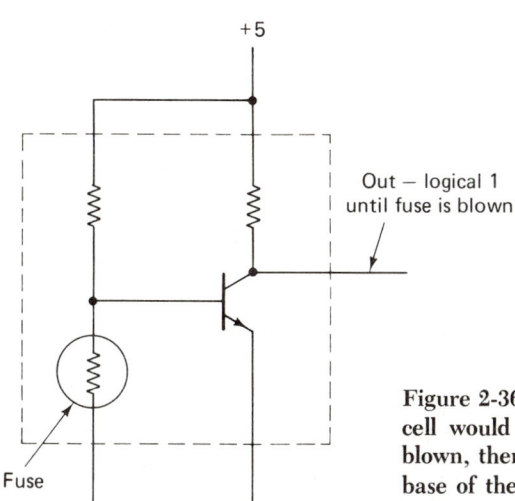

Figure 2-36 If the fuse of this cell were not blown, then the cell would have a logical 1 stored in it. If the fuse were blown, then the cell would have a logical 0 stored in it. (The base of the transistor would not be connected to ground.)

obvious; once the fuse is blown the information cannot be changed. PROMs are used often in the initial development stages of a microprocessor system. An advantage of the PROM is that it can be tailored to fit any given application without the great expense of having a ROM especially built at the factory.

2-7 Erasable Programmable Read Only Memory

This is another type of read only memory. The EPROM or EROM can be programmed like a PROM, but the information in it can be erased and the EPROM reprogrammed. The data in an EPROM is erased by exposing the device to ultraviolet (UV) light. These devices are built with a special window for this purpose, as shown in Figure 2-37. When EPROM devices are used in environments where accidental exposure to UV may occur, a special window covering is used. This covering prevents unwanted erasure of the information.

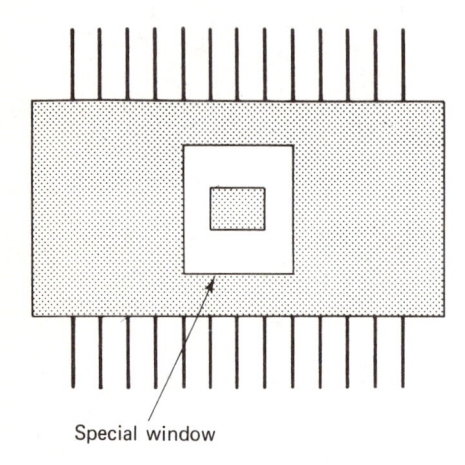

Figure 2-37 Special windows built into the device package on EPROMS provide access to ultraviolet light for erasing programs no longer needed.

Special window

As with the PROM, EPROM devices are extremely useful in the development stage of an instruction set for a microprocessor system, or any application where one-time, one-of-a-kind data is needed. It is not worth the expense to have a special ROM built for a one-of-a-kind system.

Interfacing ROMs, PROMs, and EPROMs to an I/O data bus is simpler than interfacing a RAM, because there is no data input to the device. However, we do need to disable the outputs of these devices to avoid interference with the operation of the data I/O bus. We use the same control signal that was mentioned earlier when we discussed interfacing RAMs. The control signal is connected to the chip select or enable pin of the read only memory. The chip enable signal performs the same function on a read only device as it performs on a RAM. See Figure 2-38 for illustration.

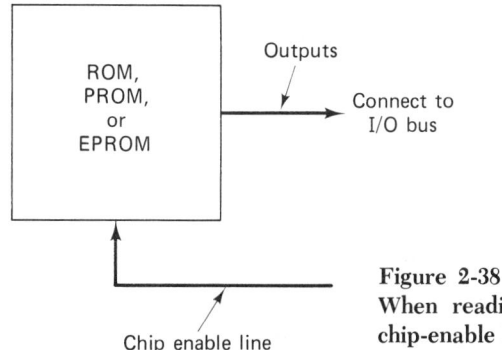

Figure 2-38 The chip is disabled when it is not being read. When reading the chip, the microprocessor will control the chip-enable line

In this chapter, we have introduced and discussed memory devices as well as memory systems. Our discussion has covered both the similarities and differences in dynamic and static memories. Some general troubleshooting techniques were presented that are applicable to both static and dynamic memories. The direct application of such techniques is only useful, however, if the troubleshooter has a sufficient working knowledge of the memory system and the type of memory in use. In other words, we should know "what should be there" from schematics, service notes, and previous study; most important, one should know how to put the particular memory system into the timing loop so that it can be checked.

Finally, it was shown how memory devices can be interfaced to a data I/O bus architecture. Anyone who wishes to become proficient in microprocessors must understand how semiconductor memories work, how they are used and, finally, how they are interfaced to microprocessors. One should be aware of common I/O memory devices, and how they differ from separate I/O memory devices. Semiconductor memories are a large part of any microprocessor system and understanding them at the level presented in this chapter is a first step in understanding how microprocessor systems function.

Review Questions

1. What are the two major types of semiconductor memories?

2. Define the following terms as they relate to semiconductor memories:
    a. Read Cycle
    b. Write Cycle
    c. Data In
    d. Data Out

3. Draw a block diagram showing the essential parts of a 1-bit semiconductor memory.

4. What do the initials RAM stand for?

5. How many storage locations are contained in a memory that has eleven address inputs and four data-in lines?

6. Define the term Read Access Time.

7. Define the term Write Access Time.

8. Draw a timing diagram showing Data Setup and Data Hold times for a RAM.

9. What is the total storage capacity in bits of a memory described as a 1024 × 8 static RAM?

10. If a RAM is organized as 64k × 1, would you think that the RAM is static or dynamic? Why?

11. Describe the function of the *chip select* pin on a memory.

12. What is meant by the term "daisy chain"?

13. Draw a block diagram of a memory system that is built from chips that are organized as 16 × 4 bit RAMs. The system is to be 64 × 8 bit RAM.

14. Explain the difference between common and separate I/O as pertains to a RAM.

3

CONSTRUCTION OF A KEYBOARD AND INTRODUCTION OF TIMED DATA INPUT TO THE MICROPROCESSOR

In this chapter we will discuss two important concepts. The first is that of timed digital signals. The second is how to enter data into a semiconductor Random Access Memory. We will realize with hardware a hexadecimal keyboard that will generate a single byte of static data. We will then discuss a means to enter that byte of data into memory.

When this chapter is completed we will have a memory system utilizing manual data entry for use with the 8080 microprocessor. This subsystem will be built entirely of standard T^{2}L devices. A complete circuit description and extensive discussion of the theory of operation will be given. The circuits presented here have been constructed and used in real applications with microprocessors.

3-1 The Keyboard and Data Transfer Functions

Let us begin by stating our objectives. We wish to enter data (digital information) into a memory. The memory is organized as a 256 × 8 bit static RAM. We will enter information into the memory manually, via a hexadecimal keyboard. (See Figure 3-1 for block diagram.)

From our discussion of semiconductor memories we recall that to write information into a RAM we must apply memory address, data-in, and write enable signals to the memory, all timed correctly. The 256 × 8 bit memory requires

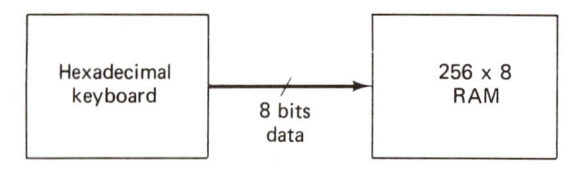

Figure 3-1 General block diagram of the keyboard system

eight address lines and eight data-in lines. Our manual keyboard data entry circuit must generate eight digital lines. These lines can be used to apply an address or data to the memory. A means to visually verify the values of the data-in and address lines to memory is useful in our microprocessor system, and we will incorporate one. In addition to constant monitoring, the display section will also provide a good debugging tool when we are ready to discuss ways to troubleshoot the microprocessor system.

A block diagram of our proposed manual data entry circuit is shown in Figure 3-2. We want to interface this memory to a microprocessor system as well as to our manual system. There we need to multiplex all of the inputs to the memory. These are Data In, Address lines, and the Write Enable signal. *Multiplexing* means to share the common input or output between two or more circuits. A

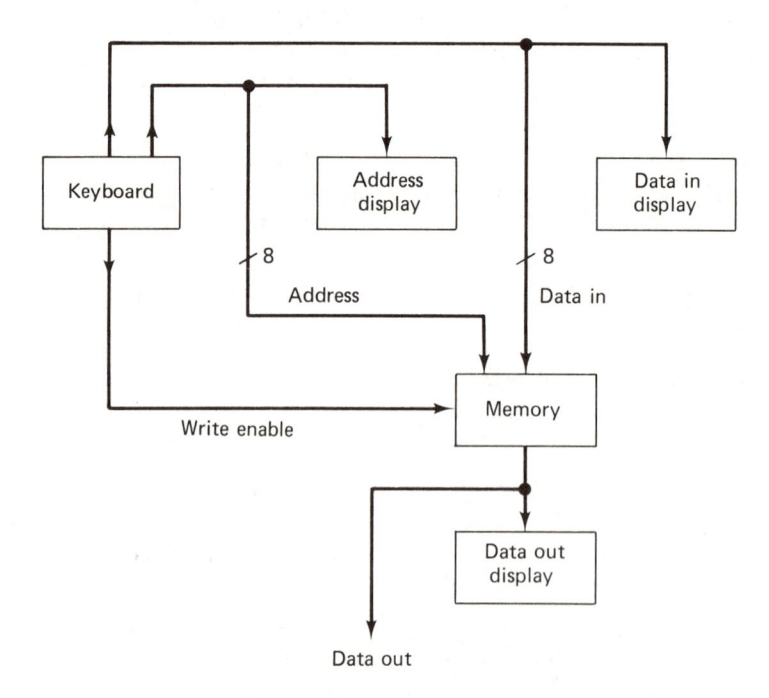

Figure 3-2 Expanded block diagram of the keyboard system

78

simplified multiplexing scheme is shown in Figure 3-3(a). Multiplexing in this way is common only to our microprocessor memory circuit. Our memory will be electrically isolated from the system data I/O buses. This is done to make understanding of microprocessor systems, components, and peripherals easier for the beginner.

Referring now to Figure 3-3(a), when the control input is a logical 0, input *1* is transferred directly to the output. When the control input is a logical 1, input *2* is transferred directly to the output. A hardware realization of this multiplexer is shown in Figure 3-3(b).

Fortunately we do not need to construct digital multiplexers from discrete logic devices because the function of multiplexing is so common that special digital devices are available now to perform this task. The multiplexer we will

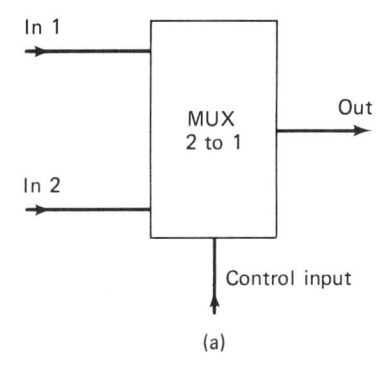

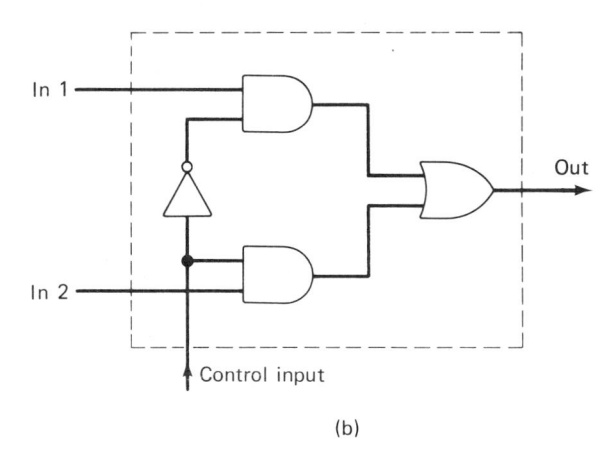

Figure 3-3 (a) Block diagram of a 2-to-1 digital multiplexer (b) Hardware realization of the block diagram in (a)

use is a 74157, shown in block diagram form in Figure 3-4. The data sheet for this device is given in Appendix A. We will use this multiplexer to share the address, data-in, and write enable signals to the 256 × 8 bit RAM. The new

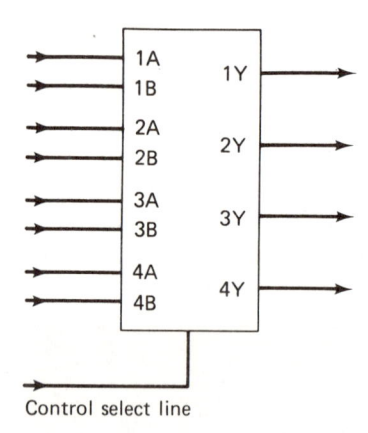

Figure 3-4 Block diagram of a 74157 Quad 2-to-1 digital multiplexer. There are 4 (2 to 1) digital multiplexers in this single IC package.

block diagram for our manual data entry circuit is shown in Figure 3-5.

A convenient feature of multiplexing is that each multiplexed system can be treated individually. So we can design our manual data entry system without adjusting any timing details of the data entry. After we enter the data manually into memory, we can flip a switch so that the multiplexers will then allow the memory—which was responding to the keyboard circuit—to respond only to the microprocessor.

Since there are 8 lines of Data In per memory word (one unique memory word per memory address), we will enter the data into the memory in two different parallel nibbles. The nibble lends itself well to hexadecimal code. For example, suppose we wish to enter the data byte (MSB)→01001000←(LSB) into a memory address. We would divide this byte into two nibbles. The nibbles would have the names LSN (least significant nibble) and MSN (most significant nibble). The LSN nibble contains the LSB (least significant bit). The MSN contains the MSB (most significant bit) of the data byte. For the data byte under consideration, the LSN would be 1000, and the MSN would be 0100. For convenience of conversing or writing these nibbles, the easiest way is the hexadecimal code. The LSN = $8_{(16)}$ and the MSN = $4_{(16)}$. The hexadecimal equivalent of this data byte would be $48_{(16)}$. The MSN is written first, at the extreme left. In this way we can describe the data byte easily, concisely, and with no ambiguity.

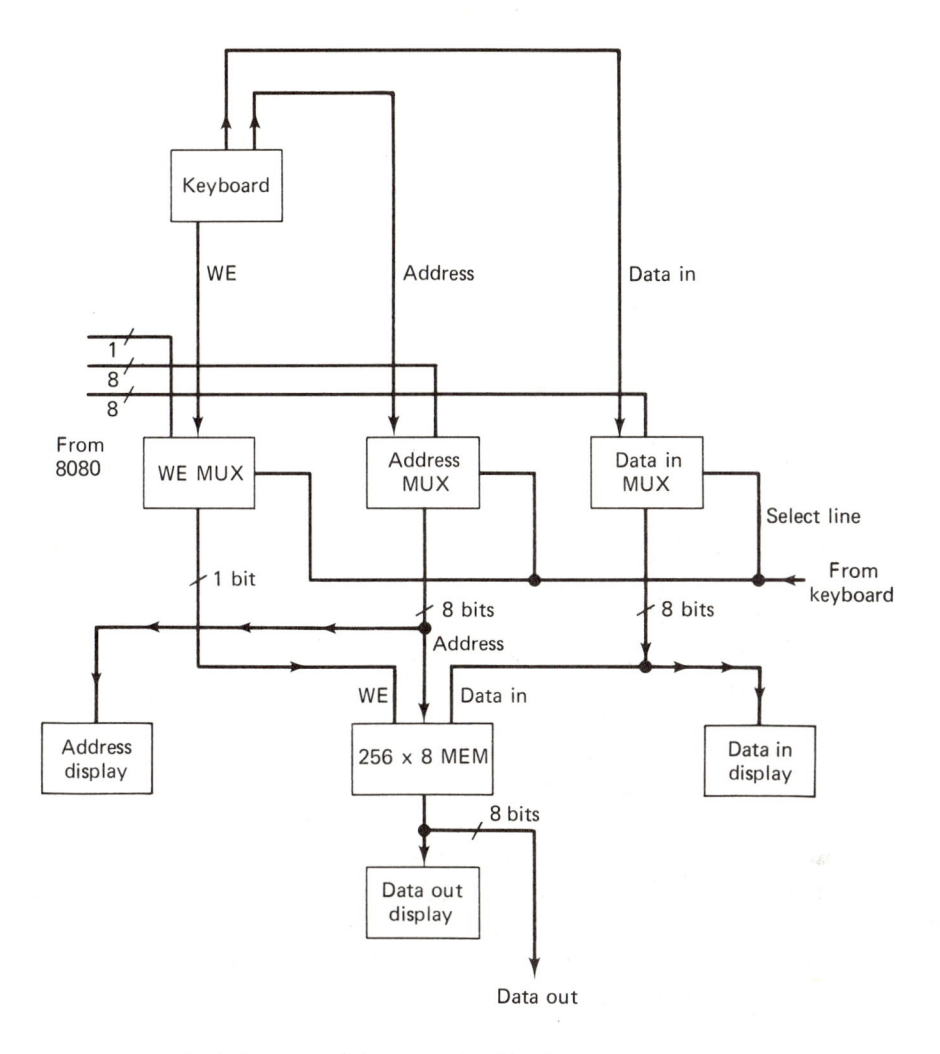

Figure 3-5 Block diagram of the entire keyboard entry system, including all multiplexing for use with a microprocessor also

Another reason for the choice of the hexadecimal system is that it lends itself well to digital hardware. A hexadecimal keyboard can be constructed that will allow data entry of two hexadecimal digits per data byte. In this way we can enter information into the memory in exactly the same way the information is written or spoken. The hexadecimal keyboard we will construct will do exactly this and we will use it to enter memory data and memory address. Many of the small microprocessor systems sold today have a hexadecimal keyboard for data entry. The single keyboard is used, and a switch determines if the keyboard is supplying address or data to the memory. The functional block diagram of the keyboard entry system shown in Figure 3-5 will be realized in digital hardware and discussed later in this chapter. The keyboard arrangement will resemble that shown in Figure 3-6.

0	4	8	C
1	5	9	D
2	6	A	E
3	7	B	F

Figure 3-6 Physical placement of the digit keys on the keyboard for use in our system

Now, we will show how to realize this block diagram of Figure 3-5 with hardware. We will begin with the details of the keyboard itself. For this we will use the same keyboard architecture that is used on most calculators. The switches of the keyboard are single pole single throw (SPST), with normally open (NO) contacts, as shown in Figure 3-7(a). The switches will be arranged in a matrix fashion as shown in Figure 3-7(b). There are 16 different switches arranged in a 4 × 4 matrix. In this way the number of signal lines can be reduced from 16 to 8. The intersection of a row line and a column line corresponds to the key being depressed. If the keys take on multiple functions (as some calculator keys do) it is easy to see why this particular key arrangement is of value. The sheer number of keys as well as the number of physical lines would become too cumbersome for a small keyboard if a way to reduce both could not be found.

With the keys arranged in this fashion there are some unique timing considerations that one must bear in mind. The technique we will use to generate hexadecimal data will call for a free running binary counter counting continually in binary from 0 to 15. During one count interval (the time between one number being generated and another being generated) there should be a static valid data word at the binary counter outputs. The idea is to store the binary counter outputs when the number we want appears at those outputs. *Latching data* is a term used to describe this process. For example, say we want to enter the number $A_{(16)}$ into memory. This number is only one nibble of the entire byte of data to be entered. We must present this number in a static or steady fashion to the data inputs of the memory. When we apply a write enable pulse the number will be stored into the memory.

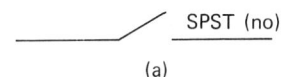

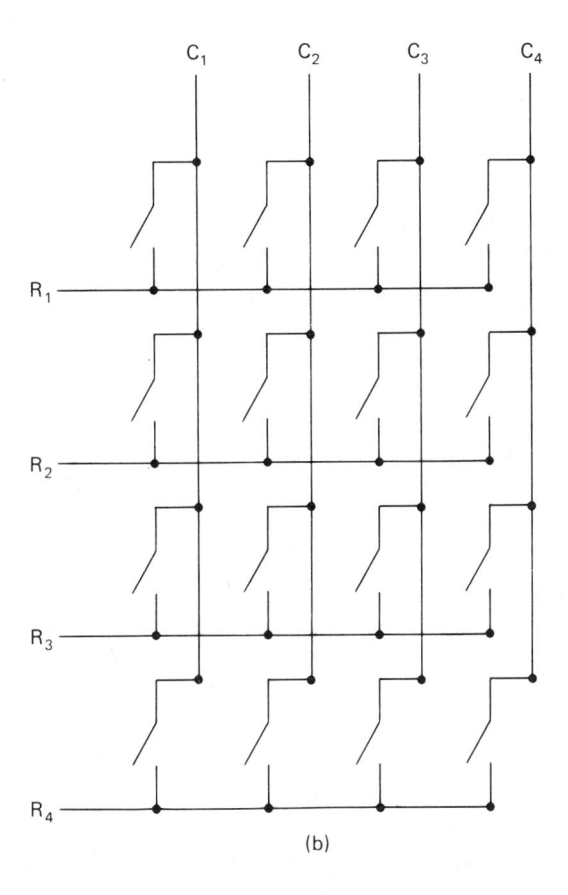

Figure 3-7 (a) Single-pole, single-throw, normally open switch used in the keyboard (b) Matrix arrangement of keyboard switches

As the counter is counting we must know somehow when the number $A_{(16)}$ is present at the counter outputs. When this is known, we can apply a strobe pulse to the latch and latch the data. Once the data is latched, the binary counter outputs can change, and we no longer concern ourselves with their output. We have the data we want stored in a latch. The data is static at the latch outputs until we again apply a strobe pulse to the latch. The problem is to apply the strobe input to the latches at the same time the data we want to enter into memory is present at the latch inputs. Figure 3-8 illustrates this timing problem.

Data to latch input

Strobe to latch

Latch output data

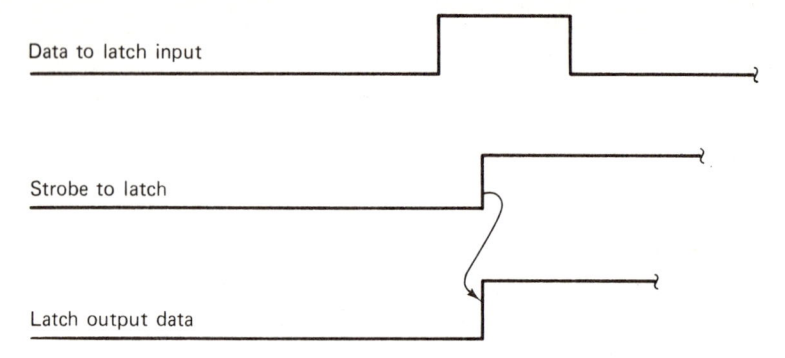

Figure 3-8 Strobe input must be applied to latch at the time when input data is present in order to latch the correct data.

There are other essential subcircuits of the keyboard circuit, but latching data at the correct instant is the main function of the timing circuit.

Let us now discuss how the keyboard and associated circuitry allows us to accomplish this task. We will approach the explanation in steps. In each step we will show the actual hardware used. When finished, each subcircuit will be integrated into a large schematic. At that point it will be a simple matter for one to understand and follow the flow of the data in the schematic. After the entire keyboard circuit has been explained, we will discuss techniques of troubleshooting this circuit.

We begin by showing in Figure 3-9 the circuit that generates the free running data, including a free-running clock. This clock is a 555 timer circuit set up in the astable, or free running, mode of operation. The data sheet for the 555 timer is given in Appendix A. The frequency of the free-running clock is set to approximately 1 kHz. This particular frequency is chosen because it is easy to generate. Any free-running frequency would have worked as well so long as we remember that there is an inherent lower limit to the frequency chosen which affects the time interval that must be allowed between key strokes. We will discuss this later. Any free-running frequency between 100 kHz and 1 kHz would be adequate for this clock in this application.

One important point to bear in mind when constructing a free-running oscillator is to keep the shape of the waveform as close to a square wave as possible. The reason for this will be shown later. For now, we try only to insure that the free-running frequency is as near a square wave as possible.

The free-running clock is an input to the 74197 binary counter. The data sheet for the 74197 binary counter is given in Appendix A. The outputs of the binary counter are the dynamic four bits of data that we will latch at the correct

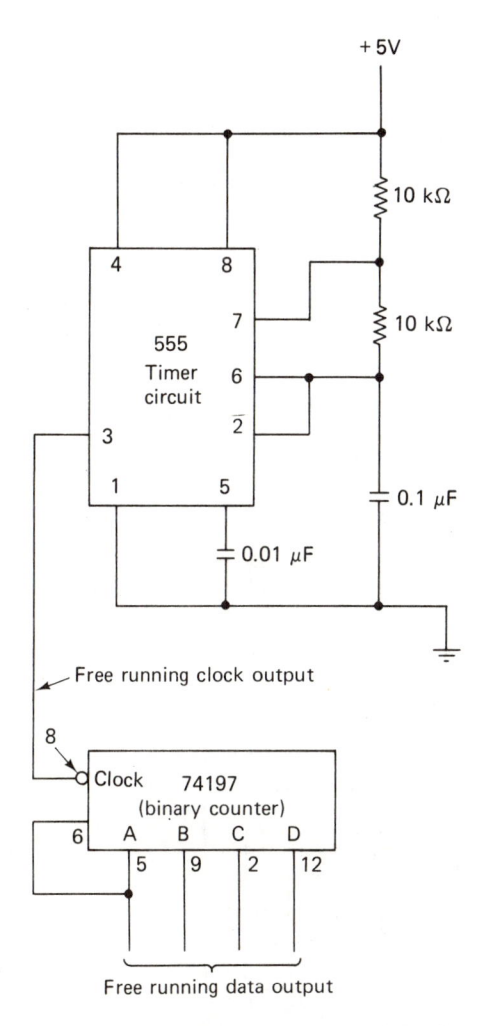

Figure 3-9 Schematic diagram of the data generator circuit

instant in time. We refer to the combination of the free-running clock and the 74197 binary counter as the *"data generation"* subcircuit. Notice in Figure 3-9 that the clock input line (pin 8 of the 74197 binary counter) has a small circle on it. This circle indicates that the counter changes state on transition of the clock as it goes from a logical 1 to a logical 0. This is referred to as the *negative transition* of the clock. The waveforms of the data generation subcircuit are shown in the timing diagram of Figure 3-10. Note how the binary outputs of the 74197 counter are referenced to the negative transition of the clock input.

85

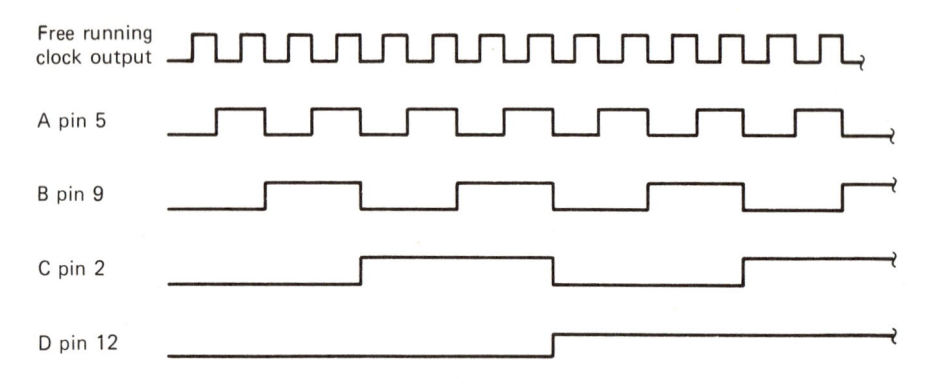

[Timing diagram showing Free running clock output, A pin 5, B pin 9, C pin 2, D pin 12]

Figure 3-10 Output of data generator circuit. Notice that data changes on the negative edge of the free-running clock.

In the next section of the circuit we will discuss *storage latches*. The latches used are 74175 and are shown in Figure 3-11. The data sheet for the 74175 latch is given in Appendix A. Notice in Figure 3-11 that there are two 4-bit or "quad"

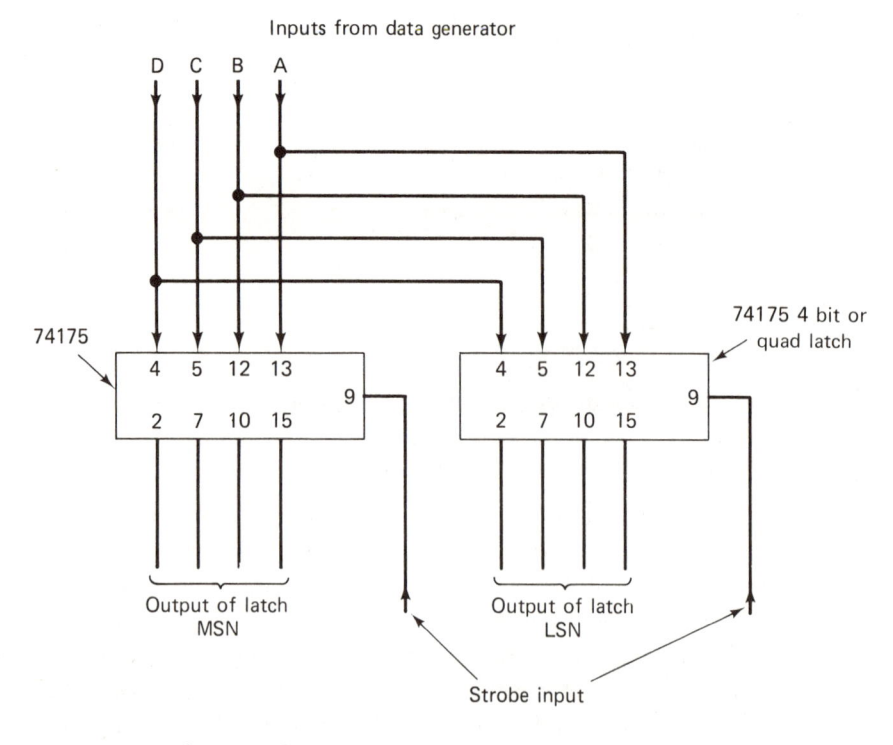

[Circuit diagram showing two 74175 quad latches receiving inputs D C B A from data generator, with outputs labeled "Output of latch MSN" and "Output of latch LSN", and a Strobe input]

Figure 3-11 The 74175 latches are used to store the data from the data generator curcuit when the strobe input goes to a logical 1 from a logical 0 level.

86

Sec. 3-1   *The Keyboard and Data Transfer Functions*   **87**

latches. One latch is for the LSN and the other is for the MSN. The data input for these storage latches comes from the data generator circuit. Note that the data input to both latches is *in parallel* which means that data for the MSN and the LSN is presented to both latch input lines at the same instant in time.

Each latch has its own strobe input. This indicates that additional circuitry must enable the correct strobe for the LSN latch or for the MSN latch. We will discuss this circuitry later. For now it is important to understand that the data is applied continously to both inputs of these 74175 latches, and when the strobe for either latch goes from a logical 0 to a logical 1 (denoted by the *absence* of a small circle on the strobe input line to the latch in the diagram) the output will reflect the input at the one instant. The output of the latch *will not* change state until another strobe is applied to it. Our circuit is now shown in block diagram form in Figure 3-12.

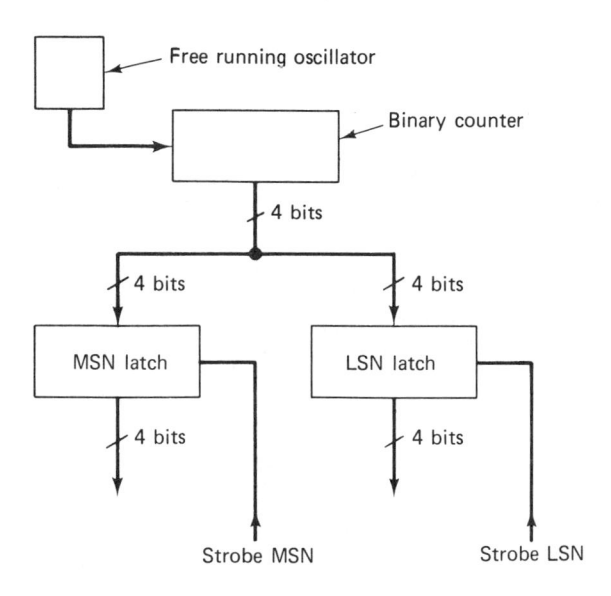

Figure 3-12 Block diagram of the data generator circuit with storage latches added. Data-in goes to both latches in parallel.

We come now to the keyboard section. We recall that the keyboard is arranged in top to bottom sequence, starting at top left with zero and going to bottom right F. The idea behind arranging the keyboard is illustrated in Figure 3-13 as follows. We apply digital signals to the $R_1 - R_4$ input lines. The digital signals applied to each row input line are active low at a different point in time. If we examine the outputs on the column lines ($C_1 - C_4$) in Figure 3-13(b) we observe that only one of the four column lines has a signal on it when any one

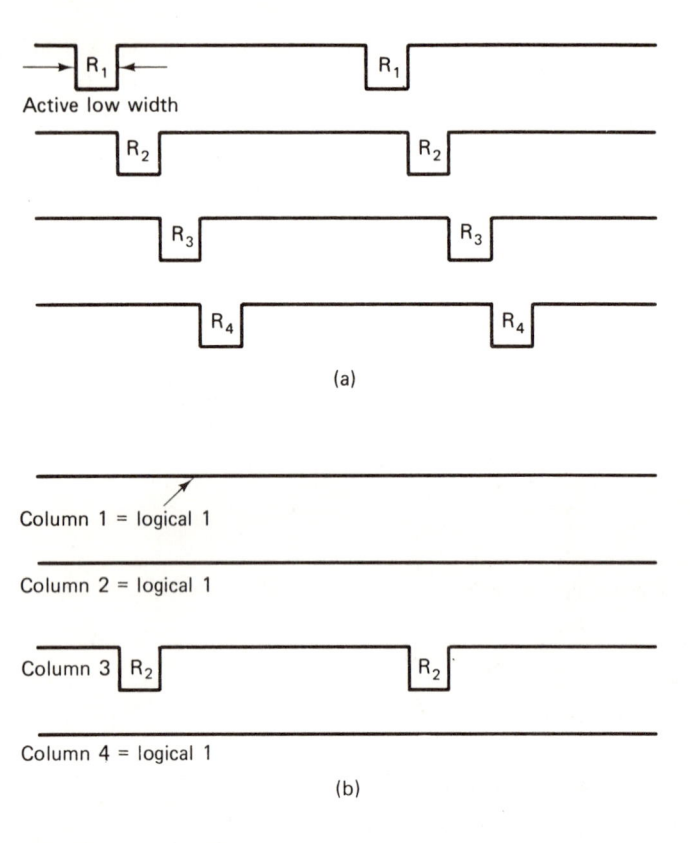

Figure 3-13 (a) Timing diagram for signals at the row input lines of the keyboard (b) Row and column line signals for R2, C3 when the switch at that matrix intersection is depressed

key is depressed. The column line that has the signal is the line that is connected to a particular row input line via the switch that has been pressed.

For example, suppose that the switch at the intersection of R_2 and C_3 (Row 2 Column 3) is depressed. This switch now supplies an electrically conductive path from the Row 2 input line to the Column 3 output line. The resulting signals on the row and the column lines are shown in Figure 3-13. We notice that only the C_3 output line has an active low signal on it, also that the signal is identical to the signal at the R_2 input line.

We will examine only one column line at a time. This is shown in Figure 3-14. We will electrically sequence through the column lines, starting with column 1 and ending with column 4. We will perform this sequencing at a rate that allows all of the four-row input lines to become active before we will examine another column output.

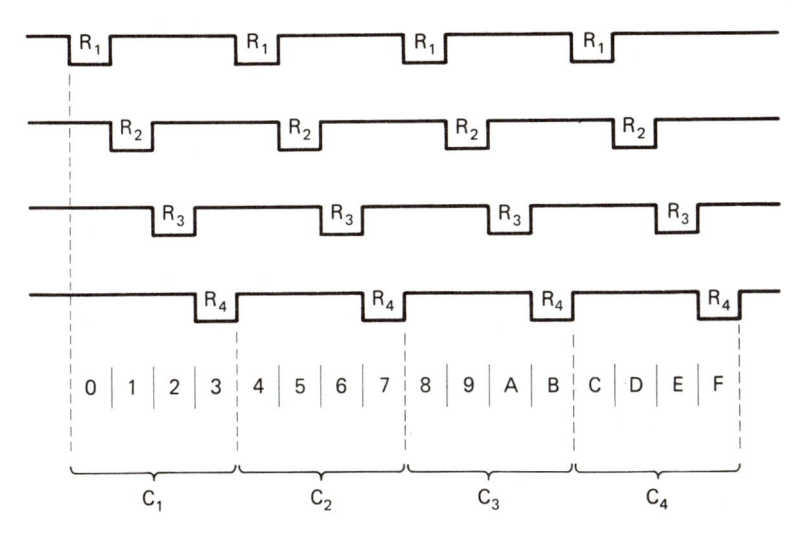

Figure 3-14 Keyboard timing diagram for digits 0-F referenced to row and column timing events

In this way we can develop sixteen possible combinations of events on the keyboard. These events are:

1.	R_1, C_1	9.	R_1, C_3
2.	R_2, C_1	10.	R_2, C_3
3.	R_3, C_1	11.	R_3, C_3
4.	R_4, C_1	12.	R_4, C_3
5.	R_1, C_2	13.	R_1, C_4
6.	R_2, C_2	14.	R_2, C_4
7.	R_3, C_2	15.	R_3, C_4
8.	R_4, C_2	16.	R_4, C_4

The designated R and C correspond to the row input line that is active low, and the column output line that is connected via a switch to that row line. (We have not shown how we actually accomplish this sequencing with hardware, and there is one more addition we must make to the list before we do so.)

Of the sixteen possible combinations of events that can be generated by the keyboard, no two events can occur at the same instant in time. The important implication of this is that we now have a means to distinguish sixteen uniquely timed events. We will assign each of these sixteen events a particular number from the data generator. The appended list of events follows:

89

1.	R_1, C_1	0		9.	R_1, C_3	8
2.	R_2, C_1	1		10.	R_2, C_3	9
3.	R_3, C_1	2		11.	R_3, C_3	A
4.	R_4, C_1	3		12.	R_4, C_3	B
5.	R_1, C_2	4		13.	R_1, C_4	C
6.	R_2, C_2	5		14.	R_2, C_4	D
7.	R_3, C_2	6		15.	R_3, C_4	E
8.	R_4, C_2	7		16.	R_4, C_4	F

This list shows that when R_1 is active low and column 1 is being examined, the data generator has at its outputs the binary number 0000. Now we have the means to detect when any of the numbers 0–F is depressed on the keyboard. The block diagram for this keyboard circuit is shown in Figure 3-15.

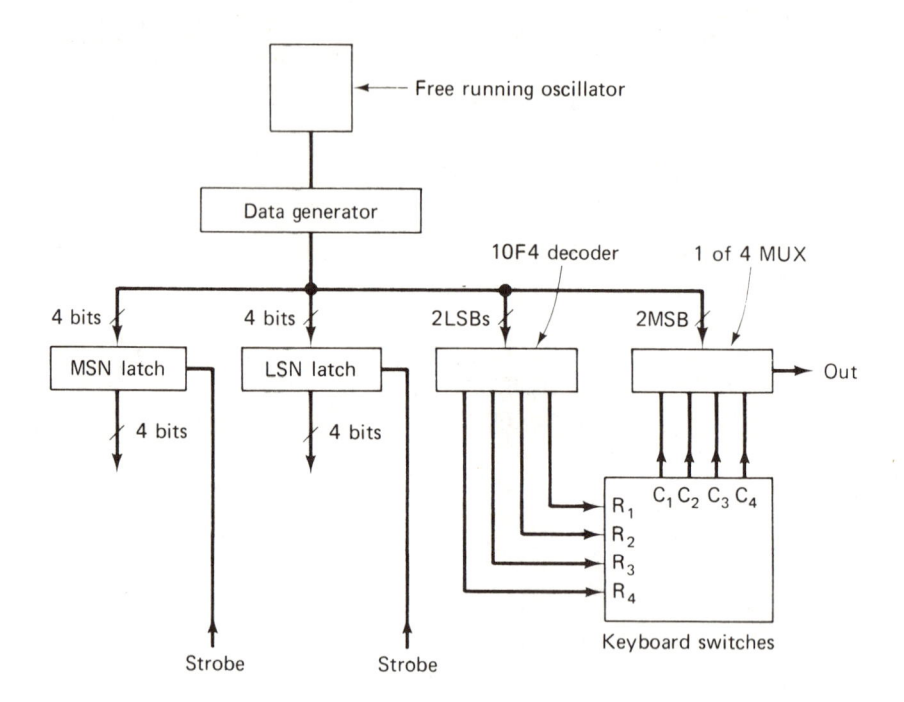

Figure 3-15 Block diagram of keyboard entry system with keyboard added

In Figure 3-16 the hardware schematic of the block diagram is shown. Here is how the keyboard circuit works. The two LSBs of the data generator outputs drive a 7442, a 1-of-10 decoder. The data sheet for the 7442 decoder is given

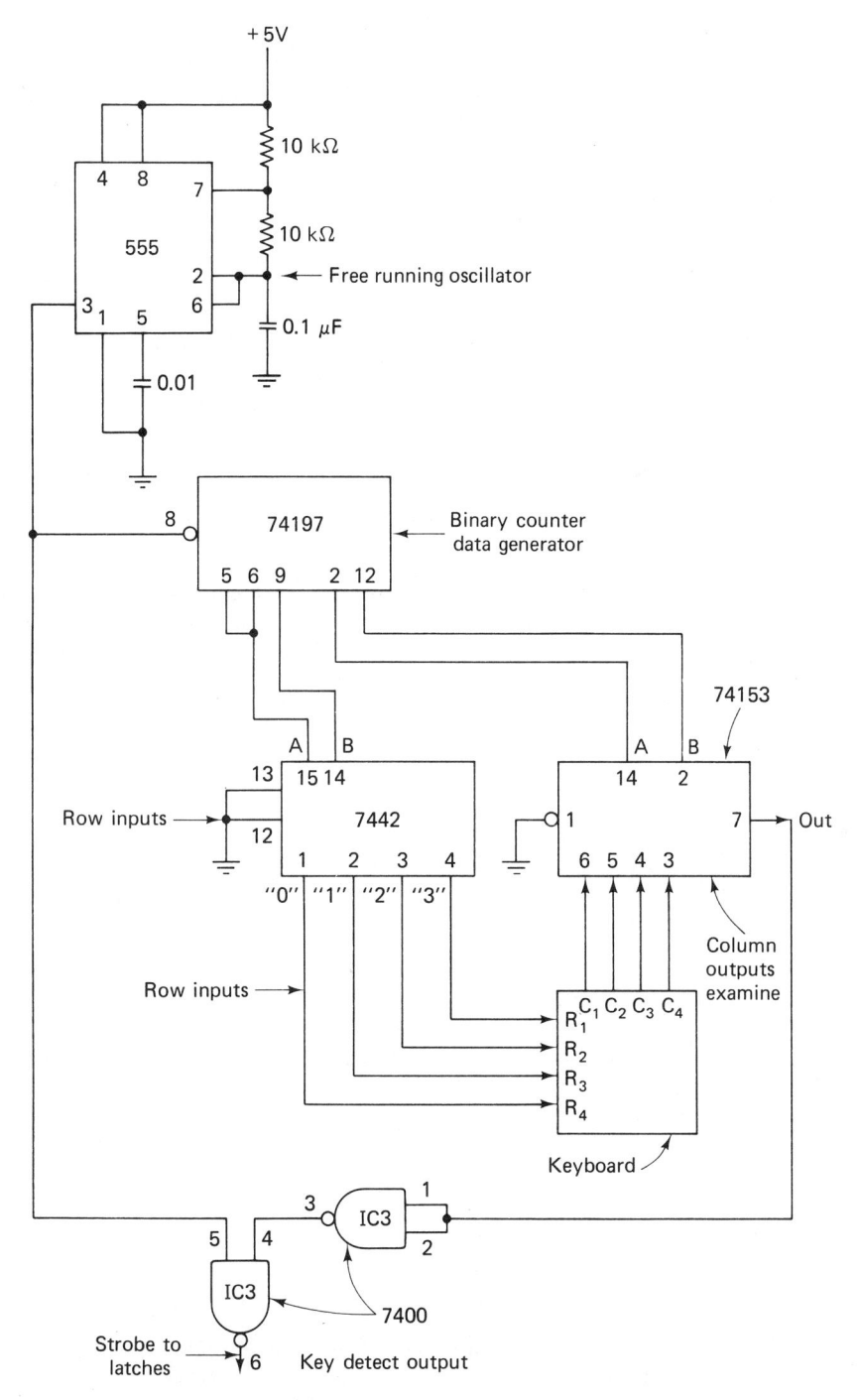

Figure 3-16 Schematic diagram of the circuits used to detect when a unique key is pressed

in Appendix A. The 7442 is used in this application as a 1-of-4 decoder. The timing waveforms for this selection of the circuit are shown in Figure 3-17. The outputs of the 7442 1-of-4 decoder are the inputs to the row lines of the keyboard.

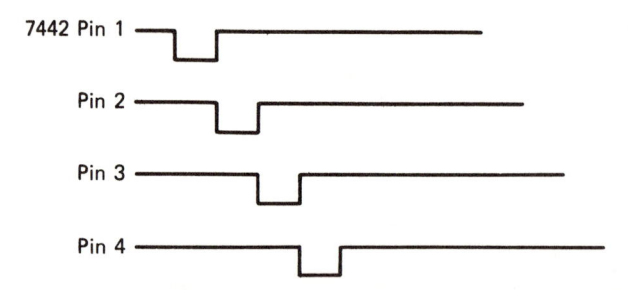

Figure 3-17 Timing diagram for the 7442 1-of-4 decoder. This device is used to generate the row line inputs for the keyboard.

The circuit used to examine the column output lines is shown in Figure 3-18. The two MSBs of the data generator circuit are the inputs of the digital multiplexer that will determine which column row will be selected. A 74153 device is used for the digital multiplexer. The data sheet for the 74153 is given in Appendix A. The inputs to the multiplexer are signals from the column output lines C_1–C_4 of the keyboard.

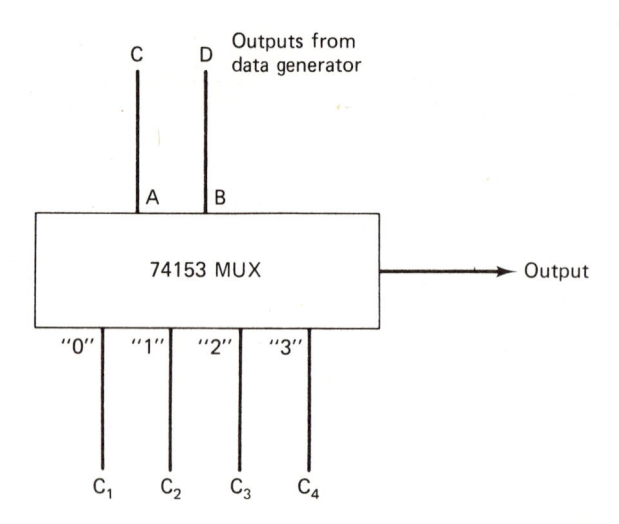

Figure 3-18 Block diagram of the 74153 1-of-4 digital multiplexer. This device is used to examine the column line outputs from the keyboard one at a time.

Sec. 3-1   *The Keyboard and Data Transfer Functions*

Since the two MSBs of the data generator circuit control which column line C_1–C_4 is examined by the multiplexer, all row input lines are active only once—when a different column line is active. The output of the 74153 multiplexer changes to logical 0 when the correct column is examined and the signal on the row input line coincides. To illustrate this, suppose we depressed the switch at the intersection of R_3 and C_2. The waveform of the 74153 output would be as shown in Figure 3-19.

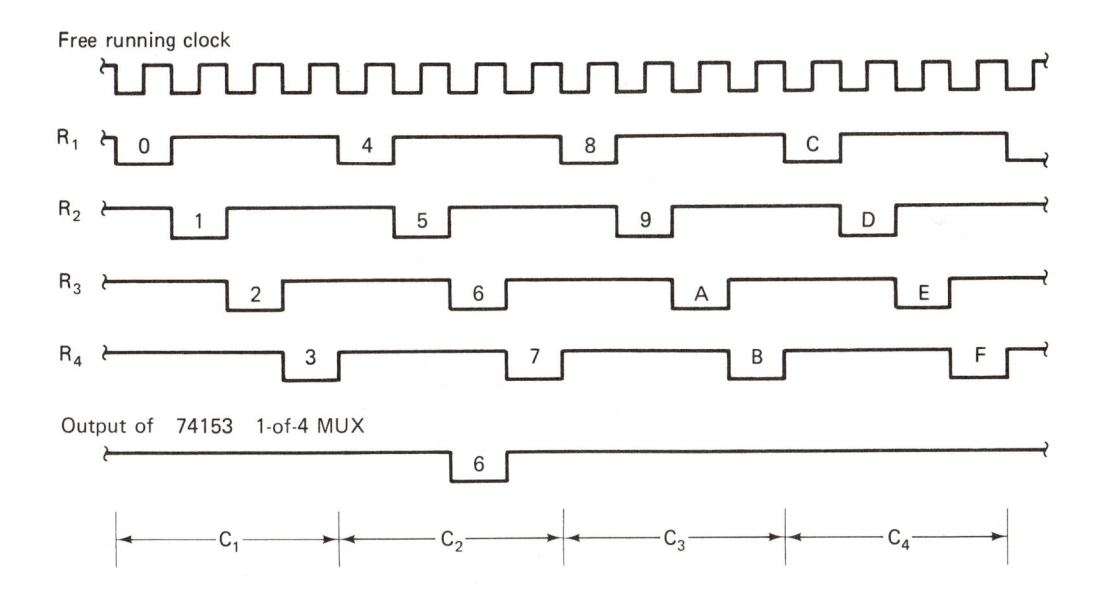

Figure 3-19 Resulting signals at the output of the 74153 (1-of-4 multiplexer) when switch at intersection of R3 and C2 is depressed

We now have a signal that is active low only at the instant that we wish to strobe data from the data generator into the latches that were shown in Figure 3-15. We will use this signal to apply the strobe pulse to the correct latch at the correct instant.

Referring to the timing diagram, Figure 3-16(a), at the output of the 74153 multiplexer we have a signal that is active low during the time that we want to strobe data into the latch. This signal is inverted by means of a 7400 NAND gate connected as an inverter integrated circuit IC3, pin 1; the resulting signal is applied to the input of the gate IC3, pin 4. The free-running clock output is connected to the input pin 5 of the same NAND gate. The output of the NAND gate IC3, pin 6 has a waveform as shown in Figure 3-20.

Clock output during the time 74153 pin 7 = logical 0

Negative going edge of clock pulse

Positive going edge of clock pulse

Output pin 7 74153 multiplexer

Output pin 3 7400 nand gate IC3

Output pin 6 7400 IC3

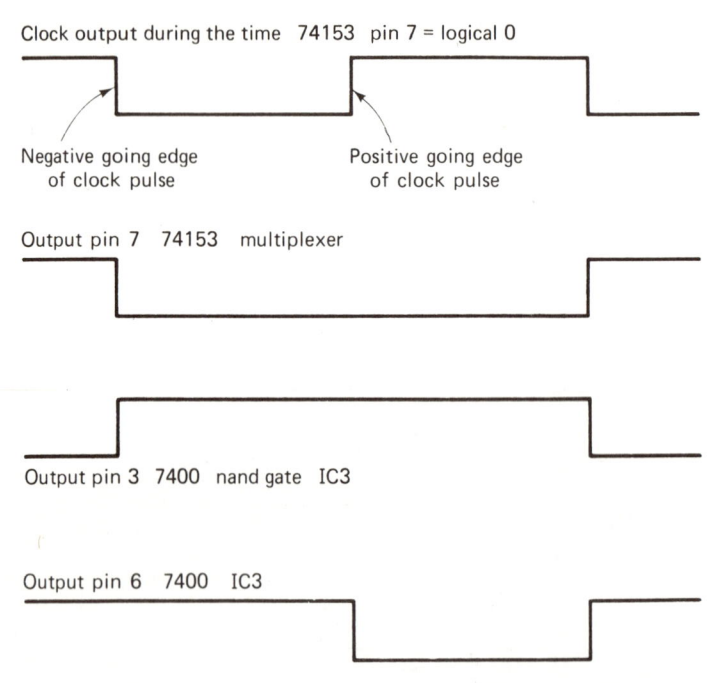

Figure 3-20 Timing diagram during the time interval when data is correct to be strobed into the 74175 quad latches. This means that the data at the output of the binary counter (data generator) matches the value of the key that is presently being pressed in the keyboard switch matrix.

We recall that it was important to have the output of the free-running clock resemble a square wave. The reason for this follows: data from the data generator changes on the negative going edge or transition of the free-running clock. This delay between the moment that data from the generator output becomes valid and the moment it is strobed into the latches is setup time for the latches. In effect, we are giving the data at the input time to stabilize before strobing it into the latches. Now that the reason for the square wave oscillator is known, one may change the shape of the oscillator output, bearing in mind the setup time required for data input to the latches. The data setup time is the same as the data setup time T_{DS} discussed in Chapter 2 for the semiconductor memory.

A complete schematic is shown in Figure 3-21. From the output of IC3 pin 6 the signal is inverted again by the 7400. The signal is now active high at IC3 pin 8 when we wish to strobe data into the latches. The problem now is: which of the two latches should be strobed? That is, are we strobing the LSN or the MSN? This problem is solved by using the JK flip-flop IC9, 74LS112. This flip flop enables the correct path for the strobe. The data sheet for this device is given in Appendix A.

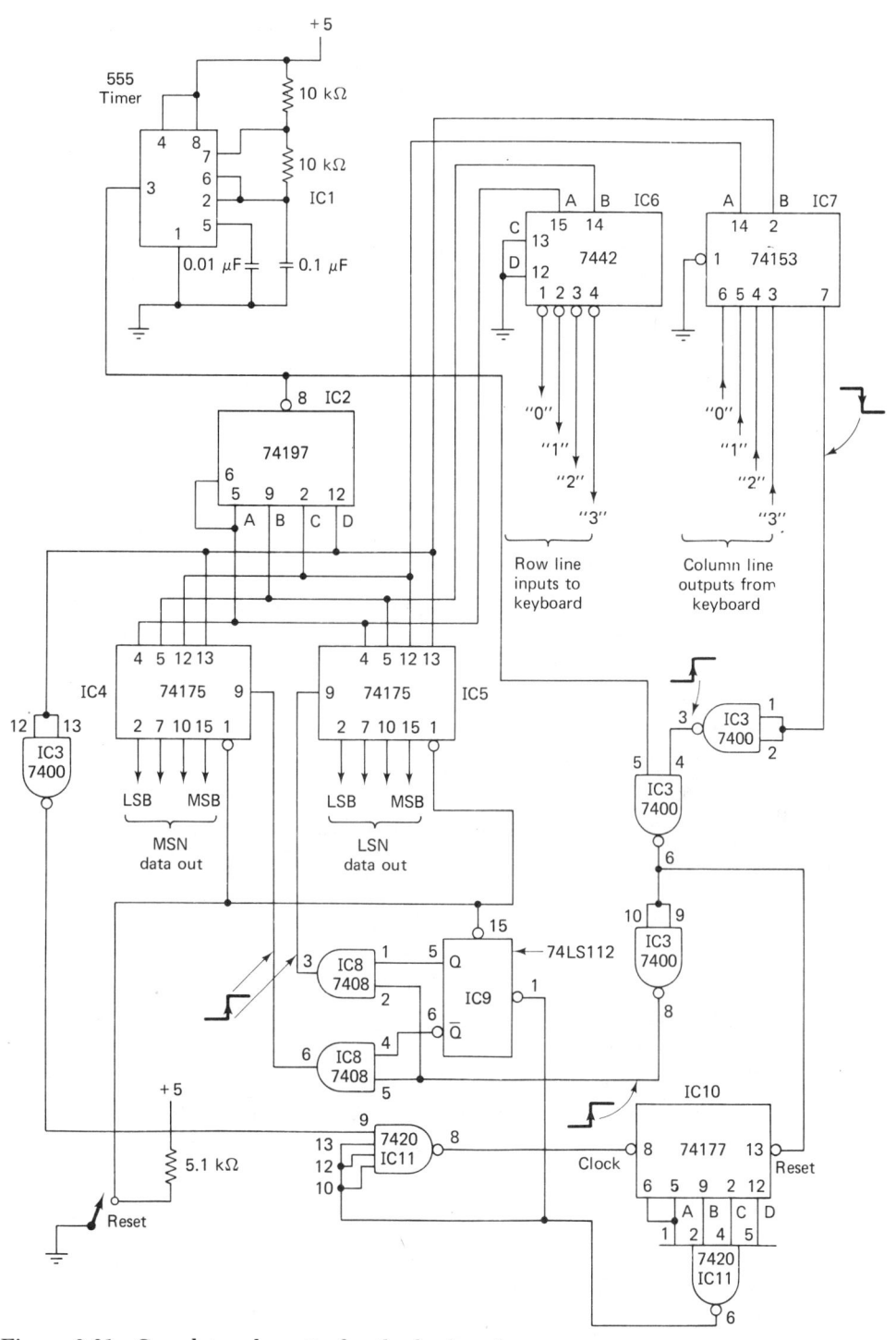

Figure 3-21 Complete schematic for the keyboard entry system, showing all ICs used and important waveforms of different signals

Notice that the Q and $\overline{Q}$ signals from the flip flop IC9 are connected to different AND gates of IC8. Assume that the flip flop is in the state where Q output = 0 and $\overline{Q}$ output = 1. This condition enables the AND gate, where output pin 6 is connected to strobe input pin 9 of the MSN latch. When the AND gate is enabled the entire path for the data strobe is complete. When the correct data is detected an active-high signal is generated at MSN latch pin 9. When this happens the data at the input of the latch is transferred to the output of the latch. Notice that as long as the switch on the keyboard is depressed the strobe signal is enabled to the latch. This means that we can strobe the same data into the latch repeatedly. See Figure 3-22 for the sequence of events that allows data to be strobed into the latch.

We have shown the complete circuit for a single nibble to be entered into a latch. To enter the second nibble we must have some means of detecting when we have released a key on the keyboard. Let us examine what happens in the circuit of Figure 3-21 when no key is depressed. This is the same condition that exists when we release a key. That is, when a key is released the circuit returns to a "no key depressed" state. The row input signals R_1–R_4 are generated continually, and column lines C_1–C_4 are being examined continually. However, no row input signal is connected to a column line output since no switch is pressed. This means that all column line outputs are logical 1. The output of the 74153 multiplexer is a logical 1. The output of the NAND gate IC3 pin 3 is a logical 0. No strobe is enabled to the latches.

We will keep track (with hardware) of how many times in succession the data generator sequences through all of its possible output codes (0–F) *and* there is no signal active low on IC3 pin 6. In effect, we are counting the number of complete data sequences where no key (switch) was pressed. After a certain number of complete data sequences without detection of a key, we let this be the equivalent of a key being released. When this is detected we enable the data strobe path to the MSN latch or the LSN latch, whichever was *not* most recently strobed. The circuit of Figure 3-23 then waits for another key to be pressed.

In our circuit we will say that if sixteen complete data sequences have happened with no key detected, (no signal active low at IC3 pin 6), then the system concludes that the key was released. So if our free-running frequency is 1 kHz (1 msec period), we must not press keys faster than indicated by the following computation:

(number of sequences) × (periods/sequence) × (period)

16 × 16 × Period = 256 × 1 msec = 256 msec

The result, 256 milliseconds, is a short time interval. If the clock frequency were slower we would have to wait longer. For example, if the clock frequency were 100 Hz, we would have to wait:

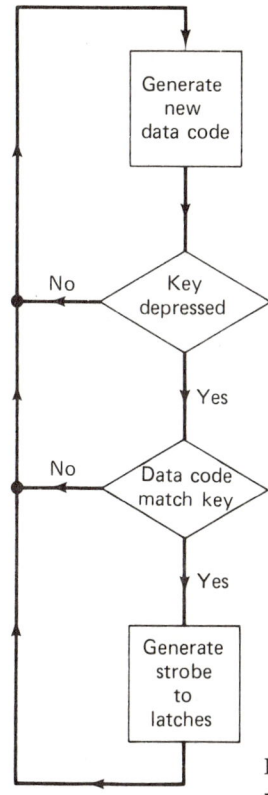

Figure 3-22 Flowchart showing sequence of events for a single nibble to be strobed into the 74175 quad latches

$16 \times 16 \times \text{Period} = 256 \times 10 \text{ msec} = 2560 \text{ msec} = 2.56 \text{ seconds}.$

Keeping this fact in mind, one is free to choose any free-running frequency desired.

We will now show how to detect the key release with hardware. We use the D output of the data generator as a sequence counter clock. Every time this signal goes from a logical 1 to a logical 0, a complete data sequence has occurred.

The 4-input NAND gate output IC11 pin 6 will be a logical 1 until all 4 outputs of the binary counter (IC10) are a logical 1. This 4-bit binary counter (IC10) is called the key release counter. It is clocked from the D output of the data generator circuit (IC2).

The key release counter is reset any time a key closure is detected. The reset input to the counter is connected to NAND gate output IC3 pin 6. This signal goes to a logical 0 each time a key closure is detected. The outputs of the key release counter will be forced to a logical 0 each time a key closure is detected.

Let us assume that a key is released. The reset input to the key release counter IC10 pin 13 will be a logical 1. The outputs of the counter will be a logical 0. The output of the 4-input NAND gate IC11 pin 6 will be a logical 1. This will enable the sequence counter clock through the NAND gate IC11 pin 9. After sixteen clock sequences without detection of a key closure, the outputs of the counter (IC10) will all be a logical 1. The output of the 4-input NAND gate IC11 pin 6 will then be a logical 0. The sequence clock will be disabled. The flip flop IC9 will be clocked. The circuit will stay in this mode until another key is pressed and a reset signal is input to the sequence counter. Figure 3-23 shows a

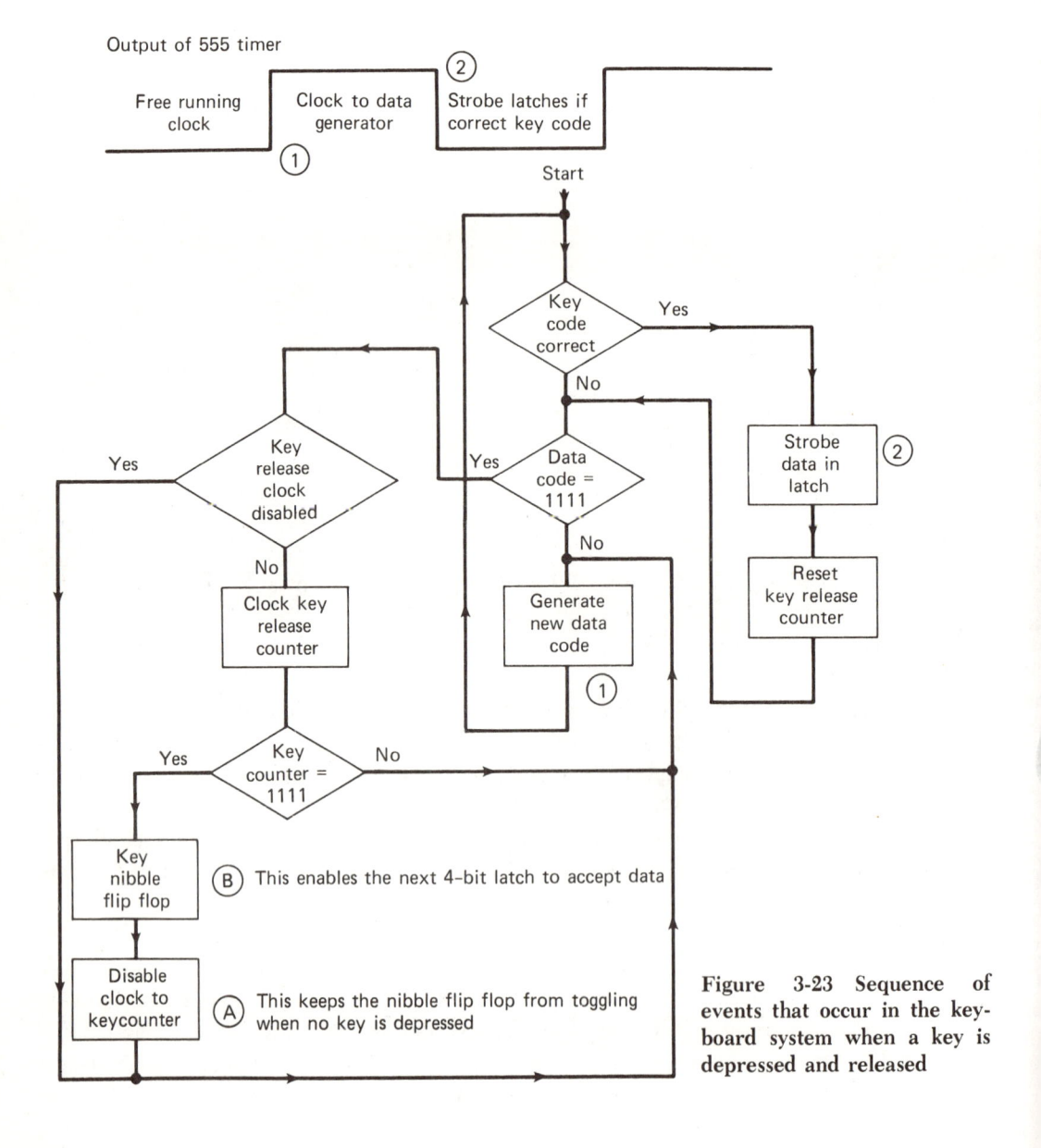

Figure 3-23 Sequence of events that occur in the keyboard system when a key is depressed and released

flowchart of the sequence of electrical events that occur in the keyboard circuit.

When we first turn on power to the system, the flip flop IC9 "comes up" in a random logic state. We want the flip flop to be in a logic state such that the latch strobe is enabled to the MSN latch. The MSN latch is strobed first. Remember we enter data as we write it. This is the condition where the flip flop is Q = logical 0, $\overline{Q}$ = logical 1. There are circuits used in industry that are called "power-on reset" circuits. These special circuits are designed to insure that flip flops and other similar digital devices stabilize in a known state when the power is turned on. We mention this fact so that anyone who encounters such flip flops for the first time will look for a power-on reset circuit. For our present purposes we will use a *momentary switch* that will ground the reset input to the flip flop. This provides manual power-on reset. We turn power on and press the reset switch. The manual entry keyboard circuit is now ready for operation, with the first nibble going to the MSN latch.

3-2 Troubleshooting the Keyboard Circuit

In this section we will show how one can determine if the keyboard circuit is operating properly. We will follow the signals through the circuit in a manner that may be used in a checkout procedure. This type of troubleshooting is directly applicable to industrial circuits. The first step in troubleshooting a circuit is to try mentally to separate the entire circuit into functional blocks. Digital circuits lend themselves well to this type of separation. One should also look up in a data book any unfamiliar devices shown in the schematics.

Based on the mental separation of circuits into functional blocks we can perform an electrical separation of blocks; that is, we troubleshoot smaller subcircuits first and determine if they are working correctly. If we can get all the subcircuits working, we will usually be able to get the entire circuit working correctly.

Let us work our way through the schematic of Figure 3-21. The problem is that the circuit is not working. We know this because we tried to enter data into an address, but the data in the display did not change. Experienced digital troubleshooters may have techniques and short cuts that allow them to find the defective component more quickly than the techniques that are shown here. This is good. Any method that works for a troubleshooter is a valid one. What is shown here is a systematic logical approach that can be used effectively even when one does not possess a good, thorough understanding of the entire system. For a beginner, such an approach is extremely useful.

The first item to check is the 555 timer. Notice that it is connected as a free-running oscillator. (It may be helpful to refer to data sheets on the 555 timer that show different circuit configurations.) We begin by checking the output to see if it is "toggling", or changing state, at the correct frequency. Again, we recall that the frequency of oscillation can be determined from the external components connected to the 555 timer. Assuming the DC power supply is normal, if the 555 timer is not oscillating there are two major possible causes:

1. The 555 timer circuit is defective
   a. One or more components are defective
   b. The device itself is defective, or
2. The output is being loaded excessively.

The troubleshooter should check the power supply, the timer circuit, the components, and the load.

If the 555 timer is oscillating at the correct frequency we then check the binary counters for proper output waveforms. The point to remember is that we are checking signals that are free running. In this way we do not have to set the system into any special mode of operation.

Next we check the waveforms for the Row input signals R_1–R_4. Here it would be easiest to use a dual-trace oscilloscope. One trace would be connected to and synchronized with the R_1 signal, and the other trace would be connected to the R_2, R_3, R_4 signals one at a time to ensure that these signals are occurring at the correct instant. When checking these signals, note if they are correct in voltage level as well as correct in time.

Next we check the keyboard. This may be done in the following way. Using a dual-trace oscilloscope, connect one trace to the R_1 output signal from the 1-of-4 decoder (7442). We reference all other signals to this signal. With no keys depressed we monitor each of the column signals C_1–C_4 with the other oscilloscope trace. The column signals should all be logical 1. If they are not all logical 1, we take three steps to find the defective switch:

1. Connect the second oscilloscope trace to the column line that has a waveform on it. This determines in which four of the sixteen switches the problem lies.
2. By referencing the waveform of the column line to the waveform of R_1, we can determine which R_1–R_4 signal is connected to the column line.
3. Once this is known, we know exactly which one(s) of the four possible switches is defective.

A flowchart of this procedure is shown in Figure 3-24.

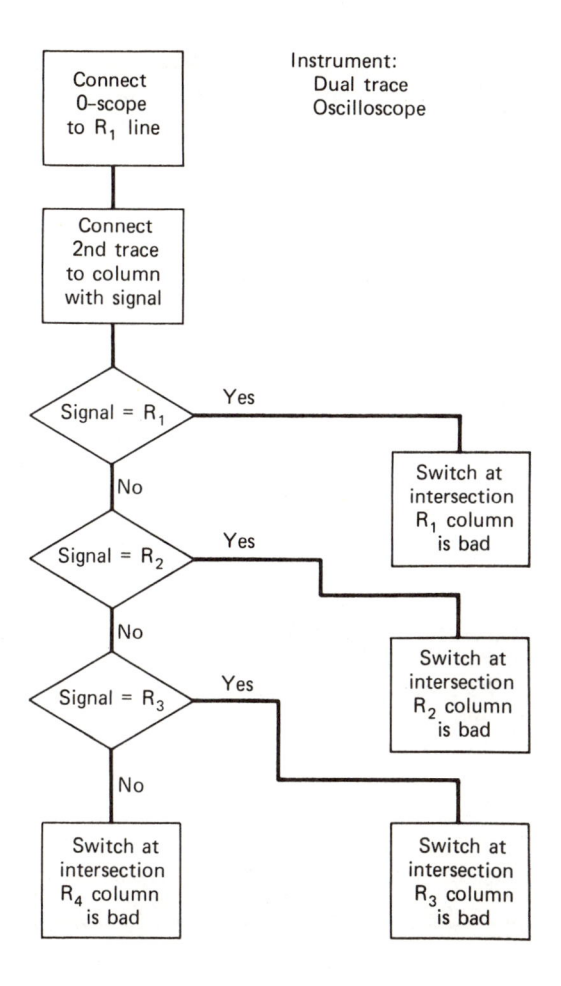

Figure 3-24 Flowchart showing how to determine if a matrix switch is "stuck" closed

If all column lines show logical 1, then we determine that all switches are making contact. To do this we:

1. Use a dual trace oscilloscope, and connect one trace to R_1 output as described earlier.
2. Connect the other trace to the column lines C_1–C_4 one at a time. When the second trace is connected, depress the four keys of that column one at a time. Monitor the column line output at the same time.

101

3. The waveform should change with respect to the R_1 signal when a different switch is depressed on the column. Examples of these waveforms are shown in Figure 3-25.

```
⎑⎑⎑⎑ Reference
  ⎑⎑⎑⎑ (a)
     ⎑⎑⎑⎑ (b)
        ⎑⎑⎑⎑ (c)
           ⎑⎑⎑⎑ (d)
```

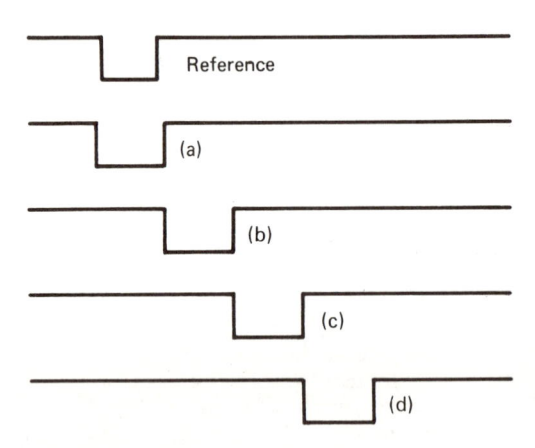

Figure 3-25 (a) Waveform when switch R1 and any column is pressed (b) Waveform when switch R2 and any column is pressed (c) Waveform when switch R3 and any column is pressed (d) Waveform when switch R4 and any column is pressed. Note the relationship of all waveforms to reference signal.

The next subcircuit to check is the output of the 1-of-4 column multiplexer. Again, the easiest way to do this is by using a dual trace oscilloscope.

1. Connect one trace to the D output of the data generator output counter. We will reference all signals to the negative going edge of this signal.
2. Connect the second trace to the output of the 1-of-4 multiplexer 74153 pin 7.
3. Then depress the keys, one at a time, starting with the key at the intersection of R_1, C_1. We proceed, pressing the keys on one column at a time.
4. Each key should move the second trace negative pulse shown on the oscilloscope farther away from the negative going edge of the D output (first trace of the oscilloscope). See Figure 3-26.

When this circuit is working we know that the keyboard is detecting the proper signal and that all data is being generated.

Now we check the circuit that strobes data into the latches. First press the reset button and examine the strobe input of the MSN latch IC4 pin 9. We should see a *positive going signal* at this input pin when we depress any key.

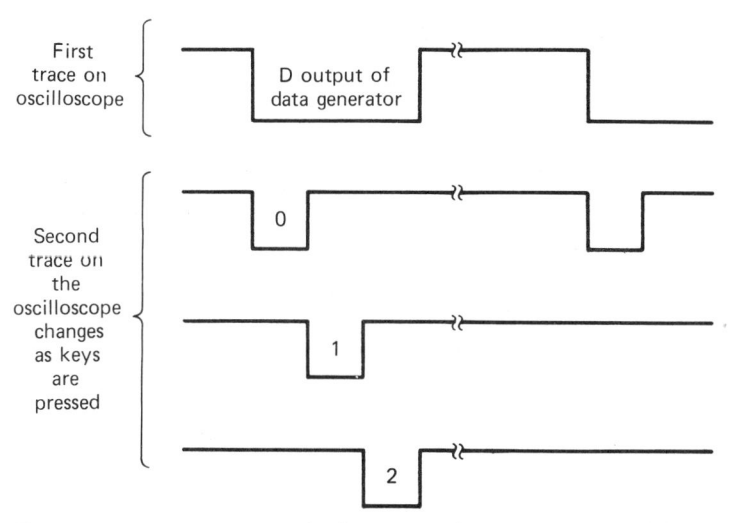

Figure 3-26 As we press the keys in order, 0,1,2,3,...F, the second oscilloscope trace should appear to move with respect to the D output of the data generator.

Release the key and examine the strobe input of the LSN latch (IC5 pin 9). Again, when any key is depressed we should see a positive going signal at the IC5 pin 9.

If there is no signal at this LSN latch, the key release detector circuit is suspect. To check the key release circuit we:

1. Depress any key and monitor the reset input to the counter. This input should have a negative going signal on it.
2. Examine the outputs of the counter. These outputs should be a logical 0. The LSB may toggle between a logical 1 and a logical 0; this is a legal state for the LSB to be in.
3. Depress any key and monitor the clock input signal to the counter. An active low clock input signal should be present.
4. When the key is released the clock input signal to the counter should go to a steady logical 1 level after approximately 256 milliseconds.
5. When any key is depressed and released the flip flop (IC9) should toggle; that is, the outputs should change state.

If one ensures that all five points mentioned are correct in the key release circuit, then there is good assurance that the circuit is operating properly. After completing these checks of the keyboard circuit satisfactorily, we should be able to latch the dynamic data being generated into the static holding latches at the correct instant in time.

3-3 Interfacing the Keyboard Circuit to Memory

Now that we have a means to generate eight bits of data, we want a way to determine what the data will be used for. That is, is this data for memory address or for input data to the memory? To determine this we again make use of digital multiplexing. This circuit is shown in block diagram form in Figure 3-27. We use

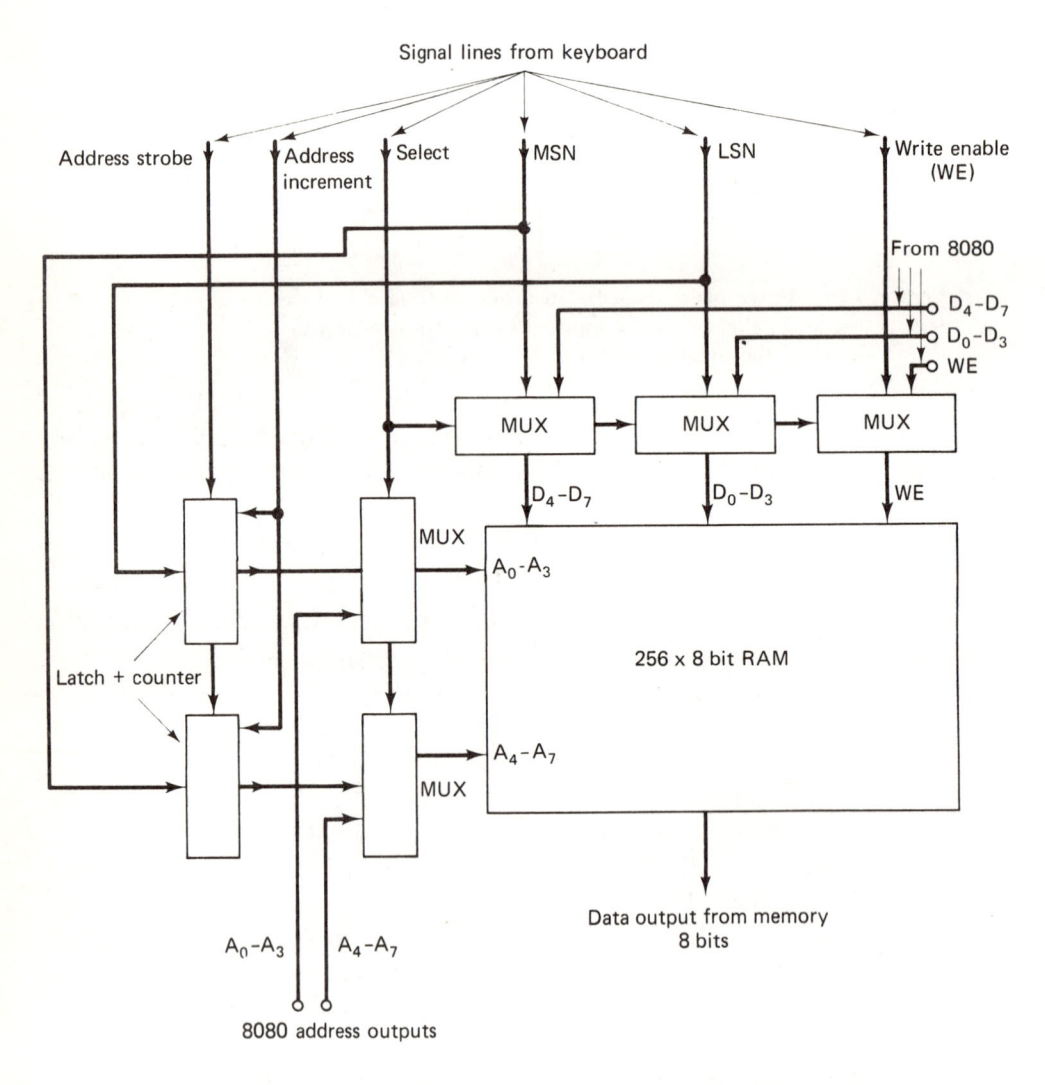

Figure 3-27 Block diagram of the entire keyboard entry system, including memory. Notice the multiplexing of DATA IN, ADDRESS, and the WE signals. One input to the multiplexer comes from the keyboard (manual), and the other input is from the 8080 system (automatic).

Sec. 3-3   *Interfacing the Keyboard Circuit to Memory*   **105**

a toggle switch to select which place data from the keyboard goes. Figure 3-28 shows the actual schematic.

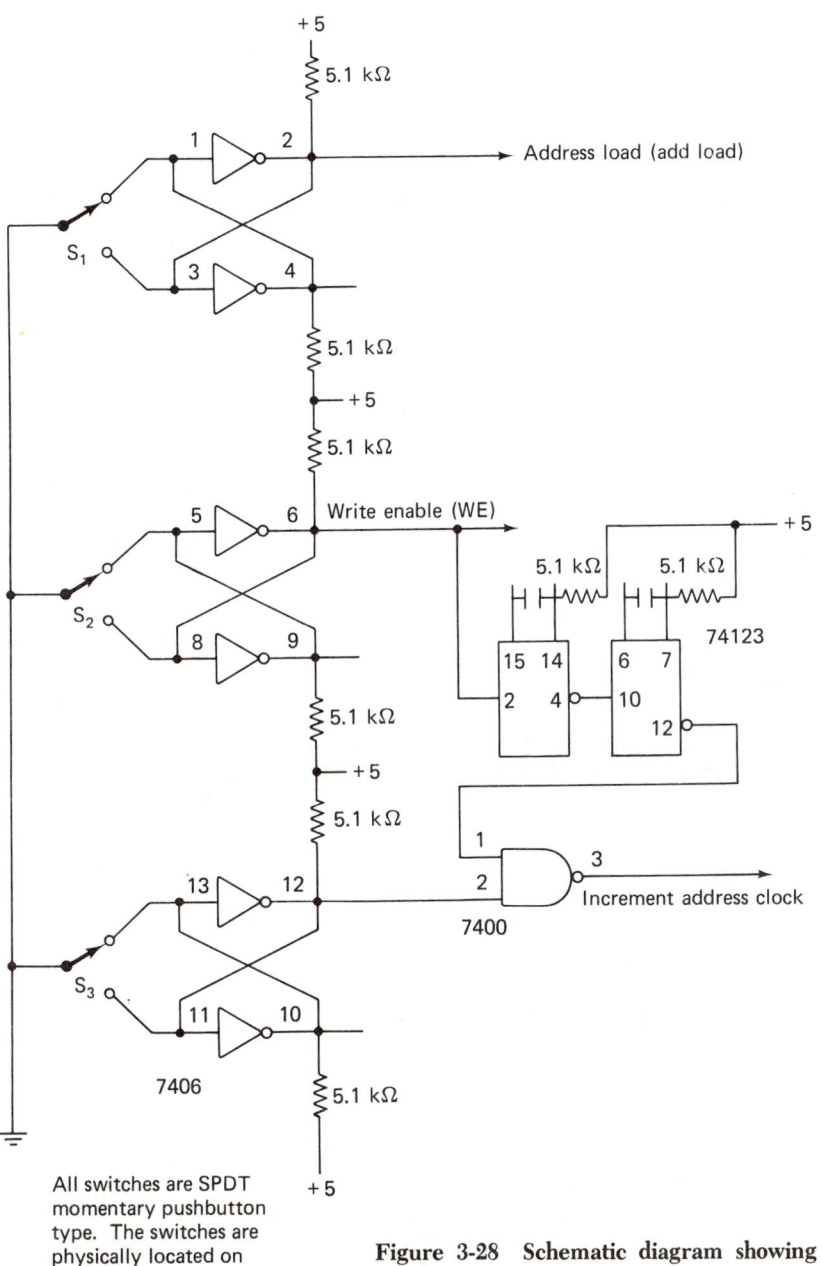

Figure 3-28 Schematic diagram showing circuits for manual address load, write enable, and address clock (increment) for the system memory.

All switches are SPDT momentary pushbutton type. The switches are physically located on keyboard

Referring to Figure 3-29, the eight bits of data from the keyboard latches are one input to the 74157 digital multiplexers (IC15, IC16). The other input lines to the multiplexers carry the eight bits from the microprocessor data bus. This bus will be discussed in detail in Chapter 4. For now, we mention only that the data bus is connected. The data select line for these multiplexers determines whether the data input lines from the manual keyboard or from the microprocessor bus are to be used for data-in to memory. If the select line carries a logical 0, the microprocessor data bus provides the inputs to memory; if the select line carries a logical 1, the manual keyboard provides the data in to memory. Note that we do *not* have to latch data in from the keyboard; the data remains static at the inputs to memory. We will apply a write pulse.

Data from the keyboard is also connected to inputs on IC18 and IC19 (74197). These two devices are called presettable binary counters. A presettable counter can have its outputs set to any of the sixteen possible states and the counter will begin counting from that state. Such counters allow us to select any address of memory to examine or store data and then increment to the next sequential location. The data sheet for the 74197 is given in Appendix A.

The outputs of the two 74197 binary counters constitute one input to the multiplexers, IC20 and IC21. The other inputs to the multiplexers are from the address bus of the microprocessor. This address bus will be discussed in detail in Chapter 4. Notice in Figure 3-29 that the select line for IC20 and IC21 is connected directly to the select line for IC15 and IC16. This allows the keyboard to provide data and address input to the memory with the select line in the logical 1 state. To present an address to memory the following steps are performed:

1. Enter address MSN and LSN into the keyboard latches.
2. Press the switch on the keyboard marked ADD LOAD. This switch is connected as shown in the schematic of Figure 3-29. When the ADD LOAD switch is depressed, the "load enable" input to the 74197 counters transfers data at the inputs of the counter to the outputs of the counter. When the switch is released, the outputs of the counter no longer respond to changes at the counter inputs. Now the address is valid at the memory address lines.

With a valid memory address we can apply data to the memory data-in lines. This is done by pressing the correct keyboard keys to latch a MSN and LSN in the keyboard latches. These two nibbles go directly to the data-in lines of the memory. We not need concern ourselves with changing the address when we change the data in the keyboard latches. We have already latched the memory address into the presettable binary counters.

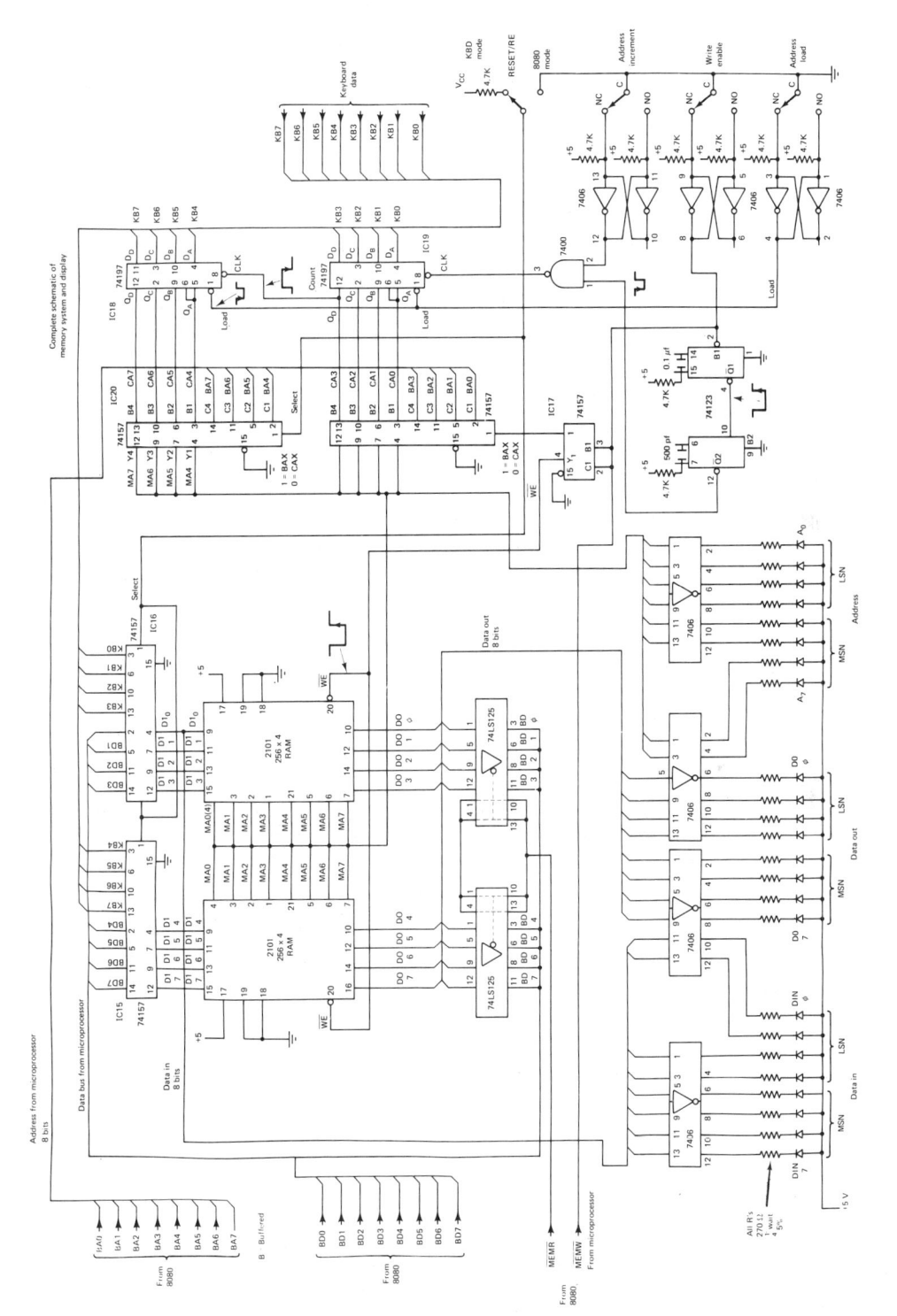

Figure 3-29 Complete schematic of memory system and display monitors

To enter data we now apply a write enable pulse to the memory. This write enable pulse is multiplexed via IC17. The other write enable pulse is generated by the microprocessor. We will show how the microprocessor does this in Chapter 4. The write enable pulse is manually applied to the memory as shown in Figure 3-29. When the write enable pulse goes to logical 1, the address counters are clocked. This increments the memory address and prepares the memory for the next byte of data to be loaded. This is handy because when we enter data we usually enter several bytes in succession. We do not have to increment the address counter between each data entry. When we examine data in memory we need a means to increment, or "step through," memory. There is a manual address increment switch for this purpose, as shown in Figure 3-29.

We now have an entire memory system in which we can enter data and examine data. The outputs of the memory are connected to tri-state buffers. The data sheet for these buffers is given in Appendix A. These buffers isolate the memory outputs from the data bus. In the microprocessor systems used in industry the outputs of memory are usually connected directly to the data bus. In our system we have isolated the memory to enhance the ease of interfacing and for easier understanding of how a memory fits into the architecture of a microprocessor system. The *disable signal* for the tri-state buffers is generated by the microprocessor and is discussed in Chapter 4.

3-4 Display Section

The next subcircuit we will discuss is the display section of the keyboard. The display enables us to monitor the address lines of memory, the data output from memory, or data input to the memory. The type of display constructed here is unique to our system, in that the signal lines used here may not all be available on different systems. For the purpose of understanding exactly what is taking place electrically at each instant in time, our system is designed to accommodate the three displays mentioned: address lines, data output, and data input to memory.

What should a display look like physically? For our display we use discrete LEDs on each signal line we wish to monitor. The LED will be "on" if the signal line is a logical 1; the LED will be "off" if the signal line is a logical 0. When installing a display one must keep in mind what type of signal is being monitored. The addition of the display should not change the characteristics of the signal line. This problem is similar to the loading of an analog circuit that occurs when a measuring instrument, such as an oscilloscope, is connected to make a measurement.

For our system we will be using standard T^2L devices with typical "fan outs" of ten. The addition of another input on the line will be acceptable. We mention

Sec. 3-4   *Display Section*   109

this fact only because some systems may use low-power T²L or CMOS, which will not readily accept additional loading on the outputs without correct buffering. One should use good judgment when installing a monitor display in a system for personal use. It is important that we know the type of logic used and how much load is already on the line to be monitored for we must avoid overloading.

If one thinks that adding an additional T²L input on a signal line will overload the line, high impedance linear voltage comparators can be used to solve the problem. An example of this type of comparator is an LM 339, which might be called a buffer. This device operates from a single power supply and has an open collector output that can drive an LED directly. The data sheet for the LM339 is given in Appendix A. Figure 3-30 shows how to connect this voltage comparator (if it must be used) to a digital signal to be monitored.

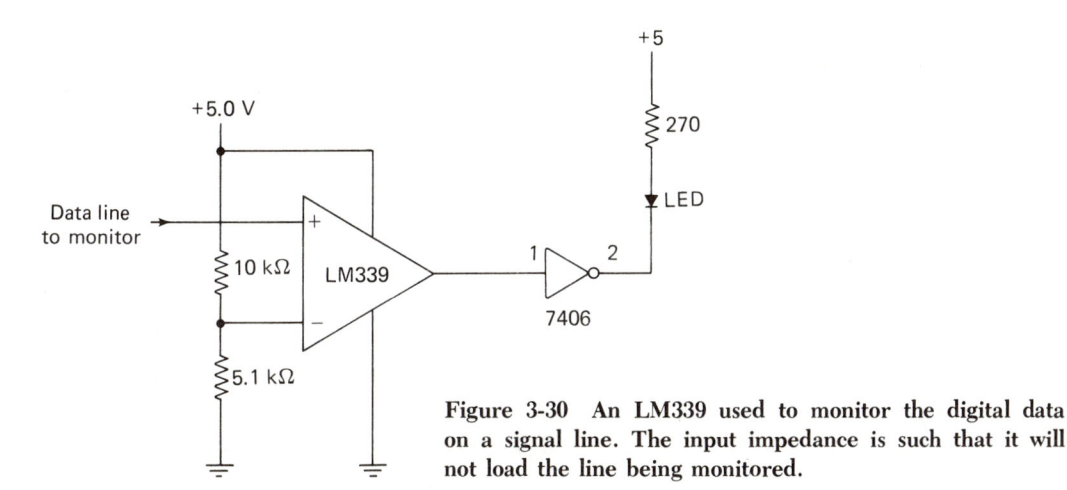

Figure 3-30 An LM339 used to monitor the digital data on a signal line. The input impedance is such that it will not load the line being monitored.

The type of monitor we will install—an inverter with open collector output—is shown in Figure 3-31. Six of these inverters are incorporated in a single

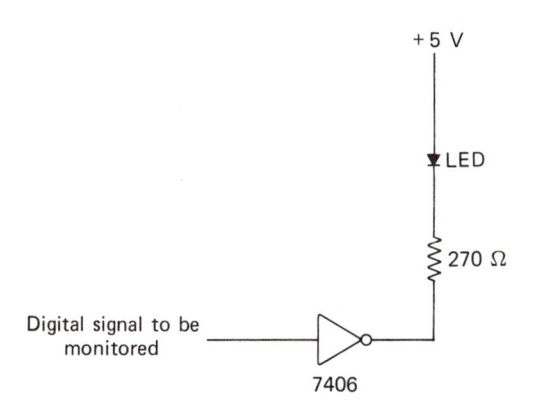

Figure 3-31 Schematic diagram of a single display monitor on a TTL line. This particular monitoring will load the signal line with one standard TTL load.

package normally. Of course one may use any type of monitor that will make the job of interrogating these signal lines easier. Our complete system with the display added was shown in Figure 3-29.

3-5 Checking the Memory System

The memory we have presented in this chapter is a small system, 256 × 8 bits. Troubleshooting this system is not difficult. Yet for a beginner who does not fully grasp the relationships between data inputs, clocks, and enabling signals, this task could be not only difficult but next to impossible without some guidance. In this section we discuss how to troubleshoot the manual entry portion of the memory and then how to make a quick check of the memory itself. Later in this book we will discuss some tricks of troubleshooting memory systems where one does not have the luxury of a manual data entry system. If necessary, we may refer to another text with more extensive discussion of troubleshooting memory systems.*

With the select line of all multiplexers at logic 1 level, we enter an address into the 74197 presettable binary counters. By watching the visual monitor it is easy to determine if the data that was entered is correct or not. Of course, this assumes that the display section of the system is working properly. If we are unsure about the display section we can check the logic levels at the outputs of the counters to determine if the data was entered correctly. If the data is not correct, we can trace the incorrect data line from the input of the memory address line to the multiplexer output and from the multiplexer input. At each point we check to be sure that the digital levels are correct. This type of troubleshooting is easy since the circuit is essentially static. This same procedure can be followed when checking the data in lines to the memory.

To check the bits of the memory, we write different data into each memory location and then check that location to see if that same data read out. For example, start at location 0 and write a 0 into this location. Then proceed to every sequential location, writing the value of that location as data into memory. This puts 00, 01, 02, 03–FF into the memory as data. We then cycle through each location and read each word to insure that the data was correct. This is like counting 1, 2, 3, 4, and so on.

This simple test does not check all bits in all locations, but it does give a quick verification of the condition of memory. Another quick check is to write all 0 s into every location in memory and then read the memory, checking for all 0 s.

---

*J. W. Coffron, *Getting Started in Digital Troubleshooting*, (Reston, Va.: Reston Publishing Company, 1979).

Then write all 1 s into the memory and read the memory, checking for all 1 s. This quick check determines whether all bits of the memory can be set to a logical 1 and a logical 0. As one gains experience in troubleshooting memories it becomes easier to determine which quick-check pattern is best suited to that system. For a beginner, the three patterns given above are adequate to check most small memory systems to find the "hard" errors. A *hard error* is one that is always there. For example, a "stuck" bit is a hard error. On the other hand, a *"soft" error* is one that is present only under a special set of electrical conditions. Soft errors usually result from heat, timing, or voltage level fluctuations. Soft errors are extremely difficult to find. One must try to reproduce the conditions under which a soft error turns into a hard error in order to find it. Until the error appears, the system works well because everything is proper. Checking reveals no error. *You have to make this error appear before you can locate it!*

In this chapter we have shown a circuit that can be used for inputting data to a memory. Our circuit uses a common keyboard timing technique employed in many keyboards in industry. The circuit is constructed using common, readily available T²L devices. This allows readers to construct their own keyboard circuit if they wish. We have also shown how to check for proper operation of this circuit. By gaining understanding of this circuit and of the timing relationships involved, one will become partially familiar with timed, strobed signals. These types of signals are very common in the 8080 microprocessor system, which will be analyzed in the remaining chapters of this text.

Review Questions

1. Describe the function of a multiplexer.
2. Draw a schematic to connect the 555 timer as a free-running oscillator with a frequency of approximately 3 kiloHertz.
3. Draw a timing diagram showing a 4-bit ripple counter's outputs referenced to the positive edge of the input clock pulse.
4. Draw the equivalent circuit of the 74175 using 7474 devices. (Look up in Appendix A or product data book.)
5. What is meant by the term "active low"?
6. Referring to the schematic of Figure 3-21, what would be the possible causes if the 555 timer output were not toggling?
7. Explain the difference between a "hard error" and a "soft error."

4

THE 8080 MICROPROCESSOR AS A CPU

In this chapter we will discuss the basic hardware required to enable an 8080 microprocessor to communicate electrically with different circuits. How these required hardware circuits achieve communication will be shown and examined in detail. The hardware will be standard T^2L devices. We will not discuss the internal architecture of the 8080 at this time. However, we will present a basic system architecture that will serve as the core of all systems and circuits shown in this book. When one is familiar with what the hardware is designed to do, it is easier to understand why that hardware is controlled in the way it is. This is the approach we shall take in this book and this chapter. So we begin by looking at what jobs the hardware must perform to make the system work.

The first element of the 8080 microprocessor to be discussed is the power supply. Three DC power supplies are needed for the operation of the 8080 device: +12 volts, −5 volts, and +5 volts. These voltages are measured with respect to ground, or 0.00 volts. The output required of each supply is;

+12 volts at approximately 200 milliamperes,
−5 volts at approximately 5 milliamperes,
+5 volts at approximately 3 amperes.

The +5 volt supply will be the highest current rated because it not only provides +5 volts (V_{CC}) for the 8080 device, but provides +5 volts for the other logic circuits in the system. The amount of current required of the +5 volt supply varies with the number of and family of logic used for the external circuits. As a

The 8080 Microprocessor as a CPU

general requirement, the +5 volt supply should be capable of supplying 2 to 3 amperes of current to a load. If one has a +5 volt supply with a higher current rating, this is even better. For those who are serious about constructing a microprocessor system of any size, it is worthwhile to purchase a very high current rated +5 volt supply to provide some reserve capacity. To get a rough, first-order approximation of how much current a power supply must deliver to a particular system, we add the supply currents of all devices used in that system, and this total becomes the amount of current the +5 volt source must produce.

The DC power must be applied constantly to the system. This is shown in Figure 4-1. One of the first troubleshooting checks that should be made on a microsystem is a voltage check of the DC power sources. *The voltage should be tested directly at the pin* of the device, not on a PC trace or at the power supply output. Testing the pin ensures that the DC power is reaching that pin. If the power input pin is not carrying the correct voltage, simply trace this defective supply backwards to find the point in the power supply path where the voltage drops off.

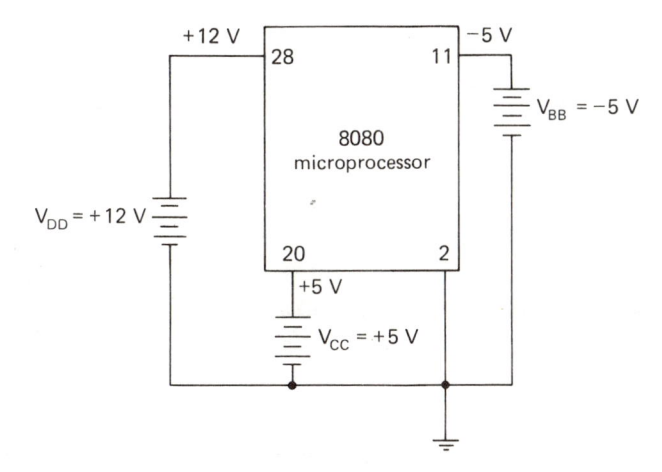

Figure 4-1 Three DC power supplies are required for the 8080. Note that they are applied to device pins 20, 28, and 11, with pin 2 serving as the common ground.

If we find that the power supplies are providing the correct voltage, the next parts of the 8080 circuit to check are the clock inputs to the device. The clock inputs are called phase 1 and phase 2, designated by ϕ_1 and ϕ_2. These two clock inputs to the device provide the internal timing and refreshing of all of the storage circuits that require them. This means that phase 1 and phase 2 clocks are free running continously at the same frequency, and differ only in phase. These ϕ_1 and ϕ_2 clocks must always be present and operational at the two clock input pins of the 8080 if the device is to operate correctly.

Let us examine the specifications of these ϕ_1 and ϕ_2 clock signals as presented in a typical data sheet for the 8080 microprocessor. The part of the data sheet that concerns the clocks is shown in Figure 4-2(a).

Symbol	Parameter	Min.	Typ.	Max.	Unit
V_{ILC}	Clock input low voltage	$V_{SS} - 1$		$V_{SS} + 0.8$	V
V_{IHC}	Clock input high voltage	9.0		$V_{DD} + 1$	V

(a)

(b)

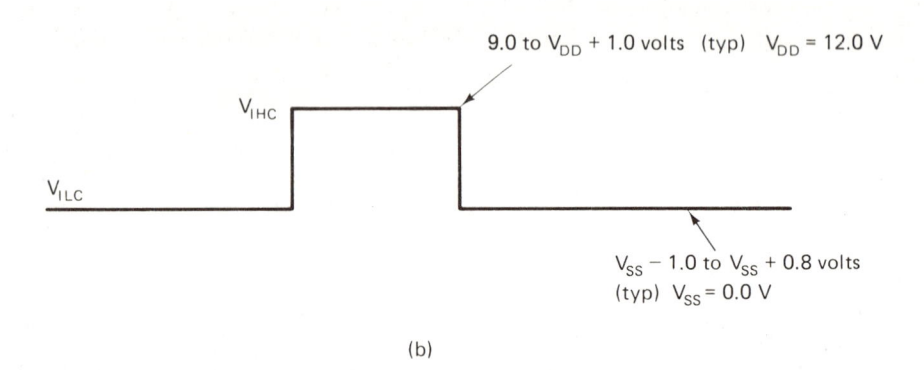

9.0 to V_{DD} + 1.0 volts (typ) V_{DD} = 12.0 V

V_{SS} − 1.0 to V_{SS} + 0.8 volts (typ) V_{SS} = 0.0 V

Figure 4-2 (a) Data sheet showing phase 1 and phase 2 DC specifications (b) V_{ILC} and V_{IHC} graphically referenced to a clock output waveform

V_{ILC} (VOLTAGE IN LOW-LEVEL CLOCK)

This voltage has the range of $V_{SS} = -1$ volt to $V_{SS} = +0.8$ volt. (V_{SS} is the voltage of the substrate, which means the clock input low voltage must be between +0.8 V and −1.0 V. The typical value is approximately 0.00 V).

V_{IHC} (VOLTAGE IN HIGH-LEVEL CLOCK)

With $V_{DD} = +12.0$ V, this voltage has the range of +9.0 volts to V_{DD} +1.0 volt, which means the clock input high voltage must be between +9.0 V and +13.0 V. It is important to check these input voltage levels when checking the clock inputs to the 8080 microprocessor. Figure 4-2(b) shows how V_{ILC} and V_{IHC} are related to the clock waveform.

The 8080 Microprocessor as a CPU

The timing waveforms of the phase 1 and phase 2 clock inputs are shown in Figure 4-3(b), with the important timing references labeled. Figure 4-3(a) shows a typical data sheet timing diagram. In discussing phase 1 and phase 2 timing here we will assume that the voltage levels for both ϕ_1 and ϕ_2 are within specifications.

AC Characteristics

$T_A = 0°C$ to $70°C$, $V_{DD} = +12 V \pm 5\%$, $V_{CC} = +5 V \pm 5\%$, $V_{BB} = -5 V \pm 5\%$, $V_{SS} = 0V$, unless otherwise noted

Symbol	Parameter	Min.	Max.	Unit
t_{CY} [3]	Clock period	0.48	2.0	μ sec
t_r, t_f	Clock rise and fall time	0	50	n sec
$t_{\phi 1}$	ϕ_1 Pulse width	60		n sec
$t_{\phi 2}$	ϕ_2 Pulse width	220		n sec
t_{D1}	Delay ϕ_1 to ϕ_2	0		n sec
t_{D2}	Delay ϕ_2 to ϕ_1	70		n sec
t_{D3}	Delay ϕ_1 to ϕ_2 leading edges	80		n sec

(a)

(b)

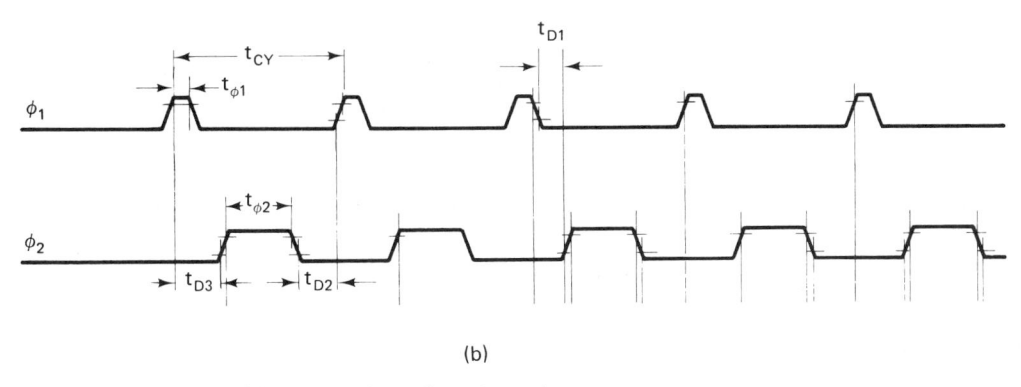

Figure 4-3 (a) Excerpt from data sheet showing timing parameters of phase 1 and phase 2 clocks (b) Timing diagram of phase 1 and phase 2 clocks

The first specification to discuss is the cycle time, which is designated as t_{CY}. Cycle time is the *period* of the clock pulse ϕ_1. This period may range from 480 nanoseconds (nsec) to 2.0 microseconds (μsec).

The *rise time* (t_r) and *fall time* (t_f) of the ϕ_1 and ϕ_2 clock edges are diagrammed in Figure 4-4. In standard practice, rise time and fall time refer to the elapsed time required for a waveform to rise from 10% to 90% of the total pulse height, and fall from 90% to 10%. Specifications for the 8080 designate that t_r and t_f be measured between the 1.0 V and 8.0 V levels, regardless of pulse height, which is usually higher than 8.0 V. These specifications apply to clock signals input to the 8080 from external clocks.

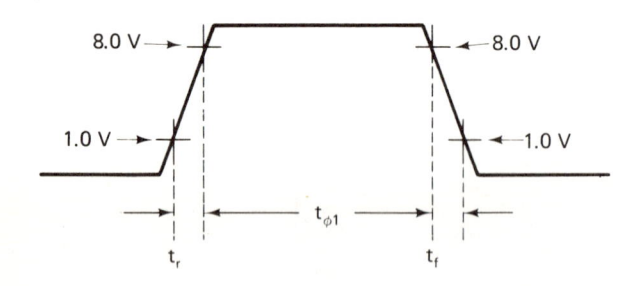

Figure 4-4 Clock waveform showing t_r and t_f measured from the 1.0 and 8.0 volt limits

The time it takes a clock signal to rise from 1.0 V to 8.0 V should be less than 50 nsec, and the time for the clock signal to fall from 8.0 V to 1.0 V should be less than 50 nsec.

$t_{\phi 1}$: This term is the minimum phase 1 pulse width. Notice in Figure 4-4 that the pulse width is measured between the two 8.0 V points on the waveform. The minimum pulse for phase 1 is 60 nsec. This and the following specifications are called out and illustrated graphically in Figures 4-3 and 4-4.

$t_{\phi 2}$: This term is the minimum pulse width for phase 2. The width is also measured between the 8.0 V points of the phase 2 pulse width. Phase 2 has a minimum pulse width of 220 nsec.

t_{D1}: This is the minimum delay time between the falling edge of phase 1 and the rising edge of phase 2. Note in Figure 4-3(b) that this delay is measured between the 1.0 V points of each clock edge.

t_{D2}: This is the minimum delay from the falling edge of phase 2 and the rising edge of phase 1. This delay is also measured between the 1.0 V points on each waveform.

t_{D3}: This is the minimum delay between the rising edge of phase 1 and the rising edge of phase 2. Note that this measurement is referenced to the 8.0 V point on the ϕ_1 edge and the 1.0 V point on the ϕ_2 edge.

One must be familiar with the timing specifications on the ϕ_1 and ϕ_2 clock inputs in order to understand the 8080 microprocessor data sheets and their relationships to the external timing circuits referenced, or clocked, by the same ϕ_1 and ϕ_2 clock inputs.

To make the timing of phase 1 and phase 2 clock inputs more meaningful, we will now consider how one can generate these with standard hardware. Once this timing circuit is explained and understood, it can be used to provide the ϕ_1 and ϕ_2 clock inputs for a real system. We will explain and design this system as we proceed through the book.

The first step in constructing a timing circuit is to know what it should do. A detailed timing diagram should be drawn and understood before proceeding with the design of the hardware system to accomplish the task desired. Let us start by drawing the timing diagrams for the ϕ_1 and ϕ_2 clocks that we will use. One must bear in mind that *all* specifications of the V_{IHC} and V_{ILC} clocks we have just discussed must be met in the design. In our design we will not run the clocks as rapidly as they can go; instead, we will choose a lower frequency that is easy to generate and is within specifications. We will also choose a frequency that does not require any special digital devices. The t_{CY} of our chosen clocks is 1 microsecond. This is within the specification for t_{CY} shown in Figure 4-3(a).

We now need a free-running clock at 1 megahertz (MH_z). We can use a variety of techniques for generating this clock frequency. Note that this frequency does not have to be exact, because the specifications are wide enough to permit some variation in the free-running clock frequency. The timing waveforms for our ϕ_1 and ϕ_2 clock inputs are shown in Figure 4-5. We can

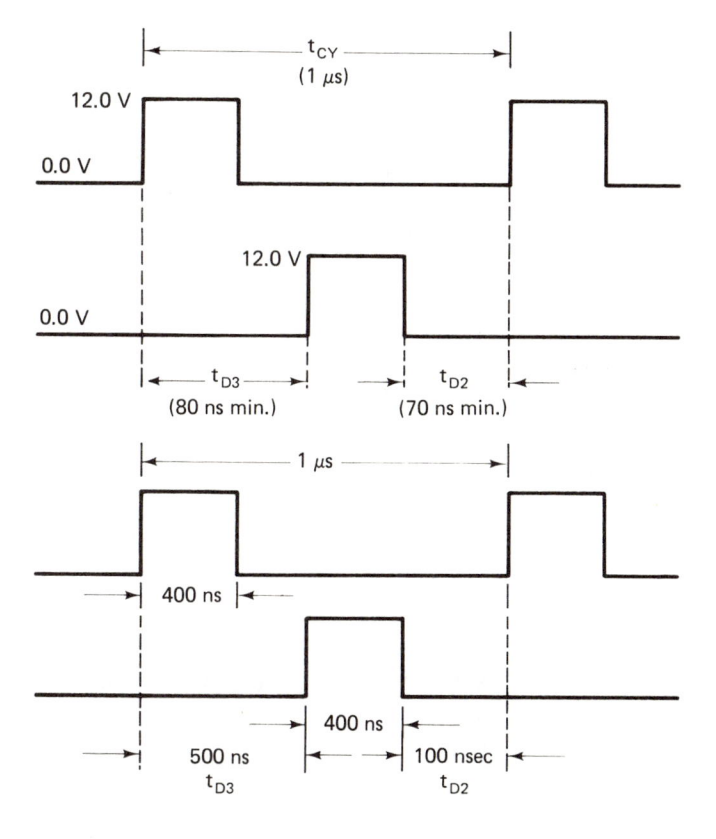

Figure 4-5 Timing of the phase 1 and phase 2 clocks for our 8080 system

compare these waveform outputs to the specifications given in Figure 4-3. A comparison of the specified and actual values is given in Figure 4-6.

8080 microsystem		Our microsystem
t_{cy}	0.48 μsec	1.0 μsec
t_{D2}	80 nsec	500 nsec
t_{D3}	70 nsec	100 nsec
$t_{\phi 1}$	60 nsec	400 nsec
$t_{\phi 2}$	220 nsec	400 nsec

Figure 4-6 Comparison of specifications between the 8080 data sheet specifications and actual values for our system

To generate these waveforms we will use standard T²L devices that are available on the market today. A block diagram of the timing generator circuit is shown in Figure 4-7. Hardware realization of the blocks shown can be done a number of ways; here we show a method that is easy to use and will work. However, if your own experience and background enable you to design your own timing generator circuit, do not hesitate to do so. The important thing in an exercise like this is that one understand what the final output should be, and *exactly* how each part of the circuit works to achieve this output. Don't hesitate to experiment.

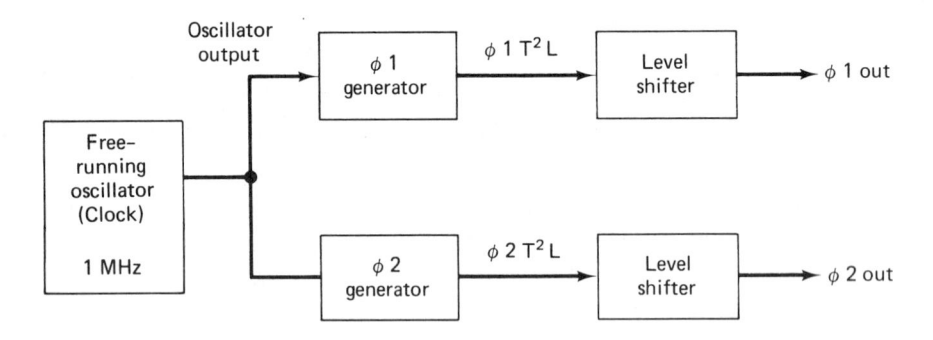

Figure 4-7 Block diagram of timing generator circuit

The free-running 1 MHz oscillator will be constructed using a 74123 dual one-shot multivibrator. The circuit for the oscillator is shown in Figure 4-8, and the data sheet for the 74123 multivibrator is given in Appendix B. In this oscillator each one-shot triggers the other. Each one-shot is connected to give an output waveform as shown in Figure 4-9. On the trailing edge of each one-shot output pulse, the other one-shot oscillator input (which is connected to this output pin) will trigger. The variable resistors R_1 and R_2 in the circuit serve to

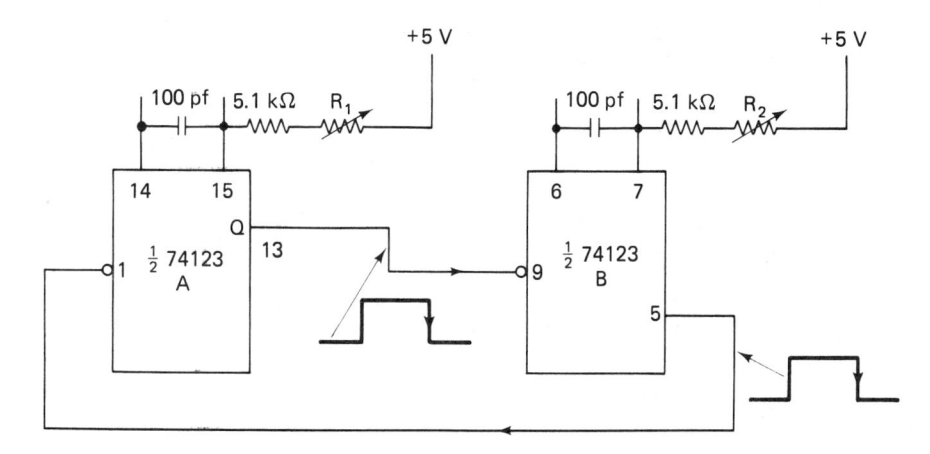

Figure 4-8 Schematic diagram of the free-running oscillator. The frequency = 1 MHz (R_1 and R_2 are used to vary the t_{CY}). The two 1-shot multivibrators A and B are contained in the same 74123 IC package. (Note that ground and V_{CC} are usually not shown on digital schematics.)

control the pulse width of each one-shot individually. By varying the resistors, the frequency of oscillation as well as the *duty cycle* can be altered. The oscillator circuit of Figure 4-8 should be adjusted to give the output waveforms shown in Figure 4-9(b).

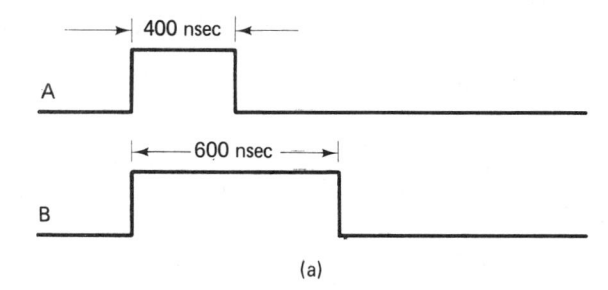

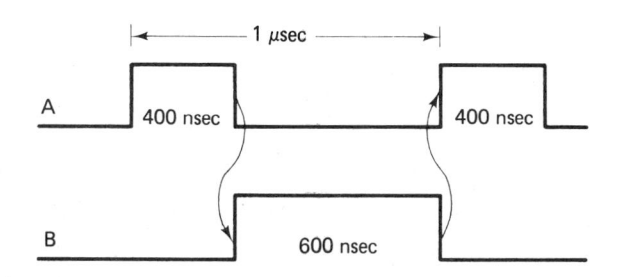

Figure 4-9 (a) Output waveforms of each 1-shot multivibrator (b) Timing diagram, showing how each 1-shot will trigger the other on the falling edge of the output

To generate the phase 1 and phase 2 signals we will again make use of one-shots. The T²L waveforms for ϕ_1 and ϕ_2 are shown in Figure 4-10. Referring to Figure 4-7, the parts now under discussion are the ϕ_1 and ϕ_2 blocks denoted on the diagram. For the phase 1 signal we will use the Q output of the same one-shot multivibrator that is used in the free-running oscillator. This will give a waveform for phase 1 as shown in Figure 4-10. The phase 2 waveform will be generated differently. For this we will use the circuit shown in Figure 4-11.

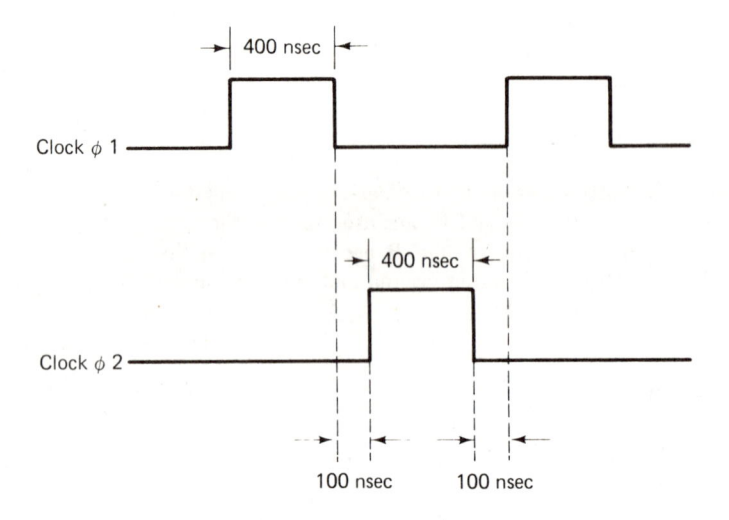

Figure 4-10 Timing of TTL phase 1 and phase 2 clocks for the 8080

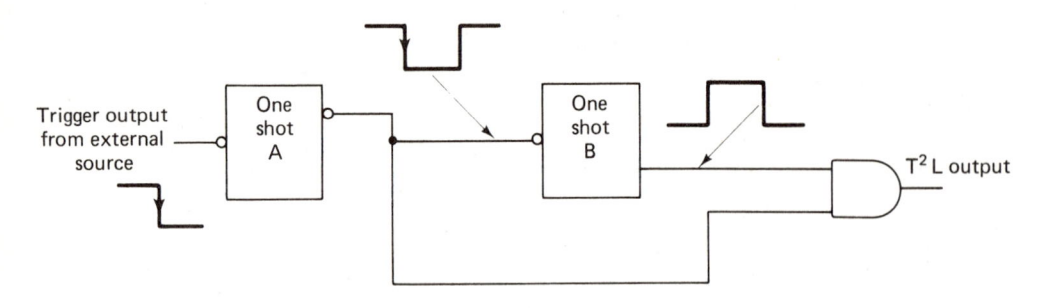

Figure 4-11 Block diagram of circuit used to generate phase 2 TTL clock input for the 8080

In this circuit both one-shots are triggered on the falling edge of the phase 1 clock signal. The resulting waveforms from these one-shots are shown in the timing diagram of Figure 4-12. Notice from the timing diagram that there is a

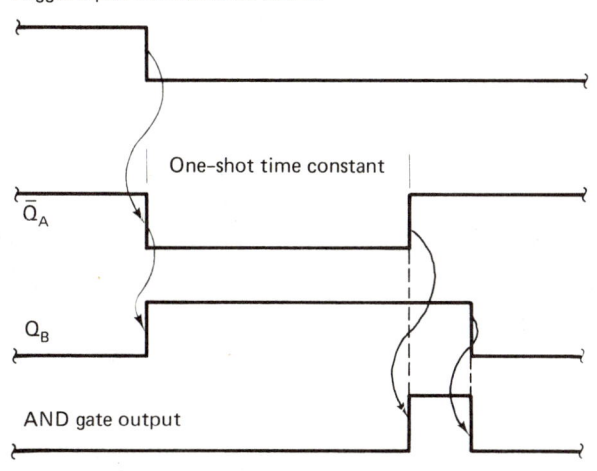

Figure 4-12 Output waveforms of one-shots used to generate TTL phase 1 and phase 2 clocks

period of overlap where both inputs to the AND gate are a logical 1. It is during this period of overlap that the output of the AND gate is a logical 1. We can adjust the rising edge of the signal at the output of the AND gate by changing the RC time constant of one-shot A. The trailing edge of the pulse at the output of the AND gate can be adjusted by changing the RC time constant of one-shot B.

We should keep in mind that it is possible to adjust the RC timing constants of one-shots A and B in such manner that *no* output pulse will be generated at the output of the AND gate. This is illustrated by the timing diagram of Figure 4-13. This fact is mentioned so that when first adjusting the RC time constants of the one-shots, one is aware that a "no output" condition of the AND gate could be due to improper adjustment and does not necessarily indicate a circuit defect.

When constructing this type of pulse generator, it is best to use an oscilloscope to adjust the output pulses of each one-shot individually. As soon as a waveform is obtained at the output of the AND gate, it is easy to monitor the output with an oscilloscope and make final adjustments on the RC time constants. It is very important to understand how the free-running oscillator circuit, the ϕ_1 circuit, and the ϕ_2 circuit work because all of the other timing circuits are referenced to these signals. Also, one should know exactly what effects to expect on the waveforms as a result of adjusting any of the four variable resistors.

Referring again to the block diagram of the timing generator circuit shown in Figure 4-7, we now have the three blocks shown in that figure constructed.

Trigger input from external source

$\overline{Q}_A$

Q_B

AND gate output

Logical 0 level

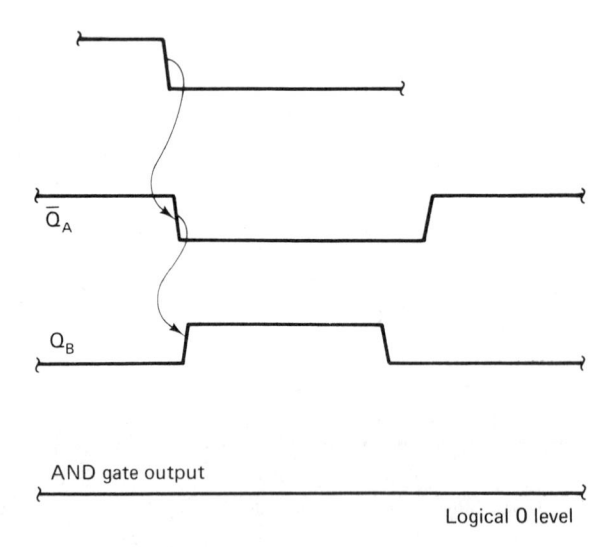

Figure 4-13 Timing diagram showing no Q_A and Q_B overlap. This condition produces a steady logical 0 level at the output of the AND gate.

We will now discuss techniques for generating the T²L to MOS level shifters. Level shifters are required to make T²L voltage levels compatible with MOS voltage levels. We will show two different techniques. Again, if you, the reader, are experienced enough to design your level shifters, don't hesitate to try. The important point is that whatever the technique used, it should be well understood.

The first technique that will be shown makes use of an additional power supply. This circuit is shown in Figure 4-14 and works as follows. The 7407 is a

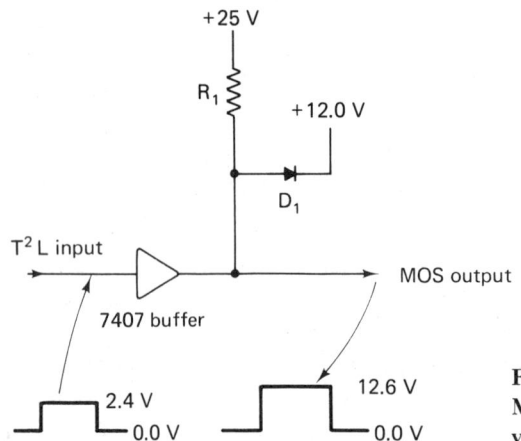

Figure 4-14 One technique for generating an MOS clock output voltage from a TTL input voltage

non-inverting buffer with an open collector output. The collector of the output transistor is pulled up to +25 V (the additional power supply output voltage) via resistor R_1. However, when the output voltage reaches approximately 12.6 V, the diode D_1 will conduct and clamp the voltage. The reason the collector is pulled up toward +25 V and clamped at +12.6 V is to take advantage of the rapid rise time as the collector voltage moves from 0 to +12.6 V. Clamping at 12 V provides a nicely shaped output waveform as shown in Figure 4-15(b). A point to remember about using this type of circuit is what when the diode D_1 conducts, the +12 V supply must sink current from the +25 V supply through R_1. Some power supplies are capable of sourcing current only (having current flow out of the supply). The +12 V supply created here must be capable of both sinking and sourcing current.

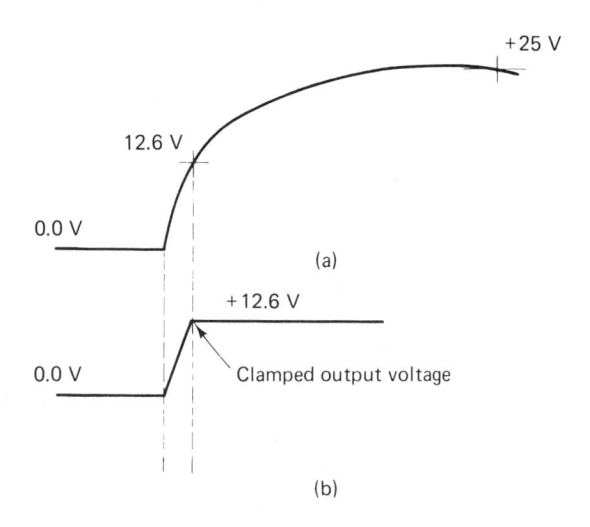

Figure 4-15 (a) Output of 7407 if no diode were clamping at 12.0 volts (b) Output waveform with clamped output. Note that we use the nearly linear portion of the signal shown in (a).

The second technique we will discuss does not require an additional power supply, and this is the one that will be used in our system. The circuit for this T²L to MOS level shifter is shown in Figure 4-16 and works as follows. The signal input is a logical 1, and the output of the 7406 inverter (labeled A) is a logical 0. The data sheet for the 7406 is given in Appendix A. The logical 0 at output A (open collector) provides a current path from the +12 V supply through R_1 and R_2. This current path turns on transistor Q_1. When Q_1 turns on, the collector voltage of Q_1 approaches the emitter voltage. The collector voltage is the output voltage of the circuit.

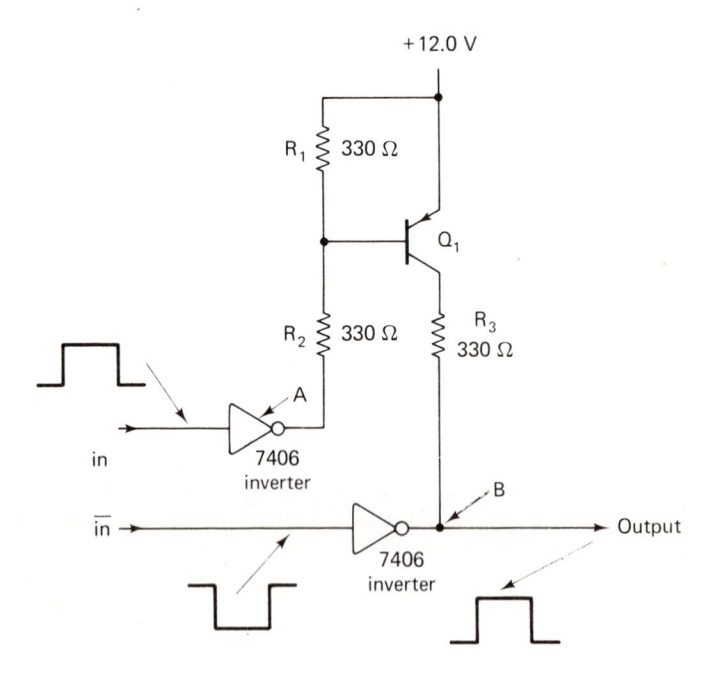

Figure 4-16 Circuit used to generate high-level clocks for phase 1 and phase 2

When the input voltage to the circuit is logical 1, inverter output B is off. When the input signal goes to logical 0, inverter A turns off and inverter B turns on. With inverter A turning off and inverter B turning on, the transistor Q_1 turns off, and the output transistor of the open collector inverter B tends to pull the output voltage toward ground. Under this condition the output voltage is approximately 0.0 V. This circuit provides both active pull-up and active pull-down for the output. Both the ϕ_1 and ϕ_2 T²L to MOS level shifters will be constructed using this circuit. The schematic of this timing circuit is shown in Figure 4-17.

The next circuit described concerns that part of the 8080 microprocessor called *status information*. The status section gives a unique binary code for each type of major job the 8080 performs. What are the major jobs? There are ten major jobs that the 8080 can perform, but for now we will concentrate on five of them. These are:

1. Reading data from memory
2. Writing data to memory
3. Writing data to some external circuit
4. Reading data from some external circuit
5. Performing an internal register manipulation

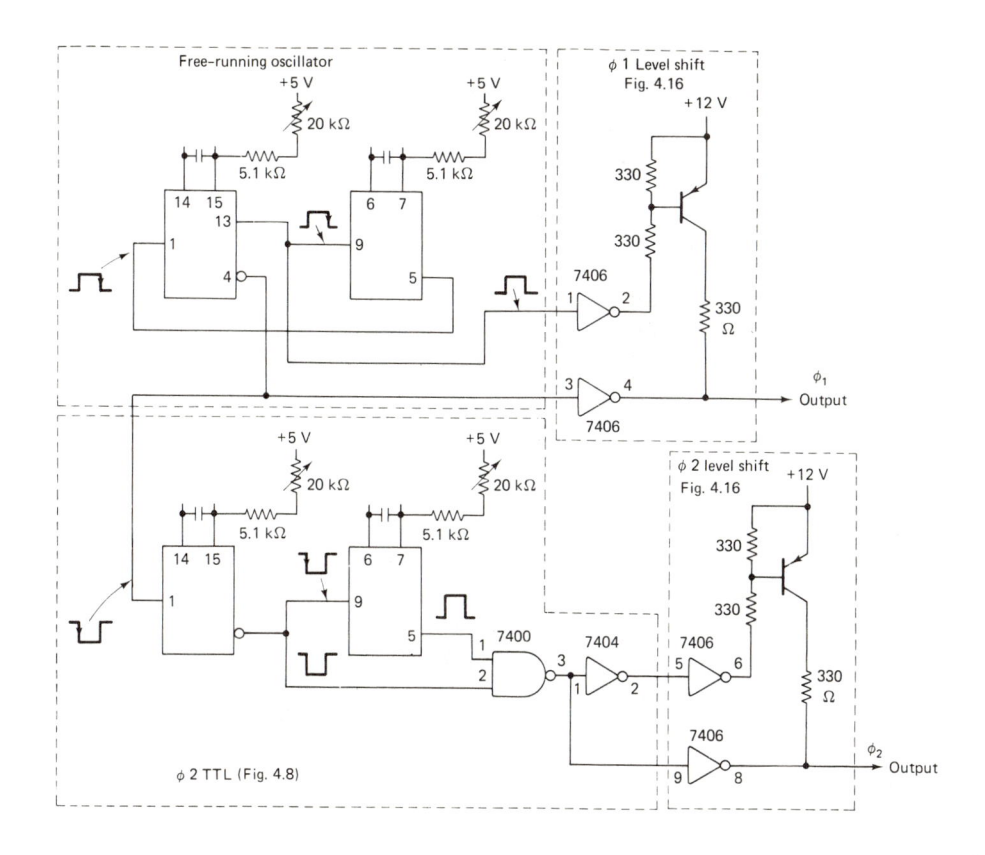

Figure 4-17 Complete timing generator schematic for phase 1 and phase 2 clocks

With these five jobs in mind we note that the 8080 central processing unit (CPU) must communicate with different satellite circuits. See Figure 4-18.

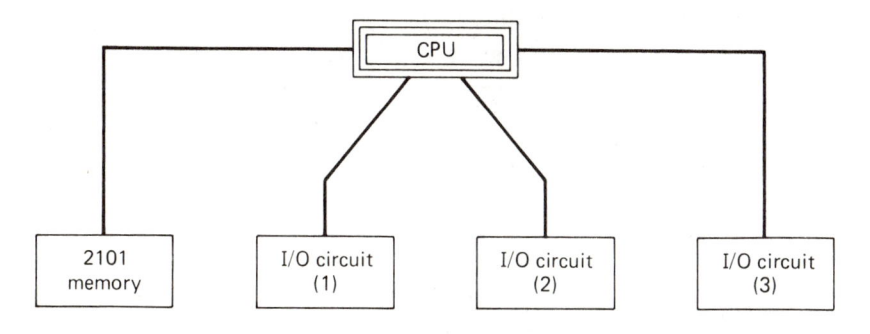

Figure 4-18 Picturial representation of the CPU with satellite circuits under its control

125

To further illustrate the communication necessary between the CPU and satellite circuits, consider the familiar tick-tack-toe game we have all played at some time in our lives. We wish to instruct our microprocessor system to play tick-tack-toe against a human opponent. How shall we proceed?

To begin, we need a game board. The game board must be able to accept human choice, and the microprocessor system must understand which choice has been made. Also, the system must keep track of all *past* choices that have been made so far in the game.

Then the system must make its choice (decision) based on past history and the human choice recently made; then it must initiate a response.

Finally, the system must be able to determine if there has been a tie or a winner, and indicate end of game.

Consider for a moment how the five jobs listed earlier relate to the three requirements of our tick-tack-toe game:

1. When the human makes a choice, the system must perform Job 4, *reading data from an external circuit*.
2. The human choice must be remembered by the system, so Job 2, *writing data to memory*, must be performed.
3. After the human choice has been made, the system must refer to history for instructions; this is Job 1, *reading data from memory*.
4. Based on the human choice and instructions from memory, the system must execute Job 5, *performing an internal register manipulation*, in order to make a decision.
5. As soon as the system makes its decision it must implement that decision by performing Job 3, *writing data to some external circuit*.

How the CPU performs this function of communication with the satellite circuits depends largely on the digital hardware used to construct the circuits. No matter what digital hardware is used, the system must have a means of determining the communication path; that is, which of the many satellite circuits will the CPU direct data to or receive data from? Part of this information is contained in the status information that is output from the CPU.

Status information is generated by the CPU according to the instruction being executed. If the instruction directed the CPU to write data to memory, the status information would indicate this. The status information is generated physically on the data bus (D_0–D_7) at a certain instant in time. Thus, it is present only for a brief interval and must be latched. Since the status data must be latched, we have to know when to latch it. The CPU must generate a signal pulse to indicate that the status information is available on the data bus. This signal from the 8080 is called the SYNC signal. The sync signal is *active high* whenever status information is available on the data bus. The sync signal has other sig-

The 8080 Microprocessor as a CPU

nificance relating to the 8080, but for now let us assume that its only function is to inform the hardware latches that status information is available on the data bus.

The timing diagram of the sync signal referenced to the ϕ_1 and ϕ_2 clocks is shown in Figure 4-19. It should be stated here that the sync signal is not always present. When it is present, it always occurs with the same relative position to ϕ_1 and ϕ_2 on the 8080. Also, when the sync signal is present, the status information is also present.

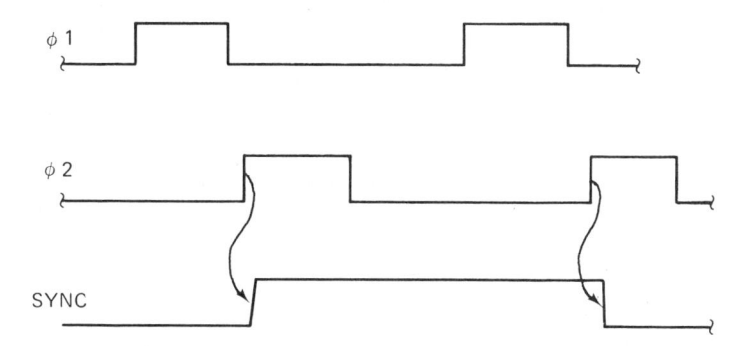

Figure 4-19 Timing diagram of the SYNC signal referenced to phase 1 and phase 2

In order to latch the status information we will construct hardware to realize the block diagram of Figure 4-20. Note first that the eight bits of data are connected to inputs of a buffer circuit. The data bus D_0–D_7 on the 8080 has an I_{OL} of 1.9 milliamperes. The I_{OH} is -150 microamperes (μA). This current specification

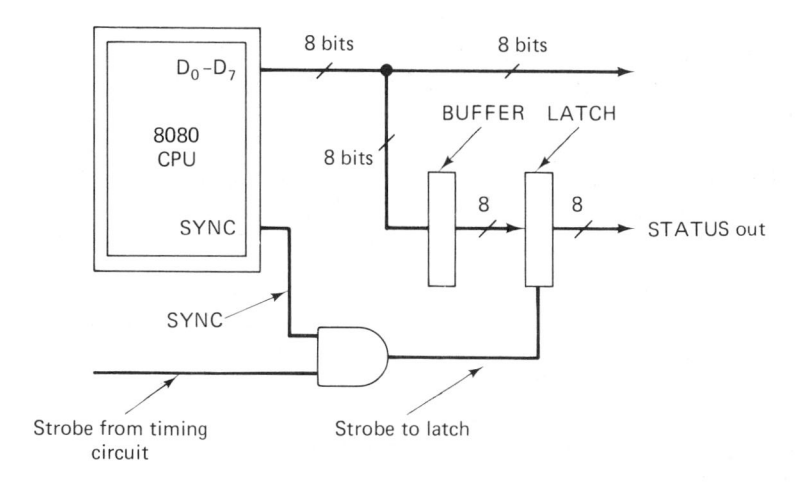

Figure 4-20 Block diagram of status latches for the 8080

of the 8080 is sufficient to drive only one standard T²L load input reliably, so it is necessary to buffer the data bus outputs. The data bus usually connects to many circuit inputs, so the cumulative effect of the parallel circuits may possibly load the data bus lines excessively.

Note that the strobe input to the latch is the logical AND of the strobe from the timing circuit and sync. This gives the timing shown in Figure 4-21. The actual hardware circuit to latch the status information is shown in Figure 4-22.

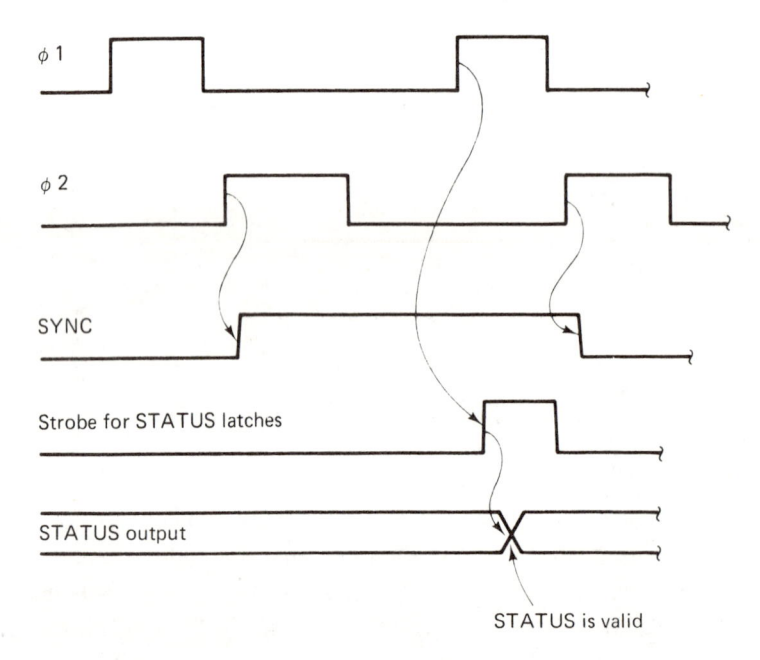

Figure 4-21 Timing diagram of status information as it is latched, referenced to phase 1, phase 2, and SYNC. The arrows indicate the edge of signal to which other signals are referenced.

We will now make use of the status information that we have just latched. With this information we will show how to accomplish with hardware the five major jobs that the CPU performs. In later chapters we will expand this job list. As we enter this discussion the reader is asked to accept for now that the CPU will give the status information and we can latch it as shown. We will also refer to other control signals generated by the 8080. We will show how to make use of these just mentioned events, given that they happen. The programming of the 8080 microprocessor will be discussed in Chapter 6. All of the different programming instructions that control the 8080 order the operation of the internal hardware and enable these events to happen in the proper sequence.

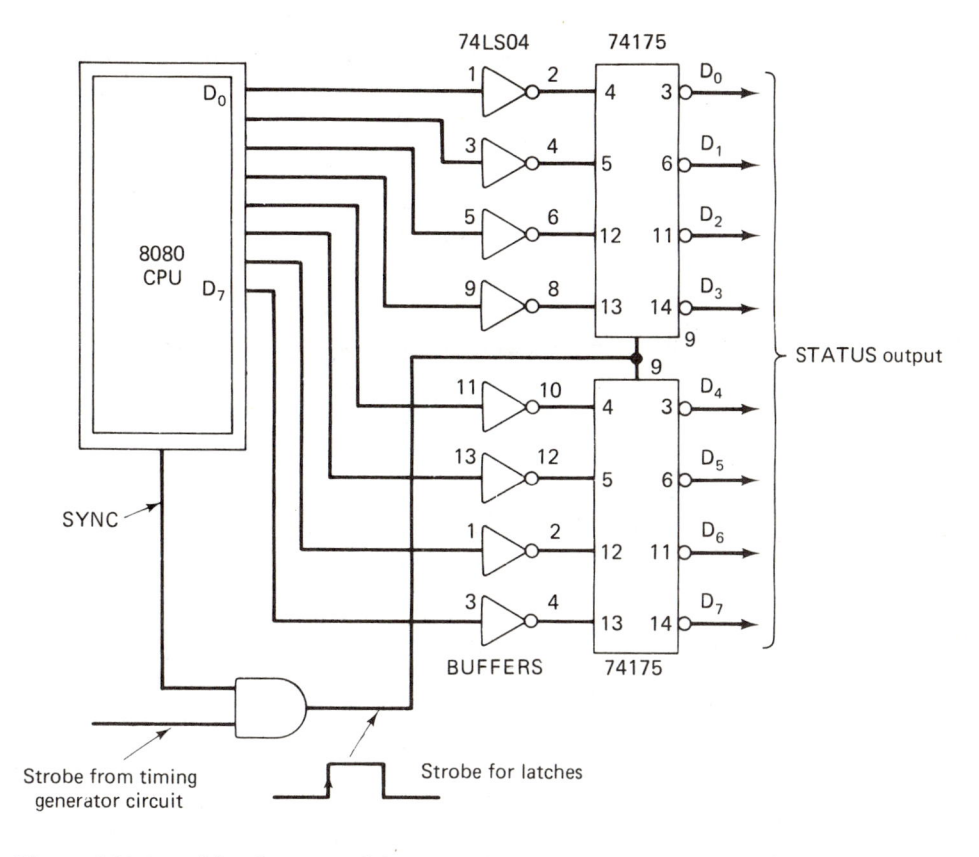

Figure 4-22 Actual hardware used for status latches in an 8080 system

Because all of the timing is internal on an 8080 chip, once the external, free-running ϕ_1 and ϕ_2 signals are established, the other timing details are fixed. A user really has no control over events internal to the 8080. At this point it is easier to think of the 8080 as a "black box" that performs in a certain manner under different conditions. (We will show later that there are some special signals that may be of use, but the detail of the internal structure of an 8080 chip is a confusion factor that need not be confronted at this point in the learning process.)

4-1 Reading Data from Memory

Let us start by discussing how the CPU performs the first job—that of reading data from memory. We want to read from memory when we are reading an instruction that has been permanently stored in memory, or when reading a value that has been temporarily stored in memory. It is important to understand that when the CPU is reading data from memory, the hardware is being used in a certain order or sequence. Once this is understood, the reasons for the CPU to generate its control signals in a certain manner will be more easily followed.

Now, what is the proper sequence of events or conditions for the CPU to read data from memory? This four-step sequence follows:

1. Memory address is stable
2. Data out from memory is enabled to the I/O bus
3. Data is accessed from memory (Read access time)
4. Data is strobed into the CPU.

In the status information there is a bit signal called MEMR. This bit is always a logical 1 whenever the CPU is performing a memory read operation. (A Status Word Chart is given in Appendix A. This chart shows all of the status word outputs for the different jobs a CPU performs.)

The address outputs A_0–A_{15} of the 8080 will be the address of memory that we wish to access. For our system only A_0–A_7 are connected to the memory. We do not use A_8–A_{15} in this application; unused address lines are left "floating." As soon as address lines A_0–A_7 are stable at the 8080 outputs, the memory will access the correct data.

Up to this point the output buffers (tri-state) have been disabled, so any other device connected in parallel to the data bus could have control of the data bus lines without interference. When the memory output buffers are enabled, the data bus is controlled by the information present at the memory output.

The data bus I/O pins D_0–D_7 on the 8080 must be buffered as discussed in the previous section. For this we will install bidirectional bus drivers on our system. This will enable data to flow in both directions on the data bus. The bus drivers will be installed as shown in Figure 4-23. Notice in this figure that the data will flow from the microprocessor to the data bus when the control line is logical 0. The control line signal is generated by the 8080. The control line will switch to logical 1 only when the 8080 is "requesting" data to be input. The signal on the control line is called DBIN.

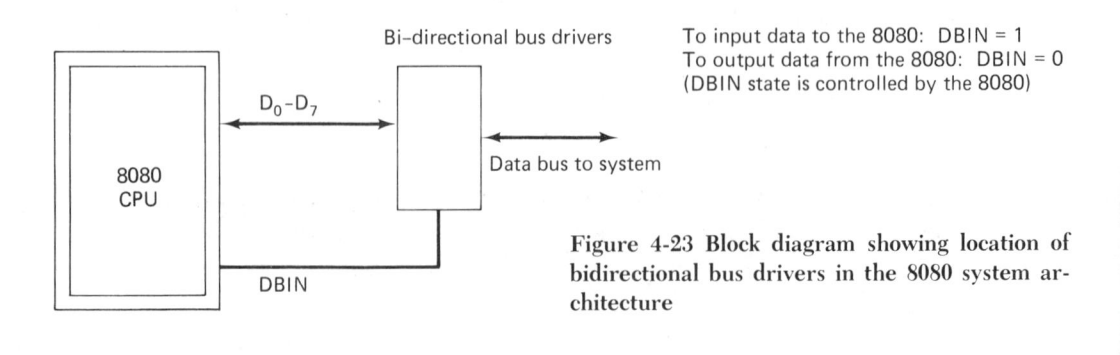

Figure 4-23 Block diagram showing location of bidirectional bus drivers in the 8080 system architecture

Sec. 4-1   *Reading Data from Memory*   131

This signal will always go to logical 1 when data is input to the CPU. Our system now looks as shown in Figure 4-24. We will use the DBIN signal to access and the $\overline{\text{MEMR}}$ signal to read data from memory. Figure 4-25 shows the hardware for a new MEMR signal that we will generate. This new signal is a logical 0 when DBIN and MEMR are both logical 1. This condition exists whenever the CPU is requesting data from memory. We use the $\overline{\text{MEMR}}$ signal

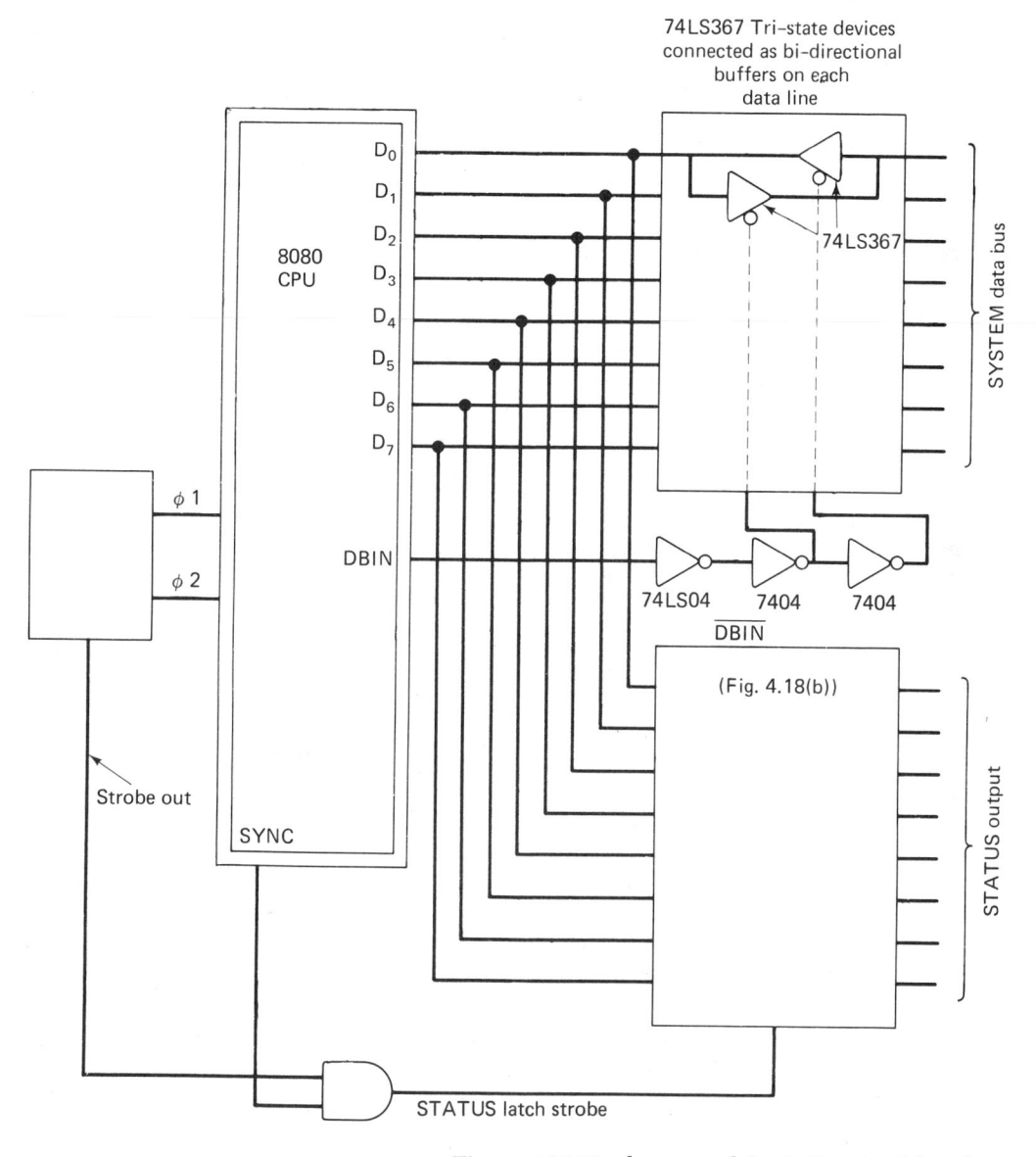

Figure 4-24 Hardware used for bidirectional bus drivers

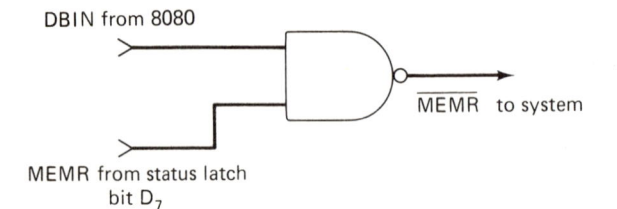

Figure 4-25 Generation of $\overline{\text{MEMR}}$ signal

to enable the output buffers from memory. The signal DBIN directly enables the data bus input lines to the CPU. The flow of data is shown in Figure 4-26. If we

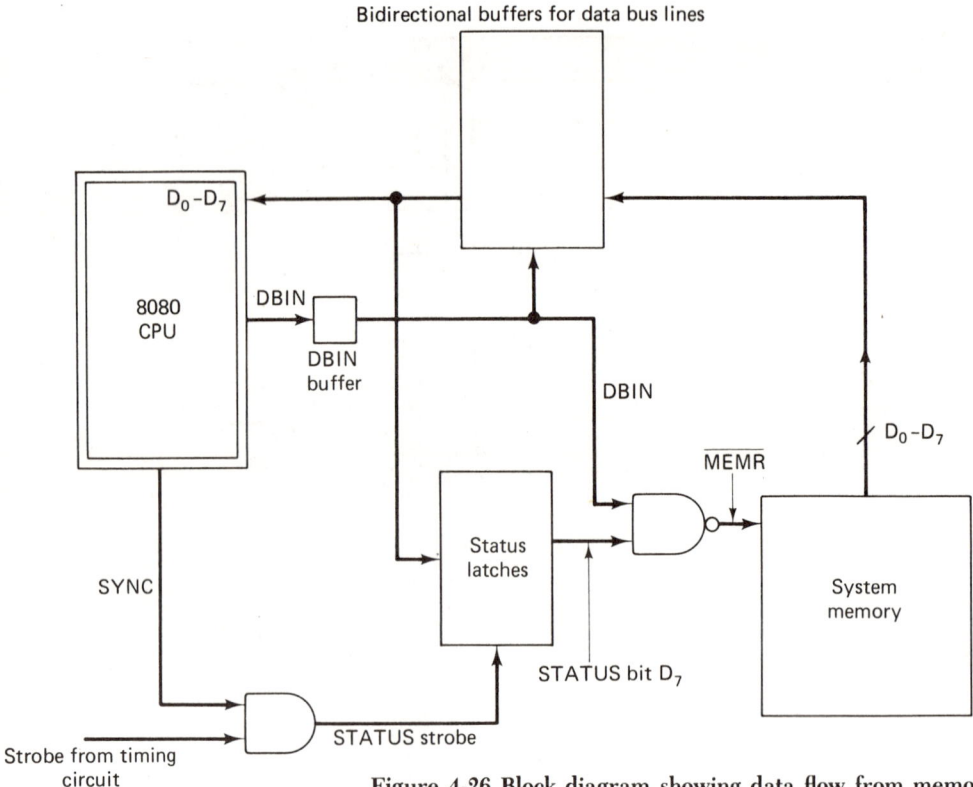

Figure 4-26 Block diagram showing data flow from memory to the bidirectional buffers to the CPU. The $\overline{\text{MEMR}}$ signal enables the tri-state buffers at the memory output to control data bus bits D_0-D_7.

examine the read from memory sequence of events as they relate to specific hardware signals, the results will look as shown in Figure 4-27.

The sequence of Figure 4-27 is logical, based on the way that memory must be accessed—that is, the address signal must be stable and the DBIN signal

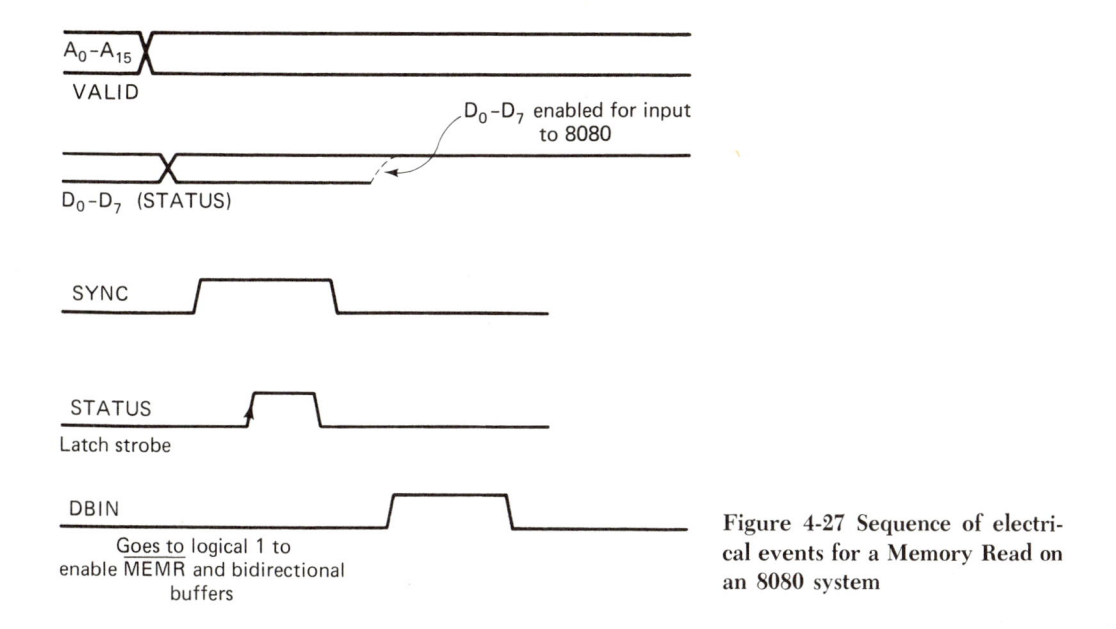

```
A₀-A₁₅  ─────⟨═══════════════════════════
VALID
                        D₀-D₇ enabled for input
                               to 8080
         ─────⟨═══════════════════════════
D₀-D₇ (STATUS)

SYNC     _____╱‾‾‾╲_____

STATUS   _____╱‾╲_____
Latch strobe

DBIN     _____╱‾‾‾╲_____
   Goes to logical 1 to
enable MEMR and bidirectional
         buffers
```

Figure 4-27 Sequence of electrical events for a Memory Read on an 8080 system

must enable data from memory. If we relate these signals to the actual timing of the 8080, the diagram appears as shown in Figure 4-28.

At the top of Figure 4-28 we see the notations t_1, t_2, t_3. These letters denote each fixed period interval as a state. A *state* is defined as the time interval between leading edges of ϕ_1. Notice that it requires three states to complete the operation of a memory read. This is what we meant when we said that the other internal timing details of the 8080 are fixed. All of the control signals will happen in the correct sequence, but we as users have no control over the internal timing that makes them happen. If we design our hardware assuming that these signals will occur, then the time it takes for them to occur is transparent to the system. By the term *transparent* we mean that even though the signals take a longer or shorter time to happen, the hardware will still work reliably. This always depends on whether the 8080 itself is operating properly of course.

In the terminology of an 8080 microprocessor the combination of states t_1, t_2, t_3 are called a machine cycle. A *machine cycle* is the entire length of time, composed of states, that it will take the 8080 to execute a single instruction. Different instructions in the 8080 require a different number of states. Thus each instruction, or job, may require a different time to complete its machine cycle. That is, the time length of one machine cycle is not fixed, but varies from instruction to instruction. The definition of a machine cycle is constant however. Other operations that require a different number of states will be discussed in the programming of the 8080 in Chapter 6.

We have now shown all of the necessary hardware required for the 8080 to

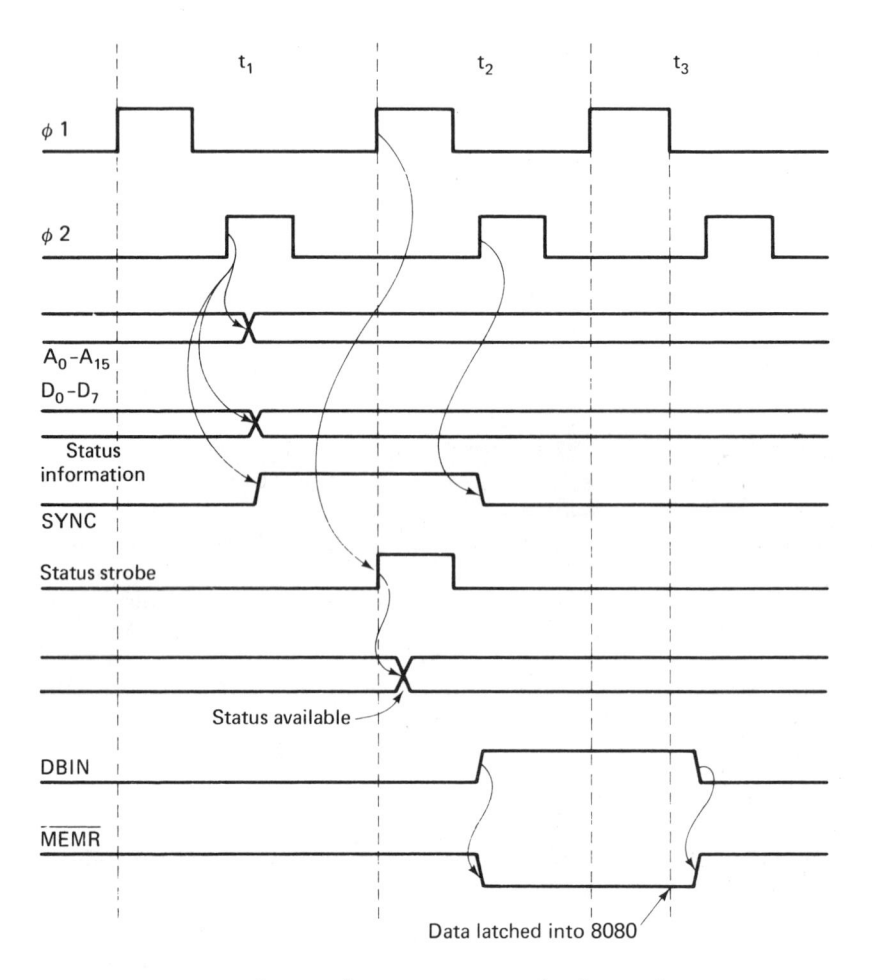

Figure 4-28 Timing of events for a Memory Read referenced to the 8080 phase 1 and phase 2 clocks

read data from memory. It should be kept in mind that the specific hardware may change, depending on the type of memory the 8080 is using: that is, dynamic, static, common I/O, or separate I/O to name a few. The overall job of reading data from memory still remains as described. When confronted with a different type of memory, one should look for the basic blocks of circuitry that perform the functions described here. In the system under construction, no matter how complicated the instructions are that the 8080 is executing, data will be read from memory in exactly the manner we have shown.

From the timing diagram of Figure 4-28 note that data from memory is latched (strobed) into the 8080 on the falling edge of ϕ_1 in the t_3 state. Data out is requested when the address lines A_0–A_7 are stable. This requires that the read-access time of the memory be less than the time between the moment the addresses become stable and the moment the data is latched into the 8080. For our circuit this is approximately 2.4 microseconds.

This number is shown in the timing diagram of Figure 4-29. If the period of ϕ_1 and ϕ_2 were shorter, the access time of our memory would have to be less. The read-access time of our memory (2101) is less than 1 microsecond, according to specifications. Thus our system has no problem responding to the 2.4 microsecond access time imposed by the cycle time of ϕ_1 and ϕ_2. If our memory had a longer read-access time than that available with the 8080 timing, the memory would send a signal to the 8080 indicating that the data requested was not valid.

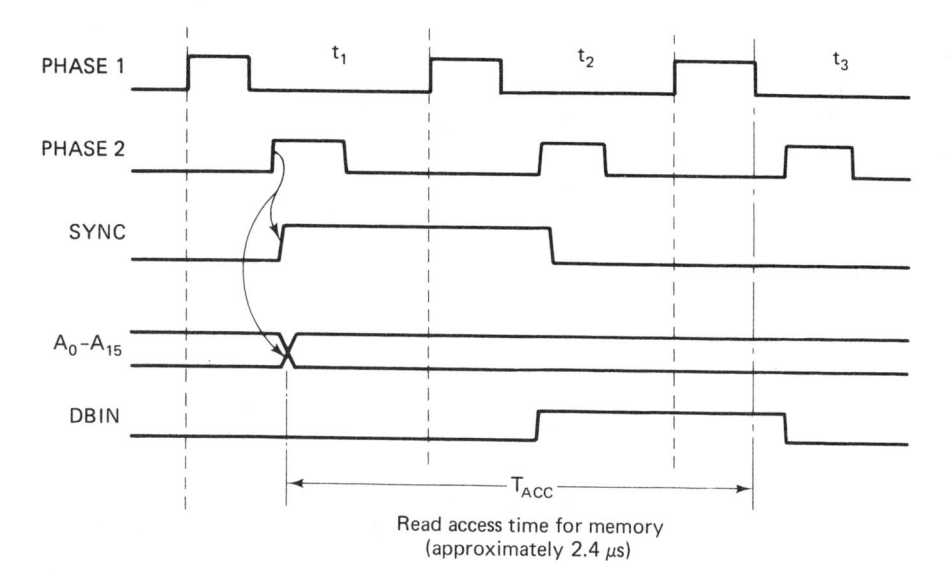

Figure 4-29 Timing diagram showing read-access time for an 8080 system

If this happened the 8080 would enter a wait state called t_w. In the *wait state* all conditions on the system buses remain frozen (static) until the memory again signals the 8080 to resume execution. (We mention this fact because one may wonder how the problem of a longer read-access time is handled.) The chapter on advanced microprocessor techniques discusses in detail how this wait signal from memory can be realized with hardware.

4-2 Writing Data to Memory

We will now discuss the procedure and hardware required to perform the second major job of the CPU—the write data into memory. Let us first review the three signals needed to write data into a memory location:

1. the address of the memory location where data will be stored
2. the data signals to the data-in lines of memory, and
3. the write enable pulse that is generated to the memory.

The timing diagram (for the microprocessor) to write data to memory is shown in Figure 4-30. Note that it is similar to Figure 4-28, the timing diagram for reading data from memory.

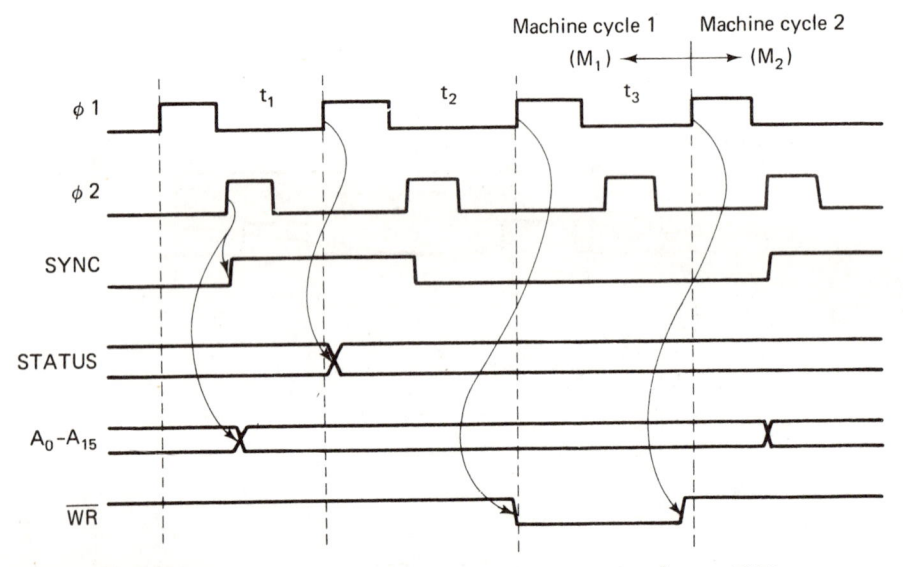

Figure 4-30 Timing diagram for a Memory Write operation for an 8080 system

Notice in Figure 4-30 that both the status information and the memory addresses are presented during t_1. The data to memory is present on the data bus at t_2. During t_3 a write pulse called $\overline{WR}$ is generated by the 8080. This is a negative going pulse timed as shown, and it is present whenever the microprocessor is writing data on the data bus to some satellite circuit, such as the memory or an I/O circuit. Using the $\overline{WR}$ signal and one of the status bits called D_4, we can generate a write-enable pulse to memory. The circuit to accomplish this is shown in Figure 4-31.

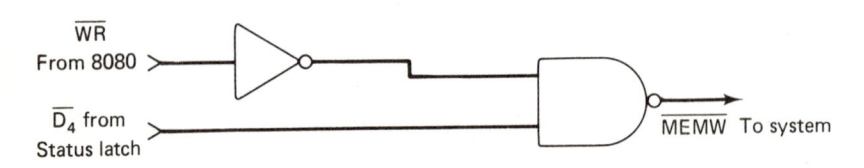

Figure 4-31 Signals used to generate MEMW pulse to memory

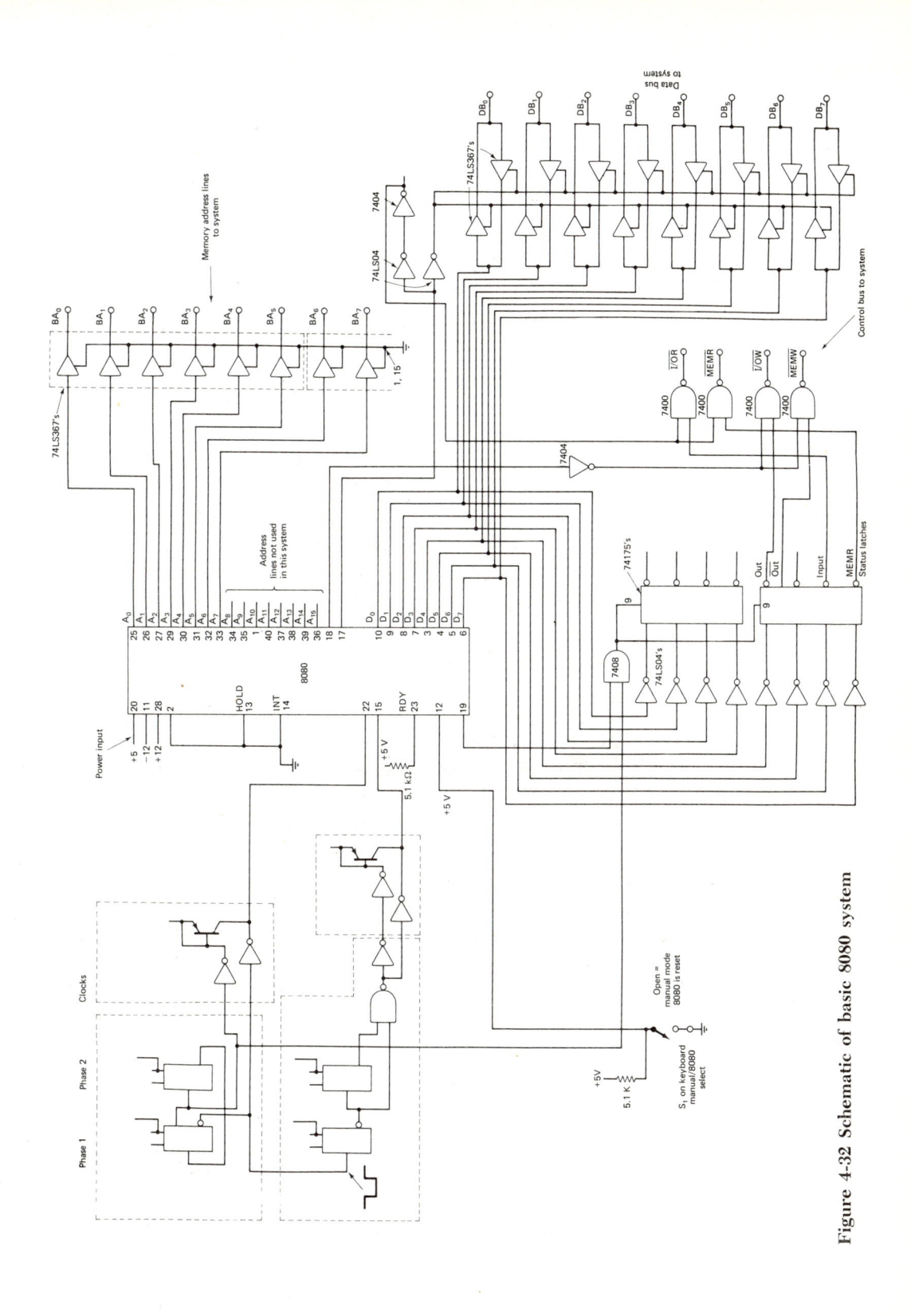

Figure 4-32 Schematic of basic 8080 system

In Figure 4-32 we see this total system for writing data to memory and reading data from memory. Notice that the ϕ_1 and ϕ_2 clocks are not shown in detail. We can safely assume that these clocks are always present on the 8080 clock input pins, even if they are not shown on the drawing.

The write-access time of the memory may be longer than the time provided by the CPU; however, this time may be extended much the same way as we described for the read-access time. In Chapter 8 we show how this can be accomplished with hardware.

4-3 Writing Data to an External Circuit

Of the 10 major jobs of a CPU, the third job is writing data to some external output circuit. We now discuss the hardware required to accomplish this data transfer. In Chapter 5 we will cover the actual design and implementation of I/O devices to communicate with the 8080 microprocessor. In that discussion we will employ the hardware that we discuss in this chapter.

To write data to an I/O device we need exactly the same type of information that is required when we write data to memory:

1. the address of the I/O device.
2. the data signals to the I/O device placed on the data bus
3. the I/O write strobe signal issued to the system.

From this list we see that the first two items are indeed similar to the list for the memory write. However, the hardware in the system cannot determine electrically whether the data on the bus is meant for the memory or for an I/O device. To determine this, the status information required for the CPU to write data to an I/O device must be different from the status information required to write data to memory. Although we use the same status information and $\overline{WR}$ signal to generate the I/O write signal that we used for the memory write, we use the status bit D_4 as shown in Figure 4-33 to generate the I/O write signal. This procedure enables the system to generate two mutually exclusive (never happen at the same time) write signals for memory write and I/O write. These

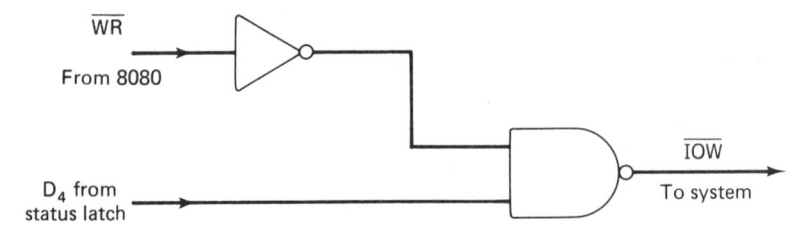

Figure 4-33 Signals used to generate $\overline{IOW}$ pulse to I/O circuits in an 8080 systems

Sec. 4-4 *Reading Data from an Extended Circuit* 139

two mutually exclusive signals are the major difference between the system performing a memory write and an I/O write.

4-4 Reading Data from an External Circuit

The fourth of the major jobs that the CPU does is read data from some external circuit, or I/O device. Again this task is similar to its counterpart of reading data from memory. To perform the I/O read function requires a four-step sequence:

1. the address of the I/O device to be read from
2. output of the I/O device is enabled onto the data bus
3. the bidirectional buffers are enabled to act on the data input to the 8080
4. the data is strobed into the 8080.

Figure 4-34, the timing diagram for this operation, shows that the bidirectional buffers are enabled by the DBIN signal just as the memory-read operation

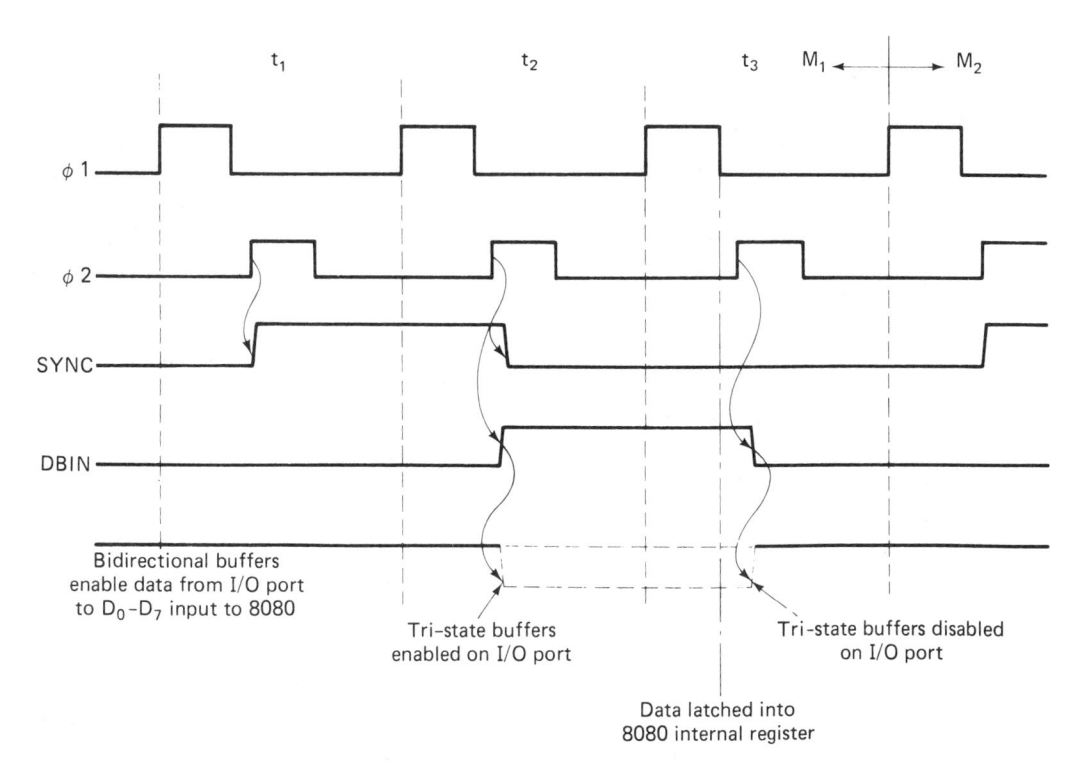

Figure 4-34 Timing diagram for an I/O Read operation in an 8080 system

was. The I/O device outputs are enabled by gating the DBIN signal with bit D_6 of the status word. The status bits are selected because they will be logical 1 only when we wish to do this operation—read in from a satellite circuit. Finally, the data on the bus is latched into the 8080 internal register on the negative going edge of the ϕ_1 clock during the t_3 state.

The problem of an I/O device not having data ready when the 8080 is strobing data in can be eliminated by the same technique used to provide a longer access time for memory—namely, by putting the 8080 into a wait state until the I/O device signals it is ready. This technique is described in detail in Chapter 9.

4-5 Performing an Internal Register Manipulation

The fifth major job of the CPU that we listed was performing an internal register manipulation. Since this type of operation does not require external memory or I/O satellite circuits, no additional hardware is required; the CPU performs these operations internally.

The four signals generated by the CPU—IOW, IOR, MEMR, and MEMW—are grouped together to form the *control bus*. This is used throughout the system to control the operation of all satellite circuits.

The total microprocessor system that we have discussed so far is shown in schematic form in Figure 4-32. Some details of the memory are omitted in this diagram; however, all of the other circuits are shown with the ICs labeled. We have used only standard T^2L devices in this system, with the exception of the microprocessor itself. If readers are unfamiliar with the characteristics of T^2L logic elements, they should review them now. In discussions throughout the rest of this text we assume that readers know the characteristics of this logic family.

In this chapter we have presented the essential subcircuits that allow the 8080 to communicate with the satellite circuits. We have also shown important timing considerations that must be remembered when one is designing or troubleshooting a microprocessor system. It is important for beginners to understand in detail the use of every part of the system presented in this chapter. The following chapters relate to the basic system building blocks presented in this chapter. In Chapter 9, where taking advantage of large-scale integration (LSI) is discussed, readers will have a good understanding of how large-scale devices integrate into the system if they understand the relationship of the functional blocks and timing sequences just examined.

Finally, one should keep in mind that the CPU will perform only limited functions; that is, the types of jobs that it will do electrically are few. No matter how complex or how long the set of instructions are that the CPU is executing,

Sec. 4-5 *Performing an Internal Register Manipulation* 141

the hardware still performs the same jobs over and over again. What really makes a microprocessor system unique is the makeup of the different I/O or satellite circuits that the CPU controls while it is performing a few electrical jobs. If one understands the hardware examples given in this chapter there will be no reason for concern when faced with another CPU that uses different hardware, because it will perform the same five jobs listed in this chapter. One should still have a good intuitive feel for "what should be there," and for what type of hardware one may expect to find in a microprocessor system—regardless of the CPU used.

Review Questions

1. What voltages are required for the 8080?
2. Why is the +5 volt supply for an 8080 system usually the highest current rated supply?
3. What are the typical voltage levels (high, low) of the phase 1 and phase 2 clock inputs?
4. Draw the waveforms of the 8080 phase 1 and phase 2 clocks. Show the important timing relationships between these two signals.
5. Draw a diagram for a 1 megahertz free-running oscillator using two one-shot multivibrators of your choice. Explain fully how the circuit you designed works.
6. What are five major jobs of the CPU?
7. What is meant by the term "status information" as related to the 8080?
8. Describe the relationship of the sync signal as referenced to the status information.
9. Describe how the status information is latched by showing timing diagrams.
10. What is the four-step sequence of electrical events required to read data from memory?
11. Describe the sequence of events required to read data from memory.
12. What is the sequence of electrical events required to write data to memory?
13. Describe how the 8080 writes data to memory.
14. What signals constitute the control bus? Where are they generated?

5

MICROPROCESSOR INPUT AND OUTPUT (I/O)

We have stated that the microprocessor is capable of controlling many satellite, or peripheral, circuits. In this chapter we will discuss different hardware techniques used by microprocessors to control such circuits. We will show specific hardware needed to perform each different type of control.

Let us begin by presenting some definitions and vocabulary that are common to microprocessor satellite (peripheral) circuits.

DATA BUS: This is the group of signal lines D_0–D_7. These data bus lines are the physical means of communication from the microprocessor to the peripheral circuits.

INPUT: Input is the condition where a peripheral circuit is sending data *to* the microprocessor via the data bus. The microprocessor is inputting data *from* the data bus.

OUTPUT: Output is the condition where a peripheral circuit is receiving data *from* the microprocessor via the data bus. The microprocessor is outputting data *to* the data bus.

I/O ADDRESS: The I/O address is a binary address similar to a memory address. Where the memory address points to the memory location that we will read data from or write data into, the I/O address points to the I/O circuit that we will read data from or write data into. On the 8080 the I/O address is the

Microprocessor Input and Output (I/O) 143

lower byte of the 16-bit memory address, bits A_0–A_7. The upper byte, bits A_8–A_{15}, are equal to the lower byte for I/O operations. Note that the memory uses these same addresses.

PORT: Port refers to any valid I/O address to which data can be transferred on the data bus.

DEVICE: Device refers to a single circuit that the microprocessor controls. A peripheral device has at least one port associated with it, and may have more.

CONTROL BUS: (The term identifies the group of signals) $\overline{\text{MEMW}}$, $\overline{\text{MEMR}}$, $\overline{\text{IOR}}$, and $\overline{\text{IOW}}$. These signals enable memory write, memory read, I/O read, and I/O write. *This group of signals controls all of data flow on the data bus lines.* That is, these signals "enable" the correct I/O port or memory address for data transfer at the proper instant in time.

The basic architecture or structure of an I/O interface is shown in Figure 5-1.

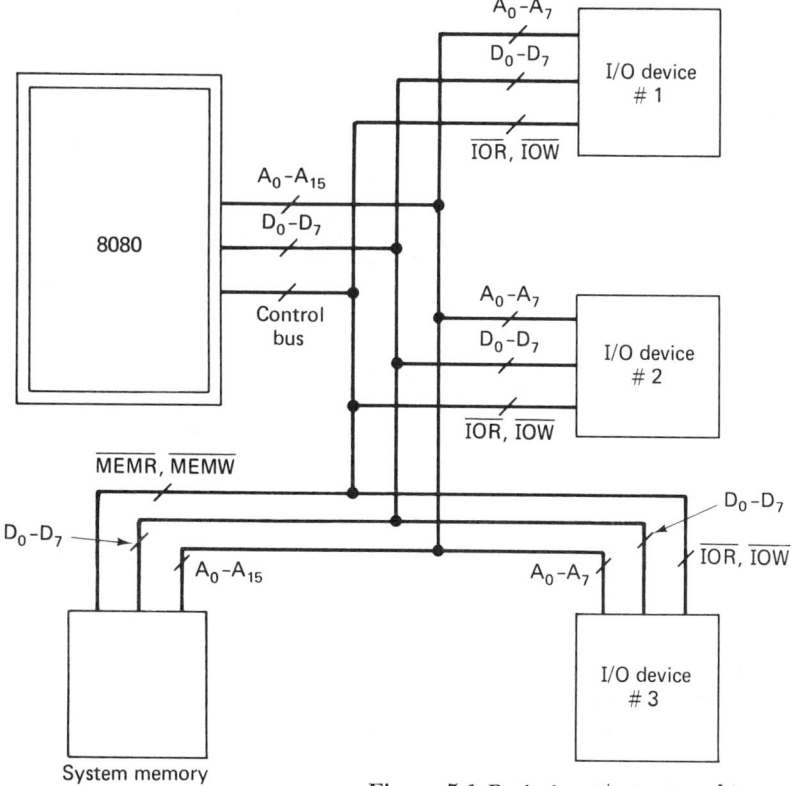

Figure 5-1 Basic input/output architecture of an 8080 system. The three busses are Address, Data, and Control.

Notice that the control bus goes to each I/O device and memory in the system. Also data bus lines D_0–D_7 go to all devices or ports in the system. Since there are so many input lines connected to the data bus, this bus is buffered, as shown in Figure 4-23.

The general architecture for I/O can be modified to suit a given application. We will discuss four general modifications of the basic I/O structure. With each modification we will discuss the special features and characteristics of this type of architecture. Hardware will also be discussed that will enable the reader to realize any of these four architectures. An understanding of these basic I/O structures will make it easy to understand the more complicated architectures that may be encountered in industry. After these interfacings have been introduced, we will discuss how reliable data communication can be established between the microprocessor and the I/O ports.

5-1 Addressed Port I/O

The four architectures of I/O that we will discuss are *ADDRESSED PORT*, *DEVICE/PORT*, *LINEAR SELECT*, and *MEMORY MAPPED*.

The first type of I/O architecture we will discuss is *addressed port*. A block diagram for addressed port I/O is shown in Figure 5-2. Each port has a unique

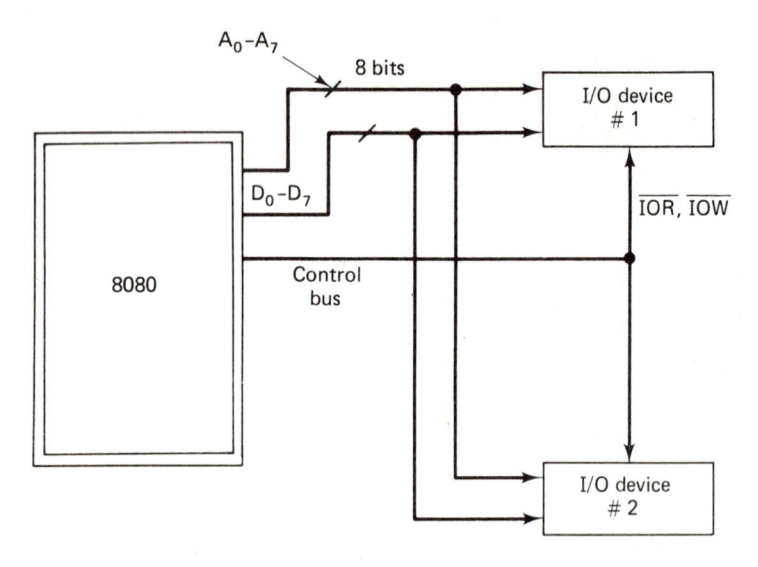

Figure 5-2 Architecture of addressed port I/O. Each I/O circuit may have more than one port. Each port has a unique select code.

Sec. 5-1   Addressed Port I/O   145

8-bit binary code or address assigned to it. An 8-bit code is "hardwired" on the port hardware. *Hardwired* is a general term that means fixed by hardware. When the address of the port is stable on the address bus (A_0–A_7) a signal is generated that is active 1 or active 0. This signal is the output of the decoding circuit on the selected I/O port. This signal output indicates to the external hardware that the port number is presently on the address bus. See Figure 5-3. Information on the data bus D_0–D_7 will be directed to input to the port, or output from the port.

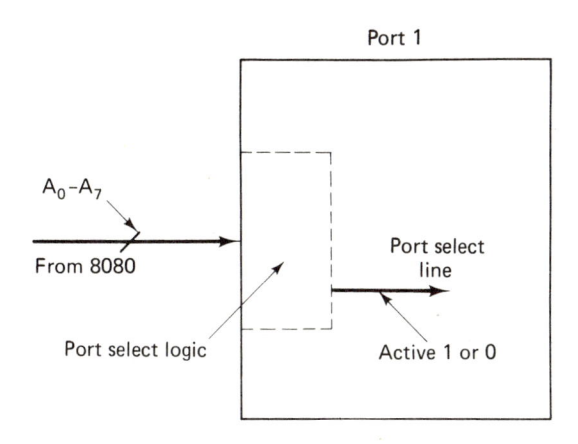

Figure 5-3 Block diagram showing the port select line. This line carries an indication to external hardware that address lines A_0-A_7 are the same as the select code for that particular I/O port.

The sequence of events for an I/O operation using addressed port I/O follows:

1. Address for the unique port is valid (A_0–A_7)
2. Data is valid on the Data Bus (D_0–D_7) for input to the selected port
3. $\overline{IOR}$ or $\overline{IOW}$ is generated by the 8080 hardware
4. The valid port enable signal is generated on the addressed I/O port

The timing diagram shown in Figure 5-4 gives another perspective on the events that take place in an I/O operation using addressed port I/O.

The port-enable signal can be used to latch the data on the bus into the active port. One should remember that all 8 bits of an I/O address need not be used.

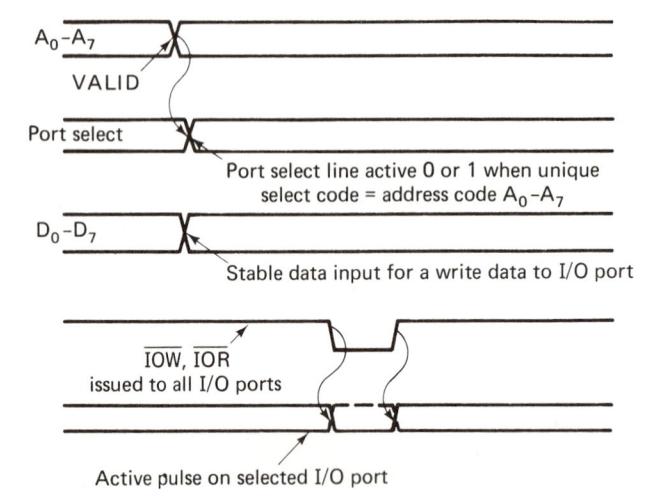

Figure 5-4 Timing diagram showing electrical events for an I/O read or I/O write operation

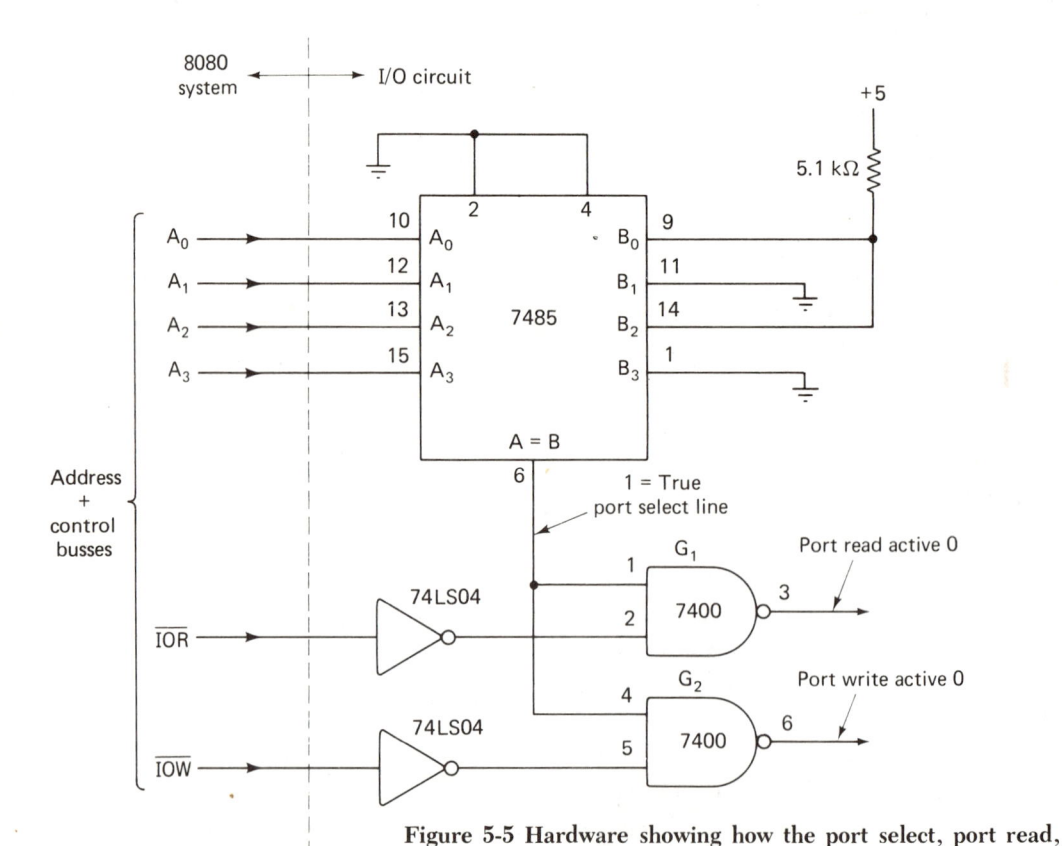

Figure 5-5 Hardware showing how the port select, port read, and port write signals can be generated using standard hardware

146

Sec. 5-1   Addressed Port I/O   147

If we have 14 unique ports to be accessed for I/O we need use only 4 of the 8 possible address bits. An example of how addressed port I/O can be implemented with hardware is shown in Figure 5-5.

In Figure 5-5 the 7485 is a 4-bit *magnitude comparator*. The data sheet for the 7485 is given in Appendix A. When the I/O address code on A_0–A_3 equals the hardwired *port select code*, the output of the 7485 pin 6 equals logical 1. This signal enables the NAND gates G_1 and G_2. When the $\overline{IOW}$ or $\overline{IOR}$ signal is generated by the system, an active-low signal unique to the selected I/O port is generated at the output of the NAND gate G_1 or G_2. Later we will discuss how these unique signals are used to latch data into the port or transfer data from the port to the data bus. For now, it is enough to know that this happens and that both actions are accomplished via the data bus (D_0–D_7).

Shown in Figure 5-6 are switches that will fix the select code of the I/O port. These *dip switches* fit into a 14- or 16-pin DIP socket made for an IC. Using this type of switch allows the port select code to be changed conveniently. This approach is used often in industry where one general I/O circuit is used in several different systems. Each system may wish to treat the I/O circuit as a different port. The DIP switch allows this to be implemented.

A question that may arise at this point is, how are signals for the I/O address

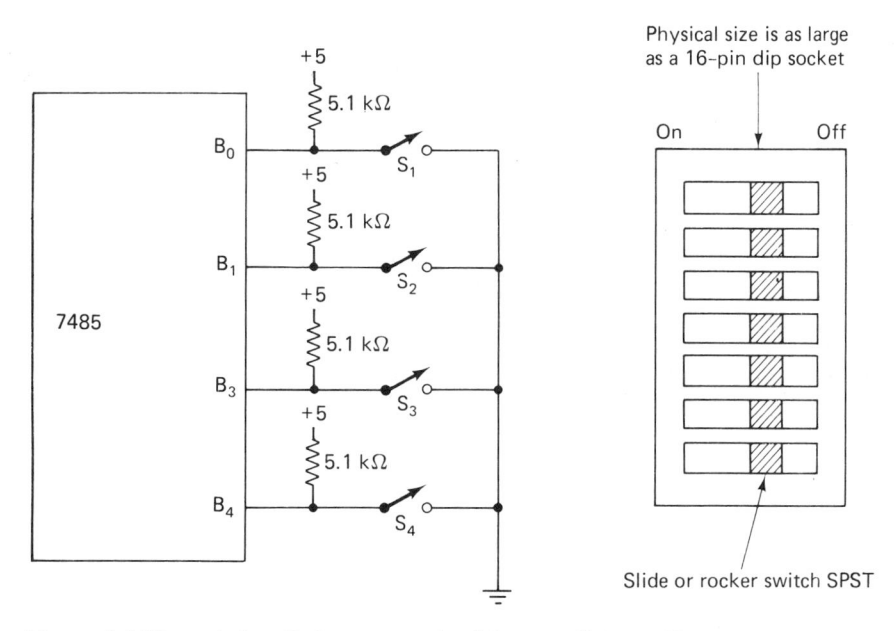

Figure 5-6 The switches S_1-S_4 are contained in a small 14 or 16 pin DIP package. These switches are SPST rocker or slide switches. The select code can be changed quite easily using this switch technique.

lines, data lines, and control bus signals generated at the correct instant in time? The answer is simply that the 8080 internal timing circuits generate these signals in the correct order. The 8080 does not generate the strobe pulse, but it does generate all the signals required to allow external circuits to generate the strobe pulses. This was covered in Chapter 4.

The fact that the 8080 generates all of these signals is a very nice feature. The hardware discussed in Chapter 4 along with the 8080, decodes instructions from the memory and from the associated output signals. If the instruction indicates that an I/O operation is to take place, the 8080 sends out the required signals to the address, data, and control lines at the correct instant in time. We will discuss more about timing in Chapter 6 where the 8080 instruction set is presented. For now, let us assume that the proper signals are generated for the system to use.

The simple 4-bit decode circuit shown in Figure 5-5 may be expanded to decode all eight bits or any subset of the eight bits by the addition of another 7485 4-bit magnitude comparator. Figure 5-7 shows how to expand the 4-bit select code to 8-bits using hardware. Another method of decoding ports is by

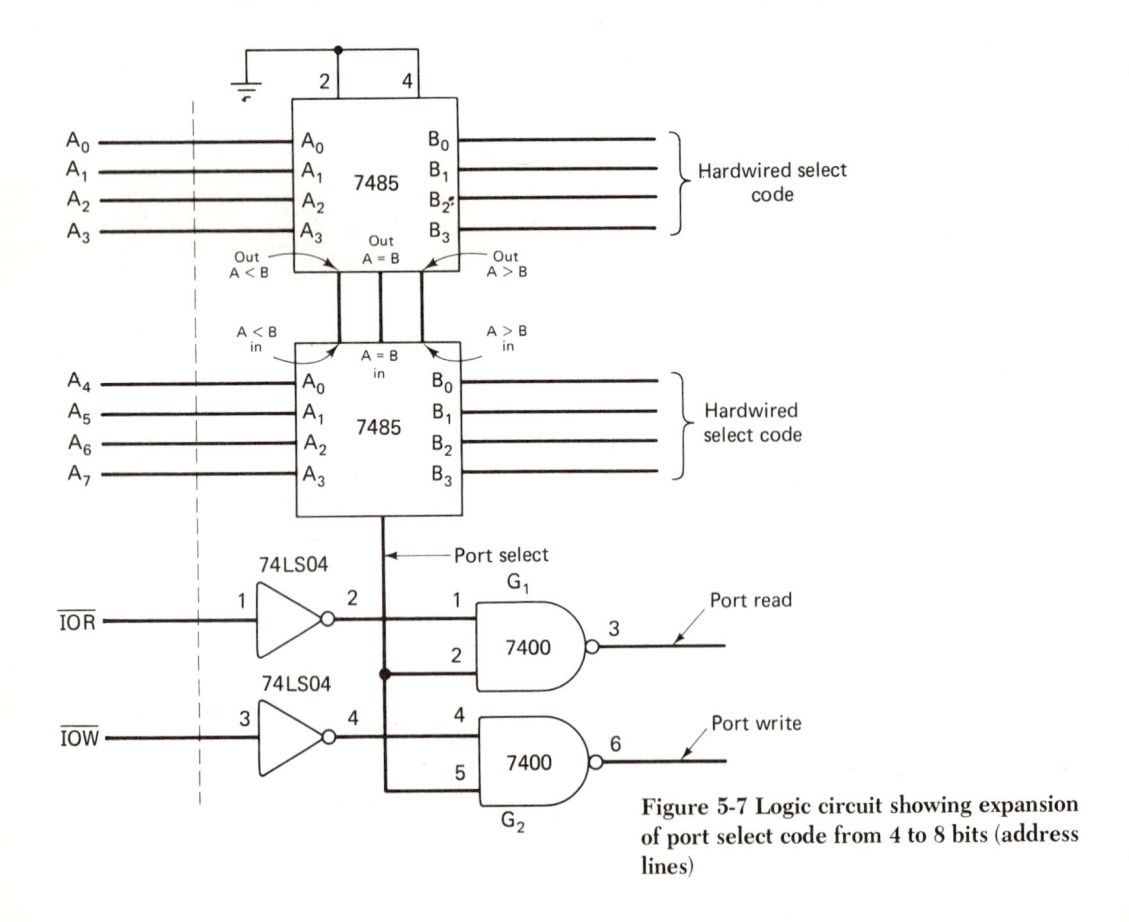

Figure 5-7 Logic circuit showing expansion of port select code from 4 to 8 bits (address lines)

Sec. 5-2 *Device/Port I/O Architecture* 149

using a 7442, 1-of-10 decoder. Only 100 select codes out of a possible 256 can be used. However, this may not be too drastic a limitation for some applications. The hardware for this type of decoder is shown in Figure 5-8.

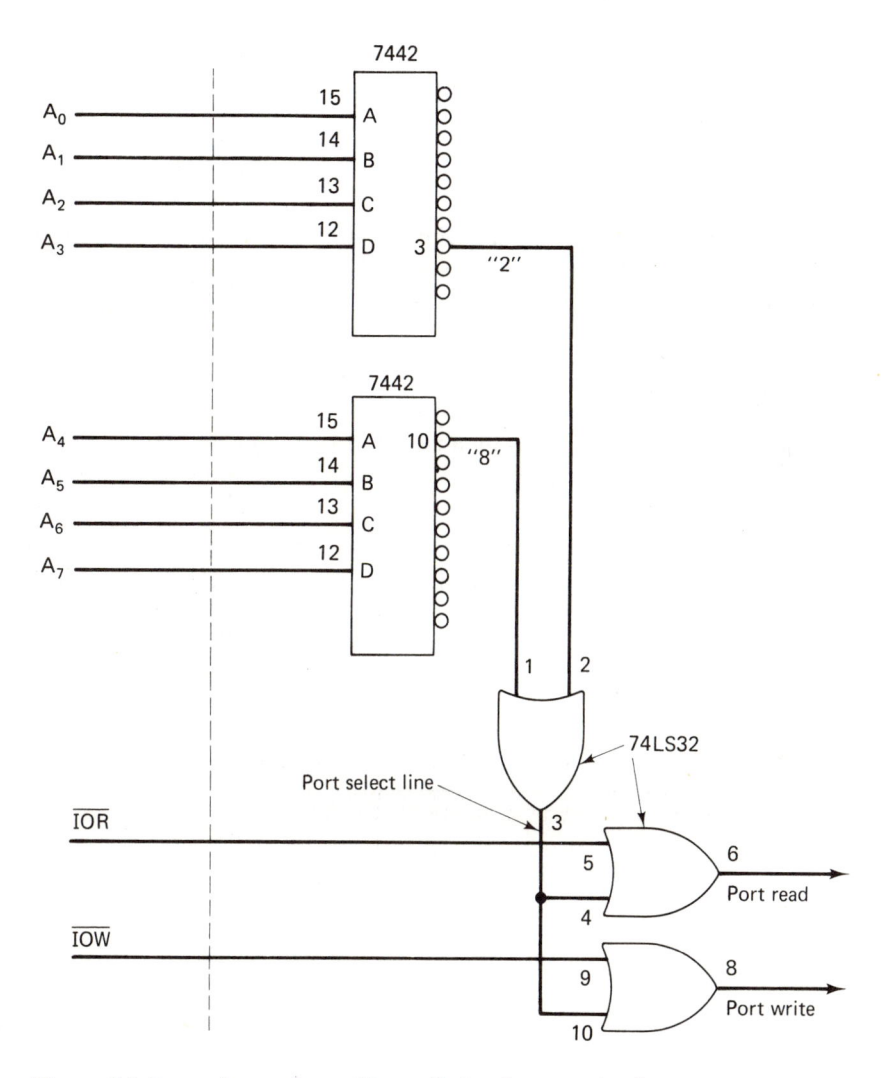

Figure 5-8 Port select code = $82_{(16)}$, all signals are active low. This scheme uses the 7442 as the decoder.

5-2 Device/Port I/O Architecture

A second type of I/O architecture is called device/port I/O. Device/port I/O is used when a single device (I/O circuit) has multiple ports to be accessed. An example of a device/port device could be a *digital voltmeter* (DVM). The input to a digital voltmeter is an *analog voltage* such as DC or AC. The output is a digital word of any number of bits. Let us say that the output of a certain digital voltmeter has a digital word output of 12 bits. This is shown in Figure 5-9.

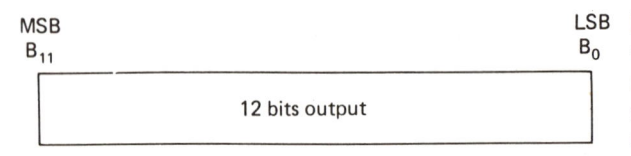

Figure 5-9 Output of this digital voltmeter requires 12 bits. The number of bits is a function of voltage resolution and output number format: i.e., binary, BCD, gray code, and so on.

To read the 12 bits of the digital voltmeter we need to transfer data to the 8080 in two 8-bit words, because the data bus can support only 8 bits of digital information at a single transfer. We will assign 8 of the 12 bits to one port and the 4 remaining bits to another port. The entire DVM is one *device* in the I/O architecture. The two 8-bit words to the device are to the ports to be accessed. A block diagram of this is shown in Figure 5-10.

The I/O address bus is divided into two groups of bits; one group is called port select, and the other is called device select. For our application we will assign bit A_0 to be the port group. The address bits A_1–A_7 will serve the device group. The division of the address lines into groups is based on the number of ports for any device. If we have five unique ports at a device address then we would need three address bits in the port group. These address bits

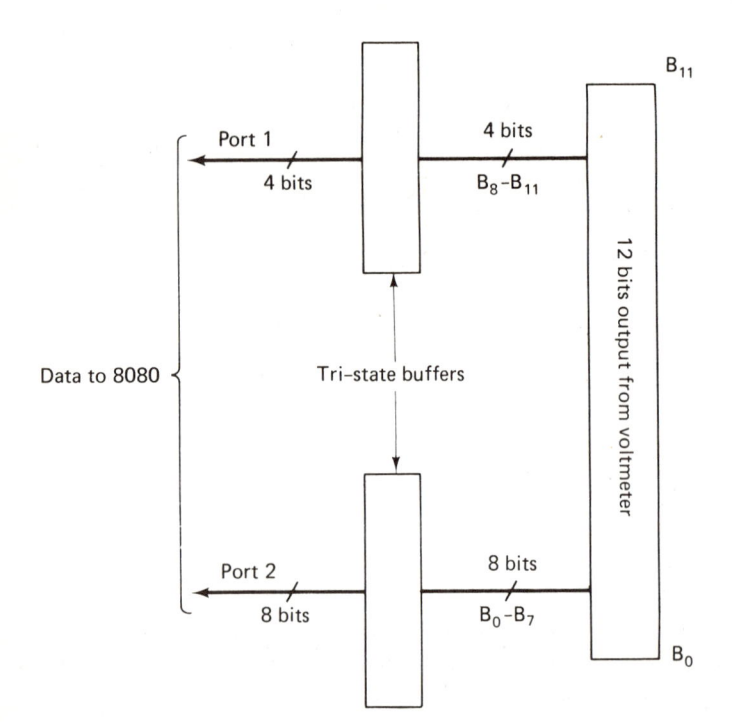

Figure 5-10 Division of the 12 output bits of data from the digital voltmeter into two separate I/O ports

Sec. 5-2 Device/Port I/O Architecture

generate unique port codes. The two bits left over we would assign to the device group. Our device port assignment is shown in Figure 5-11.

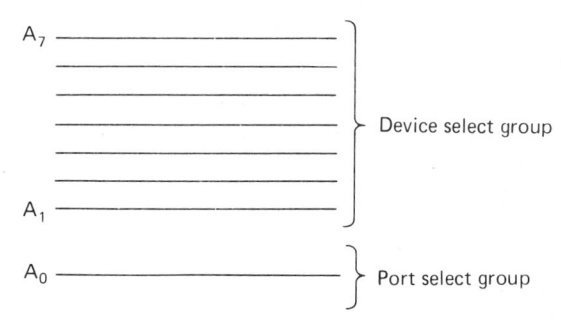

Figure 5-11 Division of the address lines into a device select group and a port select group. This is for device/port I/O architecture.

A hardware realization of this type of I/O architecture is shown in Figure 5-12. In this figure we use the 7485 *digital comparator* as the device select, and discrete logic (single function) to decode the unique ports of the device.

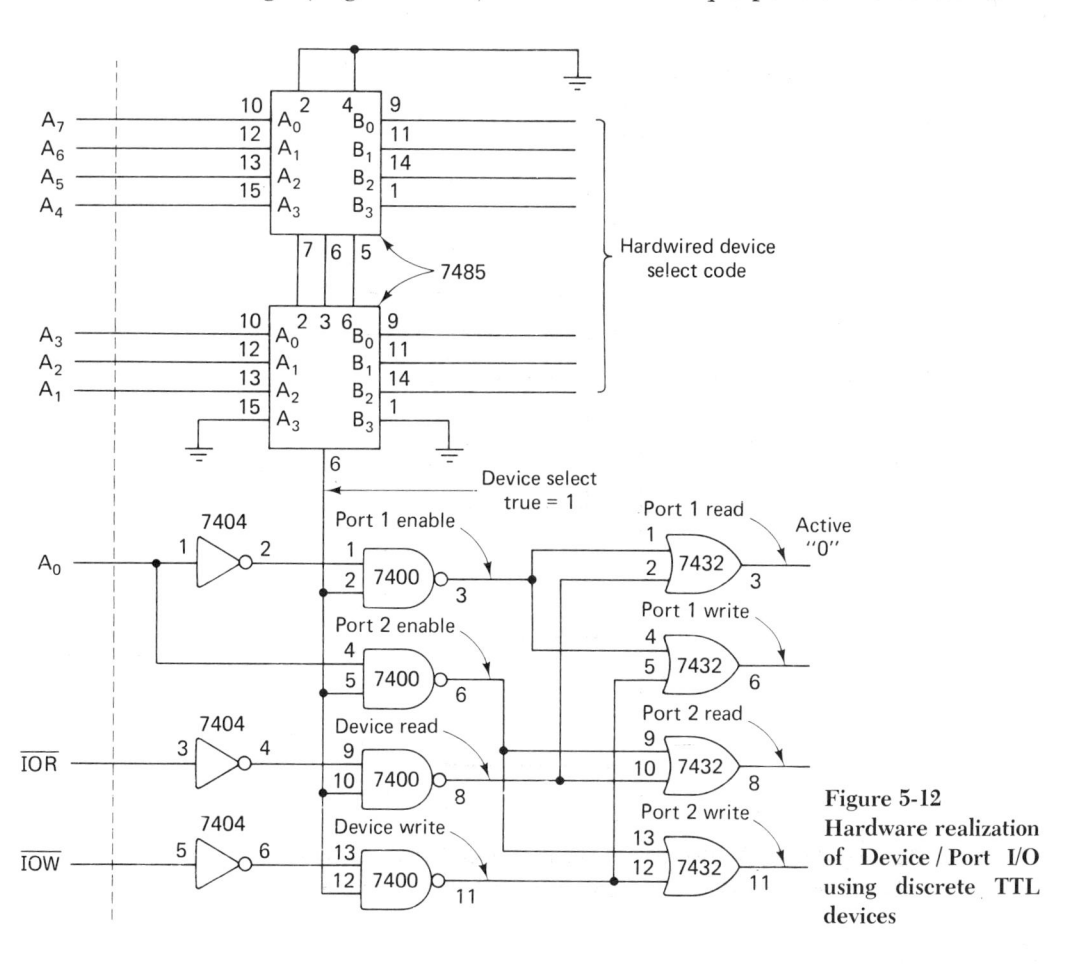

Figure 5-12 Hardware realization of Device / Port I/O using discrete TTL devices

5-3 Linear Select I/O Architecture

A third type of I/O architecture is called *linear select*. Linear select I/O is shown in block diagram form in Figure 5-13. Each line of the I/O address is used as a port select. Of course, this will limit the number of I/O ports to 8. In a small system where a few (less than 8) I/O ports are used, this type of I/O is the easiest to use. This type of I/O is the most direct to realize with hardware. A hardware realization of this type of I/O is shown in Figure 5-14.

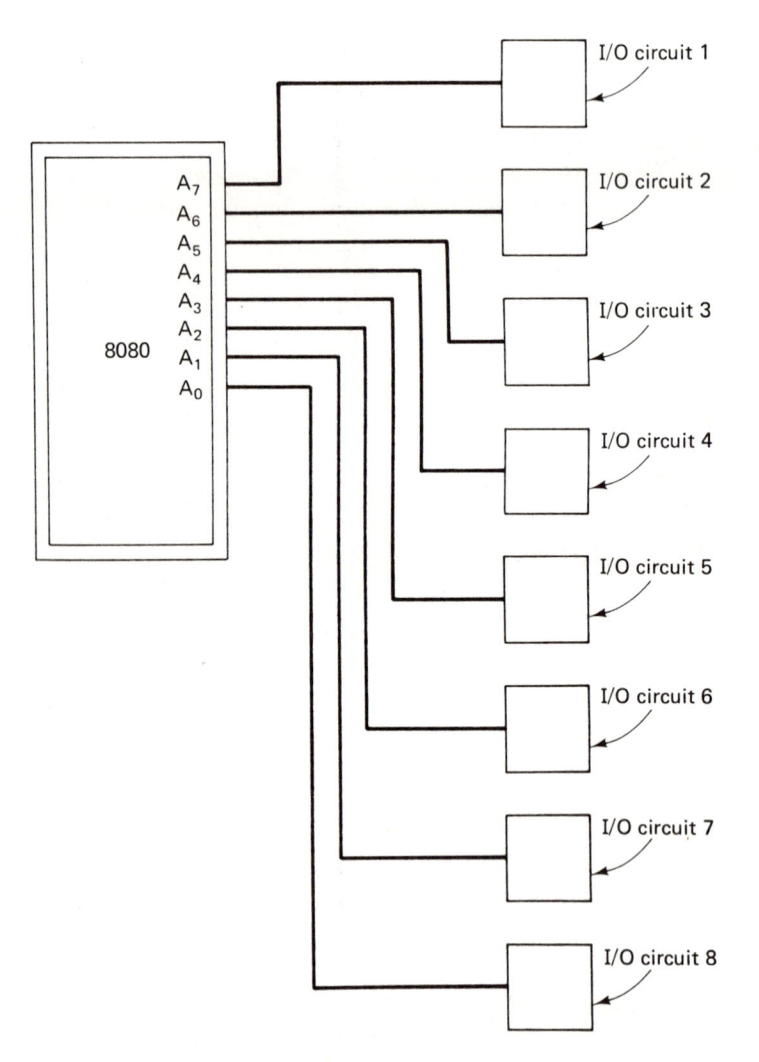

Figure 5-13 Block diagram of linear select I/O architecture. Notice that one address line goes to each I/O circuit or port.

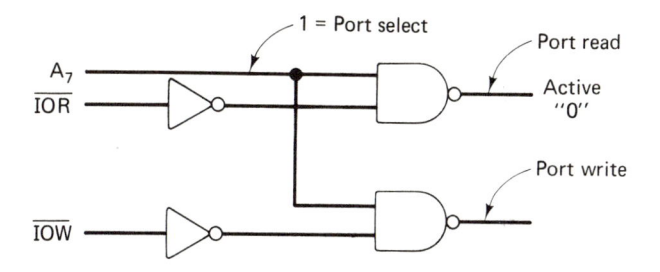

Figure 5-14 Hardware realization of linear selected I/O architecture for a single I/O port

5-4 Memory-Mapped I/O Architecture

A fourth type of I/O architecture is called *memory-mapped I/O*. To understand how this memory mapped architecture works we first review how the 8080 accesses memory. In Chapter 4 we showed the control signals required to read and write from memory. These were called $\overline{\text{MEMR}}$ and $\overline{\text{MEMW}}$. These signals are generated from the status information and selected signals from the 8080, and are present only during a memory operation. The address lines A_0–A_{15} for the memory location to be accessed are generated and controlled by the 8080.

However, with memory mapped I/O we use only A_0–A_{14} (as an example) as address lines input to memory. The 16th address bit, A_{15}, is used to signal the system that the operation is I/O and not memory. The similarity between I/O operations and memory operations was discussed in Chapter 4. The 8080 instruction for memory access and memory-mapped I/O are the same. The only difference is that the memory address determines if the operation is memory or I/O. When, for example, bit 16 is logical 1 the system will perform I/O; but when the bit is logical 0 the system performs memory operations.

Figure 5-15 shows the hardware realization of memory-mapped I/O. Notice how the $\overline{\text{IOR}}$ and $\overline{\text{IOW}}$ signals are generated now. We no longer use the $\overline{\text{IOR}}$ and $\overline{\text{IOW}}$ signals that were generated for use with the other I/O architectures. Note, too, that the INPUT and OUTPUT instructions are no longer used. Instead, all I/O operations are the same as memory instructions. The 8080 has quite a powerful instruction set related to the memory operations. With this architecture all of these memory instructions can be used for I/O. This instruction set is discussed in detail in Chapter 6. Memory-mapped I/O architecture is used in applications where a powerful I/O instruction set is needed, because it makes the programming of the system easier.

However, we do not get this added system performance for free; we have to limit the size of memory. We have reduced the available memory from 64K (16

153

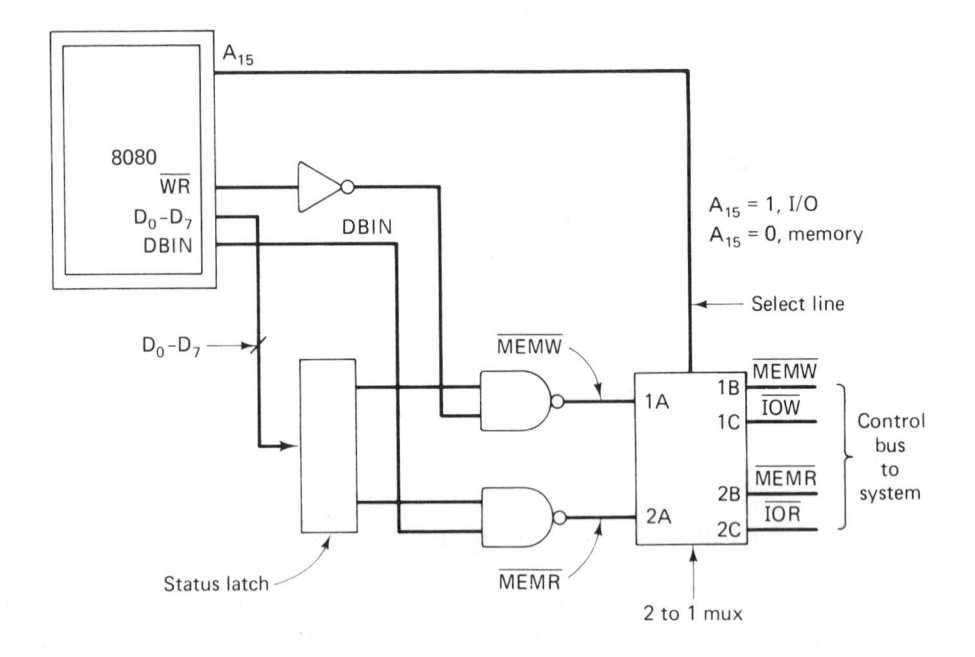

Figure 5-15 Hardware that can be used to implement memory mapped I/O architecture. Notice that the select line (A_{15}) will determine if the I/O signals are directed for memory or for I/O ports.

address lines) to 32K (15 address lines.) This loss is of little consequence in a small system, but it is of major importance in a large system where memory size is critical.

5-5 Communication between the 8080 and Various I/O Architectures

We have shown the four major types of I/O architecture used in microprocessor systems. We now discuss communication between these architectures. Only the addressed port architecture will be discussed in detail. If one is familiar with this operation, then relating this discussion to the other three architectures is an easy task.

The type of hardware used in I/O communications is truly a function of the task to be performed. What will be shown here are different ways of controlling the hardware that receives various types of inputs and returns different types of outputs. If the hardware can function within the following guidelines, then what the hardware actually does will not hamper reliable communication between the 8080 and the peripherals.

Sec. 5-5 *Communication between the 8080 and Various I/O Architectures*   **155**

The first question is, what type of hardware do we want to control? Let's take an example. As a part of our system we want to establish a power supply voltage that can be programmed to different voltage levels. To set this voltage we will be setting bits of a digital to analog converter (DAC). This is the simplest type of an I/O transfer. Data will flow directly from the 8080 to the I/O port. A block diagram of this system is shown in Figure 5-16.

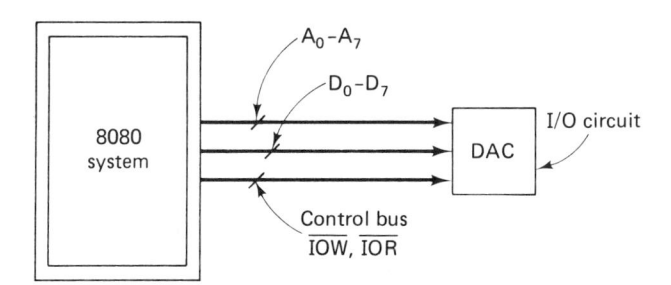

Figure 5-16 Block diagram showing data flow for the system to control the programmable power supply. Note that the I/O address, the data from the 8080, and the control bus all input to the I/O circuit.

Notice that we transfer the data to storage latches located on the I/O circuit. We see from the figure that this particular power supply requires 16 bits of information to be set to a particular voltage value. The data is to be transmitted via the data bus (D_0–D_7) in two consecutive data bytes. The destination for each byte of data is a different I/O port.

The address codes for the I/O ports are $5_{(16)}$ and $9_{(16)}$. The (16) means that this number is in hexadecimal; and it is also an indication of how many I/O address lines are used to select the I/O port. This example uses 4 address lines. If the I/O address given is $05_{(16)}$ and $09_{(16)}$ then we assume that 2 hexadecimal digits are needed. This requires 8 address lines. Our example uses only the 4 address lines A_0–A_3. The sequence of events for the 2 bytes of I/O data transfer is:

1. Address lines A_0–A_3 = $5_{(16)}$
2. Data lines D_0–D_7 = correct data to transfer for port 5
3. Write signal ($\overline{\text{IOW}}$) is generated
4. I/O port 5 enable signal becomes active (1 or 0)
5. Data D_0–D_7 is latched into the I/O circuit
   FIRST BYTE OF DATA TRANSFER IS COMPLETE
6. Address lines A_0–A_3 = $9_{(16)}$
7. Data lines D_0–D_7 = correct data to transfer for port 9
8. I/O port 9 enable signal becomes active (1 or 0)
9. Data D_0–D_7 is latched via port 9 enable signal into storage latches on the I/O circuit
   SECOND BYTE OF DATA TRANSFER IS COMPLETE

In steps 4 and 8, note that the port enable signal becomes active 1 or 0. Whether it becomes 1 or 0 depends on what type of signal is needed in the I/O circuit. This signal could vary from circuit to circuit. The actual hardware that performs this I/O transfer is shown in Figure 5-17. Remember that the data sheet for any schematic shown in this book is in Appendix A.

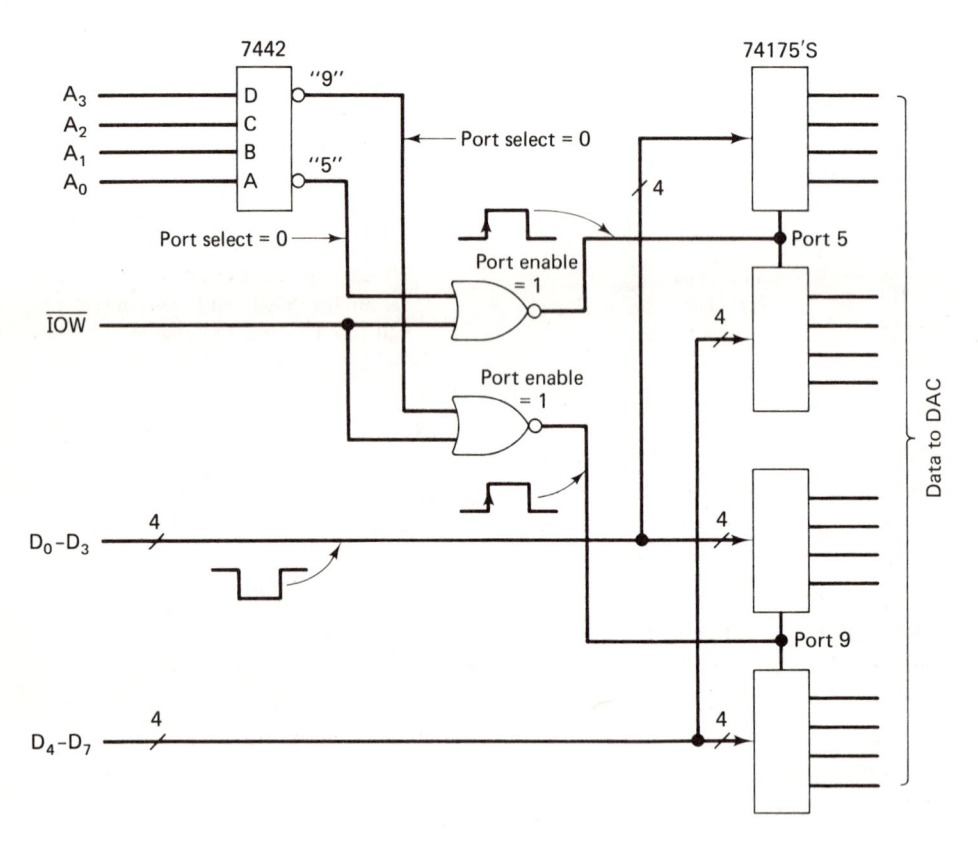

Figure 5-17 Hardware used to implement the I/O circuit for writing data to port 5 and port 9

The 8080 has no physical means of determining if the transfer just described was successful. The 8080 puts data on the data lines and generates the correct I/O address and I/O signals. Once the CPU has done this, it has finished its part of the I/O transfer. It is now up to the receiving hardware to accept this data in the correct way. Although this type of I/O transfer is simple, do not think it an unsatisfactory method; it is not. When designed properly, this transfer is both reliable and electrically fast. We point out that the 8080 cannot determine if the transfer is successful so that beginners in microprocessor circuits understand the data flow and limitations that are characteristic of each type of I/O transfer.

Sec. 5-5 *Communication between the 8080 and Various I/O Architectures* **157**

The next I/O transfer we will discuss is how the 8080 receives data from an I/O circuit. For this operation we will transfer only one byte of data from the I/O circuit to the 8080. Later in this text we will discuss how more than one byte may be transferred. The schematic diagram for 1-byte I/O transfer is shown in Figure 5-18. Notice that this looks very similar to Figure 5-17, for an output

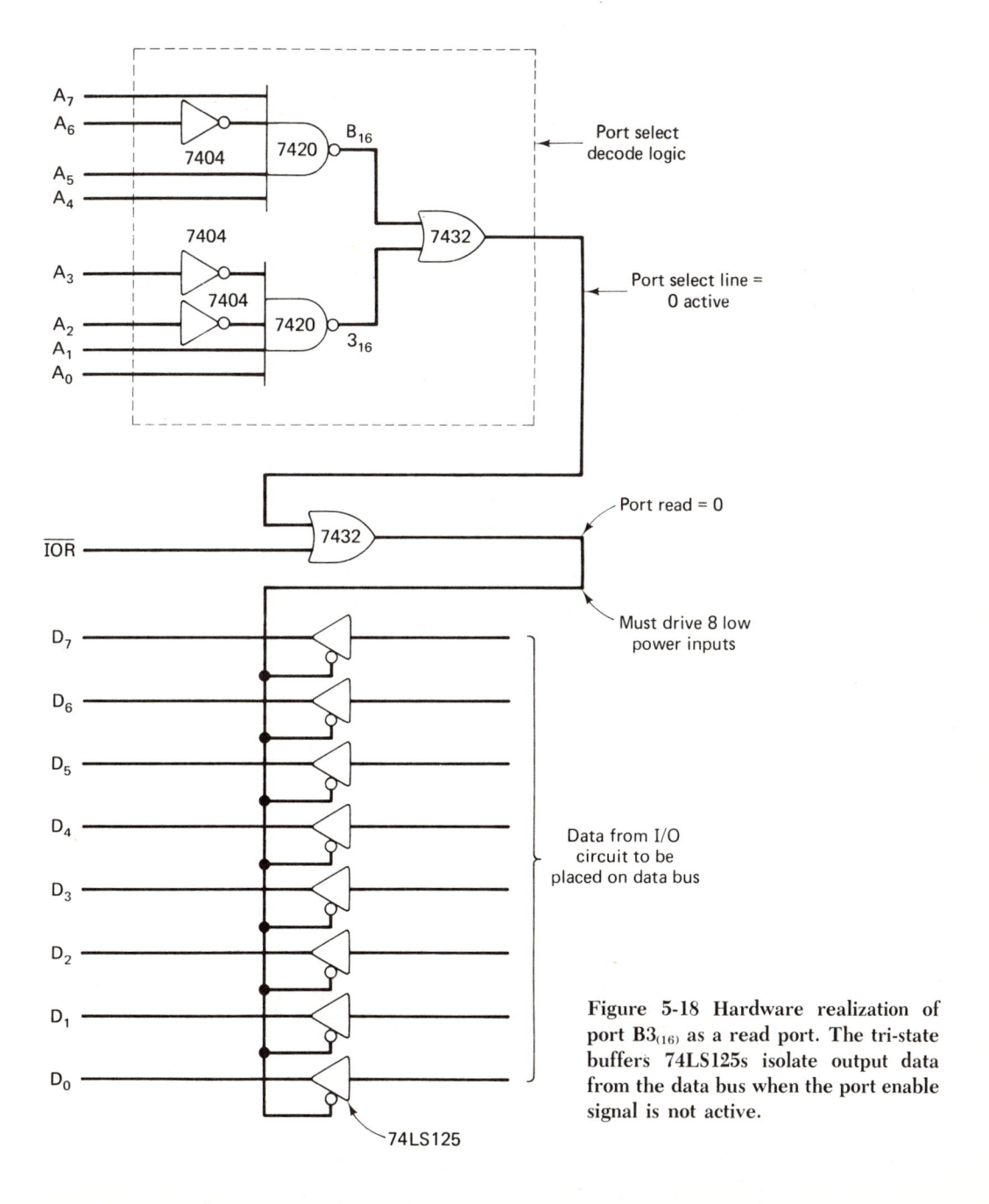

Figure 5-18 Hardware realization of port $B3_{(16)}$ as a read port. The tri-state buffers 74LS125s isolate output data from the data bus when the port enable signal is not active.

transfer; however, the tri-state output buffers have been added. These buffers are needed to isolate the output of the I/O circuit from the data bus D_0–D_7 when the I/O circuit has not yet been selected.

The address code for the I/O port is $B3_{(16)}$. We will have eight address lines to decode. This type of I/O transfer can be used in systems where the I/O circuit sends eight bits to the processor. For example, suppose one of the eight bits contains the status of a temperature transducer in a hot water system. When the temperature reaches a certain level, the output of the transducer goes to logical 1. This single status bit may be read and interpreted by the 8080 at any time; that is, the 8080 can monitor or check the I/O circuit at any convenient time. The I/O circuit is *slaved* to the 8080, which means that the I/O circuit is passive; it cannot initiate a data transfer but must wait for the 8080 to request it. This is shown in Figure 5-19.

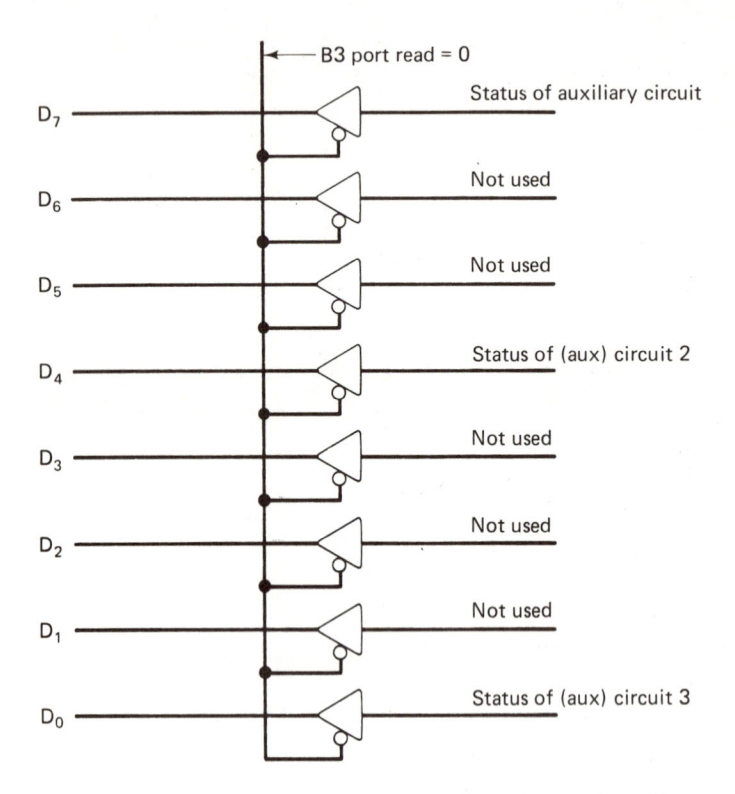

Figure 5-19 Schematic diagram showing how certain bits of a data byte can be used for monitoring status of auxiliary I/O circuits. This data byte can be input to the 8080, and decisions can be made on the status.

By addressing port B3$_{(16)}$ and checking the data, the 8080 can determine if the water temperature has reached the critical value or not. If it has, the 8080 may be instructed to perform certain operations. If not, then the 8080 can ignore the temperature signal and continue with whatever task it was doing before the data water temperature signal was input. This is a simple example, but it demonstrates how and under what conditions one can use this type of I/O port. The sequence of events for this type of transfer are:

1. Address lines A_0–A_7 = B3$_{(16)}$
2. Data lines D_0–D_7 are prepared to accept data from an I/O circuit
3. Read signal $\overline{IOR}$ is generated
4. I/O port-enable signal becomes active 1 or 0
5. Tri-state buffers are enabled for port B3$_{(16)}$
6. The data from port B3 is placed on the data bus lines D_0–D_7
7. Data is latched into the 8080
I/O TRANSFER IS COMPLETE

In step 2, where data lines D_0–D_7 are prepared to accept data, we recall that the data lines have bidirectional buffers in series with them. This was discussed in Chapter 4.

In this type of input I/O transfer the 8080 has no means of determining if the transfer was successful. The external I/O circuit must ensure that all timing specifications for I/O transfers are met. In Chapter 6 we will discuss the timing as it relates to different instructions that are being executed. There, too, all timing considerations and restrictions will be considered in detail. In this discussion we do not closely examine the restrictions because we are concerned with the basic mechanics of I/O transfers. A technician who is familiar with these basic mechanics will be in a knowledgable position to decide when timing parameters are discussed whether the restrictions would affect a particular I/O design.

The next I/O transfer we will discuss is outputting data to and inputting data from the same I/O port. Up to this point we have read and written to different I/O ports. The type of I/O transfer discussed now is really a combination of the two types of I/O transfers already covered. We can use the same port I/O address to write data and read data from one I/O circuit. We are able to do this because the 8080 system cannot input and output data at the same instant. When we are outputting data the 8080 generates the $\overline{IOW}$ signal. When we are inputting data the 8080 generates the $\overline{IOR}$ signal. We will assume that the output data will be latched into storage latches (register) on the I/O circuit. The input data will be static at the addressed I/O port. A block diagram for this type of I/O circuit is shown in Figure 5-20. The hardware realization of this block diagram is given in Figure 5-21.

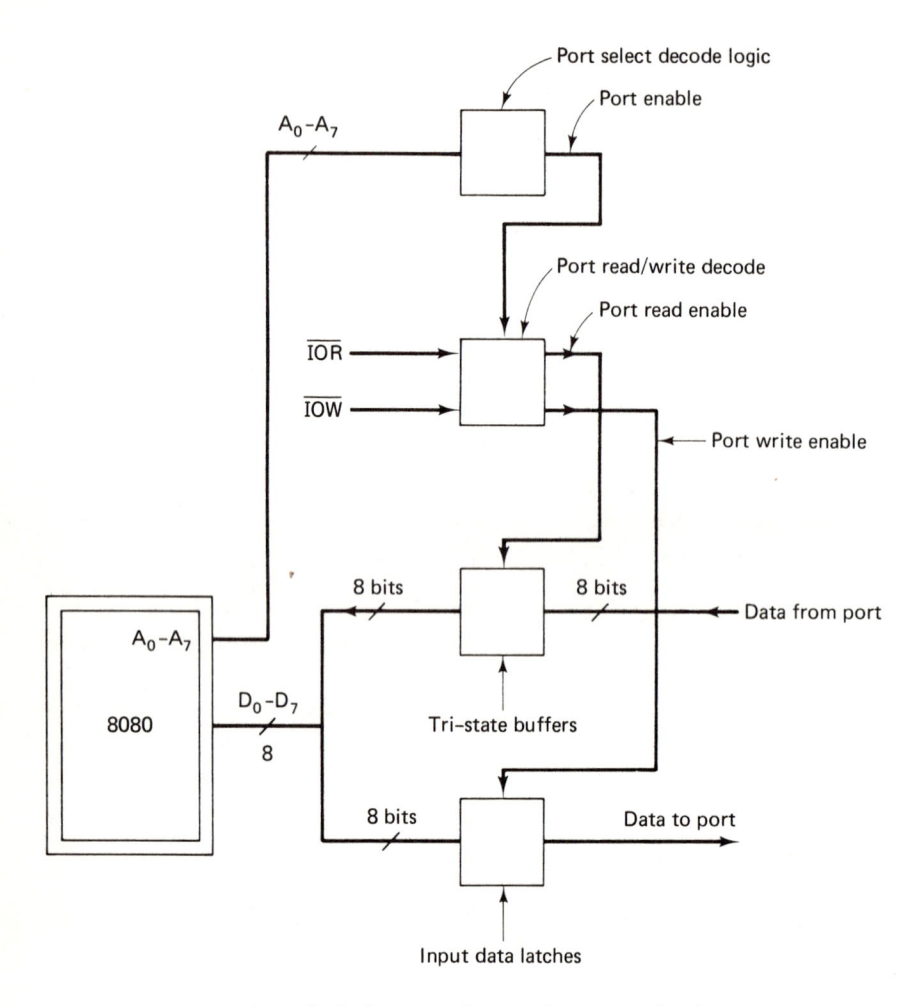

Figure 5-20 Block diagram showing how a single I/O port may be used for both reading and writing

Another type of I/O transfer includes a handshake. This *handshake* technique allows two hardware circuits to communicate reliably with each other. An example of the hardware would be a line printer with a paper tape reader or punch, or with a cassette tape reader. These devices are generally slower at handling data than microprocessors or CPU's. Suppose that a certain line printer accepts one byte of data and several milliseconds later prints out that data in the form of a letter or a number. Compared to a microprocessor, this is a great length of time, since it can execute hundreds of instructions while the line printer is printing out a single letter or number. Other methods of handshaking, or *interfacing*, are discussed in Chapter 9.

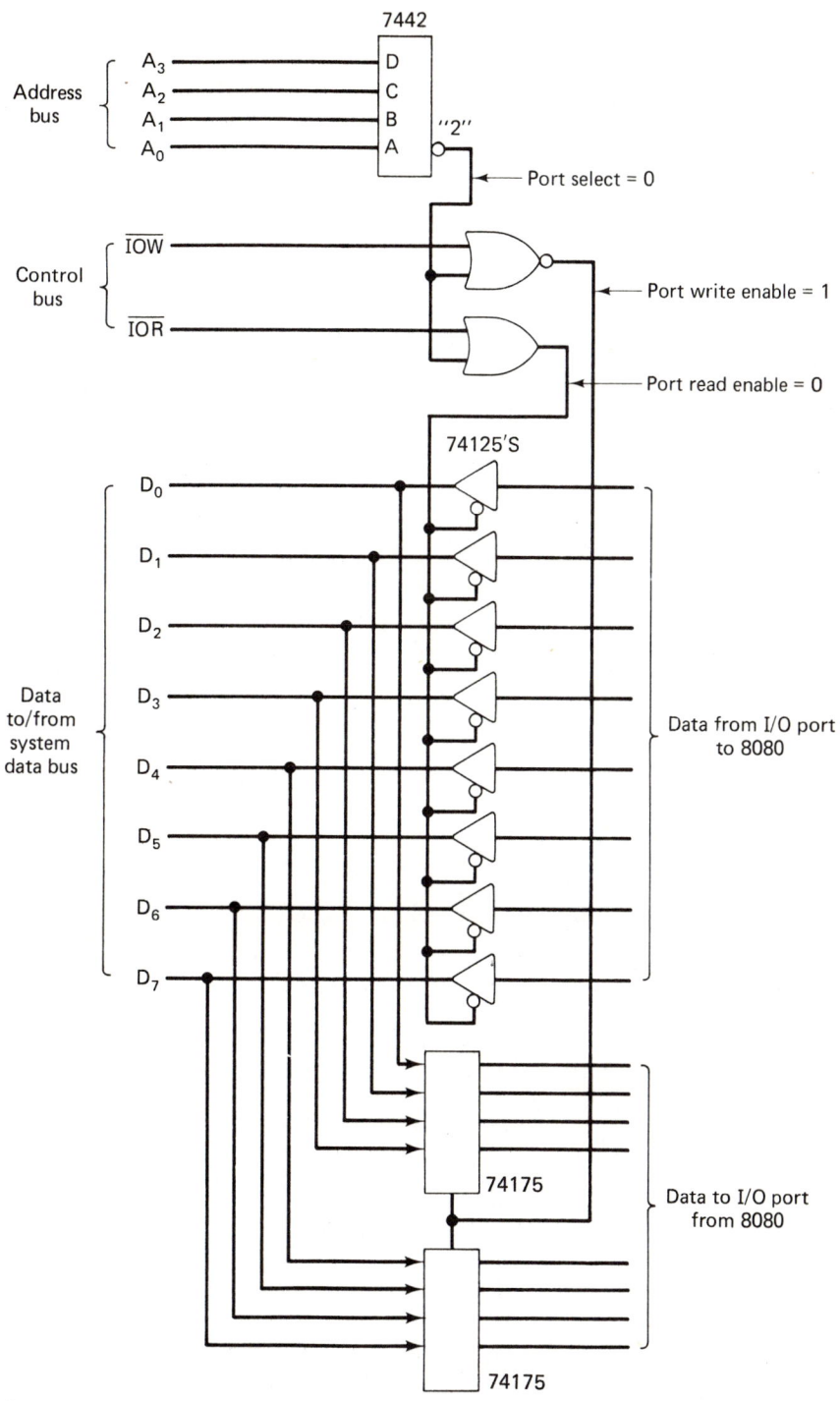

Figure 5-21 Hardware realization for reading and writing from the same I/O port select code ($2_{(16)}$)

161

Many times in microprocessor systems we wish to print a message or interface with a device that has a slower data handling than microprocessor. The slower device must have a way of indicating to the microprocessor when one state is completed and another data byte may be sent. The microprocessor sends data and waits for the I/O device to respond with the handshake "ready signal" before sending another data byte to the device. There are several methods for implementing a handshake with hardware. The technique we show here is easy to understand, highly reliable, and easy to realize with hardware.

Our example will be an I/O device that will receive data at a slower rate than the 8080 can transmit it. Two I/O ports in the device will be used: One port for data sent to the I/O device from the microprocessor, the other for the status information of the I/O circuit. The status information will indicate whether the I/O circuit is ready to accept another byte of data from the microprocessor. This I/O port is, in effect, the handshake line. The flowchart for I/O transfer is shown in Figure 5-22.

Figure 5-22 shows that after data has been sent to the I/O device, the 8080 continues to read the status port of the I/O device until the status signal indicates "yes" the I/O device is ready to continue.

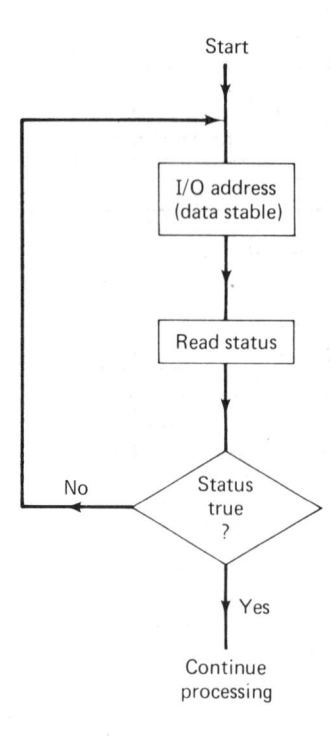

Figure 5-22 Flowchart showing an I/O transfer and waiting for status to indicate that the transfer is complete

Sec. 5-5   *Communication between the 8080 and Various I/O Architectures*   163

Several different problems can occur using this type of I/O transfer. The first problem follows. Suppose the I/O device becomes inoperative due to some circuit malfunction? If this happens, the status information for the I/O circuit may never indicate that the I/O circuit is ready to accept another data byte. The 8080 will be in a continuous loop. One way to prevent this is to have the 8080 read the status only a fixed number of times before it stops interrogating. Let us say the status is read unsuccessfully 100 times in succession. If the status does not come "true," or valid, indicating that the I/O circuit is now ready for another data byte, it may be assumed that the status may never become true. We need a way for the system to detect this.

When this is detected, the system will stop trying to input data to the device and print out, or indicate in some way, that the I/O circuit is malfunctioning. This is shown in a flowchart of Figure 5-23. This type of checking is totally

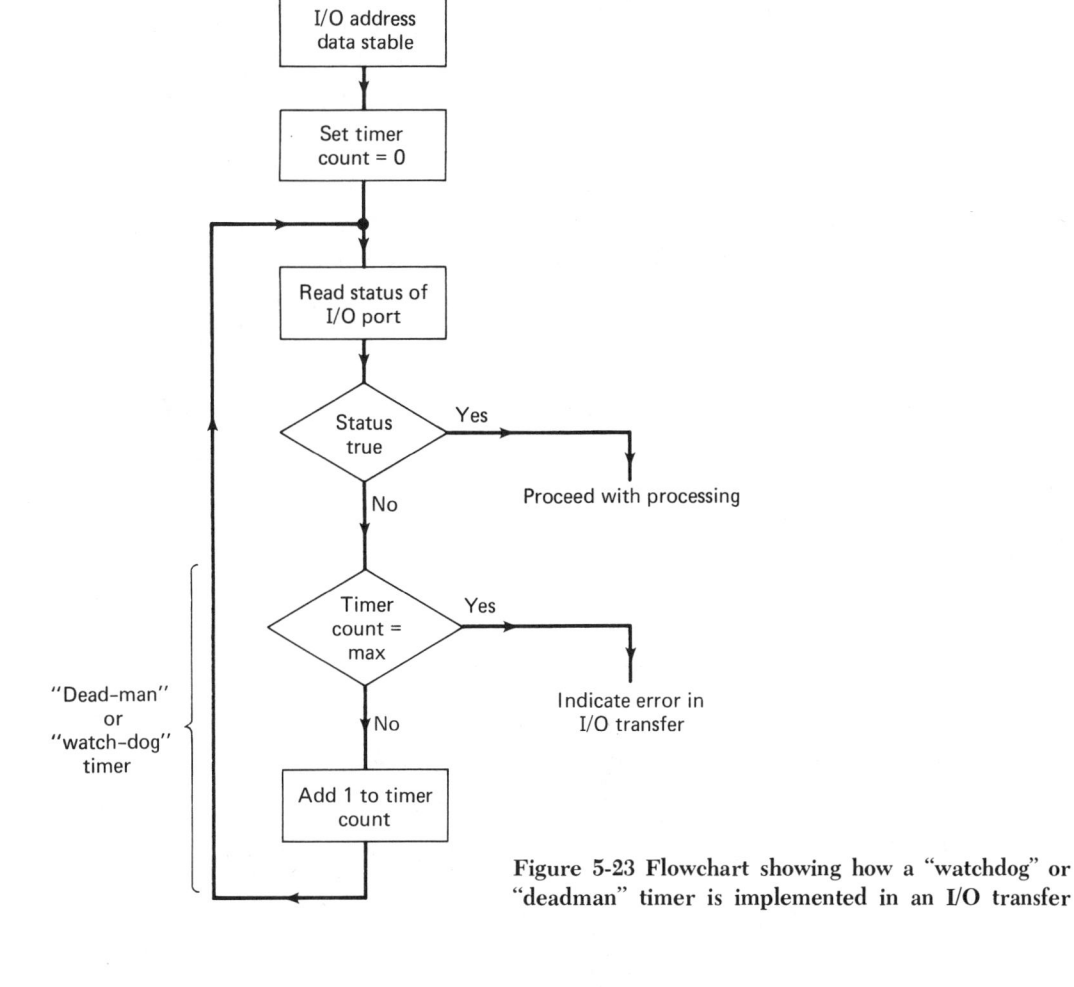

Figure 5-23 Flowchart showing how a "watchdog" or "deadman" timer is implemented in an I/O transfer

independent of the I/O structure. That is, the same I/O hardware can be used; only the way it is controlled is changed. We simply change the 8080 instructions to be executed. This monitoring of the time required for status information to become valid or true is referred to in industry as using a "dead-man timer" or "watch-dog timer."

Another problem with this type of monitoring is that the microprocessor spends most of the processing time in a non-processing loop. This is the loop where the microprocessor is reading the status port and checking whether the I/O circuit is ready to accept another data byte. Since the CPU could do many processing steps during this waiting time we should take advantage of its capability, but only if it is necessary in the application. In many I/O controlling techniques the CPU could check status and, if it is not true, go on to execute other processing steps. The CPU can come back at regular intervals to check the status port. A better method of monitoring slaved devices is by a technique called an *interrupt*, which is discussed in Chapter 9. Again, as with the "watch-dog timer," the I/O hardware is constant. The interrupt technique allows the CPU to be used more efficiently. Of course, in the beginning getting a CPU to work in any fashion requires a major effort. Therefore efficient use is low on our priority list.

In this chapter we have described four different techniques for implementing I/O architectures. These four techniques are (1) *addressed port*, (2) *device/port*, (3) *linear select*, and (4) *memory mapped*. Variations of each technique are possible. Understanding these four major techniques enables one to relate to something familiar when confronted with a variation. When designing I/O architecture, use the one that best fits the needs. For small system applications, any technique that we have discussed will work. Select the one you feel the most comfortable with. A solid understanding of these four techniques and the hardware used to realize them will better enable one to understand the control of these subsystems. Further discussion of control timing will be presented in detail in the next chapter.

Review Questions

1. What is meant by the term I/O?
2. What are the four major types of I/O architecture?
3. How many unique I/O ports can be supported by eight I/O address lines?
4. What are the main control signals for an I/O transfer?
5. Design an input port that has a select code of $03_{(16)}$.
6. Using a 7442 IC, design an output port with a select code of $92_{(16)}$.

Review Questions

7. How many I/O ports can be supported using linear select I/O with eight address lines?

8. Explain some advantages of memory mapped I/O.

9. Design an interface to an external device that has ten bits output and twelve bits input for control. The interface will be to an 8-bit data bus.

10. What is meant by the term "handshake"?

11. Design an I/O port using memory mapped I/O. Use address bit $A_{15} = 0$ to indicate a memory operation.

6

PROGRAMMING THE 8080

Up to this point we have been concerned mainly with the external hardware of the 8080 based system. We have stated that the hardware will work, assuming certain control signals from the 8080 are present. In this chapter we will discuss the program or set of instructions that allow the 8080 to generate these control signals. We will start by presenting programming elements common to many computer languages. We will then discuss the programming architecture of the 8080. This architecture discussion is especially useful because it will help relate the hardware internal to the 8080 to the software programming instructions. In discussing the 8080 instruction set we will not cover each instruction in detail. Instead, specific instructions will be discussed in depth as examples. These discussions are calculated to provide a broad base with which many instructions may be understood. The program or set of instructions that the CPU performs in order to control the hardware is known as "software." After the functions of the software instructions have been discussed, we will show detailed hardware timing diagrams. These diagrams relate electrical operations in the hardware to the sequence of events we know should happen, based on the instruction input, if the system is to operate properly.

Computer personnel are usually divided into two major categories, namely, "software" and "hardware." Hardware personnel are concerned with the actual ICs, resistors, components, and hardware that make up an electrical and physical system. Software personnel assume the hardware will work in a given way, and they write programs for the system based on these assumptions. Just from considering our system so far, it is quite easy to visualize how this can happen. Once our system is constructed and tested, we know it will work in a certain way. We concentrate our efforts at that point on controlling the system. This control is accomplished with software.

The computer language we will use to program the 8080 will be called 8080 *assembly language*. There are many different assembly languages. Each different model of computer, mini-computer, and microprocessor usually has a unique assembly language associated with it. The 8080 assembly language uses (as do most assembly languages) a set of abbreviations for each possible instruction.

These abbreviations are called mnemonics, pronounced "new-monics." An example of mnemonic that the 8080 uses is an instruction that is described as (Return if Carry is True). This description accurately describes the instruction, but is clumsy to write. The mnemonic for this instruction is (RC). Another example is an instruction that is described as (Move the Contents of the B register into the C register). The mnemonic for this instruction is simply (MOV C,B). Do not be concerned at this point about the meanings of these instructions. The main idea is to understand what a mnemonic is and why it is used.

Associated with each mnemonic is an equivalent set of the electrical 1 s and 0 s the 8080 hardware actually interprets. An example of a mnemonic and its equivalent data byte is shown in Figure 6-1. In this figure, the hexadecimal number shown is the equivalent of actual binary 1 s and 0 s that correspond to the STC mnemonic. When we are writing a program we first write the mnemonics, then we translate the mnemonics into 1 s and 0 s.

From 8080 instruction set:

Instruction name: SET CARRY BIT TO A LOGICAL 1.

Mnemonic: STC

Data byte: D_7 00110111 D_0 = $37_{(16)}$

            Actual binary data   Hexadecimal equivalent

Figure 6-1 Set carry instruction with its equivalent data byte and mnemonics

In computer programming the *list* of mnemonics is called the *source program* or *source code*. The corresponding 1 s and 0 s are called *object code*. It is a very tedious and error-prone task to convert from the source program to the object code. For small programs this task is not too difficult, but for large programs it is a tremendous job. Many computer systems have a program that will produce object code from a source program. Such a computer program is called a *compiler*. Figure 6-2 shows how a compiler program fits into the scheme of writing a computer program.

Source program written
in 8080 assembly language

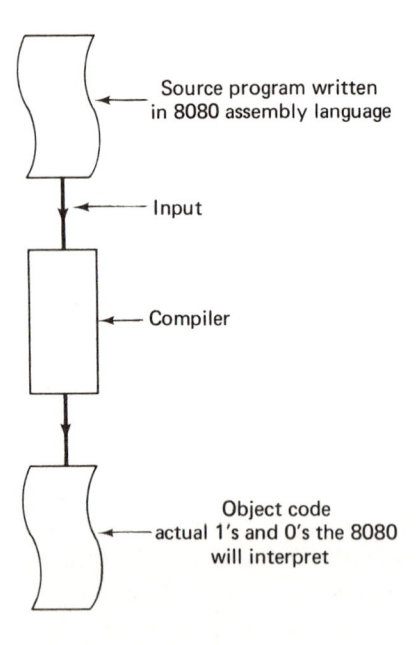

Input

Compiler

Object code
actual 1's and 0's the 8080
will interpret

Figure 6-2 Flowchart of data for converting a source program into object code by use of a compiler

6-1 Definitions

When we write 8080 assembly language programs, we first write a source program in 8080 mnemonics. We then translate the mnemonics into the binary equivalent (object code) by hand. Let us present a few definitions so we can all start on common ground.

Register: The *register* may be thought of as a unique RAM location inside the 8080 chip that is eight bits wide. We can write data into the register and read data out of the register.

Register Pair: This is a combination of two registers in the 8080. There are certain registers that are associated with one another. We can transfer data from both registers to another set of register pairs at the same time. Sixteen bits of data are transferred. To conform to 8080 convention and organization, Figure 6-3 shows the locations of the LSB and MSB in relation to the data bits D_0–D_7.

D_7	D_0
MSB	LSB

Figure 6-3 Data bits of the 8080 showing most significant bit and least significant bit

Sec. 6-1 *Definitions* 169

These definitions are sufficient to allow us to introduce an internal architecture of the 8080 that will enable us to understand the function of the instructions. This architecture is shown in Figure 6-4. In this simple architecture we notice the heavy line connecting the structure. This line may be thought of as an internal data I/O bus. Connected to this bus is an accumulator. The *accumulator* is the register where all bit manipulations of the 8-bit data byte take place. The type of bit manipulation that is possible will be shown as we discuss the instructions. Attached to the accumulator is a block labeled ALU. These initials stand for *Arithmetic Logic Unit*. The ALU, in conjunction with the accumulator, performs the bit manipulations.

Attached to the ALU is another block labeled *Condition Flags*. This block

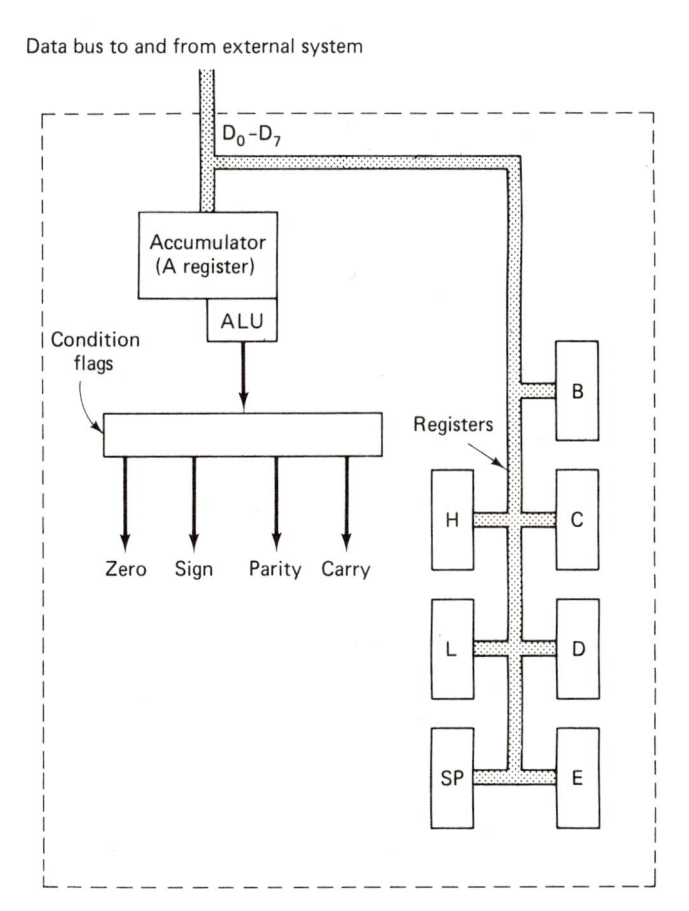

Figure 6-4 Simplified internal programming architecture for the 8080

indicates certain conditions about the data in the accumulator, or about past data in the accumulator at given points in time. The condition flags are called ZERO, SIGN, PARITY, and CARRY. The significance of these condition flags will be explained later in this chapter. The 8080 can perform certain operations based on the logical value of these flags.

Finally, in Figure 6-4 we see blocks attached to the internal bus with letter names. These blocks A, B, C, D, E, H, L, and SP, represent the internal registers of the 8080. Note that these registers are all input and output registers. This means we can transfer data between these registers and the accumulator in any order we choose. If one keeps the simple internal architecture of the 8080 in mind when reviewing the set of instructions, understanding the function or job of the instruction will be a much easier task.

6-2 8080 Instructions

Let us now discuss the 8080 instructions. One should remember that these instructions are simply eight bits of data, residing in memory, that the CPU will interpret, and, based on what these eight bits convey, perform some action. In the 8080 instruction set there are five major types of instructions. These are:

1. Data Transfer Group
2. Arithmetic Group
3. Logical Group
4. I/O Group
5. Branching Group

We will discuss selected instructions from each of these five groups in detail. Once these are covered it will be an easy matter to relate them to other instructions in that group.

We start by discussing the *Data Transfer Group*. This group of instructions moves data between 8080 internal registers and between external memory and internal registers. In discussing the data transfer group of instructions it should be noted that these are either 1-byte, 2-byte, or 3-byte instructions. This means that a single instruction will require one, two, or three consecutive bytes of memory (or addresses) to complete. This concept of 1-, 2-, or 3-byte instructions will become very clear as we proceed in this discussion.

MOV R_1, R_2. This is a 1-byte instruction meaning move the contents of Register (R_2) into Register (R_1). Register R_2 remains unchanged. Other examples of this instruction are:

Sec. 6-2   8080 Instructions   171

        MOV B,C   C→B
        MOV L,H   H→L
        MOV B,E   E→B

MOV R_1, M. This is a 1-byte instruction meaning *move contents of external memory (M)* (addressed by the H,L registers) *into the internal register* R_1. The information in memory is not changed. In this instruction the address for memory is supplied by registers H and L, where L is address lines A_0–A_7 (lower order) and H is address lines A_8–A_{15} (higher order). To use this instruction we must first set the H,L registers to the value of the address we wish to address in memory. We should not concern ourselves with the details of how the H,L registers are placed on the address lines. We must know only that this happens and make use of this information when programming.

MOV M,R_1. This is a 1-byte instruction and is the opposite of the instruction just discussed. The contents of the Register (R_1) will be stored into external memory at the address location pointed to by H,L. Remember H is the higher order address byte, L is the lower order address byte.

MVI R_1, DATA. This is a 2-byte instruction, and is a *move immediate*. Translated, it means to move the immediately following data into internal register (R_1). In memory this data resides in the byte following the instruction location. For example, suppose the instruction MVI R_1, DATA was at memory location 9A. The data to be moved into Register R_1 would be at memory location 9B. The CPU would interpret the instruction at 9A and then perform a memory read of location 9B to bring that data into the CPU. Again, one should not be concerned with how the CPU does this.

LXI RP, DATA 16 BITS. This is a 3-byte instruction. This instruction is interpreted as *load register pair immediate*. This means that a register pair (H,L), (D,E), (B,C) or (SP) will be loaded with two bytes of data from memory. The RP is the first letter of the pair (H,D,B). The first letter of the register pair also defines the higher order byte. Registers H,D,B are always the higher order bytes for the pairs. Register SP has no designation for higher or lower order bytes. It is a 16-bit register to the user. We will discuss the SP register later in this chapter.

    Data to be loaded into the register pair follows in the next two consecutive bytes of memory after the instruction. The first byte after the instruction is placed into the lower order register of the pair. The second byte is placed into the higher order register of the pair. For example, if the instruction were LXI B,

3A20, data 20 would be loaded into register C, and data 3A would be loaded into register B, where the LXI B portion is the instruction and the 203A is the sixteen bits of data to be loaded. In memory, the data would appear as shown in Figure 6-5. Assume that the instruction was at memory location F3 in memory.

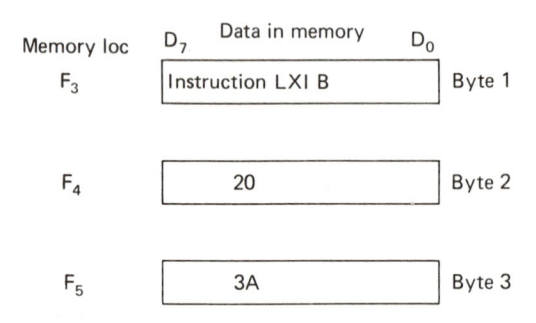

```
Memory loc   D₇  Data in memory   D₀
   F₃        | Instruction LXI B |    Byte 1

   F₄        |        20         |    Byte 2

   F₅        |        3A         |    Byte 3
```

Figure 6-5 Data arrangement in memory for the instruction LXI B,3A20

LDA ADDRESS. This is a 3-byte instruction. This instruction is interpreted to mean *load the accumulator with the data at the memory address location specified*. The point to remember here is that the address data appears as lower address byte, upper address byte. For example, if we wish to load the accumulator with data stored at memory location 00F5, the instruction would appear as LDA F500. Byte 2 of this instruction is carried by the lower order address lines, and byte 3 of this instruction is carried by the higher order address lines.

STA ADDRESS. The last instruction we will discuss in this group is the opposite of the LDA instruction. This is a 3-byte instruction also and by this instruction the contents of the accumulator are stored at the memory address specified. Again, the second byte of the instruction is carried by the lower order address lines.

The next major group of instructions that we will discuss is the *Arithmetic Group*.

ADD R₁. This is a 1-byte instruction to add the content of register R₁ to the content of the accumuator. The result is stored in the accumulator. The addition is done on eight bits, so there may be a possibility of a carry. This can happen if the sum of the two numbers is greater than 255.

ADD M. This is a 1-byte instruction to add the content of the memory location addressed by the H and L registers to the accumulator. The result is placed in the accumulator. The H and L registers must have the correct value prior to execution of this instruction.

Sec. 6-3 Logic Instructions 173

ADI DATA. This is a 2-byte instruction called an *add immediate instruction*. The second byte of this instruction is added to the content of the accumulator.

SUB R₁. This is a 1-byte instruction, to subtract the content of the specified *register* R₁ *from* the content of the *accumulator*. If the execution of this subtraction results in a borrow, then the carry flag will set to logical 1. If there is no borrow, then the carry flag will be a logical 0.

SUB M. This is a 1-byte instruction to subtract the content of memory at the address specified by the contents of the H and L registers from the content of the accumulator. The result is stored in the accumulator.

SUI DATA. This is a 2-byte instruction called a *subtract immediate*. The second byte of this instruction is subtracted from the content of the accumulator. The result is stored in the accumulator.

INR R₁. This is a 1-byte instruction called *increment register*. The value of the data in the register specified is incremented by 1 and placed back in the register.

INX RP. This is a 1-byte instruction called *increment register pair*. The register pair specified is incremented, and the result is replaced in the register pair. For example, if the H,L register pair were equal to OABC before an INX H instruction, it would equal OABD after the instruction.

These are only a few selected instructions from the Arithmetic Group so one can obtain a general idea of how the instructions work. If one can understand the operation of these instructions it will be easier to understand other instructions in this group.

6-3 Logic Instructions

The next group of instructions we will discuss is the *Logical Group*. This group of instructions performs the logical operations such as AND, OR, and Exclusive OR on data in the 8080.

ANA R₁. This is a 1-byte instruction called *AND accumulator with the content of the register specified*. Logical ANDing is done on a bit-by-bit basis. For example, if the accumulator was equal to 01001101, and the specified register was equal to 11000010, then the result of ANDing these two registers would be 01000000. This is shown in Figure 6-6. The AND instruction is often used to set

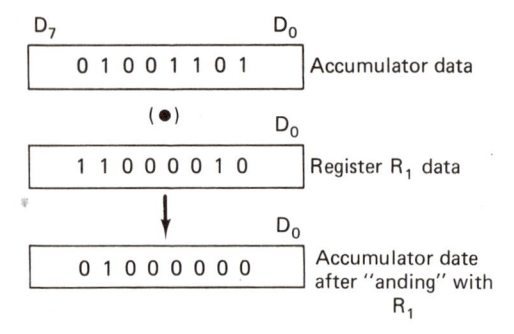

```
D₇                    D₀
┌─────────────────┐
│ 0 1 0 0 1 1 0 1 │  Accumulator data
└─────────────────┘
         (•)      D₀
┌─────────────────┐
│ 1 1 0 0 0 0 1 0 │  Register R₁ data
└─────────────────┘
          ↓       D₀
┌─────────────────┐
│ 0 1 0 0 0 0 0 0 │  Accumulator date
└─────────────────┘   after "anding" with
                      R₁
```

Figure 6-6 Diagram showing how accumulator data would appear after ANDing the accumulator with register R₁

certain bits of a byte to logical 0. This is referred to as "masking off" bits. For example, if we read a data byte and wish to examine only D_3 out of all eight bits D_0–D_7, we could "AND" the byte containing the D_3 bit with the register containing a value of 00001000. In this way only bit D_3 will be enabled to 1 if it is a 1.

ANI DATA. This is a 2-byte instruction called *and immediate*. The second byte of data is ANDed with the contents of the accumulator. The result is stored in the accumulator.

XRA R₁. This is a 1-byte instruction called *Exclusive OR with register data*. The data in the register specified is exclusive ORed bit-by-bit with the contents of the accumulator. The result is placed in the accumulator. We can use this 1-byte instruction to zero out the accumulator by specifying XRA A. Figure 6-7 shows the results of this instruction.

```
D₇              D₀
┌─────────────┐
│ 1 0 1 1 0 0 1 0 │  Accumulator
└─────────────┘       data
       (+)
┌─────────────┐
│ 1 0 1 1 0 0 1 0 │
└─────────────┘
        ↓
┌─────────────┐
│ 0 0 0 0 0 0 0 0 │
└─────────────┘
      (a)
```

A	B	C
0	0	0
0	1	1
1	0	1
1	1	0

(b)

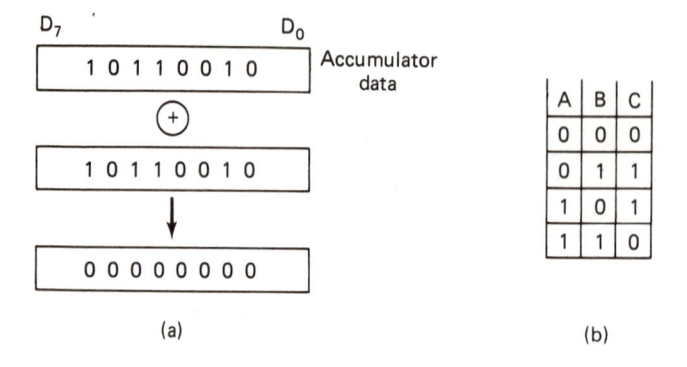

Figure 6-7 (a) Results of the XRA A instruction. The accumulator is zeroed out. (b) Truth table of the exclusive OR function

ORA R₁. This is a 1-byte instruction called *OR accumulator with register specified*. The data in the register is logically ORed with the data in the accumulator. This instruction can be used to set selected bits of a data word to logical 1.

CMP R₁. This is a 1-byte instruction called *compare accumulator with specified register*. The content of the register is subtracted from the accumulator. The content of the accumulator remains unchanged. The ZERO FLAG is set to logical 1 if the two registers are equal. The CARRY FLAG is set to 1 if the content of the accumulator is less than the content of the register. Using this instruction we can tell if the two numbers are equal, or if A is greater than R_1, or if R_1 is greater than A. This is shown in the following list.

$$A = R_1 \quad \text{ZERO FLAG} = 1$$
$$A < R_1 \quad \text{CARRY FLAG} = 1$$
$$A > R_1 \quad \text{CARRY FLAG} = 0$$

By examining these flags we know the results of this compare.

CPI DATA. This is a 2-byte instruction called *compare immediate*. The second data byte of this instruction is subtracted from the content of the accumulator. Condition flags Zero and Carry react the same as the CMP instruction discussed previously.

RAL. This is a 1-byte instruction called *rotate accumulator left*. Each bit in the accumulator is shifted one bit to the left. The Carry flag is shifted into D_0 (LSB); D_7 (MSB) is shifted into the Carry flag.

RAR. This is a 1-byte instruction called *rotate accumulator right*. Each bit of the accumulator is shifted one bit to the right. D_0 is shifted into the Carry flag. The Carry flag is shifted into D_7.

These are only a few of the instructions in this group, but knowing them enables one to better understand the other instructions.

6-4 Memory Stack

Before discussing the I/O group of instructions, we must introduce the concept of a Stack. After this discussion one should also be familiar with the structure of a stack. The *stack* is nothing more than a group of external memory locations reserved for special operations. This implies that the stack can be variable length. If we examine where the stack usually resides in memory it is the uppermost (highest numbered) addresses. This is shown in Figure 6–8. This is not the case in all systems. Two functions are associated with a stack—pushing and popping. *Pushing* the stack means to put something (we have not said what

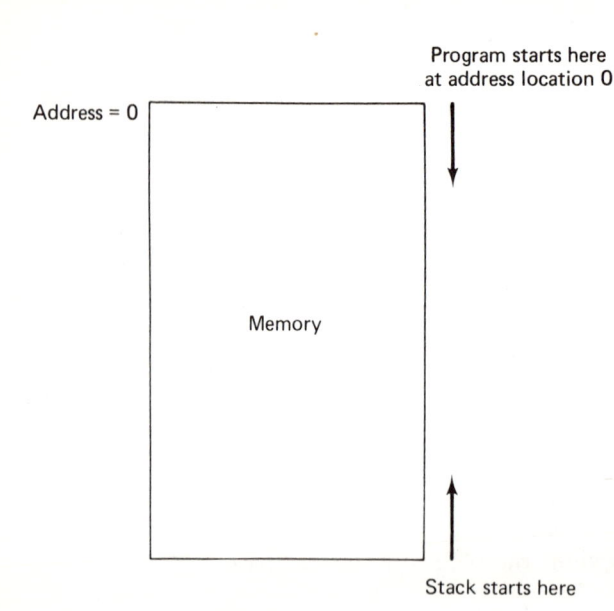

Figure 6-8 The physical location of the stack in memory. It usually resides in the uppermost memory locations, but this is not always the case. The stack grows downward in memory addresses.

the something is) on top of the stack. *Popping* the stack means to take something from the top of the stack—that is, taking something away from the top. The "something" we push onto and take away from the stack is a data byte.

In Figure 6-4, the block diagram of internal registers for the 8080, there is a 16-bit register called SP. This is the *stack pointer register*. When we "push" data onto the top of the stack, we are storing data in the top memory location as specified by the stack pointer. As we add more data to the stack, the stack pointer (address of top of stack) will get smaller. This is shown in Figure 6-9. The top of the stack is always the current stack pointer address.

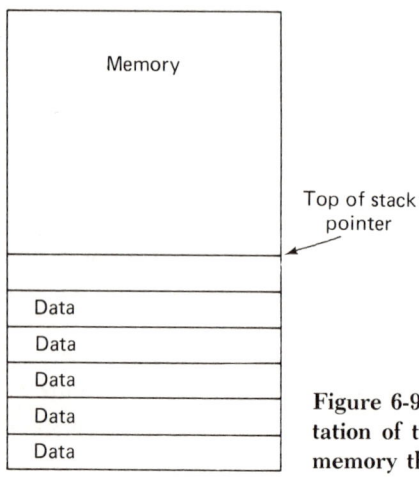

Figure 6-9 Block diagram showing the physical representation of the top-of-stack pointer. This is the address of memory that is pointed to by the SP register.

Sec. 6-4 Memory Stack

When we pop data from the top of the stack we read data from the current top address of the stack pointer and then increment the value of the stack pointer by 1. The data that was read is now removed from the stack, so the stack pointer now points to the new top-of-stack memory address. We can make a flowchart of what actually happens in the memory when we push or pop a stack. A flowchart for each procedure is shown in Figure 6-10.

POP B

↓

Data in memory location SP is stored in lower order byte of the register pair, in this case register C.

↓

SP = SP + 1
Memory address is incremented

↓

Data in memory location SP is stored in the upper order byte of the register pair, for this case register B.

↓

SP = SP + 2
New top of stack

(a)

Push B

↓

SP = SP − 1. Top stack is moved one location. Stack is growing "downward"

↓

Upper byte of register pair is stored in memory location SP.

↓

SP = SP − 1. Top of stack is moved another location "downward"

↓

Data from lower byte of register pair is stored in memory location SP.

SP is not decremented. It points to the last entry in the stack.

(b)

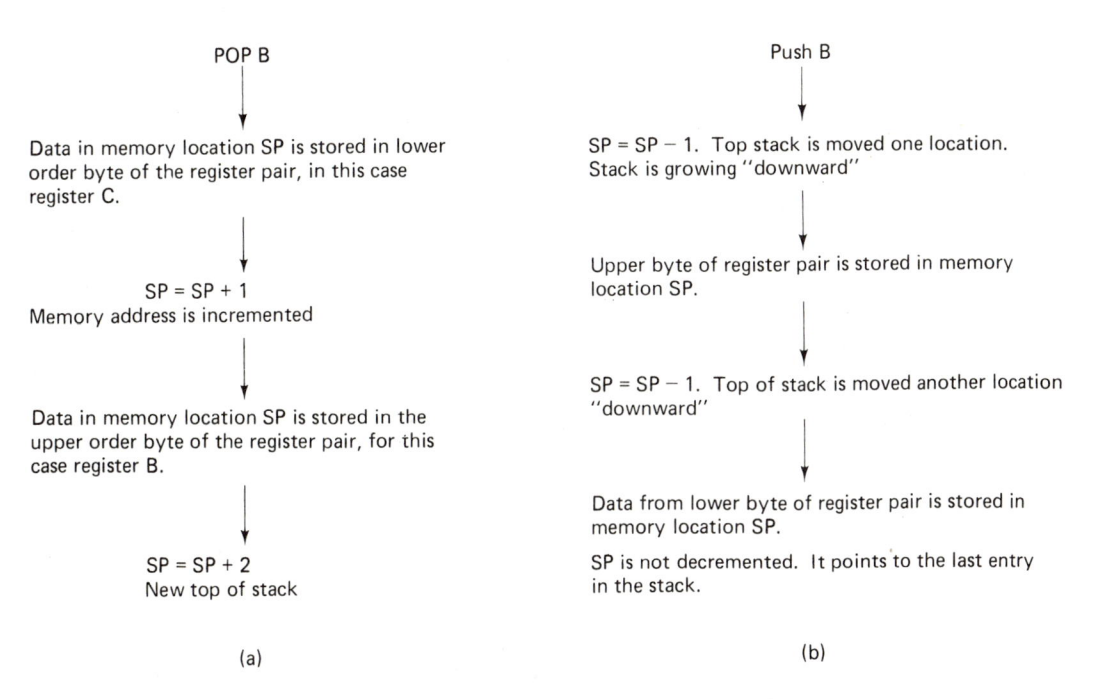

Figure 6-10 (a) Flowchart for a POP B instruction (b) Flowchart for a PUSH B instruction

When we initially turn power onto an 8080, the Stack Pointer (SP) register comes up in a random state. Before performing any stack operations the stack pointer must be set to the first top-of-stack address.

The sequence of events for a POP instruction is:

1. Data in address SP is transferred to the lower order register of the register pair.
2. SP = SP + 1
3. Data in SP + 1 is transferred to the higher order register of the register pair.
4. SP = SP + 2

The following instructions describe how the stack can be used.

PUSH RP. This is a 1-byte instruction meaning *push register pair specified to top of stack*. Since a register pair is two data bytes, we can use two data bytes from the external stack memory to save our internal registers. Let us say that the stack pointer is initially set to pair FF. When we execute a PUSH RP instruction the following operations result:

1. The higher order register of the register pair is written (saved) into memory location FE (SP-1).
2. The lower order register of the register pair is written (saved) into external memory location FD (SP-2).
3. The top of the stack pointer is now FD (SP-2).

In effect, the stack grows downward. This pushing of data bytes onto the memory stack is used to save temporary values without having to specify a unique memory location to store the data.

PUSH PSW. This is a 1-byte instruction called *push processor status word*. A processor status word is a combination of the condition flags plus some bits inserted by the 8080. When the PUSH PSW occurs, these events take place:

1. The content of the accumulator is stored into SP-1 (SP is the current top of stack address of memory)
2. The condition flags with some extra data bits are saved in SP-2
3. The new top of stack is SP-2

Since we can push data onto the stack we must have the ability to retrieve this data. When we retrieve this data we need not return it to the same register from which it was pushed. For instance if we execute a PUSH H instruction we would save the contents of the H and L registers on the stack. We could then "pop" the stack into the D and E registers by executing a POP D instruction. Now the data that was in the H and L is in the D and E registers. *The stack does not remember where the data came from. The programmer must keep track of what data was pushed onto the stack and in what order.*

To retrieve data from the external memory location stack we perform the opposite of PUSH; that is, the POP.

POP RP. This is a 1-byte instruction called POP to register pair. This moves the data byte at the top of stack into the register pair specified. The sequence of events for this instruction is:

Sec. 6-5   I/O Instructions

1. Data in address SP is transferred to the lower order register of the register pair.
2. SP = SP + 1
3. Data in SP + 1 is transferred to the higher order register of the register pair.

The new top of stack address is SP + 2.

POP PSW   This is a 1-byte instruction called *POP processor status word*. The sequence of events for this instruction is:

1. Data in SP is stored into the condition flag register. These flags are returned to the same condition as before PUSH PSW.
2. SP = SP + 1
3. The data in SP + 1 is transferred into the accumulator.
4. SP = SP + 2

The new top of stack is now SP + 2.

There are other stack operations, but if one understands how these four instructions operate on the stack, it will be an easy task to understand how the other instructions work.

6-5 I/O Instructions

Having covered the structure and operation of a stack, we now discuss the instructions used to input data from and output data to an I/O port. The input and output port numbers are the lower order address lines A_0–A_7.

IN Port.   This is a 2-byte instruction simply called *input*. The second byte of data in this instruction is the I/O port number from which data will be input. When this instruction is complete, the data from the specified port is stored in the accumulator.

OUT Port.   This is a 2-byte instruction called *Output*. The second byte of data in this instruction is the I/O port number to which data will be output. Data in the accumulator at the onset of this instruction is to be written to the output port specified.

6-6 Branching Instructions

We will now discuss three instructions from the group of instructions called the *Branching Group*. The program flow in an 8080 program is sequential through memory unless changed by a branching instruction. Some typical branching instructions follow.

JMP address. This is a 3-byte instruction called the *jump instruction*. It is further described as an unconditional jump. This means that when the program executes this instruction the 8080 always jumps to the address location specified and continues sequential execution of instructions from that new memory address. The address for the jump instruction is contained in the second and third byte of the instruction. The second byte contains the lower order address data and the third byte contains the higher order address data. As an example, suppose the jump instruction is located at memory address 003A. We want to jump to memory address 015B. Then address 003B would contain 5B and address 003C would contain 01. This data is hexadecimal.

The next instruction we will discuss allows the program to jump to a location in memory, but "remember" from where it jumped.

CALL address. This is a 3-byte instruction with the same format as the jump instruction. In fact this instruction acts just like JMP, except for one extra feature—the address of the next instruction in sequence will be pushed to the top of the stack. For example, let us say that the *Call* instruction is at memory address 001A. The memory address to jump to is in location 001B and 001C. This means the next sequential instruction to be executed will be in memory location 001D. Now the following would happen:

1. Data 00 is stored in SP-1.
2. SP = SP-2
3. Data 1D is stored in SP-2.
4. The memory address is changed to the address location specified by the call address.

A Call instruction is used to go to the subroutines in an 8080 assembly language program. Figure 6-11 illustrates how a subroutine would be used. Once we enter a subroutine we will want to return to the location where the subroutine was called. There is an instruction for doing this.

180

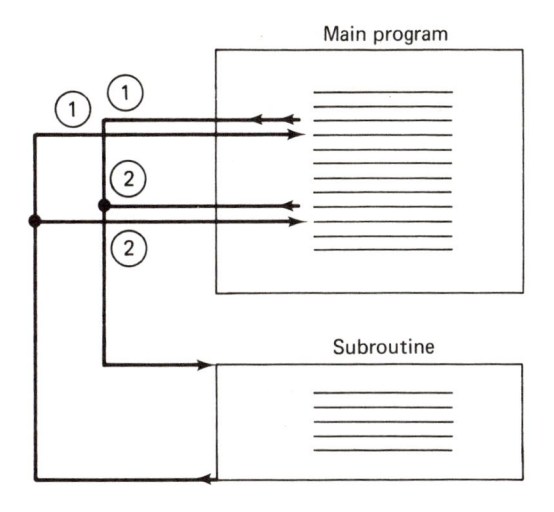

Figure 6-11 Pictorial representation of how a subroutine is used. It is a section of program that can be executed at any time. The subroutine will interrupt the main program and then return to it at the next instruction after the CALL to the subroutine. In this case the same subroutine is used twice by the main program.

RET. This is a 1-byte instruction called *Return*. When this instruction is executed the following events happen:

1. SP is popped, and the data byte is stored into lower order address lines A_0-A_7.
2. SP = SP + 1
3. SP is popped again and the data byte is stored into address lines A_8-A_{15}.
4. SP = SP + 2

We are, in effect, restoring the execution of the program to the next instruction after the Call instruction was completed.

Because a Call instruction pushes data onto the stack, we must keep a very careful record of the data on the top of stack. We can pop data from the stack at any time; also we can push data onto the stack at any time. When the 8080 performs a RET instruction it assumes that the data on the top of the stack is truly the correct memory address to return to. If we are not careful about our "housekeeping" relating to the top of the stack we may return to some memory address we do not wish. This is an important point to keep in mind when programming in the 8080 assembly language.

A complete instruction set for the 8080 is given at the end of this book with explanations for each instruction.

Before proceeding to the timing diagrams, let us draft a simple 8080 program. This draft will highlight all of the mechanical steps involved in writing a program. This is an easy example shown only to illustrate the mechanics of writing a program in 8080 assembly language. You will find very detailed programming problems worked to their final solutions in Chapters 7 and 10.

The program we will write will perform a binary to octal conversion on an 8-bit binary number. The binary number will be read in from port $C3_{16}$. The octal digits will be stored in consecutive memory locations, starting at memory location $A0_{16}$. The program will start initial execution at memory location 00. The maximum memory address is FF. Step 1 is to flowchart the problem. This flowchart is shown in Figure 6-12. Next we write the 8080 mnemonics to perform the functions in each block of the flowchart. These mnemonics are shown in Figure 6-13. Finally, we write the object code based on the mnemonics. This is shown in Figure 6-14.

The sequence of steps is personality dependent, varying with the programmer. It is here that creativity results in different (and sometimes better) ways of programming. The flowchart of Figure 6-12 is but an example of one way to structure this program.

This simple program has shown all of the required steps for writing an 8080 assembly language program. If one is fortunate enough to have a compiler, then the job of producing object code (which is the most tedious) can be eliminated. In Appendix A a complete list of all 8080 instructions with their corresponding object code is listed.

Now that we have an idea of what these five groups of instructions are supposed to do, we will discuss the hardware related to them. We will show timing diagrams for selected instructions so we know exactly what is happening electrically on all buses at any instant. The timing will now make sense, because we know what the instruction must do. The hardware must be controlled in such a way as to allow the system to perform properly. This detailed discussion of timing is another way to present to the system troubleshooter "what should be there."

First we will discuss the timing for the instruction MOV R_1,M. This is the instruction where data in memory location M, specified by the H,L register pair, is stored into the register specified by R_1. The sequence of events for this instruction is:

1. Fetch instruction
2. Fetch data from memory
3. Store data into register R_1

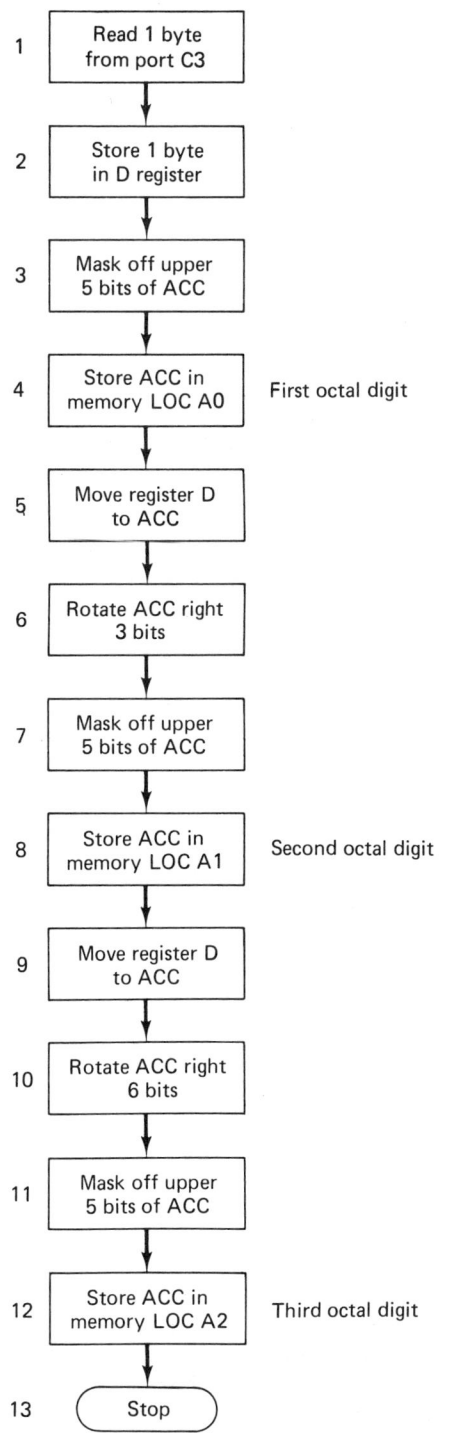

1. Read 1 byte from port C3
2. Store 1 byte in D register
3. Mask off upper 5 bits of ACC
4. Store ACC in memory LOC A0 — First octal digit
5. Move register D to ACC
6. Rotate ACC right 3 bits
7. Mask off upper 5 bits of ACC
8. Store ACC in memory LOC A1 — Second octal digit
9. Move register D to ACC
10. Rotate ACC right 6 bits
11. Mask off upper 5 bits of ACC
12. Store ACC in memory LOC A2 — Third octal digit
13. Stop

Figure 6-12 Flowchart of a binary-to-octal conversion routine

1	IN	C3
2	MOV	D, A
3	ANI	7
4	STA	00A0
5	MOV	A, D
6	RAR RAR RAR	
7	ANI	7
8	STA	00A1
9	MOV	A, D
10	RAR RAR RAR RAR RAR RAR	
11	ANI	7
12	STA	00A2
13	HLT	

Figure 6-13 8080 mnemonics for performing the binary-to-octal conversion shown in Figure 6-14

(HEX) Mem location	(HEX) Data byte	(Binary) Data byte D7 D0	Mnemonic
00	DB	11011011	IN C3
01	C3	11000011	
02	57	01010111	MOV D, A
03	E6	11100110	ANI 7
04	07	00000111	
05	32	00110010	STA 00A0
06	A0	10100000	
07	00	00000000	
08	BA	10111010	MOV A, D
09	1F	00011111	RAR
0A	1F	00011111	RAR
0B	1F	00011111	RAR
0C	E6	11100110	ANI 7
0D	07	00000111	
0E	32	00110010	STA 00A1
0F	A1	10100001	
10	00	00000000	
11	BA	10111010	MOV A, D
12	1F	00011111	RAR
13	1F	00011111	RAR
14	1F	00011111	RAR
15	1F	00011111	RAR
16	1F	00011111	RAR
17	1F	00011111	RAR
18	E6	11100110	ANI 7
19	07	00000111	
1A	32	00110010	STA 00A2
1B	A2	10100010	
1C	00	00000000	
1D	76	01110110	HLT

Figure 6-14 Translation of mnemonics shown in Figure 6-13 into binary data for loading into memory. Note in the STA instructions how the data is stored into memory.

Sec. 6-6 Branching Instructions

("Fetch" is a commonly used term that means *read the data in memory*.)

We will discuss each event in detail. First we must fetch the instruction from memory. The instruction is a single byte of data. Let us break down the fetch part of the sequence. The following sequence of events must happen when we read data from memory.

1. Address lines A_0–A_{15} are stable. These equal the address of memory where the first byte of data is stored.
2. Status information must indicate that a memory read can take place.
3. The bidirectional buffers for data lines D_0–D_7 must be enabled to let the 8080 accept data.
4. The 8080 must strobe (latch) data D_0–D_7 into its internal registers.

These events must happen. The hardware to be controlled must be put into the conditions that enable these events to happen. The timing diagram of Figure 6-15 shows the control signals generated by the 8080 and when they occur in the instruction cycle.

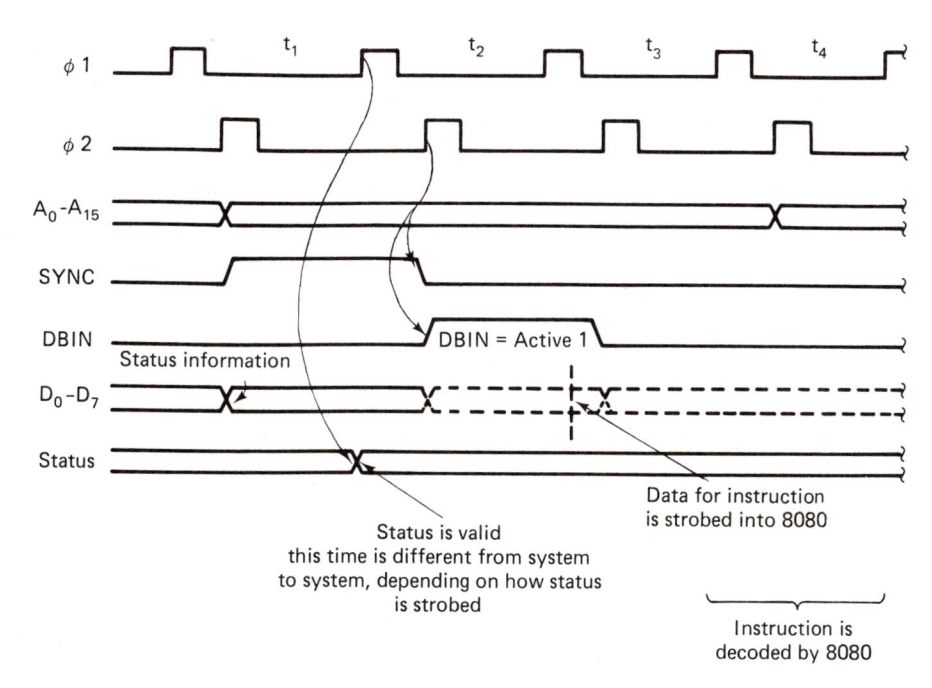

Figure 6-15 Timing diagram for an instruction Fetch cycle. Data is being read from memory. The instruction is decoded in state t_4.

In Figure 6-15 we notice that address lines A_0–A_{15} become stable in the t_1 state. Data lines D_0–D_7 contain the status information and these lines also become stable in t_1. The arrows show to what edge of the phase 1 and phase 2 clock the addresses and data are referenced. Note that status information is latched and becomes available to the control bus signals in state t_2. In state t_2 the sync signal goes to logical 0, indicating that status information is no longer valid on the data bus.

At ϕ_2, on the leading edge in t_2 the DBIN signal goes to logical 1. We recall that the DBIN signal does two things:

1. It enables the bidirectional buffers into a mode to let the 8080 accept data into its internal registers.
2. The DBIN signal enables the tri-state buffers on the memory outputs to control the data bus lines D_0–D_7.

When the instruction data is valid on the data bus it is strobed into the 8080. This action takes place on the negative going edge of $\phi 1$ in state t_3. The DBIN signal then goes to logical 0 in state t_3. The instruction is now latched into the 8080 internal registers. The 8080 now enters state t_4, which is used for internal decoding of the instruction. This fourth state is always present in the first machine cycle of any instruction. The first part of the instruction has now been completed; we have fetched the instruction from memory. Based on the instruction, the 8080 will do certain functions in the second machine cycle.

We must now fetch the second data byte from memory. This data will be stored into the internal register specified. Figure 6-16 shows the timing diagram

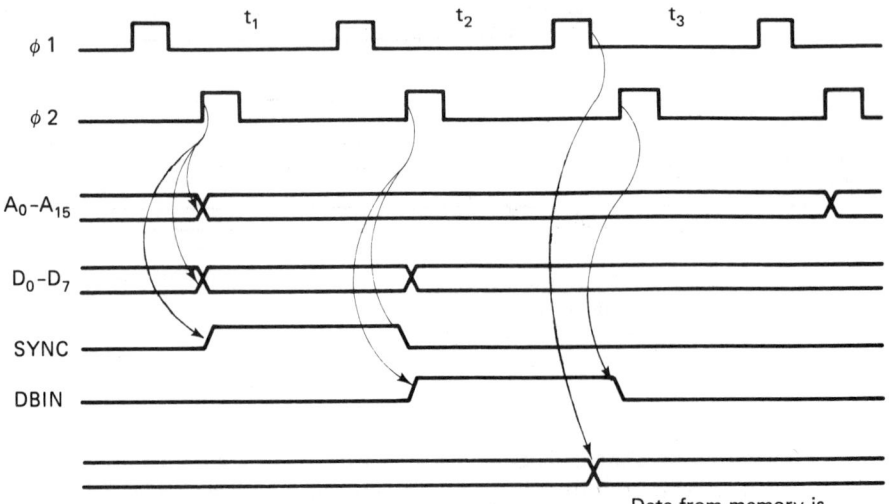

Figure 6-16 Timing diagram for a Read Data from Memory machine cycle

Data from memory is stored into internal 8080 register specified

Sec. 6-6 *Branching Instructions*

for the second machine cycle. We note that it looks almost identical to the first machine cycle. The exception is there are only three states in this machine cycle. This is logical because we pointed out in the discussion of the first machine cycle that the data from memory is latched into the 8080 in state t_3. State t_4 is used for instruction decode. We do not need to decode this data byte; we need only transfer it to the correct internal 8080 register.

```
┌─────────────────────┐
│        STA          │
└─────────────────────┘


┌─────────────────────────────────────┐
│ Lower order address bits $A_0$–$A_7$ │
└─────────────────────────────────────┘


┌──────────────────────────────────────┐
│ Higher order address bits $A_8$–$A_{15}$ │
└──────────────────────────────────────┘
```

Figure 6-17 Block diagram of the order of data bytes as they would appear in system memory

After the second machine cycle, the 8080 has finished execution of the MOV R_1, M instruction. We will now discuss the STA address instruction in detail. We recall that the STA address instruction is a 3-byte instruction to store data into the accumulator in the memory location specified by the next two data bytes. The data in memory for this instruction will look as shown in Figure 6-17. The sequence of events for execution of this instruction is:

1. Fetch instruction from memory.
2. Fetch second byte of data and store it in an internal 8080 register. This data byte will become the lower order address lines A_0–A_7.
3. Fetch third data byte from memory and store it in an internal 8080 register. This data will become the higher order address lines A_8–A_{15}.
4. Write the data from the accumulator to memory using the address in the second and third data bytes.

We notice from the list that there are four major events that must take place in this instruction. The 8080 will perform a single event per machine cycle. This means it will require four 8080 machine cycles to complete this instruction. The first three machine cycles will look as shown in Figures 6-15 (cycle 1) and 6-16 (cycles 2 and 3). The fourth machine cycle is shown in the timing diagram of Figure 6-18. This machine cycle will write data from the accumulator to the system memory.

To summarize the cycle time, the first machine cycle is the instruction fetch; this requires four states t_1–t_4. The next three machine cycles require three states each. At the end of the fourth machine cycle the instruction is complete. We can compute the execution time for this instruction or any instruction in the following way. We add the total number of states in all machine cycles and multiply this result by the period of the $\phi 1$ clock. For the STA instruction this becomes:

$$\begin{array}{cccc} t_1 + t_2 + t_3 + t_4 & t_1 + t_2 + t_3 & t_1 + t_2 + t_3 & t_1 + t_2 + t_3 \\ M_1 & M_2 & M_3 & M_4 \end{array}$$

(13 states total) × (period of one state)
13 × period of $\phi 1$ clock

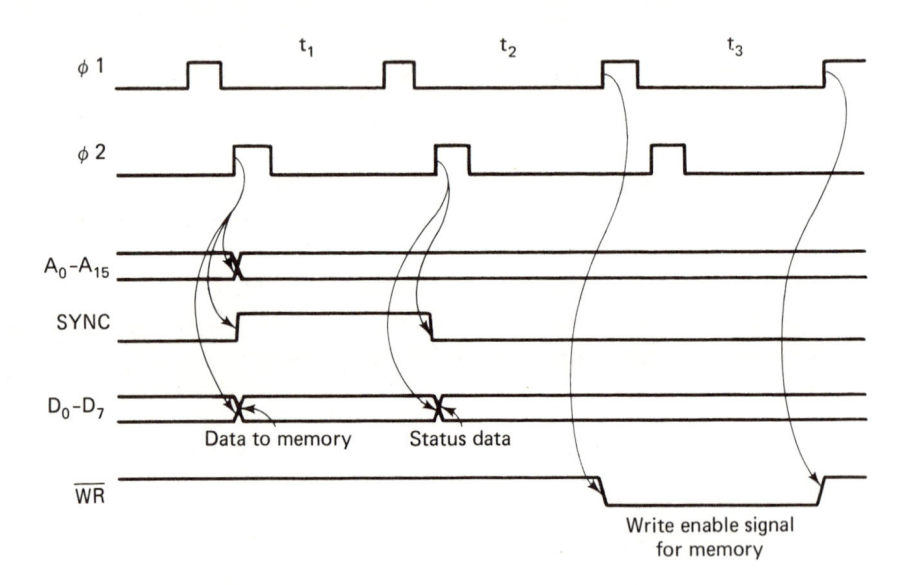

Figure 6-18 Timing diagram for the fourth machine cycle of an STA instruction. In this machine cycle the data in the accumulator is written into system memory.

In this chapter we have shown how the 8080 instructions control the actual hardware of the system. We have discussed selected instructions in detail. Understanding these instructions will enable one to comprehend other 8080 instructions. It is interesting to note that once our system hardware is operating cor-

Sec. 6-6 *Review Questions*   189

rectly we can write our software without worrying about the hardware. There are many good programming manuals for the 8080 available on the market today. These and their sources are listed in Appendix B. After reading this introduction one will be able to understand these in-depth programming manuals.

Review Questions

1. Explain the difference between "software" and "hardware" as it relates to digital electronics.
2. Draw a block diagram of the 8080 as it is used by the software.
3. What is a register pair?
4. What are the five groups of software instructions?
5. Explain what is meant by the term "1-byte," "2-byte," or "3-byte" instruction?
6. Write an 8080 program to read a byte of data from an I/O port with a select code of $43_{(16)}$, then store the data into memory location $03F2_{(16)}$.
7. What is meant by the term "machine cycle"?
8. What is a "stack" as it relates to digital electronics?
9. Explain the terms "pushing and popping" the stack.
10. List five 3-byte instructions.
11. If the period of the phase 1 clock input to the 8080 is one microsecond, how many microseconds are required to execute the following instructions?
    a. MVI A,03
    b. PUSH B
    c. IN 03
    d. CALL A100

7

MICROPROCESSOR CIRCUIT APPLICATION: Problem Definition, Relationship of Software Instructions to Hardware Operation

So far we have developed the concepts, software, and hardware that one needs in order to use an 8080 microprocessor. In this chapter we will apply these concepts to the solution of a simple problem, using the basic 8080 system that has been discussed. The application will tie the pieces together and show vividly how the software and hardware perform together to do a useful function.

In presenting this, we will first outline the basic problem. Then we will discuss a solution in general terms, without relating the solution to specific hardware. Next, we will design the hardware (I/O circuits) to solve the specific problem by means of an 8080 microprocessor. Finally, we will write an 8080 instruction program to control the hardware operation.

Remember that the hardware and software of the 8080 work in conjunction with one another. If one understands the software of the 8080, it makes the job of designing the hardware easier. This is true because for each software instruction there is associated hardware that will be controlled by that instruction. The final hardware design may be adjusted to accommodate the specific timing and unique features of the 8080 microprocessor.

7-1 Statement and Elements of the Problem

The problem we wish to solve is this. We are given the output of a certain instrument in two 8-bit binary numbers. One byte is an actual binary equivalent of a decimal number. The other 8-bit number contains scaling and range infor-

Sec. 7-1   *Statement and Elements of the Problem*   **191**

mation for the first byte. We want to read both bytes and write data based on them to a general output display I/O circuit. The display will accept up to four digits of BCD data. In addition, the display will set the decimal point based on the data input. Our system must monitor several I/O circuits and then send the outputs to a general display used by all I/O circuits. This type of system is shown in block diagram form in Figure 7-1. To keep the drawing simple in this figure, we show only the particular I/O circuit *that we will be working with* and the display I/O circuit.

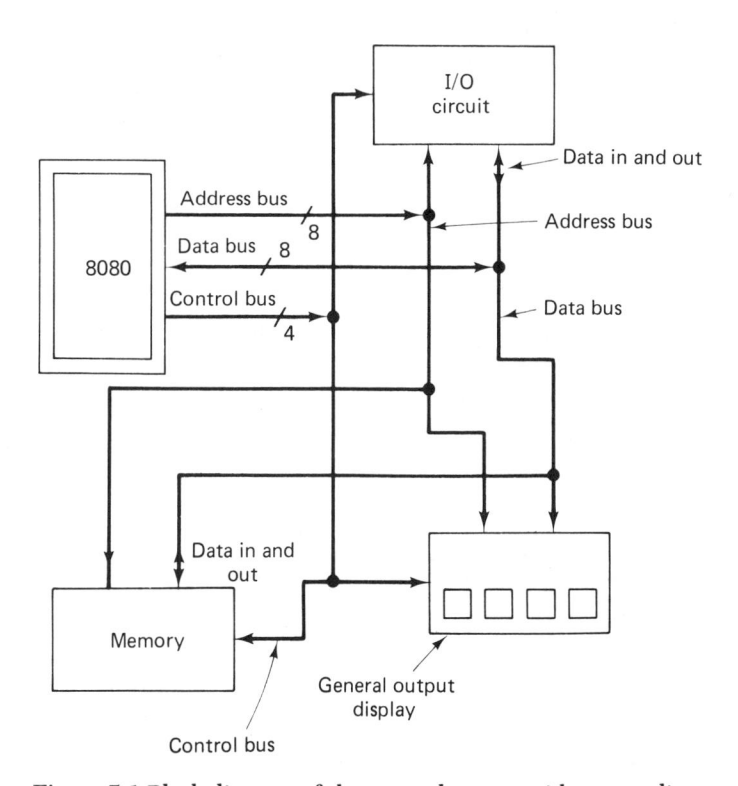

Figure 7-1 Block diagram of the general system with output display. The I/O circuit will be used as the source of the two data bytes to be read by the CPU.

From the general statement of the problem just given, let us now get a little more detailed. The important points of the problem follow:

1. Read two data bytes from the instrument I/O circuit
2. Modify these data bytes as necessary for output to general display
3. Write out the data bytes in proper form for the general display I/O circuit.

This list contains only three general points, which we will discuss in detail. As we discuss these points we will show explicitly what type of information one needs when initially designing an I/O circuit to interface with an 8080 microprocessor.

7-2 Reading Data Bytes

First, we wish to read two data bytes. What is contained in these data bytes? We stated that one data byte was a binary number, while the other contained information relating to this binary number. The first data byte will contain a number from 0 to 255 (eight bits maximum). This number can represent pressure, temperature, voltage, or any quantifiable characteristic that has the appropriate transducer connected to it to change it into electrical terms.

Let us assume that the first data byte represents temperature in degrees centigrade and that the second byte of data indicates either + or − temperature and scales the number. For example, suppose the digits in the first byte are 255. This can be .255, 2.55, 25.5 or 255. Where does the decimal point belong? That is the function of the second data byte. The actual bit placement of the first data byte is in ordinary binary notation. The bit placement for the second data byte is shown in Figure 7-2. An example of actual data from the I/O circuit is shown in Figure 7-3. The temperature shown is +15.3 degrees centigrade.

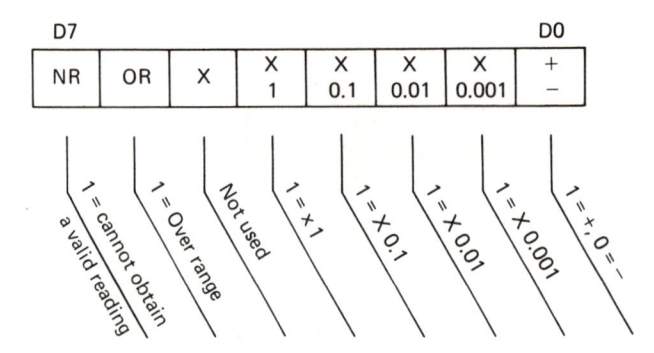

D7							D0
NR	OR	X	X 1	X 0.1	X 0.01	X 0.001	+ −

- 1 = a cannot obtain valid reading
- 1 = Over range
- Not used
- 1 = × 1
- 1 = × 0.1
- 1 = × 0.01
- 1 = × 0.001
- 1 = +, 0 = −

Figure 7-2 Bit placement for the second data byte read from the I/O circuit

D7							D0	
1	0	0	1	1	0	0	1	Byte 1

153

D7							D0	
0	0	0	0	1	0	0	1	Byte 2

× 0.1

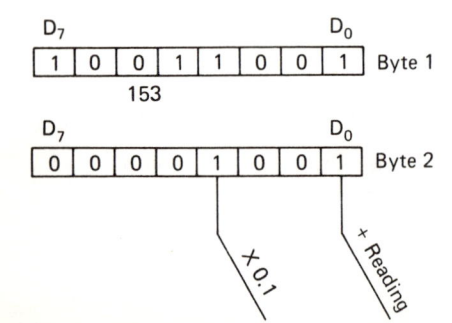

+ Reading

Figure 7-3 Actual data read from the I/O circuit. Byte 1 = 153. Byte 2 indicates that we scale the reading by multiplying byte 1 × 0.1. The data bit D_0 is a logical 1. This indicates the reading is positive. The final result is +15.3.

7-3 Modifying Data Bytes for Display

We see by examination of the bits in the second data byte that we are given all the information needed to determine the temperature from the I/O circuit. Now, we need to modify the two data bytes so that we can write BCD data to the output display. Before we can modify the data bytes, however, we must know what the output data should look like for the display to interpret it. The display will interpret two binary data bytes as four BCD digits. To indicate to the output display the position of the decimal point, + or −, and other control functions for the display a *third* data byte must be added. Figure 7-4 shows each of these three data bytes and how they are interpreted by the display I/O circuit.

D_7 ... D_0 Byte 1
BCD (LSD + 1)   BCD (LSD)
(a)

D_7 ... D_0 Byte 2
BCD (MSD)   BCD (LSD + 2)

D_7 ... D_0 Byte 3
Not used   Decimal point placement

0 0 0 = .XXXX
0 0 1 = X.XXX
0 1 0 = XX.XX
0 1 1 = XXX.X
1 0 0 = XXXX.

1 = Display blink

1 = +
0 = −

(b)

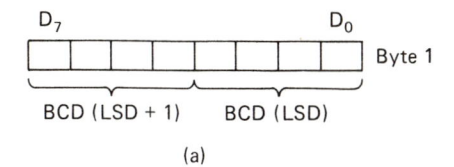

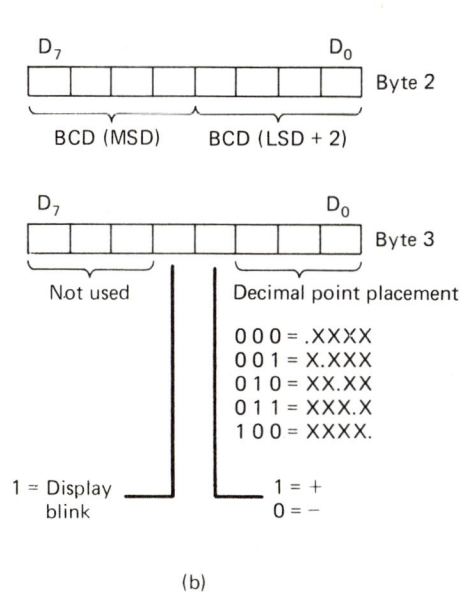

Figure 7-4 The functions of each bit in the three data bytes to output to the general output display. (a) Translating digital (binary) numbers into equivalent common decimal numbers (b) Scaling and other information carried to the output display in binary form

Suppose we wish to display the number +034.6. The MSD is 0, the LSD is 6. The places occupied by the binary and equivalent common decimal digits in the three data bytes to be output to the display circuit are shown in Figure 7-5. With this information we can decide how to modify the two data bytes from the instrument I/O circuit. The problem we are faced with is converting a binary number between 0 and 255 to a BCD equivalent with three digits. We will now discuss one possible solution to this problem without relating it to specific computer language or hardware.

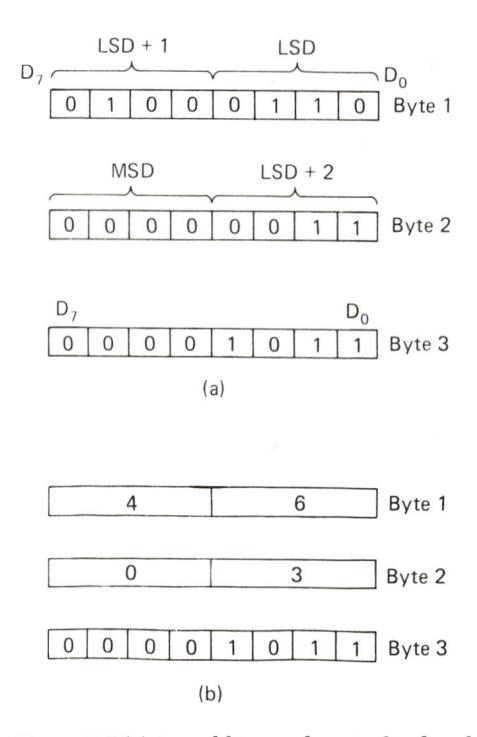

```
         LSD + 1        LSD
D₇    ⌢⏜⏜⏜⏜⌢  ⌢⏜⏜⏜⌢  D₀
     | 0 | 1 | 0 | 0 | 0 | 1 | 1 | 0 |  Byte 1

         MSD         LSD + 2
     ⌢⏜⏜⏜⏜⌢  ⌢⏜⏜⏜⌢
     | 0 | 0 | 0 | 0 | 0 | 0 | 1 | 1 |  Byte 2

     D₇                       D₀
     | 0 | 0 | 0 | 0 | 1 | 0 | 1 | 1 |  Byte 3
                (a)

     |     4     |     6     |  Byte 1

     |     0     |     3     |  Byte 2

     | 0 | 0 | 0 | 0 | 1 | 0 | 1 | 1 |  Byte 3
                (b)
```

Figure 7-5 (a) Actual binary data in the data bytes (b) Position of binary equivalent decimal data in the three bytes

The main idea behind the conversion follows. We first divide the binary number up into its component parts. These are:

        100's   10's   1's

We next determine how many 100's, 10's and 1's are contained in the number. When we know this, we know the BCD digit to assign to each display in the output. For example, the number 136 has (1 × 100's), (3 × 10's), and (6 × 1's). The number 136 will be in its binary equivalent form, but we need not concern ourselves with this. We can think of the number 136 as a decimal

Sec. 7-3 *Modifying Data Bytes for Display* 195

number. The digits to send to the display would be 0, 1, 3, 6. What we now show is a means or procedure to determine how many 100's, 10's, and 1's are contained in any number.

To determine how many 100's are contained in any number we subtract 100 repeatedly from the number and each time check for the result to be negative. For example, take the number 216. We subtract 100 and obtain 116. This result is not less than 0 (negative), so we subtract 100 again. The result is 16. This result is not less than 0 so we subtract 100 again. We obtain -84. This result is now negative, less than 0. At this point, we stop subtracting 100. Meanwhile, we have kept track of how many times we were able to subtract 100 from the number and obtain a result greater than, or equal to, 0. For this example, we did this two times. This means that our 100's digit is (2). A flowchart for this process is shown in Figure 7-6.

From Figure 7-6 we see that we must save the starting number, because this number is changed or lost when we subtract 100 from it. When we finish this

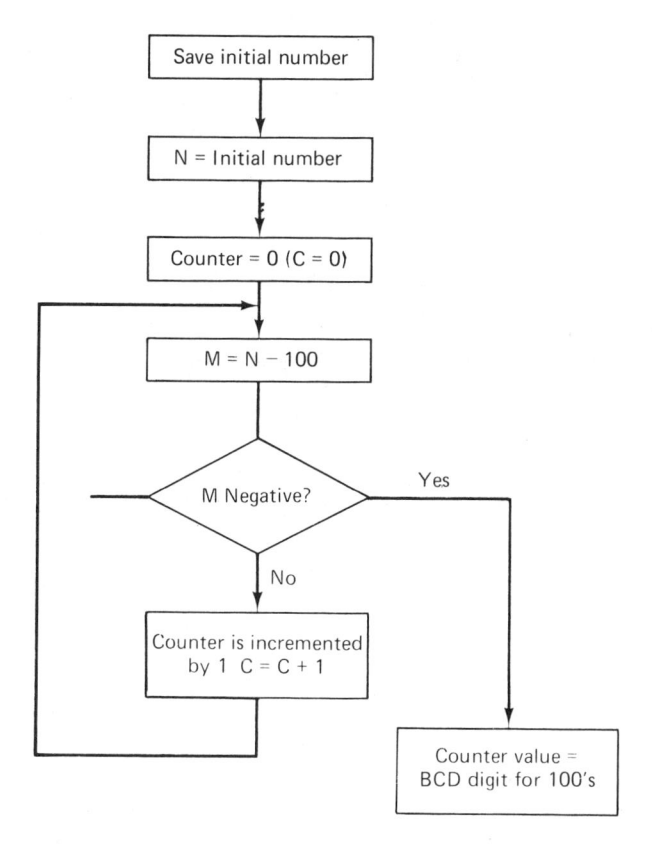

Figure 7-6 Flowchart for determining the BCD value for the 100s digit

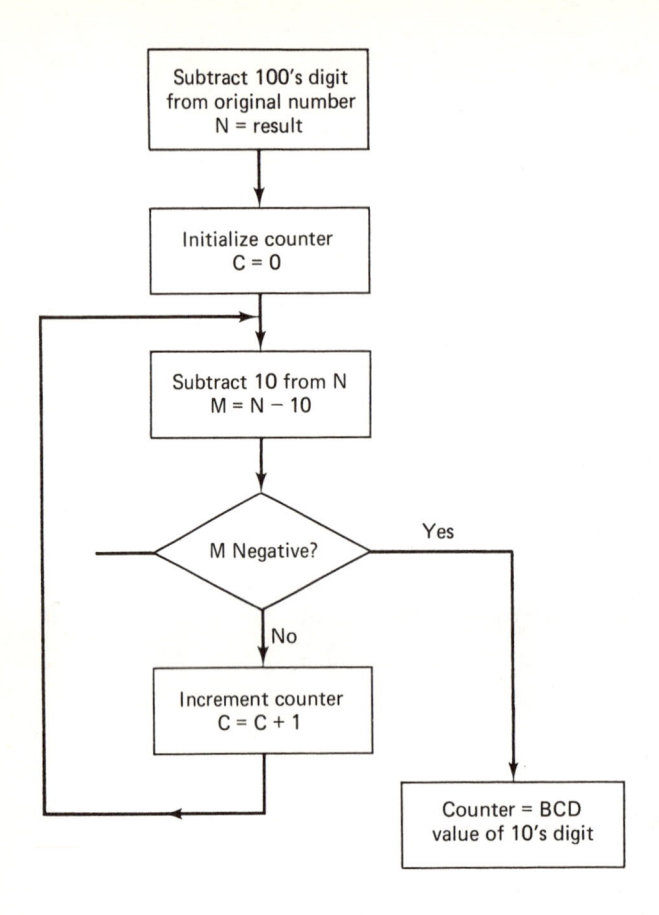

Figure 7-7 Flowchart for determining the BCD 10s digit

subtraction, the counter contains the number of times we subtracted 100 and obtained a result greater than, or equal to, 0.

After we have determined how many 100's are in the given number we can subtract this amount from the number and we will be left with the 10's and 1's. In our example we had 216 as our starting number. We have 2 × 100's so we subtract 200 from the starting number and are left with 16. We again subtract as before, except that we now use 10 instead of 100. This is shown in the flowchart of Figure 7-7.

When we finish this loop we know the decimal number of 10's in our limited number containing only 10's and 1's. To find the number of 1's we repeat the procedure, subtracting the number of 100's and 10's and then we have the number of 1's. In our example we started with the number 216. From this we subtracted 200 and were left with 16. This is our limited number containing only 10's and 1's. From this number we subtracted 10. This left us with 6. This final number is the 1's BCD digit for the output display. We now have the BCD equivalent for the entire binary number. The 1000's digit in our display will always be 0 since we have only three digits possible (0–255). The complete flow chart to convert from decimal (binary equivalent) to BCD is shown in Figure 7-8.

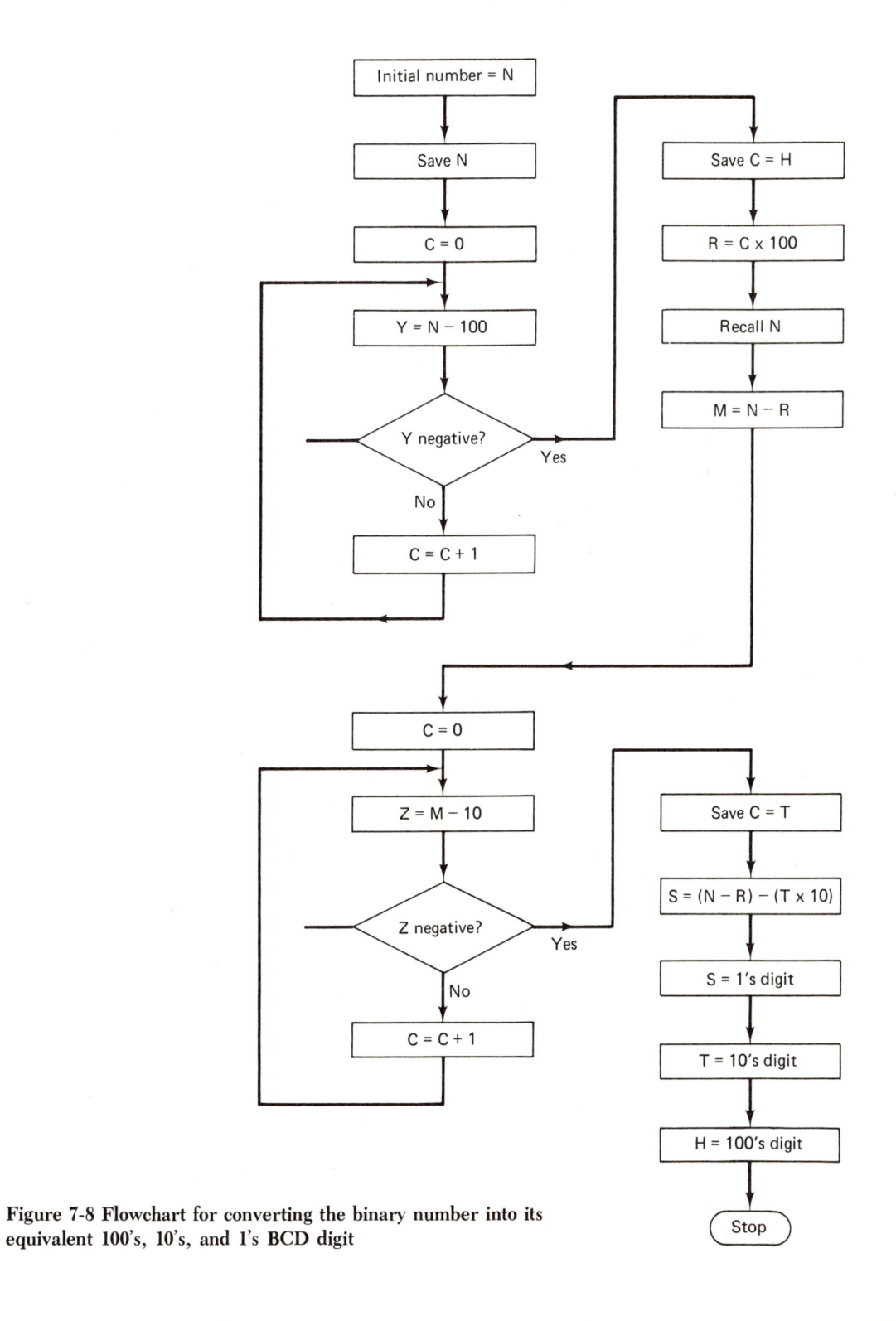

Figure 7-8 Flowchart for converting the binary number into its equivalent 100's, 10's, and 1's BCD digit

Now we turn our attention to scaling the output and determining the + or − sign. Before going through the process of converting the binary number to BCD and scaling the number, we should check to see if the reading is valid. This is shown in the two MSBs of the second data byte. If either of these two bits is logical 1, then the conversion is meaningless. This type of prechecking is called error checking. If an error exists, do not convert the number.

Two kinds of errors can occur in our system: the first is that the temperature may be greater than 255°F or "over range." This is denoted by bit D_6 of the second data byte being equal to logical 1. If this is the case, we want to indicate this type of error on the display. To do so, we output all four display digits to nines.

The second type of error occurs when the I/O circuit is unable to make a correct reading. Perhaps an oscillation or some hardware malfunction may not permit the transducer to perform adequately. This condition is indicated by bit D_7 of the second data byte being equal to logical 1. If this error occurs, we want to indicate it at the output display. For this type of error we also set all four digits equal to nine. In addition, we want the display to blink. If both bits D_6 and D_7 of the data byte are logical 1, then we use only bit D_7 as an error indication. These error conditions and indications are shown in Figure 7-9.

Now that we have checked for errors, let's discuss how we can scale the reading according to the scaling information, which is contained in bits D_1, D_2, D_3, and D_4 of the second data byte. Each bit corresponds to a decimal point position. We can relate this directly to the output display decimal point position. This relationship is shown in Figure 7-10.

The next information to consider is the + and − sign. This, too, can be related to the output display directly. It follows the rule:

If D_0 equals 1 then the output display = +
If D_0 equals 0 then the output display = −

This is further interpreted as shown in Figure 7-11.

We now have all of the information we need to chart the solution to the scaling. This flowchart is shown in Figure 7-12.

We have shown with general terms how to solve the overall problem. Let us now get to some details of the hardware. We will concentrate on the I/O circuits and use the basic system presented in Chapter 4. First, let us examine the I/O circuit from which the two data bytes will be read. This circuit is shown in Figure 7-13.

Referring to Figure 7-13, notice that there is one I/O port associated with the I/O circuit. This port is used both to read and write data. The sequence of events to read the two data bytes from the I/O port follows.

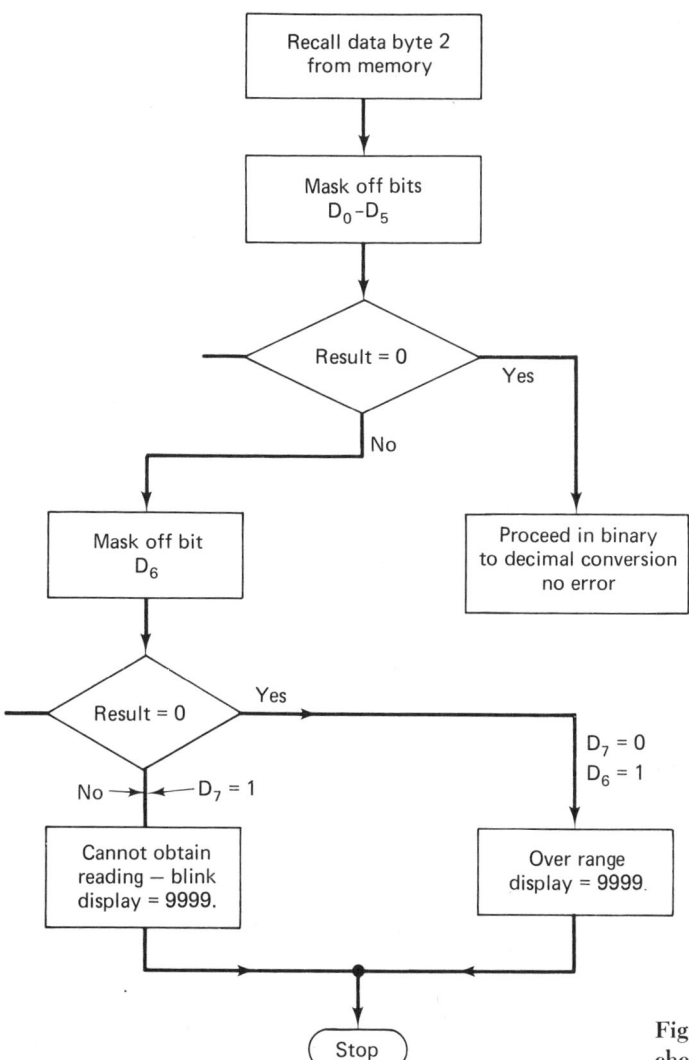

```
                    ┌──────────────────┐
                    │ Recall data byte 2│
                    │  from memory      │
                    └─────────┬────────┘
                              ▼
                    ┌──────────────────┐
                    │   Mask off bits  │
                    │      $D_0$-$D_5$ │
                    └─────────┬────────┘
                              ▼
                         ╱Result = 0╲   Yes
                         ╲          ╱──────┐
                              │No          │
                              ▼            ▼
                    ┌──────────────┐  ┌────────────────────┐
                    │ Mask off bit │  │ Proceed in binary  │
                    │     $D_6$    │  │ to decimal conversion│
                    └──────┬───────┘  │     no error       │
                           ▼          └──────────┬─────────┘
                      ╱Result = 0╲  Yes          │
                      ╲          ╱──────┐  $D_7$ = 0
                       No    $D_7$ = 1  │  $D_6$ = 1
                        │               ▼
                        ▼        ┌──────────────┐
                 ┌──────────────┐│  Over range  │
                 │Cannot obtain ││display = 9999│
                 │reading – blink│└──────┬───────┘
                 │display = 9999│       │
                 └──────┬───────┘       │
                        └────────┬──────┘
                                 ▼
                              ( Stop )
```

Figure 7-9 Flowchart for error checking before processing

Second data byte input

D_4	D_3	D_2	D_1
0	0	0	1
0	0	1	0
0	1	0	0
1	0	0	0

Byte three output

D_2	D_1	D_0	Display
0	0	0	X.XXX
0	1	0	XX.XX
0	1	1	XXX.X
1	0	0	XXXX.

Figure 7-10 Relationship between input data byte and the third data byte to be output to the general output display

Second input data byte	Third output byte	Display
D_0	D_3	
1	1	+
0	0	–

Figure 7-11 Relationship between input and output data byte for determining the sign of the number at the output display

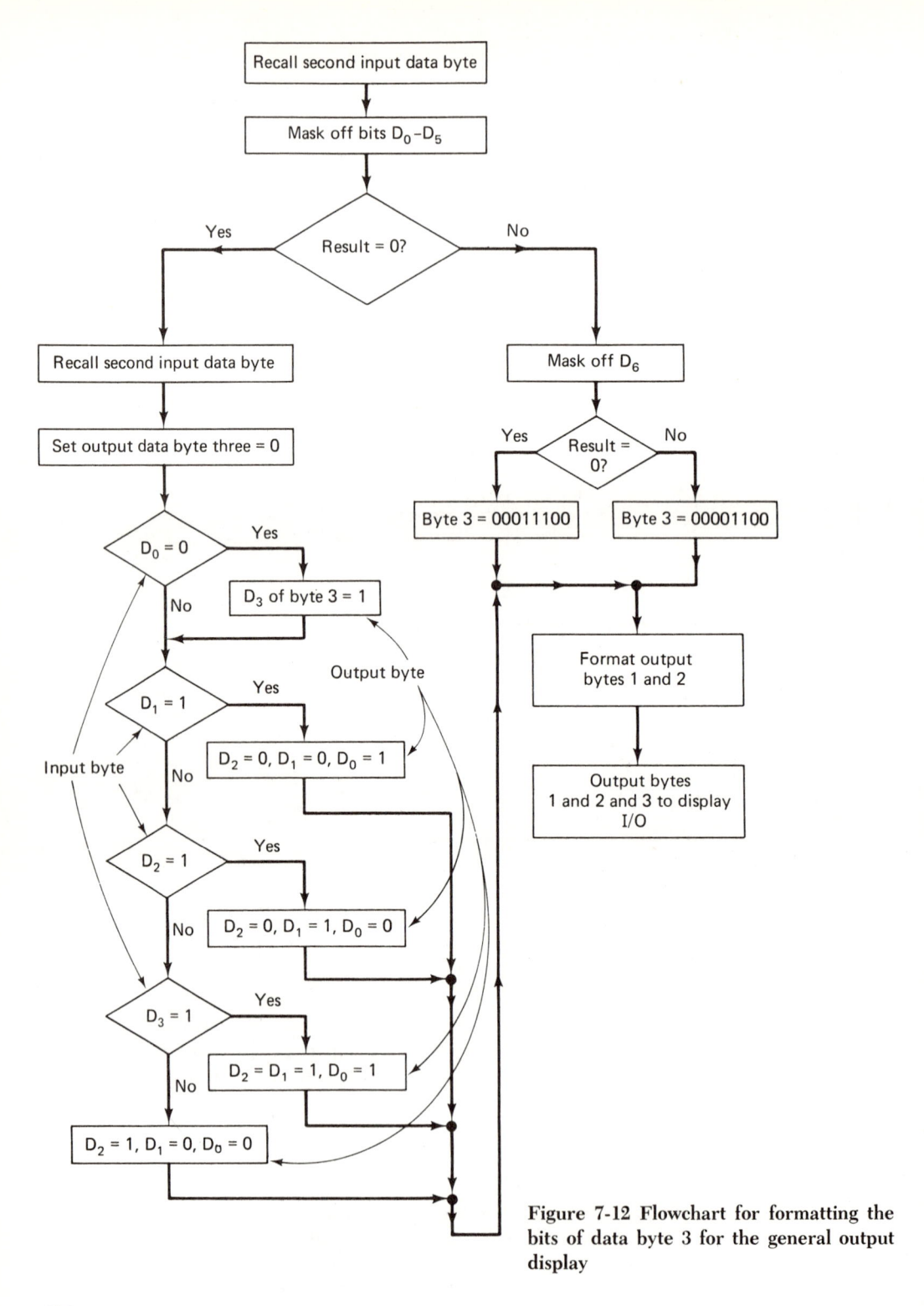

Figure 7-12 Flowchart for formatting the bits of data byte 3 for the general output display

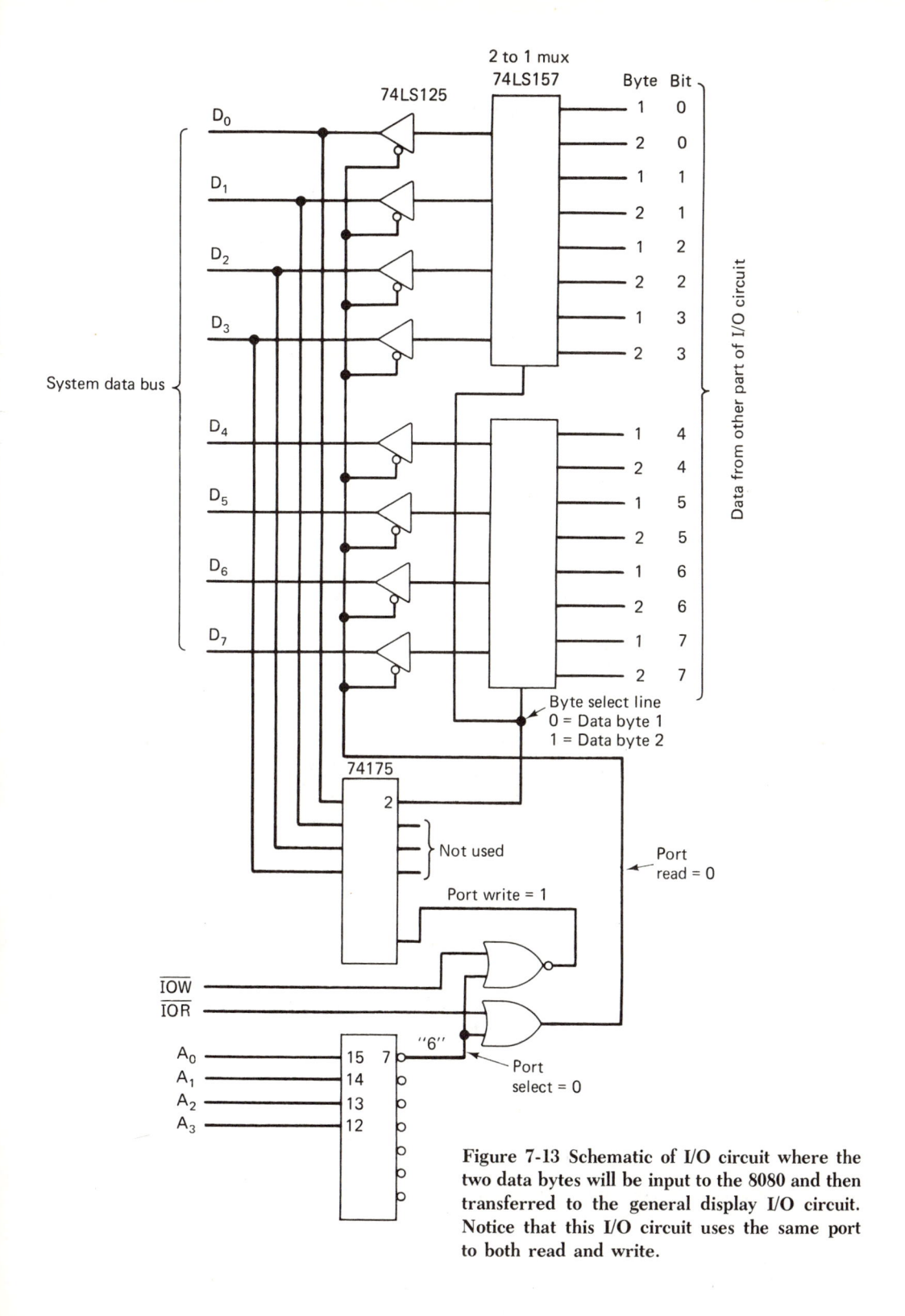

Figure 7-13 Schematic of I/O circuit where the two data bytes will be input to the 8080 and then transferred to the general display I/O circuit. Notice that this I/O circuit uses the same port to both read and write.

1. Write 00 to port 6. This strobes a 0 into the 74175 latch output pin 2. With pin 2 equal to logical 0, the quad 2-to-1 multiplexers then enable byte 1 to the I/O tri-state buffers.
2. Read port 6. This reads byte 1 of port 6 to the internal registers of the 8080.
3. Write the data byte to memory. This saves the data input to the 8080 in a location in memory.
4. Write 01 to port 6. This puts a logical 1 on output pin 2 of the 74175 latch. This logical 1 then selects the second data byte to be enabled to the tri-state output buffers.
5. Read port 6. This reads the data byte into the internal registers of the 8080.
6. Write the data to memory. This saves the data input to the 8080 in a location in memory.

Both data bytes are now stored in memory.

7-4 Writing Data in the General Output Display

Now that we have both I/O data byte values in memory we can return to them later. We turn our attention at this point to outputting the three data bytes to the general display. The hardware for this I/O circuit is shown in Figure 7-14. This I/O circuit has three ports associated with it, which are numbered A, B, and C, base 16. Port A is for the first data byte. Port B is for the second data byte. Port C is for the third data byte. We may assume that the three data bytes to be written to the ports are stored in memory.

We next focus on the sequence of writing the three bytes of data in memory to the three output ports A, B, C. This six-step sequence is:

1. Read byte 1 from memory
2. Write byte 1 to I/O port A
3. Read byte 2 from memory
4. Write byte 2 to I/O port B
5. Read byte 3 from memory
6. Write byte 3 to I/O port C.

One nice feature of listing this sequence is that we already know or assume that the hardware will perform its job. All we need do is control the hardware with the correct sequence of instructions. This feature allows us to put aside the hardware and write only the software, once we are sure that the hardware is working correctly.

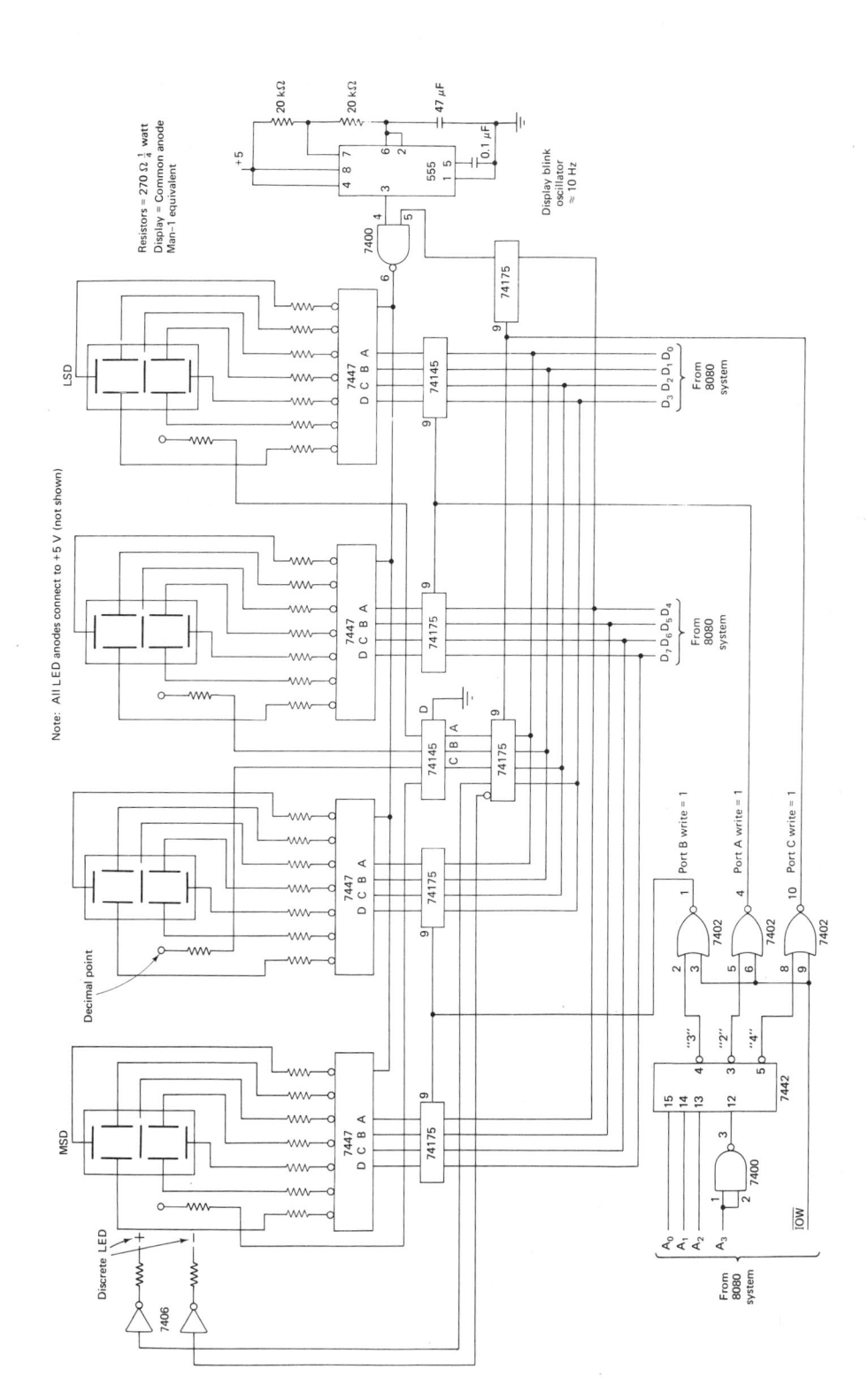

Figure 7-14 Hardware schematic for a general output display circuit. Four digits, selectable decimal point, and display blink circuit

If we re-examine the different types of jobs the CPU must perform, based on the information we have illustrated thus far, we have:

1. read data from an I/O port
2. read data from memory
3. write data to an I/O port
4. write data to memory
5. perform internal register manipulation. This is where the scaling and bit forming of the output data bytes is done.

These five jobs are identical to the five major jobs listed in Chapter 4.

We will now discuss writing the software to allow the entire problem to be solved. We will write the software in functional blocks or parts to make it easier to debug and to understand. When each block is working we will put the parts together to form the entire program. The first block of software serves to read the two data bytes from the input I/O port and store them in selected memory locations. A flowchart for this part of the program is shown in Figure 7-15.

The next block of the program is the error checking and data formatting routine. This program follows the flowchart sequence of Figure 7-12. In Figure

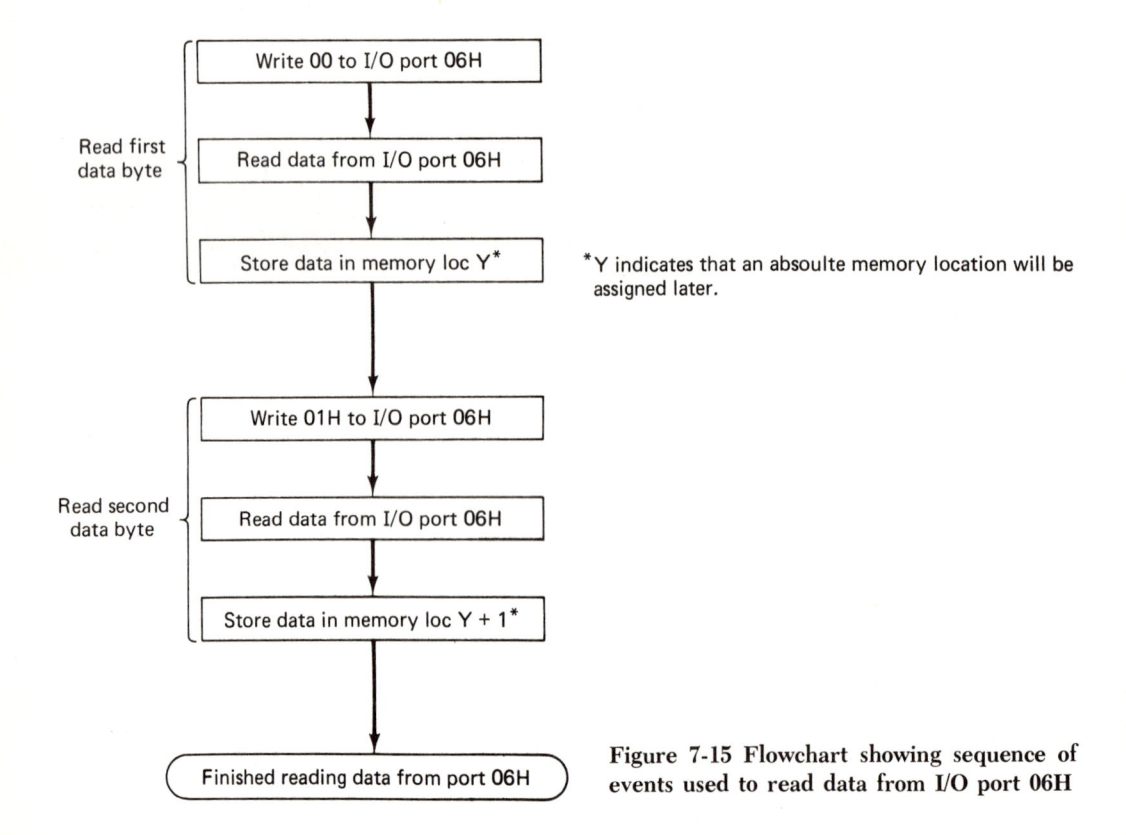

*Y indicates that an absoulte memory location will be assigned later.

Figure 7-15 Flowchart showing sequence of events used to read data from I/O port 06H

Sec. 7-4 *Writing Data in the General Output Display* 205

7-16 these two sections of the program, error checking and data formatting, are given with source statements written in 8080 assembly language.

```
ITEM   LOC    OBJECT CODE    SOURCE STATEMENTS                           PAGE   1

  1    0000    .  .  .
  2    0000    .  .  .       ;
  3    0000    .  .  .       ;
  4    0000    .  .  .       ;
  5    0000    .  .  .       ;
  6    0000    .  .  .       ;
  7    0000    .  .  .       ;
  8    0000    3E 00  .      BEGIN  MVI  A,00
  9    0002    D3 06  .             OUT  06         SELECT I/O FOR 1ST BYTE
 10    0004    DB 06  .             IN   06         READ FIRST BYTE
 11    0006    32 6B 00             STA  BYT1       STORE IN MEMORY
 12    0009    D3 06  .             OUT  06         SELECT I/O FOR 2ND BYTE
 13    000B    DB 06  .             IN   06         READ 2ND BYTE
 14    000D    32 6C 00             STA  BYT1+1     STORE IN MEM
 15    0010    E6 C0  .             ANI  300Q       MASK OF LOWER 6 BITS
 16    0012    CA 2F 00             JZ   NOERR      IF ZERO THE NO ERROR
 17    0015    E6 80  .             ANI  200Q       MASK OFF BIT D6
 18    0017    CA 1F 00             JZ   QERR       IF 0 THEN D7=0,D6=1
 19    001A    3E 1C  .             MVI  A,034Q     BYTE3=00011100 BLINK DIS
 20    001C    C3 21 00             JMP  BNEX
 21    001F    3E 0C  .      QERR   MVI  A,014Q     BYTE 3=00001100 NO BLINK
 22    0021    32 6D 00     BNEX    STA  BYT1+2     STORE BYTE 3 FOR OUTPUT IN
                                                    MEM
 23    0024    3E 99  .             MVI  A,231Q     ACC=10011001=99 BCD
 24    0026    32 6B 00             STA  BYT1
 25    0029    32 6C 00             STA  BYT1+1     ALL DIGITS=99
 26    002C    C3 6E 00             JMP  ROUT       GOTO OUTPUT SECTION OF PRO
                                                    GRAM
 27    002F    3A 6C 00     NOERR   LDA  BYT1+1     NO ERR FORMAT BYTE 3
 28    0032    47  .  .             MOV  B,A        B=2ND BYTE FROM I/O PORT
 29    0033    0E 00  .             MVI  C,00       C=BYTE 3 INITIALIZE TO 0
 30    0035    E6 01  .             ANI  01         EXAMINE BIT 1 ONLY
 31    0037    CA 3C 00             JZ   S1
 32    003A    0E 08  .             MVI  C,010Q     SET BIT D3=1 + SIGN
 33    003C    47  .  .     S1      MOV  B,A        RESTORE ACC NO MASK
 34    003D    E6 02  .             ANI  002Q       EXAMINE D1 ONLY
 35    003F    CA 49 00             JZ   T1
 36    0042    79  .  .             MOV  A,C
 37    0043    F6 01  .             ORI  001Q       BYTE 3= XXXXX001
 38    0045    4F  .  .             MOV  C,A
 39    0046    C3 67 00             JMP  Z
 40    0049    78  .  .     T1      MOV  A,B        RESTORE ACC NO MASK
 41    004A    E6 04  .             ANI  004Q       CHECK BIT D3=1
 42    004C    CA 56 00             JZ   V1         BIT NOT =1
 43    004F    79  .  .             MOV  A,C
 44    0050    F6 02  .             ORI  002Q       BYTE 3=XXXXX010
 45    0052    4F  .  .             MOV  C,A
 46    0053    C3 67 00             JMP  Z
 47    0056    78  .  .     V1      MOV  A,B        RESTORE ACC NO MASK
 48    0057    E6 08  .             ANI  010Q       CHECK BIT D3 ONLY
 49    0059    CA 63 00             JZ   U1
 50    005C    79  .  .             MOV  A,C
```

Figure 7-16 8080 program for error checking and formatting output byte 3 for general output display (part a)

```
■■■■■■■■■■■■■■■■■■■■■■■■■■■■■■■■■■■■■■■■■■■■■■■■■■■■■■■■■■■■■■■■■■■■■■■■■■■■■■
   ITEM    LOC    OBJECT CODE    SOURCE STATEMENTS                PAGE    2
■■■■■■■■■■■■■■■■■■■■■■■■■■■■■■■■■■■■■■■■■■■■■■■■■■■■■■■■■■■■■■■■■■■■■■■■■■■■■■
   51     0050   F6  03   .              ORI    003Q    BYTE 3=XXXXX011
   52     005F   4F   .   .              MOV    C,A
   53     0060   C3  67  00              JMP    Z
   54     0063   79   .   .        U1    MOV    A,C
   55     0064   F6  04   .              ORI    004Q    BYTE 3=XXXXX100
   56     0066   4F   .   .              MOV    C,A
   57     0067   79   .   .        Z     MOV    A,C     MOVE BYTE 3 TO ACC
   58     0068   32  6D  00              STA    BYT1+2  STORE IN MEM
   59     006B    .   .   .         ;
   60     006B    .   .   .         ;
   61     006B    .   .   .         ;
   62     006B    .   .   .         ;
   63     006B    .   .   .         ; LOCATIONS TO STORE DATA IN MEM FOLLOW
   64     006B    .   .   .         ;
   65     006B    .   .   .         ;
   66     006B   00   .   .       BYT1   NOP
   67     006C   00   .   .              NOP
   68     006D   00   .   .              NOP
   69     006E    .   .   .         ;
   70     006E    .   .   .         ; ROUT IS A DUMMY LOCATIONS WHERE OUTPUT DISPLAY
   71     006E    .   .   .         ; CODE WOULD EXIST IN A PROGRAM
   72     006E    .   .   .         ;
   73     006E   00   .   .       ROUT   NOP
   74     006F    .   .   .         ;
   75     006F    .   .   .              END            END STATEMENT FOR COMPILER
    0    ERRORS FOUND IN ASSEMBLY CODE .
```

Figure 7-16 (part b) 8080 program for error checking and formatting output byte 3 for general output display

Next we write the block of the program that formats the two data bytes and stores them in selected memory locations. This part of the program follows the flowchart shown in Figure 7-17. Finally, we write the section that writes out the data bytes to the general display. This section of the program follows the flowchart shown in Figure 7-18.

Now all the programming has been finished. We connect these blocks together and have a total program that resembles Figure 7-19. We have shown one solution of a problem from the initial design of the hardware system to the final writing of the software to control the hardware.

To make our system run this program we put the system into manual mode, then load the program into memory, starting at location 00. Next we load the address pointer to = 00H. Now, we start writing data bytes into memory. After all of the data bytes have been entered, we should examine all memory locations for correct data and correct when necessary.

At this point the 8080 is prepared to run the program, so we put the Manual/Run Switch into "Run" position. When this action is taken the 8080 begins executing the program, starting with memory location 000. It starts at mem-

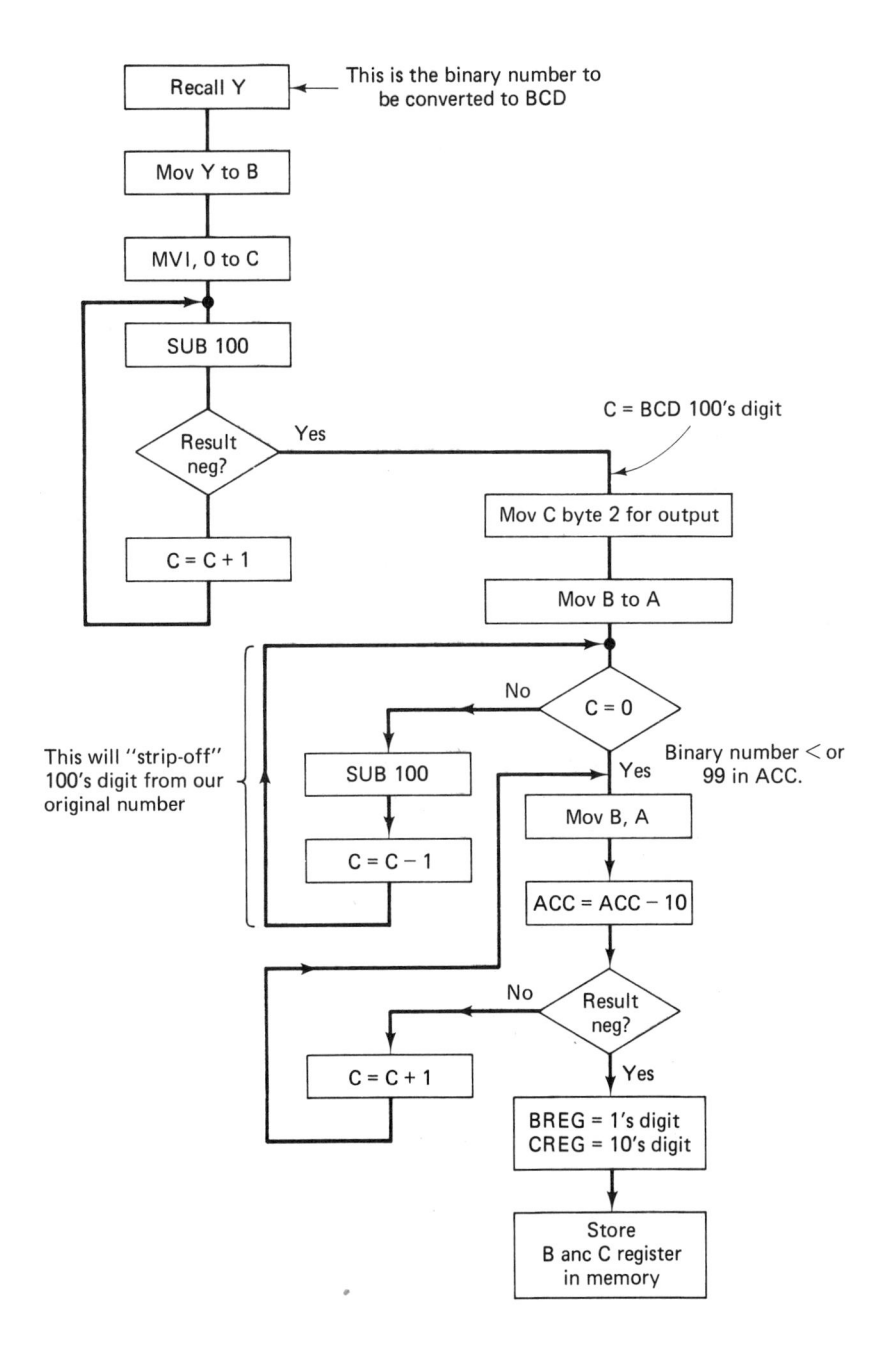

Figure 7-17 Flowchart for converting a binary number to a three-digit BCD number

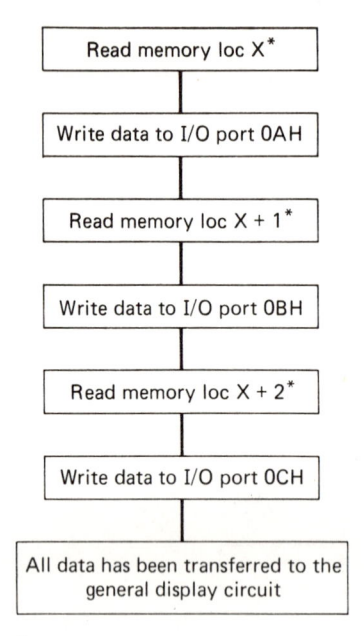

```
┌─────────────────────────┐
│   Read memory loc X*    │
└───────────┬─────────────┘
┌───────────┴─────────────┐
│ Write data to I/O port 0AH │
└───────────┬─────────────┘
┌───────────┴─────────────┐
│  Read memory loc X + 1* │
└───────────┬─────────────┘
┌───────────┴─────────────┐
│ Write data to I/O port 0BH │
└───────────┬─────────────┘
┌───────────┴─────────────┐
│  Read memory loc X + 2* │
└───────────┬─────────────┘
┌───────────┴─────────────┐
│ Write data to I/O port 0CH │
└───────────┬─────────────┘
┌───────────┴──────────────────┐
│ All data has been transferred to the │
│     general display circuit          │
└──────────────────────────────┘
```

*X indicates an absolute memory location to be assigned later

Figure 7-18 Flowchart for writing data stored in three consecutive bytes of memory to the general output display I/O circuit

ory location zero because the reset input to the 8080 is active when the system is in the manual mode. The reset function of the 8080 device is discussed in detail in Chapter 9. We mention it here so everyone will know why we load the program into memory, starting at location 0, and also how the 8080 begins to run in a known state. In Chapter 8 we will cover troubleshooting the system if the solution does not work the first time.

Review Questions

1. Referring to Figure 7-3, suppose the data in byte 1 and byte 2 are:

   Byte 1 = 10001010
   Byte 2 = 00001001

   What is the BCD equivalent of these data bytes?

2. Referring to Figure 7-4, suppose we wish to write +17.6 to the general output display. What is the actual binary data in each data byte 1 and 2?

3. Make a flowchart that shows a solution for converting a binary number to its octal equivalent.

```
ITEM   LOC    OBJECT CODE    SOURCE STATEMENTS                                          PAGE   1

  1    0000    .   .   .              ASB,HEX,8080 CONTROL PROGRAM
  2    0000    .   .   .        ;
  3    0000    .   .   .        ;
  4    0000    .   .   .        ;
  5    0000    .   .   .        ;    COMPLETE PROGRAM TO CONTROL SYSTEM OF CHAPTER 7
  6    0000    .   .   .        ;
  7    0000    .   .   .        ;
  8    0000   3E  00   .   BEGIN  MVI   A,0Q
  9    0002   D3  06   .          OUT   06            SELECT I/O FOR 1ST BYTE
 10    0004   DB  06   .          IN    06            READ FIRST BYTE
 11    0006   32  B7  00          STA   BYT1          STORE IN MEMORY
 12    0009   D3  06   .          OUT   06            SELECT I/O FOR 2ND BYTE
 13    000B   DB  06   .          IN    06            READ 2ND BYTE
 14    000D   32  B8  00          STA   BYT1+1        STORE IN MEM
 15    0010   E6  C0   .          ANI   300Q          MASK OF LOWER 6 BITS
 16    0012   CA  2F  00          JZ    NOERR         IF ZERO THE NO ERROR
 17    0015   E6  80   .          ANI   200Q          MASK OFF BIT D6
 18    0017   CA  1F  00          JZ    QERR          IF 0 THEN D7=0,D6=1
 19    001A   3E  1C   .          MVI   A,034Q        BYTE3=00011100 BLINK DIS
 20    001C   C3  21  00          JMP   BNEX
 21    001F   3E  0C   .   QERR   MVI   A,014Q        BYTE 3=00001100 NO BLINK
 22    0021   32  B9  00   BNEX   STA   BYT1+2        STORE BYTE 3 FOR OUTPUT IN
                                                      MEM
 23    0024   3E  99   .          MVI   A,231Q        ACC=10011001=99 BCD
 24    0026   32  B7  00          STA   BYT1
 25    0029   32  B8  00          STA   BYT1+1        ALL DIGITS=99
 26    002C   C3  A5  00          JMP   ROUT          GOTO OUTPUT SECTION OF PRO
                                                      GRAM
 27    002F   3A  B8  00   NOERR  LDA   BYT1+1        NO ERR FORMAT BYTE 3
 28    0032   47   .   .          MOV   B,A           B=2ND BYTE FROM I/O PORT
 29    0033   0E  00   .          MVI   C,0Q          C=BYTE 3 INITIALIZE TO 0
 30    0035   E6  01   .          ANI   01            EXAMINE BIT 1 ONLY
 31    0037   CA  3C  00          JZ    S1
 32    003A   0E  08   .          MVI   C,010Q        SET BIT D3=1 + SIGN
 33    003C   47   .   .   S1     MOV   B,A           RESTORE ACC NO MASK
 34    003D   E6  02   .          ANI   002Q          EXAMINE D1 ONLY
 35    003F   CA  49  00          JZ    T1
 36    0042   79   .   .          MOV   A,C
 37    0043   F6  01   .          ORI   001Q          BYTE 3= XXXXX001
 38    0045   4F   .   .          MOV   C,A
 39    0046   C3  67  00          JMP   Z
 40    0049   78   .   .   T1     MOV   A,B           RESTORE ACC NO MASK
 41    004A   E6  04   .          ANI   004Q          CHECK BIT D3=1
 42    004C   CA  56  00          JZ    V1            BIT NOT =1
 43    004F   79   .   .          MOV   A,C
 44    0050   F6  02   .          ORI   002Q          BYTE 3=XXXXX010
 45    0052   4F   .   .          MOV   C,A
 46    0053   C3  67  00          JMP   Z
 47    0056   78   .   .   V1     MOV   A,B           RESTORE ACC NO MASK
 48    0057   E6  08   .          ANI   010Q          CHECK BIT D3 ONLY
 49    0059   CA  63  00          JZ    U1
 50    005C   79   .   .          MOV   A,C
```

Figure 7-19 Complete 8080 program to control the hardware for the system given in this chapter (part a) (Continued next page)

```
ITEM    LOC     OBJECT CODE     SOURCE STATEMENTS                                   PAGE   2

 51     0050    F6  03          .           ORI     003Q        BYTE 3=XXXXX011
 52     005F    4F      .   .               MOV     C,A
 53     0060    C3  67  00                  JMP     Z
 54     0063    79      .   .   U1          MOV     A,C
 55     0064    F6  04      .               ORI     004Q        BYTE 3=XXXXX100
 56     0066    4F      .   .               MOV     C,A
 57     0067    79      .   .   Z           MOV     A,C         MOVE BYTE 3 TO ACC
 58     0068    32  B9  00                  STA     BYT1+2      STORE IN MEM
 59     006B    .   .   .       ;
 60     006B    .   .   .       ;
 61     006B    .   .   .       ;   NOW TO FORMAT THE BYTES 1,2 FOR DISPLAY
 62     006B    .   .   .       ;
 63     006B    .   .   .       ;
 64     006B    3A  B7  00                  LDA     BYT1        FIRST BYTE FROM I/O PORT
 65     006E    47      .   .               MOV     B,A         STORE IN B REGISTER
 66     006F    0E  00      .               MVI     C,00        INITIALIZE COUNTER=0
 67     0071    D6  64      .   BB          SUI     100         SUBTRACT 100 FROM ACC
 68     0073    FA  7A  00                  JM      AA          IF RESULT IS NEG JUMP
 69     0076    0C      .   .               INR     C           NOT NEG SO INCREMENT COUNT
 70     0077    C3  71  00                  JMP     BB          GO AGAIN UNTIL NEG
 71     007A    79      .   .   AA          MOV     A,C         BCD VALUE IN C TO ACC
 72     007B    32  B8  00                  STA     BYT1+1      BYT1+1=100'S AND 1000'S DIGIT
 73     007E    FE  00      .   DD          CPI     00Q         CHECK FOR C 100'S DIGIT =0
 74     0080    CA  8D  00                  JZ      CC
 75     0083    78      .   .               MOV     A,B
 76     0084    D6  64      .               SUI     100         STRIP OFF 100'S DIGIT
 77     0086    47      .   .               MOV     B,A         STORE ACC TEMP
 78     0087    79      .   .               MOV     A,C
 79     0088    3D      .   .               DCR     A
 80     0089    4F      .   .               MOV     C,A         DECREMENT BCD VALUE OF 100S
 81     008A    C3  7E  00                  JMP     DD
 82     008D    .   .   .       ;
 83     008D    .   .   .       ; WHEN FINISHED WITH THE ABOVE LOOP A NUMBER
 84     008D    .   .   .       ; BETWEEN 99 AND 0 IS IN THE B REGISTER
 85     008D    .   .   .       ;
 86     008D    .   .   .       ;
 87     008D    0E  00      .   CC          MVI     C,00        INITIALIZE COUNTER =0
 88     008F    78      .   .   CD          MOV     A,B         ACC = NUMBER OF 10'S +1'S
 89     0090    D6  0A      .               SUI     10          SUBTRACT 10
 90     0092    FA  9A  00                  JM      EE          IF NEGATIVE GOTO EE
 91     0095    47      .   .               MOV     B,A
 92     0096    0C      .   .               INR     C           INCREMENT COUNT
 93     0097    C3  8F  00                  JMP     CD
 94     009A    .   .   .       ;
 95     009A    .   .   .       ; WHEN THE ABOVE LOOP IS FINISHED B REGISTER=1'S
 96     009A    .   .   .       ; C REGISTER = BCD 10'S
 97     009A    .   .   .       ;
 98     009A    .   .   .       ;
 99     009A    79      .   .   EE          MOV     A,C         BCD VALUE IN ACC
100     009B    17      .   .               RAL
101     009C    17      .   .               RAL
102     009D    17      .   .               RAL
```

Figure 7-19 (part b) Complete 8080 program to control the hardware for the system given in this chapter

```
ITEM    LOC     OBJECT CODE     SOURCE STATEMENTS                          PAGE   3
 103    009E    17   .   .              RAL              SHIFT LEFT 4 BITS
 104    009F    E6   F0  .              ANI    360Q      MASK OFF LOWER 4 BITS
 105    00A1    B0   .   .              ORA    B         ACC NOW IS CORRECTLY FORMAT
                                                         TED
 106    00A2    32   B7  00             STA    BYT1      BYTE 1 FOR DISPLAY IN MEM
 107    00A5    .    .   .       ;
 108    00A5    .    .   .       ;  NOW TO PRINT OUT THE DATA TO THE DISPLAY
 109    00A5    .    .   .       ;
 110    00A5    .    .   .       ;
 111    00A5    3A   B7  00      ROUT   LDA    BYT1
 112    00A8    D3   0A  .              OUT    10        FIRST BYTE TO PORT A
 113    00AA    3A   B8  00             LDA    BYT1+1
 114    00AD    D3   0B  .              OUT    11        SECOND BYTE TO PORT B
 115    00AF    3A   B9  00             LDA    BYT1+2
 116    00B2    D3   0C  .              OUT    12        3RD BYTE TO PORT C
 117    00B4    C3   00  00             JMP    BEGIN     START OVER AGAIN
 118    00B7    .    .   .       ;
 119    00B7    .    .   .       ;
 120    00B7    .    .   .       ;  STORAGE LOCATIONS FOR DATA IN MEM FOLLOW
 121    00B7    .    .   .       ;
 122    00B7    .    .   .       ;
 123    00B7    00   .   .       BYT1   NOP
 124    00B8    00   .   .              NOP
 125    00B9    00   .   .              NOP
 126    00BA    .    .   .       ;
 127    00BA    .    .   ,       ;
 128    00BA    .    .   .              END              END STATEMENT FOR COMPILER
   0    ERRORS FOUND IN ASSEMBLY CODE .
```

Figure 7-19 (part c) Complete 8080 program to control the hardware for the system given in this chapter

211

8

STATIC STIMULUS TESTING AND OTHER TROUBLESHOOTING TECHNIQUES

Testing and troubleshooting are vital and necessary parts of manufacturing and using machines of all kinds. This has been true ever since man chipped his first crude spearhead. Unlike most of man's machines prior to the electrical age, electrical and electronic equipment defies analysis by physical examination based on sight and touch alone. This is a fact we must face when we compare electrical machinery with nonelectrical machinery. The eye cannot see magnetic or electric fields, and the ear cannot hear electrons move; the "events" or phenomena that make electrical and electronic circuits valuable to us take place on the atomic scale. Hence, all of our sensory inputs of what is taking place in a working electrical circuit are secondary indications, *not* the primary phenomena themselves.

The difficulty posed by the invisibility of basic events in electrical and electronic circuits requires that we use instruments as translators of the primary phenomena into forms that are acceptable and meaningful to our human senses. We might say that the instruments present us with symbols, visible or audible, of unseeable events, which are really another form of abstraction as discussed in Chapter 1. Whatever way we choose to make events on the atomic level "visible" to us, most people will agree that working effectively with electronics requires a high degree of mastery of abstractions. We *must* rely on instruments, and we *must* form mental pictures based on what the instruments tell us about events that we have never seen!

8-1 Troubleshooting Digital Equipment Compared with Troubleshooting Analog Equipment

Analog equipment is built to amplify, store, and process signals with a minimum of distortion. A typical application is in high fidelity recording, where sound tracks must be pure or true. Its development began to move steadily with the invention of the telephone in 1875. Digital equipment came later with the completion of the *Electronic Numerator, Integrator, And Calculator* (ENIAC) in 1946, which marked a comparable significant starting point in electronic computer development. To be noted is the fact that the troubleshooting and testing of analog equipment had already reached a high state of maturity when digital equipment arrived on the scene.

In order to make some comparisons, let's take a brief look at the nature of electronic troubleshooting. It may be subdivided as follows:

1. Component testing. This involves checking individual components to insure that they conform to their specifications.
2. Static, in-circuit testing of components and circuits. This involves both power-on and power-off checks of components and circuits for "what should be there."
3. Substitution testing of components and circuits. This involves checking to determine that the circuit is working properly with the new replacement component or circuit in place of the original.
4. Dynamic, in-circuit, operational performance tests of circuits and components. This includes signal injection and signal tracing techniques when in-use operational tests reveal a malfunction.

With regard to Item 1, seldom are *all* components tested out-of-circuit prior to manufacture and installation in either analog or digital systems. Because of this, and because of errors that may creep in during the manufacturing process, quality testing of each system is essential at the end of the production line before the product can be certified for sale.

Dynamic operational tests (Item 4) are the final authority on whether the design and manufacturing steps have been successful. These in-circuit tests answer the question, does this circuit work properly? This is true for both analog and digital systems. The basic goal is to produce stable, predictable, dependable units that are economically attractive, durable, and trouble-free in performance. Every time a digital or analog system is operated, it undergoes a dynamic test.

When a system fails this user test, it is brought to a technician who uses signal injection and signal tracing techniques to localize the trouble to a small section or area. From this point, the troubleshooter can use a combination of static tests and parts substitution to pinpoint the defect and effect the repair.

Substitution or replacement of suspected parts is the next to last step in the troubleshooting and repair process. The last step is a final operational test itself, to see if the equipment is now working properly; this is the "moment of truth" that reveals whether or not the troubleshooting process has been successful. This is equally true in both analog and digital systems.

It is in the use of static tests of digital and analog systems that differences arise. Static tests of the discrete components that have historically made up analog systems are both valuable and necessary. In fact, such tests form the backbone of much of the troubleshooting process because they are so highly effective. However, such discrete *component* testing is not possible in most digital equipment because ICs are used; the decision that an IC is defective must often be made on the basis of dynamic tests alone. Typically such tests call for all clock and control signals to be operating at normal speeds and specifications. This means that control signals are very fleeting and constantly changing. The technician has little time to select and study a particular logic level as it propagates through the system.

In the remainder of this chapter different techniques for troubleshooting a microprocessor-controlled system are discussed. Although we focus on the 8080, the techniques described can be adapted to other microprocessor devices. The complexity of a microprocessor circuit may lead one to think that simple troubleshooting techniques cannot be employed. This is not true. It is possible to troubleshoot these complex circuits in a straightforward, uncomplicated manner that will save time and produce good results.

8-2 Static Stimulus Testing

The potential power of static testing has been largely ignored in digital literature and practice. The author has effectively used a technique we shall call *Static Stimulus Testing* to take advantage of the power of static testing in digital troubleshooting and make it as productive as it has long been in analog circuits. Static stimulus testing (SST), in addition to adding a new and powerful dimension to digital troubleshooting, also vastly simplifies it by making possible the use of more basic, less exotic, and less expensive instrumentation.

Before anyone can troubleshoot the 8080 circuits with assurance he or she must have a very good understanding of what should be there. That is, one must know 1) the controlling signals that the 8080 sends out, 2) the functions of the peripherals to which the controlling signals go, and 3) the logic level that must appear at specific points to accomplish a particular function or instruction. We have delayed the discussion of troubleshooting until now so these three areas could be explained. One must understand how the microprocessor is used in order to appreciate the procedures, steps, and sequences that will be most effective in troubleshooting these circuits. In this example and in previous discussions the 8080 has operated in one way—as a controller. Since the 8080 provides all of the control signals for the circuit, we might say that all circuits are "slaved" to the 8080.

For convenience, it helps to classify digital malfunctions into two categories:

1. timing problems, and
2. faults in circuits and devices.

In any system that has been operating correctly, a timing problem is less likely than a fault in a circuit or device. Note that static stimulus testing is especially valuable for locating faults in circuits and devices, and not for solving timing problems. Static stimulus testing is especially well-adapted to troubleshooting microprocessor systems because a steady logic level can be supplied as a control signal for as long as necessary while our stimulus box substitutes for the microprocessor.

Since control signals from the 8080 occur at a rapid rate and in a non-periodic manner, easy observation of these signals with an oscilloscope is very difficult. Using the technique of SST, we will be able to reduce complex dynamic troubleshooting problems to simpler static troubleshooting ones wherever possible. Troubleshooting static (DC) voltages is much easier than troubleshooting nonperiodic, dynamic signals.

The first special troubleshooting device we will employ in static stimulus testing will be a signal injector, or "stimulus box." The signals we will inject are DC voltages of the T^2L level. The main idea is to substitute our own static control signals for those normally produced by the 8080. First, we must physically remove the 8080 from the circuit. This is readily possible if the 8080 is mounted on a socket. If the 8080 is soldered directly to a circuit board, it is worth the trouble to remove it and mount a 40-pin socket on the circuit board to receive the 8080 as a plug-in device. Fortunately, most system designers realize that the 8080 must be removed in the troubleshooting process and so design the system with a socket mount. In any case, the 8080 is removed from the circuit board for troubleshooting and our signal injector is installed in its place. The physical system is shown in Figure 8-1.

To plug the signal injector cable into the 40-pin socket may require some modification to the cable or connector. Different 40-pin sockets have different types of holes to receive the 8080, so the cable must be adaptable to the type of socket. The other end of the cable, of course, comes from our stimulus box,

Figure 8-1 Photograph of an 8080 system (a) connected to static stimulus box (b)

which has toggle switches that will force the individual output lines on the circuit board to known logic states at the operator's option. These states are static as long as the controlling switch remains in that particular position. With these outputs in known states it becomes an easy task to trace a signal from the 8080 socket pin through connecting lines and devices to its ending point. While following the signal path we can perform static checks of any logic elements that are included in it. Using our stimulus box, we can provide data bus outputs and actually transfer data to and from an IO port and memory. The power and beauty of this technique is that it permits us to hold any logic level steady for as long as we need to check all the elements in the signal path.

Our stimulus box also has a signal monitoring circuit that monitors data bus lines D_0–D_7 visually. This is particularly useful for visually monitoring data input to the 8080. Using our stimulus box, we can call for an I/O read or a memory read and actually see the data being strobed into the 8080.

These checks are static checks only, and one may object that timing parameters are not being investigated. This is true. We assume that if the system was once working correctly, the probability is that all timing specifications for this system are correct. We may be wrong, of course, because it is possible for integrated circuits to develop timing changes as a function of age and/or tempera-

Sec. 8-2   *Static Stimulus Testing*   **217**

ture. When this happens, we usually have an intermittent problem, or "soft failure." These problems are never easy to find. One must duplicate conditions in such a way that the soft failure will become a hard failure. When a hard failure does occur the technique presented here locates it in a very short period of time.

The block diagram for our stimulus box is shown in Figure 8-2. The complete

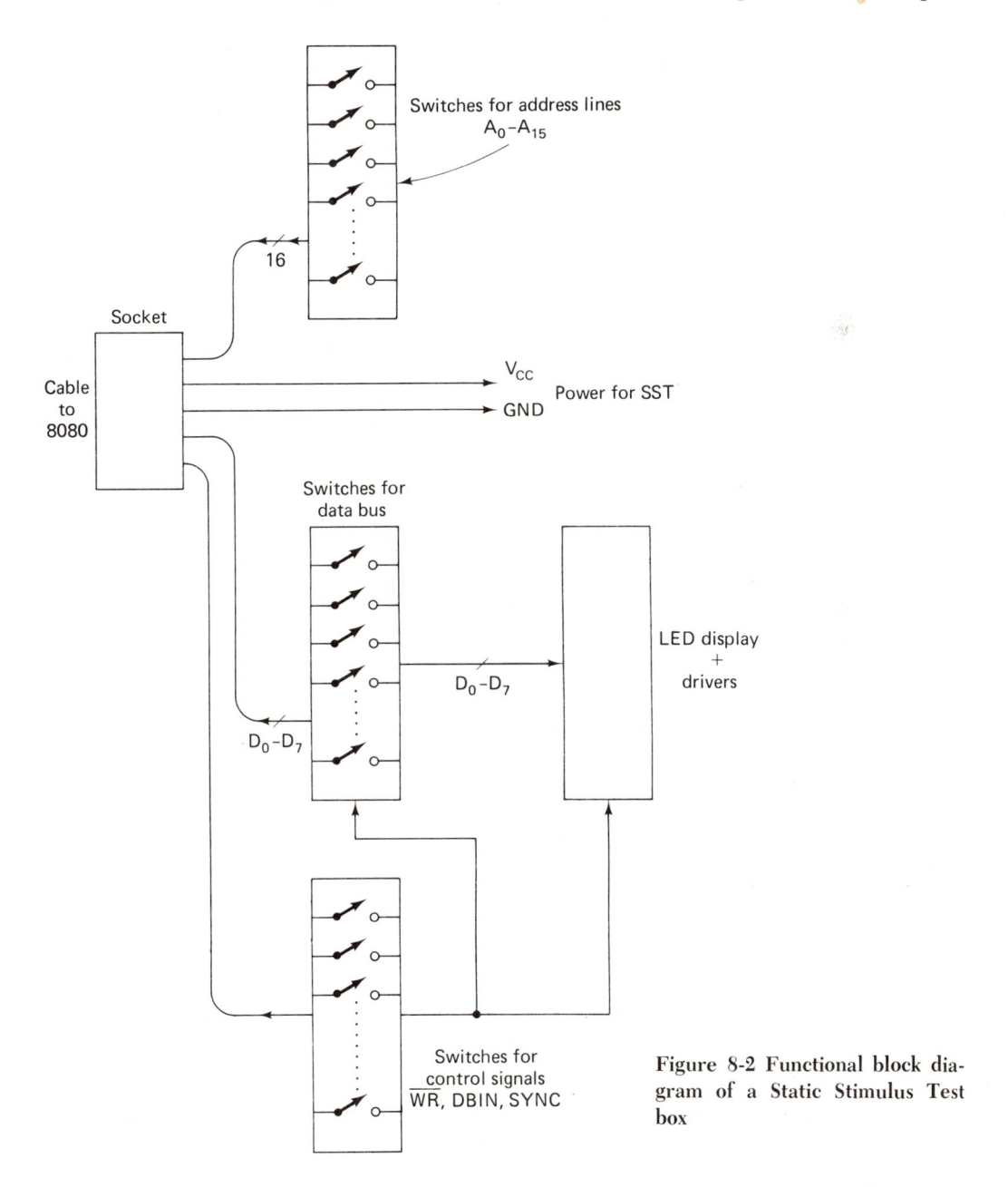

Figure 8-2 Functional block diagram of a Static Stimulus Test box

schematic for this circuit is given in Figure 8-3.* Notice that the +5 *volts* and *ground* for the box are taken from the +5 volt and ground pin of the 8080 socket. The devices used for building the stimulus box are standard T²L and CMOS devices. The hardware items are inexpensive, and one can construct the SST box in a short period of time.

Here is an example of how to use this SST box for troubleshooting a system. Suppose we want to verify that a microprocessor system can write to a specified memory location. The steps for doing this with the stimulus box are the same as for the 8080. This is why one must be familiar with the operation of the 8080 to effectively use this type of static stimulus testing. Using the stimulus box, the events for writing to memory are:

1. Set address switches and lines A_0–A_{15} to the desired memory address. When these address lines are set to proper logic levels, statically check the address inputs to memory for proper corresponding voltage levels.
2. Set data switches D_0–D_7 to the correct status word for a memory write. Status information for this operation can be obtained from the status word chart in Appendix A.
3. Set the SYNC signal to logical 1. Check to make sure that the status strobe signal is reaching the strobe input to the latches by checking for proper voltage level.
4. Set the SYNC signal to logical 0. Check to make sure the strobe signal for the latches is disabled by checking for proper voltage level.
5. Set data lines D_0–D_7 to the data we wish to write to the memory address set on A_0–A_{15} (Step 1).
6. Set the $\overline{WR}$ signal to logical 0. The memory write signal $\overline{MEMR}$ should be valid (logical 0, and logical 1, depending on the system design) at the memory R/W input line.
7. Set the $\overline{WR}$ signal to a logical 1. Now, the $\overline{MEMR}$ signal should *not* be valid. The data should now be in memory at the address set by address lines A_0–A_{15}. To further illustrate this point, let's take a specific example. We will use the system shown in Figure 8-4. This system contains the memory and all peripheral decoding logic for the 8080 to write and read data from memory. In this example we wish to write data to memory location $A3_{16}$. This corresponds to memory address (MSB)→ 10100011←(LSB) in binary.

---

*A kit is available from Creative Microprocessor Systems, P.O. Box 1538, 18615 Farragut Lane, Los Gatos, CA 95030.

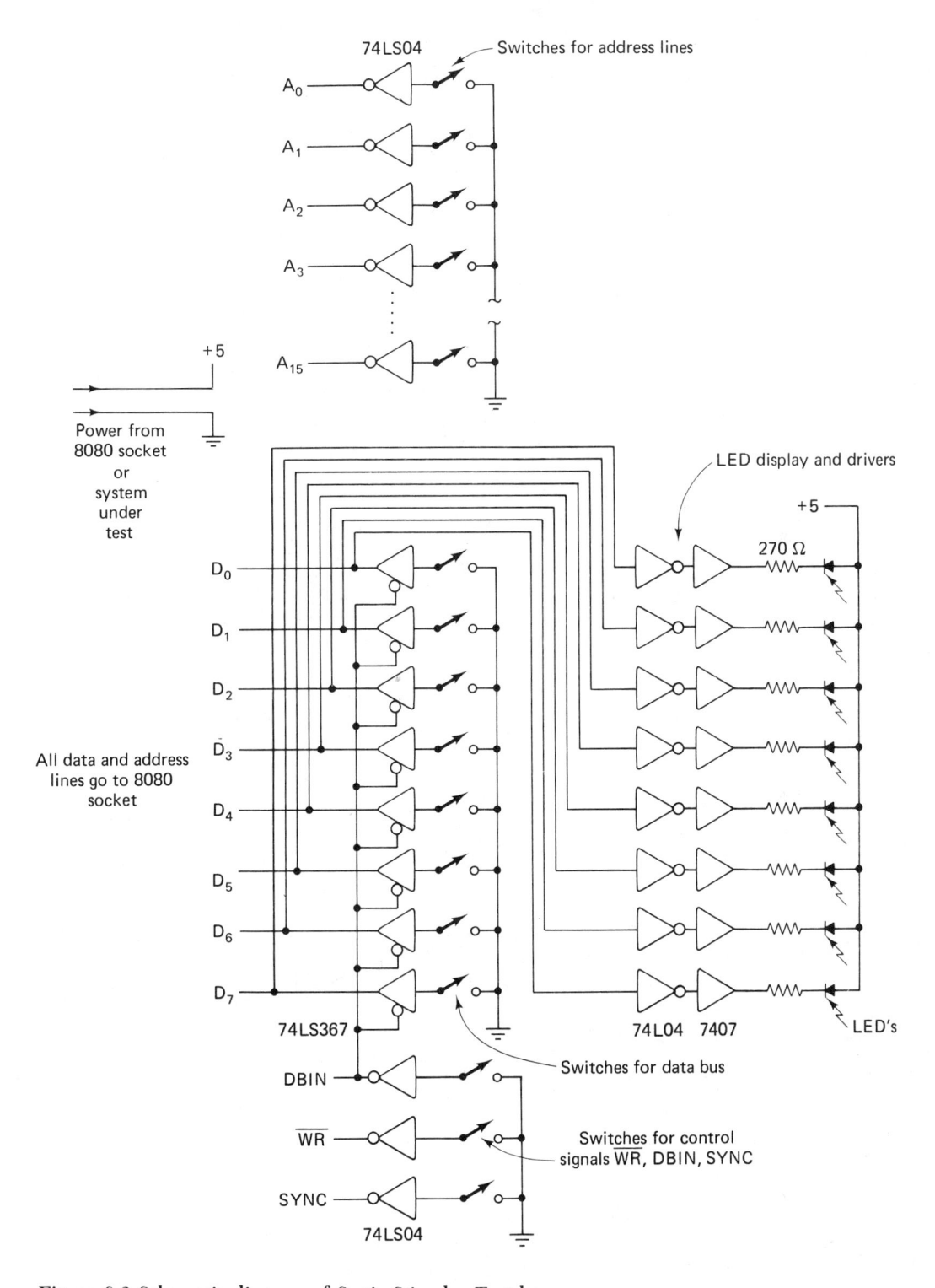

Figure 8-3 Schematic diagram of Static Stimulus Test box

Figure 8-4 Schematic of basic 8080 system

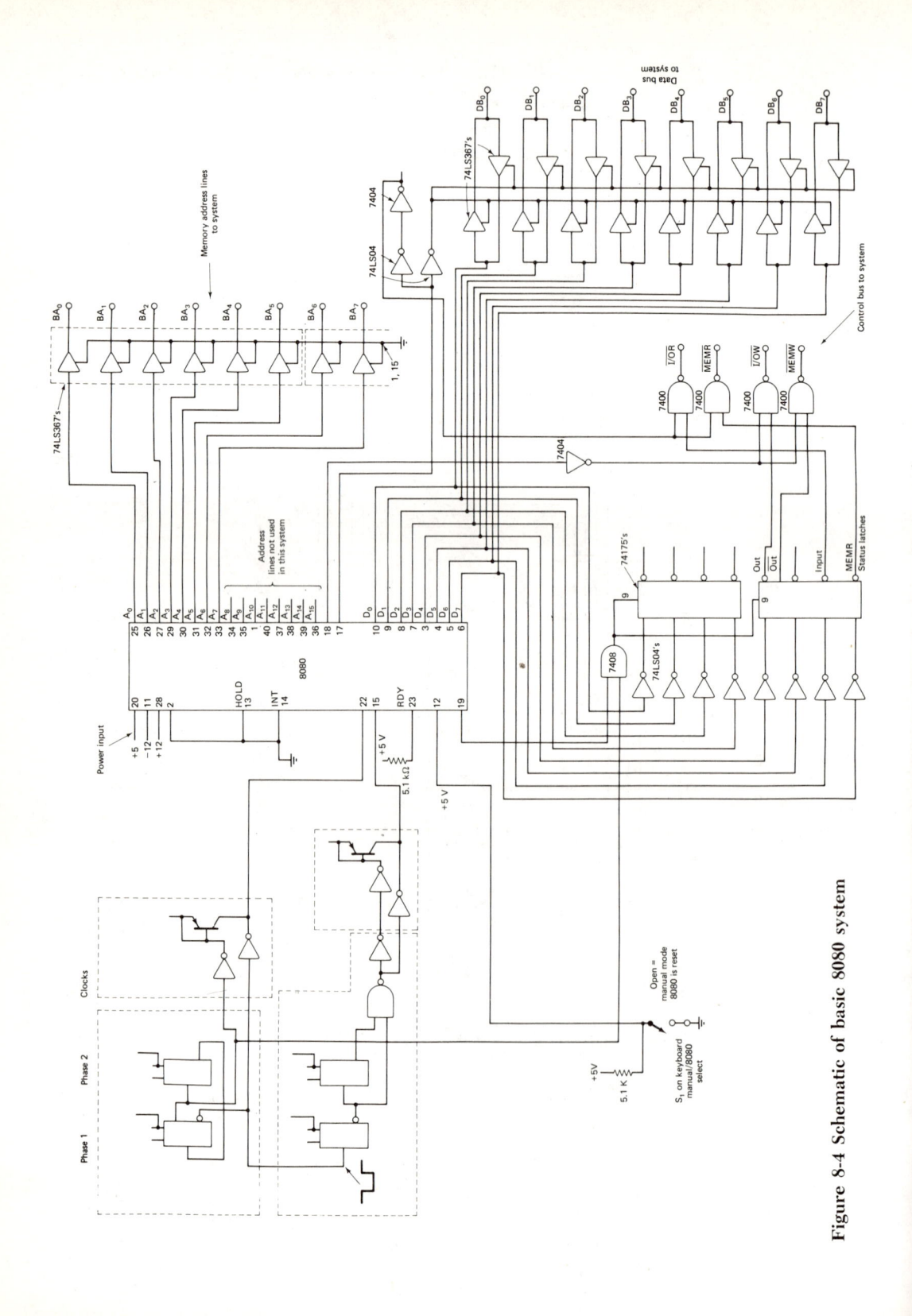

Sec. 8-2 Static Stimulus Testing

We set this binary word on the *address* (A_0–A_7) toggle switches of our SST box. We can now check all address inputs statically to insure that proper logic voltage levels are maintained to the input pins of the memory. One can see that static stimulus testing is much easier than trying to examine these address lines while the system is running a program that may access these address inputs only *one* brief moment.

When we have made certain that all address inputs to the memory are correct, we proceed to the second step required to write data to memory. We now set the *data* switches of our stimulus box for the correct status word. This status word is 00_{16}. All data switches are set to logical 0 level. Next, we set the SYNC control switch to logical 1. This action enables the status word to be strobed into the status latches. Now we return the SYNC output to logical 0. The status word will remain stable until we change it again. Now one can realize how essential it is for troubleshooters to have a sure understanding of 8080 external circuit control.

Now we have the status word correct and we can statically determine if all external circuitry is responding to the status information as it should. We check the control bus logic and follow the path for a memory write.

First, we set data switches D_0–D_7 to write some desired data word to the memory. Let us write AA_{16}. This would mean that the binary word would be 10101010. We check the data at the memory data input lines to insure that the data is actually reaching these inputs.

Second, we enable the $\overline{WR}$ control switch to logical 0. This action should cause a logical 0 to occur at the R/W input pin of the memory. Third, we return the WR switch to logical 1 level. The R/W input to the memory should now be at logical 1 level.

Notice in each step that the signals to memory can be checked in a static fashion. Further, each path for data can be enabled just as it would be if the 8080 were controlling the circuits. If all paths check good statically, then there is good assurance that the system will work dynamically under the control of the microprocessor.

We will perform a memory read operation now to determine if the data we input has actually been stored in the memory. Here it should be noted that the status information will be strobed into the status latches because of the free-running strobe input signal that is generated by the timing generator circuit. The status information will be valid when the SYNC signal goes to logical 1.

To read data from memory we will use the SST box to inject signals in the following way:

1. Set address lines A_0–A_{15} to the memory address from which we wish to read data. Let us use the same address we have written data into, $A3_{16}$.

2. Set D_0–D_7 to the correct status word for a memory read, 10000010.
3. Set the SYNC signal to logical 1. This allows the status word to be strobed into the status latches.
4. Set the SYNC signal to logical 0.
5. Set the DBIN signal to logical 1. This action does three things. First, it enables the LEDs inside the stimulus box to reflect the information on the D_0–D_7 data lines. Second, the DBIN signal enables the bidirectional buffers to allow data from memory to be input to the 8080. Finally, the DBIN signal enables the tri-state buffers on the memory circuit. This allows the memory data to control data lines D_0–D_7. We should see the data AA_{16} in binary form on the LEDs of the SST box, since this was the data we had previously written to that memory location.

Using the stimulus box, we can statically check the logic level of the various circuits, one at a time at each new step. And we can perform these same operations on the various I/O ports in the system. With this device and technique we can execute an orderly sequence of static checks of all the decoding and I/O port select signals. We can also read and write data to an I/O port. To do this we follow the same sequence of events that is used when the 8080 CPU provides control. The idea of a stimulus box can be modified to fit a particular application. Only the basic architecture is presented here. Many more "bells and whistles" can be added to make the box easier to use in any given application.

8-3 Construction and Use of a Mobile I/O Port

Another special circuit we will use is a "mobile" I/O port, which can be attached to an 8080 system via clip leads or cable. The mobile I/O port has two physical ports. One is for writing data to, and the other is for reading data from. Each port has a settable port address, so that the I/O address can be changed easily with switches. The physical unit connects as shown in Figure 8-5. We will use special 16-pin IC clips to gain physical access to the control bus and data bus for other measurements. These clips are shown in use in Figure 8-6. If one is troubleshooting a particular piece of hardware regularly, then special test points may be added to the circuit board to accommodate the use of the mobile I/O port readily. A schematic for this I/O port is shown in Figure 8-7.

Notice that this I/O port can also serve as a memory address. We simply connect the $\overline{\text{MEMR}}$ and $\overline{\text{MEMW}}$ signal from the control bus to the $\overline{\text{IOR}}$ and $\overline{\text{IOW}}$ signals input to the I/O port. With this we can write a program that will

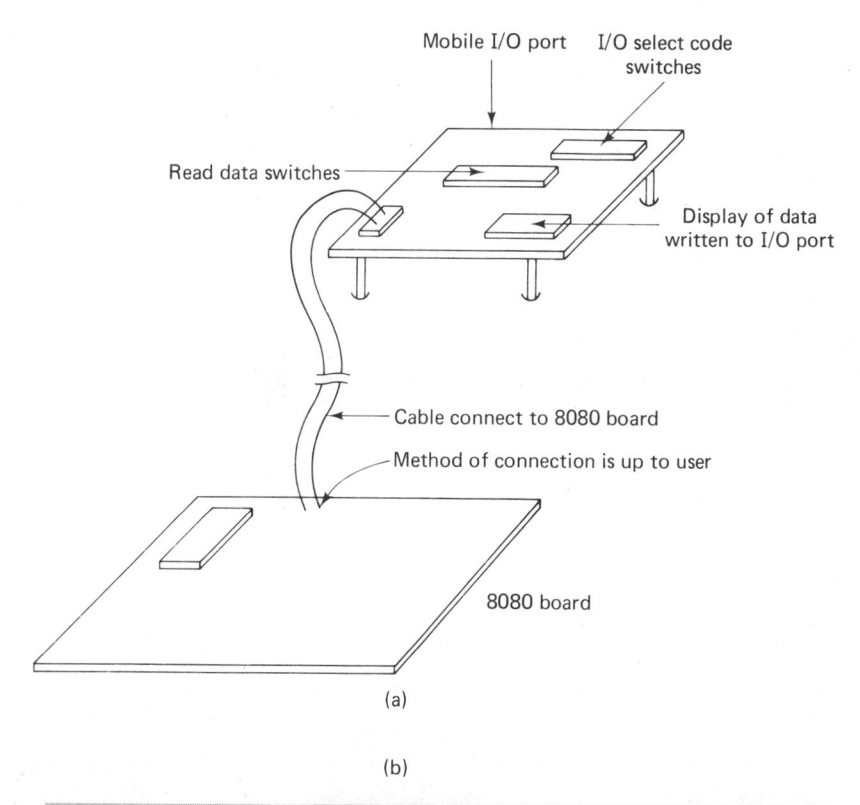

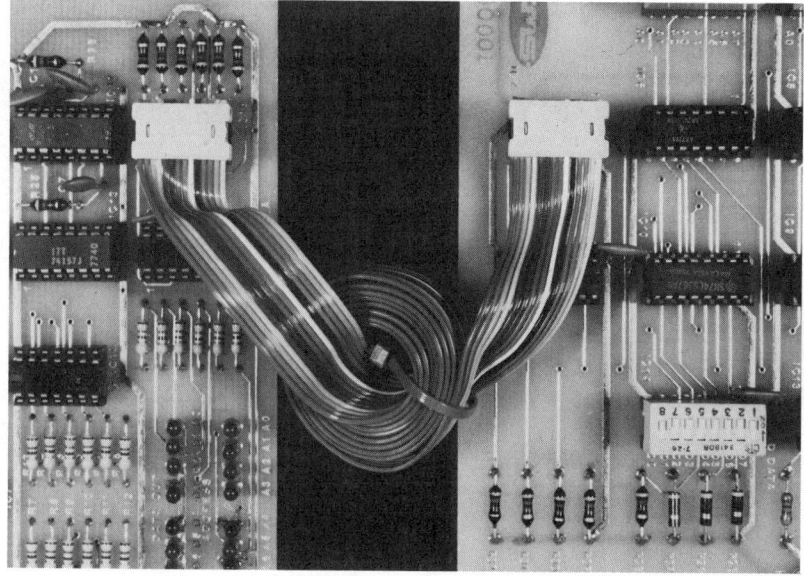

Figure 8-5 Pictorial illustration showing the mobile I/O port in use

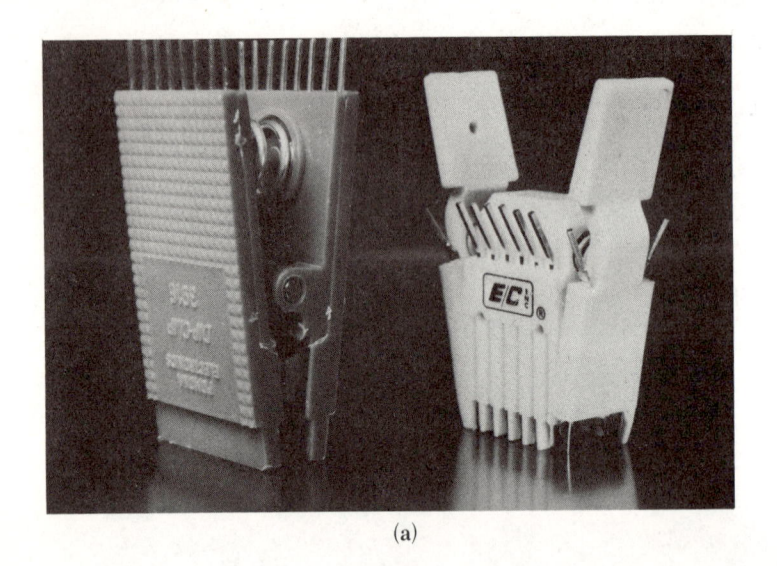

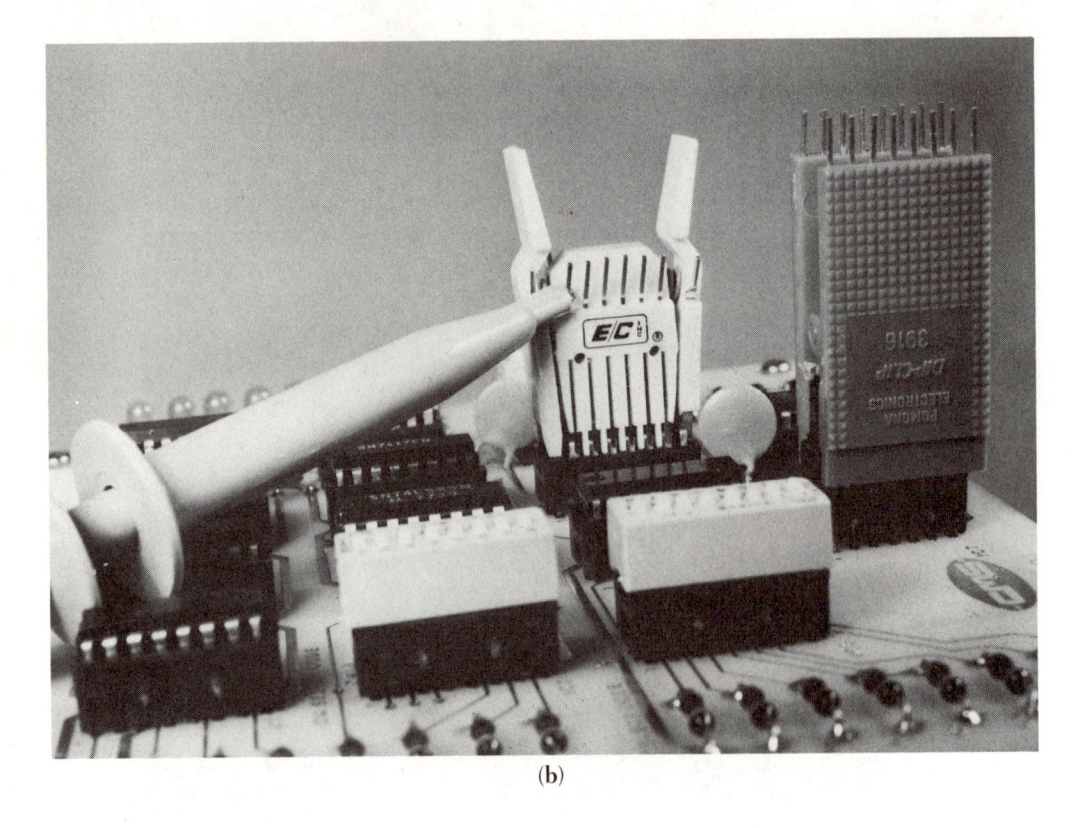

Figure 8-6 Photograph of IC clips (a) showing how they are used to gain access to test points for measurements (b)

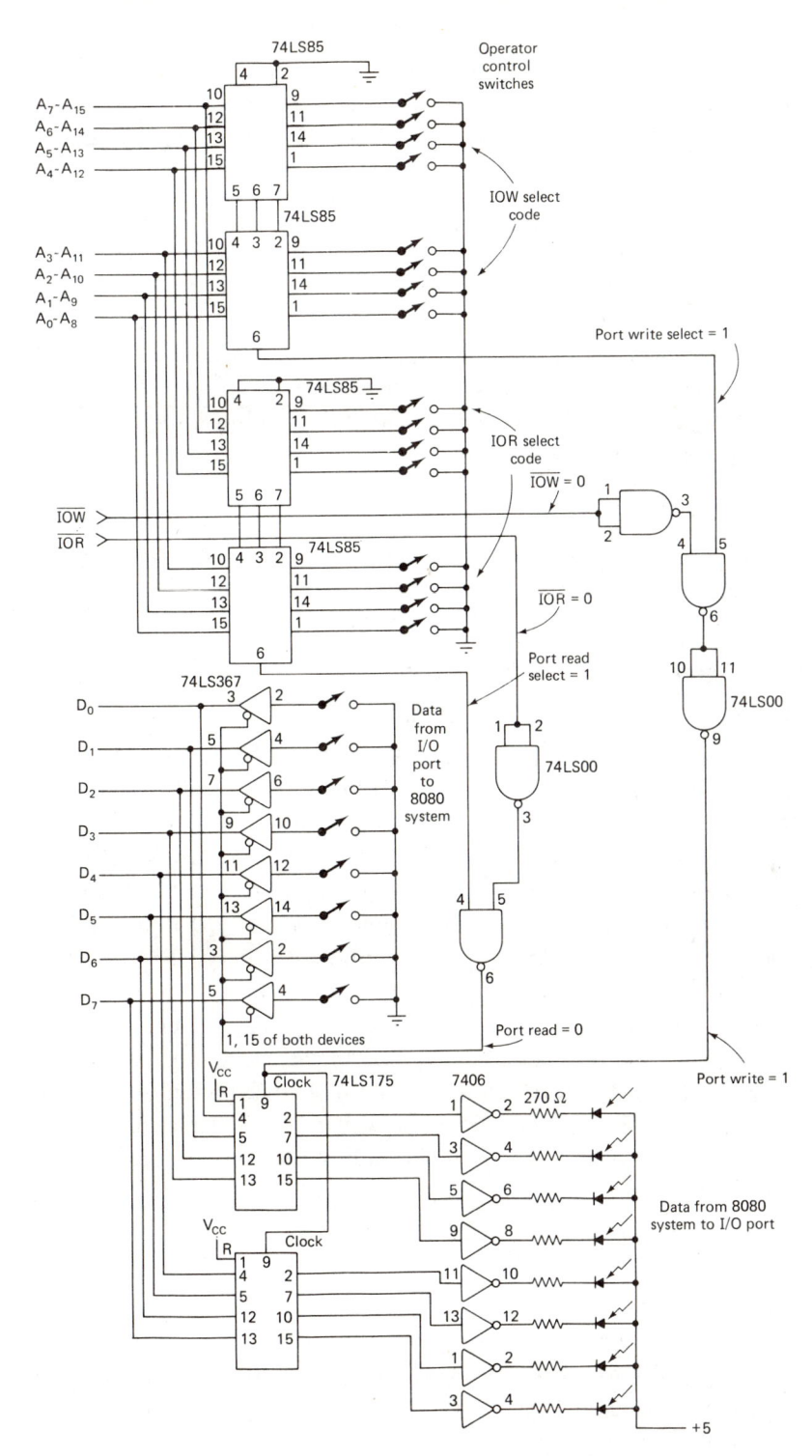

Figure 8-7 Schematic of mobile I/O port

225

read and write to the I/O port and determine if the buses are all functional. If one suspects that a particular I/O port in a system is defective the following can be done:

1. Disconnect the $\overline{IOR}$ and $\overline{IOW}$ signals input to the suspect I/O port
2. Set the mobile (test) I/O port address to the same as the suspect port
3. Set known data in the read port, and perform a read-from and then a write-to the I/O port being tested
4. This will quickly determine the hardware path used to write and read from the suspect port.

This type of mobile I/O port is very effective in systems in which the software instructions can be changed. The mobile I/O port also provides a dynamic check of all timing signals.

8-4 Troubleshooting Systems with Read Only Memory

Some microprocessor systems are entirely programmed in some type of non-changeable memory. This is ROM, PROM, or EPROM. This leads us to a third very useful tool for the microprocessor troubleshooter.

If the system is programmed in some type of ROM, the troubleshooters should program their own special "DEBUG" ROM. This ROM can be inserted into the system and it will perform certain diagnostic programs that are unique for that piece of equipment. This type of debugging tool is very effective when one is troubleshooting the same type of equipment over and over again.

For instance, if one has the responsibility for repairing a microprocessor-controlled test system, one can modify the system to change ROMs easily. This modification can be as simple as inserting a socket in a circuit board so one can unplug one ROM and plug in another. It will be well worth the effort and cost to have this flexibility in order to decrease the amount of time one spends locating and repairing problems.

We have presented three major special tools that can be used in troubleshooting of microprocessor circuits. These are:

1. a stimulus box (signal injector) for static stimulus testing
2. a mobile I/O port with selectable I/O address
3. a special software ROM for use in systems that are programmed in nonchangeable memory. That is, the entire program for the 8080 is contained in ROM.

8-5 Localizing Trouble in a Microprocessor System

Let us now show how these tools could be used to locate a problem in a microprocessor system. We will use the system we presented in Chapter 7. Suppose we had this system running the program that was shown in Figure 7-19 and found that the display was reading incorrectly. There are two major areas where the problem could be. One is the software, which could be in error. That is, our program could be performing functions in an incorrect sequence. The second area is the hardware controlled by the 8080, or the 8080 itself could be defective.

If we are troubleshooting a system that has worked properly in the past but is now malfunctioning, we suspect the hardware. We know that the order of the instructions was correct once and there is no reason to suspect that it is bad now. However, the memory may be defective, and the instructions are being modified by a malfunctioning memory. This is still a hardware problem, rather than a software error.

If we assume that we have a hardware problem, where do we start to look in the system to find the problem? There are several approaches we can take, depending on the type of memory that is operating the system. If we have a ROM memory, then we can insert our "debug" ROM and run our own diagnostic programs on our system. These diagnostics could consist of reading and writing data to specified I/O ports and to memory. Also, the special diagnostic program could read and write data to the mobile I/O port that we use as a troubleshooting aid. If our system is programmed in all ROM, then our debug ROM could include read and writes to non-existent I/O ports in the system. We could then make our mobile I/O port select the correct code for this non-existent I/O port. In this way we could check dynamically the circuits and buses required to perform memory and I/O operations.

If the system will not transfer data to and from the special I/O port, then we can install our static stimulus box and inject the correct signals to the system. While injecting these signals we can monitor the response of the I/O hardware and memory hardware to trace down the problem. We have, in effect, made a very complicated dynamic troubleshooting problem a simpler static one. When troubleshooters become practiced and knowledgeable in these techniques they can develop some innovative additions of their own to augment the troubleshooting tools and techniques we have described.

Let us now discuss a specific problem. Again we will make use of the system we designed in Chapter 7. Suppose that the output is not performing correctly; that is, the display is incorrect. The first thing we must insure is that the data we are inputting to the 8080 is correct. To do this we must examine first the digital outputs of the I/O card where these inputs are generated. We do this to insure

228 Static Stimulus Testing and Other Troubleshooting Techniques   Chap. 8

that the source of data is not in error. If it is in error we *do not* proceed further in the troubleshooting process until we have corrected this problem. Figure 8-8 shows the major areas where a problem may occur in an incorrectly working system such as we have presented.

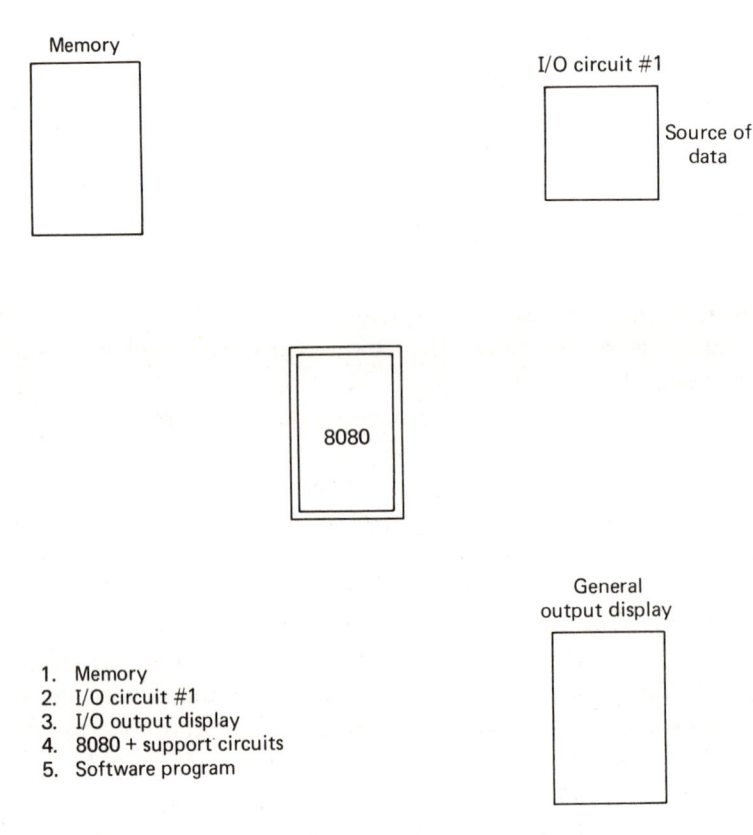

1. Memory
2. I/O circuit #1
3. I/O output display
4. 8080 + support circuits
5. Software program

Figure 8-8 Major areas where a problem may occur in a system

If we assume or find that our data source is correct, then we will check next to insure that this data is being transferred to the 8080 correctly. To do this we modify the 8080 control software (the program that is running) and insert a HLT instruction after the two bytes of data have been transferred to memory from the I/O circuit. (The modified partial program is shown in Figure 8-9.) We then switch our system into manual mode and check the data stored in memory. This procedure is outlined in the flowchart of Figure 8-10. If the data in memory is incorrect, the problem may lie in three major areas:

1. The peripheral circuits for the I/O transfer, or control (hardware), are defective

```
ITEM    LOC     OBJECT CODE     SOURCE STATEMENTS                              PAGE    1

  1     0000    .  .  .                 ASB,HEX,8080 CONTROL PROGRAM
  2     0000    .  .  .         ;
  3     0000    .  .  .         ;
  4     0000    .  .  .         ;
  5     0000    .  .  .         ;
  6     0000    3E 00 .                 MVI     A,00        ZERO TO ACC
  7     0002    D3 06 .                 OUT     06          SELECT PORT 06 FOR FIRST BYTE
  8     0004    DB 06 .                 IN      06          READ FIRST BYTE
  9     0006    32 13 00                STA     BYT1        STORE FIRST BYTE IN MEM
 10     0009    3E 01 .                 MVI     A,01        PORT 06 FOR 2ND BYTE
 11     000B    D3 06 .                 OUT     06
 12     000D    DB 06 .                 IN      06          READ 2ND BYTE TO ACC
 13     000F    32 14 00                STA     BYT1+1      STORE 2ND BYTE IN MEM
 14     0012    76 .  .                 HLT                 HALT THE SYSTEM
 15     0013    .  .  .         ;
 16     0013    .  .  .         ;
 17     0013    .  .  .         ; LOCATIONS TO STORE DATA BYTES
 18     0013    .  .  .         ;
 19     0013    00 .  .         BYT1    NOP
 20     0014    00 .  .                 NOP                 TWO LOCATIONS FOR TWO BYTES
 21     0015    .  .  .                 END                 COMPILER COMMAND TO END
  0     ERRORS FOUND IN ASSEMBLY CODE .
```

Figure 8-9 8080 program to read two bytes and store them in memory

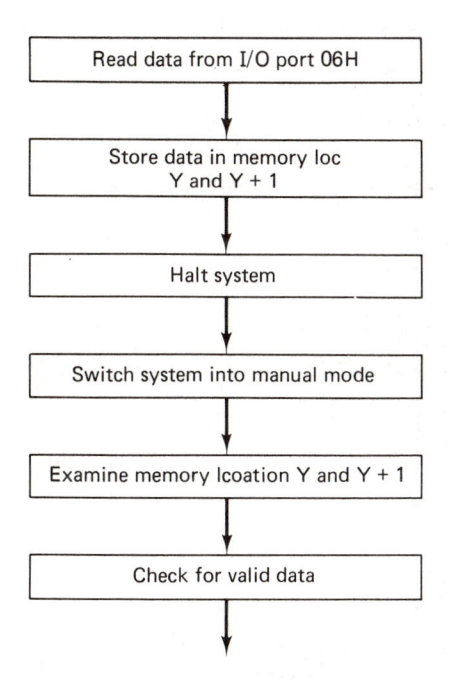

Figure 8-10 Flowchart of events to follow when performing a partial check of the program

1. The peripheral circuits for the I/O transfer, or control (hardware), are defective
2. The program is controlling the hardware in an incorrect manner (software)
3. The peripheral circuits for writing data to memory (hardware) defective

Here are some guidelines for isolating the major area of the malfunction. First, we manually write known data (all 0's) into the two memory locations where data will be transferred. We then run the partial program again, checking to see if the data in memory is changed. If it is changed but is still not correct, then we assume that the peripheral circuits for writing data into memory are working. (This is a *temporary* assumption and may prove later to be invalid.)

We now attach our own I/O port to the system, and again run the partial program except that the read and write I/O address should be changed to equal a non-existent I/O port in our system. We can change the I/O port address to $F3_{16}$, for example. The program will now be reading to port $F3_{16}$, and the select code on our manual I/O port will equal $F3_{16}$. A block diagram of this test setup is shown in Figure 8-11.

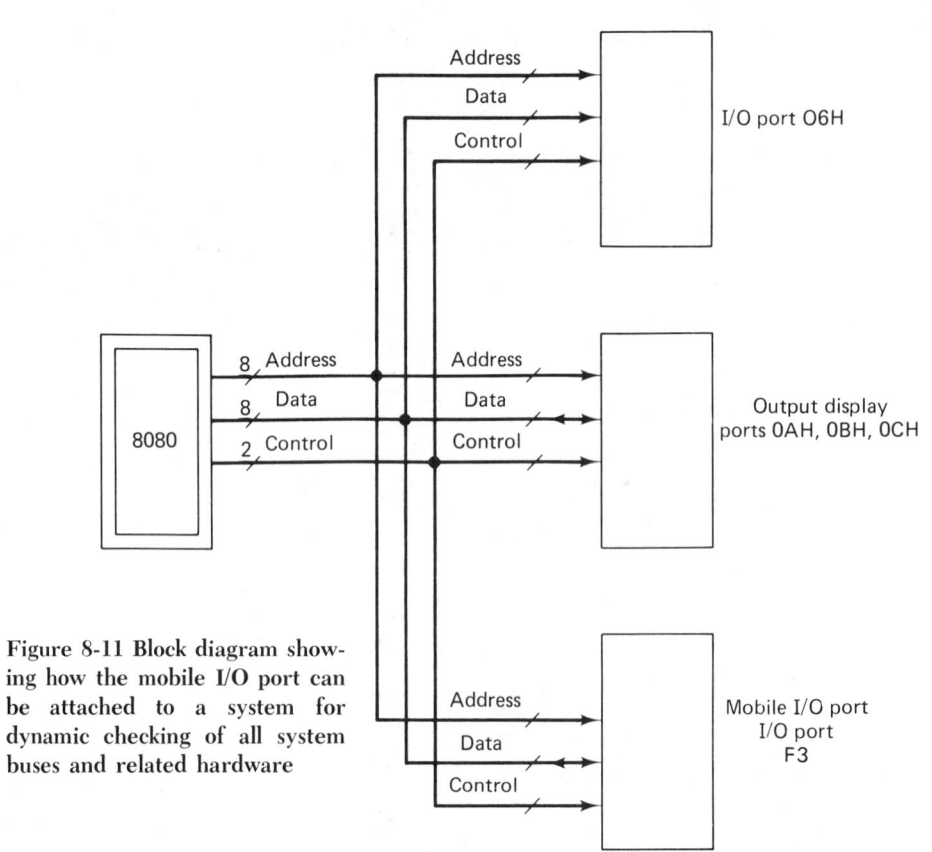

Figure 8-11 Block diagram showing how the mobile I/O port can be attached to a system for dynamic checking of all system buses and related hardware

When this is set up, we again run the partial program to examine data in memory. If the data transferred is the same as the data we sent, then we know that the problem is in the hardware and is located in the I/O circuit. There may be a case, however, where an I/O circuit is excessively loading down a data line D_0–D_7 or an address line A_0–A_7. If this happens it will be difficult to find except by installing our stimulus box. Notice that what we have been doing is troubleshooting major circuit blocks to localize the problem. Once we have determined which block is defective, then we can perform normal digital troubleshooting techniques to isolate the defective hardware.

Keep in mind that our objective is to locate the defective major block of the circuit. With the stimulus box installed we:

1. Set the switches for an I/O address of the suspect I/O port
2. Set the data switches for status word of an I/O write
3. Set the SYNC signal to logical 1. This allows the transfer of the status information from the input of the status latches to the output.
4. Set the SYNC to logical 0. Each time we do this we should examine the status hardware to insure it is working properly. If the status word is changed in the middle of a machine cycle the results are most unpredictable. Therefore we should insure that the status is strobed *only* when it is supposed to be.
5. Set the data lines to the correct data to write to the I/O port.
6. Set the $\overline{\text{WR}}$ signal to logical 0. At this point we can check all of the decoding circuits on the I/O circuit. The levels should be static and easy to examine. The key to this type of troubleshooting, as any other, is for the technician to be aware of "what should be there." Only by this knowledge may the problem be approached in a logical way that will get results.
7. Set the $\overline{\text{WR}}$ signal to logical 1. This completes the I/O transfer.

The I/O write to the addressed I/O port should have taken place now. At each step in the process one should be checking the logical levels of the hardware at the strategic points to determine if the circuits are performing correctly. By using the stimulus box we can inject a signal to statically check the hardware in the system point by point. However, to use this type of troubleshooting aid effectively, one must clearly understand how the peripheral hardware is controlled by the 8080.

If we can assume that the hardware in our system is operating properly and the malfunction is in the execution order of the instructions, we can use the following concept to find the problem area. We can write the program so as to write data to memory at selected places and halt the system at each place. For

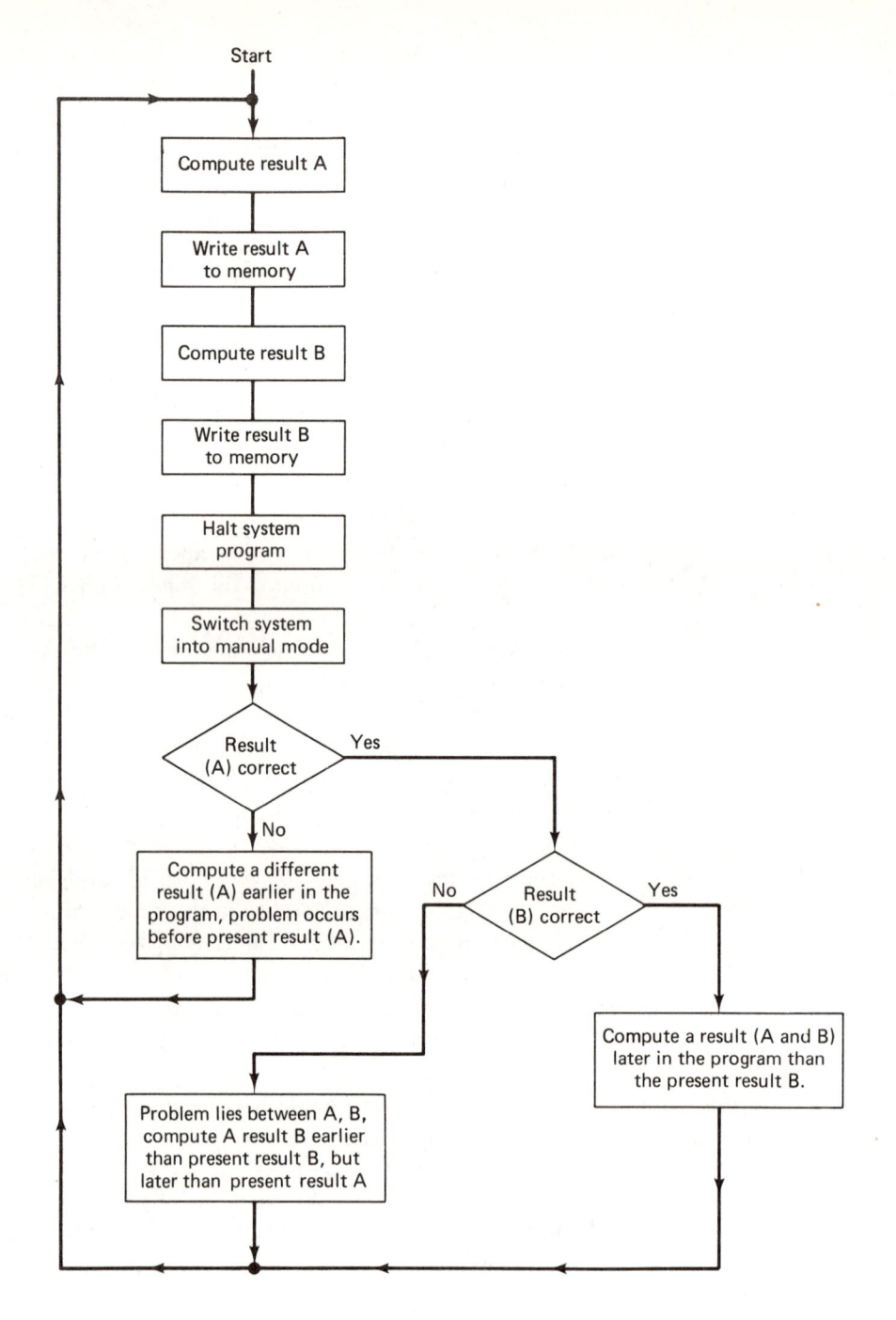

Figure 8-12 Flowchart for a search technique for finding problems in software. We find a section of code where a problem exists and continue to narrow the starting and stopping points until we are able to isolate the problem.

example, in our present program we first halt the system after writing data to memory. We then examine memory to insure that the data transfer has been done correctly.

At different points in the program we can write data that consists of intermediate results to memory and then halt to test the result. The idea is this: if we examine result A and it is correct, but result B is not correct, then the software error is between result A and result B. This is shown in the flowchart in Figure 8-12. This type of debugging is very useful when writing an 8080 program for the first time. We can narrow the number of instructions between result A and result B until we find the section of 8080 program code that is in error.

In this chapter we have shown some simple but effective tools and techniques for troubleshooting the 8080 microprocessor system. The stimulus box is an inexpensive and effective tool for troubleshooting 8080 hardware. These techniques and hardware can be modified by a technician, experimenter, or hobbyist to fit specific applications. Finally, we have shown a technique that can be used with good results when troubleshooting software errors.

Learning troubleshooting techniques for both hardware and software is essential for anyone who is serious about using microprocessors. Furthermore, the techniques we have described can be adapted to other microprocessor circuits. The emphasis here is on the concept, for once this is well understood we will find it easier to adapt to the unique situation that confronts us.

Review Questions

1. What is meant by signal injection in analog or digital equipment?
2. What are the two major categories of digital malfunctions?
3. Draw a block diagram of the hardware required for a static stimulus test box. Explain the function of each block in the diagram.
4. How can one supply adequate +5 volts and ground to the SST box if the system +5 volts supply will not handle the additional current?
5. Draw a flowchart to show how one can use the SST box to check a particular memory location in a microprocessor-controlled system.
6. What is meant by the term "mobile I/O port"?
7. How can the mobile I/O port be used to check the functions of the data bus and control bus in a microprocessor-controlled system?
8. What is the purpose of static stimulus testing in a microprocessor-controlled system?
9. What are the three main "debug" tools presented in this chapter? Can you think of any others that would be general purpose?
10. What type of diagnostic program could one put into a ROM for troubleshooting a microprocessor-controlled system?

9

TAKING ADVANTAGE OF LSI: ADVANCED FEATURES OF AN 8080 SYSTEM

In this chapter special LSI (Large Scale Integration) devices that have been designed specifically for use with an 8080 microprocessor are discussed. These devices are the hardware one is most likely to encounter in industry. Systems designed around the 8080 use these special LSI devices to reduce the number of integrated circuit packages required to realize a system design. The number of devices required to realize a design is called the "can count." These LSI devices do reduce the can count in a system, often dramatically.

We have waited to introduce these devices until after we have firmly established how an 8080 is supported by its peripheral circuits. These surrounding circuits have been described previously as using standard T^2L and MOS devices for the most part. This was done to establish a good understanding of what is basically required to enable the 8080 to work, and because not everyone has access to these special LSI circuits when designing an 8080 system. Now as we introduce and show how these special devices work, one will easily understand what purpose they serve in the system and how impressively these LSI devices reduce the overall size, complexity, and cost of the final system.

9-1 8224 Clock Generator and Driver

The first LSI device we will discuss is the *8224 clock generator and driver*. This device performs all of the functions of generating the correct phase 1 and phase 2 timing and generates the high level phase 1 and phase 2 clock outputs. The pinout and block diagram for this device is shown in Figure 9-1.

PIN CONFIGURATION

```
RESET   [ 1      16 ] V_CC
RESIN   [ 2      15 ] XTAL 1
RDYIN   [ 3      14 ] XTAL 2
READY   [ 4  8224 13 ] TANK
SYNC    [ 5      12 ] OSC
φ2(TTL) [ 6      11 ] φ1
STSTB   [ 7      10 ] φ2
GND     [ 8       9 ] V_DD
```

BLOCK DIAGRAM

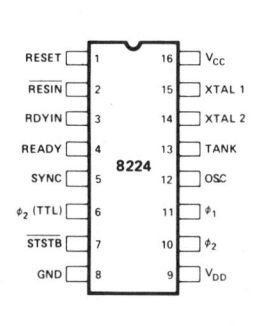

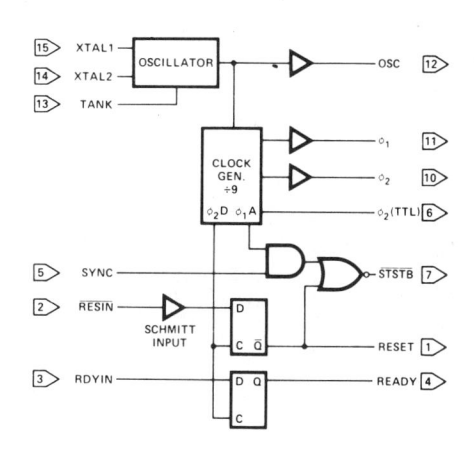

PIN NAMES

RESIN	RESET INPUT
RESET	RESET OUTPUT
RDYIN	READY INPUT
READY	READY OUTPUT
SYNC	SYNC INPUT
STSTB	STATUS STB (ACTIVE LOW)
φ1	8080
φ2	CLOCKS

XTAL 1	CONNECTIONS FOR CRYSTAL
XTAL 2	
TANK	USED WITH OVERTONE XTAL
OSC	OSCILLATOR OUTPUT
φ2 (TTL)	φ2 CLK (TTL LEVEL)
V_CC	+5V
V_DD	+12V
GND	0V

Figure 9-1 Logic diagram and block diagram of the 8224 clock driver © Intel 1978

In the block diagram the top left block represents the *oscillator*. There are three input lines to this block, labled XTAL1, XTAL2, and TANK. The lines XTAL1 and XTAL2 are for external connections to the crystal, whose oscillating frequency determines the cycle time t_{CY} of the $\phi 1$ clock. To determine the oscillating frequency of the external crystal the following formula may be used:

Basically, Frequency = 1/period

In this case, Frequency of crystal = $9/t_{CY}$

(See Figure 9-3 for relationship of crystal frequency and clock frequency;

Crystal frequency = 9 × clock frequency.)

The units of this are correct because t_{CY} is the period for phase 1. The inverse of the period is frequency. For example, suppose we want a t_{CY} of 500 nsec. The frequency of the external crystal needed is calculated by:

$$\text{Frequency of crystal} = 9t_{CY}$$
$$= 9\ (1/500 \times 10^9)$$
$$= 9\ (2 \times 10^6)$$
$$= 18 \times 10^6, \text{ or 18 megahertz}$$

The tank input external to the oscillator block is used only when *overtone mode crystals* are used. An overtone crystal oscillates at a harmonic of its base frequency. When a crystal is made to do this it has a lower "gain," and it is harder to make oscillate correctly than a crystal that is designed to oscillate at its fundamental frequency. For overtone crystals an external LC (inductance-capacitance) network must be added to insure proper oscillation of the crystal at the desired frequency. The external LC network can be calculated by the following formula.

$$LC = 1/(2\ \Pi F)^2$$

Here, LC is the external inductance-capacitance network and F is the frequency of oscillation for the crystal. The output of the oscillator block is buffered and connected to an external pin. This gives the system a free-running T²L clock at the frequency we have selected. Figure 9-2 shows how the external crystal and tank circuit are connected for both overtone and fundamental crystals.

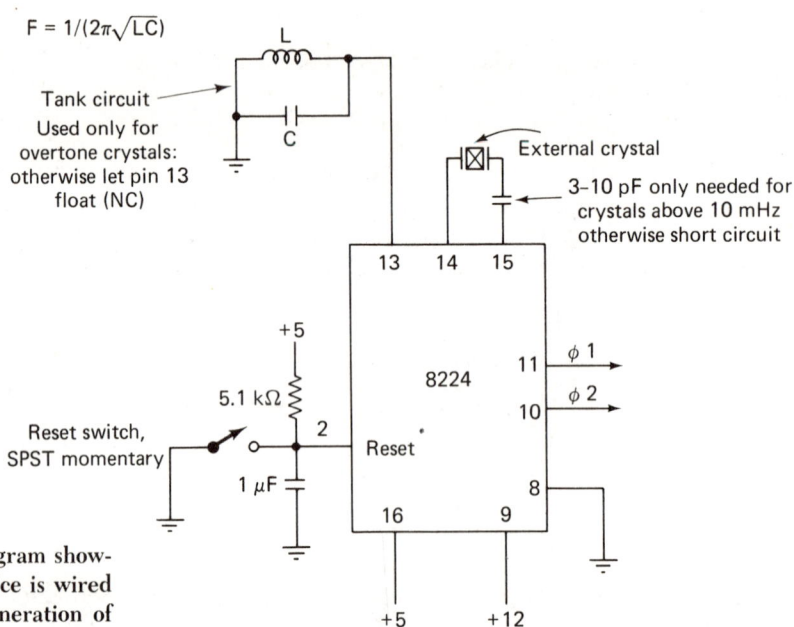

Figure 9-2 Circuit diagram showing how the 8224 device is wired up in a circuit for generation of the phase 1 and phase 2 clocks for the 8080

Sec. 9-1 8224 Clock Generator and Driver

Referring again to Figure 9-1, the next block in the diagram is the *clock generator* block. The clock generator provides the correct timing for the ϕ 1 and ϕ 2 clocks, plus added timing to be discussed later.

The waveforms for the $\phi1$ and $\phi2$ clocks always have the same position relative to one another, because the clock generator uses a digital counter to generate waveforms. To illustrate how these waveforms look, let us assume that the free-running oscillator frequency is 10 mHz. The period is $1/10 \times 10^6$ or 100 nsec. This produces the waveforms shown in Figure 9-3.

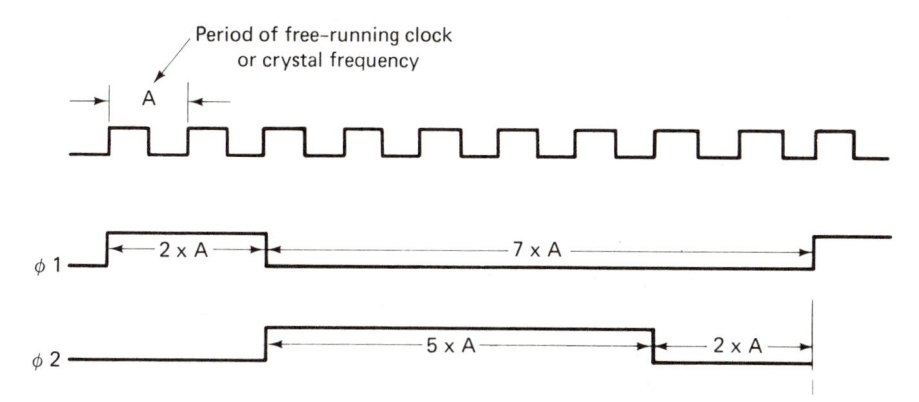

Figure 9-3 Waveforms for phase 1 and phase 2 clocks out of the 8224 device. The positions of phase 1 and phase 2 relative to one another are the same regardless of the free-running oscillator frequency.

Note that the ϕ 1 waveform is at a high level for 2 free-running clock periods. The $\phi1$ wave is always at a low level for 7 free-running clock periods. The $\phi2$ clock is at logical 1 level for 5 free-running clock periods. The phase 2 clock is at logical 0 for 4 free-running clock periods. Now it can be seen why the formula for calculating the crystal frequency states that this frequency is nine times our desired 8080 frequency. The total number of free-running (crystal) clock periods during a single $\phi1$ clock period equals nine: 2 free-running clock periods for a high logical 1 level, and 7 free-running clock periods for a low logical 0 level.

The block diagram (Figure 9-1) also shows the $\phi1$ and $\phi2$ clock signals as being buffered and level-shifted. This allows the user to connect these outputs directly to the $\phi1$ and $\phi2$ inputs of the 8080 chip.

We notice also from the block diagram of Figure 9-1 that a signal called $\overline{STSTB}$ is generated. This is the *Status* (ST) *Strobe* (STB) signal that goes to the status latches in the system. Notice that the SYNC signal is input to the 8224 device to gate the $\overline{STSTB}$ signal out at the proper time. The $\overline{STSTB}$ signal is one free-running clock period in duration. It occurs relative to $\phi1$ as shown in Figure 9-4.

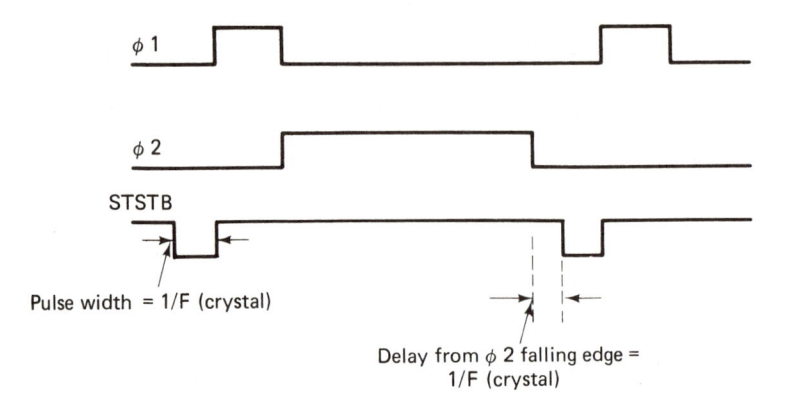

Figure 9-4 Timing of status strobe ($\overline{\text{STSTB}}$) signal output relative to phase 1 and phase 2 clocks. These are all outputs from the 8224 device to the 8080 and status latches.

The next signal we will discuss is the $\overline{\text{RESIN}}$ input signal to the 8224. This special signal is used with a power-on reset. The $\overline{\text{RESIN}}$ input to the 8224 allows a very simple power-on reset circuit to be installed. Earlier in this text we mentioned that many systems employ a power-on reset for presetting the logic into known states *after* power has been turned on. On the 8080 this is accomplished with the RESET input. When the RESET input goes to logical 1 on the 8080, selected internal registers are set to known states. Figure 9-5 shows this circuit.

When power is turned off, the capacitor discharges. When power is turned on, capacitor voltage rises to +5 volts at a rate determined by the external RC network. When voltage across the capacitor reaches a certain level, a Schmitt trigger in the 8224 changes state, and the 8080 system resumes normal operation.

While the capacitor is charging, the reset input to the 8080 is logical 1. This is the condition for the 8080 to reset. Also, an external switch can be used to reset the 8080 at any time.

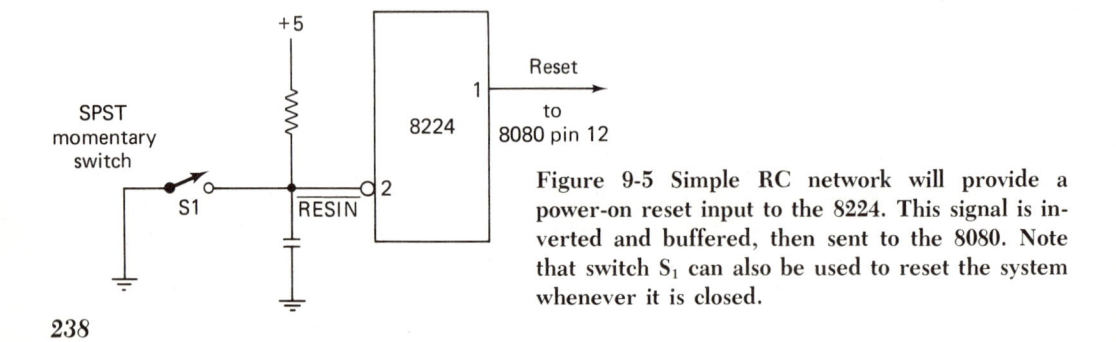

Figure 9-5 Simple RC network will provide a power-on reset input to the 8224. This signal is inverted and buffered, then sent to the 8080. Note that switch S_1 can also be used to reset the system whenever it is closed.

Sec. 9-2 *The 8228 System Controller and Bus Driver*

The function of the last signal called RDYIN will be discussed later in this chapter. Readers should be aware that this input and output is available on the 8224 package.

One may realize the tremendous savings in PC board space and can count that may be achieved by use of an 8224 LSI device. Note too, that a special crystal called the 8801 has been designed for use with the 8224. Data sheets for this and other crystals are available from the individual manufacturers.

9-2 The 8228 System Controller and Bus Driver

The next LSI device we will discuss is the *8228 System Controller and Bus Driver*—a very powerful device. In the 8228, all the logic is internal to the device. The block diagram, pin names, and pinout for this device are shown in Figure 9-6. There are three major logic blocks inside this 8228 device. The first block is called the *bidirectional bus driver*. (In Chapter 4 we discussed how such bus drivers operated and how they could be constructed using discrete logic.) Again there is a great reduction in circuitry and in can count.

The second major logic block is the *status latch*. This is an 8-bit latch that strobes in status information when the $\overline{STSTB}$ signal that is generated from the

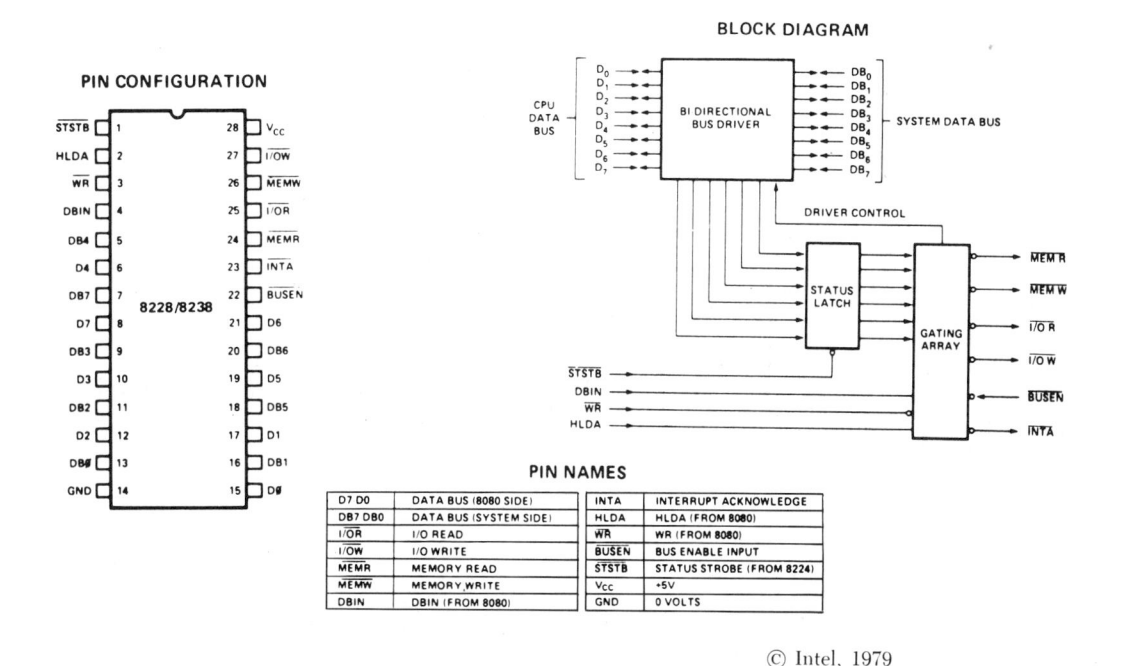

© Intel, 1979

Figure 9-6 Pinout and logic diagram for the 8228 system controller

8224 clock generator is input. The status latch does not have any inputs or outputs that the user can control. This leads us to the third major logic block in the 8228 chip.

This logic block is the decoding for the control bus called *Gating Array*. The four control bus signals $\overline{\text{MEMR}}$, $\overline{\text{MEMW}}$, $\overline{\text{IOR}}$, $\overline{\text{IOW}}$ are outputs of this logic block. The inputs to this block are the $\overline{\text{WR}}$ signal and the DBIN signals, both from the 8080, plus the outputs from the status latch (which is internal to the chip). By connecting all three logic blocks together, the 8228 LSI performs the function of many discrete IC's. Compare this device to the number of devices we used to realize this function with discrete logic in Figure 4-32 of Chapter 4.

At this point it is easy to understand how devices such as the 8224 and 8228 fit into an overall 8080 system. After we have realized these same functions with discrete logic, one has a good understanding of how these composite devices can be used to reduce circuitry. In Figure 9-7 the same system presented in Chapter

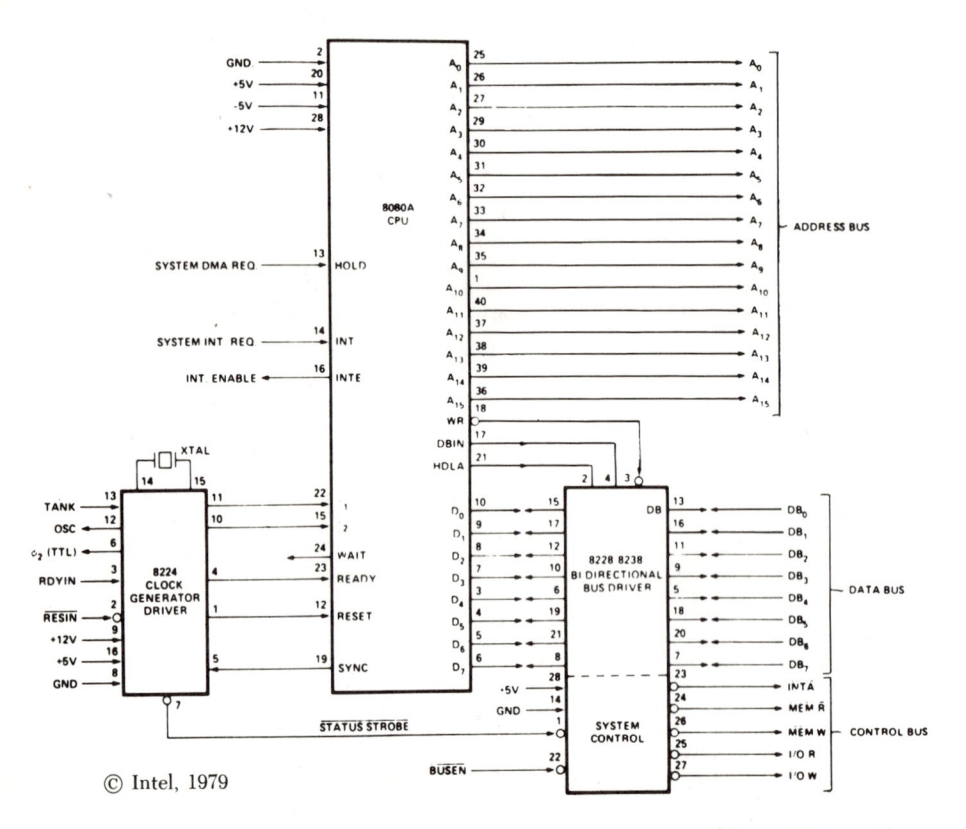

© Intel, 1979

Figure 9-7 Schematic diagram showing how the 8228 system controller and the 8224 clock generator are used in conjunction with the 8080 to form the basic system

Sec. 9-3   The 8212 8-Bit Input/Output Port   241

4 is now realized with only *three chips*—the 8224 clock generator, the 8080 CPU, and the 8228 controller-bus driver.

9-3 The 8212 8-Bit Input/Output Port

Two other devices apply to a general 8080 system. The first is the 8212 8-BIT INPUT/OUTPUT PORT. The main section of this device includes the 8 latches and tri-state buffers. The pinout and block diagram for this device is shown in Figure 9-8. Probably the easiest way to understand how this device can be used is to show an I/O port realized with an 8212 LSI device. This circuit is shown in Figure 9-9. Notice again how the use of this 8-bit I/O port can reduce the

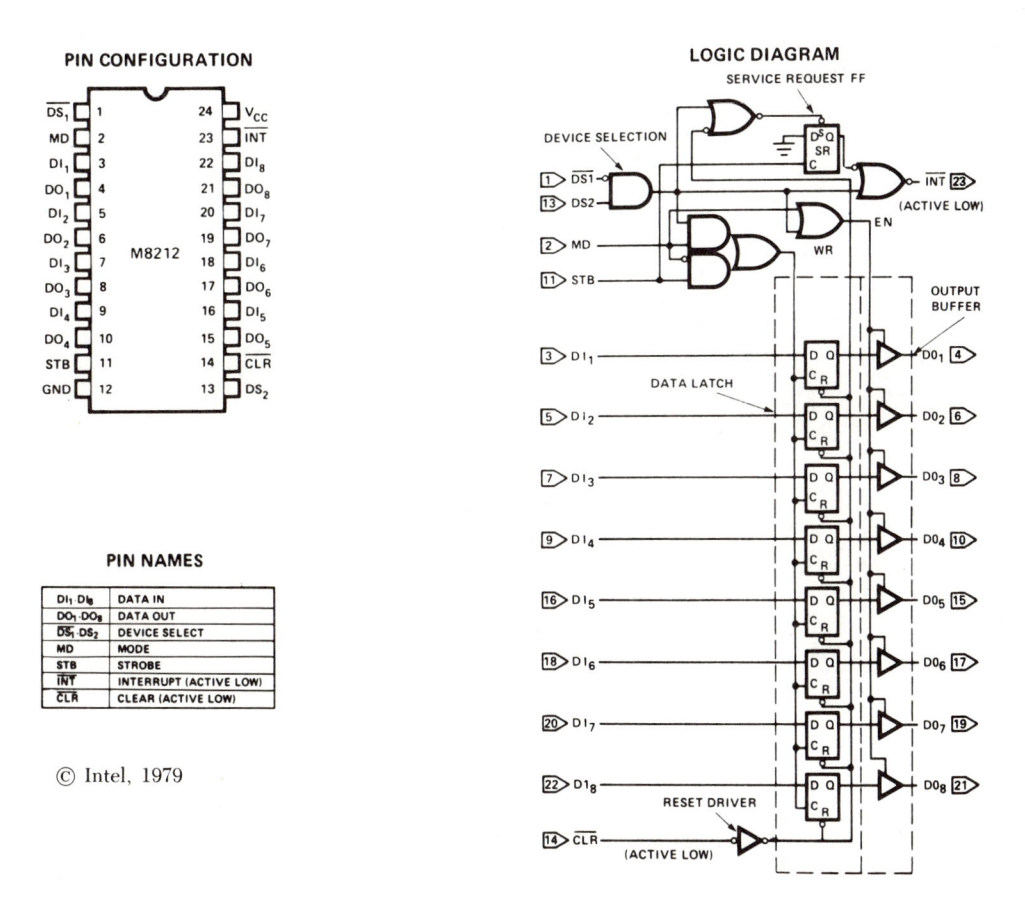

Figure 9-8 Pinout and logic diagram for the 8212 I/O port

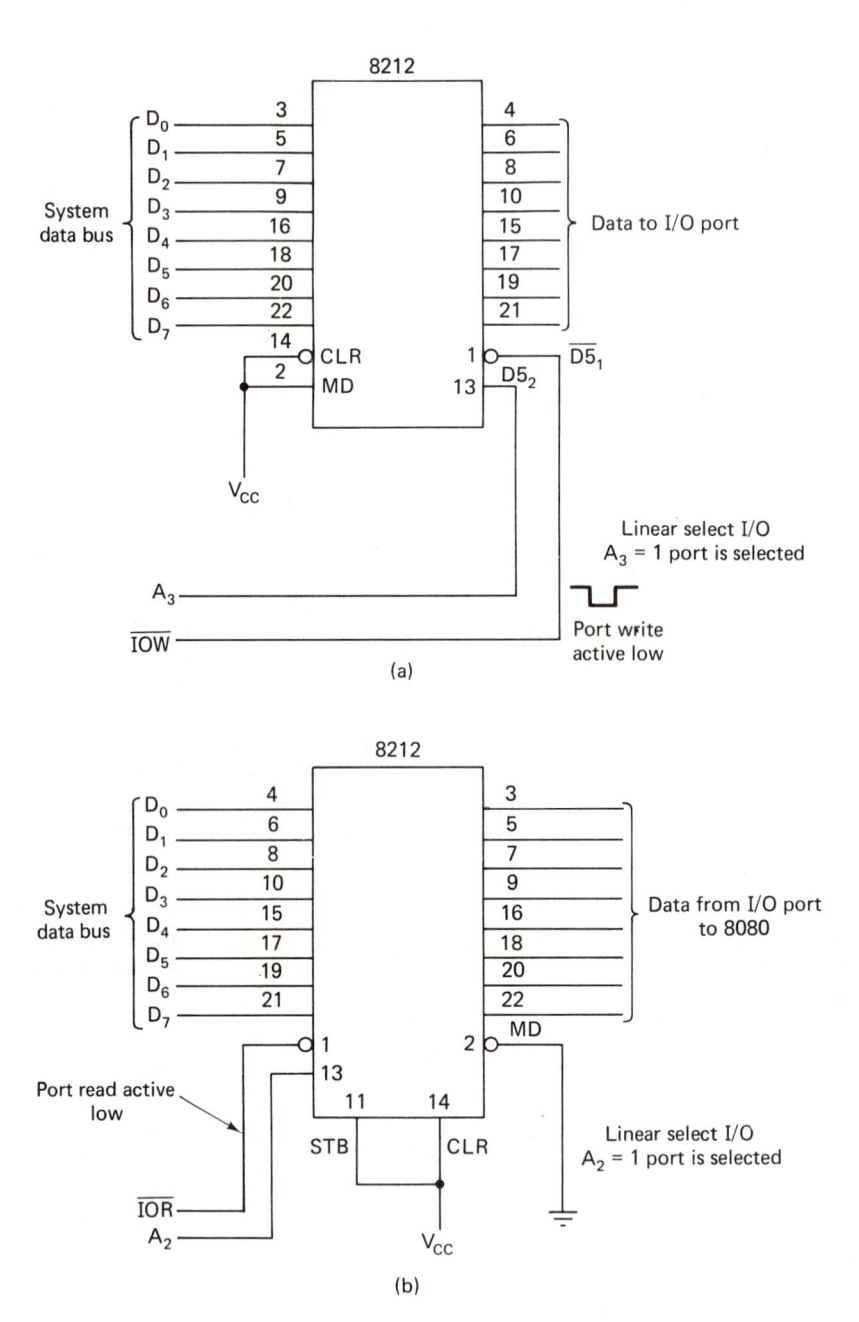

Figure 9-9 (a) Schematic diagram showing how the 8212 device can be connected as an output port (b) Schematic diagram showing how the 8212 device can be connected as an input port

Sec. 9-4 4-Bit Parallel Bidirectional Bus Driver   243

number of devices required to realize a certain logic function. In effect, we are further reducing the can count of the logic system.

It is important to understand that not all of the capability of a digital device need be used in order to justify its use in a logic design. We did not use some of the logic of the 8212 I/O port in this application. The discussion of the extra logic internal to the 8212 device was purposely omitted here. If one understands the internal logic of an 8-bit I/O port and knows that there is more capability that can be used, this is sufficient for a beginner. When one is confronted with troubleshooting an 8212 device in industry, it will be a straightforward task to determine how the device is being used, and what its function is in the overall system.

9-4 4-Bit Parallel Bidirectional Bus Driver

The final device we will discuss in this chapter is the 8216 4-bit parallel Bidirectional Bus Driver. These devices can be used in I/O circuits, memory interfaces, or as bidirectional drivers for the 8080 data lines. The pinout and block diagram for this device is shown in Figure 9-10.

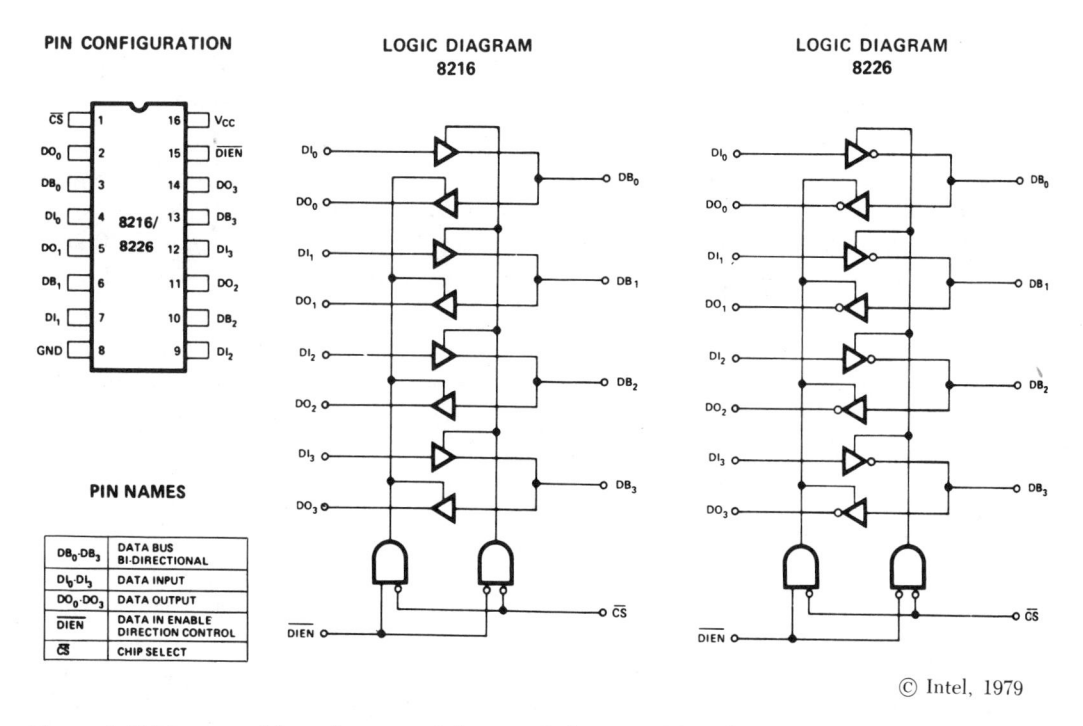

© Intel, 1979

Figure 9-10 Pinout and logic diagram of the 8216 bidirectional bus driver

It should be pointed out that the application of these devices is extremely user-dependent. If one feels that any of the LSI devices discussed can be used in a system to perform a certain function, then use it! Think of these special devices as logic blocks that do not have a final use until the designer gives them a function in a system.

Again in the block diagram of Figure 9-10 note that the device has control inputs called $\overline{\text{DIEN}}$ and $\overline{\text{CS}}$. These signals can be virtually any digital signal in a system. (The important point is to understand the function of these control inputs relating to the 8216 device. Figure 9-11 shows an application of the 8216 circuit so the reader may see one way the device might be used.) This circuit interfaces to a memory device that has separate I/O. The 8216 is used to allow the separate I/O of the memory device to communicate with a system data bus. The concept of separate and common I/O for memories was discussed in Chapter 2.

Finally, let us show an entire system constructed that uses the special digital devices discussed in this chapter wherever possible. In order to make a comparison between a system using these special devices and a system that does not, we will construct the same system that was discussed in Chapter 7. These two schematics are presented in Figures 9-12 and 9-13 so comparison can be made easily. When the can count is reduced, the ease of troubleshooting the system is usually improved. This is dependent on the technician's understanding of the components in the system, of course. The system reliability may also be improved. The point is, that when using these special devices or troubleshooting systems with these special devices in them, one must study the schematics and know how these special devices fit into the total system.

We have introduced four special devices designed for use in the 8080 system. Many other special digital devices are available. The few introduced here relate directly to our small system design. In preceding chapters we realized these same digital functions using discrete logic. Now by the use of special devices we have reduced the can count impressively, and it has been an easy matter to "fit" these special devices into our coverage of a general microprocessor system.

9-5 Advanced Microprocessor Concepts

In preceding chapters we discussed basic microprocessor circuits, and the information given was sufficient to allow one to build, troubleshoot, and analyze circuits designed around the 8080. When an 8080 is used in a more complex design, some additional capability that the 8080 possesses can be used. We have

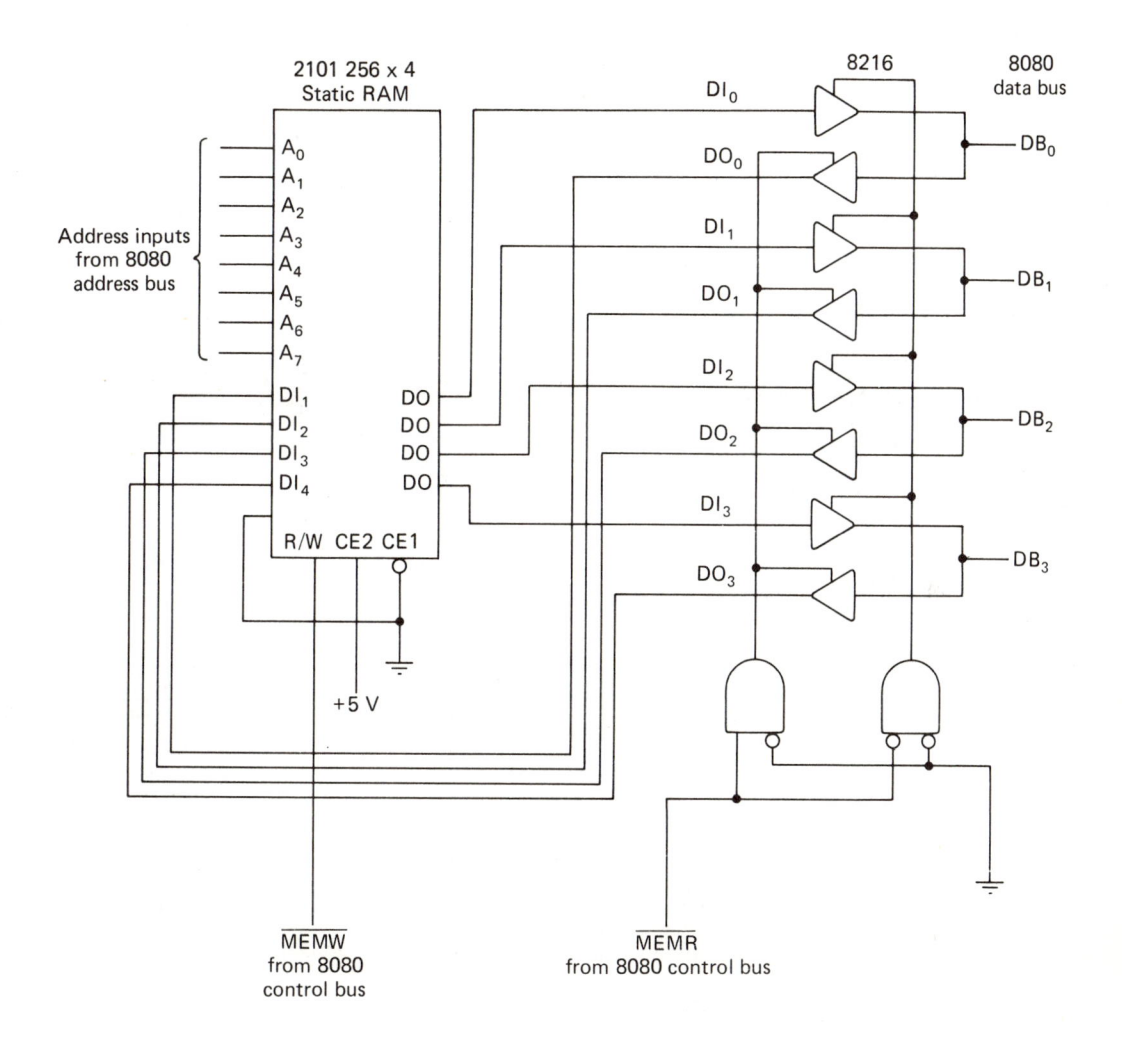

Figure 9-11 Schematic diagram showing how the 8216 device can be used to interface a memory with separate I/O to a data bus for common I/O

waited to present some of this additional capability because it is not easily understood by the beginner in microprocessor circuits. One must have a good, sound understanding of how to make the 8080 do something before these advanced concepts can be made to fit into the total mental picture of an 8080 system. In other words, if one does not understand the basics of microprocessors first, the study of advanced concepts will be of little or no value.

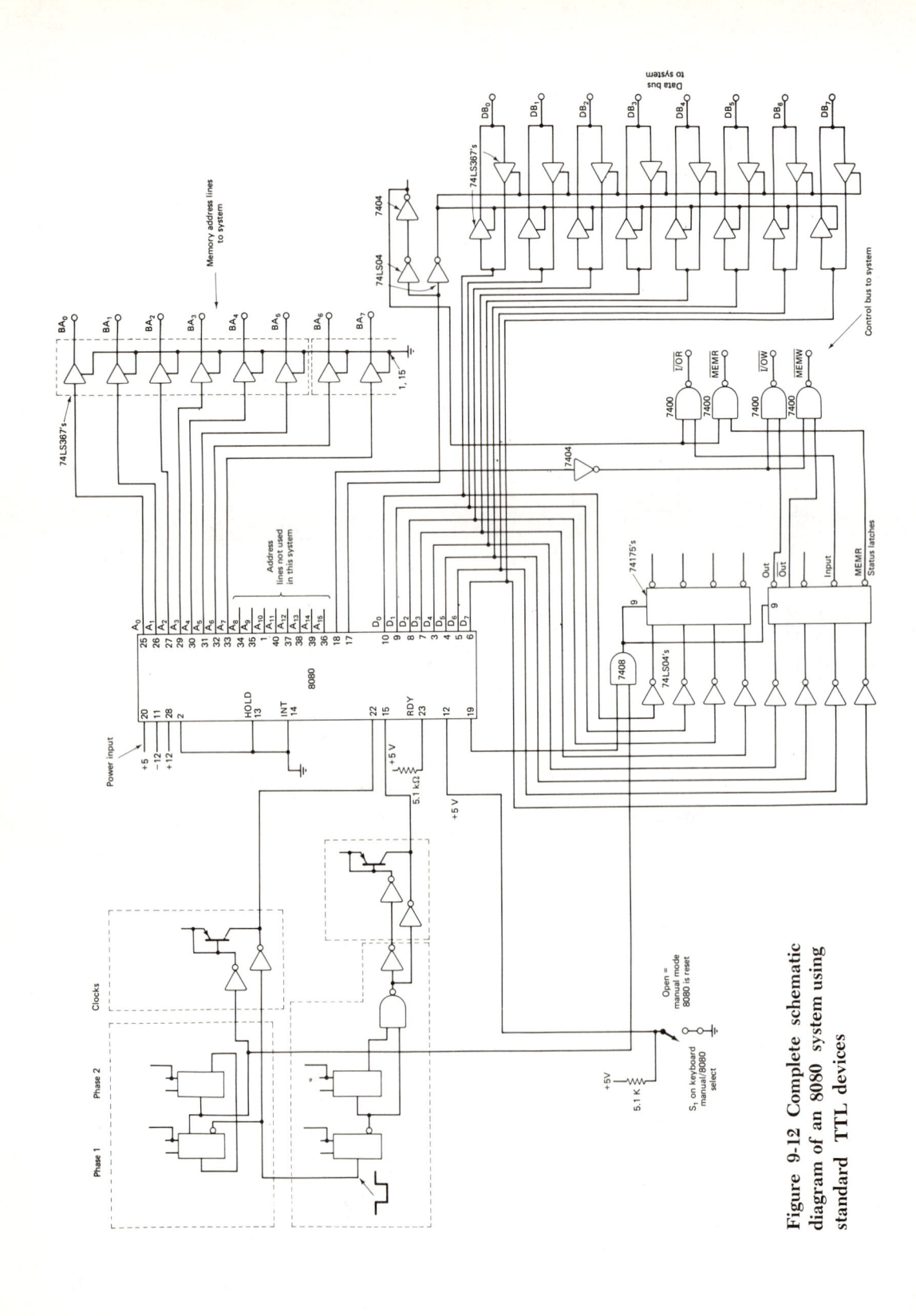

Figure 9-12 Complete schematic diagram of an 8080 system using standard TTL devices

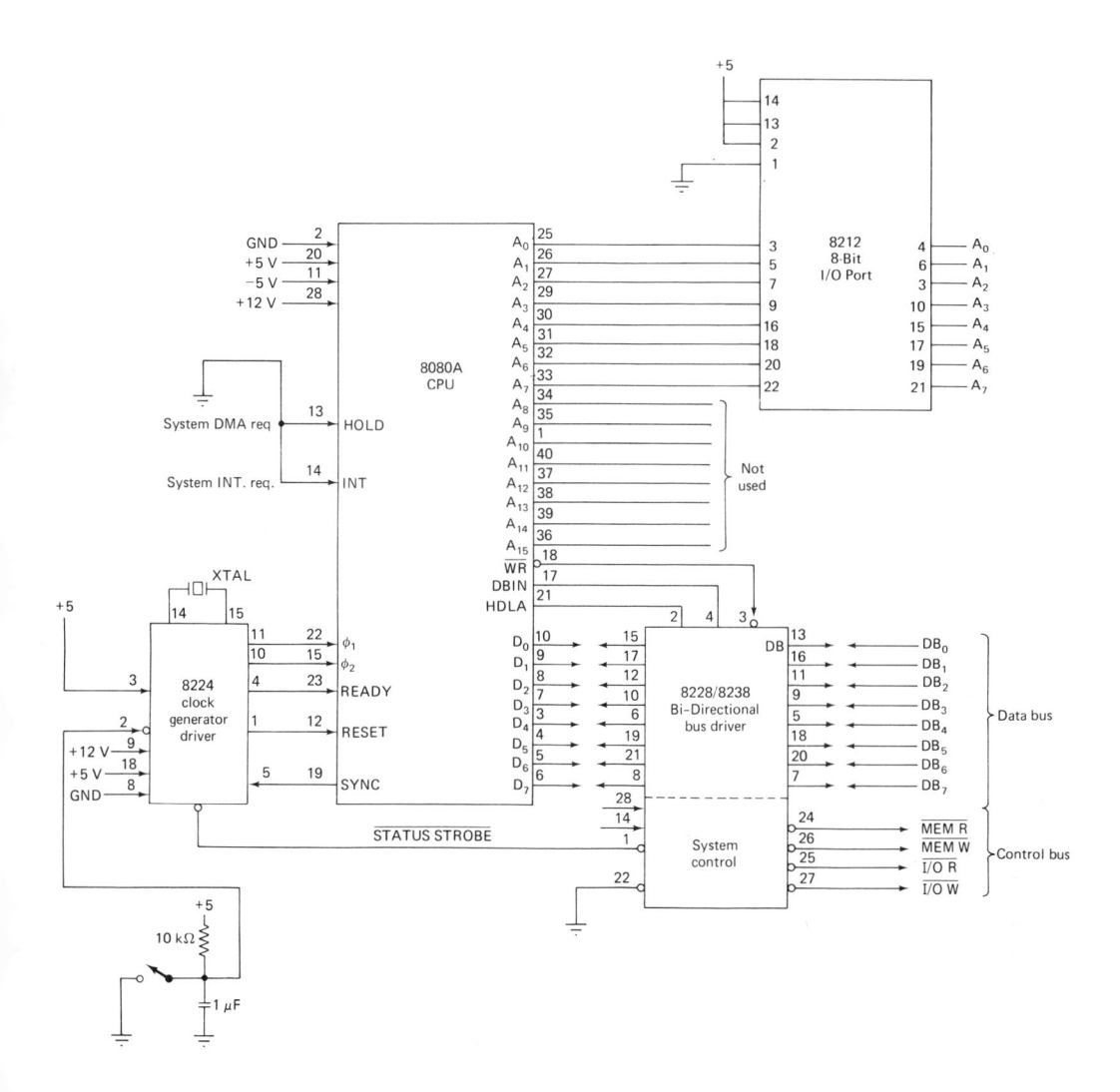

Figure 9-13 Complete diagram of an 8080 system using special devices designed for use with an 8080 CPU. Note how the use of these special devices greatly reduces package count.

9-6 Extending Read and Write Access Time

The first advanced concept to be discussed is that of extending the access time for reading and writing to memory. In Chapter 4 it was stated that when memory access time (read access or write access) was greater than the time allowed by the 8080 for this function, then the time may be extended. This discussion will show how that is accomplished. Let us review how the 8080 accesses memory by studying the timing diagram in Figure 9-14. Let us say that the t_{CY} of a microprocessor system is equal to 500 nanoseconds. Referring to the timing diagram of Figure 9-14, this allows about 1 microsecond to access data in memory.

Suppose we wish to use a memory that has an access time of 2 μsec. We could slow the entire system down, of course, to accommodate a memory of this slow access time. So the first solution to the problem of how to access a slower memory *is to slow the system down*. This involves slowing the overall t_{CY} from 500 nsec to approximately 1 μsec. This method eliminates the need for any special circuits.

The second solution to this problem is to slow the system down only when the system is accessing memory. This method enables the system to run at a faster rate for other functions, such as decision making, logical functions with the accumulator, or internal register manipulation. The advantage of this flexible type of solution over the first one is apparent. However, if it is not a critical matter for the system to run at a slower rate, then the first solution would be the easier to realize with hardware.

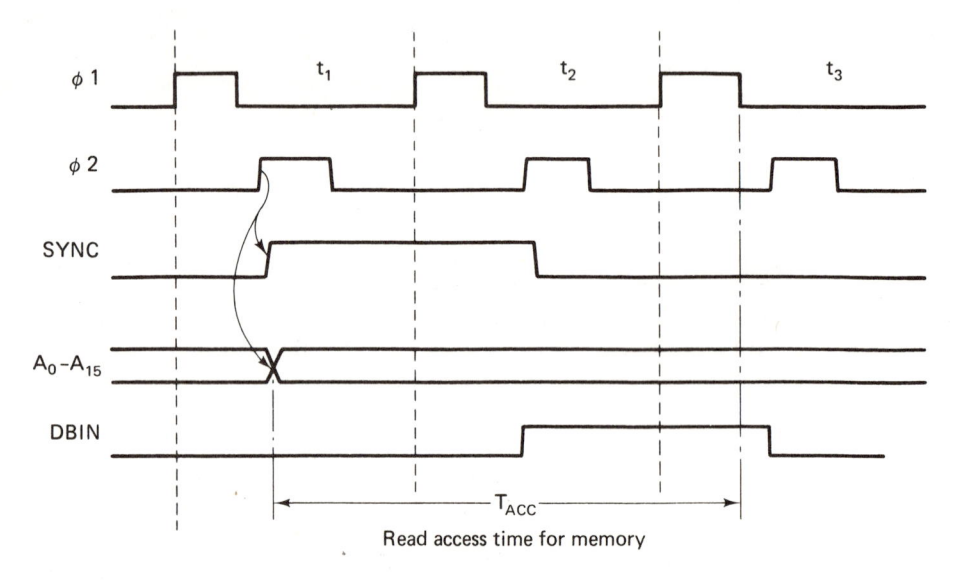

Figure 9-14 Timing diagram showing Read access time for an 8080 system

Sec. 9-6 *Extending Read and Write Access Time* 249

For this discussion let us assume that the overall system must run at a t_{CY} of 500 nsec, but the memory we wish to access requires two μsec for memory read or write. The point to be stressed is that the one μsec allowed by the system for memory access is not enough time. We will show two different ways to solve this problem, and both involve the same concept. That concept is to allow the 8080 to enter a wait state (t_W), while the memory is responding to the request to read or write from the 8080.

The 8080 is, in effect, idling during this wait time. All signals during the wait time will remain stable. It is similar to setting the system up for a memory read or write and then stopping the system momentarily so the memory can have enough time to respond.

The wait state has a minimum duration of one t_{CY}, or one state cycle. The wait time consists of an integer number of state cycles. There are very strict sequences of electrical events that must be followed by the system hardware when the 8080 is preparing to enter a wait state. These timing rules have to do with the internal timing of the 8080. There is an input line to the 8080 called READY. The READY input to the 8080 must be *active low* prior to the falling edge of phase 2 in state t_2 of a memory read or memory write cycle. This is shown by the timing diagram of Figure 9-15. In other words, the system must request a wait state electrically before the falling edge of φ 2 in state t_2. To accomplish this the status information (which indicates a memory read or write)

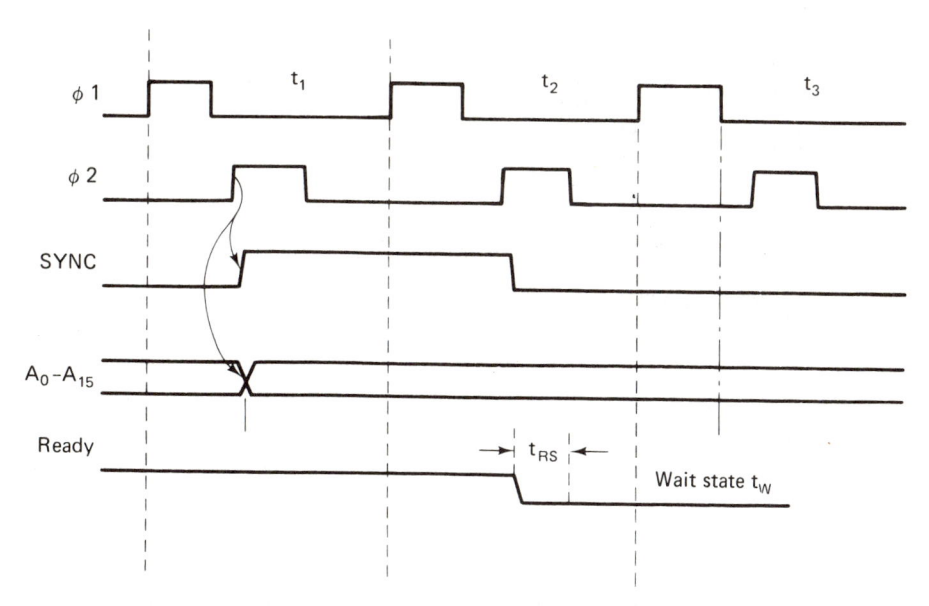

Figure 9-15 Timing diagram showing the relationship of the READY input with respect to the phase 1 and phase 2 clock inputs to the 8080

must be decoded as soon as it is available. In some microprocessor systems the address lines are "decoded" by the system to request a wait; that is, when certain address codes are present, the system requests a wait.

The system decodes the status information for a memory read or memory write, then sends the decoded information to the memory strobed by the leading edge of phase 2. This is shown in Figure 9-16. The memory hardware has been

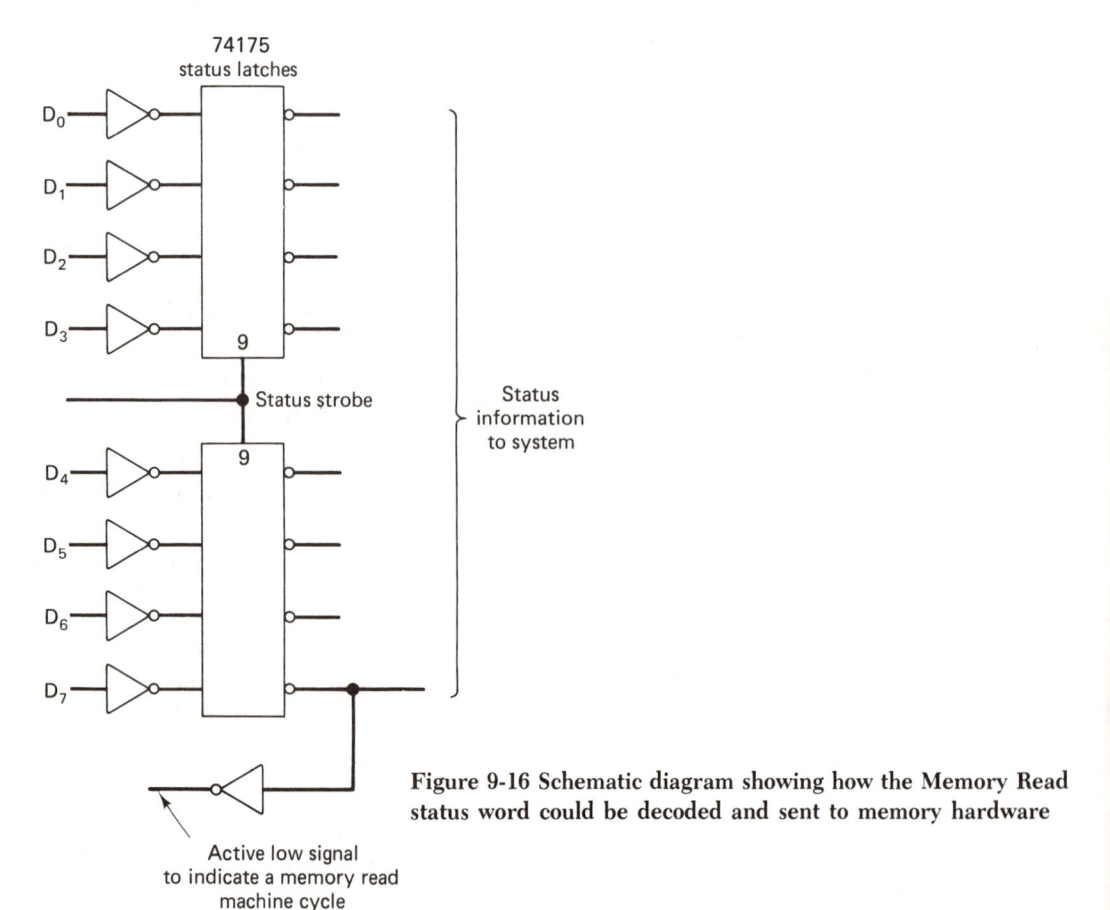

Figure 9-16 Schematic diagram showing how the Memory Read status word could be decoded and sent to memory hardware

sent the electrical signal indicating that the 8080 will be requesting a read or write in the next state cycle. The memory now issues a signal to the 8080 indicating that the 8080 must enter a fixed delay or wait state at the appropriate time. When the memory has had its 2 μsec for read or write access, it releases the 8080 from the wait state to resume normal operation. The timing of the request from memory to allow the 8080 to enter a wait state must be synchronized externally to the 8080 device. Figure 9-17 shows how this synchronization may appear. One technique for realizing a wait request with actual hardware is shown in Figure 9-18.

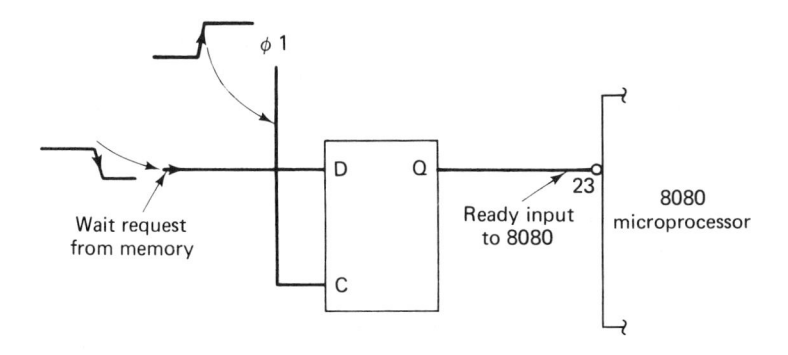

Figure 9-17 Schematic diagram showing how a Wait request could be implemented with hardware in an 8080 system

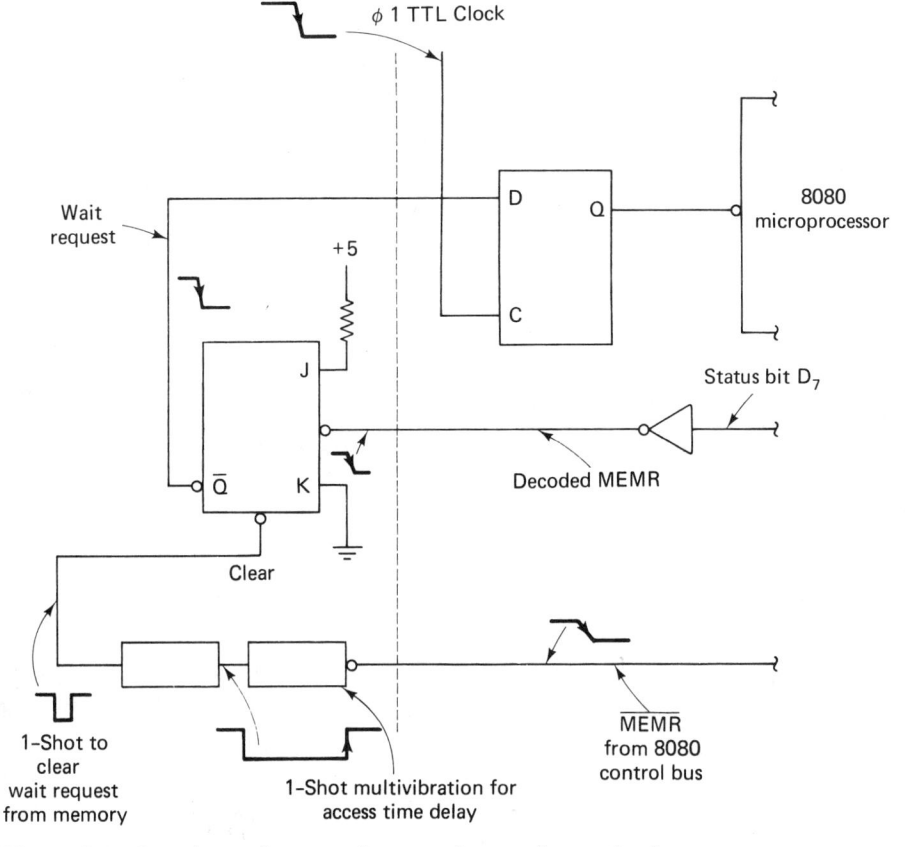

Figure 9-18 Complete schematic diagram showing how a fixed delay (Wait) is issued from memory hardware to the 8080 system. The Memory Read request is decoded and sent to memory hardware where 1-shots provide a fixed delay for memory access time.

251

The 8224 clock generator and driver (Figure 9-1) discussed earlier in this chapter synchronizes the external request for a wait when it is issued from memory. Figure 9-19 shows the section of the 8224 device that performs this function.

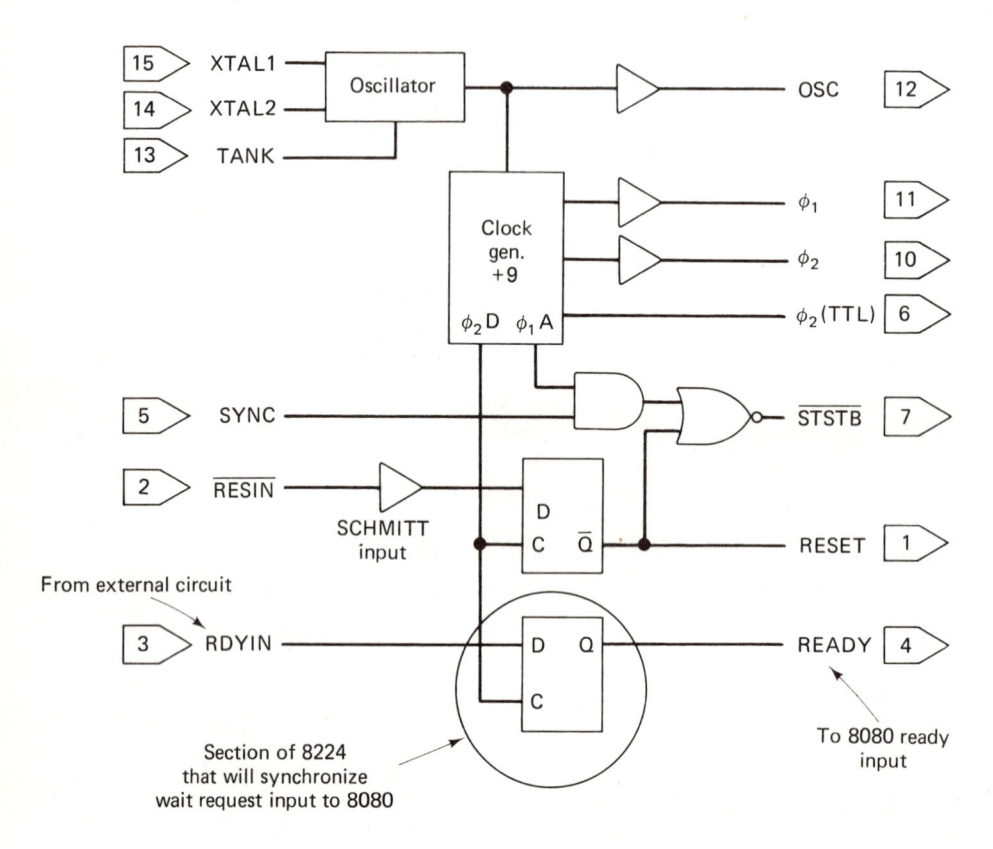

Figure 9-19 Schematic of the 8224 clock driver showing the section of the device used to synchronize the external wait request to the 8080

The hardware circuit shown here uses a 1-shot multivibrator to delay program execution and request the 8080 to enter a wait state. In some systems the delay or wait state may be of variable length. This variable time wait is required because some memories need to be refreshed, but a request for memory access may occur at the same time this memory is being refreshed. The 8080 can be designed to wait for both the refresh and the extended access time. This is not the case with all dynamic memory systems, and we mention it only as an example of one situation where a variable delay may occur.

The hardware needed to realize variable wait time is shown in Figure 9-20. Here the circuit allows the external hardware to take as long as necessary to

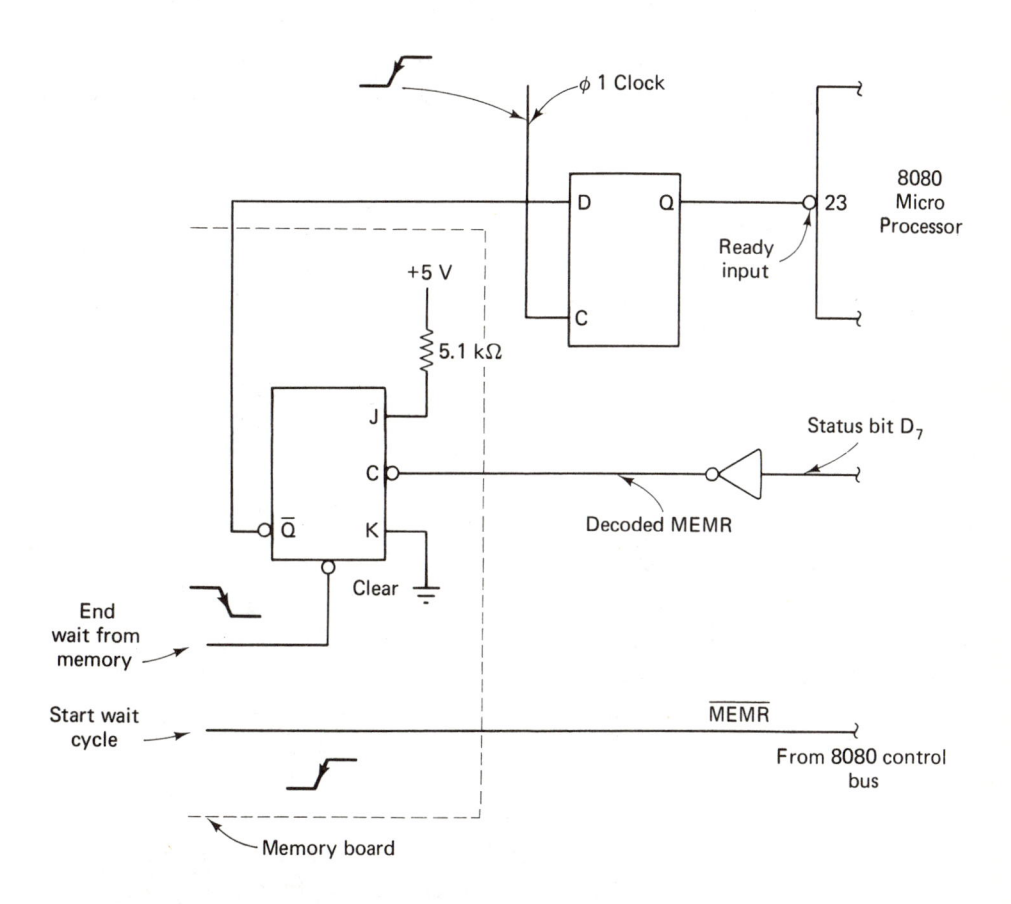

Figure 9-20 Schematic diagram showing how a variable length delay could be implemented for a memory system. The memory board can take as long as necessary for access. When the memory system is ready to continue, it pulls the clear input to the flip flop to logical 0. This action ends the wait period of the 8080.

complete its task. When the hardware is finished, a signal is sent to the 8080 indicating that normal execution may resume.

The concept of causing the 8080 to enter a wait state can also be used by the I/O circuits. For this application the status words that would indicate an I/O read or I/O write are decoded.

9-7 Interrupting the 8080

The next concept we will introduce is that of an Interrupt. We mentioned earlier that to process I/O data transfers with I/O devices that run slower than the CPU two main methods are employed. One method is to output or input a

253

data byte to the slower I/O device and have the CPU enter a wait loop until the slower device is ready to transfer another data byte. This is shown by the flowchart in Figure 9-21.

A second method for handling a slow I/O transfer is for the CPU to output or input data from the slow I/O device and then continue processing other information. When the slow device is again ready to accept or send data to the CPU the I/O device issues an INTERRUPT signal to the CPU. The interrupt signal indicates to the CPU electrically that some external I/O device requires the attention of the CPU.

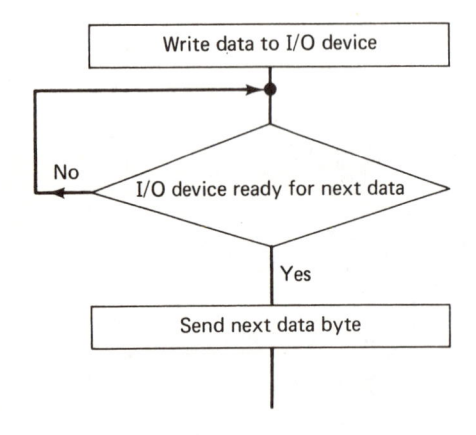

Figure 9-21 Flowchart showing how a Wait loop could be used for servicing I/O devices that operate at a slower rate than the 8080

In very complex systems the CPU may operate by a series of interrupts; that is, every I/O device in the system can interrupt the CPU when it needs attention for the data transferring. If the CPU were servicing ten I/O devices in an interrupt mode, then the CPU must have some means of keeping track of which device is presently being serviced and which device is next to be online. This type of operation is enabled partially with software and partially with hardware. The interrupt requests are issued from hardware; the software determines what the CPU services when the interrupt request is honored.

Now we will discuss how such interrupt signals are received by the 8080 and what is affected when an interrupt occurs. Finally, we will show what the external hardware must provide when it issues an interrupt request to the CPU. We will discuss these interrupts as they occur in a small system. With this understanding one will be on partially familiar ground when relating to interrupt handling in large systems.

The 8080 has an input pin labled INT, which enables the external circuits to interrupt. The INT input is *asynchronous* to any 8080 internal clocking. This means that a request to interrupt can occur at any moment during program execution. However, the internal logic of the 8080 does not honor the interrupt

Sec. 9-7 *Interrupting the 8080* 255

request until the last cycle of the present operating instruction has been executed.

For example, if the 8080 were performing a MVI R1 data instruction, which requires two machine cycles to complete, and an interrupt request occurred during either of the two cycles, that INT would be delayed until t_1 of the machine cycle following t_3 of the second cycle of the MVI R1. This is shown in Figure 9-22.

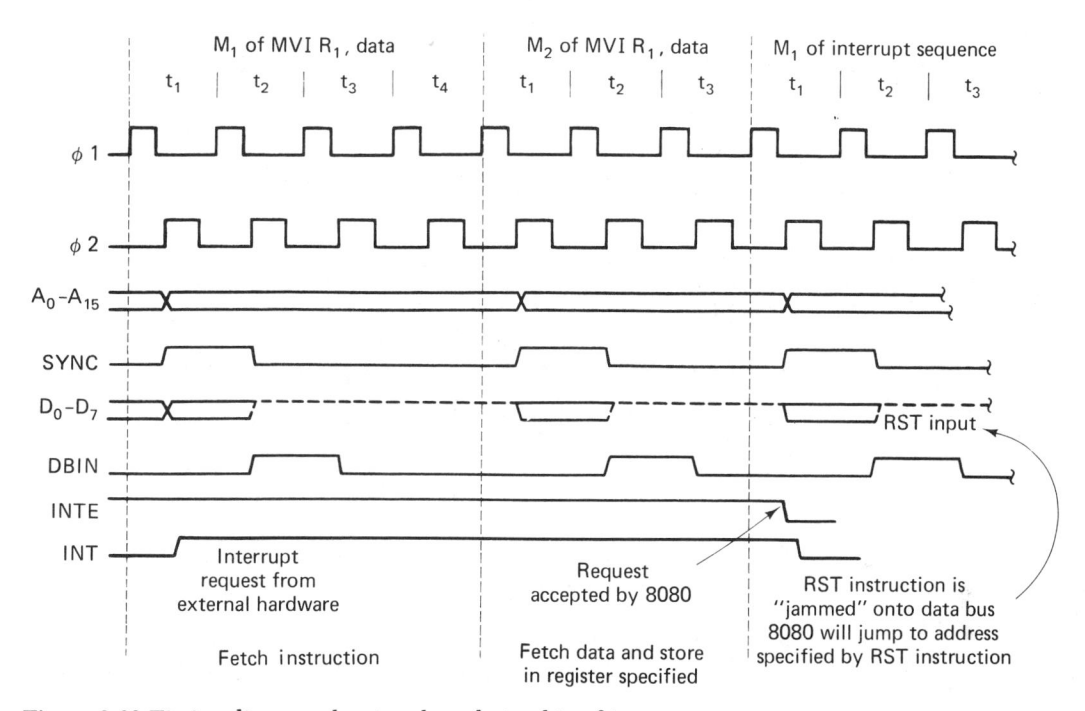

Figure 9-22 Timing diagram showing the relationship of important signals for an interrupt request to an 8080 CPU

Let us examine what happens when the 8080 honors an interrupt request.

Machine cycle one
1. Status information is sent to the data bus and latched in the status latches
2. Program counter registers are output on address lines A_0–A_{15}
3. The program counter is not incremented at this time. (In normal program execution a 1 would be added to the program counter.)
4. A single bit of status information called INTA (interrupt acknowledge) goes to logical 1 level. This indicates to external hardware that the 8080 has honored an interrupt request.

When the INTA status bit (D_0) goes to logical 1, the external hardware must use this bit to do the following: During the t_3 state of this same cycle the external hardware must place one of eight special hardware codes on data bus lines D_0–D_7. These special codes are interpreted as instructions by the 8080. Notice that the major difference between an interrupt machine cycle and a normal cycle is that the instruction for the 8080 normally comes from memory during time t_3, but in an interrupt the instruction is placed, or "jammed" onto the data bus during cycle time t_3. The external hardware uses control signal INTA to jam the special code onto the data bus. This is shown in Figure 9-23.

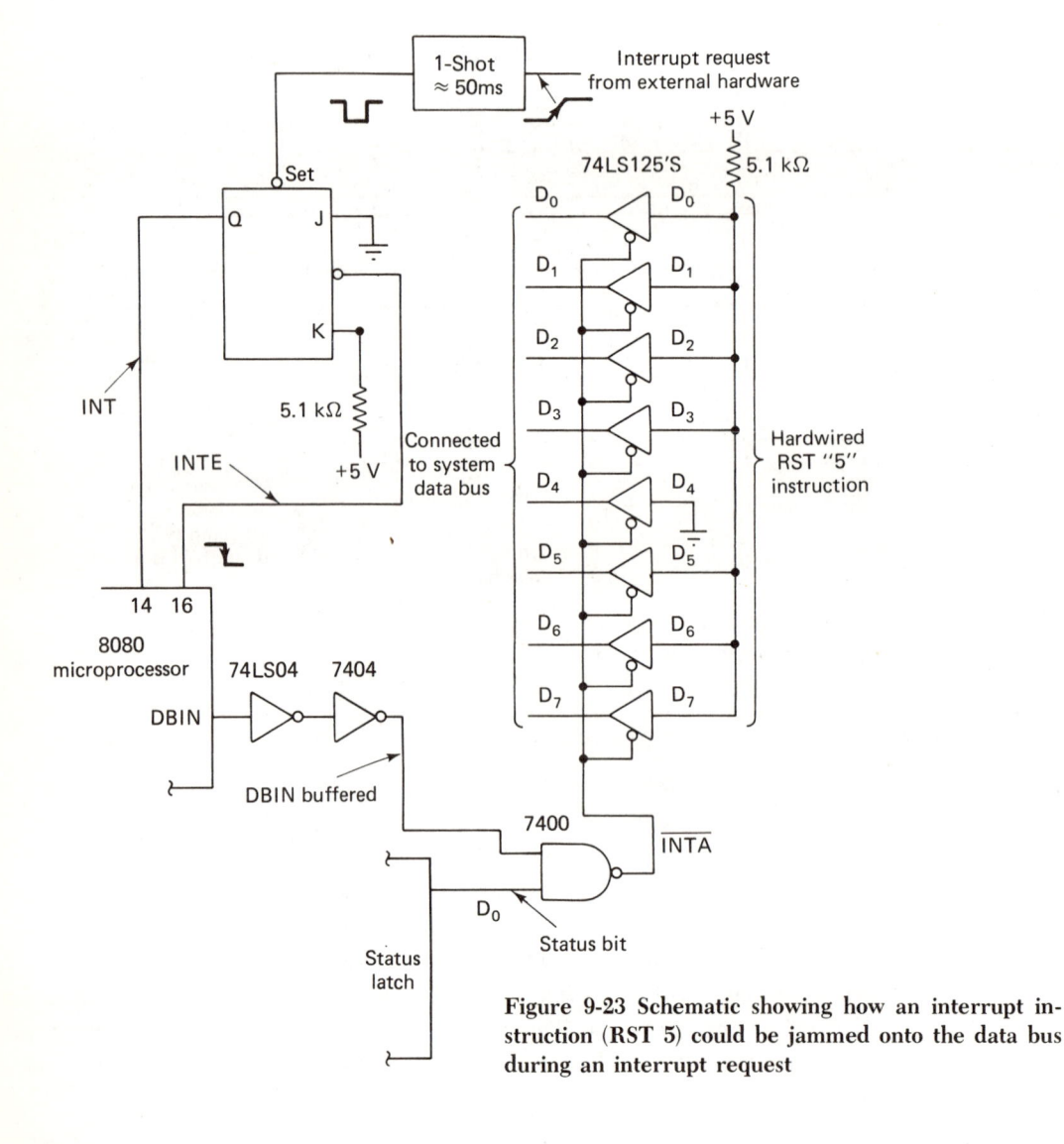

Figure 9-23 Schematic showing how an interrupt instruction (RST 5) could be jammed onto the data bus during an interrupt request

Sec. 9-7 Interrupting the 8080

The special codes that are placed on the data bus are called restart (RST) instructions. They are further designated as RST N instructions. The value of N can be 0, 1, 2, 3, 4, 5, 6, 7. The data bits for each of these instructions are shown in Figure 9-24.

D_7	D_6	D_5	D_4	D_3	D_2	D_1	D_0	RST
1	1	0	0	0	1	1	1	0
1	1	0	0	1	1	1	1	1
1	1	0	1	0	1	1	1	2
1	1	0	1	1	1	1	1	3
1	1	1	0	0	1	1	1	4
1	1	1	0	1	1	1	1	5
1	1	1	1	0	1	1	1	6
1	1	1	1	1	1	1	1	7

Figure 9-24 Actual data bits for each RST instruction that can be jammed onto the 8080 data bus during an interrupt request

When RST N instructions are interpreted by the 8080, the CPU performs a CALL direct to one of eight fixed-memory address locations. These locations are:

RST instruction	Location in memory called
RST 0	$0_{(10)}$
RST 1	$8_{(10)}$
RST 2	$16_{(10)}$
RST 3	$24_{(10)}$
RST 4	$32_{(10)}$
RST 5	$40_{(10)}$
RST 6	$48_{(10)}$
RST 7	$56_{(10)}$

During a normal CALL instruction you recall that the content of the program counter is pushed onto the top of the stack. This same operation takes place in the RST CALL. This means that the address in memory that was about to be executed (prior to the interrupt request) is pushed onto the top of the stack.

The 8080 CPU will now execute the instructions at the memory locations selected by RST CALL. The program at these memory locations can contain calls to other memory addresses where the software routine for communication with the I/O device that requested the interrupt can take place.

When the first external interrupt occurs, the 8080 is automatically put in the DI (disable interrupt) mode. This allows the first interrupt to complete before being interrupted again by another external I/O circuit. However, one may wish the first interruption to be interrupted; if this is the case, then an EI (enable interrupt) instruction is required in the software that handles the interrupt in progress.

When an interrupt occurs we usually want to save the condition of the status flags on the CPU. This requires a PUSH PSW instruction to be contained in the interrupt software. It should be one of the first instructions in the sequence to insure that the status flags are not disturbed or changed before they are saved. To return to normal program execution—running the same program that was being executed prior to an interrupt request, the system executes a simple RET instruction. We recall that the RET will POP the stack and continue execution from the address on the top of the stack. That address is the one that was pushed onto the stack at the time of the interrupt.

Figure 9-25 illustrates the major points concerning interrupts. One can see that the interrupt subroutine is not much different from a CALL subroutine sequence of operation. The major difference lies in the manner in which the

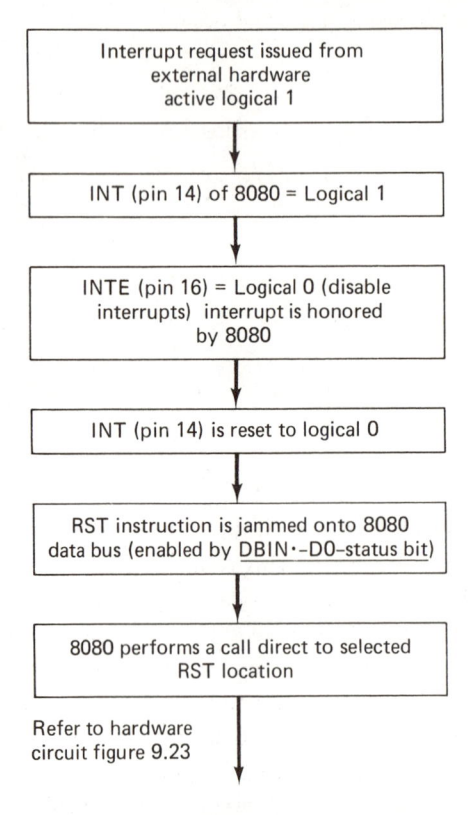

```
┌─────────────────────────────────┐
│   Interrupt request issued from │
│        external hardware        │
│         active logical 1        │
└─────────────────────────────────┘
                │
                ▼
┌─────────────────────────────────┐
│  INT (pin 14) of 8080 = Logical 1│
└─────────────────────────────────┘
                │
                ▼
┌─────────────────────────────────┐
│ INTE (pin 16) = Logical 0 (disable│
│   interrupts)  interrupt is honored│
│            by 8080              │
└─────────────────────────────────┘
                │
                ▼
┌─────────────────────────────────┐
│  INT (pin 14) is reset to logical 0│
└─────────────────────────────────┘
                │
                ▼
┌─────────────────────────────────┐
│ RST instruction is jammed onto 8080│
│ data bus (enabled by DBIN·–D0–status bit)│
└─────────────────────────────────┘
                │
                ▼
┌─────────────────────────────────┐
│ 8080 performs a call direct to selected│
│          RST location           │
└─────────────────────────────────┘
 Refer to hardware
 circuit figure 9.23
```

Figure 9-25 Flowchart showing important events that occur during an interrupt request to an 8080 CPU

subroutine address is read by the 8080. For a normal CALL the address of the subroutine is two consecutive locations in memory. For an interrupt RST Call subroutine the address is supplied by external hardware. Also, there are only eight possible subroutine locations for a RST Call.

9-8 Priority Interrupt

In some systems each I/O device is assigned a priority related to another. This means that some I/O devices have higher priority than others. If two I/O devices try to interrupt the CPU at the same time, the device with the higher priority will interrupt first. In some instances a high priority device may not be interrupted except by a higher priority I/O device.

The assigning of priority to I/O devices is not the job of the CPU. The CPU does not know what device interrupted it, only that an interrupt has occurred. The interrupt software determines whether the present I/O device may be interrupted by another device, and the external hardware decodes the priority of each I/O device. The point to be stressed is that the CPU does not deal with priority or non-priority interrupts; it deals only with interrupts. The external hardware and software determine if an interrupt request is priority or non-priority.

These two special hardware features of waiting and interrupting the 8080 that we have discussed are used often in medium to large systems. The 8080 user should be aware of how these features work. For many small systems these features need not be used. In industrial applications one may expect to encounter these two special features frequently in microprocessor systems.

We have also discussed four special LSI circuits that will be encountered in industry. These special circuits and features were chosen for discussion because they are the most likely second step of a beginning test on microprocessors. Technicians in the field will be faced with some of these advanced features sooner or later when working with microprocessors in industry.

Review Questions

1. What is the function of the 8224 clock generator in an 8080 system?
2. Why is there a reset input on the 8224?
3. What is the advantage of using an 8228 system controller over discrete logic? Can you think of any time where discrete logic would be better to use than the 8228?
4. Design an I/O port to both read and write data to the data bus using an 8212 device.
5. What is a bidirectional driver? Design a single bit bidirectional driver using discrete logic.

6. Why would we need to extend the read access time in a microprocessor-controlled system?

7. Design an interrupt circuit that will jam an RST 3 code on the data lines during an interrupt.

8. Describe what sequence of electrical events takes place when the 8080 is interrupted by external hardware.

9. What is meant by the term "priority interrupt"?

10

AN ADVANCED MICROPROCESSOR APPLICATION

In this chapter we will discuss the design of a complete microprocessor system. We will interface the 8080 system shown in Chapter 4 with an external circuit. This external circuit, it should be noted, will perform its function at a rate independent of the 8080 system. That is, the external circuit *will not* depend on the microprocessor to start and stop it. In effect, the external circuit will be *asynchronous* to the microprocessor.

Our goal is to write an 8080 program, construct the necessary hardware to extract data from this asynchronous I/O circuit, yet not interrupt the normal operation of the I/O circuit. Further, we must adjust for the fact that voltage levels for the I/O circuit that we have chosen to communicate with are not compatible with our system. This gives an opportunity to show a technique that may be used to "get around" this common interface problem. The main point that will be stressed in our explanation is how to enable the 8080 system to communicate with external circuits that are *not* designed to interface to an 8080 or any other microprocessor. After this discussion, one should have an intuitive feel for the kinds of problems to expect when doing this type of microprocessor interface.

10-1 Statement of the Problem

The I/O circuit that we will interface with is a digital clock chip. The clock chip will be connected as a free-running, four-digit clock. It will have its own power supply and output display. The I/O clock circuit will operate and display the correct time even when the microprocessor system is powered down or inoperative. This is essential for this type of I/O circuit; that is, it should always be doing its job. The microprocessor will only monitor the outputs.

Many large computer systems have a system clock. This system clock is used for automatic scheduling of programs or for accurately recording when data was taken by the system. It can be used to perform some system operation automatically such as saving memory on a magnetic tape during a period when the system is not in heavy use. These types of clocks are designed to be interfaced to a computer. Our clock is not. Our clock has been designed only to display the time visually. A block diagram of our system for this discussion is shown in Figure 10-1.

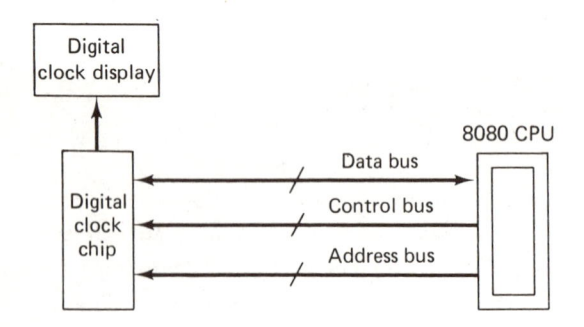

Figure 10-1 Block diagram of an 8080 monitoring the time from a digital clock chip

We will be "taking" data from the C10 clock circuit and inputting this data to the 8080. We will then output the "massaged" data to the general output display. This display will be the same one used in the microprocessor system in Chapter 7.

10-2 The MM5314 Digital Clock Chip

Before designing the interface for the clock, we must review the operating characteristics of the clock. We will use the National Semiconductor MM5314 digital clock chip, whose data sheet is included in Appendix A. This device operates in a "stand alone" mode—that is, when it is keeping correct time and not interfaced to an 8080 system. The 5314 clock chip uses multiplexed 7-segment outputs. This means that the display digits have their segments A–G connected in parallel. Our system will also use four display digits as shown in Figure 10-2.

The 7-segment data for each digit is valid when the *digit enable* signal for a specified digit is active. The digit enable signals turn power on to the selected digit. See Figure 10-3 for a timing diagram showing digit enable timing.

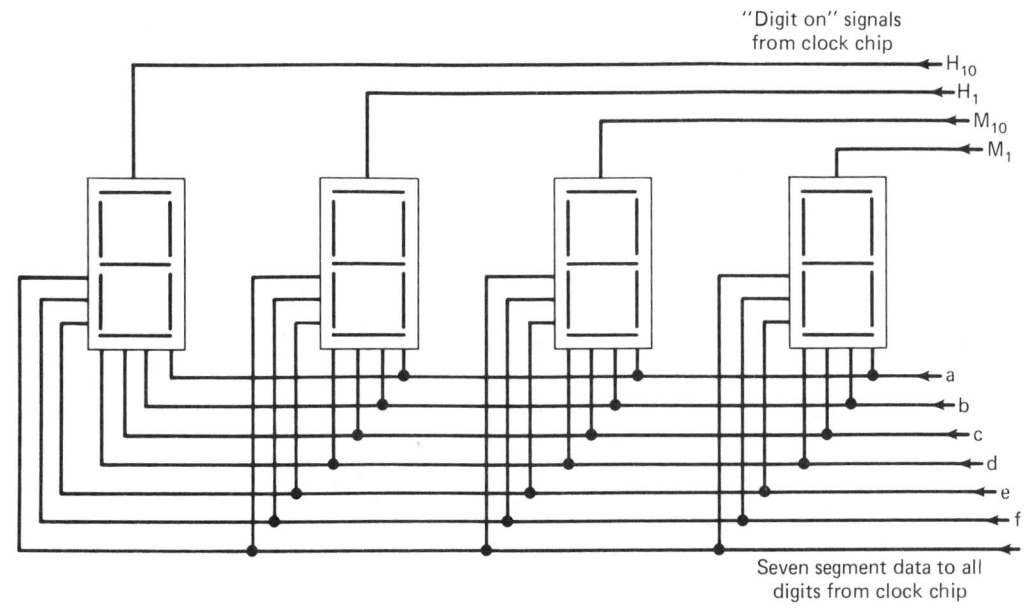

Figure 10-2 Schematic diagram showing how all digits of the display are multiplexed. The seven-segment data is applied to all digits at the same time. The Digit Enable turns on only the correct digit for which the seven-segment data is intended.

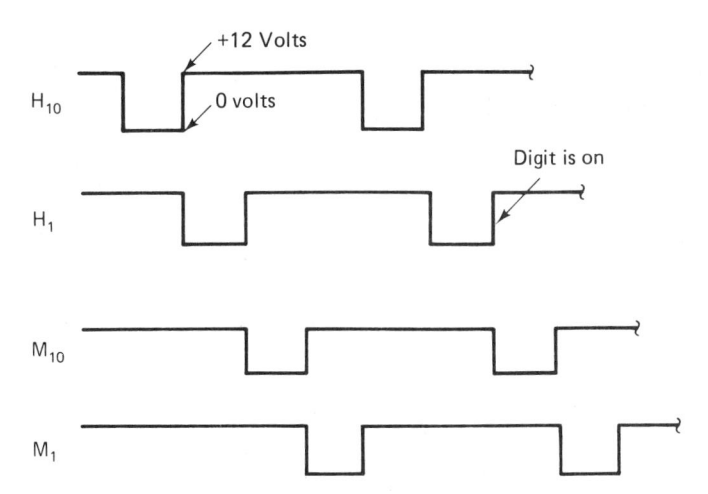

Figure 10-3 Timing diagram showing how Digit Enables are active during different times. When the Digit Enable is active 1, the display is turned on. During this time seven-segment data is used for this digit only.

All of the multiplexing is internal to the clock chip. An external resistor-capacitor network determines the multiplexing frequency. The output structure of the digit enable signal is shown in Figure 10-4 and the output structure for the

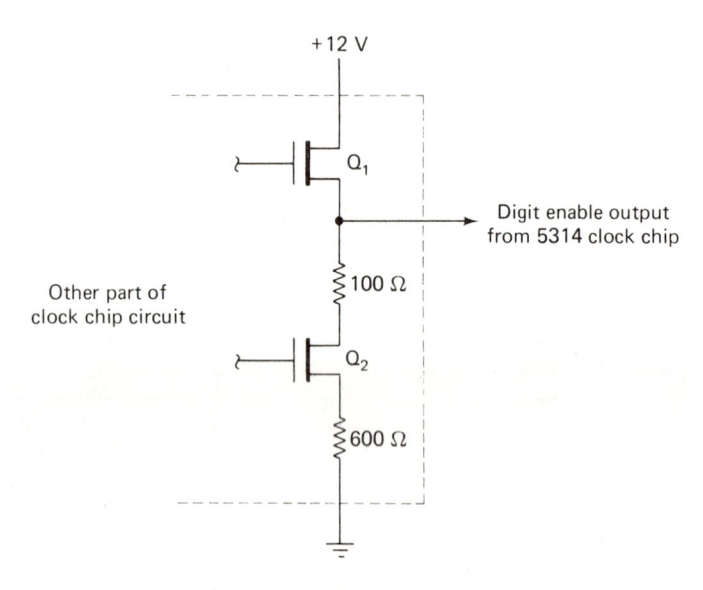

Figure 10-4 Schematic diagram showing the output structure of the 5314 digital clock chip for a Digit Enable line. There are six enable lines, but we use only four of them: the 10s hours (H10), the 1s hours (H1), the 10s minutes (M10) and the 1s minutes (M1).

7-segment data is shown in Figure 10-5. These outputs must be made to drive some type of output display. We will use an LED 7-segment common anode display. The schematic diagram for this type of display is shown in Figure 10-6.

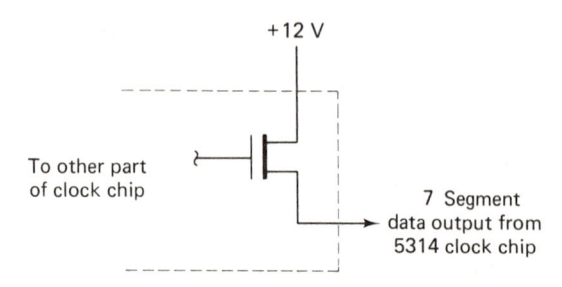

Figure 10-5 Schematic diagram showing output structure of the 5314 digital clock chip for the seven-segment data lines

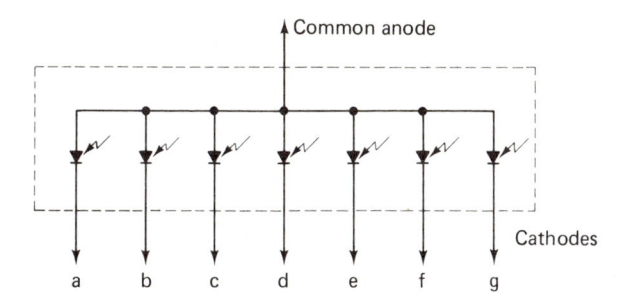

Figure 10-6 Schematic diagram showing how the common anode display is connected internally. Anode connects to +12 V via the Digit Enable signal. Cathodes connect to ground through current limiting resistor via the seven-segment data lines of the 5314 clock chip

The digit enable signals will be used to turn +5 volts on and off to the anodes of the display. The 7-segment outputs will be used to ground the cathodes of the light-emitting diodes in the display. A schematic for one digit-enable circuit and one 7-segment output circuit is shown in Figure 10-7.

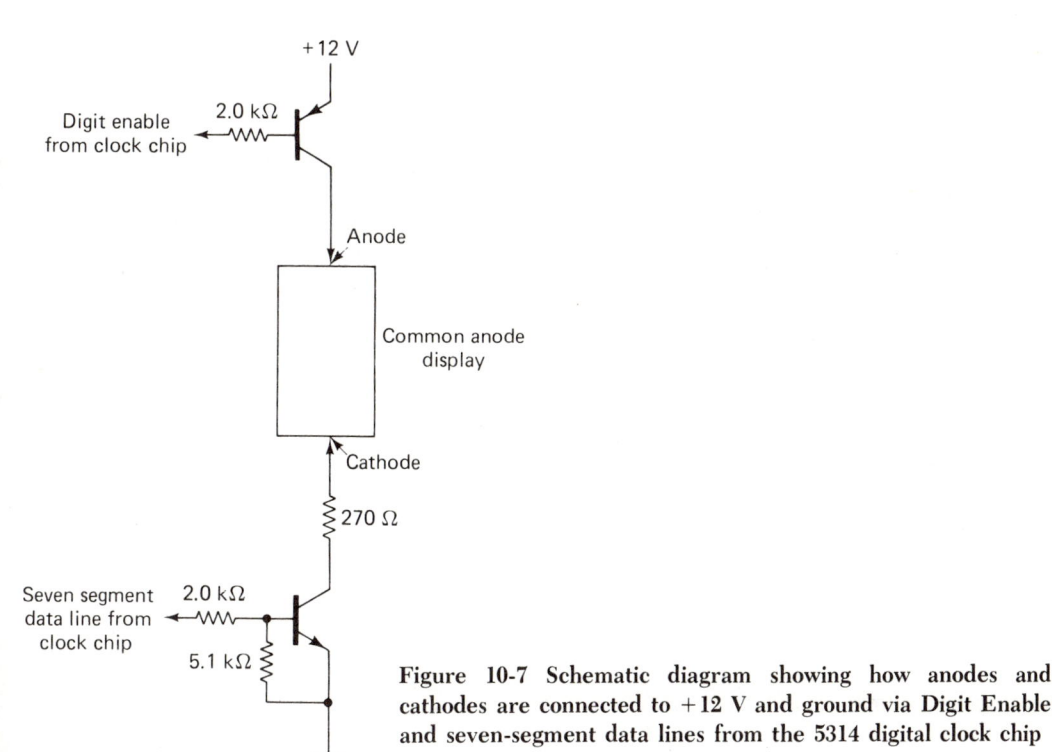

Figure 10-7 Schematic diagram showing how anodes and cathodes are connected to +12 V and ground via Digit Enable and seven-segment data lines from the 5314 digital clock chip

265

10-3 I/O Interface to the 5314 Clock Chip

The complete schematic for the 5314 to run as a "stand alone" digital clock is shown in Figure 10-8. Our job is to monitor the 7-segment data outputs to obtain the time of day. The first problem in the interface is the difference in voltage levels between the 5314 digital clock and the 8080 system. These digital clock outputs swing between +12.0 V and 0.0 V. The 8080 system requires voltage levels between +5.0 V and 0.0 V. Implied in this is the fact that *we must not affect the operation of the clock by our design of the level shifters.*

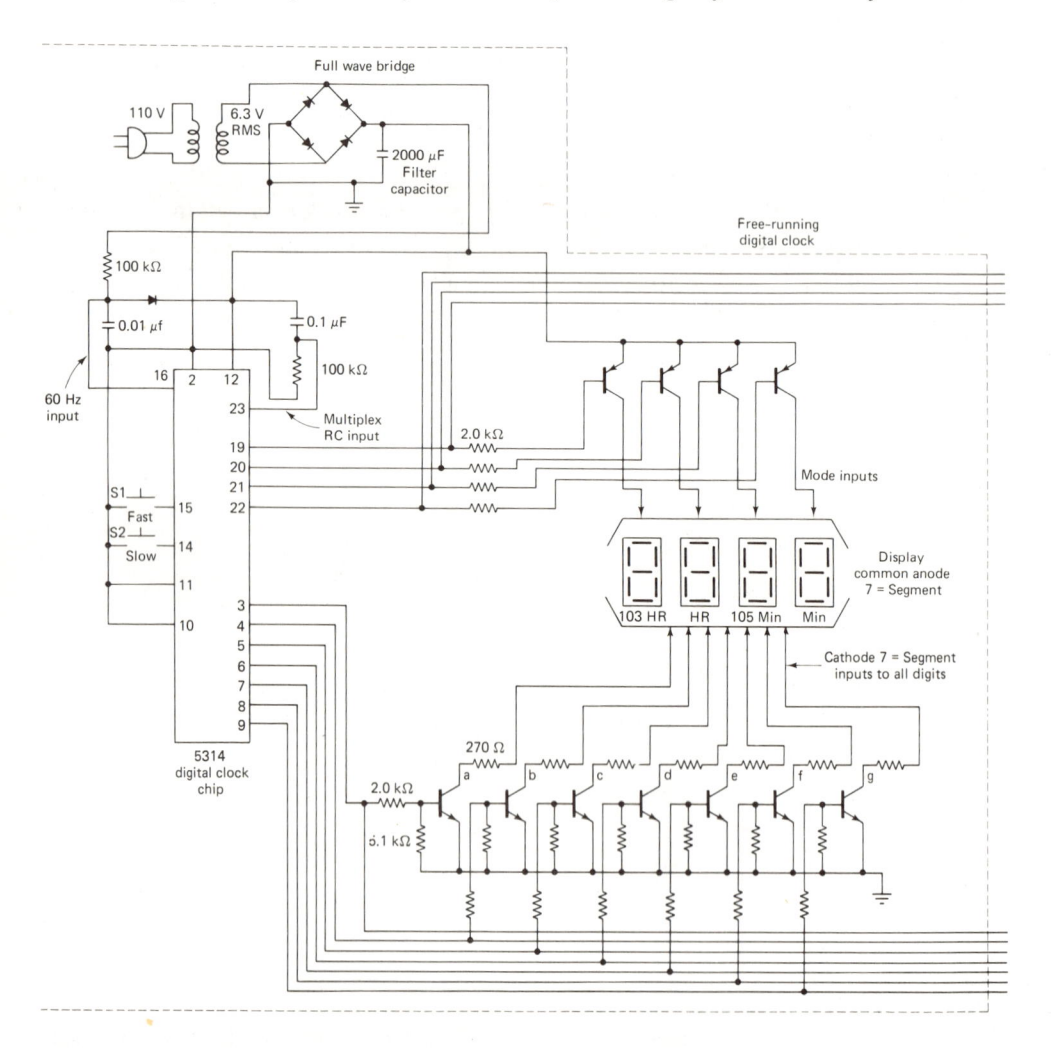

Figure 10-8 Schematic diagram of stand-alone digital clock using the 5314 digital clock chip

266

Sec. 10-3 I/O Interface to the 5314 Clock Chip

We will use CMOS inverters (CD4049) as level shifters and buffers between the MOS levels of the clock chip and the TTL voltage levels of the 8080 system. That is shown in Figure 10-9. The supply voltage of the CD4049 inverters is connected to +5.0 V. The input current (typically 10 picoamperes) is such that it will not overload the outputs of the 5314 digital clock chip.

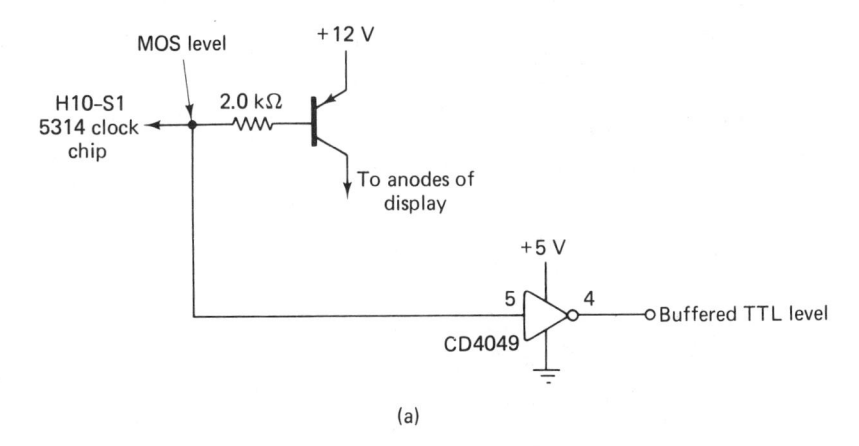

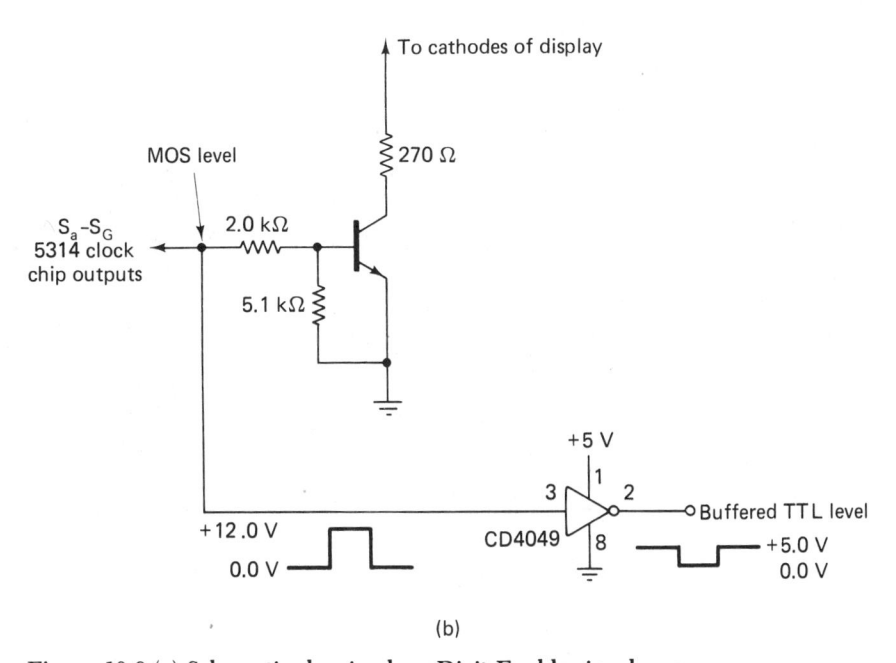

Figure 10-9 (a) Schematic showing how Digit Enable signals are level-shifted and buffered using the CD4049 CMOS device (b) Schematic diagram showing how the seven-segment data lines are level-shifted and buffered using the CD4049 CMOS device

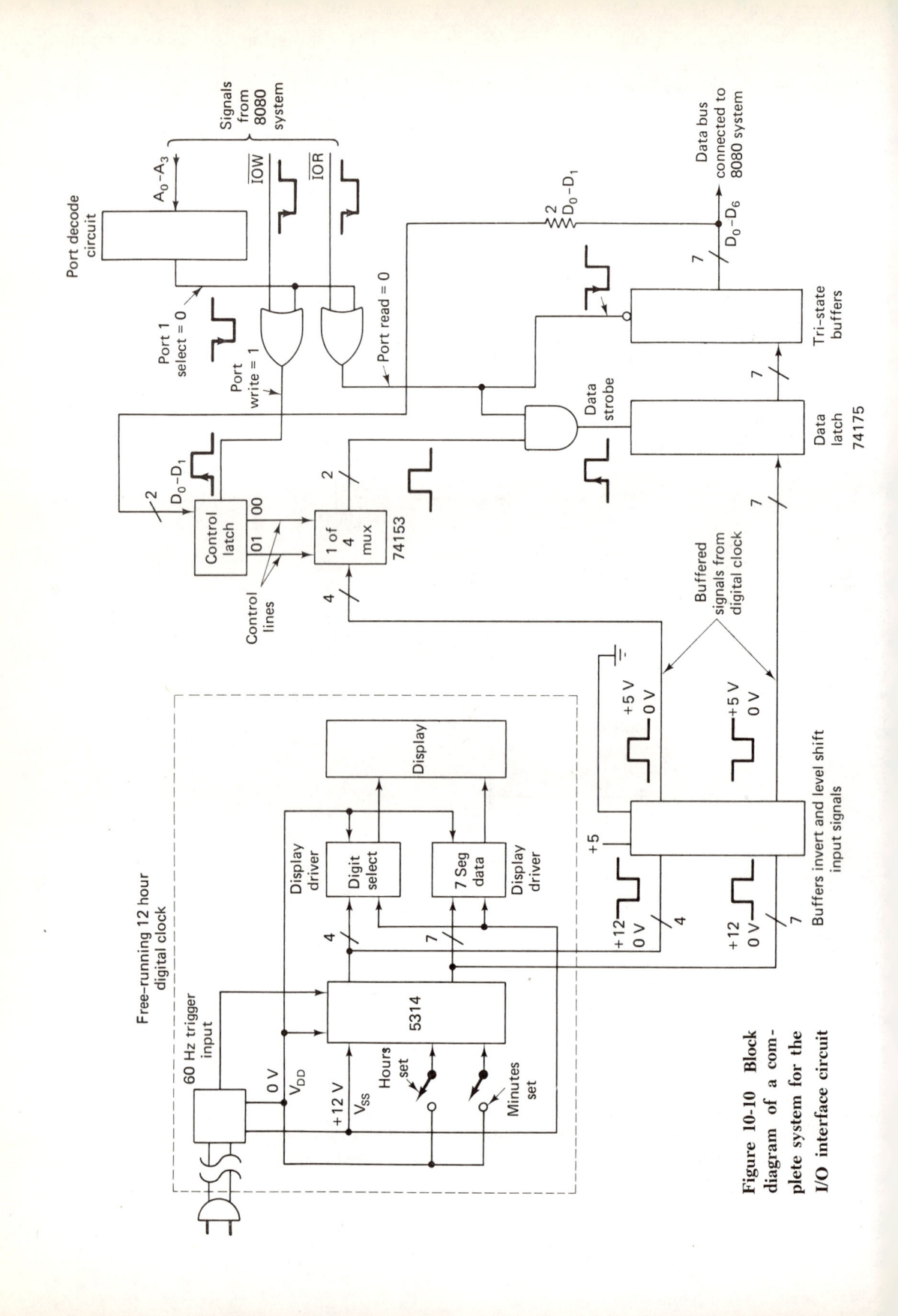

Figure 10-10 Block diagram of a complete system for the I/O interface circuit

Sec. 10-3   I/O Interface to the 5314 Clock Chip   269

Let us assume that the CD4049 will perform both the level shift and buffering satisfactorily. Now, we need to input one digit at a time from the clock display to the 8080. This presents a problem, because the data for each digit is valid (static) only for a brief period of time due to the multiplexing of the display outputs. We must design a circuit that takes the dynamic data from the digital clock chip and converts it to static data. A block diagram of this circuit is shown in Figure 10-10.

In this circuit the digit enable signals H10, H1, M10, and M1 are inputs to a 1-of-4 digital multiplexer, 74153. These input signals have been level-shifted and buffered. The output of the miltiplexer is connected to the *strobe* input of the 74175 storage latches. The input signals for the latches are level-shifted and buffered 7-segment outputs of the digital clock. The control inputs to the 1-of-4 digital multiplexers are D_0–D_1 of the data bus. For example, if we write 00 to port 1 we enable the M1 (minutes) digit to the D inputs of the latches.

When the strobe is active (active 1), the data present at the latch inputs is the correct data for the M1 digit. The data at the output of the latches is now static data. The timing diagram of Figure 10-11 shows the timing of the important signals in the block diagram of Figure 10-10.

Finally, the outputs of the latches are inputs to the tri-state buffers. These buffers enable the outputs onto the data bus when we read port 2. The sequence

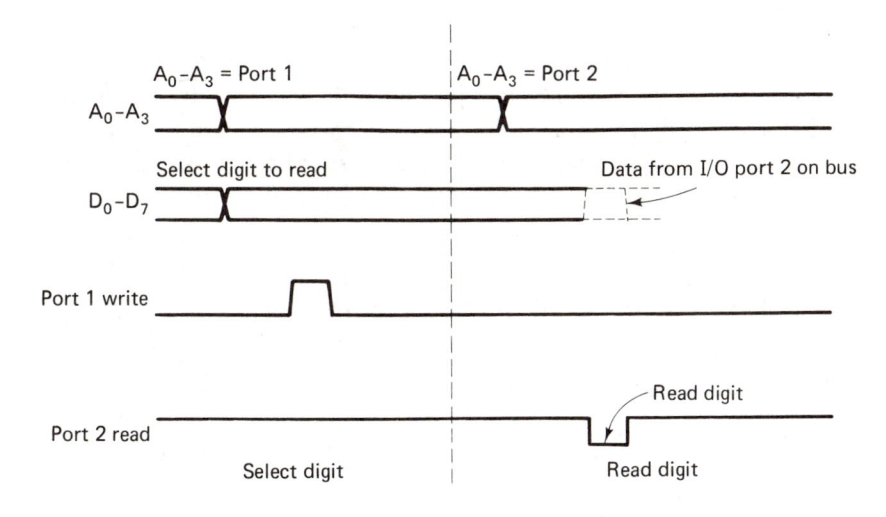

Figure 10-11 Timing diagram showing the sequence of events for selecting the correct digit to read, and actual transfer of data to the 8080 from the I/O port

of events for reading a selected digit based on the block diagram of Figure 10-10 is:

1. Write to port 1, data = 0, 1, 2, 3;
   0-digit M1
   1-digit M10
   2-digit H1
   3-digit H10
   This selects the digit to be read.
2. Wait long enough for the digit enables to complete an entire cycle. This means we must wait for a period equal to the time from one M1 enable to another M1 enable. This insures that at least one digit enable has occurred to strobe the latches. This is called *updating the latches*. Wait time is dependent on the multiplexing frequency that was set by the external RC network.
3. Read port 1. This transfers the 7-segment data into the accumulator of the 8080. Notice that when we read port 1, the strobe to the data latches is gated off. This prevents data from changing while we are reading the data in the latches. If it did change, then we have the possibility of reading bad data.

The complete schematic for this I/O interface is shown in Figure 10-12. We have used a 7442 as our port decoder. When the port address equals $01_{(16)}$, the state 1 output of the 7442 is active low. The $\overline{IOW}$ is also an active low signal. We obtain a logical 1 output of the NOR gate 7402 only when the $\overline{IOW}$ is logical 0 and port 1 is addressed. This condition occurs when we are writing data to port 1.

The same type of decoding takes place when we are reading port 1. The output of the OR gate is active low only when the $\overline{IOR}$ is active and port 01 is addressed. When these signals are logical 0 the tri-state buffers enable data from the storage latches to be placed on the data bus. We now have our communication interface from the asynchronous digital clock circuit to the 8080.

10-4 Software to Control the System

Our task now is software development. Originally we wished to write data to a general purpose display, as described in Chapter 7. Let us review briefly how this display worked. The display shows four BCD digits, so the data for this display is output in three bytes. Each byte is written to a different I/O port. A summary of the three data bytes is shown in Figure 10-13.

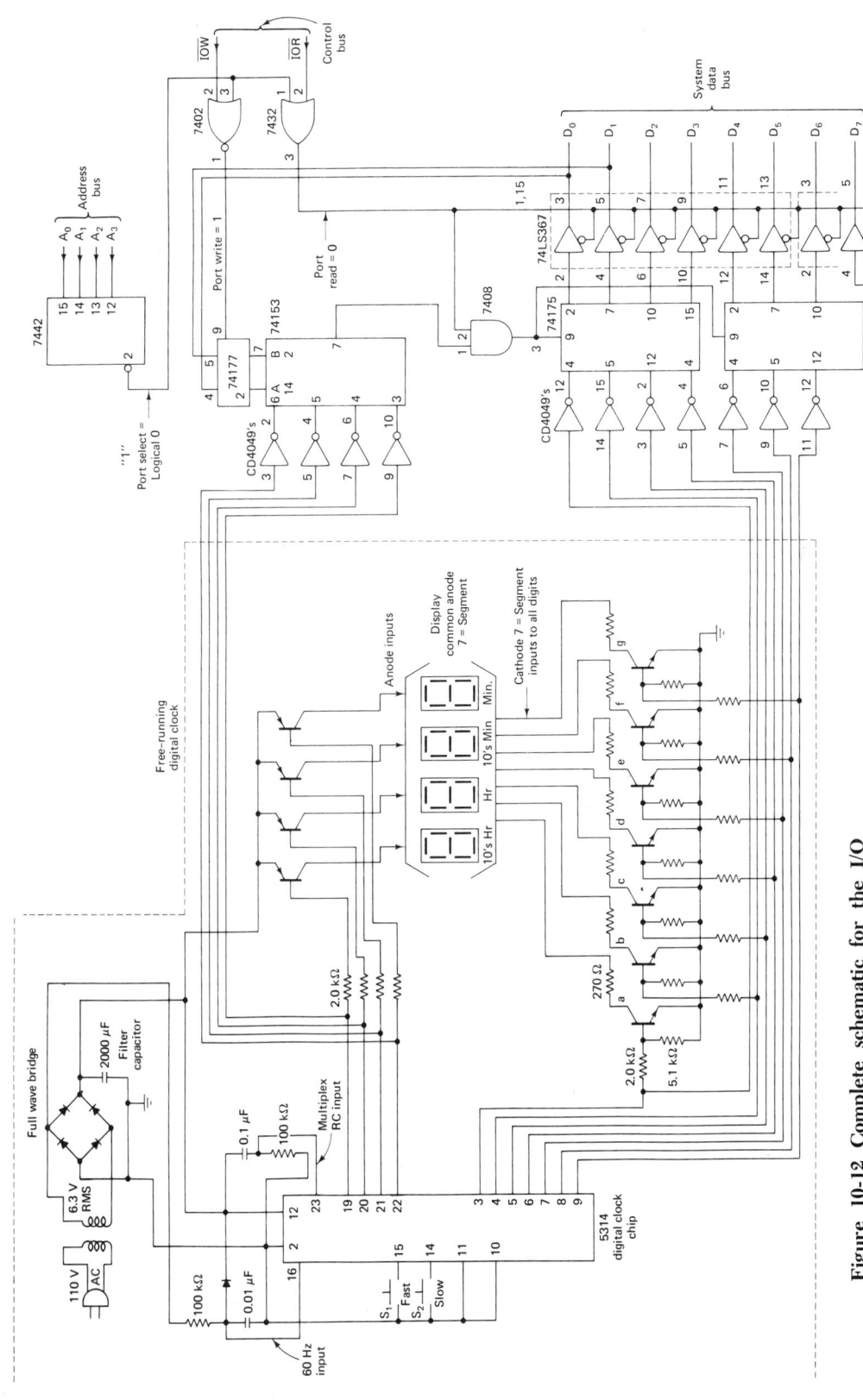

Figure 10-12 Complete schematic for the I/O circuit for monitoring digital clock outputs

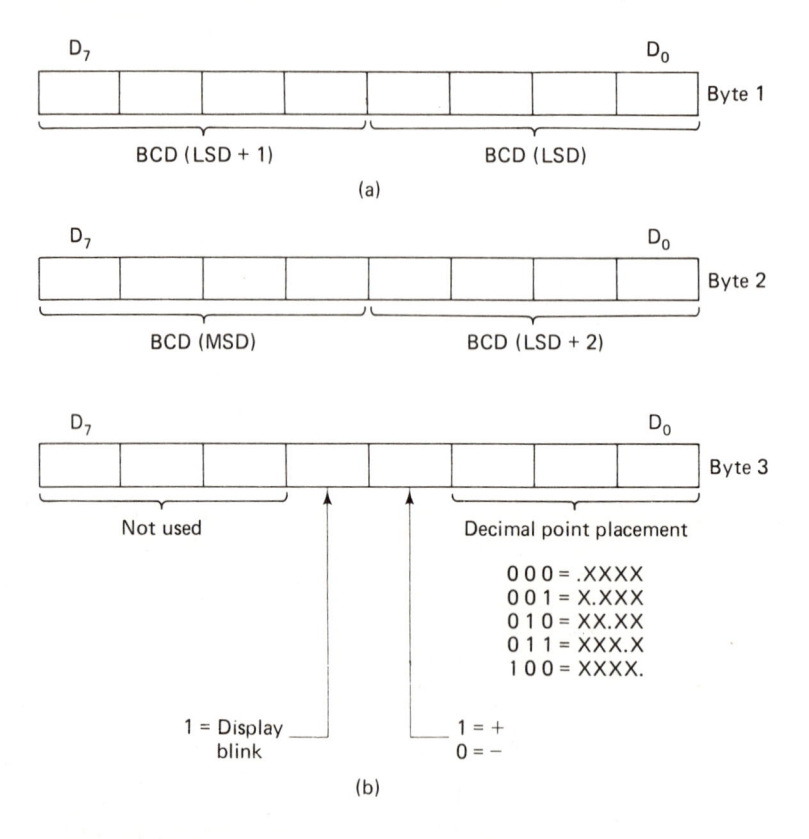

Figure 10-13 The functions of each bit in the three data bytes for output to the general output display: (a) Translating digital (binary) numbers into equivalent common decimal numbers (b) Scaling and other information carried to output display in binary form

Next we must take the 7-segment data of each digit input and "massage" it to fit the data format of the general output display. Figure 10-14 shows an overall task flowchart for our software. Let us discuss a section at a time. First, we read the four data bytes coming in from the digital clock. Then each byte is stored in four consecutive temporary memory locations. When writing our program we do not know how much memory our program is going to require, so instead of defining the location in memory for temporary storage, we simply reserve a location mentally for later assignment.

The first section of our program is written as shown in Figure 10-15. This first section of the program reads the data from the digital clock. We must examine how the data looks, and we see that it is actual 7-segment data that represents a BCD digit. There is a unique 7-segment code for each BCD digit; this is shown

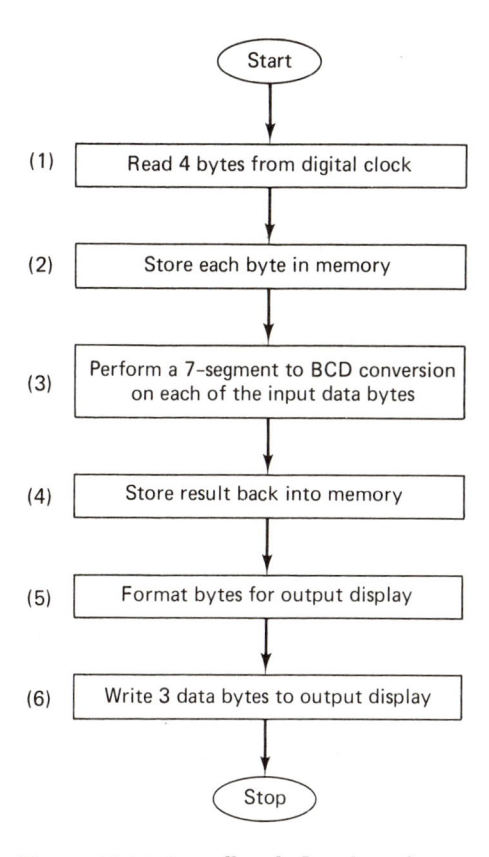

```
                    ┌───────┐
                    │ Start │
                    └───┬───┘
                        ▼
     (1)  ┌──────────────────────────────┐
          │ Read 4 bytes from digital clock │
          └──────────────┬───────────────┘
                         ▼
     (2)  ┌──────────────────────────────┐
          │  Store each byte in memory   │
          └──────────────┬───────────────┘
                         ▼
     (3)  ┌──────────────────────────────────────┐
          │ Perform a 7-segment to BCD conversion │
          │   on each of the input data bytes    │
          └──────────────┬───────────────────────┘
                         ▼
     (4)  ┌──────────────────────────────┐
          │ Store result back into memory │
          └──────────────┬───────────────┘
                         ▼
     (5)  ┌──────────────────────────────┐
          │ Format bytes for output display │
          └──────────────┬───────────────┘
                         ▼
     (6)  ┌──────────────────────────────┐
          │ Write 3 data bytes to output display │
          └──────────────┬───────────────┘
                         ▼
                    ┌───────┐
                    │ Stop  │
                    └───────┘
```

Figure 10-14 Overall task flowchart for events associated with controlling the 8080 and digital clock interface

in Figure 10-16. The logical 0 indicates that a segment is illuminated. This is how data appears at the output of the clock chip. We must convert this 7-segment data into BCD data. In effect, we are performing a 7-segment to BCD conversion.

Notice that we are converting with software as opposed to hardware. We could have converted the 7-segment data to BCD data with hardware in the I/O circuit. Then we would have read BCD data directly into the 8080. The tradeoffs between software and hardware vary from application to application. In our instance we would need to add more hardware to the I/O circuit. We have chosen to perform the 7-segment to BCD conversion in software. The point is that there are different solutions to any problem.

Our technique of conversion will be to compare the 7-segment data that is input to the 8080 from the clock I/O circuit against a table of known 7-segment codes. In effect, we will be using a "look-up table." The software will keep the

```
ITEM    LOC    OBJECT CODE    SOURCE STATEMENTS                    PAGE   1

  1    0000      .    .   .              ASB,HEX,8080 CONTROL PROGRAM
  2    0000      .    .   .          ;
  3    0000      .    .   .          ;
  4    0000      .    .   .          ;
  5    0000      .    .   .          ; READ DATA FROM I/O PORT
  6    0000      .    .   .          ;
  7    0000     3E   00   .              MVI   A,00       ZERO INTO ACC
  8    0002     D3   01   .              OUT   01         SETUP FOR MINUTE DIGIT
  9    0004     CD   31  00              CALL  WAIT       WAIT FOR DATA STABLE
 10    0007     DB   01   .              IN    01         READ MINUTE DIGIT
 11    0009     32   38  00              STA   TIME       STORE DATA IN MEM
 12    000C     3E   01   .              MVI   A,01       SETUP FOR 10'S MINUTE
 13    000E     D3   01   .              OUT   01
 14    0010     CD   31  00              CALL  WAIT       WAIT FOR DATA STABLE
 15    0013     DB   01   .              IN    01         READ 10'S MINUTE DIGIT
 16    0015     32   39  00              STA   TIME+1     STORE IN MEM
 17    0018     3E   02   .              MVI   A,02       SETUP FOR HOUR DIGIT
 18    001A     D3   01   .              OUT   01
 19    001C     CD   31  00              CALL  WAIT       WAIT FOR DATA STABLE
 20    001F     DB   01   .              IN    01         READ HOUR DIGIT
 21    0021     32   3A  00              STA   TIME+2     STORE IN MEM
 22    0024     3E   03   .              MVI   A,03       SETUP FOR 10'S HOURS
 23    0026     D3   01   .              OUT   01
 24    0028     CD   31  00              CALL  WAIT       WAIT FOR DATA STABLE
 25    002B     DB   01   .              IN    01         READ 10'S HOURS DIGIT
 26    002D     32   3B  00              STA   TIME+3     STORE IN MEM
 27    0030     76    .   .              HLT              STOP EXECUTION OF PROGRAM
 28    0031      .    .   .          ;
 29    0031      .    .   .          ;
 30    0031      .    .   .          ; SUBROUTINE WAIT
 31    0031      .    .   .          ;
 32    0031     3E   FF   .      WAIT    MVI   A,255      SETUP WAIT LOOP
 33    0033     3D    .   .      WAIT 1  DCR   A          DECREMENT ACC
 34    0034     C2   33  00              JNZ   WAIT 1     JUMP IF ACC NOT ZERO TO WAIT
 35    0037     C9    .   .              RET              WAITED FOR 255 LOOPS RETURN
                                                          TO MAIN PROGRAM
 36    0038      .    .   .          ;
 37    0038      .    .   .          ;
 38    0038      .    .   .          ;
 39    0038      .    .   .          ; LOCATIONS TO STORE DATA TIME (4)
 40    0038      .    .   .          ;
 41    0038      .    .   .          ;
 42    0038     00    .   .      TIME    NOP
 43    0039     00    .   .              NOP
 44    003A     00    .   .              NOP
 45    003B     00    .   .              NOP
 46    003C      .    .   .          ;
 47    003C      .    .   .          ;
 48    003C      .    .   .              END              END FOR COMPILER
   0   ERRORS FOUND IN ASSEMBLY CODE .
```

Figure 10-15 8080 program to read seven-segment data from the digital clock I/O port and store the data into memory locations 38, 39, 3A, and 3B

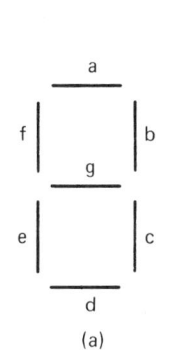

	D_7		D_0	Digit value
0 0	0 0 0	0 0 0		0
0 0	1 1 1	0 0 1		1
0 0	1 0 0	1 0 0		2
0 0	1 1 0	0 0 0		3
0 0	0 1 1	0 0 1		4
0 0	0 1 0	0 1 0		5
0 0	0 0 0	0 1 1		6
0 1	1 1 1	0 0 0		7
0 0	0 0 0	0 0 0		8
0 0	0 1 1	0 0 0		9
0 1	1 1 1	1 1 1		Blank

Figure 10-16 (a) Diagram showing seven-segment data LEDs inside a typical display (b) Actual data the 8080 interprets for the digit value shown

systems comparing the data input to the 8080 from the clock against known data in the look-up table. When the system finds a match the software will indicate which element of the table was correct and can then determine which BCD number this entry represents. The use of a look-up table is one way of converting the 7-segment to binary coded decimals. We keep mentioning that there is more than one way to solve most problems, so that readers do not think the method described is the only way. The fun begins when one can implement a self-inspired solution and perhaps improve on an example given in a text.

Our conversion will work like this. The system will read the first byte of 7-segment data from memory. It will then initialize an internal register to zero and will then compare data from memory against the first entry in the look-up table. The first entry in the look-up table corresponds to the digit zero. The second entry is one, the third is two, and so on. The last entry in the table corresponds to a blank. *Remember—a blank digit is legal* (valid) *output from the clock chip.*

We compare against the first entry in the table. If the entry matches the data, we know the digit was zero. But suppose that the entry did not match. The machine would increment an internal counter and compare the 7-segment data against the second entry in the table. Notice that the internal counter value will equal the BCD value of the entry we are comparing against.

Next, when a match occurs, the system transfers the contents of the internal counter to the memory address location where it had initially stored the 7-segment data. If the 7-segment data matches with a "blank" the system stores a zero into the memory location. However, it is possible that there will be no match at all. If the system read bad data from our I/O circuit, we do not want to print this to the display. Also, we want the display to reflect the fact that the system had bad data in at least one digit. If this condition exists the system will make the display flash. This can be done by setting a particular bit in the third output byte written to the display. A flowchart for the 7-segment to BCD conversion is shown in Figure 10-17.

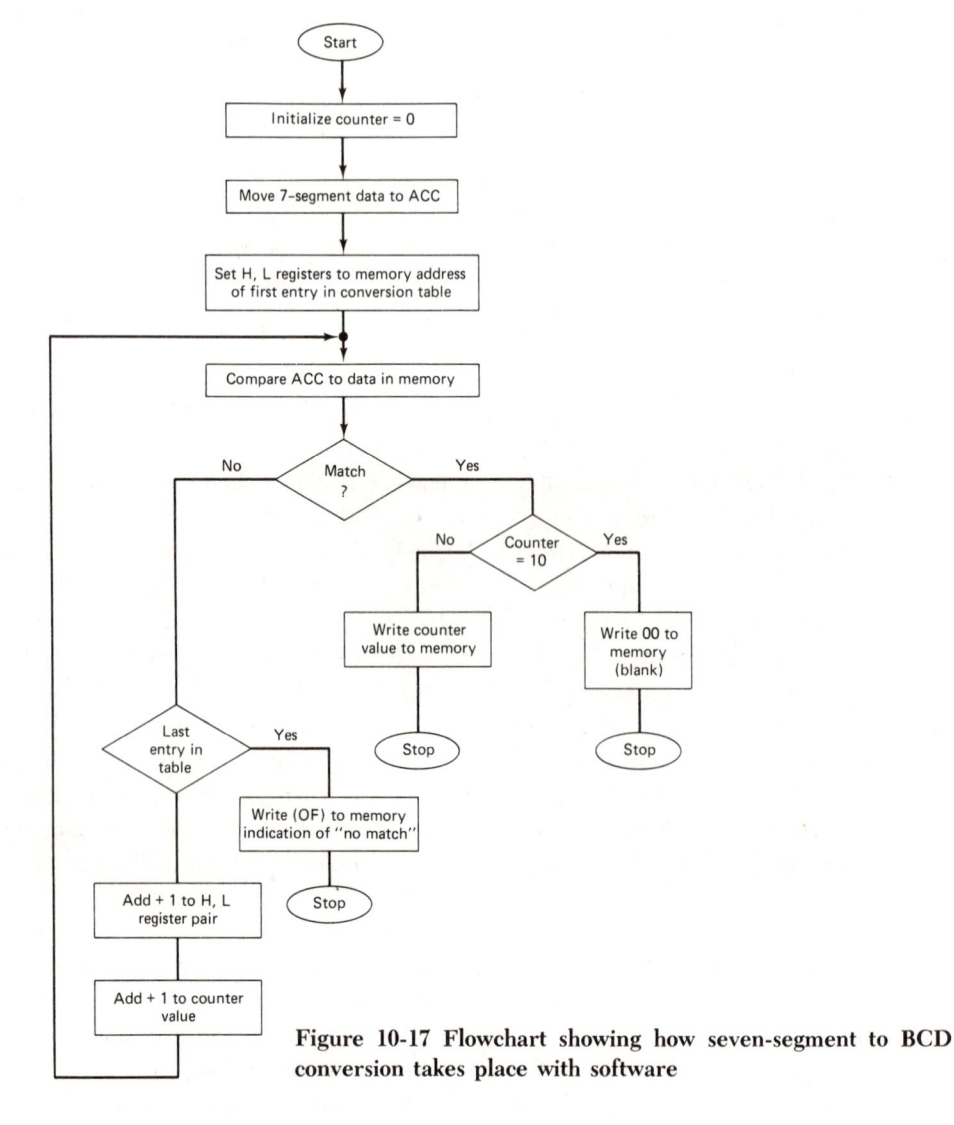

Figure 10-17 Flowchart showing how seven-segment to BCD conversion takes place with software

The fifth programming step is to re-format the BCD data stored in the four temporary memory locations into the three bytes needed for the output display. We recall that the data byte format for the display looks as shown in Figure 10-13. We will read a BCD digit and check for errors with this digit. If we perform the 7-segment to BCD conversion but the data does not match any entries in the look-up table, we will store 0F in the memory location. When formating these data bytes for writing to the display first check to see if the data equals a 0F. If it does, then we know to set the bit that will flash the display. The flowchart for formatting this data is shown in Figure 10-18.

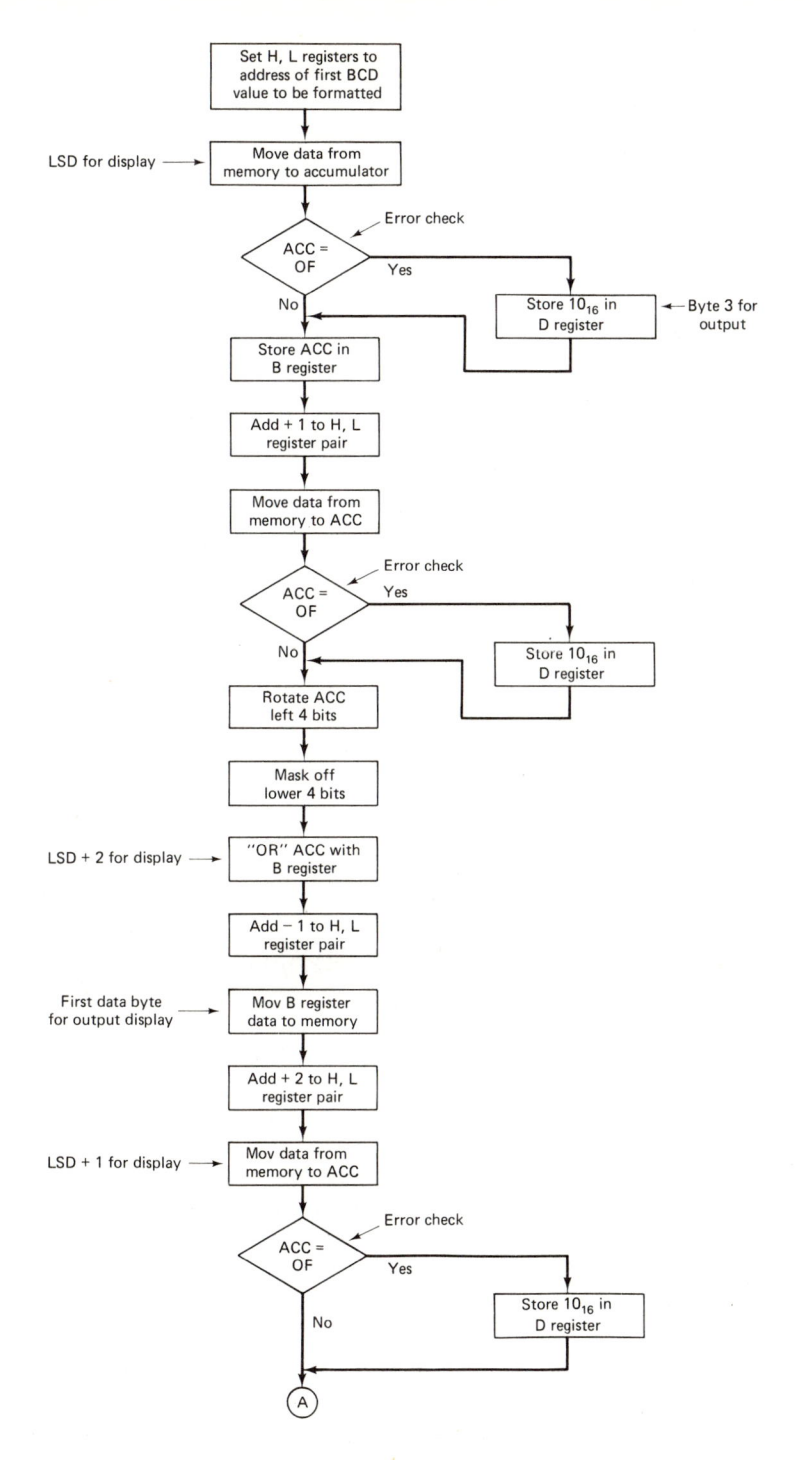

Figure 10-18 Flowchart for formating BCD data into three data bytes needed for output to general output display (part a) (Continued next page)

277

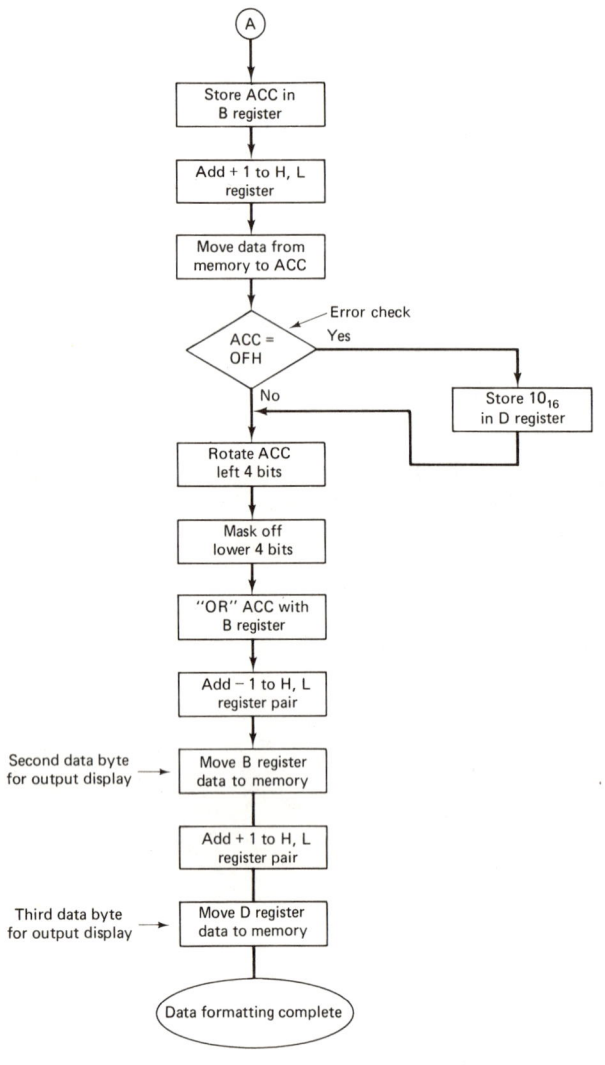

Figure 10-18 (part b) Flowchart for formatting BCD data into three data bytes needed for output to general output display

When one byte is formatted it is stored in the same memory address where we stored the first 7-segment data. When the formatting has been completed the three data bytes to be printed to the display are located in the first three of the four memory locations in which we stored the 7-segment data from the I/O port. This actual program is presented in Figure 10-19.

```
ITEM   LOC    OBJECT CODE   SOURCE STATEMENTS                                    PAGE   1

   1   0000     .   .   .              ASB,HEX,8080 CONTROL PROGRAM
   2   0000     .   .   .      ;
   3   0000     .   .   .      ;
   4   0000     .   .   .      ;
   5   0000     .   .   .      ;
   6   0000    16  00   .              MVI   D,00       INITIALIZE D REGISTER
   7   0002    3A  3F  00              LDA   TIME       MOV FIRST BYTE TO ACC
   8   0005    FE  0F   .              CPI   15         ERROR CHECK OF BYTE
   9   0007    CC  3C  00              CZ    ERROR      CALL ERROR IF MATCH
  10   000A    47   .   .              MOV   B,A        STORE IN B REGISTER
  11   000B    3A  40  00              LDA   TIME+1     NEXT DATA TO ACC
  12   000E    FE  0F   .              CPI   15         ERROR CHECK
  13   0010    CC  3C  00              CZ    ERROR      CALL ERROR IF MATCH
  14   0013    17   .   .              RAL
  15   0014    17   .   .              RAL
  16   0015    17   .   .              RAL
  17   0016    17   .   .              RAL              SHIFT LEFT 4 BITS
  18   0017    E6  F0   .              ANI   360Q       MASK OFF LOWER 4 BITS
  19   0019    B0   .   .              ORA   B          DATA BYTE FORMATTED
  20   001A    32  3F  00              STA   TIME       FIRST DATA BYTE FOR DISPLAY
  21   001D     .   .   .      ;
  22   001D     .   .   .      ;
  23   001D     .   .   .      ; FORMAT SECOND DATA BYTE
  24   001D     .   .   .      ;
  25   001D    3A  41  00              LDA   TIME+2     MOVE THIRD BYTE TO ACC
  26   0020    FE  0F   .              CPI   15         ERROR CHECK
  27   0022    CC  3C  00              CZ    ERROR      CALL ERROR IF MATCH
  28   0025    47   .   .              MOV   B,A        STORE IN B REGISTER
  29   0026    3A  42  00              LDA   TIME+3     4TH BYTE TO ACC
  30   0029    FE  0F   .              CPI   15         ERROR CHECK
  31   002B    CC  3C  00              CZ    ERROR      CALL ERROR IF MATCH
  32   002E    17   .   .              RAL
  33   002F    17   .   .              RAL
  34   0030    17   .   .              RAL
  35   0031    17   .   .              RAL
  36   0032    E6  F0   .              ANI   360Q       SHIFT AND MASK OFF 4 LOWER
                                                        BITS
  37   0034    B0   .   .              ORA   B          SECOND DATA BYTE FORMATTED
  38   0035    32  40  00              STA   TIME+1     2ND DATA BYTE FOR DISPLAY
  39   0038    7A   .   .              MOV   A,D
  40   0039    32  41  00              STA   TIME+2     3RD DATA BYTE FOR DISPLY
  41   003C     .   .   .      ;
  42   003C     .   .   .      ;
  43   003C     .   .   .      ; SUBROUTINE ERROR SETS THE D REGISTER TO BLINK
                                                        DISPLAY
  44   003C     .   .   .      ;
  45   003C     .   .   .      ;
  46   003C    16  10   .      ERROR   MVI   D,16       SET BIT TO BLINK DISPLAY
  47   003E    C9   .   .              RET
  48   003F     .   .   .      ;
  49   003F     .   .   .      ;
  50   003F     .   .   .      ; FOUR LOCATIONS TO STORE TIME DATA
  51   003F     .   .   .      ;
  52   003F     .   .   .      ;
  53   003F    00   .   .      TIME    NOP
  54   0040    00   .   .              NOP
  55   0041    00   .   .              NOP
  56   0042    00   .   .              NOP
  57   0043     .   .   .              END              END STATEMENT FOR COMPILER
   0   ERRORS FOUND IN ASSEMBLY CODE .
```

Figure 10-19 8080 program to format BCD data into three data bytes to be written to general output display. The four BCD digits are stored in memory locations 3F, 40, 41, and 42 of this program (part a).

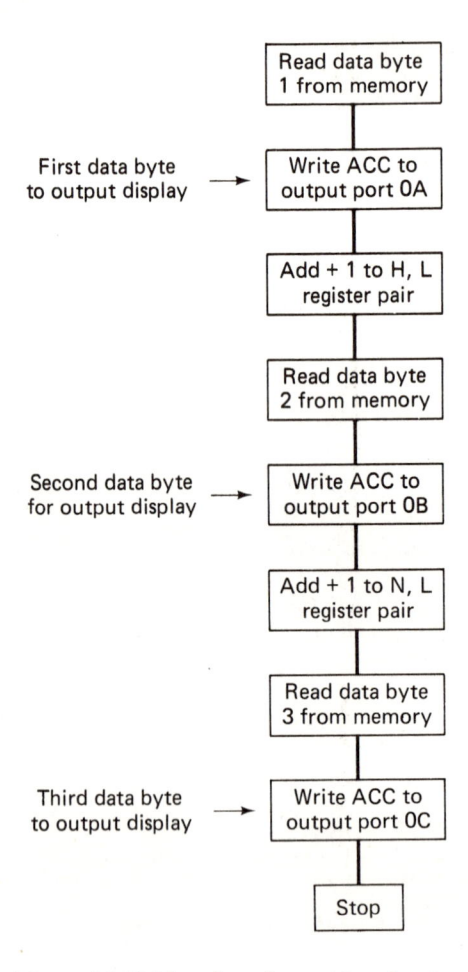

```
                    ┌──────────────────┐
                    │ Read data byte   │
                    │ 1 from memory    │
                    └──────────────────┘
                             │
First data byte     ┌──────────────────┐
to output display → │ Write ACC to     │
                    │ output port 0A   │
                    └──────────────────┘
                             │
                    ┌──────────────────┐
                    │ Add + 1 to H, L  │
                    │ register pair    │
                    └──────────────────┘
                             │
                    ┌──────────────────┐
                    │ Read data byte   │
                    │ 2 from memory    │
                    └──────────────────┘
                             │
Second data byte    ┌──────────────────┐
for output display →│ Write ACC to     │
                    │ output port 0B   │
                    └──────────────────┘
                             │
                    ┌──────────────────┐
                    │ Add + 1 to N, L  │
                    │ register pair    │
                    └──────────────────┘
                             │
                    ┌──────────────────┐
                    │ Read data byte   │
                    │ 3 from memory    │
                    └──────────────────┘
                             │
Third data byte     ┌──────────────────┐
to output display → │ Write ACC to     │
                    │ output port 0C   │
                    └──────────────────┘
                             │
                         ┌───────┐
                         │ Stop  │
                         └───────┘
```

Figure 10-20 Flowchart for writing the three data bytes to general output display

Last, we must write the three data bytes to the output display. The flowchart for this operation is shown in Figure 10-20. The actual 8080 program to perform this function is given in Figure 10-21. A complete 8080 program to perform the entire sequence of reading, comparing, formatting, and writing out data is shown in Figure 10-22, which follows on the next four pages.

```
=========================================================
  LOC    OBJECT CODE    SOURCE STATEMENTS
=========================================================

0000    .    .    .    ;
0000    3A   10   00        LDA   TIME      LOAD FIRST BYTE INTO ACC
0003    D3   0A   .         OUT   10        WRITE FIRST BYTE TO PORT A
0005    3A   11   00        LDA   TIME+1    2ND BYTE INTO ACC
0008    D3   0B   .         OUT   11        WRITE 2ND BYTE TO PORT B
000A    3A   12   00        LDA   TIME+2    THIRD BYTE TO ACC
000D    D3   0C   .         OUT   12        WRITE THIRD BYTE TO PORT C
000F    76   .    .         HLT             HALT THE SYSTEM
0010    .    .    .    ;
0010    .    .    .    ;
0010    .    .    .    ;   LOCATIONS TO STORE TIME BYTES (3)
0010    .    .    .    ;
0010    .    .    .    ;
0010    00   .    .   TIME  NOP
0011    00   .    .         NOP
0012    00   .    .         NOP           3 LOCATIONS TO STORE DATA TIM
```

Figure 10-21 8080 program to write three formated data bytes to general output display. Note the three locations for the data stored in memory. This data was stored there by some other program. This partial program will take this data and write it to the display.

```
ITEM   LOC    OBJECT CODE    SOURCE STATEMENTS                              PAGE   1

   1   0000    .  .  .                  ASB,HEX,8080 CONTROL PROGRAM
   2   0000    .  .  .          ;
   3   0000    .  .  .          ;
   4   0000    .  .  .          ;
   5   0000    .  .  .          ; COMPLETE PROGRAM FOR THIS CHAPTER
   6   0000    .  .  .          ;
   7   0000    .  .  .          ;      FIRST READ DATA FROM I/O PORT 01H
   8   0000    .  .  .          ;
   9   0000    .  .  .          ;
  10   0000   3E 00  .                  MVI   A,00       ZERO INTO ACC
  11   0002   D3 01  .                  OUT   01         SETUP FOR MINUTE DIGIT
  12   0004   CD 33 00                  CALL  WAIT       WAIT FOR DATA STABLE
  13   0007   DB 01  .                  IN    01         READ MINUTE DIGIT
  14   0009   32 3A 00                  STA   TIME       STORE DATA IN MEM
  15   000C   3E 01  .                  MVI   A,01       SETUP FOR 10'S MINUTE
  16   000E   D3 01  .                  OUT   01
  17   0010   CD 33 00                  CALL  WAIT       WAIT FOR DATA STABLE
  18   0013   DB 01  .                  IN    01         READ 10'S MINUTE DIGIT
  19   0015   32 3B 00                  STA   TIME+1     STORE IN MEM
  20   0018   3E 02  .                  MVI   A,02       SETUP FOR HOUR DIGIT
  21   001A   D3 01  .                  OUT   01
  22   001C   CD 33 00                  CALL  WAIT       WAIT FOR DATA STABLE
  23   001F   DB 01  .                  IN    01         READ HOUR DIGIT
  24   0021   32 3C 00                  STA   TIME+2     STORE IN MEM
  25   0024   3E 03  .                  MVI   A,03       SETUP FOR 10'S HOURS
  26   0026   D3 01  .                  OUT   01
  27   0028   CD 33 00                  CALL  WAIT       WAIT FOR DATA STABLE
  28   002B   DB 01  .                  IN    01         READ 10'S HOURS DIGIT
  29   002D   32 3D 00                  STA   TIME+3     STORE IN MEM
  30   0030   C3 3E 00                  JMP   NEXT       NEXT IS THE 7SEG TO BCD CON
                                                         VERT
  31   0033    .  .  .          ;
  32   0033    .  .  .          ;
  33   0033    .  .  .          ; SUBROUTINE WAIT
  34   0033    .  .  .          ;
  35   0033   3E FF  .          WAIT    MVI   A,255      SETUP WAIT LOOP
  36   0035   3D  .  .          WAIT1   DCR   A          DECREMENT ACC
  37   0036   C2 35 00                  JNZ   WAIT1      JUMP IF ACC NOT ZERO TO WAIT
  38   0039   C9  .  .                  RET              WAITED FOR 255 LOOPS RETURN
                                                         TO MAIN PROGRAM
  39   003A    .  .  .          ;
  40   003A    .  .  .          ;
  41   003A    .  .  .          ;
  42   003A    .  .  .          ; LOCATIONS TO STORE DATA TIME (4)
  43   003A    .  .  .          ;
  44   003A    .  .  .          ;
  45   003A   00  .  .          TIME    NOP
  46   003B   00  .  .                  NOP
  47   003C   00  .  .                  NOP
  48   003D   00  .  .                  NOP
  49   003E    .  .  .          ;
  50   003E    .  .  .          ;
```

Figure 10-22 Complete 8080 program for reading, comparing, formatting, and writing data to output display from the digital clock I/O port

```
================================================================================
ITEM   LOC    OBJECT CODE    SOURCE STATEMENTS                         PAGE   2
================================================================================
 51    003E     .    .   .    ; THIS SECTION OF CODE WILL CONVERT
 52    003E     .    .   .    ; 7 SEGMENT DATA IN MEM LOC TIME-TIME+3
 53    003E     .    .   .    ; TO BCD DATA AND STORE IN TIME-TIME+3
 54    003E     .    .   .    ;
 55    003E     .    .   .    ;
 56    003E     3A   3A  00   NEXT    LDA   TIME       FIRST DATA TO BE CONVERTED
 57    0041     CD   65  00           CALL  CONV       CONV WILL RETURN BCD IN ACC
 58    0044     32   3A  00           STA   TIME       STORE BCD INTO MEM
 59    0047     3A   3B  00           LDA   TIME+1     SECOND DATA TO CONV
 60    004A     CD   65  00           CALL  CONV
 61    004D     32   3B  00           STA   TIME+1     STORE BCD DATA INTO MEM
 62    0050     3A   3C  00           LDA   TIME+2     3RD DATA BYTE TO CONV
 63    0053     CD   65  00           CALL  CONV
 64    0056     32   3C  00           STA   TIME+2     STORE BCD DATA INTO MEMJ
 65    0059     3A   3D  00           LDA   TIME+3     4TH DATA BYTE TO CONVERT
 66    005C     CD   65  00           CALL  CONV
 67    005F     32   3D  00           STA   TIME+3     BCD DATA TO MEM
 68    0062     C3   8B  00           JMP   FORMA      FORMA WILL FORMAT DATA FOR
                                                       DISPLAY
 69    0065     .    .   .    ;
 70    0065     .    .   .    ;
 71    0065     .    .   .    ; CONV SUBROUTINE WILL CONVERT THE 7SEGMENT
 72    0065     .    .   .    ; DATA IN ACC AND RETURN BCD DATA IN ACC
 73    0065     .    .   .    ;
 74    0065     .    .   .    ;
 75    0065     0E   00  .    CONV    MVI   C,00       INITIALIZE COUNTER
 76    0067     21   80  00           LXI   H,TABLE    H,L POINT TO FIRST ENTRY IN
                                                       TABLE
 77    006A     BE   .   .    L001    CMP   M          COMPARE FIRST ENTRY WITH ACC
 78    006B     CA   7E  00           JZ    VAL        JMP IF MATCH TO VAL
 79    006E     0C   .   .            INR   C          INCREMENT COUNTER
 80    006F     23   .   .            INX   H          INCREMENT TABLE POINTER
 81    0070     47   .   .            MOV   B,A        TEMP STORE OF ACC
 82    0071     79   .   .            MOV   A,C        COUNTER TO ACC
 83    0072     FE   0C  .            CPI   12         IF COUNT =12 NO MATCH IN
                                                       TABLE
 84    0074     CA   7B  00           JZ    NOMA       JMP IF C=12 TO SET ERROR BITS
 85    0077     78   .   .            MOV   A,B        RESTORE ACC TO ORIGINAL VALUE
 86    0078     C3   6A  00           JMP   L001       TRY TO MATCH NEXT ENTRY IF NOT
                                                       LAST
 87    007B     .    .   .    ;
 88    007B     .    .   .    ;
 89    007B     3E   F0  .    NOMA    MVI   A,360Q     SET ERROR CODE
 90    007D     C9   .   .            RET              BACK TO MAIN PROGRAM
 91    007E     .    .   .    ;
 92    007E     .    .   .    ;
 93    007E     .    .   .    ;
 94    007E     79   .   .    VAL     MOV   A,C        BCD DATA TO ACC
 95    007F     C9   .   .            RET              BACK TO MAIN PROGRAM
 96    0080     .    .   .    ;
 97    0080     .    .   .    ; TABLE IS THE 7 SEGMENT LOOK UP TABLE
 98    0080     .    .   .    ; EACH ENTRY CORRESPONDS TO A BCD DIGIT
```

```
ITEM   LOC    OBJECT CODE    SOURCE STATEMENTS                         PAGE   3

 99    0080     .    .   .   ; POSSIBLE FROM THE DIGITAL CLOCK OUTPUT PORT.
100    0080     .    .   .   ;
101    0080     .    .   .   ;
102    0080     .    .   .   ;
103    0080    40    .   .   TABLE  DB    100Q      DIGIT 0
104    0081    79    .   .          DB    171Q      DIGIT 1
105    0082    24    .   .          DB    044Q      DIGIT 2
106    0083    30    .   .          DB    060Q      DIGIT 3
107    0084    19    .   .          DB    031Q      DIGIT 4
108    0085    12    .   .          DB    022Q      DIGIT 5
109    0086    03    .   .          DB    003Q      DIGIT 6
110    0087    78    .   .          DB    170Q      DIGIT 7
111    0088    00    .   .          DB    000Q      DIGIT 8
112    0089    18    .   .          DB    030Q      DIGIT 9
113    008A    7F    .   .          DB    177Q      BLANK DIGIT
114    008B     .    .   .   ;
115    008B     .    .   .   ;
116    008B     .    .   .   ; THE Q AFTER NUMBER MEANS OCTAL VALUE
117    008B     .    .   .   ; THESE ENTRYS ARE OBTAINED FROM THE
118    008B     .    .   .   ; TABLE IN FIGURE 10-16 B.
119    008B     .    .   .   ;
120    008B     .    .   .   ;
121    008B     .    .   .   ; THE FOLLOWING SECTION OF CODE WILL
122    008B     .    .   .   ; FORMAT THE BCD DATA INTO THREE BYTES
123    008B     .    .   .   ; FOR THE OUTPUT DISPLAY.  THE FORMATTED DATA
124    008B     .    .   .   ; WILL BE STORED IN MEMORY LOCATIONS TIME-TIME+2.
125    008B     .    .   .   ;
126    008B    16   00       FORMA  MVI   D,00      INITIALIZE D REGISTER
127    008D    3A   3A   00         LDA   TIME      MOV FIRST BYTE TO ACC
128    0090    FE   0F   .           CPI   15        ERROR CHECK OF BYTE
129    0092    CC   CA   00          CZ    ERROR     CALL ERROR IF MATCH
130    0095    47    .   .           MOV   B,A       STORE IN B REGISTER
131    0096    3A   3B   00          LDA   TIME+1    NEXT DATA TO ACC
132    0099    FE   0F   .           CPI   15        ERROR CHECK
133    009B    CC   CA   00          CZ    ERROR     CALL ERROR IF MATCH
134    009E    17    .   .           RAL
135    009F    17    .   .           RAL
136    00A0    17    .   .           RAL
137    00A1    17    .   .           RAL                SHIFT LEFT 4 BITS
138    00A2    E6   F0   .           ANI   360Q      MASK OFF LOWER 4 BITS
139    00A4    B0    .   .           ORA   B          DATA BYTE FORMATTED
140    00A5    32   3A   00          STA   TIME      FIRST DATA BYTE FOR DISPLAY
141    00A8     .    .   .   ;
142    00A8     .    .   .   ;
143    00A8     .    .   .   ; FORMAT SECOND DATA BYTE
144    00A8     .    .   .   ;
145    00A8    3A   3C   00          LDA   TIME+2    MOVE THIRD BYTE TO ACC
146    00AB    FE   0F   .           CPI   15        ERROR CHECK
147    00AD    CC   CA   00          CZ    ERROR     CALL ERROR IF MATCH
148    00B0    47    .   .           MOV   B,A       STORE IN B REGISTER
149    00B1    3A   3D   00          LDA   TIME+3    4TH BYTE TO ACC
150    00B4    FE   0F   .           CPI   15        ERROR CHECK
```

Figure 10-22 (cont'd.)

```
ITEM    LOC     OBJECT CODE    SOURCE STATEMENTS                          PAGE   4

151     00B6    CC  CA  00             CZ     ERROR     CALL ERROR IF MATCH
152     00B9    17                     RAL
153     00BA    17                     RAL
154     00BB    17                     RAL
155     00BC    17                     RAL
156     00BD    E6  F0                 ANI    360Q      SHIFT AND MASK OFF 4 LOWER
                                                         BITS
157     00BF    B0                     ORA    B         SECOND DATA BYTE FORMATTED
158     00C0    32  3B  00             STA    TIME+1    2ND DATA BYTE FOR DISPLAY
159     00C3    7A                     MOV    A,D
160     00C4    32  3C  00             STA    TIME+2    3RD DATA BYTE FOR DISPLAY
161     00C7                    ;
162     00C7                    ;
163     00C7                    ; NOW TO WRITE THE 3 DATA BYTES OUT TO
164     00C7                    ; THE GENERAL OUTPUT DISPLAY
165     00C7                    ;
166     00C7                    ;
167     00C7    C3  CD  00             JMP    OUTA
168     00CA                    ;
169     00CA                    ;
170     00CA                    ;
171     00CA                    ;
172     00CA                    ; SUBROUTINE ERROR SETS THE D REGISTER TO BLINK
                                                        DISPLAY
173     00CA                    ;
174     00CA                    ;
175     00CA    16  10           ERROR MVI    D,16      SET BIT TO BLINK DISPLAY
176     00CC    C9                     RET
177     00CD                    ;
178     00CD                    ;
179     00CD                    ; THE FOLLOWING SECTION OF CODE WILL OUTPUT THE
180     00CD                    ; DATA IN MEMORY LOCATIONS TIME-TIME+2
181     00CD                    ; TO THE GENERAL OUTPUT DISPLAY
182     00CD                    ;
183     00CD                    ;
184     00CD    3A  3A  00      OUTA   LDA    TIME      LOAD FIRST BYTE INTO ACC
185     00D0    D3  0A                 OUT    10        WRITE FIRST BYTE TO PORT A
186     00D2    3A  3B  00              LDA   TIME+1    2ND BYTE INTO ACC
187     00D5    D3  0B                  OUT   11        WRITE 2ND BYTE TO PORT B
188     00D7    3A  3C  00              LDA   TIME+2    THIRD BYTE TO ACC
189     00DA    D3  0C                  OUT   12        WRITE THIRD BYTE TO PORT C
190     00DC    76                      HLT             HALT THE SYSTEM
191     00DD                    ;
192     00DD                    ;
193     00DD                           END              END STATEMENT FOR COMPILER
  0   ERRORS FOUND IN ASSEMBLY CODE .
```

10-5 Troubleshooting the System

Let us assume now that we have loaded the program, but our system is not operating correctly. What do we do? First, we separate the problem, if we can, into either a hardware problem or a software problem. If this is a hardware problem, what is malfunctioning? If this is a software problem, what instruction or group of instructions is incorrect? We will now proceed through a troubleshooting sequence for determining just this type of information.

To begin, let us determine if information from the clock I/O circuit is reaching the 8080 and being stored in memory correctly. To do this we modify our program of Figure 10-21 and insert a HLT instruction after the fourth data byte from the I/O circuit has been read. (We could put the HLT instruction after the first data byte was read in.) When the system halts we manually examine the data in memory. This indicates to us if data is being transferred correctly. If not, we need to know if the hardware or the software is preventing the data transfer. Here is where our own R/W, mobile I/O port serves as a handy troubleshooting tool. Set the mobile I/O port to read address 4 and write address 5. Then write a small program to read data from port 4 and write data to port 5. We physically connect our own mobile I/O port to the address bus, data bus, $\overline{IOR}$, and $\overline{IOW}$ signals as was discussed in Chapter 8. If this transfer works we know that the 8080 and its peripheral circuits are controlling the hardware correctly and that the I/O port is defective.

If the I/O transfer still does not work, we assume that the hardware is inoperative. Remove the 8080 from the circuit and install our "static stimulus" troubleshooting box. When the SST box is installed, apply an I/O address of 1, then statically examine the I/O circuit decoder enable. The 7442 of Figure 10-12 should have a logical 0 at pin 2. This can be verified by voltage measurement. We now set the correct status word on the data bus. We then make the SYNC signal go to logical 1. In this condition the status information is latched into the status latches. We then examine the status latches to insure that the status word is being strobed in correctly. Remember—this strobe is free running and is generated from the $\phi 1$ and $\phi 2$ free-running clocks.

Now switch the SYNC signal to logical 0. The status word data should stay in the status latches. Next we change the data on the data bus to 0D. Then switch the $\overline{WR}$ signal from the 8080 to logical 0. At this point, we should detect an I/O write signal at the I/O port that is addressed. Through the use of our stimulus box and mobile I/O port, we can write data into memory or to an I/O port. We can also read data from memory or from an I/O port. This static troubleshooting makes the isolation of the fault much easier.

Now let us assume that when we examined the 7-segment data in memory it was correct. We could modify our program to halt after this data had been con-

Sec. 10-5 Troubleshooting the System

verted to BCD data. If the 7-segment data were correct, but the BCD data were incorrect, we would suspect the software of being faulty. But perhaps we have entered the wrong instruction. Let us examine this section of the program that resides in memory. The program in memory should agree with the written list of instructions.

When one is developing software and is unsure if the program flow is correct, the following steps may be taken. Write a few lines of code (program instructions) at a time and after these lines of code are executed, write the new data (or intermediate result) to a known memory location. One can then halt the system and examine that particular location of memory. If the data is correct at this location, this will give good evidence that the program is doing what it is supposed to *up to the point where we wrote data to memory.*

If the BCD data in memory checks good, then we can halt the system just after the three data bytes for the display I/O circuit have been stored in memory. We again examine memory to determine if these data bytes are correct. If these bytes are in error we can further subdivide this section of program and examine intermediate results.

Let us assume that these output data bytes are correct. We now run the entire program, but the display is still in error. We should examine the display closely to see if we can learn anything from it. If only one digit is in error we may assume that the hardware path for that digit has a malfunction. We could also install our static stimulus box and statically exercise and check all hardware paths to the output display. We should exercise these paths in the same electrical sequence that the 8080 would. This will duplicate as closely as possible the same type of electrical signals that the 8080 produces.

In this chapter we have discussed a technique for interfacing an asynchronous I/O circuit to the 8080 system architecture. This interfacing technique can be used for a variety of I/O circuits. If one understands this type of I/O interface, then relating this discussion to other I/O circuits will be an easier task.

Finally, we concluded by showing a technique for debugging or troubleshooting both software and hardware problems. We used the troubleshooting tools presented in Chapter 8, plus a good understanding of the timing and control signals related to the 8080 microprocessor. This type of troubleshooting is very effective for debugging a system during the initial checkout phase.

Hopefully, at this point this introduction to microprocessor systems has enlarged your knowledge and widened your understanding of them. Real expertise comes with practice of course. We are all victims of a bad memory at times, and we forget things that we need to know. With the refreshing that comes with practice, we forget less as time goes on and our command of facts and skills grows. So it is with microprocessors. There is a large and growing field out there, with many opportunities for accomplishment and self-satisfaction.

Review Questions

1. What is meant by the term multiplexed 7-segment data?
2. Draw a block diagram for the 5314 digital clock chip and explain the function of each block.
3. What is the purpose of MOS to TTL level shifters?
4. Design a TTL to MOS level shifter.

APPENDIX A

Data sheets for devices
used in this text

The 8080 8-Bit N-Channel Microprocessor

- Organization and Functional Block Diagrams
- Specifications Characteristics and Data Sheets
- Functional Pin Definition and Configuration
- Status Information Definition and Word Chart
- Instruction Set
- Condition Flags and Standard Rules
- Symbols and Abbreviations
- Physical Dimensions

ABSOLUTE MAXIMUM RATINGS*

Temperature Under Bias . . . . 0°C to +70°C
Storage Temperature . . . . -65°C to +150°C
All Input or Output Voltages
   With Respect to V_{BB} . . . . -0.3V to +20V
V_{CC}, V_{DD} and V_{SS} With Respect to V_{BB} -0.3V to +20V
Power Dissipation 1.5W

*COMMENT: Stresses above those listed under "Absolute Maximum Ratings" may cause permanent damage to the device. This is a stress rating only and functional operation of the device at these or any other conditions above those indicated in the operational sections of this specification is not implied. Exposure to absolute maximum rating conditions for extended periods may affect device reliability.

D.C. CHARACTERISTICS

$T_A = 0°C$ to $70°C$, $V_{DD} = +12V \pm 5\%$, $V_{CC} = +5V \pm 5\%$, $V_{BB} = -5V \pm 5\%$, $V_{SS} = 0V$, Unless Otherwise Noted.

Symbol	Parameter	Min.	Typ.	Max.	Unit	Test Condition
V_{ILC}	Clock Input Low Voltage	$V_{SS}-1$		$V_{SS}+0.8$	V	
V_{IHC}	Clock Input High Voltage	9.0		$V_{DD}+1$	V	
V_{IL}	Input Low Voltage	$V_{SS}-1$		$V_{SS}+0.8$	V	
V_{IH}	Input High Voltage	3.3		$V_{CC}+1$	V	
V_{OL}	Output Low Voltage			0.45	V	I_{OL} = 1.9mA on all outputs,
V_{OH}	Output High Voltage	3.7			V	I_{OH} = -150µA.
$I_{DD(AV)}$	Avg. Power Supply Current (V_{DD})		40	70	mA	
$I_{CC(AV)}$	Avg. Power Supply Current (V_{CC})		60	80	mA	Operation T_{CY} = .48 µsec
$I_{BB(AV)}$	Avg. Power Supply Current (V_{BB})		.01	1	mA	
I_{IL}	Input Leakage			±10	µA	$V_{SS} \leq V_{IN} \leq V_{CC}$
I_{CL}	Clock Leakage			±10	µA	$V_{SS} \leq V_{CLOCK} \leq V_{DD}$
I_{DL} [2]	Data Bus Leakage in Input Mode			-100 -2.0	µA mA	$V_{SS} \leq V_{IN} \leq V_{SS}+0.8V$ $V_{SS}+0.8V \leq V_{IN} \leq V_{CC}$
I_{FL}	Address and Data Bus Leakage During HOLD			+10 -100	µA	$V_{ADDR/DATA} = V_{CC}$ $V_{ADDR/DATA} = V_{SS} + 0.45V$

CAPACITANCE

$T_A = 25°C$ $V_{CC} = V_{DD} = V_{SS} = 0V$, $V_{BB} = -5V$

Symbol	Parameter	Typ.	Max.	Unit	Test Condition
C_ϕ	Clock Capacitance	17	25	pf	f_c = 1 MHz
C_{IN}	Input Capacitance	6	10	pf	Unmeasured Pins
C_{OUT}	Output Capacitance	10	20	pf	Returned to V_{SS}

NOTES:
1. The RESET signal must be active for a minimum of 3 clock cycles.
2. When DBIN is high and $V_{IN} > V_{IH}$ an internal active pull up will be switched onto the Data Bus.
3. ΔI supply / ΔT_A = -0.45%/°C.

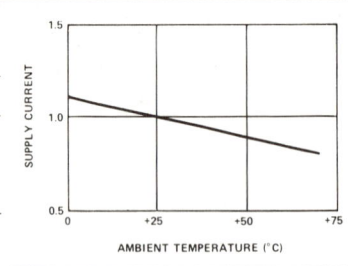

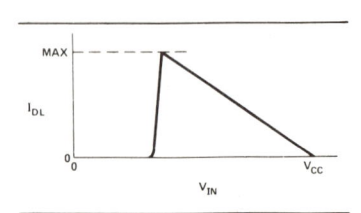

© Intel, 1979

A.C. CHARACTERISTICS (8080A)

$T_A = 0°C$ to $70°C$, $V_{DD} = +12V \pm 5\%$, $V_{CC} = +5V \pm 5\%$, $V_{BB} = -5V \pm 5\%$, $V_{SS} = 0V$, Unless Otherwise Noted

Symbol	Parameter	Min.	Max.	-1 Min.	-1 Max.	-2 Min.	-2 Max.	Unit	Test Condition
t_{CY}[3]	Clock Period	0.48	2.0	0.32	2.0	0.38	2.0	μsec	
t_r, t_f	Clock Rise and Fall Time	0	50	0	25	0	50	nsec	
$t_{ø1}$	ø1 Pulse Width	60		50		60		nsec	
$t_{ø2}$	ø2 Pulse Width	220		145		175		nsec	
t_{D1}	Delay ø1 to ø2	0		0		0		nsec	
t_{D2}	Delay ø2 to ø1	70		60		70		nsec	
t_{D3}	Delay ø1 to ø2 Leading Edges	80		60		70		nsec	
t_{DA}[2]	Address Output Delay From ø2		200		150		175	nsec	$C_L = 100$ pF
t_{DD}[2]	Data Output Delay From ø2		220		180		200	nsec	
t_{DC}[2]	Signal Output Delay From ø2 or ø2 (SYNC, WR, WAIT, HLDA)		120		110		120	nsec	$C_L = 50$ pF
t_{DF}[2]	DBIN Delay From ø2	25	140	25	130	25	140	nsec	
t_{DI}[1]	Delay for Input Bus to Enter Input Mode		t_{DF}		t_{DF}		t_{DF}	nsec	
t_{DS1}	Data Setup Time During ø1 and DBIN	30		10		20		nsec	

WAVEFORMS (Note: Timing measurements are made at the following reference voltages: CLOCK "1" = 8.0V "0" = 1.0V; INPUTS "1" = 3.3V, "0" = 0.8V; OUTPUTS "1" = 2.0V, "0" = 0.8V.)

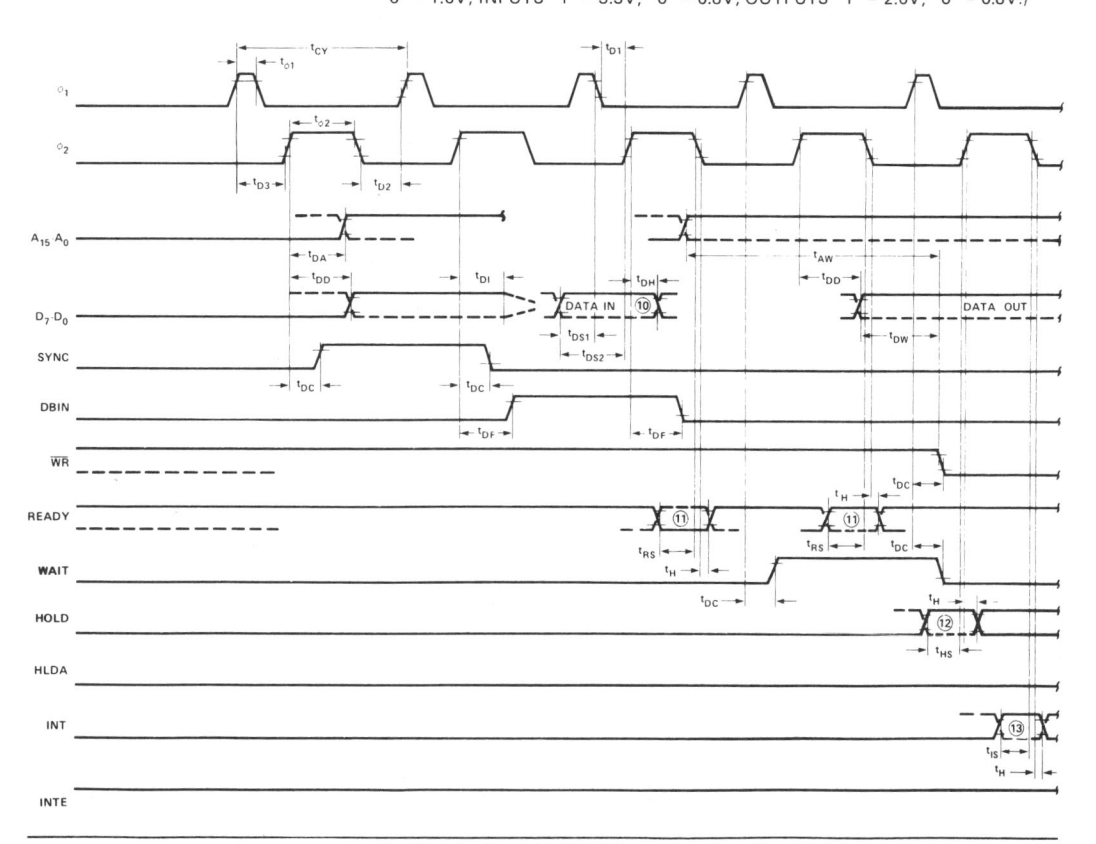

© Intel, 1979

291

A.C. CHARACTERISTICS (8080A)

$T_A = 0°C$ to $70°C$, $V_{DD} = +12V \pm 5\%$, $V_{CC} = +5V \pm 5\%$, $V_{BB} = -5V \pm 5\%$, $V_{SS} = 0V$, Unless Otherwise Noted

Symbol	Parameter	Min.	Max.	-1 Min.	-1 Max.	-2 Min.	-2 Max.	Unit	Test Condition
t_{DS2}	Data Setup Time to $\varnothing_2$ During DBIN	150		120		130		nsec	
t_{DH}[1]	Data Holt time From $\varnothing_2$ During DBIN	[1]		[1]		[1]		nsec	
t_{IE}[2]	INTE Output Delay From $\varnothing_2$		200		200		200	nsec	$C_L = 50$ pF
t_{RS}	READY Setup Time During $\varnothing_2$	120		90		90		nsec	
t_{HS}	HOLD Setup Time to $\varnothing_2$	140		120		120		nsec	
t_{IS}	INT Setup Time During $\varnothing_2$	120		100		100		nsec	
t_H	Hold Time From $\varnothing_2$ (READY, INT, HOLD)	0		0		0		nsec	
t_{FD}	Delay to Float During Hold (Address and Data Bus)		120		120		120	nsec	
t_{AW}[2]	Address Stable Prior to WR	[5]		[5]		[5]		nsec	
t_{DW}[2]	Output Data Stable Prior to WR	[6]		[6]		[6]		nsec	
t_{WD}[2]	Output Data Stable From WR	[7]		[7]		[7]		nsec	$C_L = 100$ pF: Address, Data
t_{WA}[2]	Address Stable From WR	[7]		[7]		[7]		nsec	$C_L = 50$ pF: WR, HLDA, DBIN
t_{HF}[2]	HLDA to Float Delay	[8]		[8]		[8]		nsec	
t_{WF}[2]	WR to Float Delay	[9]		[9]		[9]		nsec	
t_{AH}[2]	Address Hold Time After DBIN During HLDA	−20		−20		−20		nsec	

NOTES: (Parenthesis gives -1, -2 specifications, respectively)
1. Data input should be enabled with DBIN status. No bus conflict can then occur and data hold time is assured. $t_{DH} = 50$ ns or t_{DF}, whichever is less.
2. Load Circuit.

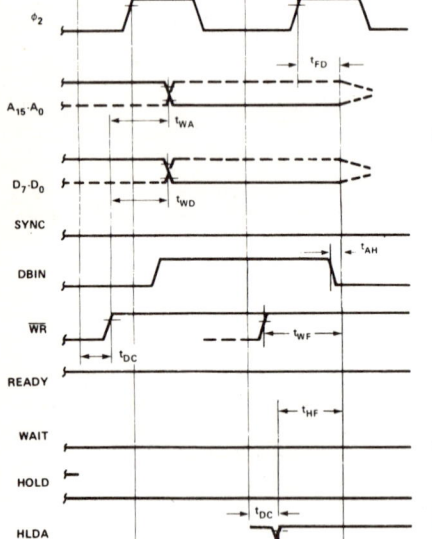

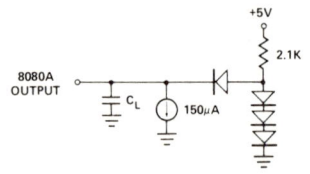

3. $t_{CY} = t_{D3} + t_{r\varnothing2} + t_{\varnothing2} + t_{f\varnothing2} + t_{D2} + t_{r\varnothing1} \geq 480$ ns (−1: 320 ns, −2: 380 ns).

TYPICAL Δ OUTPUT DELAY VS. Δ CAPACITANCE

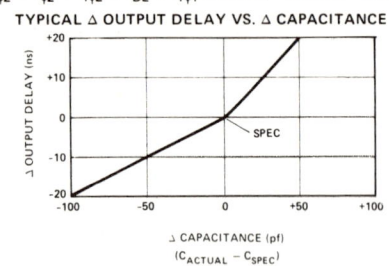

4. The following are relevant when interfacing the 8080A to devices having $V_{IH} = 3.3V$:
   a) Maximum output rise time from .8V to 3.3V = 100ns @ C_L = SPEC.
   b) Output delay when measured to 3.0V = SPEC +60ns @ C_L = SPEC.
   c) If $C_L \neq$ SPEC, add .6ns/pF if $C_L >$ C_{SPEC}, subtract .3ns/pF (from modified delay) if $C_L < C_{SPEC}$.
5. $t_{AW} = 2 \, t_{CY} − t_{D3} − t_{r\varnothing2} − 140$ ns (−1: 110 ns, −2: 130 ns).
6. $t_{DW} = t_{CY} − t_{D3} − t_{r\varnothing2} − 170$ ns (−1: 150 ns, −2: 170 ns).
7. If not HLDA, $t_{WD} = t_{WA} = t_{D3} + t_{r\varnothing2} + 10$ns. If HLDA, $t_{WD} = t_{WA} = t_{WF}$.
8. $t_{HF} = t_{D3} + t_{r\varnothing2} − 50$ns.
9. $t_{WF} = t_{D3} + t_{r\varnothing2} − 10$ns.
10. Data in must be stable for this period during DBIN $\cdot T_3$. Both t_{DS1} and t_{DS2} must be satisfied.
11. Ready signal must be stable for this period during T_2 or T_W. (Must be externally synchronized.)
12. Hold signal must be stable for this period during T_2 or T_W when entering hold mode, and during T_3, T_4, T_5 and T_{WH} when in hold mode. (External synchronization is not required.)
13. Interrupt signal must be stable during this period of the last clock cycle of any instruction in order to be recognized on the following instruction. (External synchronization is not required.)
14. This timing diagram shows timing relationships only; it does not represent any specific machine cycle.

© Intel, 1979

8080A CPU FUNCTIONAL BLOCK DIAGRAM

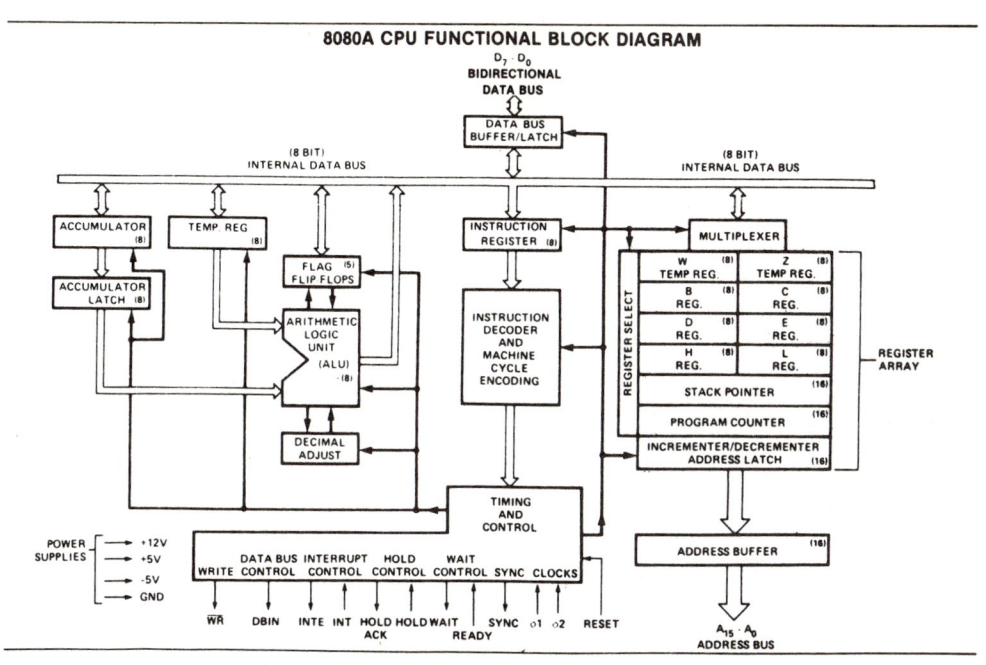

8080A/8080A-1/8080A-2

PIN DESCRIPTION

The following describes the function of all of the 8080A I/O pins. Several of the descriptions refer to internal timing periods.

A_{15}-A_0 (output three-state)

ADDRESS BUS; the address bus provides the address to memory (up to 64K 8-bit words) or denotes the I/O device number for up to 256 input and 256 output devices. A_0 is the least significant address bit.

D_7-D_0 (input/output three-state)

DATA BUS; the data bus provides bi-directional communication between the CPU, memory, and I/O devices for instructions and data transfers. Also, during the first clock cycle of each machine cycle, the 8080A outputs a status word on the data bus that describes the current machine cycle. D_0 is the least significant bit.

SYNC (output)

SYNCHRONIZING SIGNAL; the SYNC pin provides a signal to indicate the beginning of each machine cycle.

DBIN (output)

DATA BUS IN; the DBIN signal indicates to external circuits that the data bus is in the input mode. This signal should be used to enable the gating of data onto the 8080A data bus from memory or I/O.

READY (input)

READY; the READY signal indicates to the 8080A that valid memory or input data is available on the 8080A data bus. This signal is used to synchronize the CPU with slower memory or I/O devices. If after sending an address out the 8080A does not receive a READY input, the 8080A will enter a WAIT state for as long as the READY line is low. READY can also be used to single step the CPU.

WAIT (output)

WAIT; the WAIT signal acknowledges that the CPU is in a WAIT state.

$\overline{WR}$ (output)

WRITE; the $\overline{WR}$ signal is used for memory WRITE or I/O output control. The data on the data bus is stable while the $\overline{WR}$ signal is active low ($\overline{WR}$ = 0).

HOLD (input)

HOLD; the HOLD signal requests the CPU to enter the HOLD state. The HOLD state allows an external device to gain control of the 8080A address and data bus as soon as the 8080A has completed its use of these buses for the current machine cycle. It is recognized under the following conditions:
- the CPU is in the HALT state.
- the CPU is in the T2 or TW state and the READY signal is active.

As a result of entering the HOLD state the CPU ADDRESS BUS (A_{15}-A_0) and DATA BUS (D_7-D_0) will be in their high impedance state. The CPU acknowledges its state with the HOLD ACKNOWLEDGE (HLDA) pin.

HLDA (output)

HOLD ACKNOWLEDGE; the HLDA signal appears in response to the HOLD signal and indicates that the data and address bus

© Intel, 1979

will go to the high impedance state. The HLDA signal begins at:
- T3 for READ memory or input.
- The Clock Period following T3 for WRITE memory or OUTPUT operation.

In either case, the HLDA signal appears after the rising edge of ϕ_1 and high impedance occurs after the rising edge of ϕ_2.

INTE (output)
INTERRUPT ENABLE; indicates the content of the internal interrupt enable flip/flop. This flip/flop may be set or reset by the Enable and Disable Interrupt instructions and inhibits interrupts from being accepted by the CPU when it is reset. It is automatically reset (disabling further interrupts) at time T1 of the instruction fetch cycle (M1) when an interrupt is accepted and is also reset by the RESET signal.

INT (input)
INTERRUPT REQUEST; the CPU recognizes an interrupt request on this line at the end of the current instruction or while halted. If the CPU is in the HOLD state or if the Interrupt Enable flip/flop is reset it will not honor the request.

RESET (input)[1]
RESET; while the RESET signal is activated, the content of the program counter is cleared. After RESET, the program will start at location 0 in memory. The INTE and HLDA flip/flops are also reset. Note that the flags, accumulator, stack pointer, and registers are not cleared.

V_{SS} Ground Reference.
V_{DD} +12 ± 5% Volts.
V_{CC} +5 ± 5% Volts.
V_{BB} -5 ±5% Volts (substrate bias).
ϕ_1, ϕ_2 2 externally supplied clock phases. (non TTL compatible)

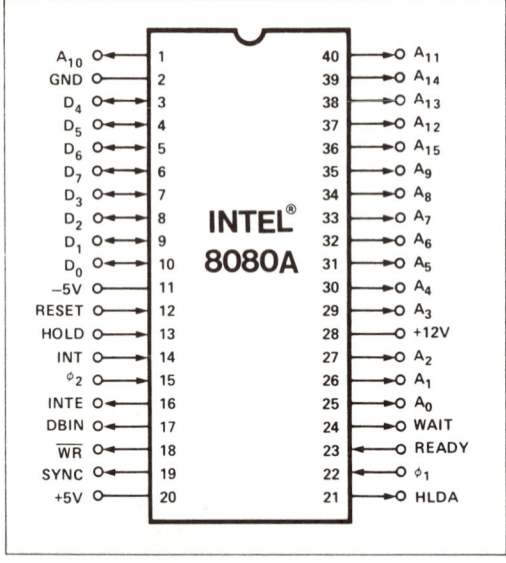

Figure 1. Pin Configuration

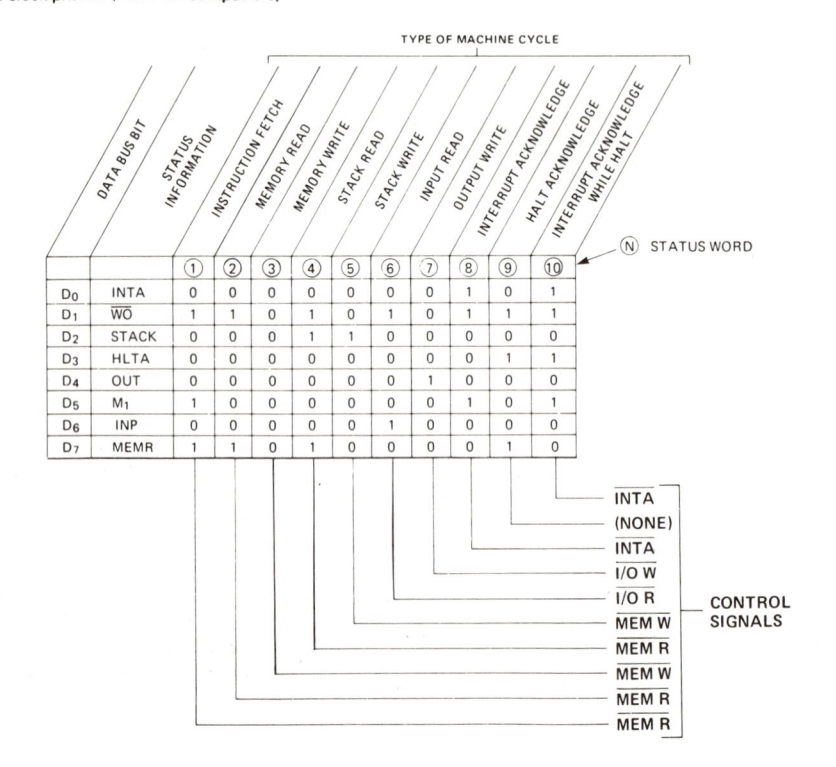

© Intel, 1979

INSTRUCTION SET

The accumulator group instructions include arithmetic and logical operators with direct, indirect, and immediate addressing modes.

Move, load, and store instruction groups provide the ability to move either 8 or 16 bits of data between memory, the six working registers and the accumulator using direct, indirect, and immediate addressing modes.

The ability to branch to different portions of the program is provided with jump, jump conditional, and computed jumps. Also the ability to call to and return from subroutines is provided both conditionally and unconditionally. The RESTART (or single byte call instruction) is useful for interrupt vector operation.

Double precision operators such as stack manipulation and double add instructions extend both the arithmetic and interrupt handling capability of the 8080A. The ability to increment and decrement memory, the six general registers and the accumulator is provided as well as extended increment and decrement instructions to operate on the register pairs and stack pointer. Further capability is provided by the ability to rotate the accumulator left or right through or around the carry bit.

Input and output may be accomplished using memory addresses as I/O ports or the directly addressed I/O provided for in the 8080A instruction set.

The following special instruction group completes the 8080A instruction set: the NOP instruction, HALT to stop processor execution and the DAA instructions provide decimal arithmetic capability. STC allows the carry flag to be directly set, and the CMC instruction allows it to be complemented. CMA complements the contents of the accumulator and XCHG exchanges the contents of two 16-bit register pairs directly.

Data and Instruction Formats

Data in the 8080A is stored in the form of 8-bit binary integers. All data transfers to the system data bus will be in the same format.

D_7 D_6 D_5 D_4 D_3 D_2 D_1 D_0

DATA WORD

The program instructions may be one, two, or three bytes in length. Multiple byte instructions must be stored in successive words in program memory. The instruction formats then depend on the particular operation executed.

One Byte Instructions

| D_7 D_6 D_5 D_4 D_3 D_2 D_1 D_0 | OP CODE |

TYPICAL INSTRUCTIONS

Register to register, memory reference, arithmetic or logical, rotate, return, push, pop, enable or disable Interrupt instructions

Two Byte Instructions

| D_7 D_6 D_5 D_4 D_3 D_2 D_1 D_0 | OP CODE |
| D_7 D_6 D_5 D_4 D_3 D_2 D_1 D_0 | OPERAND |

Immediate mode or I/O instructions

Three Byte Instructions

D_7 D_6 D_5 D_4 D_3 D_2 D_1 D_0	OP CODE
D_7 D_6 D_5 D_4 D_3 D_2 D_1 D_0	LOW ADDRESS OR OPERAND 1
D_7 D_6 D_5 D_4 D_3 D_2 D_1 D_0	HIGH ADDRESS OR OPERAND 2

Jump, call or direct load and store instructions

For the 8080A a logic "1" is defined as a high level and a logic "0" is defined as a low level.

© Intel, 1979

8080A/8080A-1/8080A-2

8080 INSTRUCTION SET
Summary of Processor Instructions

Mnemonic	Description	D7	D6	D5	D4	D3	D2	D1	D0	Clock[2] Cycles
MOVE, LOAD, AND STORE										
MOV r1,r2	Move register to register	0	1	D	D	D	S	S	S	5
MOV M,r	Move register to memory	0	1	1	1	0	S	S	S	7
MOV r,M	Move memory to register	0	1	D	D	D	1	1	0	7
MVI r	Move immediate register	0	0	D	D	D	1	1	0	7
MVI M	Move immediate memory	0	0	1	1	0	1	1	0	10
LXI B	Load immediate register Pair B & C	0	0	0	0	0	0	0	1	10
LXI D	Load immediate register Pair D & E	0	0	0	1	0	0	0	1	10
LXI H	Load immediate register Pair H & L	0	0	1	0	0	0	0	1	10
STAX B	Store A indirect	0	0	0	0	0	0	1	0	7
STAX D	Store A indirect	0	0	0	1	0	0	1	0	7
LDAX B	Load A indirect	0	0	0	0	1	0	1	0	7
LDAX D	Load A indirect	0	0	0	1	1	0	1	0	7
STA	Store A direct	0	0	1	1	0	0	1	0	13
LDA	Load A direct	0	0	1	1	1	0	1	0	13
SHLD	Store H & L direct	0	0	1	0	0	0	1	0	16
LHLD	Load H & L direct	0	0	1	0	1	0	1	0	16
XCHG	Exchange D & E, H & L Registers	1	1	1	0	1	0	1	1	4
STACK OPS										
PUSH B	Push register Pair B & C on stack	1	1	0	0	0	1	0	1	11
PUSH D	Push register Pair D & E on stack	1	1	0	1	0	1	0	1	11
PUSH H	Push register Pair H & L on stack	1	1	1	0	0	1	0	1	11
PUSH PSW	Push A and Flags on stack	1	1	1	1	0	1	0	1	11
POP B	Pop register Pair B & C off stack	1	1	0	0	0	0	0	1	10
POP D	Pop register Pair D & E off stack	1	1	0	1	0	0	0	1	10
POP H	Pop register Pair H & L off stack	1	1	1	0	0	0	0	1	10
POP PSW	Pop A and Flags off stack	1	1	1	1	0	0	0	1	10
XTHL	Exchange top of stack, H & L	1	1	1	0	0	0	1	1	18
SPHL	H & L to stack pointer	1	1	1	1	1	0	0	1	5
LXI SP	Load immediate stack pointer	0	0	1	1	0	0	0	1	10
INX SP	Increment stack pointer	0	0	1	1	0	0	1	1	5
DCX SP	Decrement stack pointer	0	0	1	1	1	0	1	1	5
JUMP										
JMP	Jump unconditional	1	1	0	0	0	0	1	1	10
JC	Jump on carry	1	1	0	1	1	0	1	0	10
JNC	Jump on no carry	1	1	0	1	0	0	1	0	10
JZ	Jump on zero	1	1	0	0	1	0	1	0	10
JNZ	Jump on no zero	1	1	0	0	0	0	1	0	10
JP	Jump on positive	1	1	1	1	0	0	1	0	10
JM	Jump on minus	1	1	1	1	1	0	1	0	10
JPE	Jump on parity even	1	1	1	0	1	0	1	0	10

Mnemonic	Description	D7	D6	D5	D4	D3	D2	D1	D0	Clock[2] Cycles
JPO	Jump on parity odd	1	1	1	0	0	0	1	0	10
PCHL	H & L to program counter	1	1	1	0	1	0	0	1	5
CALL										
CALL	Call unconditional	1	1	0	0	1	1	0	1	17
CC	Call on carry	1	1	0	1	1	1	0	0	11/17
CNC	Call on no carry	1	1	0	1	0	1	0	0	11/17
CZ	Call on zero	1	1	0	0	1	1	0	0	11/17
CNZ	Call on no zero	1	1	0	0	0	1	0	0	11/17
CP	Call on positive	1	1	1	1	0	1	0	0	11/17
CM	Call on minus	1	1	1	1	1	1	0	0	11/17
CPE	Call on parity even	1	1	1	0	1	1	0	0	11/17
CPO	Call on parity odd	1	1	1	0	0	1	0	0	11/17
RETURN										
RET	Return	1	1	0	0	1	0	0	1	10
RC	Return on carry	1	1	0	1	1	0	0	0	5/11
RNC	Return on no carry	1	1	0	1	0	0	0	0	5/11
RZ	Return on zero	1	1	0	0	1	0	0	0	5/11
RNZ	Return on no zero	1	1	0	0	0	0	0	0	5/11
RP	Return on positive	1	1	1	1	0	0	0	0	5/11
RM	Return on minus	1	1	1	1	1	0	0	0	5/11
RPE	Return on parity even	1	1	1	0	1	0	0	0	5/11
RPO	Return on parity odd	1	1	1	0	0	0	0	0	5/11
RESTART										
RST	Restart	1	1	A	A	A	1	1	1	11
INCREMENT AND DECREMENT										
INR r	Increment register	0	0	D	D	D	1	0	0	5
DCR r	Decrement register	0	0	D	D	D	1	0	1	5
INR M	Increment memory	0	0	1	1	0	1	0	0	10
DCR M	Decrement memory	0	0	1	1	0	1	0	1	10
INX B	Increment B & C registers	0	0	0	0	0	0	1	1	5
INX D	Increment D & E registers	0	0	0	1	0	0	1	1	5
INX H	Increment H & L registers	0	0	1	0	0	0	1	1	5
DCX B	Decrement B & C	0	0	0	0	1	0	1	1	5
DCX D	Decrement D & E	0	0	0	1	1	0	1	1	5
DCX H	Decrement H & L	0	0	1	0	1	0	1	1	5
ADD										
ADD r	Add register to A	1	0	0	0	0	S	S	S	4
ADC r	Add register to A with carry	1	0	0	0	1	S	S	S	4
ADD M	Add memory to A	1	0	0	0	0	1	1	0	7
ADC M	Add memory to A with carry	1	0	0	0	1	1	1	0	7
ADI	Add immediate to A	1	1	0	0	0	1	1	0	7
ACI	Add immediate to A with carry	1	1	0	0	1	1	1	0	7
DAD B	Add B & C to H & L	0	0	0	0	1	0	0	1	10
DAD D	Add D & E to H & L	0	0	0	1	1	0	0	1	10
DAD H	Add H & L to H & L	0	0	1	0	1	0	0	1	10
DAD SP	Add stack pointer to H & L	0	0	1	1	1	0	0	1	10

NOTES: 1. DDD or SSS: B 000, C 001, D 010, E 011, H 100, L 101, Memory 110, A 111.
2. Two possible cycle times, (6/12) indicate instruction cycles dependent on condition flags.

*All mnemonics copyright ©Intel Corporation 1977

© Intel, 1979

8080A/8080A-1/8080A-2

Summary of Processor Instructions (Cont.)

Mnemonic	Description	D7	D6	D5	D4	D3	D2	D1	D0	Clock[2] Cycles
SUBTRACT										
SUB r	Subtract register from A	1	0	0	1	0	S	S	S	4
SBB r	Subtract register from A with borrow	1	0	0	1	1	S	S	S	4
SUB M	Subtract memory from A	1	0	0	1	0	1	1	0	7
SBB M	Subtract memory from A with borrow	1	0	0	1	1	1	1	0	7
SUI	Subtract immediate from A	1	1	0	1	0	1	1	0	7
SBI	Subtract immediate from A with borrow	1	1	0	1	1	1	1	0	7
LOGICAL										
ANA r	And register with A	1	0	1	0	0	S	S	S	4
XRA r	Exclusive Or register with A	1	0	1	0	1	S	S	S	4
ORA r	Or register with A	1	0	1	1	0	S	S	S	4
CMP r	Compare register with A	1	0	1	1	1	S	S	S	4
ANA M	And memory with A	1	0	1	0	0	1	1	0	7
XRA M	Exclusive Or memory with A	1	0	1	0	1	1	1	0	7
ORA M	Or memory with A	1	0	1	1	0	1	1	0	7
CMP M	Compare memory with A	1	0	1	1	1	1	1	0	7
ANI	And immediate with A	1	1	1	0	0	1	1	0	7
XRI	Exclusive Or immediate with A	1	1	1	0	1	1	1	0	7
ORI	Or immediate with A	1	1	1	1	0	1	1	0	7
CPI	Compare immediate with A	1	1	1	1	1	1	1	0	7
ROTATE										
RLC	Rotate A left	0	0	0	0	0	1	1	1	4
RRC	Rotate A right	0	0	0	0	1	1	1	1	4
RAL	Rotate A left through carry	0	0	0	1	0	1	1	1	4
RAR	Rotate A right through carry	0	0	0	1	1	1	1	1	4
SPECIALS										
CMA	Complement A	0	0	1	0	1	1	1	1	4
STC	Set carry	0	0	1	1	0	1	1	1	4
CMC	Complement carry	0	0	1	1	1	1	1	1	4
DAA	Decimal adjust A	0	0	1	0	0	1	1	1	4
INPUT/OUTPUT										
IN	Input	1	1	0	1	1	0	1	1	10
OUT	Output	1	1	0	1	0	0	1	1	10
CONTROL										
EI	Enable Interrupts	1	1	1	1	1	0	1	1	4
DI	Disable Interrupt	1	1	1	1	0	0	1	1	4
NOP	No-operation	0	0	0	0	0	0	0	0	4
HLT	Halt	0	1	1	1	0	1	1	0	7

NOTES: 1. DDD or SSS B=000 C=001 D=010 E=011 H=100 L=101 Memory=110 A=111
2. Two possible cycle times (6/12) indicate instruction cycles dependent on condition flags

© Intel, 1979

The following is a summary of the instruction set:
8080/85 CPU INSTRUCTIONS IN OPERATION CODE SEQUENCE

OP CODE	MNEMONIC	OP CODE	MNEMONIC	OP CODE	MNEMONIC	OP CODE	MNEMONIC	OP CODE	MNEMONIC	OP CODE	MNEMONIC
00	NOP	2B	DCX H	56	MOV D,M	81	ADD C	AC	XRA H	D7	RST 2
01	LXI B,D16	2C	INR L	57	MOV D,A	82	ADD D	AD	XRA L	D8	RC
02	STAX B	2D	DCR L	58	MOV E,B	83	ADD E	AE	XRA M	D9	—
03	INX B	2E	MVI L,D8	59	MOV E,C	84	ADD H	AF	XRA A	DA	JC Adr
04	INR B	2F	CMA	5A	MOV E,D	85	ADD L	B0	ORA B	DB	IN D8
05	DCR B	30	SIM	5B	MOV E,E	86	ADD M	B1	ORA C	DC	CC Adr
06	MVI B,D8	31	LXI SP,D16	5C	MOV E,H	87	ADD A	B2	ORA D	DD	—
07	RLC	32	STA Adr	5D	MOV E,L	88	ADC B	B3	ORA E	DE	SBI D8
08	—	33	INX SP	5E	MOV E,M	89	ADC C	B4	ORA H	DF	RST 3
09	DAD B	34	INR M	5F	MOV E,A	8A	ADC D	B5	ORA L	E0	RPO
0A	LDAX B	35	DCR M	60	MOV H,B	8B	ADC E	B6	ORA M	E1	POP H
0B	DCX B	36	MVI M,D8	61	MOV H,C	8C	ADC H	B7	ORA A	E2	JPO Adr
0C	INR C	37	STC	62	MOV H,D	8D	ADC L	B8	CMP B	E3	XTHL
0D	DCR C	38	—	63	MOV H,E	8E	ADC M	B9	CMP C	E4	CPO Adr
0E	MVI C,D8	39	DAD SP	64	MOV H,H	8F	ADC A	BA	CMP D	E5	PUSH H
0F	RRC	3A	LDA Adr	65	MOV H,L	8G	SUB B	BB	CMP E	E6	ANI D8
10	—	3B	DCX SP	66	MOV H,M	91	SUB C	BC	CMP H	E7	RST 4
11	LXI D,D16	3C	INR A	67	MOV H,A	92	SUB D	BD	CMP L	E8	RPE
12	STAX D	3D	DCR A	68	MOV L,B	93	SUB E	BE	CMP M	E9	PCHL
13	INX D	3E	MVI A,D8	69	MOV L,C	94	SUB H	BF	CMP A	EA	JPE Adr
14	INR D	3F	CMC	6A	MOV L,D	95	SUB L	C0	RNZ	EB	XCHG
15	DCR D	40	MOV B,B	6B	MOV L,E	96	SUB M	C1	POP B	EC	CPE Adr
16	MVI D,D8	41	MOV B,C	6C	MOV L,H	97	SUB A	C2	JNZ Adr	ED	—
17	RAL	42	MOV B,D	6D	MOV L,L	98	SBB B	C3	JMP Adr	EE	XRI D8
18	—	43	MOV B,E	6E	MOV L,M	99	SBB C	C4	CNZ Adr	EF	RST 5
19	DAD D	44	MOV B,H	6F	MOV L,A	9A	SBB D	C5	PUSH B	F0	RP
1A	LDAX D	45	MOV B,L	70	MOV M,B	9B	SBB E	C6	ADI D8	F1	POP PSW
1B	DCX D	46	MOV B,M	71	MOV M,C	9C	SBB H	C7	RST 0	F2	JP Adr
1C	INR E	47	MOV B,A	72	MOV M,D	9D	SBB L	C8	RZ	F3	DI
1D	DRC E	48	MOV C,B	73	MOV M,E	9E	SBB M	C9	RET Adr	F4	CP Adr
1E	MVI E,D8	49	MOV C,C	74	MOV M,H	9F	SBB A	CA	JZ	F5	PUSH PSW
1F	RAR	4A	MOV C,D	75	MOV M,L	A0	ANA B	CB	—	F6	ORI D8
20	RIM	4B	MOV C,E	76	HLT	A1	ANA C	CC	CZ Adr	F7	RST 6
21	LXI H,D16	4C	MOV C,H	77	MOV M,A	A2	ANA D	CD	CALL Adr	F8	RM
22	SHLD Adr	4D	MOV C,L	78	MOV A,B	A3	ANA E	CE	ACI D8	F9	SPHL
23	INX H	4E	MOV C,M	79	MOV A,C	A4	ANA H	CF	RST 1	FA	JM Adr
24	INR H	4F	MOV C,A	7A	MOV A,D	A5	ANA L	D0	RNC	FB	EI
25	DCR H	50	MOV D,B	7B	MOV A,E	A6	ANA M	D1	POP D	FC	CM Adr
26	MVI H,D8	51	MOV D,C	7C	MOV A,H	A7	ANA A	D2	JNC Adr	FD	—
27	DAA	52	MOV D,D	7D	MOV A,L	A8	XRA B	D3	OUT D8	FE	CPI D8
28	—	53	MOV D,E	7E	MOV A,M	A9	XRA C	D4	CNC Adr	FF	RST 7
29	DAD H	54	MOV D,H	7F	MOV A,A	AA	XRA D	D5	PUSH D		
2A	LHLD Adr	55	MOV D,L	80	ADD B	AB	XRA E	D6	SUI D8		

D8 = constant, or logical/arithmetic expression that evaluates to an 8 bit data quantity.
Adr = 16-bit address

D16 = constant, or logical/arithmetic expression that evaluate to a 16 bit data quantity

ALL MNEMONICS © *1974, 1975, 1976, 1977 INTEL CORPORATION*

© Intel, 1979

54/74 FAMILIES OF COMPATIBLE TTL CIRCUITS

PIN ASSIGNMENTS (TOP VIEWS)

QUADRUPLE 2-INPUT POSITIVE-NAND GATES

00

positive logic:
$Y = \overline{AB}$

See page 6-2

SN5400 (J)
SN54H00 (J)
SN54L00 (J)
SN54LS00 (J, W)
SN54S00 (J, W)

SN7400 (J, N)
SN74H00 (J, N)
SN74L00 (J, N)
SN74LS00 (J, N)
SN74S00 (J, N)

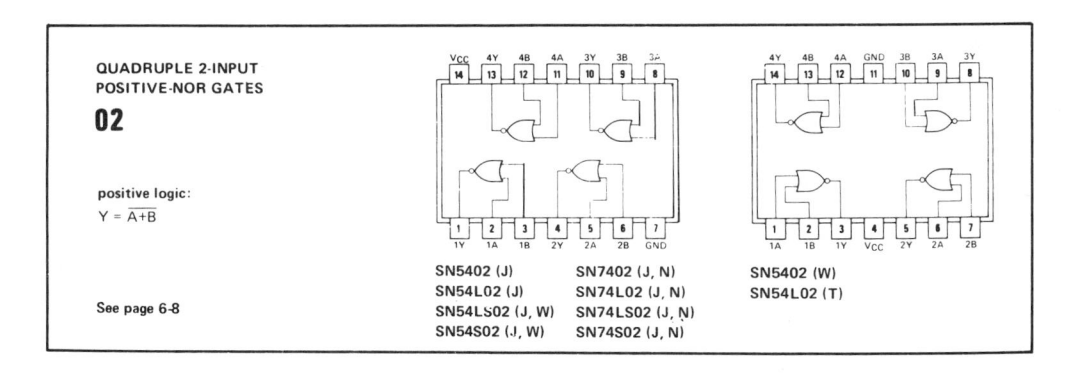

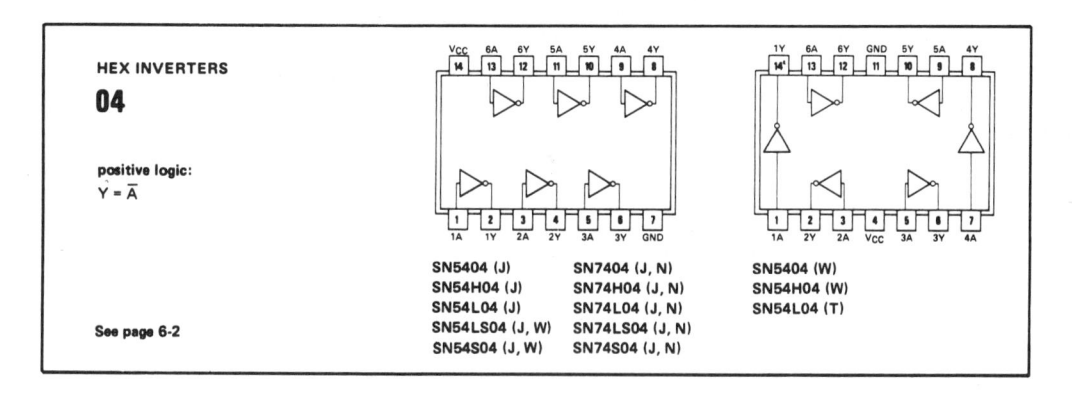

SN5400 (W)
SN54H00 (W)
SN54L00 (T)

QUADRUPLE 2-INPUT POSITIVE-NOR GATES

02

positive logic:
$Y = \overline{A+B}$

See page 6-8

SN5402 (J)
SN54L02 (J)
SN54LS02 (J, W)
SN54S02 (J, W)

SN7402 (J, N)
SN74L02 (J, N)
SN74LS02 (J, N)
SN74S02 (J, N)

SN5402 (W)
SN54L02 (T)

HEX INVERTERS

04

positive logic:
$Y = \overline{A}$

See page 6-2

SN5404 (J)
SN54H04 (J)
SN54L04 (J)
SN54LS04 (J, W)
SN54S04 (J, W)

SN7404 (J, N)
SN74H04 (J, N)
SN74L04 (J, N)
SN74LS04 (J, N)
SN74S04 (J, N)

SN5404 (W)
SN54H04 (W)
SN54L04 (T)

© Texas Instruments Incorporated, 1979

299

**HEX INVERTER BUFFERS/DRIVERS
WITH OPEN-COLLECTOR
HIGH-VOLTAGE OUTPUTS**

06

positive logic:
Y = $\overline{A}$

See page 6-24

SN5406 (J, W)   SN7406 (J, N)

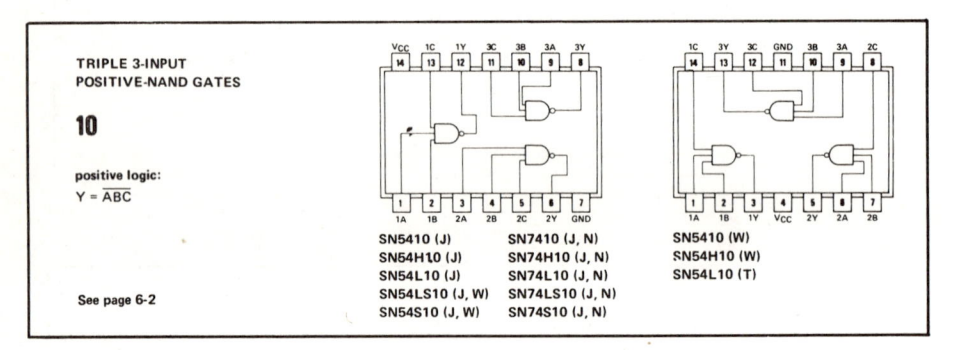

**QUADRUPLE 2-INPUT
POSITIVE-AND GATES**

08

positive logic:
Y = AB

SN5408 (J, W)   SN7408 (J, N)
SN54LS08 (J, W)   SN74LS08 (J, N)
SN54S08 (J, W)   SN74S08 (J, N)

See page 6-10

**TRIPLE 3-INPUT
POSITIVE-NAND GATES**

10

positive logic:
Y = $\overline{ABC}$

SN5410 (J)   SN7410 (J, N)   SN5410 (W)
SN54H10 (J)   SN74H10 (J, N)   SN54H10 (W)
SN54L10 (J)   SN74L10 (J, N)   SN54L10 (T)
SN54LS10 (J, W) SN74LS10 (J, N)
SN54S10 (J, W)   SN74S10 (J, N)

See page 6-2

© Texas Instruments Incorporated, 1979

DUAL 4-INPUT POSITIVE-NAND GATES

20

positive logic:
Y = $\overline{ABCD}$

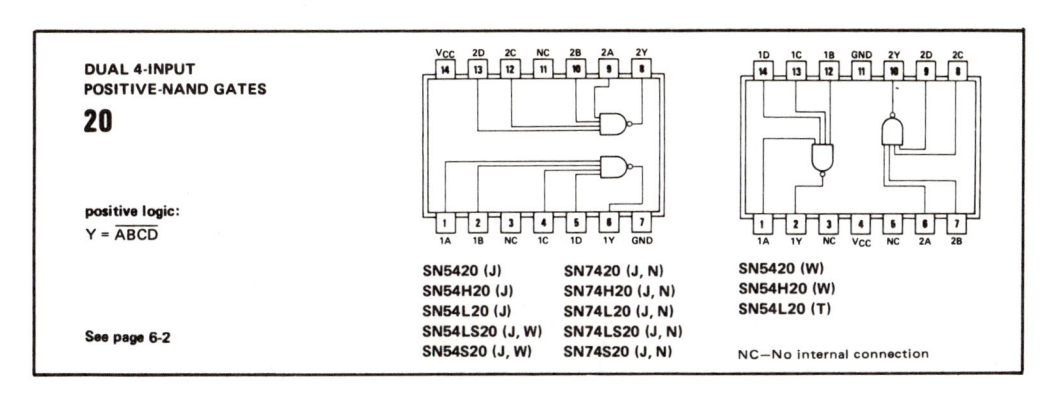

See page 6-2

SN5420 (J)
SN54H20 (J)
SN54L20 (J)
SN54LS20 (J, W)
SN54S20 (J, W)

SN7420 (J, N)
SN74H20 (J, N)
SN74L20 (J, N)
SN74LS20 (J, N)
SN74S20 (J, N)

SN5420 (W)
SN54H20 (W)
SN54L20 (T)

NC—No internal connection

---

4 LINE-TO-10 LINE DECODERS

42 BCD-TO-DECIMAL

43 EXCESS-3-TO-DECIMAL

44 EXCESS-3-GRAY-TO-DECIMAL

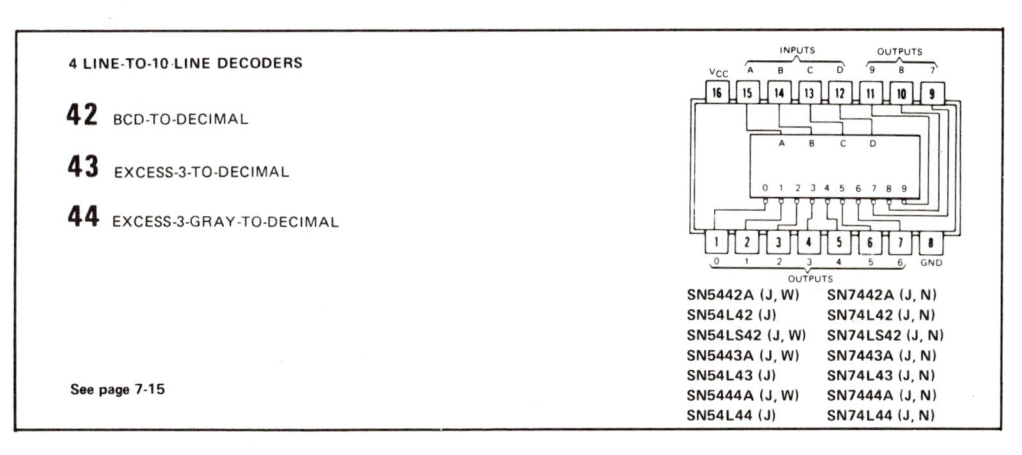

See page 7-15

SN5442A (J, W)   SN7442A (J, N)
SN54L42 (J)   SN74L42 (J, N)
SN54LS42 (J, W)   SN74LS42 (J, N)
SN5443A (J, W)   SN7443A (J, N)
SN54L43 (J)   SN74L43 (J, N)
SN5444A (J, W)   SN7444A (J, N)
SN54L44 (J)   SN74L44 (J, N)

DUAL J-K NEGATIVE-EDGE-TRIGGERED FLIP-FLOPS WITH PRESET AND CLEAR

112

FUNCTION TABLE

INPUTS					OUTPUTS	
PRESET	CLEAR	CLOCK	J	K	Q	$\overline{Q}$
L	H	X	X	X	H	L
H	L	X	X	X	L	H
L	L	X	X	X	H*	H*
H	H	↓	L	L	Q_0	$\overline{Q}_0$
H	H	↓	H	L	H	L
H	H	↓	L	H	L	H
H	H	↓	H	H	TOGGLE	
H	H	H	X	X	Q_0	$\overline{Q}_0$

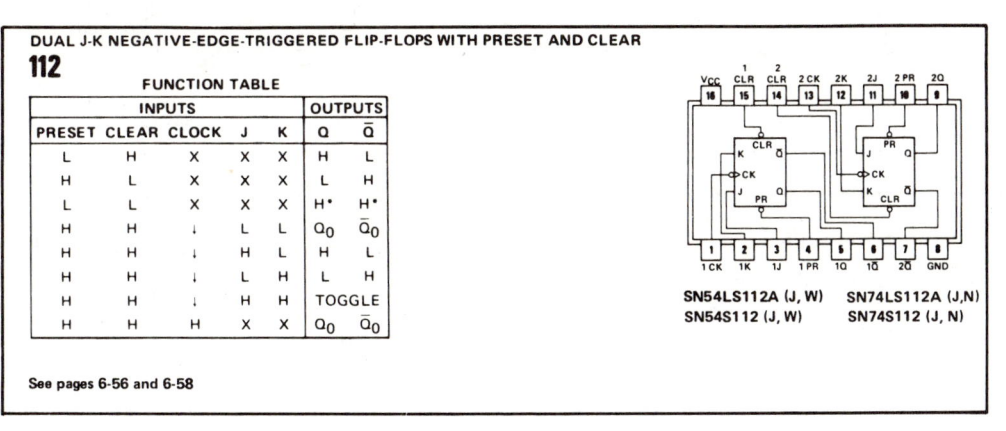

SN54LS112A (J, W)   SN74LS112A (J, N)
SN54S112 (J, W)   SN74S112 (J, N)

See pages 6-56 and 6-58

© Texas Instruments Incorporated, 1979

QUAD D-TYPE FLIP-FLOPS

175 COMPLEMENTARY OUTPUTS
COMMON DIRECT CLEAR

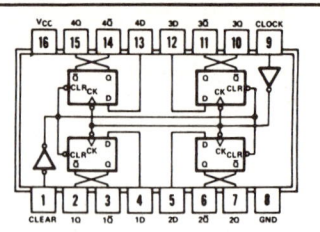

SN54175 (J, W)   SN74175 (J, N)
SN54LS175 (J, W) SN74LS175 (J, N)
SN54S175 (J, W)   SN74S175 (J, N)

PRESETABLE COUNTERS/LATCHES

176 DECADE (BI-QUINARY)

177 BINARY

SN54176 (J, W)   SN74176 (J, N)
SN54177 (J, W)   SN74177 (J, N)

QUAD DATA SELECTORS/MULTIPLEXERS

257 NONINVERTED 3-STATE OUTPUTS

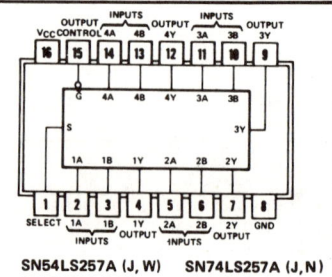

SN54LS257A (J, W) SN74LS257A (J, N)
SN54S257 (J, W)   SN74S257 (J, N)

HEX BUS DRIVERS

367 NONINVERTED DATA OUTPUTS
4-LINE AND 2-LINE ENABLE INPUTS
3-STATE OUTPUTS

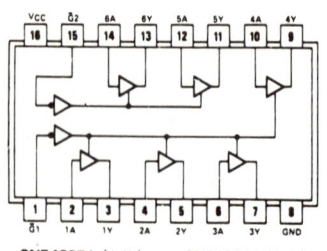

SN54367A (J, W)   SN74367A (J, N)
SN54LS367A (J, W) SN74LS367A (J, N)

© Texas Instruments Incorporated, 1979

POSITIVE-NAND GATES AND INVERTERS WITH TOTEM-POLE OUTPUTS

switching characteristics at $V_{CC} = 5$ V, $T_A = 25°C$

TYPE	TEST CONDITIONS#	t_{PLH} (ns) Propagation delay time, low-to-high-level output			t_{PHL} (ns) Propagation delay time, high-to-low-level output		
		MIN	TYP	MAX	MIN	TYP	MAX
'00, '10	$C_L = 15$ pF, $R_L = 400$ Ω		11	22		7	15
'04, '20			12	22		8	15
'30			13	22		8	15
'H00	$C_L = 25$ pF, $R_L = 280$ Ω		5.9	10		6.2	10
'H04			6	10		6.5	10
'H10			5.9	10		6.3	10
'H20			6	10		7	10
'H30			6.8	10		8.9	12
'L00, 'L04, 'L10, L20	$C_L = 50$ pF, $R_L = 4$ kΩ		35	60		31	60
'L30			35	60		70	100
'LS00, 'LS04	$C_L = 15$ pF, $R_L = 2$ kΩ		9	15		10	15
'LS10, 'LS20			8	15		13	20
'LS30			3	4.5		3	5
'S00, 'S04	$C_L = 15$ pF, $R_L = 280$ Ω		4.5			5	
'S10, 'S20	$C_L = 50$ pF, $R_L = 280$ Ω		4	6		4.5	7
'S30, 'S133	$C_L = 15$ pF, $R_L = 280$ Ω / $C_L = 50$ pF, $R_L = 280$ Ω		5.5			6.5	

#Load circuits and voltage waveforms are shown on pages 3-10 and 3-11.

supply current¶

TYPE	I_{CCH} (mA) Total with outputs high		I_{CCL} (mA) Total with outputs low		I_{CC} (mA) Average per gate (50% duty cycle)
	TYP	MAX	TYP	MAX	TYP
'00	4	8	12	22	2
'04	6	12	18	33	2
'10	3	6	9	16.5	2
'20	2	4	6	11	2
'30	1	2	3	6	2
'H00	10	16.8	26	40	4.5
'H04	16	26	40	58	4.5
'H10	7.5	12.6	19.5	30	4.5
'H20	5	8.4	13	20	4.5
'H30	2.5	4.2	6.5	10	4.5
'L00	0.44	0.8	1.16	2.04	0.20
'L04	0.66	1.2	1.74	3.06	0.20
'L10	0.33	0.6	0.87	1.53	0.20
'L20	0.22	0.4	0.58	1.02	0.20
SN54L30	0.11	0.33	0.29	0.51	0.20
SN74L30	0.11	0.2	0.29	0.51	0.20
'LS00	0.8	1.6	2.4	4.4	0.4
'LS04	1.2	2.4	3.6	6.6	0.4
'LS10	0.6	1.2	1.8	3.3	0.4
'LS20	0.4	0.8	1.2	2.2	0.4
'LS30	0.35	0.5	0.6	1.1	0.48
'S00	10	16	20	36	3.75
'S04	15	24	30	54	3.75
'S10	7.5	12	15	27	3.75
'S20	5	8	10	18	3.75
'S30	3	5	5.5	10	4.25
'S133	3	5	5.5	10	4.25

¶Maximum values of I_{CC} are over the recommended operating ranges of V_{CC} and T_A; typical values are at $V_{CC} = 5$ V, $T_A = 25°C$.

schematics (each gate)

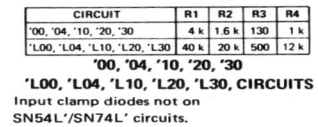

'00, '04, '10, '20, '30 CIRCUITS

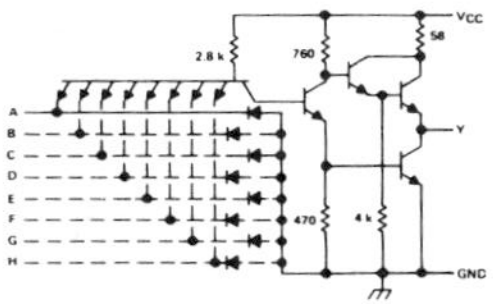

'H00, 'H04, 'H10, 'H20, 'H30 CIRCUITS

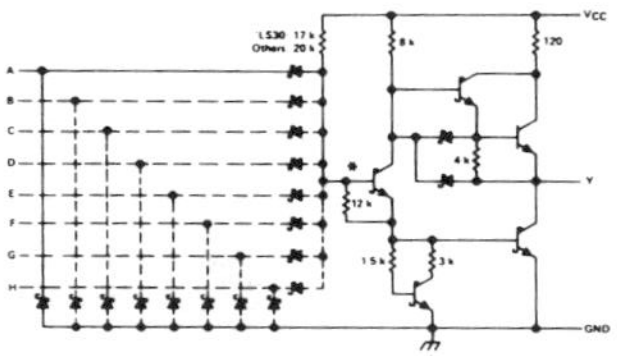

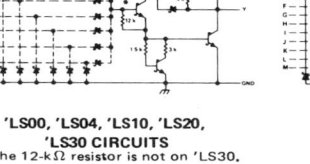

'LS00, 'LS04, 'LS10, 'LS20, 'LS30 CIRCUITS
*The 12-kΩ resistor is not on 'LS30.

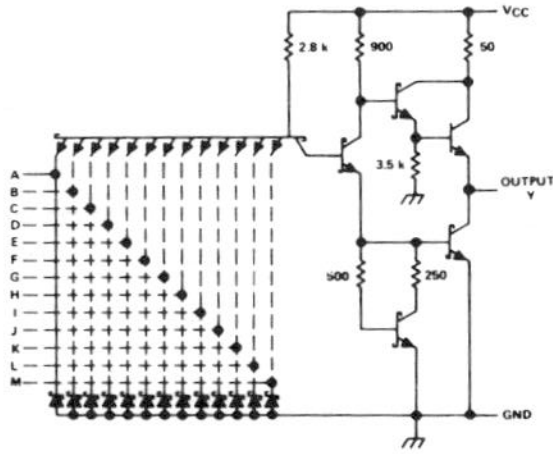

'S00, 'S04, 'S10, 'S20, 'S30, 'S133 CIRCUITS

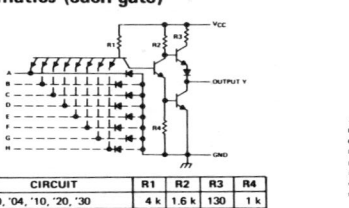

CIRCUIT	R1	R2	R3	R4
'00, '04, '10, '20, '30	4 k	1.6 k	130	
'L00, 'L04, 'L10, 'L20, 'L30	40 k	20 k	500	12 k

Input clamp diodes not on SN54L'/SN74L' circuits.

Resistor values shown are nominal and in ohms.

© Texas Instruments Incorporated, 1979

GATES WITH 3-STATE OUTPUTS

recommended operating conditions

		SERIES 54 SERIES 74 '125, '126, '425, '426			SERIES 54LS SERIES 74LS 'LS125A, 'LS126A			SERIES 54S SERIES 74S 'S134			UNIT
		MIN	NOM	MAX	MIN	NOM	MAX	MIN	NOM	MAX	
Supply voltage, V_{CC}	54 FAMILY	4.5	5	5.5	4.5	5	5.5	4.5	5	5.5	V
	74 FAMILY	4.75	5	5.25	4.75	5	5.25	4.75	5	5.25	
High-level output current, I_{OH}	54 Family			−2			−1			−2	mA
	74 Family			−5.2			−2.6			−6.5	
Low-level output current, I_{OL}	54 Family			16			12			20	mA
	74 Family			16			24			20	
Operating free-air temperature, T_A	54 Family	−55		125	−55		125	−55		125	°C
	74 Family	0		70	0		70	0		70	

electrical characteristics over recommended operating free-air temperature range (unless otherwise noted)

PARAMETER		TEST FIGURE	TEST CONDITIONS†		SERIES 54 SERIES 74 '125, '126, '425, '426			SERIES 54LS SERIES 74LS 'LS125A, 'LS126A			SERIES 54S SERIES 74S 'S134			UNIT
					MIN	TYP‡	MAX	MIN	TYP‡	MAX	MIN	TYP‡	MAX	
V_{IH}	High-level input voltage	1, 2			2			2			2			V
V_{IL}	Low-level input voltage	1, 2		54 Family			0.8			0.7			0.8	V
				74 Family			0.8			0.8			0.8	
V_{IK}	Input clamp voltage	3	V_{CC} = MIN,	I_I = §			−1.5			−1.5			−1.2	V
V_{OH}	High-level output voltage	1	V_{CC} = MIN, V_{IL} = V_{IL} max,	V_{IH} = 2 V, I_{OH} = MAX	2.4	3.3		2.4			2.4	3.4		V
V_{OL}	Low-level output voltage	2	V_{CC} = MIN, V_{IH} = 2 V, V_{IL} = V_{IL} max	I_{OL} = MAX I_{OL} = 12 mA Series 74LS	2.4	3.1	0.4 0.4		0.25 0.35 0.25	0.4 0.5 0.4	2.4	3.2	0.5 0.5	V
I_{OZ}	Off-state (high-impedance state) output current	19	V_{CC} = MAX, V_{IH} = 2 V, V_{IL} = V_{IL} max	V_O = 2.4 V V_O = 0.4 V V_O = 0.5 V			40 −40			20 −20			50 −50	µA
I_I	Input current at maximum input voltage	4	V_{CC} = MAX	V_I = 5.5 V V_I = 7 V			1			0.1			1	mA
I_{IH}	High-level input current	4	V_{CC} = MAX	V_{IH} = 2.4 V V_{IH} = 2.7 V			40			20			50	µA
I_{IL}	Low-level input current	5	V_{CC} = MAX	V_{IL} = 0.4 V V_{IL} = 0.5 V			−1.6			0.4			−2	mA
I_{OS}	Short-circuit output current♦	6	V_{CC} = MAX	54 Family 74 Family	−30 −28		−70 −70	−40 −40		−225 −225	−40 −40		−100 −100	mA
I_{CC}	Supply current	7	V_{CC} = MAX					See table on next page						mA

† For conditions shown as MIN or MAX, use the appropriate value specified under recommended operating conditions.
‡ All typical values are at V_{CC} = 5 V, T_A = 25°C.
§ I_I = −12 mA for SN54'/SN74' and −18 mA for SN54LS'/SN74LS' and SN54S'/SN74S'.
♦ Not more than one output should be shorted at a time, and for SN54LS'/SN74LS' and SN54S'/SN74S', duration of the short circuit should not exceed one second.

© Texas Instruments Incorporated, 1979

POSITIVE-NAND GATES AND INVERTERS WITH TOTEM-POLE OUTPUTS

recommended operating conditions

		54 FAMILY / 74 FAMILY	SERIES 54 / SERIES 74 '00, '04, '10, '20, '30			SERIES 54H / SERIES 74H 'H00, 'H04, 'H10, 'H20, 'H30			SERIES 54L / SERIES 74L 'L00, 'L04, 'L10, 'L20, 'L30			SERIES 54LS / SERIES 74LS 'LS00, 'LS04, 'LS10, 'LS20, 'LS30			SERIES 54S / SERIES 74S 'S00, 'S04, 'S10, 'S20, 'S30, 'S133			UNIT
			MIN	NOM	MAX	MIN	NOM	MAX	MIN	NOM	MAX	MIN	NOM	MAX	MIN	NOM	MAX	
Supply voltage, V_{CC}		54 Family	4.5	5	5.5	4.5	5	5.5	4.5	5	5.5	4.5	5	5.5	4.5	5	5.5	V
		74 Family	4.75	5	5.25	4.75	5	5.25	4.75	5	5.25	4.75	5	5.25	4.75	5	5.25	
High-level output current, I_{OH}		54 Family			−400			−500			−100			−400			−1000	µA
		74 Family			−400			−500			−200			−400			−1000	
Low-level output current, I_{OL}		54 Family			16			20			2			4			20	mA
		74 Family			16			20			3.6			8			20	
Operating free-air temperature, T_A		54 Family	−55		125	−55		125	−55		125	−55		125	−55		125	°C
		74 Family	0		70	0		70	0		70	0		70	0		70	

electrical characteristics over recommended operating free-air temperature range (unless otherwise noted)

PARAMETER	TEST FIGURE	TEST CONDITIONS†	SERIES 54 / SERIES 74 '00, '04, '10, '20, '30			SERIES 54H / SERIES 74H 'H00, 'H04, 'H10, 'H20, 'H30			SERIES 54L / SERIES 74L 'L00, 'L04, 'L10, 'L20, 'L30			SERIES 54LS / SERIES 74LS 'LS00, 'LS04, 'LS10, 'LS20, 'LS30			SERIES 54S / SERIES 74S 'S00, 'S04, 'S10, 'S20, 'S30, 'S133			UNIT
			MIN	TYP‡	MAX	MIN	TYP‡	MAX	MIN	TYP‡	MAX	MIN	TYP‡	MAX	MIN	TYP‡	MAX	
V_{IH} High-level input voltage	1, 2		2			2			2			2			2			V
V_{IL} Low-level input voltage	1, 2				0.8			0.8			0.7			0.7			0.8	V
														0.8				
V_{IK} Input clamp voltage	3	V_{CC} = MIN, I_I = §			−1.5			−1.5						−1.5			−1.2	V
V_{OH} High-level output voltage	1	V_{CC} = MIN, V_{IL} = V_{IL} max, I_{OH} = MAX	2.4	3.4		2.4	3.5		2.4	3.3		2.5	3.4		2.5	3.4		V
			2.4	3.4		2.4	3.5		2.4	3.2		2.7	3.4		2.7	3.4		
V_{OL} Low-level output voltage	2	V_{CC} = MIN, V_{IH} = 2 V		0.2	0.4		0.2	0.4		0.15	0.3		0.25	0.4			0.5	V
		Series 74LS I_{OL} = 4 mA		0.2	0.4		0.2	0.4		0.2	0.4		0.25	0.5			0.5	
														0.4				
I_I Input current at maximum input voltage	4	V_I = 5.5 V			1			1			0.1			0.1			1	mA
		V_I = 7 V																
I_{IH} High-level input current	4	V_{IH} = 2.4 V			40			50			10			20			50	µA
		V_{IH} = 2.7 V																
I_{IL} Low-level input current	5	V_{IL} = 0.3 V			−1.6			−2			−0.18			−0.4			−2	mA
		V_{IL} = 0.4 V																
		V_{IL} = 0.5 V																
I_{OS} Short-circuit output current♦	6	V_{CC} = MAX	−20		−55	−40		−100	−3		−15	−20		−100	−40		−100	mA
			−18		−55	−40		−100	−3		−15	−20		−100	−40		−100	
I_{CC} Supply current	7	V_{CC} = MAX										See table on next page						mA

†For conditions shown as MIN or MAX, use the appropriate value specified under recommended operating conditions.
‡All typical values are at V_{CC} = 5 V, T_A = 25°C.
§I_I = −12 mA for SN54/SN74', −8 mA for SN54H'/SN74H', and −18 mA for SN54LS'/SN74LS' and SN54S'/SN74S'.
♦Not more than one output should be shorted at a time, and for SN54H'/SN74H', SN54LS'/SN74LS', and SN54S'/SN74S', duration of short-circuit should not exceed 1 second.

© Texas Instruments Incorporated, 1979

256 X 4 BIT STATIC RAM

- 256 x 4 Organization to Meet Needs for Small System Memories
- Single +5V Supply Voltage
- Directly TTL Compatible: All Inputs and Output
- Statis MOS: No Clocks or Refreshing Required
- Simple Memory Expansion: Chip Enable Input
- Inputs Protected: All Inputs Have Protection Against Static Charge
- Low Cost Packaging: 22 Pin Plastic Dual In-Line Configuration
- Low Power: Typically 150 mW
- Three-State Output: OR-Tie Capability
- Output Disable Provided for Ease of Use in Common Data Bus Systems

2101A-2	250 ns Max.
2101A	350 ns Max.
2101A-4	450 ns Max.

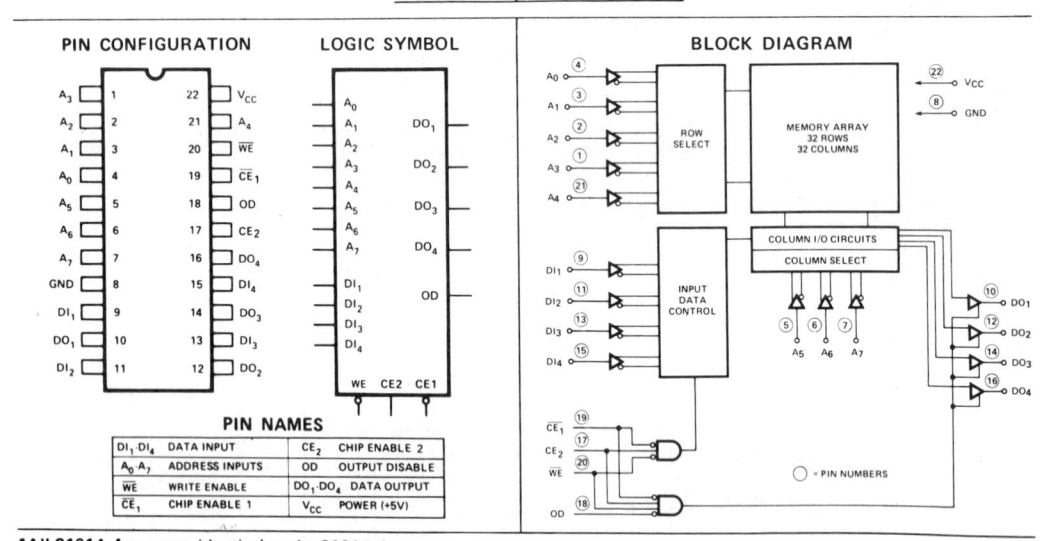

PIN CONFIGURATION / LOGIC SYMBOL / BLOCK DIAGRAM

DI_1-DI_4	DATA INPUT	CE_2	CHIP ENABLE 2
A_0-A_7	ADDRESS INPUTS	OD	OUTPUT DISABLE
WE	WRITE ENABLE	DO_1-DO_4	DATA OUTPUT
$\overline{CE}_1$	CHIP ENABLE 1	V_{CC}	POWER (+5V)

*All 8101A-4 specs are identical to the 2101A-4 specs.

3-26

WAVEFORMS

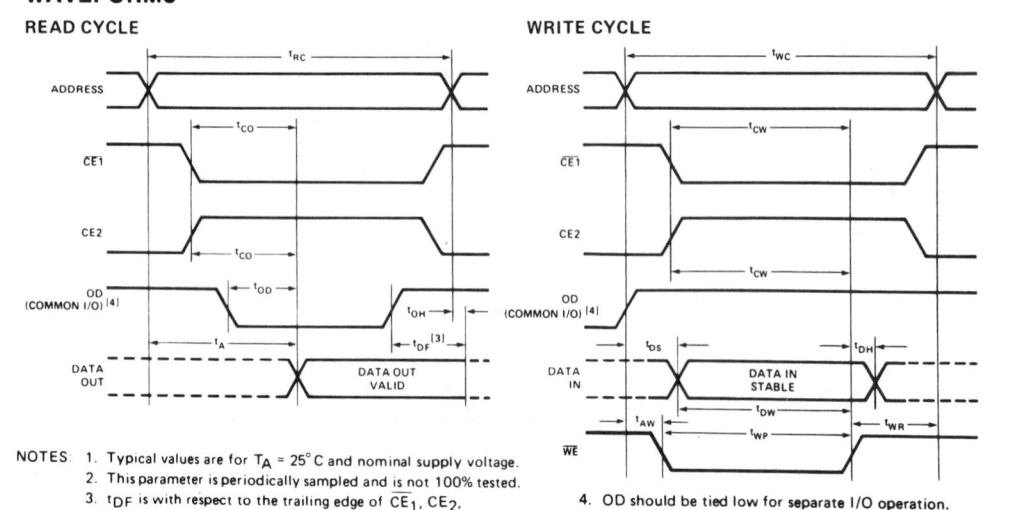

READ CYCLE

WRITE CYCLE

NOTES:
1. Typical values are for $T_A = 25°C$ and nominal supply voltage.
2. This parameter is periodically sampled and is not 100% tested.
3. t_{DF} is with respect to the trailing edge of $\overline{CE}_1$, CE_2, or OD, whichever occurs first.
4. OD should be tied low for separate I/O operation.

© Texas Instruments Incorporated, 1979

74157

SN54157, SN54LS157, SN54S157 . . . J OR W PACKAGE
SN54L157 . . . J PACKAGE
SN74157, SN74L157, SN74LS157, SN74S157 . . . J OR N PACKAGE
(TOP VIEW)

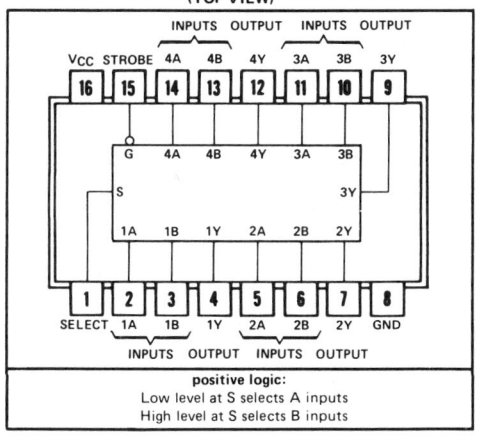

Pinout (top view):
- 16: V_CC
- 15: STROBE
- 14: 4A
- 13: 4B
- 12: 4Y
- 11: 3A
- 10: 3B
- 9: 3Y
- 1: SELECT
- 2: 1A
- 3: 1B
- 4: 1Y
- 5: 2A
- 6: 2B
- 7: 2Y
- 8: GND

positive logic:
Low level at S selects A inputs
High level at S selects B inputs

features

- Buffered Inputs and Outputs
- Three Speed/Power Ranges Available

TYPES	TYPICAL AVERAGE PROPAGATION TIME	TYPICAL POWER DISSIPATION
'157	9 ns	150 mW
'L157	18 ns	75 mW
'LS157	9 ns	49 mW
'S157	5 ns	250 mW
'LS158	7 ns	24 mW
'S158	4 ns	195 mW

FUNCTION TABLE

INPUTS				OUTPUT Y	
STROBE	SELECT	A	B	'157, 'L157, 'LS157, 'S157	'LS158, 'S158
H	X	X	X	L	H
L	L	L	X	L	H
L	L	H	X	H	L
L	H	X	L	L	H
L	H	X	H	H	L

H = high level, L = low level, X = irrelevant

functional block diagram   '157, 'L157

© Texas Instruments Incorporated, 1979

SN54176, SN54177 . . . J OR W PACKAGE
SN74176, SN74177 . . . J OR N PACKAGE
(TOP VIEW)

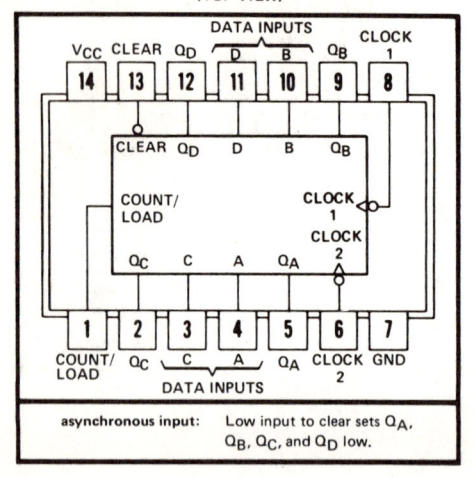

SN54177, SN74177

```
          DATA INPUTS      CLOCK
    VCC CLEAR QD  D   B  QB   1
    ┌───┬───┬───┬───┬───┬───┬───┐
    │14 │13 │12 │11 │10 │ 9 │ 8 │
    │                            │
    │     CLEAR QD  D   B  QB    │
    │                            │
    │     COUNT/        CLOCK    │
    │     LOAD            1      │
    │                    CLOCK   │
    │      QC   C   A   QA  2    │
    │                            │
    │ 1 │ 2 │ 3 │ 4 │ 5 │ 6 │ 7 │
    └───┴───┴───┴───┴───┴───┴───┘
    COUNT/ QC   C   A  QA CLOCK GND
    LOAD       DATA INPUTS    2
```

asynchronous input: Low input to clear sets QA, QB, QC, and QD low.

SN54177, SN74177
FUNCTION TABLE
(See Note A)

COUNT	QD	QC	QB	QA
0	L	L	L	L
1	L	L	L	H
2	L	L	H	L
3	L	L	H	H
4	L	H	L	L
5	L	H	L	H
6	L	H	H	L
7	L	H	H	H
8	H	L	L	L
9	H	L	L	H
10	H	L	H	L
11	H	L	H	H
12	H	H	L	L
13	H	H	L	H
14	H	H	H	L
15	H	H	H	H

H = high level, L = low level

NOTE A: Output QA connected to clock-2 input.

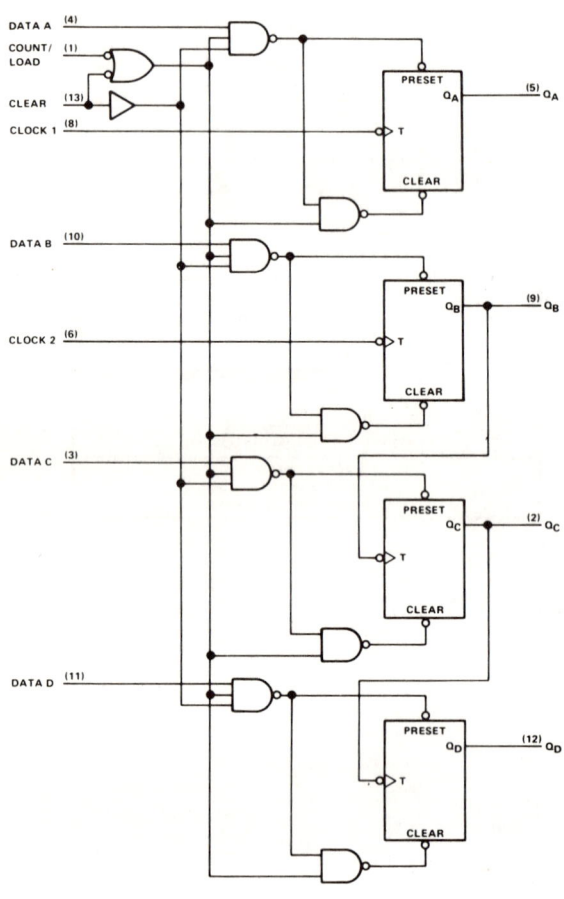

- Performs BCD, Bi-Quinary, or Binary Counting
- Fully Programmable
- Fully Independent Clear Input
- Guaranteed to Count at Input Frequencies from 0 to 35 MHz
- Input Clamping Diodes Simplify System Design

© Texas Instruments Incorporated, 1979

DUAL RETRIGGERABLE MONOSTABLE MULTIVIBRATORS WITH CLEAR

123
FUNCTION TABLE

INPUTS			OUTPUTS	
CLEAR	A	B	Q	$\bar{Q}$
L	X	X	L	H
X	H	X	L	H
X	X	L	L	H
H	L	↑	⊓	⊔
H	↓	H	⊓	⊔
↑	L	H	⊓	⊔

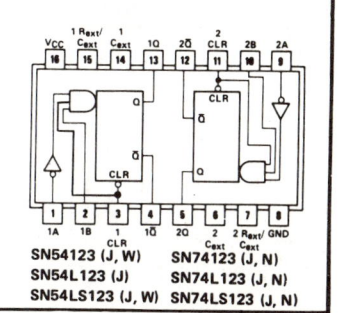

SN54123 (J, W)   SN74123 (J, N)
SN54L123 (J)   SN74L123 (J, N)
SN54LS123 (J, W) SN74LS123 (J, N)

QUADRUPLE BUS BUFFER GATES WITH THREE-STATE OUTPUTS

125

positive logic:
Y = A
Output is off (disabled) when C is high.

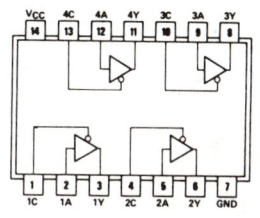

SN54125 (J, W)   SN74125 (J, N)
SN54LS125A (J, W)   SN74LS125A (J, N)

© Texas Instruments Incorporated, 1979

TYPES SN54122, SN54123, SN54L122, SN54L123, SN54LS122, SN54LS123, SN74122, SN74123, SN74L122, SN74L123, SN74LS122, SN74LS123
RETRIGGERABLE MONOSTABLE MULTIVIBRATORS

- D-C Triggered from Active-High or Active-Low Gated Logic Inputs
- Retriggerable for Very Long Output Pulses, Up to 100% Duty Cycle
- Overriding Clear Terminates Output Pulse
- Compensated for V_{CC} and Temperature Variations
- '122, 'L122, 'LS122 Have Internal Timing Resistors

SN54122, SN54LS122 . . . J OR W
SN54L122 . . . J OR T
SN74122, SN74L122, SN74LS122 . . . J OR N
(TOP VIEW) (SEE NOTES 1 THRU 4)

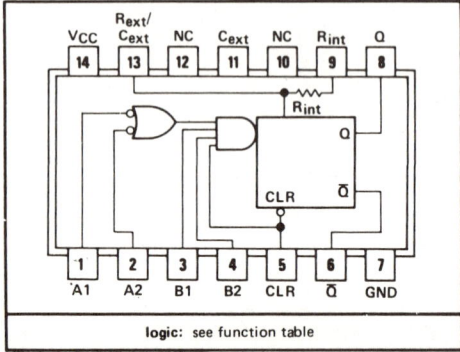

logic: see function table

NC—No internal connection.

SN54123, SN54LS123 . . . J OR W
SN54L123 . . . J
SN74123, SN74L123, SN74LS123 . . . J OR N
(TOP VIEW) (SEE NOTES 1 THRU 4)

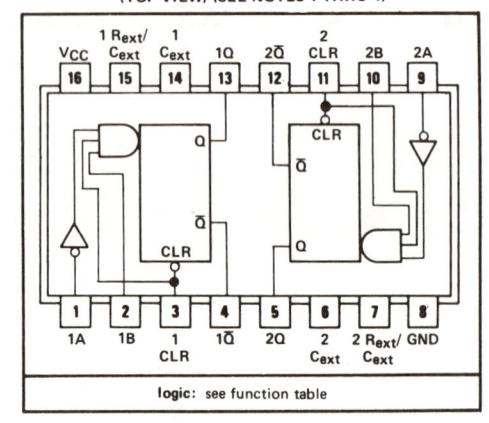

logic: see function table

'122, 'L122, 'LS122 FUNCTION TABLE

INPUTS				OUTPUTS	
CLEAR	A1	A2	B1	B2	Q	Q̄
L	X	X	X	X	L	H
X	H	H	X	X	L	H
X	X	X	L	X	L	H
X	X	X	X	L	L	H
H	L	X	↑	H	⊓	⊔
H	L	X	H	↑	⊓	⊔
H	X	L	↑	H	⊓	⊔
H	X	L	H	↑	⊓	⊔
H	↓	↓	H	H	⊓	⊔
H	↓	H	H	H	⊓	⊔
H	H	↓	H	H	⊓	⊔
↑	L	X	H	H	⊓	⊔
↑	X	L	H	H	⊓	⊔

'123, 'L123, 'LS123 FUNCTION TABLE

INPUTS		OUTPUTS	
CLEAR	A	B	Q	Q̄
L	X	X	L	H
X	H	X	L	H
X	X	L	L	H
H	L	↑	⊓	⊔
H	↓	H	⊓	⊔
↑	L	H	⊓	⊔

See explanation of function tables on page 3-8.

description

These d-c triggered multivibrators feature output pulse width control by three methods. The basic pulse time is programmed by selection of external resistance and capacitance values (see typical application data). The '122, 'L122, and 'LS122 have internal timing resistors that allow the circuits to be used with only an external capacitor, if so desired. Once triggered, the basic pulse width may be extended by retriggering the gated low-level-active (A) or high-level-active (B) inputs, or be reduced by use of the overriding clear. Figure 1 illustrates pulse control by retriggering and early clear.

The 'LS122 and 'LS123 are provided enough Schmitt hysteresis to ensure jitter-free triggering from the B input with transition rates as slow as 0.1 millivolt per nanosecond.

NOTES: 1. An external timing capacitor may be connected between C_{ext} and R_{ext}/C_{ext} (positive).
2. To use the internal timing resistor of '122, 'L122 or 'LS122, connect R_{int} to V_{CC}.
3. For improved pulse width accuracy and repeatability, connect an external resistor between R_{ext}/C_{ext} and V_{CC} with R_{int} open-circuited.
4. To obtain variable pulse widths, connect an external variable resistance between R_{int} or R_{ext}/C_{ext} and V_{CC}.

© Texas Instruments Incorporated, 1979

TYPES SN54122, SN74122, SN54123, SN74123, SN54L122, SN74L122, SN54L123, SN74L123
RETRIGGERABLE MONOSTABLE MULTIVIBRATOR

TYPICAL APPLICATION DATA FOR '122, '123, 'L122, 'L123

For pulse widths when $C_{ext} \leq 1000$ pF, See Figures 4 and 5.

The output pulse is primarily a function of the external capacitor and resistor. For $C_{ext} > 1000$ pF, the output pulse width (t_W) is defined as:

$$t_W = K \cdot R_T \cdot C_{ext} \left(1 + \frac{0.7}{R_T} \right)$$

where

K is 0.32 for '122, 0.28 for '123,
0.37 for 'L122, 0.33 for 'L123

R_T is in kΩ (internal or external timing resistance.

C_{ext} is in pF

t_W is in nanoseconds

To prevent reverse voltage across C_{ext}, it is recommended that the method shown in Figure 2 be employed when using electrolytic capacitors and in applications utilizing the clear function. In all applications using the diode, the pulse width is:

$$t_W = K_D \cdot R_T \cdot C_{ext} \left(1 + \frac{0.7}{R_T} \right)$$

K_D is 0.28 for '122, 0.25 for '123,
0.33 for 'L122, 0.29 for 'L123

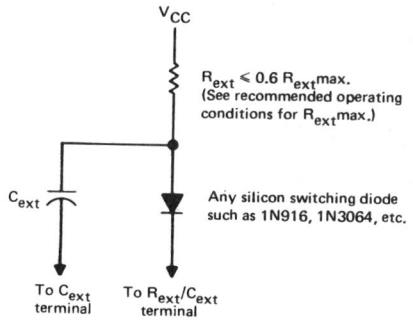

TIMING COMPONENT CONNECTIONS
FIGURE 3

'122, '123
TYPICAL OUTPUT PULSE WIDTH
vs
EXTERNAL TIMING CAPACITANCE

FIGURE 4

TIMING COMPONENT CONNECTIONS WHEN $C_{ext} > 1000$ pF AND CLEAR IS USED
FIGURE 2

Applications requiring more precise pulse widths (up to 28 seconds) and not requiring the clear feature can best be satisfied with the '121 or 'L121.

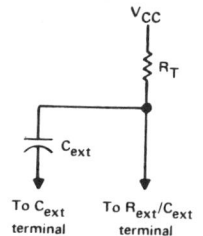

'L122
TYPICAL OUTPUT PULSE WIDTH
vs
EXTERNAL TIMING CAPACITANCE

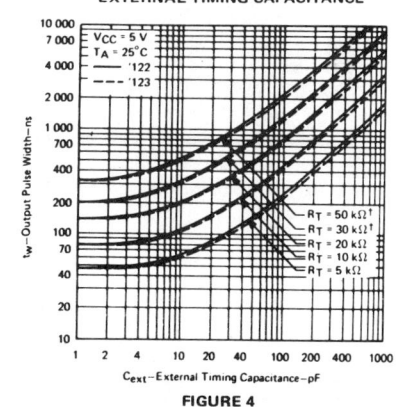

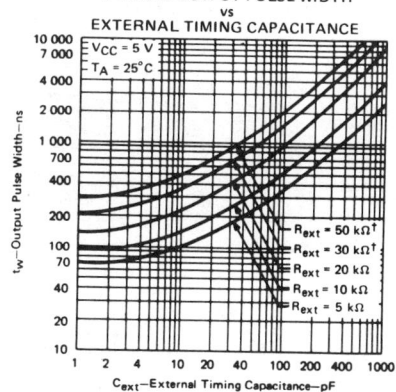

FIGURE 5

†These values of resistance exceed the maximum recommended for over the full temperature range of the SN54' and SN54L' circuits

© Texas Instruments Incorporated, 1979

TYPES SN54LS122, SN74LS122, SN54LS123, SN74LS123
RETRIGGERABLE MONOSTABLE MULTIVIBRATORS

TYPICAL APPLICATION DATA FOR 'LS122, 'LS123

The basic output pulse width is essentially determined by the values of external capacitance and timing resistance. For pulse widths when $C_{ext} \leq 1000$ pF, see Figure 7.

When $C_{ext} > 1000$ pF, the output pulse width is defined as:

$$t_W = 0.45 \cdot R_T \cdot C_{ext}$$

where

R_T is in kΩ (internal or external timing resistance.)

C_{ext} is in pF

t_W is in nanoseconds

For best results, system ground should be applied to the C_{ext} terminal. The switching diode is not needed for electrolytic capacitance applications.

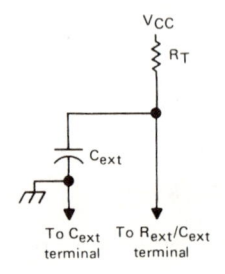

TIMING COMPONENT CONNECTIONS
FIGURE 6

'LS122, 'LS123
TYPICAL OUTPUT PULSE WIDTH
vs
EXTERNAL TIMING CAPACITANCE

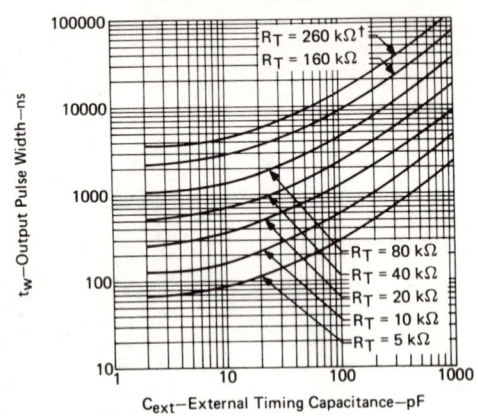

† This value of resistance exceeds the maximum recommended for use over the full temperature range of the SN54LS circuits.

© Texas Instruments Incorporated, 1979

TYPES SN54122, SN54123, SN74122, SN74123
RETRIGGERABLE MONOSTABLE MULTIVIBRATORS

recommended operating conditions

	SN54' MIN	SN54' NOM	SN54' MAX	SN74' MIN	SN74' NOM	SN74' MAX	UNIT
Supply voltage, V_{CC}	4.5	5	5.5	4.75	5	5.25	V
High-level output current, I_{OH}			−800			−800	µA
Low-level output current, I_{OL}			16			16	mA
Pulse width, t_w			40			40	ns
External timing resistance, R_{ext}	5		25	5		50	kΩ
External capacitance, C_{ext}		No restriction			No restriction		
Wiring capacitance at R_{ext}/C_{ext} terminal			50			50	pF
Operating free-air temperature, T_A	−55		125	0		70	°C

electrical characteristics over recommended free-air operating temperature range (unless otherwise noted)

PARAMETER		TEST CONDITIONS†	'122 MIN	'122 TYP‡	'122 MAX	'123 MIN	'123 TYP‡	'123 MAX	UNIT
V_{IH}	High-level input voltage		2			2			V
V_{IL}	Low-level input voltage				0.8			0.8	V
V_{IK}	Input clamp voltage	V_{CC} = MIN, I_I = −12 mA			−1.5			−1.5	V
V_{OH}	High-level output voltage	V_{CC} = MIN, I_{OH} = −800 µA, See Note 1	2.4	3.4		2.4	3.4		V
V_{OL}	Low-level output voltage	V_{CC} = MIN, I_{OL} = 16 mA, See Note 1		0.2	0.4		0.2	0.4	V
I_I	Input current at maximum input voltage	V_{CC} = MAX, V_I = 5.5 V			1			1	mA
I_{IH}	High-level input current Data inputs	V_{CC} = MAX, V_I = 2.4 V			40			40	µA
	Clear input				80			80	
I_{IL}	Low-level input current Data inputs	V_{CC} = MAX, V_I = 0.4 V			−1.6			−1.6	mA
	Clear input				−3.2			−3.2	
I_{OS}	Short-circuit output current♦	V_{CC} = MAX, See Note 5	−10		−40	−10		−40	mA
I_{CC}	Supply current (quiescent or triggered)	V_{CC} = MAX, See Notes 6 and 7		23	28		46	66	mA

† For conditions shown as MIN or MAX, use the value specified under recommended operating conditions.
‡ All typical values are at V_{CC} = 5 V, T_A = 25°C.
♦ Not more than one output should be shorted at a time.

NOTES: 5. Ground C_{ext} to measure V_{OH} at Q, V_{OL} at $\overline{Q}$, or I_{OS} at Q. C_{ext} is open to measure V_{OH} at $\overline{Q}$, V_{OL} at Q, or I_{OS} at $\overline{Q}$.
6. I_{CC} is measured (after clearing) with 2.4 V applied to all clear and A inputs, B inputs grounded, all outputs open, C_{ext} = 0.02 µF, and R_{ext} = 25 kΩ. R_{int} of '122 is open.
7. I_{CC} is measured in the triggered state with 2.4 V applied to all clear and B inputs, A inputs grounded, all outputs open, C_{ext} = 0.02 µF, and R_{ext} = 25 kΩ. R_{int} of '122 is open.

switching characteristics, V_{CC} = 5 V, T_A = 25°C, see note 8

PARAMETER¶	FROM (INPUT)	TO (OUTPUT)	TEST CONDITIONS	'122 MIN	'122 TYP	'122 MAX	'123 MIN	'123 TYP	'123 MAX	UNIT
t_{PLH}	A	Q	C_{ext} = 0, R_{ext} = 5 kΩ, C_L = 15 pF, R_L = 400 Ω		22	33		22	33	ns
	B				19	28		19	28	
t_{PHL}	A	$\overline{Q}$			30	40		30	40	ns
	B				27	36		27	36	
t_{PHL}	Clear	Q			18	27		18	27	ns
t_{PLH}		$\overline{Q}$			30	40		30	40	
t_{wQ} (min)	A or B	Q			45	65		45	65	ns
t_{wQ}	A or B	Q	C_{ext} = 1000 pF, R_{ext} = 10 kΩ, C_L = 15 pF, R_L = 400 Ω	3.08	3.42	3.76	2.76	3.03	3.37	µs

¶ t_{PLH} ≡ propagation delay time, low-to-high-level output
t_{PHL} ≡ propagation delay time, high-to-low-level output
t_{wQ} ≡ width of pulse at output Q
NOTE 8: Load circuit and voltage waveforms are shown on page 3-10.

© Texas Instruments Incorporated, 1979

Clocks

For additional application information, see AN-143 at the end of this section.

MM5309, MM5311, MM5312, MM5313, MM5314, MM5315 digital clocks

general description

These digital clocks are monolithic MOS integrated circuits utilizing P-channel low-threshold, enhancement mode and ion implanted, depletion mode devices. The devices provide all the logic required to build several types of clocks. Two display modes (4 or 6-digits) facilitate end-product designs of varied sophistication. The circuits interface to LED and gas discharge displays with minimal additional components, and require only a single power supply. The timekeeping function operates from either a 50 or 60 Hz input, and the display format may be either 12 hours (with leading-zero blanking) or 24 hours. Outputs consist of multiplexed display drives ($\overline{\text{BCD}}$ and 7-segment) and digit enables. The devices operate over a power supply range of 11V to 19V and do not require a regulated supply. These clocks are packaged in dual-in-line packages.

features

- 50 or 60 Hz operation
- 12 or 24-hour display format
- Leading-zero blanking (12-hour format)
- 7-segment outputs
- Single power supply
- Fast and slow set controls
- Internal multiplex oscillator
- For features of individual clocks, see Table I

applications

- Desk clocks
- Automobile clocks
- Industrial clocks
- Interval Timers

TABLE I.

FEATURES	MM5309	MM5311	MM5312	MM5313	MM5314	MM5315
$\overline{\text{BCD}}$ Outputs	X	X	X	X		X
4/6-Digit Display Mode	X	X		X	X	X
Hold Count Control			X	X	X	X
1 Hz Output				X	X	
Output Enable Control	X	X			X	
Reset		X				X

connection diagrams (Dual-In-Line Packages)

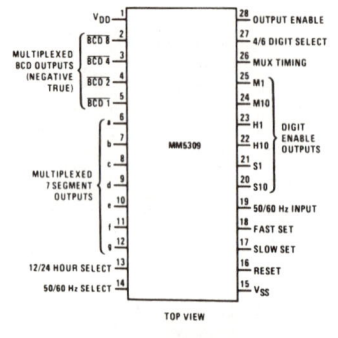

Order Number MM5309N
See Package 23

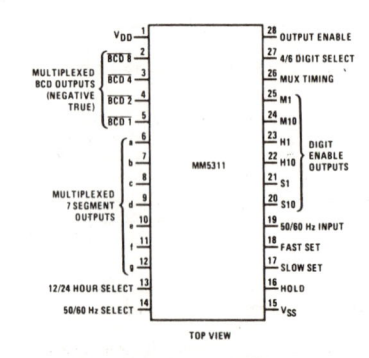

Order Number MM5311N
See Package 23

314

© National Semiconductor, 1979

absolute maximum ratings

Voltage at Any Pin	V_{SS} + 0.3 to V_{SS} − 20V
Operating Temperature	−25°C to +70°C
Storage Temperature	−65°C to +150°C
Lead Temperature (Soldering, 10 seconds)	300°C

electrical characteristics

T_A within operating range, V_{SS} = 11V to 19V, V_{DD} = 0V, unless otherwise specified.

PARAMETER	CONDITIONS	MIN	TYP	MAX	UNITS
Power Supply Voltage	V_{SS} (V_{DD} = 0V)	11		19	V
Power Supply Current	V_{SS} = 14V, (No Output Loads)			10	mA
50/60 Hz Input Frequency		dc	50 or 60	60k	Hz
50/60 Hz Input Voltage					
Logical High Level		V_{SS}−1	V_{SS}	V_{SS}	V
Logical Low Level		V_{DD}	V_{DD}	V_{SS}−10	V
Multiplex Frequency	Determined by External R & C	0.100	1.0	60	kHz
All Logic Inputs	Driven by External Timebase	dc		60	kHz
Logical High Level	Internal Depletion Device to V_{SS}	V_{SS}−1	V_{SS}	V_{SS}	V
Logical Low Level		V_{DD}	V_{DD}	V_{SS}−10	V
$\overline{BCD}$ and 7-Segment Outputs					
Logical High Level	Loaded 2 kΩ to V_{DD}	2.0		20	mA source
Logical Low Level				0.01	mA source
Digital Enable Outputs					
Logical High Level				0.3	mA source
Logical Low Level	Loaded 100 Ω to V_{SS}	5.0		25	mA sink

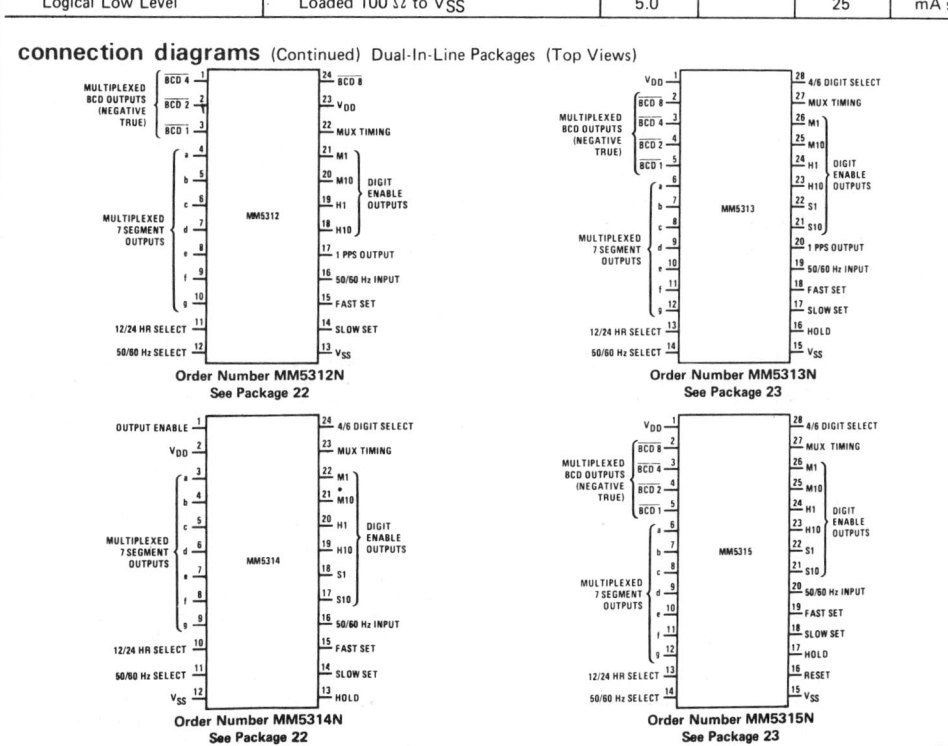

connection diagrams (Continued) Dual-In-Line Packages (Top Views)

Order Number MM5312N
See Package 22

Order Number MM5313N
See Package 23

Order Number MM5314N
See Package 22

Order Number MM5315N
See Package 23

© National Semiconductor, 1979

MM5309, MM5311, MM5312, MM5313, MM5314, MM5315

functional description

A block diagram of the MM5309 digital clock is shown in *Figure 1*. MM5311, MM5312, MM5313, MM5314 and MM5315 clocks are bonding options of MM5309 clock. Table I shows the pin-outs for these clocks.

50 or 60 Hz Input: This input is applied to a Schmitt Trigger shaping circuit which provides approximately 5V of hysteresis and allows using a filtered sinewave input. A simple RC filter such as shown in *Figure 10* should be used to remove possible line voltage transients that could either cause the clock to gain time or damage the device. The shaper output drives a counter chain which performs the timekeeping function.

50 or 60 Hz Select Input: This input programs the prescale counter to divide by either 50 or 60 to obtain a 1 Hz timebase. The counter is programmed for 60 Hz operation by connecting this input to V_{DD}. An internal depletion device is common to this pin; simply leaving this input unconnected programs the clock for 50 Hz operation. As shown in *Figure 1*, the prescale counter provides both 1 Hz and 10 Hz signals, which can be brought out as bonding options.

Time Setting Inputs: Both fast and slow setting inputs, as well as a hold input, are provided. Internal depletion devices provide the normal timekeeping function. Switching any of these inputs (one at a time) to V_{DD} results in the desired time setting function.

The three gates in the counter chain *(Figure 1)* are used for setting time. During normal operation, gate A connects the shaper output to a prescale counter (÷50 or ÷60); gates B and C cascade the remaining counters. Gate A is used to inhibit the input to the counters for the duration of slow, fast or hold time-setting input activity. Gate B is used to connect the shaper output directly to a seconds counter (÷60), the condition for slow advance. Likewise, gate C connects the shaper output directly to a minutes counter (÷60) for fast advance.

Fast set then, advances hours information at one hour per second and slow set advances minutes information at one minute per second.

12 or 24-Hour Select Input: This input is used to program the hours counter to divide by either 12 or 24, thereby providing the desired display format. The 12-hour display format is selected by connecting this input to V_{DD}; leaving the input unconnected (internal depletion device) selects the 24-hour format.

Output Multiplexer Operation: The seconds, minutes, and hours counters continuously reflect the time of day. Outputs from each counter (indicative of both units and tens of seconds, minutes, and hours) are time-division multiplexed to provide digit-sequential access to the time data. Thus, instead of requiring 42 leads to interconnect a 6-digit clock and its display (7 segments per digit), only 13 output leads are required. The multiplexer is addressed by a multiplex divider decoder, which is driven by a multiplex oscillator. The oscillator and external timing components set the frequency of the multiplexing function and, as controlled by the 4 or 6-digit select input, the divider determines whether data will be output for 4 or 6 digits. A zero-blanking circuit suppresses the zero that would otherwise sometimes appear in the tens-of-hours display; blanking is effective only in the 12-hour format. The multiplexer addresses also become the display digit-enable outputs. The multiplexer outputs are applied to a decoder which is used to address a programmable (code converting) ROM. This ROM generates the final output codes, i.e., $\overline{BCD}$ and 7-segment. The sequential output order is from digit 6 (unit seconds) through digit 1 (tens of hours).

Multiplex Timing Input: The multiplex oscillator is shown in *Figure 2*. Adding an external resistor and capacitor to this circuit via the multiplex timing input (as shown in *Figure 4a*) produces a relaxation oscillator. The waveform at this input is a quasi-sawtooth that is squared by the shaping action of the Schmitt Trigger in *Figure 2*. *Figure 3* provides guidelines for selecting the external components relative to desired multiplex frequency.

Figure 4 also illustrates two methods of synchronizing the multiplex oscillator to an external timebase. The external RC timing components may be omitted and this input may be driven by an external timebase; the required logic levels are the same as 50 or 60 Hz input.

Reset: Applying V_{DD} to this input resets the counters to 0:00:00.00 in 12-hour format and 00:00:00.00 in 24-hour formats leaving the input unconnected (internal depletion pull-up) selects normal operation.

4 or 6-Digit Select Input: Like the other control inputs, this input is provided with an internal depletion pull-up device. With no input connection the clock outputs data for a 4-digit display. Applying V_{DD} to this input provides a 6-digit display.

Output Enable Input: With this pin unconnected the $\overline{BCD}$ and 7-segment outputs are enabled (via an internal depletion pull-up). Switching V_{DD} to this input inhibits these outputs. (Not applicable to MM5312, MM5313, and MM5315 clocks.)

Output Circuits: *Figure 5a* illustrates the circuit used for the $\overline{BCD}$ and 7-segment outputs. *Figure 5b* shows the digit enable output circuit. *Figure 6* illustrates interfacing these outputs to standard and low power TTL. *Figures 7 and 8* illustrate methods of interfacing these outputs to common anode and common cathode LED displays, respectively. A method of interfacing these clocks to gas discharge display tubes is shown in *Figure 9*. When driving gas discharge displays which enclose more than one digit in a common gas envelope, it is necessary to inhibit the segment drive voltage(s) during inter-digit transitions. *Figure 9* also illustrates a method of generating a voltage for application to the output enable input to accomplish the required inter-digit blanking.

© National Semiconductor, 1979

functional description (Continued)

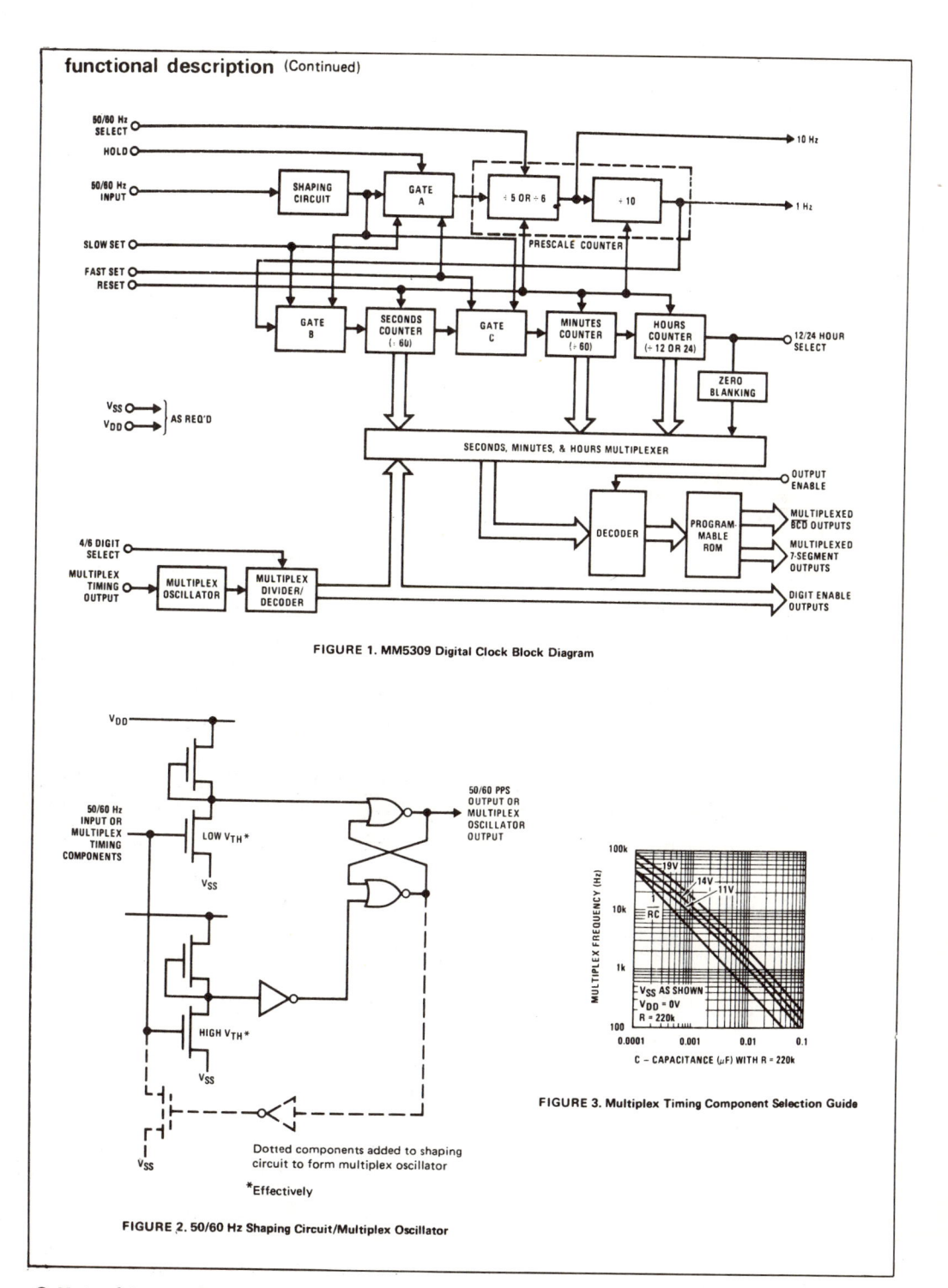

FIGURE 1. MM5309 Digital Clock Block Diagram

FIGURE 2. 50/60 Hz Shaping Circuit/Multiplex Oscillator

Dotted components added to shaping circuit to form multiplex oscillator

*Effectively

FIGURE 3. Multiplex Timing Component Selection Guide

© National Semiconductor, 1979

APPENDIX B

Useful Information

- Software sources
- Parts list for the Memory Board, CPU Board, and Keyboard
- Additional details related to the Static Stimulus Tester
- Additional details related to the Mobile I/O Port
- Supply source for Hardware Trainer designed around this textbook

Detailed instructions for assembly of the STATIC STIMULUS TESTER may be obtained for $3.00 from Creative Microprocessor Systems, P.O. Box 1538, Los Gatos, CA 95030, or a complete assembly kit may be obtained at a reasonable price from the same organization.

Software Sources

The primary sources of software information used in this textbook are:

- MCS-80
  Intel Users Manual (with introduction to MCS-85)
- Assembly Language Programming Manual

Both of these manuals above are published by:

INTEL CORPORATION
3065 Bowers Ave.
Santa Clara, California 95051

PARTS LIST FOR THE MEMORY

(FOR A SINGLE SYSTEM)

Description	Quantity
74157 Quad 2-to-1 MUX	5
74123 Dual 1-shot multivibrator	1
74LS125 Quad tri-state driver	2
2101 256 × 4 static RAM	2
74177 4-bit binary up-counter	2
7406 Hex buffer, open collector	5
7400 Quad 2-input NAND gate	1
SPDT Toggle switch	1
SPDT Momentary pushbutton switch	3
270 Ω 1/4-watt resistor	24
4.7 kΩ 1/4-watt resistor	9
LED, small, 50 mA maximum (red)	24
47 μF Capacitor, 25 VDC (or greater)	3
0.1 μF Capacitor, 10 VDC (or greater)	1
500 pF Capacitor, 10 VDC (or greater)	1
14-pin DIP socket	9
16-pin DIP socket	11

PARTS LIST FOR THE KEYBOARD
(for a single system)

Description	Quantity
555 Timer	1
7442 BCD-to-decimal decoder	1
74153 Dual 1-of-4 MUX	1
74177 Binary up-counter	2
74175 4-bit latch	2
7400 Quad 2-input NAND gate	1
7408 Quad 2-input AND gate	1
7420 Dual 4-input NAND gate	1
74LS112 Dual J-K flip-flop	1
SPST Momentary switch	1
Hexadecimal keyboard	1
4.7 kΩ resistor	1
10 kΩ resistor	2
0.01 μF Capacitor	1
0.1 μF Capacitor	1

PARTS LIST FOR THE CPU BOARD
(for a single system)

Description	Quantity
74123 Dual 1-shot multivibrator	2
5.1 kΩ resistor, 1/4 watt	4
330 Ω resistor, 1/4 watt	6
7406 Hex inverter, open collector	1
7404 Hex inverter	1
7400 Quad 2-input NAND gate	1
8080 Microprocessor	1
2N2907 Transistor, PNP	2
74LS367 Tri-state buffer	5
74175 Quad latch	2
74LS04 Hex inverter	2
7408 Quad 2-input AND gate	1

THE POWER SUPPLY
(for a single system)

The power supply must furnish
    +5 volts   @   2 amperes (or greater)
    −5 volts   @   100 mA (or greater)
    +12 volts   @   500 mA (or greater)

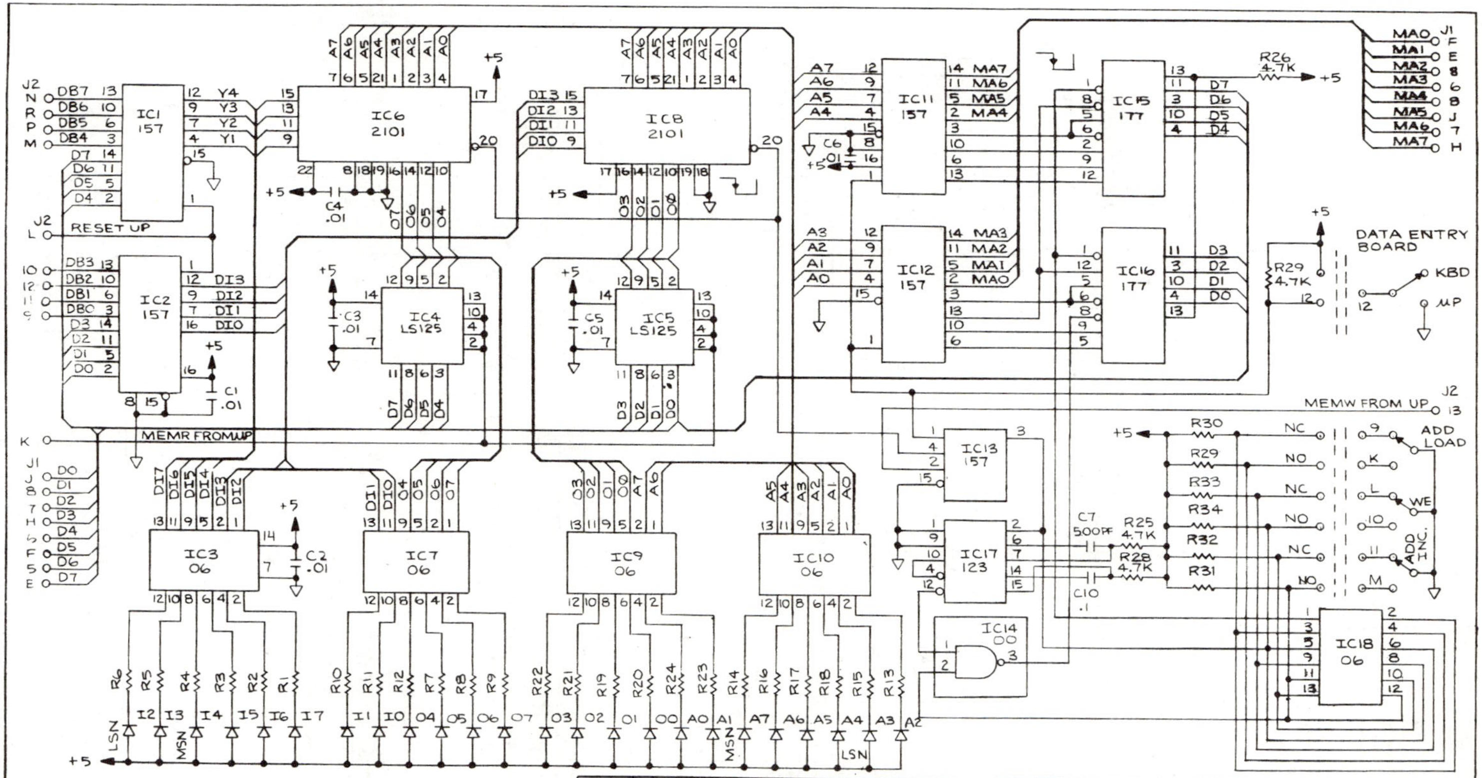

NOTES (UNLESS OTHERWISE SPECIFIED):
1. ALL RESISTORS ARE IN OHMS 1/4W 5%
2. ALL CAPACITORS ARE IN MICROFARADS.
3. C1, C9, C11, C12, C13, C14, C15, C16 ARE 0.01 DECOUPLING CAPS.

REF. DESIG.	DEVICE	+5	GND
IC1, 2, 11, 12, & IC13	74157	16	8
IC3, 7, 10, & IC18	7406	14	7
IC4, & IC5	74LS125		
IC6, & IC8	2102		
IC14	7400	14	7
IC15 & IC16	74177	14	7
IC17	74123	16	8

MEMORY BOARD TITLE	CREATIVE MICROPROCESSOR SYSTEMS
NEXT ASSM	PN
DRAWN BY	SHEET 1 OF 1
ENGINEER	B

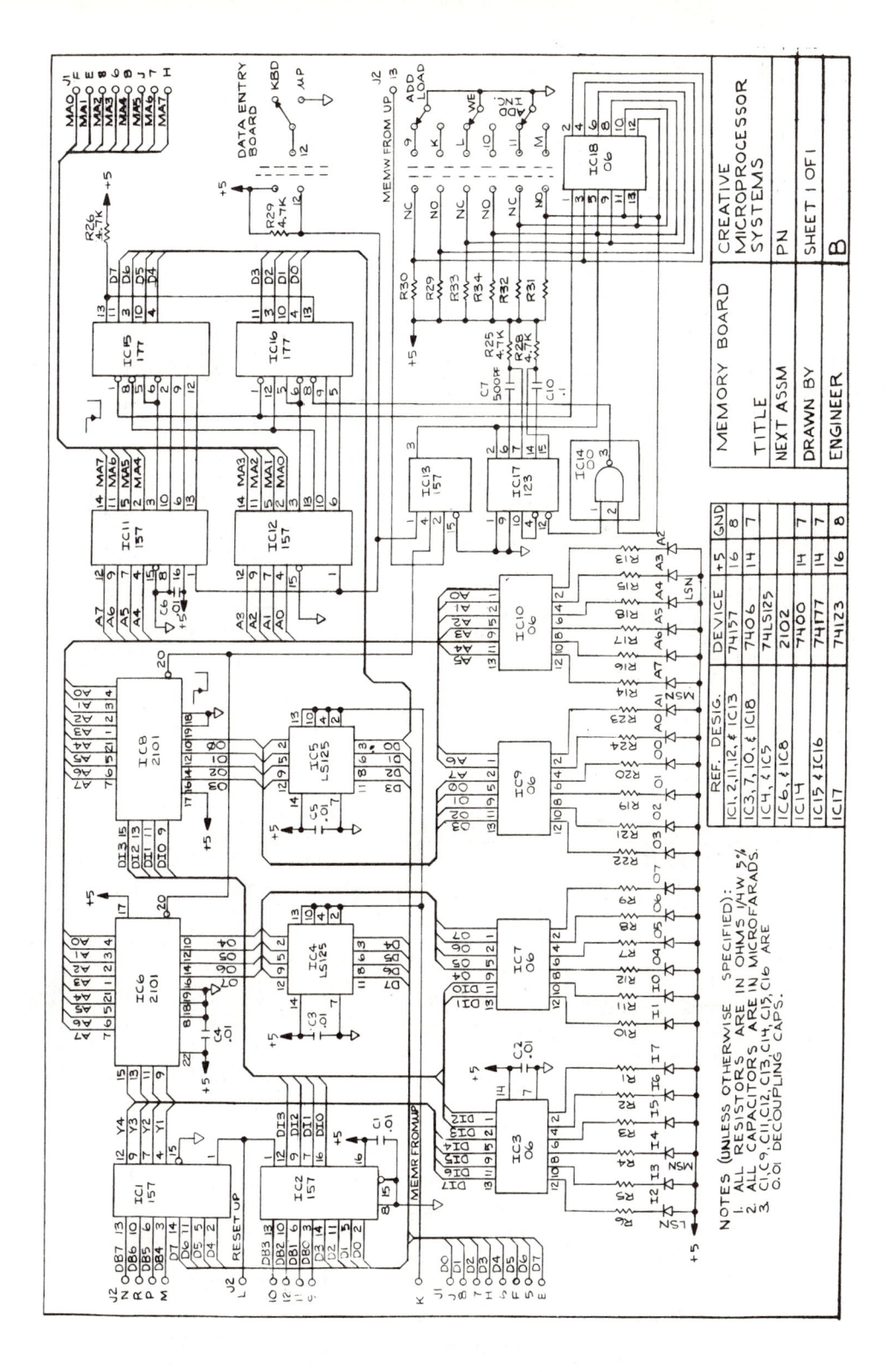

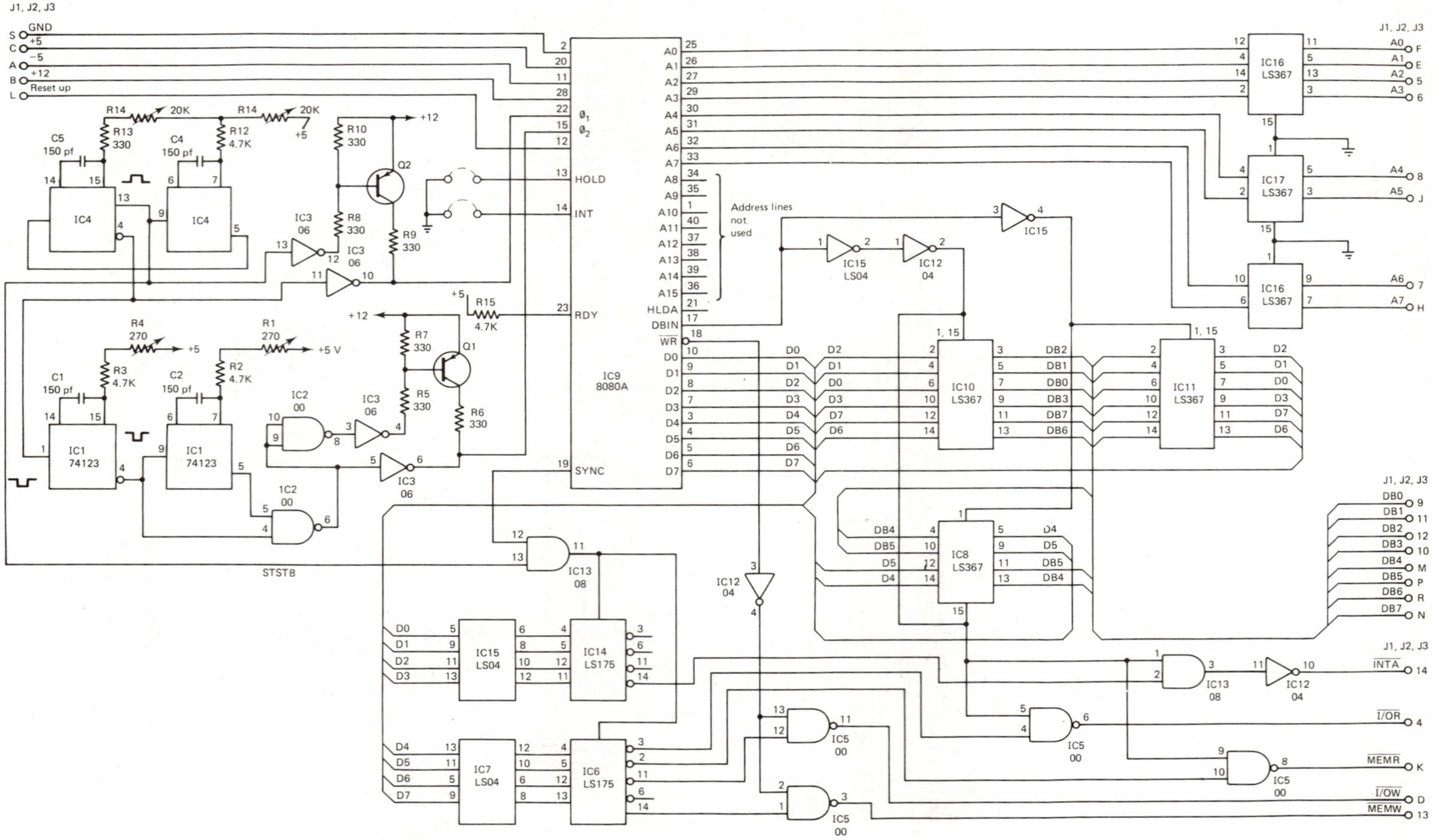

© Creative Microprocessor Systems, 1979

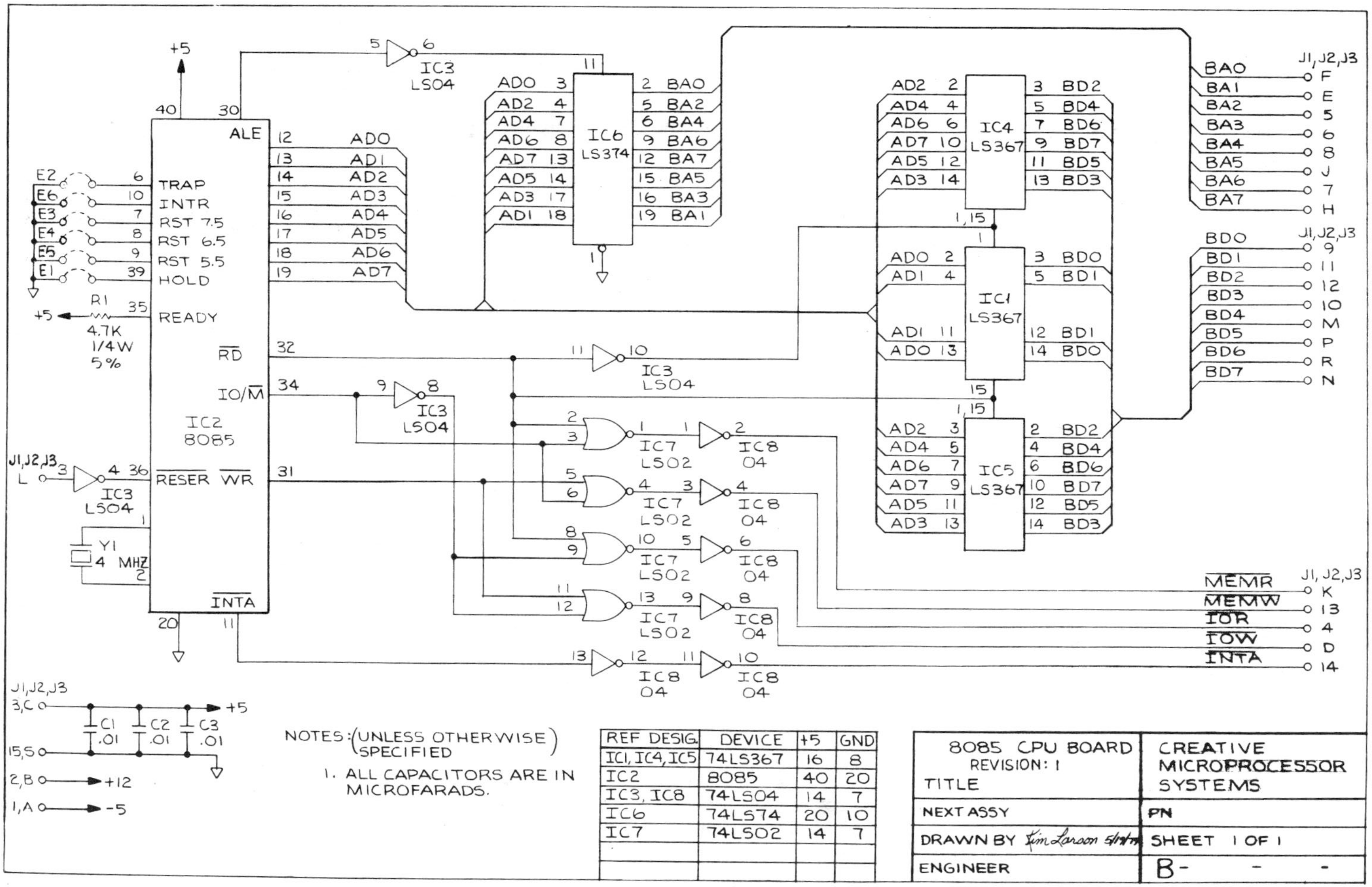

© Creative Microprocessor Systems, 1979

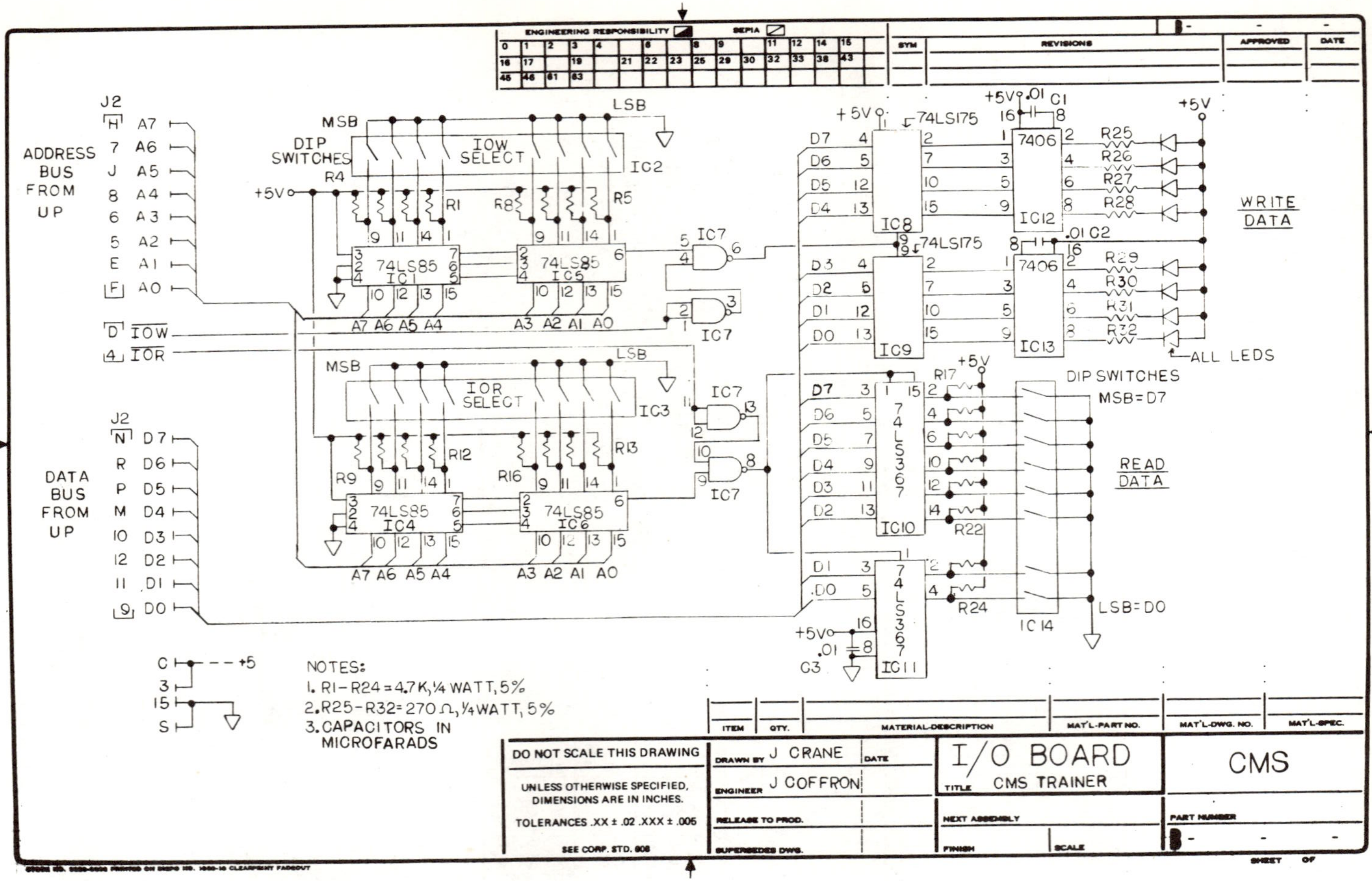
ADDRESS BUS FROM UP
DATA BUS FROM UP
J2
DIP SWITCHES
IOW SELECT
IOR SELECT
MSB
LSB
74LS85
74LS175
7406
74LS367
WRITE DATA
READ DATA
ALL LEDS
DIP SWITCHES MSB=D7
LSB=D0
NOTES:
1. R1-R24=4.7K, ¼ WATT, 5%
2. R25-R32=270 Ω, ¼ WATT, 5%
3. CAPACITORS IN MICROFARADS
DO NOT SCALE THIS DRAWING
UNLESS OTHERWISE SPECIFIED, DIMENSIONS ARE IN INCHES.
TOLERANCES .XX ± .02 .XXX ± .005
SEE CORP. STD. 808
DRAWN BY J CRANE
ENGINEER J COFFRON
I/O BOARD
TITLE CMS TRAINER
CMS

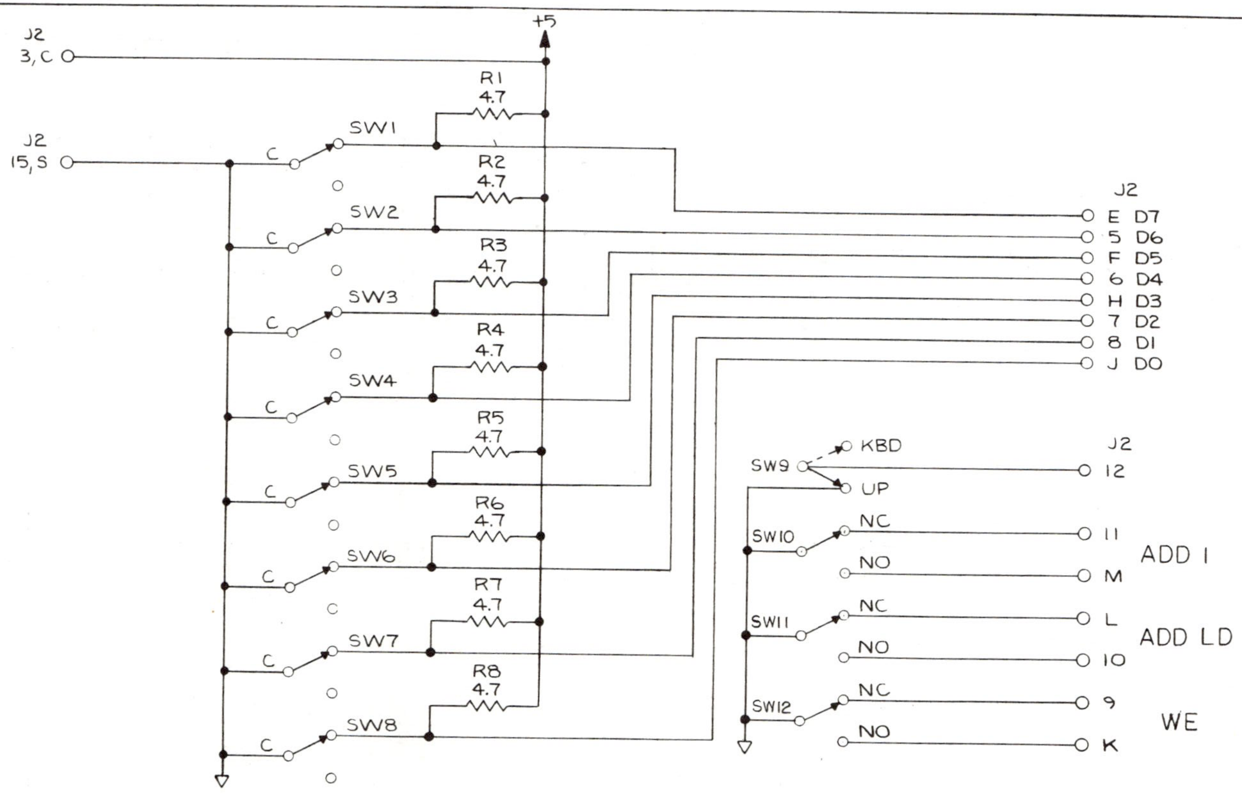

© Creative Microprocessor Systems, 1979

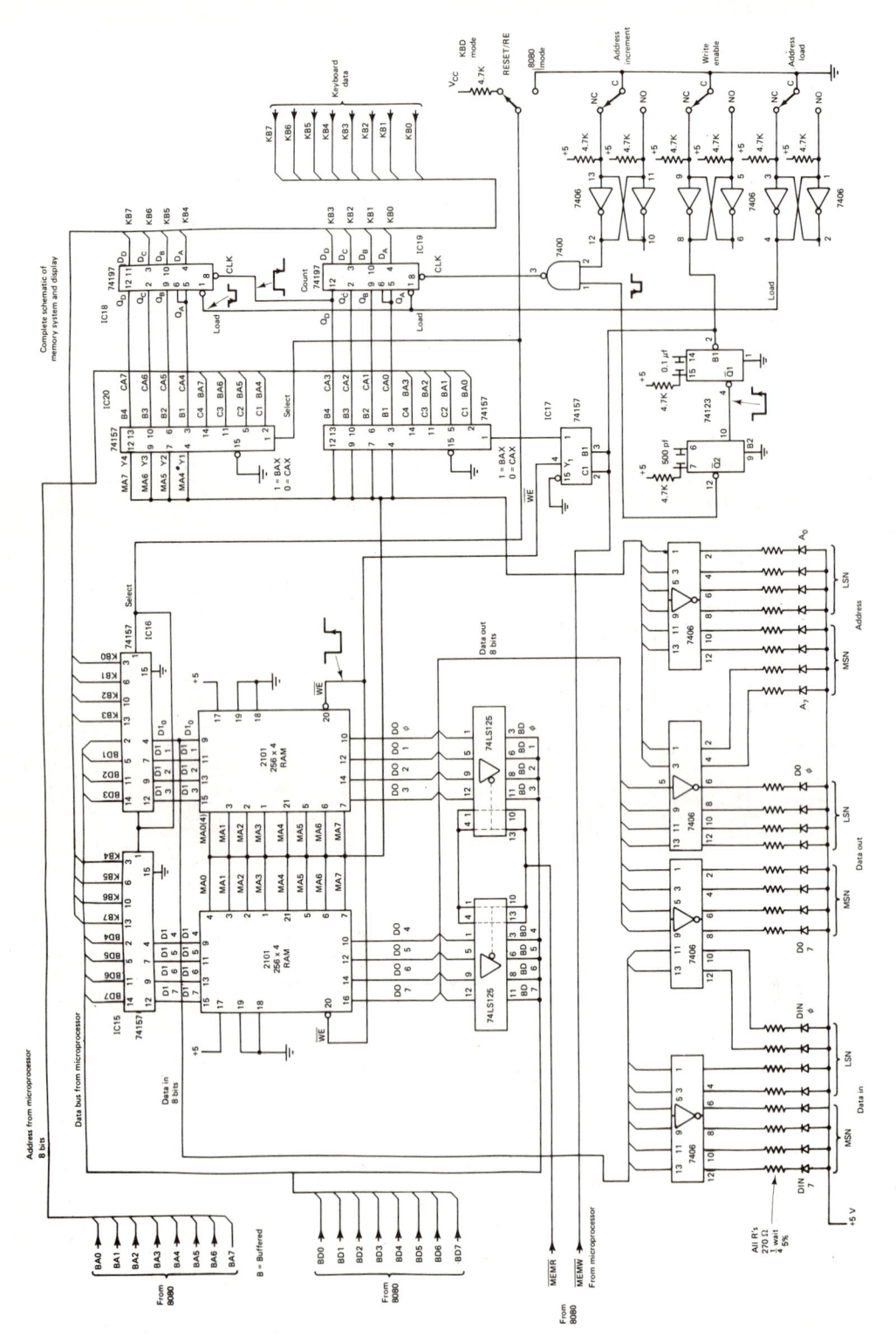

© Creative Microprocessor Systems, 1979

© Creative Microprocessor Systems, 1979

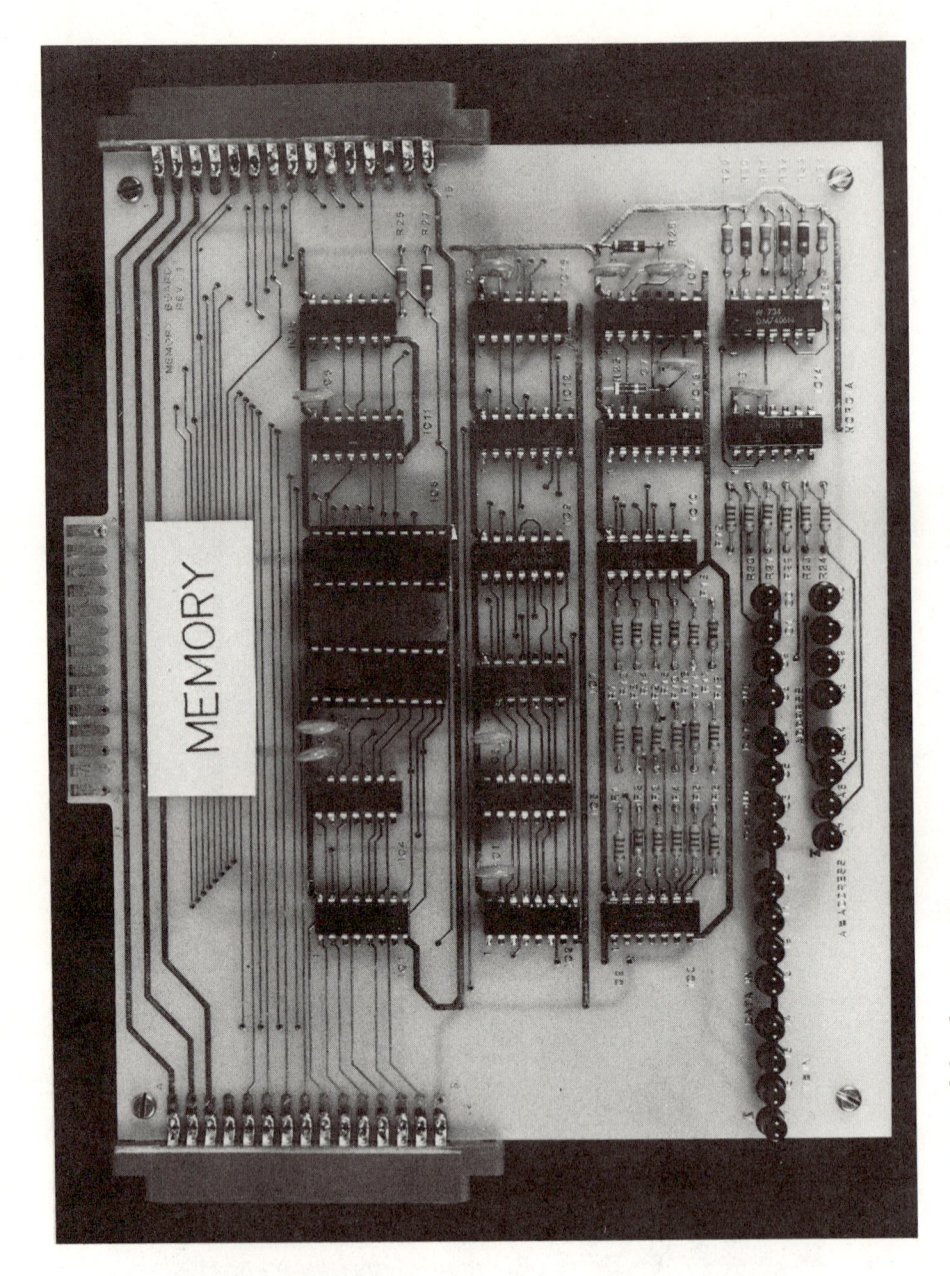

Memory Board for the CMS Trainer

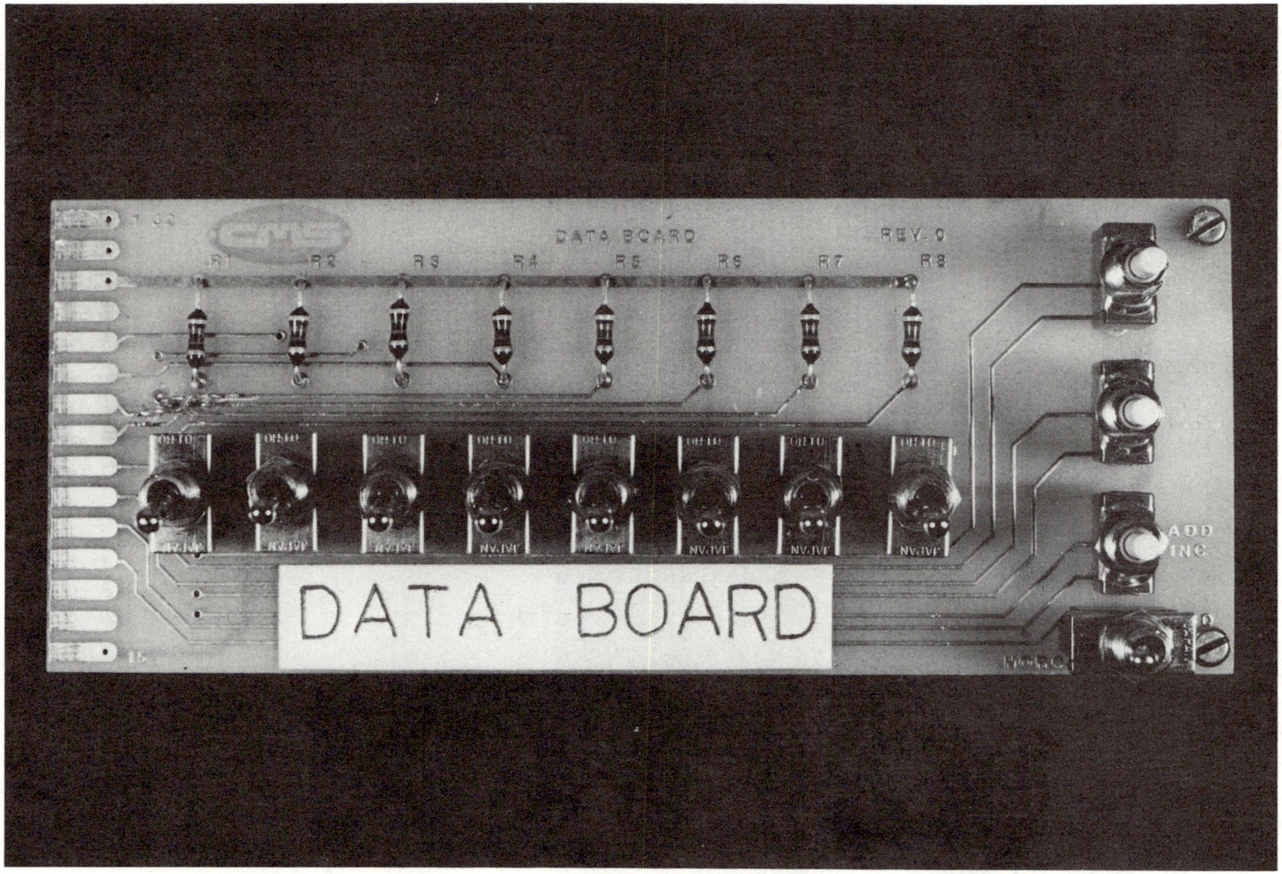

Data Entry Board for the CMS Trainer

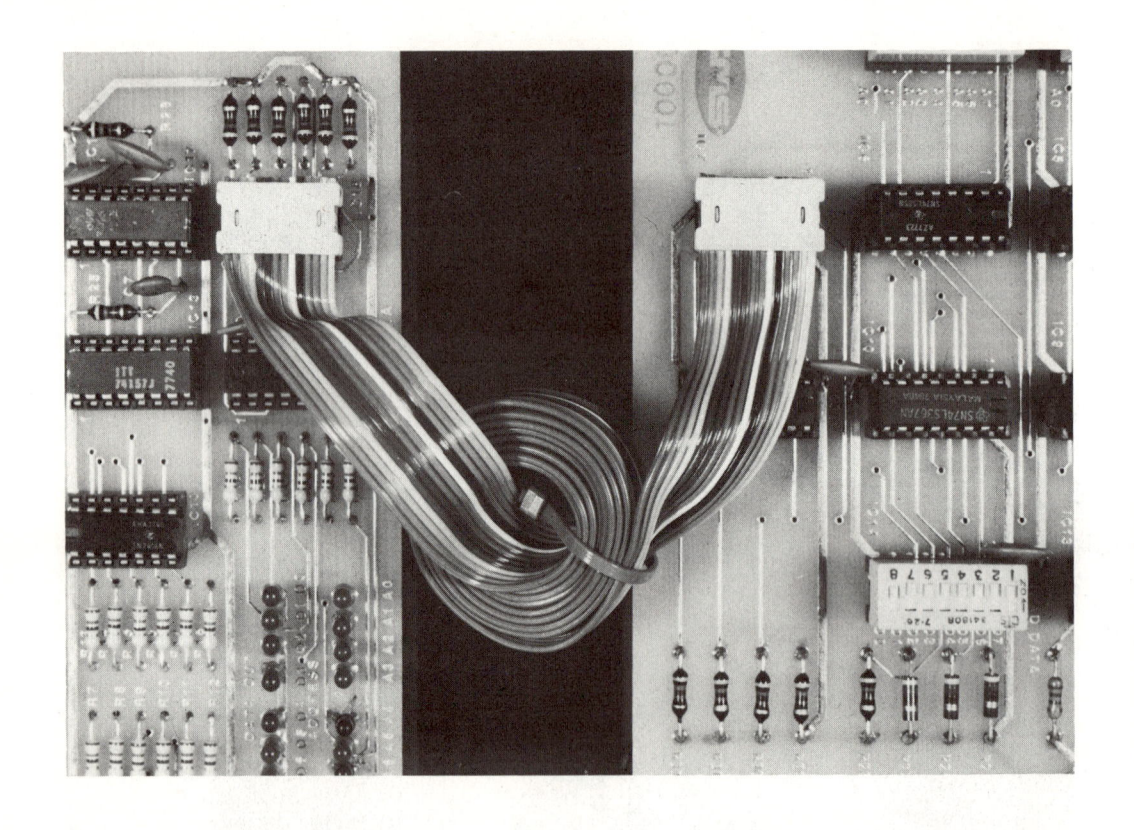

General Purpose I/O Board for the CMS Trainer

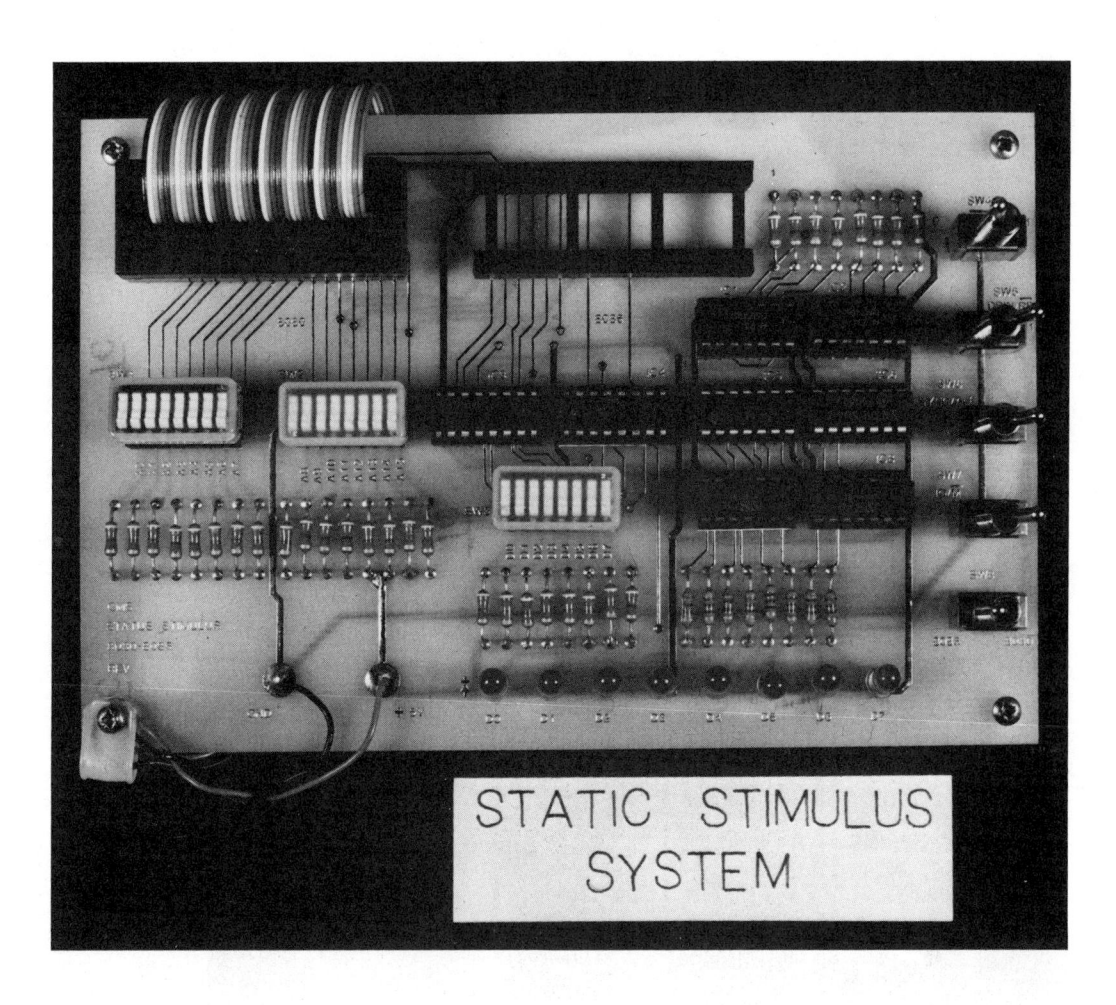

8080/8085 CMS Static Stimulus Tester

8080 CPU Board for the CMS Trainer

INDEX

A

Add instruction   172
Address decoding   43
Addressed port I/O   144-149
ADI instruction   173
Advanced application   261–287
Advanced microprocessor concepts   244–249
ALU definition   169
ANA instruction   174
ANI instruction   174
Application   261, 290
Arithmetic Logic Unit   169

B

Basic 8080 system   137
Bi-directional data drivers   130
Binary to octal conversion   183
Bit   12
Bit definitions   272
Bit placement   192
Block diagram
    memory   52
    software   169
Branching instructions   180–189
Buffer; Buffering   15, 130, 267
Bus driver, 8216   243
Bus (*See* data bus, etc.)
Byte   13, 192

C

Calculating size of memory   37
CALL instruction   180
CD4049 device   267
Chip select   49
Clock diagram
    for construction   117
    for microprocessor   113
    for MM5314 digital   262
    free-running   113
Clock generator 8224   234
Clock input voltage   113–114
CMOS buffering   267
CMP instruction   175
Codes, object   167
    octal/hexadecimal to binary   16–21
Common I/O   13, 17
Communicating with memory   65, 73
Comparator   147
Compiler   167
Condition flags   169
Control bus   140, 143
Control bus signals   140
Control software   270
Conversion
    of codes   16
    TTL to MOS   122
    voltage   122
CPI instruction   175

333

CPU data input   274
   functions of   124
   I/O   142
   main jobs of   124
   memory read with   129
   read access time   135
   read from I/O   139
   write to I/O   138
   writing to memory   135
Creative Microprocessor Systems   218, 321–332
Current
   for microprocessor   112
   logical 0/1 input   26
   short circuit in   112
Current sink   15
Current source   15
Current supply   28
Cycle
   fetch   185
   read   36
   write   36

D

Daisy chain, definition of   48
Data Buffering   130
Data bus   142
Data bytes
   bit placement   192
   modifying   193–202
   reading   192
Data, generator keyboard   85
   hold time   47
   input for memory   36
   input for the CPU   274
   output for memory   36
   setup time   48
   transfer functions + keyboard   77–99
Data sheets reading of   21–30
DBIN for the 8080   130
DC power for the 8080   112
DC power supply   12
Debugging memory with the SST   221
Decoding of address   43
Definitions   168–170
   ALU   169
   bit   272
   CPU   9
   daisy chain   48
   delay times   116
   device   143
   EPROM   9
   hardware   32

memory read/write   36
   microprocessor   6
   of input   142
   of machine cycle   133
   of output   142
   of RST instruction   257
   of software   32
   PROM   72
   RAM   8
   register   169
   time/state   133
Destructive read   63
Device, definition of   143
   digital   21–30
   memory   65–71
   microprocessor   65–71
   static memory   35–52
   tri-state   15
Device port I/O   149–151
Digit enable line, for MM5314   262
Digital clock interface, to 8080   266
Digital comparator   147
Display monitor   79
Display section   109
Drivers
   8216 bus   243
   bi-directional   130
Dynamic memory   59
Dynamic memory column line   62
Dynamic memory model   59
Dynamic memory refresh   63
Dynamic memory row decode   61
Dynamic memory row line   61
Dynamic memory systems   59–65

E

Electronic systems   10–12
EPROM   9, 74–75
Error checking   206
Examples;
   8216 bus driver   243
   8080 8-bit N-channel   289–317
   8080 as CPU   112–129
   8080 communication with   154–164
   8080 DBIN for   130
   8080 DC power   112
   8080 interrupting   253
   8080 programming   166–167
   8080 ready input to   249
   8080 schematic of system   137
   8080 sync for   127
   8212 8-bit I/O port   241–243
   8224 clock generator/driver   234–239

Index

8228 system controller 239–241
of basic system 65–68, 137
internal architecture of system 169
programming 184, 234–259
schematic diagram of system 247

F

Fall time 116
Fan out 27
Fetch cycle 185
Flags, condition 169
Flowchart task 273
Free-running clocks 113
Functions, of CPU 124

G

Generator 8224 clock 234
Generator data keyboard 185

H

Hardware 217
definition of 32
IC test clips 224
operation of and software 190
schematic diagram of 90
SST 217
Hexadecimal code 16

I

IC clips 224
Information useful 318–332
Input data, to CPU 274
Input, definition of 142
Input diode voltage 23
I/O 149–151
common 13, 70
communication with 8080 155–165
linear select 152
memory mapped 153
reading data 139, 159
sequence of events 145
write 202–206, 203
writing data 138, 159, 203
I/O address 142
I/O addressed port 144
I/O architecture 153–154
I/O circuit, schematic of 201, 268, 271
I/O device port 151
I/O instructions 179–189
I/O port
8212 chip 241
port, mobile 222

INR instruction 173
Instructions 170–175
ADI 173
ANA 173
ANI 174
branch 180
CALL 180, 257
CMP 175
CPI 175
IN 179
INR 173
INX 173
JMP 180
LDA 172
LXI 171
MOV 170
MVI 171
ORA 175
OUT 179
POP 178
PUSH 178
RAL 175
RAR 175
RET 181
RST 181
RST 257
STA 172
SUB 173
SUI 173
timing for 186
Internal register manipulation 140–141
Interrupt priority 259
Interrupting, jamming an address 254
Interrupting the 8080 253
INX instruction 173
IOR signal 140
IOW signal 140
Isolation by halves 140

J

Jamming an interrupt address 254
JMP instruction 180

K

Key entry time 97
Keyboard 77–99, 81
data generator 85
display section 108–110
interfacing to memory 104–108
matrix 83
schematic diagram of 90
storage latches 86

Index

Keyboard, continued
    timing diagram for   88
    troubleshooting   99–103

L

Latches   86, 127
LDA instruction   172
Level shifter   122
Linear select I/O   152
Logical 0
    input current   26
    input voltage   23
    output voltage   24
Logical 1
    input current   26
    input voltage   23
    output voltage   24
LXI instruction   171

M

Machine cycle definition   133
Magnitude comparator   147
Main jobs of the CPU   124
Major system problem areas   228
March pattern   136
Memory, block diagram of   44, 50, 52
    calculating the size of   37
    checking   110–111
    common I/O   70
    communicating with   65, 73
    constructing a system   38
    debugging with SST   221
    dynamic   59
    input to   274
    main job of   124
    RAM   8, 41, 47
    read only (ROM)   8
    reading data from   129–135
    ROM   72
    separate I/O   36, 65
    size of   37
    static   35
    troubleshooting   53, 57, 221
Memory column   40
Memory-mapped I/O   153
Memory read, definition of   36
Memory read destructive   63
Memory read, with CPU   129
Memory row   40
Memory stack   175–179
Memory system   107
    and display monitors   107
    writing data to   135–138

Memory write, definition of   36
    timing diagram   136
MEMR signal   131, 132, 140, 143
MEMW signal   140, 143
Microprocessor, clock   113, 117
    DC power   112
    definition   6
Microprocessor system, nature of   7–10
MM5314 digital clock chip   262–265, 266–270
Mobile I/O port   222–226, 230
MOS   6
MOV Instruction   170
Multiplexing   78
MVI Instruction   171

N

Nibble   13

O

Object code   167
Octal code   16
Octal to binary conversion   16
ORA Instruction   175
OUT Instruction   179
Output, definition of   142
Output display port   191

P

Passive pull-up   14
Phase 1 and phase 2 clock inputs   113
POP instruction   178
Popping the stack   176
Port   143
    read signal   146
    select line   145
Power supply   12, 112
Priority interrupt   259
Programming   166
    examples of   184
PROM   72–74
PUSH instruction   178
Pushing the stack   175

R

RAL instruction   175
RAM   41
    definition of   8
RAR instruction   175
Read from I/O   139
    from signal port   146
Read access time   44

Index 337

Read cycle   36
Reading
    data bytes   192
    data from external circuit   139–140
    data I/O   159
Register, definition of   169
Register pair, definition of   169
Reset, 8080 with 8224   238
Return instruction (RET)   181
Rise time   116
ROM   72
    definition of   8
    troubleshooting   226
RST instruction   257

S

Schematic diagrams
    of 8080 system   137, 247
    of clock generator   119
    of hardware   90
    of I/O circuit   201, 268, 271
    of memory display   107
Semiconductor memory   35–75
Separate I/O   68
Sequence of events for I/O   145
Short circuit   27
Signals
    control bus   140
    DBIN   130, 132, 140, 186
    $\overline{\text{IOR}}$ 140
    $\overline{\text{IOW}}$ 140
    $\overline{\text{MEMR}}$ 131, 132, 140
    $\overline{\text{MEMW}}$ 140
    port read   146
    $\overline{\text{RESIN}}$ 238
    $\overline{\text{STSTB}}$ 237
Sink current   15
Software
    definition of   32
    functions and hardware   169
    to control system   270–285
Source current   15
Source program   167
SST
    hardware for   217
    using the system   221, 214
STA instruction   172
Stack
    popping the   176
    pushing the   175
Stack pointer   176
State time   133
Static electrical parameters   21–30

Static memory devices   35–52
Static Stimulus Testing   214, 221
Status information   127
Status latches   127
Storage latches, for keyboard   86
Storage locations, for RAM   47
Stuck key   101
SUB instruction   173
Subroutines   180
SUI instruction   173
Supply current   28
Symbolism, in computer technology   30–33
SYNC for the 8080   127
System
    resetting   238
    troubleshooting the   286
System controller, 8228   239
Systems, electronic   10

T

Task flowchart   273
t_{D1} 116
t_{D2} 116
t_{D3} 116
Testing, Static Stimulus   214–222
Time extending the read access   248–253
    of fall   116
    of rise   116
    state definition   133
Timing diagrams   88 (fig) 186
Timing waveforms, clock   115–117
Tri-state device   15
Tri-state impedance   50
Troubleshooting   99, 212, 213, 227
    digital/analog   213–214
    localizing   227–233
    memory systems   53–58, 111, 221
    ROM system   226
    the keyboard   99
    the system   286–287
TTL to MOS voltage conversion   122

U

Useful information   318–332
Using the SST   221

V

Vocabulary of microprocessor systems   12–16
Voltage
    clock input   114
    diode input   23
    logical output   23–24
Voltage conversion   122

W

Wait request 251
Wait states 248
Watch-dog timer 163
Write access time 46
Write cycle 36
Write pulse width 47
Writing data to I/O 159, 203
    to external circuit 138–139
    to output display 202–208